The Skillful Teacher

Building Your Teaching Skills
Fifth Edition

Jon Saphier

Robert Gower

RESEARCH FOR BETTER TEACHING, INC.
One Acton Place • Acton • Massachusetts 01720-3945

The Skillful Teacher *fifth edition*
Copyright © 1979, 1982, 1985, 1987, and 1997 by Jon Saphier and Robert Gower

RESEARCH FOR BETTER TEACHING, INC.
One Acton Place
Acton, Massachusetts 01720-3945
978.263.9449 *voice*
978.263.9959 *fax*
rbteach@tiac.net *email*

To order copies of this book, or to request permission to reprint for any purpose, please contact Research for Better Teaching, Inc. See the RBT Publications listing at the end of this volume.

Library of Congress Catalog Card Number: 96–72496

ISBN 1–886822–06–9

10 9 8 7 6

Interior Design: Mary H. DeGarmo, *Research for Better Teaching, Inc.*
Cover Design: *Heaton Weiss, Inc.*
Editor, Revised Edition: Beverly Miller
Indexer: Elizabeth Parson
Project Manager, Revised Edition: Evelyn Ford-Connors

CONTENTS

Preface

We have written this book to assist teachers in their efforts to build greater competence in teaching skills. Our values are obvious. We believe that many things are important for good schools: curriculum is important; parent involvement is important; having a clean, safe building is important. But of all the things that are important to having good schools, nothing is as important as the teacher and what that person knows, believes, and can do. That is where the rubber meets the road in our business. Everything, literally everything, else we do is in service of empowering that relationship and what can happen in the learning environment teachers create for students with the resources they have.

We believe that a teacher's skill makes a difference in student performance, not only in achievement scores on tests (as important as that might be), but in students' sense of fulfillment in school and their feelings of well-being. We do not mean to imply that being skillful substitutes for other human qualities; but we will argue that, whatever else teachers do, they perform in the classroom and their actions set the stage for students' experiences. Therefore, only a skillful performance will do.

As the chapters of this book unfold, our exploration of teaching will be guided by three key concepts: comprehensiveness, repertoire, and matching.

> *Comprehensiveness* refers to our efforts to understand teaching as a whole. We are working toward the day when one might say, "These are the areas that make up teaching. Know how to handle these things and you have all the basic tools for the job."

> *Repertoire* represents the fact that there is more than one way for teachers to handle any basic area of teaching. Repertoire is a concept that challenges us to develop a variety of strategies and behaviors for dealing with teaching situations.

> *Matching* is an idea that directs us to think about what behavior to pick from our expanding repertoires in light of the situation, the group, or the characteristics of individual students.

The structure of this book will rotate through these three ideas again and again. As each new area of teaching is defined and described, we will take it through the range of options we have uncovered for handling it. Then we will address the issue of matching for that area and what is known about it.

We have built the framework of *The Skillful Teacher* upon a large number of very specific teaching behaviors and situations so that it can be useful immediately as a tool for self-improvement, staff development, supervision, and teacher evaluation. The framework ties theory directly to practice. Examples are provided extensively to illustrate the teaching performances being discussed. It is our hope that in this way readers will be able to understand their own teaching (or the teaching of another) more fully and accurately; and, more important, they will be able to control their own teaching so that it serves better their ends and the needs of their students.

Preface to the Fifth Edition

Readers of previous editions will see that many of the chapters are updated and expanded, especially Clarity and Expectations. Major new chapters on Classroom Climate and Assessment appear, reflecting their importance in our professional knowledge base.

Current research is used to update chapters where the structure of our knowledge has not changed, but research has deepened. Occasionally, however, readers will see sections where the references are from the 1970s. This is not because the knowledge is obsolete or we did not apply diligence in updating some chapters! These are situations where important areas of knowledge have lost their magnetism and are rarely studied anymore. Yet, they remain important variables in teaching and learning. One example is the degree of structure students experience about choice and decision making (see Learning Experiences chapter). Though out of fashion for researchers, knowing how to match structure to students can make a difference in successful learning.

We know that experienced teachers have tremendous Personal Practical Knowledge about how to teach their subjects and about how to adjust to the needs of different children (Edwards 1994).[1] Much of our work in schools over the years has been facilitating teachers' working together in collaborative settings, forming study groups, and doing action research together. These are routes to increasing teacher capacity that translate directly into better learning experiences for children.

Teachers' Personal Practical Knowledge is a hugely underutilized resource for school improvement in the country. Putting it to work requires structures of time and space one rarely sees: for example, bringing a task force of teachers together monthly to "polish lessons" on specific concepts.[2] In this approach, the task force develops progressive versions of the lesson, actively experiments and observes one another, and then presents the final result to their peers. Thus all the teachers of a given concept have the benefit of their colleagues' finest thinking and active experimentation. The lessons emerging from this kind of collaboration are refined and effective; they have the commitment and ownership of the teachers; and they are available for each teacher's direct personal use with students. Working groups of teachers developing authentic assessments can also serve as dynamic professional learning experiences that draw on the Personal Practical Knowledge of teachers.

But it is also true that because we have not acknoweldged the existence or complexity of our Public Knowledge Base on pedagogy itself, each generation of teachers has had to reinvent it; and most of us have gone our entire careers without discovering dozens of powerful tools and approaches that would have empowered our teaching. We hope this book is a step in remedying that situation.

---

[1] Edwards, John. "Thinking, Education and Human Potential." In J. Edwards, ed., *Thinking: International Interdisciplinary Perspectives*. Melbourne: Hawker Brownlow, Education, 1994.

[2] Steven, Harold W., and Stigler, James W. *The Learning Gap*. New York: Summit Books, 1992.

We hold teaching to be a complex human endeavor requiring high-level thinking, decision making, and the capacity to form, consider, and weigh multiple alternatives. Reflection and decision making are central to our concept of the teacher's role. To make informed decisions, however, we all need a full bank of available options to choose from, especially tried and tested options. We need systematic professional education that brings all the alternatives to our attention over time and enables us to acquire competence in using them. Then we will have the capacity to make decisions from both main sources of teacher knowledge: (1) our Personal Practical Knowledge and that of our colleagues and (2) the accumulated Public Pedagogical Knowledge Base of the field. *The Skillful Teacher* is an attempt to organize and make available to all this second resource for teacher decision making—the repertoires of strategies and approaches that comprise our common Public Pedagogical Knowledge Base.

Yet having access to rich resources for learning is no guarantee the learning will take place. Thus in this edition, we add two new chapters on teacher learning. The first, Chapter 19, profiles optimal conditions for teacher learning. We address such dilemmas as the balance between teacher autonomy and school cohesion, administrators' leadership, and teachers' ownership. In Chapter 20 we delve into the underlying beliefs teachers bring to their work, to their students, and to their own professional development. These beliefs have a powerful effect on teachers' willingness to stretch, to learn, and to persevere. Some colleagues have urged us to place this chapter first in the book as it is in a sense our constitution, our own framing set of beliefs. Perhaps they are correct. For the nonce, we will leave it at the end because it also serves to summarize the book. It acknowledges the crucial role our personal compasses of values play in the nature and direction of our teaching.

Acknowledgments

A book that attempts to synthesize as much information as this one is obviously indebted to a host of authors and thinkers. The bibliography at the end of each chapter should indicate the range of individuals who have influenced our thinking.

We are especially grateful to the many educators in Brookline, Cambridge, Carlisle, Concord, and Newton, Massachusetts whose participation in our early observational studies contributed to the original conceptual framework fo this book. Specifically, Jinny Chalmers, Susan-Jo Russell, Suzanne Stuart, and Risa Whitehead opened their classrooms to us and held many important discussions with us about teaching. Kim Marshall's detailed critique helped enormously in editing an earlier edition into more lucid, jargon-free prose, and Roland Barth performed a similar and much appreciated task.

We extend our immeasurable gratitude to the team of Research for Better Teaching colleagues and consultants—Louise Thompson, Mary Ann Haley, Alexander Platt, Paula Rutherford, Fran Prolman, Deborah Reed, Greg Ciardi, Ken Chapman, Sandra Spooner, Marcia Booth, and Caroline Tripp. They filtered a constant flow of refinements and suggestions from the teachers and administrators in the districts where they work. This feedback added greatly to the book's substance and clarity. The critical readings and edits of several chapters expertly done by Peggy MacNeill MacMullen, Louise Thompson, Fran Prolman, Lynn Stuart, Bena Kallick, Art Costa, and Bob Garmston were also most helpful.

The in-house production process was skillfully guided by Mary DeGarmo, Evelyn Ford-Connors, Deborah Reed, and Roberta Spang. Mary DeGarmo contributed countless hours and a great aesthetic sense to each stage of the production process, and her dedication to the project is greatly appreciated. We also thank the new edition's editor, Beverly Miller, for her high quality work, as well as John and Christine Glade for their editorial and design contributions to previous editions. Also we appreciate the addition of an index to this edition by Elizabeth Parson.

Finally, we especially want to thank our wives and families for their continuing support and understanding of the often demanding schedules of our work to advance the professionalization of teaching.

About the Authors

Jon Saphier is the Founder and Executive Director of Research for Better Teaching, Inc., an organization dedicated to the professionalization of teaching. Dr. Saphier is a nationally recognized consultant on supervision, evaluation, staff development, and school culture. He was a classroom teacher at both secondary and elementary levels for ten years. He has served as a team leader, staff developer in a large urban school system, university instructor, and supervisor of student teachers. Since 1980 Dr. Saphier has been a full-time consultant working in-depth on long-term projects for instructional improvement in school districts

Bob Gower is presently Professor of Education in the Graduate School of Education at the University of Massachusetts at Lowell, where he is an advisor in the doctoral program, "Leadership in Schooling." He has been a public and private school teacher, K–8 school principal, manager of training for a large computer company, and consultant for public schools. Dr. Gower is currently involved in long-term, school-based staff development projects in a number of Boston area schools.

How do we bring to a conscious level the fact that you and I are using them [teaching skills] daily? You can't transmit something that isn't conscious, that's simply intuitive. I know that when I used to train teachers directly I would say, "Let me take that reluctant group. Now watch what I do and then you do it." And I found that teacher picked up all my bad habits, and missed what really made that lesson go because I had not articulated it.

> Madeline Hunter
> Association for Supervision and Curriculum Development
> National Conference
> Houston 1977

  🐾   🐾   🐾   🐾   🐾   🐾   🐾   🐾   🐾   🐾   🐾   🐾   🐾   🐾   🐾   🐾   🐾   🐾

Understanding Practice is the single most important precondition for improving practice and the hallmark of a professional.

> Roland Barth
> *The Principal and the Profession of Teaching*
> Paper prepared for the California Commission
> on the Teaching Profession
> April 1985

1

Introduction

What Is Skill in Teaching?
Everything You Always Wanted
  to Know About Teaching
Parameters of Teaching
Plan of This Book
Uses of This Book

I'd ask to know what I was walling in or walling out.

Robert Frost, "Mending Wall"

What Is Skill in Teaching?

Teaching is one of the most complex human endeavors imaginable. Both as teachers ourselves and as students and researchers of teaching, we have been awed by the immensity of the task of understanding teaching. We know that a good teacher is many things, among them a caring person. But a good teacher is also a skillful practitioner, meaning adept at certain specifiable, observable actions. Being skillful means you can *do* something that can be seen; it means different levels of skill may be displayed by different individuals; and it means, above all, that you can *learn how* to do it and can continue to improve at it.

Skillful teachers are made, not born. They have the skills they use, and we can look at what they are doing in the classroom and say what is skillful about it. Many skillful teachers do not have the terms or the concepts for describing what they already do. They just "know" what to do, and seem to do it effortlessly and naturally—intuitively, some might say. To us, this effortlessness is an unconscious, automatic kind of knowing—"tacit knowledge" Michael Polanyi (1966) calls it. The limitation of it

> **Skillful teachers are made, not born.**

is that this kind of knowing is acquired only by a few—not God-given at birth, we want to repeat, but learned by them unpredictably over time in many different ways. And they can't pass it on to the rest of us because they can't say what they do.

There are some people, of course, who are not cut out to be teachers, just as some of us are not cut out to be race-car drivers. No amount of skill training is going to make some of us able race-car drivers. But the great majority of us who are not born with a feel for the road in our fingertips can still be taught the skills of race-car driving; we can become very competent at it, and we can continue to improve.

Being skillful in teaching and our attitude about that is an important theme of this book. As we develop that theme we want to be clear that we are not "walling out" from our conception of teaching certain important things, like being a human being. We value teachers who can feel a hurt, who know how to laugh and how to love. Being skillful is not in competition with being a thinking, feeling being. But we are highlighting the skillful part of being a good teacher in this book. There is more to good teaching than skill, but there's no good teaching without it.

Our image of skillful teachers is of people who are aware of the complexity of the job, people who try to be *conscious and deliberate* about what they do. They don't do what they do just because that's the way it has always been done, or because that's the cultural expectation for how it shall be done. They do what they do because they've thought about it and it seems like the best thing to do. They make choices from a repertoire of options. They want to control and regulate their teaching to have a positive effect on students, so they are willing to monitor what they do, get feedback, and try different things.

Skillful teachers are *determined* that students will succeed. If students are not succeeding, they examine their programs, their curricula, and their own teaching to see if they must adjust.

In addition to being determined, skillful teachers are *clear:* clear about what is to be learned, clear about what achievement means, clear about what they are going to do to help students attain it. And if that doesn't work, they will make another plan that is also technically clear and well thought out.

Finally, skillful teachers are *learners*—"always a student of teaching," as Joyce, Clark, and Peck (1981) say. Skillful teachers, though confident and competent, constantly reach out to the world around, to the research, to colleagues, with an assertive curiosity that says, "I don't know it all. No one does or ever will, but I am always growing, adding to my knowledge and skills and effectiveness." To skillful teachers, that openness and reaching out is an important element of professionalism.

So what, then, are the skills of teaching and how will we address them?

Everything You Always Wanted to Know About Teaching

Are the following among the things you'd like to know?

1. How do I get students to pay attention and stay on task? (*Attention*)

2. How do I keep the flow of events moving with smooth, rapid transitions? (*Momentum*)

3. How do I get the most out of my space and furniture? (*Space*)

4. How do I time events and regulate schedules so that students get the most productive learning time? (*Time*)

5. What procedural routines are important, and how do I get maximum mileage out of them? (*Routines*)

6. How do I deal with very resistant students? (*Discipline*)

7. What does it take to enable students to understand things clearly? (*Clarity*)

8. How do I make lessons more efficient and effective? *(Principles of Learning)*

9. How can I embed the teaching of thinking into my lesson designs? *(Models of Teaching)*

10. How do I communicate to students that "what we're doing is important; that they can do it well; and that I won't give up on them"? *(Expectations)*

11. How do I build good personal relationships with students? *(Personal Relationship Building)*

12. How do I build a climate of inclusion, risk taking, and ownership for students? *(Classroom Climate)*

13. What should I teach, and how should I frame my objectives? *(Objectives)*

14. How can I adjust for students' learning styles? *(Learning Experiences)*

15. How do I know what students have really learned? *(Assessment)*

16. How do I build/adjust curriculum for maximum effectiveness? *(Curriculum Design)*

17. What are the important big picture outcomes I want for my students? *(Overarching Objectives)*

If these questions are on your list, this may be the right book for you. There is a chapter on each question, and each question is clearly important. They are about areas with which all teachers deal, regardless of the age, subject, or grade taught. In a way, they define teaching; they *are* teaching. They are important things with which teachers inescapably come to grips, consciously or unconsciously. They summarize virtually all the decisions, actions, and situations a teacher has to handle with students in classrooms.

There are a lot of other important areas in which teachers need to function, too—like working effectively with colleagues, with parents, and in political and union forums; but they are not the subject of this book. *The Skillful Teacher* focuses on the classroom instructional skills of interactive teaching.

How will we go about answering the questions above? We will do so by drawing on the existing knowledge base about teaching, the stunning and rich knowledge base that has lain scattered on the barren littoral of cynicism, confusion and obscurity like a 1,000-piece jigsaw puzzle, complete, but waiting to be assembled.

The knowledge base tells us that there are many ways to handle the job implicit in each question (e.g., gaining attention to task—forty or more ways; choosing a model of teaching—twenty or more models; choosing and writing objectives—five kinds). But it also tells us *what they are*. The knowledge base about teaching is not a set of prescriptions, a list of behaviors known to produce effective learning (though there are a few of these). Nor could it nor will it ever be! The knowledge base tells us what our options are for dealing with each area, each major job of teaching, each question above. It further tells us that effective teaching lies in choosing appropriately from among our options to match given students, situations, or curricula. *In successful teaching, matching is the name of the game.*

> ## In successful teaching, matching is the name of the game.

To illustrate this, let's take a simple management situation—dealing with intrusions. Consider this situation: A teacher instructing a small group has an interruption from a student (Jimmy) who's stuck on an item on a worksheet; Jimmy has come to the teacher for help. There are several options for how the teacher can handle this, bearing in mind the need to keep the momentum of the group going but also to not leave Jimmy idle or frustrated: (1) wave Jimmy off; (2) wave Jimmy in but signal him to be silent until there is an appropriate pause to give help; (3) redirect Jimmy to another student for help; (4) teach students not to interrupt to begin with during instructional groups.

No one of these options is inherently "better" teaching. You can surely imagine various conditions under which each one would be the most appropriate response. For instance, if Jimmy doesn't have the confidence or social skills to approach another student for help, then waving in may be better than redirecting. On the other hand, if Jimmy is overly dependent on the teacher, waving him off may be best, especially if there is confidence that he *can* do it himself if he tries again. The teacher's success in handling Jimmy will depend upon whether the teacher knows the options available for dealing with the situation, and can choose the best response by matching the options to that specific situation.

If, in a similar manner, there are many ways of dealing with each of the major areas of teaching identified in our list of questions, then skillful teaching involves continually broadening one's repertoire in each area and picking from it appropriately to match given students, groups, situations, or curricula. *The knowledge base about teaching to which we are referring is the available repertoire of moves and patterns of action in each of the above areas, available for anyone to learn, to refine, and to do skillfully.* In this book we will present the specific options we have discovered for each area, illustrate them with examples, and offer what is known about how to do the matching.

Parameters of Teaching

We're going to call these areas of teaching "parameters." *Parameter* is a technical word. In science it means "a constant whose value varies with the circumstances of its application." Applied to teaching, what's constant is the job—e.g., maintaining attention or communicating expectations—and what varies is the way to do that job in different circumstances.

Each question in our earlier list represents one parameter of teaching; the label we will use for that parameter is the italicized word in parentheses following the question. Each parameter encompasses the many teaching responses and performance options that comprise the available repertoire within that particular area. In addition, since these parameters together make up teaching, it is important to recognize how the parameters are related to each other.

Some of the parameters have skills associated with them that are very specific. We will call such skills "moves," because they represent an action or a remark that takes but a second of time to perform. Moves are quick, discrete, and observable behaviors. They can be counted if you so desire. Many teaching skills can be explained in terms of moves, and many of them turn out to be related to classroom management: *attention, momentum, expectations, personal relationship building.* Those parameters that consist of moves occupy the bottom tier of the diagram in FIGURE **1.1**.

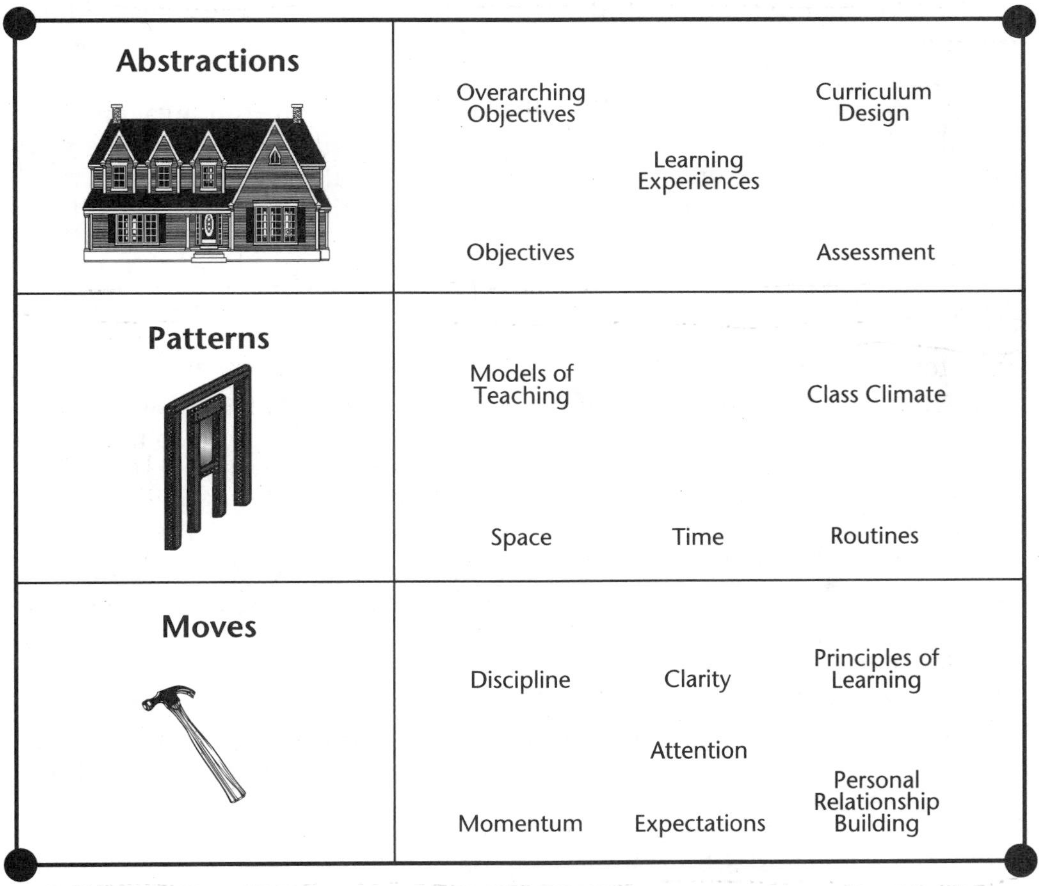

Abstractions	Overarching Objectives		Curriculum Design
		Learning Experiences	
	Objectives		Assessment
Patterns	Models of Teaching		Class Climate
	Space	Time	Routines
Moves	Discipline	Clarity	Principles of Learning
		Attention	
	Momentum	Expectations	Personal Relationship Building

FIGURE 1.1: THREE KINDS OF KNOWLEDGE THAT COMPRISE PROFESSIONAL TEACHING
This is one of a number of different ways to group units of knowledge about teaching.

Other parameters involve teaching skills that can't be performed or seen in a second. We consider being able to implement a model of teaching—for instance, Hilda Taba's nine-step Inductive Model—a skillful performance. A teacher skilled at that model orchestrates a series of events and follows certain specifiable principles for reacting to students. The whole performance unfolds over time according to a certain regular and recognizable pattern. Being able to perform the pattern is the skill. It's a package: a cohesive, planned package that is greater than the sum of its discrete parts. To understand teaching (and to expand one's repertoire as a skillful teacher) one needs to be able to see moves as they stand alone and patterns of moves which make sense only when you look at them as purposeful packages. It's a different kind of analysis, and to understand teaching one must understand both. The parameters that are patterns we group together in the middle tier of the diagram in Figure **1.1**.

As if that weren't enough, some of the important things teachers do skillfully are hard to see at all! Some of these are covert decisions and can only be inferred if we're observing a class; others take place before school, during planning or after school during the correcting of students' work. These skills generally involve choosing objectives, designing learning experiences, organizing curriculum, and assessing student learning. These areas of knowledge and skill consist of abstractions which are not immediately available for direct observation at all, but which nevertheless shape and account for what's going on in a classroom at almost all times. These parameters of teaching occupy the top tier of the diagram in Figure **1.1**.

So, we wind up with three kinds of parameters for skillful teaching, three kinds of knowledge that comprise skillful teaching: Moves, Patterns, and Abstractions. It is interesting to note that as an external observer of someone else's teaching you can only see these different types of teaching skills by looking in different ways. Classroom Management Parameters are mostly moves. They are low inference, meaning you can see and count them directly when they happen. For instance, you don't have to do much inferring to identify this Attention move: "Johnny, come on now. Get back to work." The Pattern-like Parameters, on the other hand, require medium-inference skills to see. As an observer you'd have to watch for a while and put together the behaviors you see over time to identify the pattern. The Abstract Parameters require high-inference skills to see, not to the teacher who is performing them, but to an external observer who has to put quite a few things together and make a mental leap to infer, say, what the objective is in a given lesson. To understand skillful teaching, it is necessary to recognize these different types of knowledge, and assimilate different ways of looking at teaching skills.

The parameters for skillful teaching can be grouped in another way besides the size of the units of knowledge they contain (Moves, Patterns, Abstractions). They could be grouped according to their function. The *Management Parameters*—Attention, Momentum, Space, Time, Routines, and Discipline—are the foundation of teaching—the *sine qua non*. If those jobs aren't being handled, no learning can take place. They contain the prerequisite skills for good teaching. The *Instructional Parameters*—Clarity, Models of Teaching, and Principles of Learning—deliver the goods; their skills come to life during interactive learning time in classrooms. The *Motivational Parameters*—Classroom Climate, Personal Relationship Building, and Expectations—help students generate the investment and put forth the effort that leads to successful learning. The *Curriculum Parameters* contain skills that provide the blueprints for instruction. They stand behind and above instruction, motivation, and management. Management skills support and make possible instruction. Curriculum skills design instruction. Motivational skills empower instruction. And Instructional skills themselves deliver the goods. Altogether, these parameters delineate teaching: teaching is *all* of them.

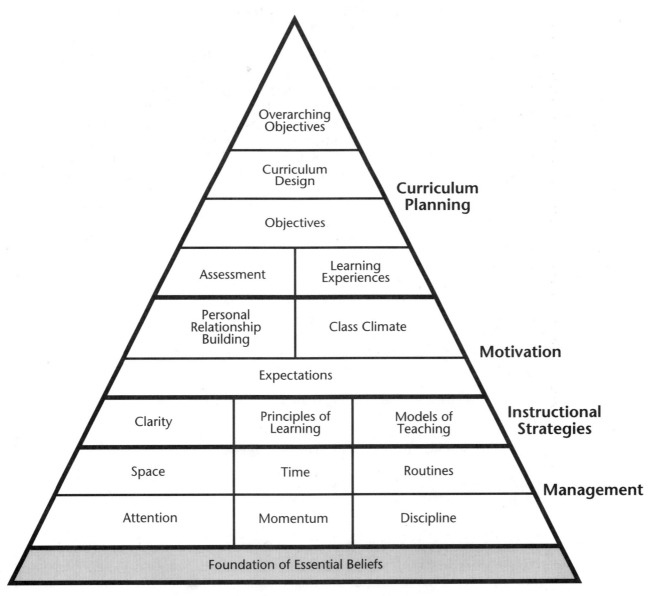

FIGURE 1.2: MAP OF PEDAGOGICAL KNOWLEDGE
The basic parameters of teaching can be organized into this simple functional structure.

FIGURE **1.2** illustrates the functional organization of the Parameters of Teaching. Readers will notice the entry "Foundation of Essential Beliefs" underneath the triangle. In the Expectations chapter of this book we will make the case that one of the most important of these beliefs is: "All students can learn rigorous academic materials at high standards." We will further make the case that the presence of this belief in individual teachers is the foundation of the drive to increase one's repertoire of teaching skills.

Other beliefs in this foundation include the role of interdependence among educators in getting the job done for students, acknowledgment of the importance of collegial behavior to strong school cultures, the belief in professional knowledge as based on repertoires and matching rather than lists of effective teaching behaviors, and belief in the need for constant learning. These beliefs will be discussed in the final chapter of the book.

Plan of This Book

The Skillful Teacher moves from the here and now concerns of the Management Parameters, those most pressing and immediate needs for many of us, to parameters that address why we went into teaching to begin with—good instruction and caring about kids. We move then into Instructional Parameters, Motivational Parameters, and finally to Curriculum Parameters, the design skills for those most important decisions about what education is for, what shall be taught, and how we shall know if it has been learned. Thus, the chapters move from the specific and discrete to the complex, from those parts of teaching that are moves, to patterns of moves, to decisions about design.

Each chapter addresses a different parameter. We frequently start by describing why the parameter is important and how it relates to the bigger picture of teaching and learning. Then we define concepts and categories useful for understanding the parameter and go inside each category to lay out the repertoire of ways teachers handle pertinent situations. We do this with examples as often as possible. Next we usually examine what is known about matching teacher choices to students, situations, or curricula. At the end of each chapter is a Checking page which lists all the key concepts of the parameter in a format designed to help teachers analyze their own repertoires and decisions. Finally there is often a Quiz which readers can use to review and anchor their study of the chapter.

It is not absolutely necessary to read the chapters in order, but there are certain cumulative benefits that make that desirable. Good discipline, for example, builds on a foundation of teachers' skills with Attention, Momentum, Expectations, and Personal Relationship Building. If you're struggling with a difficult class and turn to the Discipline chapter, you will find references back to the four Management Parameters listed above; they're the first place to check when working with difficult students.

Uses of This Book

Our audience is teachers as well as those who work with teachers around instruction—supervisors, evaluators, and staff developers. It is a professional book, a book we hope will be picked up by professional teachers and used to examine what they do. Even experienced teachers should check their skills against the repertoires available in each parameter to see if there are things that would add to their range, their effectiveness, and their ability to match the diverse needs we face these days.

We also desire through this book to build a common language and concept system for talking about teaching—not a dictionary of jargon, but at least a set of important and meaningful ideas about teaching that all educators can begin to use in common. If we can better understand each other, speaking and writing in clear and meaningful terms, then we can expect observation write-ups and evaluations of teaching to be more useful; supervision conferences to be more specific and productive; and staff development programs to be more focused.

We might also expect some of the barriers of isolation and loneliness between teachers to come down. We might expect teacher talk in teachers' rooms and other meeting places to be more open, more mutually helpful, and more about instruction. With a common professional knowledge base, discussing problems with each other might seem less an admission of personal inadequacy (a notion rooted in the "intuitive" teacher myth—if good teaching is intuitive and you're having problems, then there must be something wrong with you) and more a matter of a professional problem to tackle with knowledge and skills.

In undergraduate teacher education courses, in student teaching, and in graduate seminars, this same focus on skills and on the development of common technical understandings should find a place. To recall an earlier theme, technical understanding of teaching casts no aspersions on the importance of humanism or child development or detailed knowledge of age- and grade-specific content, methods, and materials. Student teachers in the primary grades, for example, would do well to know about Cuisenaire rods and how to use them to teach place value. Likewise, student teachers in high school social studies would do well to know about the Amherst "Problems in American Civilization" Series and its uses. But teacher training (and in-service training) already deal with these things. In our development as a profession it is time to deal with teaching itself. ❧

Source Materials

Joyce, B. R., C. Clark, and L. Peck. *Flexibility in Teaching*. New York: Longmans, 1981.

Polanyi, M. *The Tacit Dimension*. Garden City, N.Y.: Doubleday and Co., 1966.

Attention

How do I get students to pay attention and stay on task?

Desisting
Alerting
Enlisting
Acknowledging
Winning

The Attention parameter concerns teachers' skills in getting and keeping students on task during classroom time, that is, engaging and involving students in legitimate curriculum activities. (In contrast to time spent on task, off-task time includes behaviors such as setting up, getting ready, fooling around, waiting, daydreaming, socializing, and many others whose details need not concern us just yet.) Many researchers have timed students in classrooms to see how much time they spend on task, and then correlated on-task time with achievement (e.g., Bennett 1978; Rosenshine 1978). It is not surprising that they get fairly consistent positive correlations: the more time students spend seriously engaged in learning activities, the likelier they are to master the material. In this chapter we will examine the moves teachers make within the Attention parameter to maximize on-task time in the classroom.

> *Engaging and involving students on task is the sine qua non for curriculum implementation.*

In many ways, Attention is the bellwether parameter among the group of Management Parameters. Unless students are paying attention to the instruction, it does not matter how good the lesson may be otherwise. Engaging and involving students on task in large group, small group, or individual learning experiences is what Attention is all about—indeed, what management is all about. It is the precondition for instruction, the *sine qua non* for curriculum implementation.

The Repertoire of Attention Moves

Skillful teachers make certain moves to engage students' attention: to capture it initially, to maintain it, and to recapture or refocus it when it wanders off course. This is the general class of moves referred to by the parameter label "Attention." Within this general class of Attention moves it is possible to distinguish five categories of teacher behaviors: Desisting, Alerting, Enlisting, Acknowledging, and Winning. The skillful teacher's repertoire for getting and keeping students on task includes each of these categories of moves.

Desisting

Desisting moves carry the message, "Get with it." They are corrective and direct. They tell the students that they're doing something that they shouldn't be doing, and imply what the students *should* do (reengage the task). Among the various Desisting moves teachers make, individual moves vary in the degree to which they are corrective and direct. Some moves are more forceful or stronger means of conveying to students that they should "get with it" than others. The list below identifies the various types of Desisting moves we can observe teachers making—ordered from most forceful to least forceful—and gives an example of each.

1. *Punish:* "Well then, you'll have to miss recess if you can't get it done now."

2. *Exclude:* "Leave the group, Foster."

3. *Threaten:* "Stop it now, or leave the group."

4. *Sharp Sarcasm:* "Did you leave your head at home again, Grant?"[1]

5. *Judgmental Reprimand:* "Can't you stop being such a pain?" "Why don't you act like a fourth grader?"

6. *Order:* "Get back to work, now." "Sit on your hands until you're absolutely sure you're not going to touch anyone."

7. *Specific Verbal Desist:* Teacher names the behavior to stop and gives the student the appropriate replacement behavior: "Stop the tapping, Jim, and get back to your handwriting."

8. *General Verbal Desist:* Vaguer language stops a behavior: "Harry, cut it out."

9. *Mild Sarcasm:* Teacher says to a student who is whispering to his girlfriend, "Brendan, I'm glad you've found a new friend."

10. *Private Desist:* Either specific or general, but spoken softly so only the student addressed has his attention drawn to the teacher.

11. *Bring in Group Pressure:* "Fred, none of us can leave for gym until you're with us—" Classmates chime in, "Yeah, Fred, come on!"

12. *Peer Competition:* "John's ready. Are you, Beth?"

13. *Move Seat:* "Jimmy, move over to table four, please."

14. *"I"-message:* "It frustrates me when you talk to kids like that while I'm trying to teach, Clare. I feel as if all the work I put into preparing this lesson is down the drain."

---

[1] Though we will argue that any move in the continuum can be appropriate given the student or the situation, the one exception we pose is sarcasm. We feel strongly that sarcasm is always at least a small killer of relationships (and sometimes not so small). For distinguishing the sometimes fine line between sarcasm and humor, we use the following question as a litmus test: "Did it hurt?" If it did, it's sarcasm. If not, it's humor.

15. *Remove Distraction:* Without speaking to him, Mr. Glade walks by Kenneth and picks up the eraser Ken was playing with. He puts it in his pocket and walks down the aisle, continuing the discussion with the class.

16. *Offer Choice:* Observing Ken playing with the eraser, Mr. Glade says quietly, "Ken, you can put it away or give it to me."

17. *Urge:* "C'mon, Jill, will you please get in gear?" "OK, let's sit down and be good listeners."

18. *Reprimand:* "What are you supposed to be doing, Shelly?"

19. *Flattery:* "You're too conscientious to waste your time this way." "Back to work, handsome!"

20. *Signals:* Bell ring, raised hand, piano chord, etc.; or without breaking the flow of talk with one student, the teacher holds up a hand in a "stop" gesture to a third student, signaling him to cease interrupting (or whatever he's doing) and perhaps implying by facial expression and body language, "Wait a minute, I'll be right with you."

21. *Pause and Look:* Teacher looks at the child—the long look.

22. *Name Dropping:* Dropping a student's name into the flow of conversation (but not to call on the student) for purposes of attention: "Now the next problem—Jess—that we're going to tackle has some of the same elements—Jess—but the exponents are simpler."

23. *Offer Help:* "How can I help you with this, Charlie?" "Do you need help, Charlie?"

24. *Touch:* Teacher places a hand gently on the student's shoulder or some other neutral place—may or may not be accompanied by the teacher's stopping the activity and making eye contact.

25. *Proximity:* Being or moving physically near to the student with wandering attention (or whose attention is likely to wander).

Alerting

Alerting moves are often targeted at a group of students as opposed to individuals, and have the effect of keeping the students on their toes, minimizing distractions. There is no direct message conveyed in these moves; rather, they serve generally to keep the group alert and in anticipation. As with Desisting moves, the various Alerting moves teachers make differ in the degree of force expressed in the move. The continuum of Alerting moves, from most forceful to least forceful, includes:

1. *Startle:* Noticing that attention is wandering as a group listens to a cassette, the teacher abruptly hits the "stop" button and pops a question: "Why do you suppose Jefferson felt that way about Hamilton?"

2. *Using Student's Name in an Instructional Example:* "President John Lynn sits impeached and convicted. Who then would become president? And we thought life was tough under Lynn! Now V.P. Christiane Baker becomes president. It's time to pack our bags and move to Canada!"

3. *Redirecting Partial Answer:* Teacher redirects a question to another student for completion of the answer.

4. *Pre-Alert:* "That's right. Now try this next one, Holly. Check her, Dwayne, and see if she gets it right." "Now try this next one, Holly. Dwayne will help you if you run into trouble." (Both moves pre-alert Dwayne that he may have to answer. This is a way of focusing two students on one question.)

5. *Unison:* "6 x 6 is—Jane? That's right. 8 x 8 is—everybody!"

6. *Looking at One, Talking to Another:* Teacher looks at one student but talks to another student. (Lasts but a moment.)

7. *Incomplete Sentences:* "—and so, as we all know, the thing that we put at the end of a sentence is a—" Teacher may or may not display open hands and raised eyebrows at the group, or use hand gestures, to encourage someone to respond.

8. *Equal Opportunity:* Teacher makes sure everyone gets called on or is checked, and students know from past experience that it will happen and could happen to them at any moment.

9. *Random Order:* Teacher calls on students out of sequence of their seating pattern so they can't predict when they'll be called on.[2]

10. *Circulation:* Teacher physically moves around the room.

11. *Wait Time:* Teacher pauses and allows a brief silence if a student doesn't answer a question immediately. (This means having the patience to endure what may seem like an uncomfortable pause for five seconds, during which time the student may be able to generate a response if we don't jump in with cues or help. While the silence is going on, all other students are induced to focus on that question too, perhaps in anticipation that it will be referred to them.)

12. *Eye Contact:* Teacher makes eye-to-eye contact with the students in the group.

13. *Freedom from Visual and Auditory Distraction:* Teacher arranges the room so that small groups face into a corner or away from the main visual field in the room, or so that instructional or work areas are separated from noisy areas. Alternatively, the teacher directs the class to "close your eyes and listen."

---

[2] Brophy and Evertson (1978) found that random order questioning negatively correlated with achievement in low socioeconomic status schools, but not in high socioeconomic status schools. They reasoned that random order questioning generates higher anxiety and such anxiety is a mismatch for low socioeconomic status students, whom they feel may need more stability and support in their learning environment and less unpredictability.

Enlisting

We call the third category of attention-getting moves Enlisting moves because their purpose is to enlist or "sign up" an individual student's or an entire group's voluntary involvement in curriculum activities. Enlisting moves serve to captivate students and sweep them away in the interest or excitement of the activity. They capture students' attention by emphasizing the appeal or attractiveness of the activity. Enlisting moves include:

1. *Voice Variety:* Teacher varies speaking tone, pitch, volume, or inflection to emphasize points and add interest.

2. *Gesture:* Teacher uses hand or body movements to emphasize points or add interest.

3. *Piquing Student's Curiosity:* "Now, I wonder what made that happen?"

4. *Suspense:* "Wait until you see what's in the box!"

5. *Challenge:* "This next one will fool all of you!"

6. *Making Student a Helper:* "Jim, will you hold up those letters for the group to see, please?" (Jim's attention has been wandering.)

7. *Props:* Teacher uses physical objects related to the content.

8. *Personification:* "Now boys and girls, let's see if we can fool the staircase on our way up and get to the top without it hearing us." "Now, if Mr. W were to walk through the door right now and look for things that started with his sound, what would he find to make him feel at home?"

9. *Connecting with Student's Fantasies:* "If you had a million dollars, how many one hundred dollar bills could you have?"

Acknowledging

Sometimes students are inattentive for reasons that have nothing to do with what's going on in school or how skillful the teacher is. Some outside event is weighing on them (or exciting them). For example:

- their best friend refused to sit next to them on the bus coming in this morning

- their parents have just separated

- the championship game is this afternoon, and they're playing in it.

At such times, merely acknowledging out loud to students your understanding of what's on their mind can enable them to pay more attention in class. It is very validating (and rare) to have one's feelings really heard, and simply acknowledging those feelings can, indeed, facilitate attention. For example: "I know you're excited about the hockey game tonight—especially with three stalwarts right here in our midst. But I'm asking you to put that on the shelf for a while, gang, because today's review is very important."

Another example: Seven-year-old Jennifer is distracted during reading group; her glance shifts repeatedly to the place she left to come to group (a display of dolls from foreign lands which she was arranging). In a flash, the teacher sizes this up and, knowing that Jennifer realizes that lunch will immediately follow reading, figures out that the child is feeling that she'll never be able to finish arranging the dolls. (After lunch can seem like forever to a seven year old.) So, the teacher makes an Acknowledging move: "Jennifer, I know it's important to you to get all the dolls neatly arranged. You can devote yourself to that entirely, right before we go to lunch, I promise. Only now you need to work with us on this reading because we won't be doing this later. I'll make sure you get back there." Getting the dolls arranged may not seem important from an adult point of view, but such seemingly trivial matters can be consuming to children and block their involvement unless teachers perceive and respond.

Here is one more example. Perceiving that Mary is concerned about something, the teacher makes this Acknowledging move: "You're afraid you'll miss your turn at the listening station, Mary?" Mary nods. "Look, take your time and do this paper well. I'll see to it that you get your turn as soon as you're done, even if we've passed you on the sign-up sheet."

Sometimes the teacher just asks, "Brenda, what's on your mind? You don't seem with us this morning." Further probing and active listening may or may not release this block. However, sometimes just talking about what's on the student's mind, without any solution from the teacher, will be unburdening enough to permit the student to reenter "here-and-now" tasks.

Winning

Winning moves are similar to Enlisting moves in that they are positive and tend to attract rather than force students' attention to the learning experience. However, we have distinguished Winning from Enlisting moves because Winning moves focus students on the teacher, whereas Enlisting moves focus students' attention more on the activity. Winning moves rely upon the teacher's "winning" personality to mediate attention. The continuum of Winning moves that we can observe teachers making includes:

1. *Encouragement:* Teacher prompts students' ongoing work, usually by means of voice qualities and facial expressions.

2. *Enthusiasm:* "That's a really interesting topic for a paper, Bob!"

3. *Praise:* "Oh, that's fine work, Angie."

4. *Humor (without sarcasm):* Teacher jokes in a positive, supportive manner that is mutually enjoyable by students.

5. *Dramatizing:* Teacher acts out or performs material related to the lesson, or directs students to dramatize experiences. Alternate version: teacher switches into a role and speaks a line of dialogue through the persona of a character whose identity he or she has assumed, even if just for a single sentence: "Well, here I go into

the den of smiling vipers." (The teacher has become newly elected President Abraham Lincoln entering his first cabinet meeting where all the officers think they'd be a better President than he, and are, in fact, plotting to get rid of him.)

Analyzing Attention Behavior

One could order the types of moves from all five categories along a single continuum whose rule is: authority to nonauthority; or alternately, force to attraction (see FIGURE 2.1). Moves and categories at the upper end of the continuum employ the most teacher authority, most directly and firmly applied. As one travels down the continuum, the authority component becomes less and less dominant.

Thus, the Attention parameter involves a more or less continuous scale of values along a functional attribute, the functional attribute being moves whose end is to engage, continue, or reengage students' attention in the learning experience. It is this functional orientation that accounts for the merging of "praise," "enthusiasm," and "gesture"—variables previously studied by others for their own merit—into a larger parameter. We recognize that focusing students' attention is probably not the only thing "praise" or "enthusiasm" accomplishes (enhanced self-image? motivation?), and certainly not the only function with which these behaviors could be associated. We think, however, that from a functional point of view these moves at least logically do focus attention and, furthermore, that attention is a logical and necessary mediator to other outcomes with which the moves might be associated (e.g., achievement, motivation). Therefore, linking them within a coherent Attention parameter is productive for understanding teaching.

We suggest that teachers reproduce the Attention Continuum and use it to profile their own teaching performance. Which Attention moves do you use? How many and which of the five categories do you use? What does your profile reveal about your Attention performance? Some teachers have had colleagues or supervisors observe them to gather examples of Attention moves in their notes and later, using the notes as evidence, check off on the continuum the moves the teacher made. A teacher's self-profile or the pattern of Attention moves shown from such an analysis can be used to examine the appropriateness of the teacher's performance of Attention behaviors, which leads to the issue of matching.

Matching with the Attention Parameter

The Attention Continuum is an objective list; that is, no judgments are implied about moves at the bottom being better moves than moves at the top, or vice versa. We are arguing, in fact, that all the moves have a place and each may be appropriate in a given context. (The one exception to this statement, in our personal opinions, is sarcasm, which is always at least a small killer of relationships.)

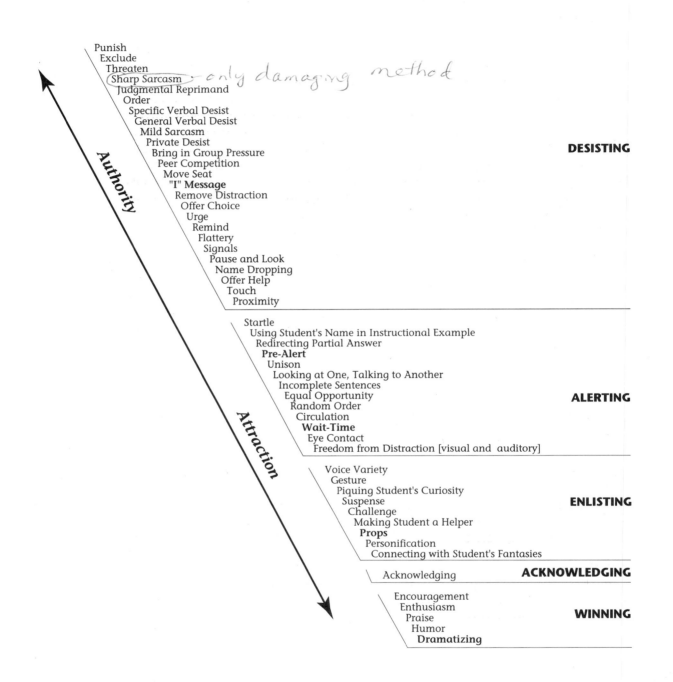

Punish
Exclude
Threaten
Sharp Sarcasm — only damaging method
Judgmental Reprimand
Order
Specific Verbal Desist
General Verbal Desist
Mild Sarcasm
Private Desist
Bring in Group Pressure
Peer Competition
Move Seat
"I" Message
Remove Distraction
Offer Choice
Urge
Remind
Flattery
Signals
Pause and Look
Name Dropping
Offer Help
Touch
Proximity

DESISTING

Startle
Using Student's Name in Instructional Example
Redirecting Partial Answer
Pre-Alert
Unison
Looking at One, Talking to Another
Incomplete Sentences
Equal Opportunity
Random Order
Circulation
Wait-Time
Eye Contact
Freedom from Distraction [visual and auditory]

ALERTING

Voice Variety
Gesture
Piquing Student's Curiosity
Suspense
Challenge
Making Student a Helper
Props
Personification
Connecting with Student's Fantasies

ENLISTING

Acknowledging

ACKNOWLEDGING

Encouragement
Enthusiasm
Praise
Humor
Dramatizing

WINNING

Authority

Attraction

Figure 2.1: Attention Continuum
This array of Attention moves offers a wealth of repertoire to the classroom teacher.

Experienced teachers with good repertoires on this parameter may be observed to respond to different students in consistent but different ways. For example, the following descriptions illustrate how Mrs. T skillfully matches her Attention moves to individual students.

Mrs. T knows that Daryl looks for power conflicts; he invites tests of will with her or any other authority figure. When she uses almost any of the Desisting moves with him he gets worse. For instance, he takes a "specific verbal desist" as a challenge to tap his pencil even louder and see what he can goad Mrs. T into doing. So, she has learned to use Alerting and Enlisting moves with him. If he really gets out of hand, she will move firmly and remove him; but she often avoids the necessity for doing that, and does get Daryl to pay attention, by "challenging" him with a question, by "pre-alerting" him, or by using a "making student a helper" move. For instance, she uses the last move when she sees him tapping the pencil and says, "—and so there really were four pyramids for the kings. Daryl, will you advance the filmstrip to the next frame so I can point to things from the front?"

Another student, Marsha, is a different sort of child. Although she also engages in frequent off-task behavior, Enlisting moves just seem to over-stimulate her. Mrs. T explains, "It's as if she interprets Enlisting and Winning moves as 'I-wanna-be-your-friend' or 'I-wanna-play' messages from me. She gets carried away with the interaction and focuses too much on me." While she looks for other ways and other opportunities to meet this need for closeness that Marsha seems to have, during work times Mrs. T uses mid-range Desisting moves consistently with Marsha when she's off task. And it works.

Different students—different needs—different moves: skillful teachers deliberately match their moves to students.

Some experienced teachers are intuitive about the way they differentiate these moves across their students—and they are known as effective class-room managers. They may not be able to explain why, nor may their evaluators. It's just known that they've "got it"—whatever it is. Perhaps it is a subconscious acuteness at matching Attention moves to various students.

Whether or not we have this intuitive flair, all of us can benefit from reflecting about the patterns of inattention we see among our students and comparing them with the patterns of moves we seem to be making in response. We may discover that we are ignoring part of our repertoire because we get so irritated at Louise—or that our repertoire could be enlarged—or that we could do better matching if we looked for the reason behind the inattention. Talking about a student (or a group) with a colleague, with the Attention parameter's continuum of behaviors in front of us, can be a very productive activity. ❧

Attention Quiz

The following questions and vignettes are designed to enable you to review, remember, and remind yourself of the choices you have when trying to gain, maintain, or regain student's attention.

Choose True or False and tell why you chose that answer.

1. It's more effective to use attention moves at the "Winning" end of the continuum.   T (F)
   Depends on student - match moves to student

2. Sharp sarcasm is a move that is not endorsed by the authors. *Can be hurtful*   (T) F

3. An "I-Message" is when I tell students what I want them to do. *makes the message about the teacher + how she feels.*   (T) F

4. I would choose to use the move "offer help" as a gentle way of getting students who were fooling around back on task   (T) F

5. Alerting moves are primarily used to maintain students' attention.   (T) F

Some of the Attention moves seem very similar or are more easily confused. This part of the test is designed to help you more effectively discriminate between them. In each case you are asked to tell the difference between the moves.

1. What is the difference between "flattery" in Desisting and "praise" in Winning?

2. What is the difference between "equal opportunity" and "random order"? Both of these are Alerting moves. *Equal opportunity -- everyone will have a turn; random order - teacher calls on students*

3. What is the difference between "humor" in Winning and "mild sarcasm" in Desisting? *Humor in winning has no sarcasm & is meant for group to enjoy; mild sarcasm is directed to a particular student*

4. What is the difference between "suspense" and "challenge," both in Enlisting? *Suspense -- something to look forward to; Challenge -- makes it a game students try to win.*

5. What is the difference between "move seat" and "exclude," both in Desisting? *Exclude = excluding from all students; move seat = move to another group of students*

6. What is the difference between "pause and look" in Desisting and "looking at one, talking to another" in Alerting? *Looking at one, talking to another lasts just a moment + teacher keeps talking; pause & look means teacher stops talking*

7. What is the difference between "proximity" in Desisting and "circulation" in Alerting? *Proximity - moving yourself near student not paying attention; circulation = teacher physically moves around room.*

8. What is the difference between "name dropping" in Desisting and "using student's name in an instructional example" in Alerting? *Using student's name makes the example about the student; name dropping doesn't tell it's just inserting a student's name just to get hing the attention w/o making the example about him*

9. What is the difference between "general and specific verbal desist" and "order," both in Desisting? *Specific + general verbal desist a student to stop something; order names something to do.*

25

Give examples of how you might apply these moves.

1. Give an example of how you might use "making student a helper."

2. You are presenting new information to your class. Wes has gotten up three times to sharpen his pencil. You decide to send him an "I-Message." What would you say?

3. Give an example of how you might use a "prop" in a lesson to enlist students' attention in the content of the lesson.

4. Give an example of a "pre-alert."

5. Tell how you might use both "random order" and "equal opportunity" to maintain students' attention.

Consider the situation and match your response based on the student, situation, or objective.

1. You're teaching a particularly difficult section of a high school calculus class. You are asking questions of individual students and at the same time you want to maintain the attention of the rest of the class. A good choice of Attention move would be:

   Wait Time   Voice Variety

   Unison   Circulation

2. It's the last period of the day on a particularly hot day. Students have been working hard and they are tired. A good choice of Attention moves would be:

   Startle   Challenge

   Acknowledging   Encouragement

3. You're getting ready to read aloud a selection from a novel students will be reading. A good choice of Attention move would be:

   Pre-Alert   Dramatizing

   Threaten   Eye Contact

4. In the middle of your lesson, students from another class are having a field day on the playground right outside your windows. A good choice of Attention move would be:

   Order   Remind

   Incomplete Sentences   Freedom from Distraction

5. Students are just completing a small group activity where they have been talking to one another. You want to get the attention of the whole group before you move on to another activity. A good choice of Attention move would be:

   Voice Variety   Signal

   General Verbal Desist Order

Source Materials on Attention

Bennett, N. "Recent Research on Teaching: A Dream, a Belief, and a Model." *Journal of Education* 160, no. 3 (August 1978).

Brophy, J. E., and C. M. Evertson. *Learning From Teaching*. Boston: Allyn & Bacon, 1978.

Church, John, in collaboration with Joe Hasenstab. *Teaching with T.E.A.C.H.* Emerson, N.J.: Performance Learning Systems, 1985.

Martin, D. L. "Your Praise Can Smother Learning." *Learning* (February 1977): 43–51.

McKenzie, R., and A. M. Schadler. "Effects of Three Practice Modes on Attention, Test Anxiety, & Achievement in a Classroom Association Learning Task." Paper presented at the American Educational Regional Association, Boston, Mass., 1980.

Redl, F., and D. Wineman. *Controls from Within*. Glencoe, Ill.: Free Press, 1952.

Rosenshine, B. V. "Academic Engaged Time, Content Covered, and Direct Instruction." *Journal of Education* 160, no. 3 (August 1978).

Rowe, M. B. "Wait Time and Rewards as Instructional Variables: Their Influence on Language, Logic and Fate Control." Paper presented at the National Association for Research on Science Teaching, Chicago, Ill., April 1972.

Tanner, L. *Classroom Discipline*. New York: Holt, Rinehart, and Winston, 1978.

3

Momentum

How do I keep the flow of events moving with smooth, rapid transitions?

Provisioning

Overlapping

Fillers

Intrusions

Lesson Flexibility

Notice

Subdividing

Anticipation

The concept of Momentum pertains to the smooth, ongoing flow of events in the classroom (Kounin 1970). Teaching is full of pitfalls to momentum. When these pitfalls occur, students' concentration is broken. They are distracted from or prevented from becoming involved in learning activities. They experience "downtime," time spent waiting for things to get ready, get started, or get organized. When momentum is not maintained, students become bored or look for things to do, potentially filling their time by daydreaming or engaging in disruptive behavior. On the other hand, when momentum is properly kept up, students experience smooth and rapid transitions from one event to another. Movement of students and equipment happens without bottlenecks, traffic jams, conflicts, arguments, or pushing and shoving. Observing such a room, one has the feeling that things are "moving along." In this chapter we will examine the behaviors teachers perform to maintain momentum and keep things moving along in the classroom.

In a general sense, many parameters relate to the concept of momentum. For instance: Attention does, insofar as students are kept interested or at least focused on learning experiences; Routines does, in that efficient design of routines for recurrent procedures expedites organizing and setting up, and speeds transitions; Expectations for work does in that teacher persistence and clarity about how things are to be done enable students to work more automatically, and make students individually efficient at moving from one thing to another.

Other parameters of teaching also bear on momentum: Personal Relationship Building does, in that students' regard for the teacher makes them less likely to resist or disrupt the way "things-spozed-to-be"; Space does, in that effective arrangement of space facilitates students' finding things and getting involved, and minimizes distractions; Time does, in that appropriate schedules provide for the ebb and flow of pupils' available energy and attention span, avoiding unreasonable demands.

Still further, one could look at the Curriculum Parameters of Objectives, Assessment, and Learning Experiences for aspects that relate to momentum: mismatched material (too hard, too easy), inappropriately presented, can lead to bored or frustrated pupils who will certainly break the momentum of classroom flow!

In a broad sense, then, we can see that any mismatch of curriculum or instruction to students tends to break momentum. But to cast momentum so broadly is to subsume all of teaching under its umbrella. Indeed, any parameter of teaching, whatever the primary purpose of the behaviors it considers, does have a secondary effect on momentum. However, we believe that it is valuable to focus on aspects of teaching that relate *primarily* to maintaining momentum in the classroom. Therefore, we will narrow our definition of Momentum to eight key subparameters or kinds of teacher behavior *whose primary purpose is to keep things moving along,* and which, when improperly done or ignored, break the orderly flow of events.

Categories of Momentum

The eight categories of Momentum are an eclectic group, comprising items that pertain to maintaining or at least enabling student involvement in learning experiences, as all Management Parameters do. But unlike the behaviors in other Management Parameters, which can be associated with other missions, these eight do not fit any other parameter and are primarily aimed at momentum. They are called provisioning, overlapping, fillers, intrusions, lesson flexibility, notice, subdividing, and anticipation.

Provisioning

Provisioning means having things ready to go—the space and the materials. With adequate Provisioning, one does not see the teacher call a group of students together and then leave them for a minute to fetch something needed for the lesson from the closet. One does not see students run out of needed materials during learning experiences so that they have to stop what they are doing and solicit new stocks from the teacher. (This does not preclude pupils' restocking themselves from known and easily accessible storehouses or supply points. It is when the supply point is out of paper, for example, that momentum suffers.) One *does* see materials out and organized before the start of lessons and the space arranged as necessary before instruction begins; one does see the room equipped with those things the students will need or are likely to need for the activities that may predictably occur over the day.

Provisioning, like much of good management, becomes conspicuous by its absence. Nevertheless, there are many observable signs of good Provisioning. For example, for lessons: audiovisuals, charts, or demonstration equipment are set up in advance; the teacher writes information on the board behind a pulled-down map, so that the information is readily available when the map is raised; handouts are stacked near the site of a planned lesson. For the room itself: activities, kits, games, listening stations, books, manipulatives, and problem cards are laid out in an orderly and visible fashion for pupils to find and engage; supply points are adequately stocked; a CD-ROM is placed next to the computer. Next to it is a pad of paper with a note giving location codes for three different areas students are assigned to research today. When skillfully done, a small amount of teacher time spent provisioning the environment during the school day results in a maximum amount of time available for focus on students.

Overlapping

We borrow this term from Kounin (1970) and expand on his definition: Overlapping is the ability to manage two or more parallel events simultaneously with evidence of attention to both. "Manage" here includes two aspects of teaching performance. First is *keeping in touch* with what is going on in several groups, areas, or activities at once (the teacher may be involved in one, more than one, or circulating among several sites); keeping in touch implies knowing the nature of the activity, the appropriate pupil behavior within the activity, and the current quality of the pupil's performance. Second is making moves to *help pupils over blockages*. Blockages may come from pupils' not understanding directions, pupils' not knowing what to do next, pupils' inability to resolve interpersonal disagreements (e.g., about sharing materials, or about how to proceed next as a group), pupils' encountering material above their frustration level, pupils' attention wandering, or pupils' finishing an activity and needing help making or planning transitions to the next activity.

> ## "Withitness" is a prerequisite.

"Withitness"—teachers' having eyes in the back of their heads, seeing the whole room and letting pupils know that they know what's going on—is a prerequisite for Overlapping (Kounin 1970). This "withitness" is necessary, of course, for noticing and responding to misbehavior in its early stages. But, in contrast to its disciplinary application, it is also the basis for Overlapping several simultaneous instructional events, as it enables teachers to keep in touch with the flow of all of the events.

Building on "withitness," teachers make moves to keep momentum going when they notice a blockage or potential blockage. For instance, below are a few examples of moves that maintain momentum by helping pupils avoid or work through blockages.

> The teacher, seeing a student nearing the end of an art project, says, "Where are you going to put it to dry, Jimmy?" Jimmy replies, "Under the woodworking table." The teacher responds, "OK, fine. After that you can finish the book you started this morning." The teacher has provided a focus for the closure of the activity and the transition to the next activity.

> As a pupil across the room appears stuck on his lab experiment, the teacher says, "Mark, ask Jane for some help if you're stuck."

> As the teacher sees a child using the last of the paint, he gestures for her to come over and reminds her to refill the paint jars when she's finished.

> When the teacher sees a group arguing over the position of a senator on a bill, she says to them, "Where could you find out for sure?" This is a way of directing the students back into constructive involvement.

The point of Overlapping is that all of these moves to maintain the momentum of groups and individuals are made *while* the teacher may be instructing a punctuation skill group, tutoring a pupil in reading, inspecting a pupil's lab report, or engaging in some other primary focus. The teacher makes the management move without leaving, interrupting, or seeming to remove attention from the primary focus but for an instant. It is an accomplishment to perform Overlapping effectively at any time, and especially so when the teacher has a primary active role in a particular learning experience.

Fillers

It happens during the course of a day that teachers are caught with groups of students for short periods (from one to ten or fifteen minutes) where nothing is planned. Sometimes this happens in awkward places where standard classroom resources are not available: e.g., outside waiting for a late bus; in the hallway waiting for a late class to come out of a specialist's room (gym, music); in an instructional group just ended where students have had it with work, yet when there isn't enough time to assign them anything else or even to let them choose and start some other activity around the room before it will be time to line up for lunch. In such situations, what does the teacher do to prevent the disruption of momentum?

Some may be inclined to comment, Why does the teacher have to do anything? The students will just have to sit and wait, that's all. Students should know how to wait: it's an occasional and unavoidable occurrence in life. It's not up to the teacher to entertain them at these times. Yes, we would answer . . . a consummation devoutly to be wished. But it doesn't always work that way. For some groups not so in command of themselves, and for some situations, relying upon students to patiently sit and wait can be an unreasonable expectation—and may result in disruptions. In such instances, teachers may pull out a Filler to hold the class together for those few minutes. Below are some examples.

> Since the clock in her room is wrong, Mrs. M arrives with her first-grade class five minutes early for gym. There's no use trekking all the way back to the room; they'd just have to turn right around and return. So she asks the children to sit against the wall and move close together so they can all see and hear her. "While we wait for the other class to finish up: raise your hand if you can think of a word that rhymes with…fish." (She calls on three students who give different rhyming words.) "You're clicking this morning…Now…one that rhymes with…lamp." (She calls on two more students.)

Another example:

> Surprisingly, tables 1 and 4 have finished their earth science experiments and write-ups early and put their equipment safely away, and ten minutes remain in the period. The teacher, Mr. L, knows the remaining tables will be asking questions and he'll need to be available for them. But to prevent downtime for tables 1 and 4 and fooling around (a distinct possibility with this freshman class), he

quickly writes eight science vocabulary words on the board and calls up those two tables. He gets them seated and started on a twenty-question review game in 45 seconds, and is then back circulating among the experimenters.

Sometimes Fillers are not as directly curriculum relevant as were the above examples. Primary teachers may just play "Simon Says." A fifth-grade teacher may say, "OK, without anyone looking at their watches, raise your hand when you think 1 1/2 minutes is up. Go!" (This "feel of time" game is a good way to quiet a noisy bus for a few minutes.) Secondary teachers may begin chatting with a class about current events or school teams. None of these is necessarily a waste of time, but it is worth distinguishing between Fillers that pass the time and Fillers that bring in something of the current curriculum.

Intrusions

Sometimes a teacher's day can seem like a series of intrusions punctuated by moments of instruction. These intrusions take many forms: pupils wanting work corrected, wanting help, wanting directions clarified, or wanting disputes arbitrated; adult visitors; incoming messengers; public address announcements. Every intrusion has the potential to disrupt momentum; but teachers can handle intrusions in a way that minimizes their distracting influence on student's involvement with learning experiences. We find that there are four basic levels of performance that describe a teacher's ability to deal with intrusions:

> *A teacher's day can seem like a series of intrusions punctuated by moments of instruction.*

1. *Allows intrusions to fracture momentum.*

2. *Deals with intrusions in a uniform way:* For instance, the teacher never allows students from outside an instructional group to ask questions (that is, doesn't tolerate intrusions of any kind); or always refers intruders to peers for help; or always has intruders wait nearby until an appropriate moment to help them arises.

3. *Deals with intrusions in a variety of ways*: The teacher uses different ways at different times.

4. *Matches response to intrusion to the characteristics of the students involved, or to the particular situation:* For example, this may mean that the teacher knows that Jane (the child she's working with) has fragile concentration and that even a delayed response to an intruder will lose Jane for good. (Maybe it took 15 minutes to get Jane started!) At other times, it is the intruder's characteristics to which the teacher adjusts, sending off Charlie to get help from a peer because she knows that Charlie can handle that, but holding John in close while signaling him to

be silent until she can briefly and quietly help him because she knows John doesn't have the confidence to approach a peer. (Perhaps later in the month she'll call over a particular child to help John when he intrudes for help.) In summary, the matching may be to the student or students in the group (those intruded upon, or to the intruder).

Sometimes the teacher matches the response to the situation rather than to the student(s). For example, the case of a fast-paced verbal game involving a large group may prompt the teacher to brook no intrusions at all, even from a student the teacher would normally accommodate, in order to preserve the momentum of the game.

As with all of the areas of teaching we will examine in this book, Intrusions remind us that the better we can match our responses to students or situations, the more effective we will be.

Lesson Flexibility

What do teachers do when lessons or planned activities are bombing? How do they control momentum? We can distinguish four levels of teacher performance:

1. *Presses on with the lesson anyway.*

2. *Drops the lesson and switches to something else.*

3. *Keeps the objective and tries to teach it another way:* Varies the format of the lesson.

4. *Matches a new format to the needs of the group and/or adjusts it for characteristics of individuals.*

Here is an example of the last. A group of students is full of energy, charged up after a fun gym period. They are having trouble settling down for paper-and-pencil exercises on contractions. The teacher, sensing this, draws a grid on the board, puts contractions in it, and calls the students up where they play a modified "concentration" game in which they can actively participate. The teacher has matched a new lesson format to the on-the-spot needs of the students. Momentum has been maintained by allowing the students to *productively* expend their energies.

Notice

Momentum can be broken if pupils are not prepared for transitions (Arlin 1979): if they are abruptly directed to cease one activity and begin another without time to come to some satisfactory closure point in what they are doing. This is especially true when pupils are heavily invested in their activity, as is often the case with creative-expressive endeavors. They resent having to stop what they are immersed in much as a sound sleeper resents being rudely awakened.

Teachers anticipate and soften these transitions by giving pupils advance Notice of when a transition is coming, so they can get ready for it. Even with advance Notice some pupils have a hard time separating from their activities: "Just one more problem"..."Just let me finish painting this side"... "Just...." (School isn't the only place we meet this issue in life.) Teachers may simply hustle pupils along at this point: "Come on, I told you five minutes ago to get ready. Now let's go!" Or, they may discriminate how they handle this kind of resistance with different pupils. With regard to how teachers move pupils along when time has run out, we can distinguish these four levels of performance:

1. *No way:* "laissez-faire" (lets pupils deal with it themselves), or erratically urges children.

2. *One way:* For instance, always pushes children along.

3. *Presses with different degrees of fervor in different circumstances.*

4. *Presses different students in different ways matched to perceived characteristics of the students:* For example, the teacher says to Jenny, "By the count of three have your book away and be on your way to the door," because the teacher knows Jenny is testing adult consistency in line with her dominant power issue. But for Noah, the teacher may allow a minute or two extra and quietly help him put things away since he has such a hard time investing, and he did a really nice job this morning, so the teacher wants to preserve its positive associations for him.

Subdividing

When groups of students travel through the room during transitions between activities or between phases of an activity (to line up, to get their coats, to go to the library, to get microscopes, to hand in papers), they sometimes get clogged in physical bottlenecks. These jam-ups result in crowding and general unpleasantness, and at the very least cause downtime while students wait for the crowd to thin. Subdividing (or Fragmentation, as Kounin calls it) means predicting these times and acting to prevent the jam-ups by dividing the groups into smaller units (individuals, pairs, tables, teams, children wearing sneakers) who move one at a time under the teacher's direction. Meanwhile, those students not in the unit currently moving are occupied with finishing tasks, putting away materials, or other aspects of the transition (perhaps a "Filler").

Some teachers use their Subdividing moves to reinforce items of recent curriculum. For instance, they dismiss students for the bus by asking multiplication facts or spelling words, calling on individuals and allowing them to exit if they get the answer... "your ticket" some teachers call it.

The kinds of Subdividing described above are most appropriate for primary-age children. Older students who can manage themselves in situations involving potential jam-ups may simply be allowed to proceed. In this case, efficient teacher moves might include detailing several students to pass out materials to the rest; storing materials at access points that accommodate several students "getting them" at once; sequencing and/or pacing activities so that small units of students naturally come up for materials (or pass the potential jam-up/downtime point) at different times—thus the sequential nature of the plan for the activities anticipates and precludes physical bottlenecks.

Anticipation

Consider this incident: The teacher has given the class advance notice to get ready to go down to the auditorium where a brass quintet will play for a middle school audience. "I hate concerts!" says Georgette. One minute passes—some children are putting things away. Two minutes—a few children are gathering by the door. Georgette is looking nobody in the eye and appears sullen. "Georgette, will you go down to the auditorium and see if the seats are set up for us?" says the teacher. Georgette goes. The class quickly lines up at the door and the teacher sets off with them. They meet Georgette halfway there; she reports that the seats are set up and joins the class without protest as they proceed to the auditorium.

> *Skilled teachers anticipate trouble spots and make moves to sidestep them.*

Skilled teachers perform this way every day. They anticipate trouble spots—incidents that will break momentum—and make moves to sidestep them. They move students out of the way of temptation, give resistant individuals face-saving ways to get out of self-made corners, anticipate situations or combinations of personalities that will break momentum and alter them—always before the trouble starts. Here are a few more examples of situations that benefit from a teacher's use of Anticipation.

When children are called to the rug or to a class meeting after cleanup, the teacher may anticipate that some will finish before others, that an ever larger group will slowly be assembling in the meeting area and waiting without focus (the meeting won't start until they're all there). The same may happen with a junior high class that filters into the room in dribs and drabs before the bell and at the bell is dispersed all over the room. In both cases, by anticipating what is likely to happen, the teacher can arrange to be present at the meeting area doing something of interest to absorb the children as they arrive (riddles, general chatter, a game, a brain teaser, writing something of interest on the board, holding a novel object). Some groups left without a focus at a time like this will provide one of their own...wrestling, arguing, or other momentum breakers. A teacher who can recognize the potential of the group will anticipate these times and be there to greet them with some engaging activity as they arrive.

Realizing that a small group will require much help and teacher time as they do follow-up work on a new geometry skill, the teacher will be sure the rest of the class are doing things they can handle comfortably, both in terms of procedures/directions and content. Otherwise, the teacher may feel "nibbled to death by ducks" as Bob Hope would say, becoming overloaded with demands for attention and help. As a result, the students will experience downtime, and momentum will falter. So on the spot the teacher assigns a page of practice proofs from the previous section of the text (ones they can handle easily) to the bulk of the class, and calls up four individual students for a ten-minute review of the new concepts taught.

Anticipation is a difficult skill to observe, and for teachers to notice themselves applying, because those who excel at it typically perform Anticipation moves spontaneously and intuitively rather than pre-planning them. But teachers who experience difficulty in this area can often benefit from running advance "mental movies" of the day they have planned, expecially if they do so out loud in the company of a colleague who's helping them problem-solve momentum issues. In this way, potential stumbling blocks to momentum may surface and steps can be taken to avoid them.

At this point, readers may be getting foggy over the distinction between Fillers and Anticipation. They are, indeed, related. Anticipation is the quality of mind that warns a teacher that without a Filler at this moment, for this group, there may be trouble. But Fillers are only one particular response showing Anticipation. Anticipation is a bigger category than Fillers. It is a kind of thinking, usually spontaneous, and often tacit, that says, "If I don't do X, momentum will break down here." X may be many things besides a Filler. For example, Mrs. R, in ending a class meeting of first graders, picks children for the clay area first, then assigns other children to other areas. She does this because clay is the most popular activity and everyone wants to go there. She anticipates that if she doesn't deal with clay first and get it off everyone's mind, as well as reassure all children that they'll eventually get a chance there, it will be on everyone's mind while she tries to get kids to choose from among the other activity areas. Thus, the sequence in which she fills activity stations reflects her Anticipation of what would happen if she didn't deal with clay first.

At its most general level, Anticipation is a quality of mind inherent in all seven situations described in this chapter (Intrusions, Fillers, Notice, Lesson Flexibility, Overlapping, Provisioning, and Subdividing). But teachers possessing that quality exercise it in many subtle movements outside the boundaries of those seven. So we need a general grab-bag category to hold and describe such situations, and this is it.

Reviewing Momentum

As you have seen, the Momentum parameter is clearly concerned with those teacher behaviors whose primary purpose is to keep things moving in the classroom. Within each of the eight subparameters, teachers perform a variety of moves specifically aimed at maintaining classroom momentum. The more skillfully teachers select from their Momentum repertoire to match their moves to the needs and characteristics of the students or situations involved, the more smoothly and efficiently transitions are made and the more successfully momentum is maintained. ❧

Checking on Momentum

Consider a recent class you taught or observed. For items 1, 2, 3, 6, 7, and 8, circle whether each behavior: was displayed when appropriate (YES); was not displayed but could have been (NO); or was not applicable (N/A). For items 4 and 5, circle the behavior observed.

1. Provisioning: space and materials ready to go   N/A   NO   YES

2. Overlapping: keeps track of several activities and helps students over blockages   N/A   NO   YES

3. Fillers: makes constructive use of short unexpected waiting times with students   N/A   NO   YES

4. Intrusions:

   fracture momentum
       uniform way of handling
           variety of ways
               matches responses
              N/A

5. Lesson Flexibility:

   presses on
       drops & switches
           varies format
               matches new format
              N/A

6. Notice: gives advance notice at transitions   N/A   NO   YES

7. Subdividing: breaks moving groups into smaller units   N/A   NO   YES

8. Anticipation: anticipates and circumvents blocks to momentum   N/A   NO   YES

Momentum Quiz

1. Summarize the Momentum parameter in your own words.

   keeping things moving in the classroom

2. Match each subparameter to the item that most clearly relates to it.

   A. Provisioning   a. "Try another way"

   B. Overlapping   b. Distracting interruptions

   C. Fillers   c. Physical bottlenecks

   D. Intrusions   d. Managing two groups at once

   E. Lesson Flexibility   e. "Simon says…"

   F. Notice   f. Anticipating transitions

   G. Subdividing   g. Set up equipment in advance

   H. Anticipation   h. Anticipate trouble spots

3. Describe some examples of:

   Provisioning: *having materials ready charts are prewritten make sure enough supplies for each student*

   Fillers: *Simon Says… rhyming…*

   Dealing with Intrusions: *students seek help from other students*

4. Describe ways of Subdividing when students are doing the following.

   Getting equipment from a supply table: *send small groups over to supply table at different times*

   Handing in papers: *Students hand in papers depending on color worn, beginning letter of name, etc.*

5. What is called for to prevent loss of momentum when several small groups are working in different parts of the room?

Withitness

6. Complete the comment a teacher using Overlapping might say in each of these situations.

A. A student across the room is obviously having difficulty with a worksheet. The teacher says:

John, see if Laura needs some help w/ that worksheet.

B. A student has completed her spelling workbook before the other students have finished theirs. The teacher says:

Write a word that rhymes with 5 of spelling word.

7. Which subparameter does each of these scenes illustrate?

A. Students are returning from gym in ones and twos, a few at a time. The teacher is in the room holding several novel objects and asking the returning students what they are used for.

This is an example of: *Anticipation*

B. A teacher says, "Boys and girls, we will be going to the lunch room in five minutes. Be sure your desks are clear and your books are ready to take to your locker."

This is an example of: *Notice*

C. A group of students is obviously bored during a grammar lesson. The teacher who was lecturing stops and faces the group. She then asks the students to come to the front of the room, to act out several parts of speech, and to tell how these parts behave in sentences.

This is an example of: *Lesson Flexibility*

8. How is Momentum related to the Attention parameter?

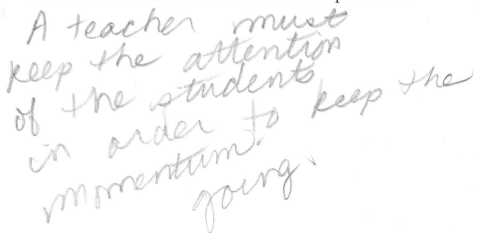

A teacher must keep the attention of the students in order to keep the momentum going.

44

Source Materials on Momentum

Arlin, M. "Teacher Transitions Can Disrupt Time Flow in Classrooms." *American Educational Research Journal* (Winter 1979): 42–56.

Doyle, W. "Making Managerial Decisions in Classrooms." In Classroom Management, *78th Yearbook of the National Society for the Study of Education*, Daniel L. Duke (ed.), Chicago: University of Chicago Press, 1979, 75–115.

Kounin, J. *Discipline and Classroom Management*. New York: Holt, Rinehart, and Winston, 1970.

Pierson, C., and J. Mansuggi, *Creating & Using Learning Games*. Palo Alto, Calif.: Learning Handbooks, 1975.

Space

How do I get the most out of
my space and furniture?

Matching Space to Instruction

Ownership and Privacy

Recommendations on
Using Space

Architects, interior decorators, and environmental engineers all believe that the way things are arranged in space (including the space itself) makes a difference in how people function. These professionals make their living helping people to be happier and to function more efficiently through better use of the physical environment. We need to apply their insights to education for similar payoffs—increased satisfaction and productivity.

In this chapter on the Space parameter of teaching, we will explore ways in which teachers can make the most advantageous use of classroom and school space. There are two equally important but different ways of looking at teachers' use of Space. One is to look at the way arrangements of furniture, materials, and space support the kind of instruction going on. What are the goals of the lesson? What kind of learning environment does it ask for? How does the use of Space support the lesson? Since lesson goals and lesson forms change, Space arrangements can be expected to change also. There are a variety of Space arrangements teachers can use, and those arrangements can be rationally matched to the active form of instruction.

> *The way things are arranged in space makes a difference in how people function.*

The second way of looking at Space focuses not on its varying uses but on how certain *constant* space-related issues of student life are handled: ownership and privacy. Different students have different needs in these areas, and there are things teachers can do to match to those individual needs. We will look at Space in both of these ways.

Matching Space to Instruction

Teachers experience a wide variety of office arrangements when they confer with school principals. Some principals speak to teachers across a desk; some have the teacher's chair next to the desk so that the conversation takes place across the corner of the desk. Other principals have their desk in a corner facing a wall, and turn their chair around to confer. Still others leave their desk and confer with teachers around a coffee table where two or three chairs are set.

Each of those arrangements sends a different message about authority, and uses physical setting to set the climate for the kind of interaction the principal desires. Likewise, teachers' arrangements of classroom space send messages about their image of the learner and the kind of learning they intend. Jacob Getzels (cited in Lewis 1979) has associated four such images with four different patterns of classroom space:

1. He ties the "empty learner" image to the *rectangular* room arrangement: "In these classroom designs, which were the standard in the early 1900s and continue to be the most prevalent today, the teacher's function is to fill the learners with knowledge. Hence all desks face front in evenly spaced rows toward the front of the class and the source of knowledge, the teacher and his or her desk."

2. Getzels next connects the image of the "active learner" to the *square* room arrangement: "In these rooms furniture is movable, arrangements are changed, the teacher's desk joins those of the children and the learner becomes the center."

3. Getzels' third model is the "social learner" and the *circular* classroom: "Learning was perceived as occurring through interpersonal actions and reactions." It is in such a shape that many of today's affective education programs occur. One commercial affective education curriculum guide even calls its program "The Magic Circle." Children learn about their own feelings, the feelings of others, and study levels and consequences of interactions.

4. Getzels' final model is the "stimulus-seeking learner" and the *open* classroom: "Where learning centers, communally owned furniture, private study spaces, and public areas replace classrooms, halls, and traditional school furniture. The learner is seen as a 'problem finding and stimulus seeking organism.'"

Learners are, of course, all of these things. It is appropriate that students in school should sometimes be good receivers of information, sometimes active learners within teacher-planned tasks, sometimes heavily involved with each other in discussion, and sometimes shapers of their own activities (the "stimulus seeking" learner). No one of these physical environments is the best; they are simply different and exist for different purposes. When we look for variety in the way teachers arrange their class space, it is not random change and variety for the sake of variety that we look for. Rather, it is patterns of space that support different forms of learning appropriate to a particular lesson's goal.

> **Patterns of space support different forms of learning.**

[Handwritten margin note: Space arrangement should be matched deliberately to the instruction]

Teachers can change Space arrangements quite quickly for different purposes. One high school teacher we know sometimes has four different arrangements for four successive periods. The changes are made easily and quickly because the students know the basic formats and do all the moving of desks in one or two minutes, usually between classes. The teacher spends time at the beginning of the year explaining these formats to the students and doing a bit of practice arranging them, so the students can set up quickly from then on.

On one day we observed, the first class (seniors) started with desks in rows for a recitation and presentation lesson on Russian short stories. The second class (juniors) quickly rearranged the desks into clusters of six and began "committee work," that is, cooperative teamwork on planning and preparing analyses of various American playwrights' works. The teacher signaled the format as students were entering the room, asking the first few students to set up for "committees" as they came in. Others then joined in. The third class (sophomores), again on signal, quickly put the desks in a large circle around the perimeter of the room for a discussion of a class book writing project involving elementary school children in a neighboring school. As a class, they were going to make some decisions and lay out a schedule for the project. The next period a new class (also sophomores) had a drill and practice lesson analyzing themes for variety in sentence pattern. Their desks were arranged, as you may have guessed, facing the teacher.

Some basic arrangements lend themselves more easily to this kind of flexibility. For example, "Mr. Orr's grade five class sat at individual desks placed around the perimeter of the room [perhaps facing the wall]. The open area at the center of the room was used for more of the formal instruction and for small group activities" (Winne and Marx 1982, p. 496). This type of arrangement gives students some privacy and insulation from visual distraction when they are doing individual work. For a class meeting, all they have to do is turn their chairs around and they're in a circle...the same for total group instruction. They can go to tables in the middle for small group work, either with a teacher or in cooperative groups.

As we look at our use of Space, we can note whether it is a rational use. That is, have we arranged things *deliberately* to best support the kind of instruction under way? If the answer is yes, we can go on to ask whether we vary the arrangement when our instruction changes. In this manner, our use of classroom space can be classified according to one of the following statements:

- *No teacher impact on space*: Teacher takes it the way it comes (from custodian, from previous period's teacher, from tradition).
- *Space arranged by teacher according to a conventional design*, and used conventionally, consistently, but without variation.
- *Space rearranged periodically but experimentally*, without clear rationale, mostly just for change itself.
- *Space arrangement constant but appropriate for instruction.*
- *Space used flexibly for different instructional purposes at different times, matched to curricular goals.*

Within a given arrangement of space, the placement of materials can further support instructional goals. We find primary grade teachers are often particularly thoughtful about the placement of various items in relation to each other. For example, art materials may be placed near a creative writing area to encourage painting as a follow-up to creative writing. This kind of attention to location and activity flow, though, applies equally well to senior high school. A display of nineteenth-century American art may be placed over the supply table where students periodically go for assignment sheets and to turn in papers in an English class. The display might serve as a stimulus for a unit on American authors of the period. References and connections to the pictures can be made when the instruction starts.

Ownership and Privacy

Lewis (1979) raises the issue of what spaces belong to the students in a classroom or a school. She provides the following list:

Desk	Probably the most valued and protected space. In very traditional classrooms it may be the child's only source of personal space. In more open classes it may be shared with others, or no longer be a part of the school furniture.
Locker	Often shared with others. Considered a convenience space.
Special Class Seat	In music, art, library, if seats are assigned, a certain degree of ownership will be attached to the seat.
Chair	Often individuals and the group will recognize individual ownership of chairs. Robert Sommer (1969) notes: "People who remain in public areas for long periods—whether at a habitual chair at a weekly conference or on a commuter train—can establish a form of tenure. Their rights to this space will be supported by their neighbors even when they are not physically present."
Boys' or Girls' Bathroom	Definitely a child's space and not a teacher's. A private retreat for tears, anger, fights, secrets, mischief and daydreams. In some schools it becomes the communal news center for the underground student communication network. In some secondary schools it may become the property of a group of students or it may be locked by the administration.
Playground	Child owned and shared with other children. Powerfully real and memorable considering the relatively limited time spent in recess.
Hall	A no-man's-land in most schools. A public avenue. Perhaps the sense of ownership would be similar to that felt for one's lane or street at home. In secondary school, the hub of socializing.

Classroom	A wide range of possible feeling here. In some rooms children feel a sense of ownership for the whole room or sections of it. In other rooms the desk may be the only owned space.
School Building	Feelings of ownership increase with the years spent in the building. Variations in intensity also depend upon school philosophies, building dimensions, and the degree to which children participate in school activities. (Lewis 1979, p. 130)*

Having a place of your own—not just a cubby or a mailbox—but a workplace to occupy that is regularly yours is a strongly felt need by many students. One of the authors consulted on a weekly basis in a school system for several years without such a space, and it drove him crazy!

Left on their own, junior and senior high school students regularly take the same desk in any given class. It becomes "their" seat. College students and adults do the same. As teachers plan classroom space, they should consider whether they have adequately met students' needs for ownership of space. That need varies considerably with individuals, as does their need for privacy.

Private spaces restrict visual distraction and noise—places like carrels or, at the most private, individual practice rooms. There are students who benefit greatly from having such places created for them or put at their disposal. Skillful teachers look for these individuals and match them with spatial arrangements that suit their needs. As they look at their classrooms and other school facilities (libraries, media centers), they ask themselves if enough private spaces have been provided to accommodate such students, because there are always some of them.

> *Placement of materials can support instructional goals.*

Recommendations on Using Space

The literature on use of school space is sparse and the research is even thinner. A series of interviews we once conducted showed support for the following ten recommendations. They are not what we could call a scientific knowledge base, but rather a useful conventional wisdom. They can serve as a checklist from which to survey one's classroom and make judgments. As with checklists in general, it reminds us to ask questions we might otherwise forget.

1. Materials students use should be visibly stored and accessible to facilitate efficient getting and putting away.

2. Avoid dead space, meaning, open purposeless space whose use lends itself to random or illegitimate student activity.

*Reprinted by permission of the publisher from Yamamato, K., ed., *Children in Time and Space*. (New York: Teachers College Press, 1977 by Teachers College, Columbia University. All rights reserved.) Excerpts from pp. 128–169.

3. In some settings, for reasons of safety or control, it may be appropriate for space to be arranged so the teacher can see all of it with no blind spots. (In other settings this guideline may be inconsistent with goals relating to trust, privacy, and independence.)

4. Vertical space (walls, dividers, closets, and movable cabinet doors) should be employed productively—for example, , for display, learning stations, or storage of materials-—effectively increasing usable space in the classroom. Hanging artifacts or displays from the ceiling, or multilevel use of space in addition to the floor (lofts, for example, or other erected structures), can further increase effective usable space within a room.

5. Dividers placed on a diagonal with respect to the 90-degree orientation of the walls can channel student movement and visual fields in interesting and deliberate directions.

6. Have a display area where students' work, art, and various other kinds of products can easily be seen and examined.

7. Keep active areas distant from quiet areas in a room to minimize distraction and interference.

8. Keep adjacent activity areas far enough apart, or clearly bounded from their immediate neighbor, so as to prevent distraction and interference.

9. Have clear traffic paths connecting functional areas of the room that do not necessitate students' walking through one area (and disturbing things there) to get to another.

10. Empty furniture absorbs energy. Therefore if you have fewer students than chairs in a secondary class, don't let the kids spread out around the periphery of the room with empty chairs between them and you. Either eliminate the empty chairs or move the students forward where they can be in contact with you and with each other.

Overall, the message we get from reviewing the literature on Space and classrooms is to be deliberate about its use. We can make our instructional spaces more attractive, more efficient, and more flexible; in short, we can control and change these spaces to best support instruction even as we move from lesson to lesson. 🐦

Checking on Space

Mark the descriptions that apply to these aspects of the use of Space in your classroom. N/A means "not applicable."

1. Which of the following describes the classroom arrangement:

   no teacher impact

   conventional

   varies experimentally

   uniform but supports instruction

   flexible, varies to support instruction

2. Is ownership and privacy provided for?　　　　N/A　　NO　　YES

3. Are private spaces made available for
   those individual students who need them?　　N/A　　NO　　YES

4. Are the following used?

   • visible, accessible storage　　　　　　　N/A　　NO　　YES

   • no dead space　　　　　　　　　　　　　N/A　　NO　　YES

   • no teacher blind spots　　　　　　　　　N/A　　NO　　YES

   • use of vertical space　　　　　　　　　　N/A　　NO　　YES

   • diagonal dividers　　　　　　　　　　　　N/A　　NO　　YES

   • display area　　　　　　　　　　　　　　N/A　　NO　　YES

   • active separated from quiet　　　　　　　N/A　　NO　　YES

   • boundaries between areas　　　　　　　　N/A　　NO　　YES

   • clear traffic patterns　　　　　　　　　　N/A　　NO　　YES

   • empty furniture effects minimized　　　　N/A　　NO　　YES

Space Quiz

This activity is intended to help you arrange your space to be congruent with your mastery objectives and the activities you have planned to reach them. Read each situation and explain or draw a map of how you might arrange the room and why. You might have several different arrangements in the course of one period.

1. You are a high school math teacher. Your objective is that students will successfully solve equations with binomials and polynomials. In the course of one 50-minute period, you have them go over their homework, hear a presentation from you on the new material, and begin to practice their homework on the new material while you circulate and give help when needed.

2. You are a second-grade teacher. You have twenty-four students. During the morning 3-hour block of time you want to have your students: (a) in a whole group to begin the day; (b) in cooperative groups of four for review and practice; (c) in learning buddies to work on a new assignment; (d) together for whole group instruction; (e) at learning centers to which students can go to practice when they have finished their assigned work.

3. You teach seventh- and eighth-grade science. You have a large room of which two-thirds is furnished with fixed lab tables. The remaining third has movable student desks and blackboards. You have lab stations and student desks for twenty-four students. Today is a lab prep for a lab on saturated solutions. You want students to review their homework, hear a brief summary from you on the definition of saturated solutions, hear the objective of the lab and the directions, and work with their lab group of four to plan how they will approach their task tomorrow.

4. You are teaching advanced placement American history to thirty students. You are in a room with six tables and five chairs at each table. The room is large enough so that you can move the tables to the wall and have room to arrange the chairs in other configurations. During the five days of classes this week you have the following activities planned: *Day 1*: Lecture and discussion; *Day 2*: Conferencing with individual students about their semester research paper, while remainder of the class meets in topic groups to compare bibliographies, outlines, idea, and problems; *Day 3*: Progress reports from each topic group, review of lecture and reading from Day 1, checking for understanding in learning buddies; *Day 4*: 20-minute video, each student writes a five-sentence reaction to the central theme of the video, meet in groups of three to compare ideas and reach consensus on a three-sentence reaction; and *Day 5*: Test. Draw the configuration of this room for each day, matching your arrangement with the activity/ activities for that day.

DAY 1   DAY 2

DAY 3   DAY 4

DAY 5

5. You are a fourth-grade teacher. You have twenty-eight students this year in a room that can comfortably hold twenty-six. You started using cooperative learning last year and want to continue this year, so you need some way to easily get students into cooperative groups of two, three or four. You also like to do a lot of checking for understanding with partners, sometimes partners that they can turn to and other times with partners they have to get up and move to. You have five computers in the room and you usually set up four learning centers which students go to for individual practice. You like to do whole group instruction, followed by smaller practice groups that you can circulate among and help. Draw some options for configuring this room to meet you needs. If you don't think you can meet them all, explain why.

Source Materials on Space

Abramson, P. *Schools for Early Childhood*. New York: Educational Facilities Laboratory, 1970.

Gross, R., and J. Murphy, *Educational Change and Architectural Consequences*. New York: Educational Facilities Laboratory, 1968.

Kohn, J. *The Early Learning Center*. New York: Educational Facilities Laboratory, 1970.

Kritchevsky, S., E. Prescott, and I. Walling. *Physical Space*. Washington, D.C.: NAEYC, 1969.

Lewis, B. V. "Time and Space in Schools." In *Children in Time and Space*, K. Yamamato (ed.), New York: Teachers College Press, 1977, 128–169.

Marshall, K. *Opening Your Class with Learning Stations*. Palo Alto, Calif.: Learning Handbooks, 1975.

School Review. Learning Environments Whole Issue 82, no. 4 (August 1974).

Winne, P. H., and R. W. Marx, "Students and Teachers View of Thinking Process For Classroom Learning." *Elementary School Journal* (May 1982): 496.

Zefferblatt, S. M. "Architecture and Human Behavior: Toward Increased Understanding of a Functional Relationship." *Educational Technology*, (August 1972): 54–57.

5

Time

How do I time events and regulate schedules so that students get the most productive learning time?

Allocation
Time to Learn
Instructional Time
Beginning and Ending Minutes
Pacing and Rhythm

Time is the currency of life, and teachers run the bank for their students about six hours a day—an enormously powerful position. They run the bank even for "free choice" times where the options available are those offered or allowed by the teacher.

When students do what, in what order, and for how long is largely under teacher's control; and we know from recent research that controlling it well has a big impact on student learning. This includes time spent in places other than the classroom too, places like the cafeteria. How long students spend in each of the environments school offers and the quality of that time is something faculty members control. This chapter is about being as deliberate as possible in managing student time use for maximum learning. It draws on the growing knowledge base of the field to help us be better time managers for our students.

> *Time is the currency of life, and teachers run the bank for their students.*

The issues of time management for students center around *allocation*, *efficiency*, and *pacing*.

Allocation

A superficial look at the research on student time use may prompt one to say, "So what else is new?" Obviously, if students spend more time on math and lose less time fooling around they will learn more math! But there is something new, and there are insights—perhaps surprises—for all of us when we start getting accurate data on how our students are really spending class time. Through the 1970s, time-on-task research worked its way through a series of more refined and powerful concepts as represented in FIGURE 5.1.

Starting with *Time in School*, each of the concepts of the chart includes and subsumes the one(s) below and inside its circle.

- *Time in School* is self-explanatory.
- *Allocated Learning Time* means time scheduled for academic work in a given area.

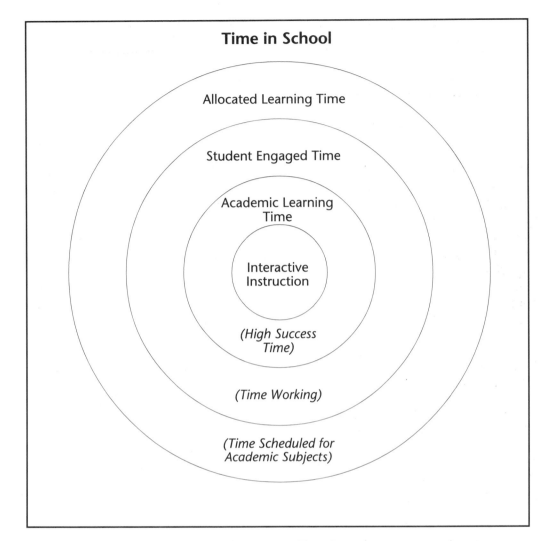

FIGURE 5.1: TIME-ON-TASK RESEARCH
Each concept in this diagram includes and subsumes the one(s) below and inside it.

> ◗ *Student Engaged Time* is the number of minutes students are actually working or attending during academic periods, and not daydreaming, fooling around, or getting organized.

> ◗ *Academic Learning Time* is the time students spend engaged with a high rate of success. The high success rate distinguishes it from Student Engaged Time and makes it a subset of Engaged Time.

> ◗ *Interactive Instruction* is time spent directly with a teacher getting instruction (one to one, small group, or large group), as opposed to time spent alone doing seatwork or projects or working with a group that's not interacting directly with an instructor.

Of the time spent in school, a portion is allocated for academics. Research has found little difference between Time in School across schools, but very big differences in Allocated Learning Time across schools and between classes. For example, as cited by Caldwell et al. (1982), Dishaw reports:

...time actually allocated for fifth-grade math ranged from 18 minutes to 80 minutes; allocated fifth-grade reading time ranged from 51 minutes to 195 minutes. Allocated time may also vary enormously within a class; for example, in one study (Dishaw 1977) one fifth-grade student spent 39 minutes each day on math while another student spent 75 minutes. These differences in actual allocated time suggest that some students may have two to four times as much opportunity to learn specific academic content as other students.

Time scheduled for different subjects should reflect some consensus across a school about what is important and what the priorities are within those things that are important, for there are surely many of them. Is it fair that because of a particular elementary teacher's talents and inclinations, her class gets a great reading and writing program but practically nothing else? One of the needs this Time parameter brings up is to look at students' school experience from a long-range point of view. Over the years, what amount of time is spent learning what subjects as a student goes through school? Is there some consistency and rationale to this expenditure of time? If not, then we are not really in control of the education we are delivering. If not, we do not even *know* what we are delivering.

While such wide variances might not show up in a similar analysis of allocated time in high school, they probably would for the next category.

Of the time allocated for academics, students are only engaged or attending for a portion of that time—on average about 75 percent of it. But there, also, the range of student engaged time is very big—50 to 90 percent (Fisher et al. 1978). It is the percentage of student engaged time as a percentage of allocated time that seems important, not just the absolute number of minutes.

Several studies indicate that engagement rates are significantly related to student achievement (Anderson 1975; Fisher et al. 1978). Thus variations in engagement rates are highly predictive of student achievement, accounting for as much as three-fifths of the variations in achievement (Bloom 1974). Reanalysis of the Stallings and Kaskowitz data (Rim and Coller 1978) showed that classrooms with more engaged time in reading or math generally showed higher achievement in that subject. However, gains in student achievement did not always directly vary with engaged time. For some grade levels and subjects the relationship between student achievement and engaged time leveled off and then became negative when engaged time was larger than a certain value." (Caldwell et al. 1982)

The above makes sense, given that some students master new material very quickly. For them, part of the engaged time can be wasted practicing material they already know.

About 25 percent of time allocated for academics seems, inescapably, to go into management tasks (getting papers, setting up equipment) and student inattention (daydreaming). Even the best classroom managers seem able to reduce this only slightly by squeezing 5 percent back from inattention. Thus, a 75 percent engagement rate is considered good. When students start falling below this, teachers should reexamine their management strategies and work to get engagement back up.

We also need to examine the *teacher's* engaged rate. What percentage of allocated time is the *teacher engaged with students* as opposed to preparing materials, correcting papers, or doing other management tasks? Research is clear that this percentage should be high (Stallings 1980). A major study of secondary school teachers found the average engaged rate to be 73 percent. Teachers who had lower rates of interaction with students had classes with significantly smaller achievement gains (or no gain at all), especially for low-performing students. This is true even if students are on task most of the time. As Stallings (1980) explains:

> The students are on-task, but the teacher is not teaching. In those classrooms where no gain was being made, the students were doing written assignments 28 percent of the time and reading silently 22 percent of the time, and teachers were doing classroom management tasks more than 27 percent of the time.

Finally, students experience a high rate of success for only a portion of the engaged time. That time is called "Academic Learning Time" in the literature (why not call it "high-success time"?) and as before, the amount of it students experience across classrooms varies hugely—in basic skill work, for example, anywhere from 16 minutes per day in a group of low-average classes to 111 minutes per day in a group of high-average classes. High- and low-average does not refer to the ability level of the students, by the way. It refers to the *teacher's* ability to get more Academic Learning Time for students. High-average teachers provide "more than twice as much academic learning time as in the average case and more than six times as much as in the low-average case" (Caldwell et al. 1982). These startling figures prompt us to take a careful look at how our students are experiencing school time, because high-success time correlates strongly with achievement, and data show that teachers who do study their time use make significant changes (Stallings 1980) and get better student learning.

> **Twenty-five percent of time allocated for academics seems, inescapably, to go into management tasks and student inattention.**

One of the authors once studied the time usage of students in five classrooms of a K-5 school using a technique adapted from Engel (1977). He scanned the class every five minutes, making a notation for each student on a class roster. The notation captured what the student was doing, and with what level of attention or involvement. From these data, a color bar graph was constructed for each student with colors coded to study activities showing student time use over a whole morning. Coded cross marks in black were overlaid on the color bar to indicate degrees of inattention or noninvolvement. Putting all the bars together on one graph for the class gave the teachers an enormous amount of data, both on individual students and on patterns across the class. One teacher was losing a great deal of time in classroom management: passing out papers, setting up in the morning, getting ready for transitions, etc. Another teacher had students with a low level of involvement due to social chatter at table groups—quiet, unobtrusive, but persistent and interfering with their work. Another teacher found her students were involved pretty consistently with individual tasks and projects, but sometimes received only 5 minutes of direct teacher instruction in the course of the day. All these teachers made changes to increase their effectiveness after they saw the data. The changes involved more attention to momentum, rearranging space, rescheduling their own instructional time, and clarifying their expectations for student behavior. The point we wish to make is that the obvious was not so obvious to them until they directly faced objective data about their own students and their own classes. When they had the data, they were able to improve their own effectiveness. Academic Engaged Time and student time spent in Interactive Instruction may sound obvious enough to you and me, but you may find some new priorities emerging when you get the numbers on your own classes.

Leinhardt et al. (1981) comment that "teachers must be vigilant in their search for children who are losing out. While the average off-task rate was 15 percent, some students were off-task more than 30 percent of the time. While the average amount of teacher instruction (in reading) was 16 minutes a day, the range was from 1.4 minutes per day to 35 minutes per day (within the same class). While the average time spent in silent reading was 14 minutes per day, some students spent no time at all reading silently. Fortunately, teachers can dramatically change the experience and performance of those students who seem to be losing out without changing things for those who are not." But first the teacher must become aware of who they are, and how the time is being lost.

Time to Learn

Benjamin Bloom's work on Mastery Learning has added another important concept to our knowledge base about time—time to learn. The idea is that most students can learn anything if they have the prerequisite pieces of knowledge and skill in place and are given adequate time to learn it. Giving them adequate time to learn doesn't mean giving them material and just waiting until they've gone over it long enough to absorb it; it means task analysis of new learnings, careful ongoing assessment, and reteaching loops for items and to students, who need it—and for only those who do.

The view of time from Mastery Learning puts teachers on the spot along with students. We can't just blame the students if learning isn't taking place. We must examine our own determination and be able to prove we are offering students appropriate-size bites of new learning; for instance, not leaving them in the dust with Chapter 2 if they haven't yet grasped the items in Chapter 1.

Mastery Learning is a form of individualizing instruction, but individualizing means more than self-paced here, more than marching through programmed material. It means clear and comprehensive sequences of instruction laid out in advance, broken down into pieces, and with options for how to deliver instruction of those pieces to students. Above all, it means monitoring what students know and not giving up until they have met mastery criteria.

Finally it means planning reteaching loops[1] and simultaneous extension activities for students who "got it" the first time around. Such a two-ringed circus presents management and planning challenges that are a stretch for teachers unused to managing multiple events in a classroom. It is also a good example of how the parameters of teaching are interdependent and ever present. Our brief examination of Time to Learn has led us back to Momentum, Space, Objectives, Learning Experiences, and Classroom Climate.

Instructional Time

Another area researchers have looked at is how much Interactive Instruction students experience, meaning time with a teacher actively working on material as opposed to seatwork, written assignments, or silent reading. For Interactive Instruction the findings have indicated: the more, the better (Stallings and Kaskowitz 1974). The point is simply that when teachers are teaching, students are more likely to be learning—and that workbooks and other solo assignments that occupy students' class time don't teach—not a very surprising finding when one considers the importance of teacher feedback, knowledge of results, degree of guidance, and other Principles of Learning we have considered previously. This finding has led some (Rosenshine 1981) to advocate the Direct Instruction pattern of teaching for whole class groups as the most efficient form of instruction. This recommendation really misses the point. Research is convincing that the proportion of Interactive Instruction time is important, but the Direct Instruction pattern is only one way to get it, and suitable only to one kind of teaching—skills. All the Models of Teaching in Chapter 10 can provide interactive teaching time. Peer tutoring can provide interactive teaching time. It is the attributes of Interactive Instruction that are important any way you get them, and those attributes are, it seems to us, clear explanation, prompt feedback, knowledge of results, and appropriate degree of guidance.

---

[1] For a detailed discussion of reteaching loops and the critical need to make being in one a valued event rather than a confirmation of one's dullness, see the Classroom Climate chapter.

Furthermore, there are learnings for which the Direct Instruction pattern is clearly not the only or the best way—like teaching students to evidence positions (see Jurisprudential Model in Chapter 10); like teaching the scientific method (see Discovery Model in Chapter 10). So, we urge our readers to put the current vogue for Direct Instruction in perspective. Direct Instruction is effective for teaching skills, and it works to the degree that it provides high proportions of Interactive Instruction time. But there are other learnings besides skills, and two dozen other models that can provide Interactive Instruction.

> *When teachers are teaching, students are more likely to be learning.*

Now, having said that, it is time to return to the point and ask ourselves and the teachers with whom we work if there really is enough direct teacher contact with students, regardless of the Model of Teaching in use. Individualized programs are at high risk here. If poorly managed, students, though active and involved, may get only a few minutes a day with the teacher and that is not enough. If that is happening to you, then either you need to do more group work or manage individualization so students get more feedback and guidance.

But how much time-with-teacher is enough? Rosenshine (1981) concludes, "Currently, the need for students to spend 60 to 75 percent of their time working alone is a fact of classroom life. Whether this percentage can be reduced, or whether instruction can be organized so students are more engaged when working alone, are major areas for future research." Thus, we can infer that 25 to 40 percent of a student's academic time directly involved with a teacher would be pretty good. There are certainly many classrooms where the figures are nowhere near that.

We must also remember that what goes on during the Interactive Instruction may or may not capture the essential attributes of good Direct Instruction. Leinhardt et al. (1981) found in a sample of classrooms that 14 of the 16 minutes of teacher instruction in reading went for "general instruction"—which sounds like presentation and direction giving. Of the remaining 2 minutes, students spent 1 minute completing a task in the teacher's presence, and 1 minute getting explanations of modeling of correct elements of reading. Thus, even within Direct Instruction time it is possible for students to get very little in direct feedback and clarification.

All of this leads us to wonder what accounts for the large differences in engaged time, high-success time, and interactive instruction time we find in different classes? What do the high-average teachers do that the others don't?

Skill at the Management Parameters (Attention, Momentum, Space) is a large part of it. Research from Kounin to Evertson and Brophy correlates student achievement with these teacher skills. They work to get more student engaged time and less time lost in management and disciplining. Thus, with more time spent in actual learning, one would expect better test results. It is interesting to note, however, that no matter how good a manager one is, "nonengaged time seems inevitable. In average classrooms, students are not engaged about 16 minutes per hour of allocated time in reading and math; the three high teachers reduced this amount to 12 minutes per hour. In classrooms of both average and high teachers, students spend eight to nine minutes in interim and wait time. Thus, the difference between the teachers who had the highest academic engaged minutes and the average teacher was about four minutes of nonengaged minutes per hour, and most of this difference occurred because the high teachers reduced off-task time to about four minutes per hour" (Rosenshine 1981). But the high teachers also allocated more time to the subject. So after Management skills we can add another to our list of reasons for the variation across classes in academic engaged time: clarity and deliberateness about priorities for time allocation.

Variance in high success time must be traced to the appropriateness of assignments, the diagnostic acuteness of the teacher, the adequacy of instruction and direction giving before students are turned loose on individual task—in other words, the teacher's skill at Clarity, Structuring Learning Experiences, and Matching Objectives to individuals and groups. But this is not much help if we are looking at Time as a parameter and wondering what skills are particular to managing it well. So far, we seem to be saying that good time management comes from handling a number of *other* parameters well. And, indeed, to a great extent it does. If you see students who are on task, productive, and experiencing success, you are seeing more than good time management; you are seeing successful education. Seen this broadly, good use of student time is a criterion for good teaching, an outcome of *all* the things that go into good education. But there are some skills that are distinctly part of efficient time management itself. Let's look at those aspects of the Time parameter that allow it to stand on its own as an area of teacher skill.

> ## *What happens at the beginning and end of a class period is best remembered.*

Beginning and Ending Minutes

In the Principle of Learning called "Sequence," we stated that what happens at the beginning and end of a class period or a lesson is best remembered. Teachers should therefore pay particular attention to what happens in these two slugs of time. We're talking about *short* slugs of time here—probably around 5 minutes. In what way should teachers take advantage of them?

The first lesson is simply not to waste them. Do not, if at all possible, let them be eaten up by organization and management—passing back papers, getting furniture arranged, getting kids seated, waiting for latecomers. Do not let the class end limply with students working on their own, starting homework, cleaning up, or socializing. Clean up the 5 minutes *before* the last 5 minutes and use the last 5 minutes to do something with the students: pull them together and have them highlight important points in today's lesson, lab, or whatever. Get them reviewing, summarizing, highlighting, or in some way engaging something important in those minutes.

Teachers with good Momentum skills are in the best position to take advantage of the opening minutes. Teachers who regularly summarize with students are likely to take advantage of closing minutes. But summarizing is not the only way to use closing minutes well. Giving assignments slowly and carefully, posing challenging dilemmas for students to ponder ("end without closure"), getting personal involvement or commitments from students on controversial issues or on contracts may be appropriate uses, too. The main point is to use it, not lose it. Give some sharp focus and purpose to the beginning and ending minutes.

Pacing and Rhythm

Matching has been an important theme with each parameter. We have advanced the notion that a parameter contains a repertoire and that skillfulness comes in matching choices from it to individuals, groups, and curricula. So it is with pacing and scheduling. The same pace will not work equally well for all classes. Carolyn Evertson (1982) found that the way teachers paced activities varied greatly and corresponded to their success with high- and low-performing classes, but made quite a difference in low-performing groups. Students in low-performing classes have a clear tendency to drop in and out of participation, especially during seatwork periods. Some students refuse to participate at all. Evertson provides descriptions and commentary on two junior high teachers' classrooms to show how differences in pacing affect low-performing students.* We start with Teacher B:

> (The teacher has just put the seatwork assignment on the board.) Marie says, "I don't have a book." The teacher says, "Look on those shelves," pointing. Marie says, "Those aren't ours." The teacher says, "Some of them are." Marie gets herself a book. Chico raises his hand and says, "I need help." About five students start the assignment right away. (There are 12 students present.) The others are talking, have their hands raised, or are going to the teacher's desk. The teacher says, "Come on up, Randy," when she calls on him. When he gets there, "Larry, leave him alone." Larry stands and visits by the teacher's desk. Chico puts his hand up again. The teacher says, "Chico, what do you need?" He says, "Help." The teacher says, "Okay, wait a second." Larry sits down by the teacher's desk and looks on as she tells him something. Chico calls out, "Miss ___ , are you going to help me?" She says, "Yes, Chico, but come up here." He says, "Aw, Miss, it's too far." The teacher ignores him, and he goes to the teacher's desk. (At this point, five students are at the teacher's desk.)

*Reprinted with permission. Evertson, C. "Differences in Instructional Activities in Higher- and Lower-Achieving Junior High English and Math Classes." *Elementary School Journal* 82/4 (1982): 329-350. © 1982 University of Chicago Press. All rights reserved.

This classroom description shows rather dramatically the difficulty students in a lower-performing class can have in getting started and participating successfully in an activity. At one point, five students were at the teacher's desk and most of them were waiting for help. (The teacher eventually helped nine students at her desk during this seatwork activity.) Having so many students in such close proximity to each other frequently created problems and led to misbehavior to which the teacher was forced to respond.

The dialogue also illustrates the poor task orientation which generally characterizes the lower-performing classroom. Chico's behavior here is typical of many slow students. He did not take academic activities seriously; he was not willing to begin work on learning tasks; and he was not interested in participating. Poor task orientation on the part of one student also can lead to disruptive behavior from others, as we find when we continue this activity:

> While the teacher is trying to work with Marie, Marie follows Chico's lead in teasing the teacher. She grabs the stapler. The teacher says loudly, "Uh uh, come on Marie." Later, Marie grabs her paper away from the teacher, wads it up, saying, "You wrote on my paper. You're not supposed to write on my paper." Marie sits down. Billy, meanwhile, has continued to play around and talk to Larry. The teacher says sharply, "Billy, you come up here!" Larry says loudly, "That's exactly what Miss ___ says, and it works for her, too." As Billy scoots his desk up, Larry sings, "Row, row, row your desk."

When the teacher had to give individual attention to so many students, she could not monitor the class efficiently, and it was more difficult for the students to get the teacher's attention according to the prescribed procedure.

> Chico, who has his hand up, calls out, "Miss, I can't wait forever." The teacher says, "Just a minute."—Mark yells loudly, "Miss!" The teacher ignores him and continues helping Marie. Then she goes to Pam, who has had her hand up for a long time. A girl calls out from the front of the room, "I need help." She has her hand up, but she calls out. The teacher looks at her and says, "Okay, I'll be there in a second."

It should be noted that two of these students here do not simply call out; they have their hands raised. However, they know that simply raising their hands is not as effective a signal as calling out. The teacher did not consistently enforce (in fact, hardly enforced at all) the rule against calling out under these circumstances.

> Chico calls out, "What time is it?" Billy tells him what time it is. The teacher ignores them both. Billy and Chico are trading epithets like, "Dumbhead." The teacher, helping the girls near the front, ignores them. Then, she looks up and says, "Chico, do you need something else to do?" Chico says, "No." The teacher says, "Then be quiet."

A basic conflict existed in lower-performing classes between two demands of the teacher: the need to help students and the need to control inappropriate, disruptive behavior. In this example, the teacher did not want to interrupt her interchange with the girls near the front, but she was finally forced to respond when their off-task behavior threatened to become disruptive.

The comparatively high achievement gain of Teacher F's lower-performing class recommends it for closer examination. Teacher F allocated considerably more time for checking and discussion of work (13.7 minutes) and the presentation of material—lecture or introduction to seatwork (14.4 minutes)—and considerably less time for the final seatwork activity (22.5 minutes) than was characteristic of the lower-performing classes in general. In addition, the lecture or introductory phase of seatwork was structured differently, frequently punctuated by two or more very brief, highly focused seatwork activities. In this class, the lecture or introduction to the final seatwork activity usually exhibited the following pattern:

> Teacher F goes to the board, where there are 25 numbers written, and begins rounding off the first one. He has the students do this on paper. He says, "I want you to do the first five." They are in columns of five. He continues, "Then put your pencils down." They are writing these numbers down and he moves around the room. He stops the class (after about 6 minutes) and asks David what his answers were. David frowns and says that he didn't get anything. "Who can help him out?" asks the teacher. Robert says, "I got it." The teacher moves on to the rest of the column and then goes on to the A column which should be rounded to the nearest hundredth. The students then do this column. Kermit calls out, "Are we going to have homework, too?" The teacher says, "I'll assign that in a minute." Kermit says, "Well, we don't have time to work on it if we're going to do all of these." Teacher F says, "Oh, we are not going to do all of these." The teacher goes to the board and asks for the students' attention and begins to go through the second column. He asks Jackie to help him round off the first, and she says she didn't get it. He says, "I just asked you to help." She looks at it and begins to try it. He walks her through the problem. (At this point, when there are approximately 10 minutes left, the teacher gives the seatwork assignment.)

Following is another instance of a lecture or discussion interrupted by brief seatwork periods.

> [The teacher] says that they will be talking about addition of decimals. He says that this is not really much different than adding whole numbers. The teacher has Johnny write the first problem out for him. He says to him, "Tell me what to put down." Johnny adds three and two and says that it's five. Then he adds six and nine and says that it's 15; put down the five and carry the one. The teacher then asks him, "Where do I put the one? Down here?" Johnny says, "No, you put the one over the eight." Then he adds the eight and gets nine. He tells him to put the decimal between the nine and the five. When he's through, the teacher says, "Very good." The teacher then starts asking them review questions on decimals. As he asks questions, he reminds students to "Raise your hands and tell me what place the

decimal is in." The teacher calls on Gracie to do the second example on the board. She declines, and then the teacher goes on to call on Edward. Edward works through the problem and then says, "Tell me what's wrong." The teacher says to him, "Well, let's find out. How can we tell?" The students call out that they can subtract to check. At 9:28 the teacher puts up a third example. He tells the class that they'll be doing the assignment on their papers, and that they should go ahead and do number three to see if they can get it right. The teacher starts walking around checking to see if students are getting the problem right. There's some quiet talking in the room and the teacher is still walking around. At 9:41 the teacher says, "Let's look up here." (He works the problem on the board. After that, he assigns them another problem to do at their seats and walks around checking them.)

Teacher F copes with the problem of sustaining seatwork in his lower-performing classes by incorporating some of the seatwork into the lecture (or introduction to seatwork) in very brief segments, placing the responsibility for maintaining lesson continuity with the students for only a very brief period of time. The advantages of this format appear clear. First, a very brief seatwork activity is more likely to have a high task orientation than an extended activity. Surrounding seatwork periods with lecture allows the more easily maintained lesson continuity of the lecture to help support seatwork. Second, these brief seatwork activities incorporated into the lecture enable the teacher to provide more immediate feedback than extended seatwork activities. The teacher can thus modify his or her explanations during the lecture, if necessary, rather than interrupt a long seatwork activity, as frequently happens in the lower-performing classes.

In summary, the lower-performing class of Teacher F presents an important contrast with Teacher B's lower-performing class. Teacher B had a significantly longer seatwork period and shorter checking and lecture activities, possibly adding to her difficulties, inasmuch as seatwork is often a problematic activity in lower-performing classes. In contrast, Teacher F minimized this problem in his lower-performing class by reducing the length of independent seatwork activity, which contributed significantly to the higher task orientation of his class, as determined by observer ratings. The comparison suggests that long, extended seatwork activities are counterproductive, adding to management problems and minimizing good task orientation in low-performing classes.

Many teachers in junior and senior high school have both high- and low-performing classes in their schedule. Are they able to make adjustments, such as Teacher F above did, and pace classes differently for different groups? That is what we mean by "Pacing and Rhythm" in the heading to this section. One can look to see teachers structure time for certain individuals, as Teacher F did for a whole class. And the reasons for varying it certainly go beyond the global word "ability." In the Evertson study, "ability" really meant achievement on C.A.T. tests. So what we had was a distinction between high- and low-*performing* classes. There are many reasons for high and low performance besides native ability with its implication about intelligence. Very capable but impulsive or disturbed students may learn best when their pacing is regulated for short bursts of highly focused activities. Skillful teachers look to create such arrangements for those who need it, while the rest of the class may be paced quite differently.

We should be able to look at how a teacher handles pacing and decide which of the following applies:

- *no pattern to pacing*
- *stable routine*
- *variations for teachable moments*
- *flexibility for changing curriculum priorities*
- *matching to individuals and groups* 🦢

Checking on Time

1. Does time allocation per subject match teacher and school priorities?　　　YES　　NO

2. Is student engaged time above 75 percent of the time allocated for academics?　　　YES　　NO

3. Does the teacher interact with students for 75 percent or more of allocated academic time (as opposed to using class time for organization and management tasks—correcting papers, preparing materials)?　　　YES　　NO

4. Do students get adequate time to learn with reteaching when necessary?　　　YES　　NO

5. Is high-success time adequate for students' independent work?　　　YES　　NO

6. Do individual students get enough interactive instruction time with teachers?　　　YES　　NO

7. Are beginning and ending minutes used fruitfully?　　　YES　　NO

8. Scheduling and pacing shows:
   - no pattern to pacing　　　YES　　NO
   - stable routine　　　YES　　NO
   - variations for teachable moments　　　YES　　NO
   - flexibility for changing curriculum priorities　　　YES　　NO
   - matching to individuals and groups　　　YES　　NO

Review of Concepts Defining Time in School

Briefly define the following concepts:

1.   Allocated Learning Time

2.   Student Engaged Time

3.   Academic Learning Time

4.   Interactive Instruction

Time Quiz

Check your understanding of the research on time management in schools by taking the True/False quiz below. Place a **T** *before those statements which are true and an* **F** *before those statements which are false.*

_____ 1. Most students can learn anything if they have the prerequisite knowledge and skill in place and are given adequate time to learn.

_____ 2. The amount of time students spend working on meaningful and appropriately matched tasks is significantly related to achievement.

_____ 3. Approximately 25 percent of time allocated for academics seems to go into organization and management tasks.

___T___ 4. When teachers are working directly with students (as opposed to preparing materials, correcting papers or doing management tasks) there are gains in student achievement.

_____ 5. Teachers who study their use of time can make significant changes and get better student learning.

_____ 6. When teachers are skilled in the management parameters (Attention, Momentum, Space, Time, Routines) student achievement rises because less time is lost in management and discipline.

_____ 7. What happens at the beginning and at the end of a lesson tends to be best remembered by students.

_____ 8. Pacing a lesson so that low-performing students have short bursts of focused activities may be an appropriate rhythm for these students, especially in heterogeneous classes.

_____ 9. When students have "high success time," their achievement increases.

Time Problems

Many areas in the knowledge base on teaching have an impact on time—momentum, routines, expectations, discipline, clarity, attention, space and others can all aid in giving teachers more productive time or taking away from what is presently available. The activity below is designed to show the interaction between other parameters of teaching and problems that present themselves initially as time loss or poor time on task.

In each of these situations, write what the teacher might do to become more efficient in the use of time.

1. At the beginning of the period the teacher spends 5 minutes taking attendance, talking to students who were absent the day before, and writing the objectives and itinerary on the board.

2. At the end of the period the teacher spends 5 minutes giving the homework assignment, collecting the papers from the day's class, and having the students straighten their chairs.

3. Each day in math class, the teacher spends 15-20 minutes having different students write each of the problems on the board and explaining their solution to the rest of the class.

4. Each day in this class, time is taken away from instruction by students who don't have a pencil, forgot their book, or didn't do their homework.

5. This teacher conducts a full-class review for a test by calling on students individually to answer questions. This activity takes the entire period of the day before the test.

6. In a 50-minute science class, the teacher shows a 30-minute videotape on volcanoes. Students answer questions in a whole group discussion for 15 minutes after the videotape and spend the last 5 minutes copying their homework assignment from the board.

7. This all-day kindergarten teacher spends 10 minutes of class time helping his students zip up their jackets, tie their hoods, and put on their boots for recess.

8. In getting ready for a seventh-grade life science lab, students go to the front of the room to pick up the solution, dissecting tools, specimens, and notebooks they need for the experiment. After 8 minutes all students have needed materials.

9. In an English class the teacher conferences with every student for 5 minutes while the remainder of the class does seatwork. This process takes two consecutive class periods.

10. In this learning center for special education students, the teacher has five students, all with different individual education plans. While working with the students one at a time she is frequently interrupted by the other four students who are attempting to do their seatwork and run into problems.

11. In physical education the teacher often loses the first 5 minutes of the 35-minute period because the class does not arrive on time.

12. When this fifth-grade teacher is working with a small group of students, students who finish their seatwork early often interrupt because they have nothing to do.

13. This teacher is meeting with a series of literature groups during the morning in a fifth grade. She is having problems with transitions and often loses time when she finishes one group and calls up another.

14. This teacher often starts class by having students compare homework answers in pairs. But students who were absent or who have brought no homework have nothing to do. If he makes them third wheels in functioning pairs, some of them tend to be disruptive.

15. This group of low-achieving students meets the last period of the day. They seem tired and are slow to respond to directions and the lecture-recitation format the teacher has planned for them.

16. In band class time is lost at the beginning of the period while students set up and tune their instruments. When the teacher stops them during their performance to make corrections, students talk to each other or fool around with their instruments.

17. In a K-6 school, the art teacher is often interrupted by students who are sent to pick up materials for other classes. In addition, she has five classes each day, usually from different grade levels. She loses time at the beginning of each class trying to make the switch in materials and in her lesson plan. How can she maximize student engaged time?

18. Teachers in this high school are changing from 50-minute classes each day to 80-minute classes two out of every three days. They are worried about what they will do to occupy their students for 80 minutes and what they will do if a student is absent and doesn't have class for two or three days.

19. This middle school is changing from grouping students in low, middle, and high achievement groups to heterogeneous groups for all subjects. Teachers are worried about how they will meet the needs of all of their students.

20. In this high school, students who play on athletic teams often miss their last class of the day so they can get to their games. Teachers are worried about how these students will keep up with the rest of the class.

Source Materials on Time

Anderson, L. W. "Student Involvement in Learning and School Achievement." *California Journal of Educational Research* 26 (March 1975): 53–62.

Bloom, B. S. "Time and Learning." *American Psychologist* 29 (September 1974): 682–688.

Caldwell, J. H., W. G. Huitt, and A. O. Graeber, "Time Spent in Learning." *The Elementary School Journal* 82/5 (1982): 371–480.

Dishaw, M. "Descriptions of Allocated Time to Content Areas for the A-B Period." *Beginning Teacher Evaluation Study Technical Note Series, Technical Note IV-2a*. San Francisco: Far West Laboratory for Educational Research and Development, 1977.

Engel, B. S. *Informal Evaluation*. Grand Forks, N.D.: University of North Dakota Press, 1977.

Evertson, C. "Differences in Instructional Activities in High and Low Achieving Junior High School Classes." Paper presented at the Annual Meeting of the American Educational Research Association, Boston, Mass., April 1980.

Evertson, C. "Differences in Instructional Activities in Higher- and Lower-Achieving Junior High English and Math Classes." *Elementary School Journal* 82/4 (1982): 329–350.

Fisher, C. W. et al. *Teaching Behaviors, Academic Learning Time and Student Achievement: Final Report on Phase III-B, Beginning Teacher Evaluation Study*. San Francisco: Far West Regional Laboratory, 1978.

Hillerich, R. L. "That's Teaching Spelling???" *Educational Leadership* (May 1982): 615–517.

Karweit, N., and R. E. Slavin, "Measurement and Modelings Choices in Studies of Time and Learning." *Educational Research Journal* 18/2 (Summer 1981): 157–172.

Leinhardt, G., N. Zigmond, and W. M. Corley. "Reading Instruction and Its Effects." *American Educational Research Journal* 18/3 (Fall 1981): 343–361.

Powell, M., and M. Dishaw, "A Realistic Picture of Reading Instructional Time." *Reading Research Quarterly* (1981).

Rim, E., and A. Coller. *In Search of Nonlinear Process-Product Functions in Existing Schooling Effects Data: A Reanalysis of the First-Grade Reading and Mathematics Data from the Stallings and Kaskowitz Follow Through Study*. Philadelphia: Research for Better Schools, Inc., 1982.

Rosenshine, B. V. "How Time is Spent in Elementary Classrooms." *Journal of Classroom Interaction* 17/1 (Winter 1981): 16–25.

Stallings, J. A. "Allocated Academic Learning Time Revisited, or Beyond Time on Task." *Educational Researcher* 9/11 (December 1980).

Stallings, J. A., and D. H. Kaskowitz. "Follow Through Classroom Observation Evaluation, 1972–1973." Menlo Park, Calif.π: Stanford Research Institute, 1974.

6

Routines

What procedural routines are important, and how do I get maximum mileage out of them?

Clear Communication and Standards
Matching Routines to Purposes

Where would we be without routines in our daily lives: routines for getting up and ready for the day; routines for finding and storing important items at home and at work; routines for doing certain recurring tasks? By "routine," we mean any recurring event or situation for which there could conceivably be a regular procedure.

Clearly, routines are essential to our daily lives. We all have hundreds of routines that we practice unconsciously; they become layered one upon another, operate automatically, and free us for the more thoughtful and interesting projects we may wish to address. The same applies to the role of routines in the organization of classroom life. Good routines are important, even vital, to successful classrooms. When they are poorly thought out—or not thought out at all—the results are seen in disorganization, poor momentum, and often discipline problems.

Classroom routines need to be *efficient*, and they need to be *clear*. The students need to know what the routines are and how to do them. We will highlight those two notions in this chapter, plus the idea that routines can teach. Routines themselves can be curriculum, by virtue of their particular purposes and the learnings embedded in them.

The Routines parameter encompasses a variety of kinds of classroom routines. Some routines pertain to *housekeeping* (e.g., attendance; lunch and milk counts; getting and/or maintaining supplies; organizing boots and coats; clean-up; snack distribution). Other routines pertain to operational features of *class business* (e.g., making announcements; noise-level control; leaving the room; turn taking and population limits; what to do with the first ten minutes of the day or of the period; how to carry chairs, scissors, pencils, etc.). Still others pertain to *work habits and work procedures* (e.g., how to sit; how to study spelling words; use of lab equipment; procedures for using an easel; what form to use on book reports; a timetable and milestone chart of events to be checked by the teacher when students are preparing an oral report or a term paper). When skillfully performed, all of these routines are valuable ways of organizing and managing a class.

> **Routines can teach by virtue of the learnings embedded in them.**

Clear Communication and Standards

To get the most out of routines, teachers need to communicate them clearly. The first set of questions to ask about the use of routines concerns expectations: Do the students know clearly what's expected of them in the way of procedures and routines? Do they know what they're supposed to do?

Teacher behaviors that account for *good communication* of routines are similar to those for communicating expectations for work. Good communication of routines is:

- ▶ *direct:* routines are explicitly brought to students' attention.
- ▶ *specific:* all important details are explained.
- ▶ *repeated* to make sure students absorb them.
- ▶ *communicated with positive expectancy*—a "you can do it" flavor.
- ▶ *modeled.*
- ▶ *tenacious* in persistently (within reason) addressing routines until students master them.
- ▶ *consistent:* especially in that the teacher reacts whenever expectations for routines aren't met.

Similarly, the same kind of thinking applied within the Expectations parameter also goes into examining the *appropriateness of the standards* inherent in the routines, and how the standards are adjusted (matched) for individuals and groups. Therefore, as with standards for Expectations, standards for Routines can be viewed along the scale below (see the Expectations chapter for expanded definitions):

- ▶ *none* exist
- ▶ *few consistent* standards are used.
- ▶ *low:* teacher demands less of students than she or he might.
- ▶ *too high:* teacher demands too much of students.
- ▶ *average:* standards are appropriate for most students.
- ▶ *inspirational and vague:* teacher motivates students, but the standards for their behavior are unclear.
- ▶ *high but reasonable:* standards are very demanding but attainable by students.

As with academic work, it is in our interest and that of our students to match standards for routines to the needs of individual students or groups. (See the Expectations chapter for a discussion of various levels of matching standards.)

Now, with those issues under our belt, we're ready to move into new ground: What about the routines themselves? Why *are* they as they are, and how much mileage is being gotten out of them?

Matching Routines to Purposes

The nature of classroom routines is determined by the teacher by abdication, by negotiation, or directly. Seven levels of performance that describe teachers' use of routines can be distinguished:

1. *No conventions or procedures* for relevant events: ad hoc teacher reactions.

2. *A few conventions erratically followed.*

3. *Stable routines* for most relevant events, usually established through training.

4. *Stable and highly efficient routines* for all relevant events.

5. *Varied routines:* the teacher modifies, experiments, uses alternative forms.

6. *Routines matched to the group.*

7. *Routines matched to characteristics of individuals* and mapped to goals for them.

This scale spans a range of answers to the question: Why are our routines the way they are? They may serve efficiency and, indeed, this is a valid and common orientation among teachers. They may serve a general goal— giving students security through the predictability of certain recurring events. They may map to more specific goals for groups or for the class as a whole, such as having students routinely record books they have read in a register so that they take some responsibility for a form of record keeping and get to see and participate in building a cumulative index of their books read; or assigning teams to areas of the room for clean-up so that the children have to come to grips with group responsibility, handling the division of labor, and dealing with individuals who won't carry their weight.

Routines may be created or adjusted by teachers in the service of objectives for specific individuals. For example, in a primary-grade class, Tim may start each day by taking down a few chairs and then moving into woodworking or clay—something with a motor emphasis; whereas Josh's starting routine may be worked out to reflect academics and time in a private space. In an older class in which students are routinely expected to check the noteboard for morning assignments or for feedback from previous work, Clara may need a personal "greet" and escort over to the noteboard, or a folder of her own in which this information is placed. Tenth-grader Margaret may be asked to end each study hall with a log entry on what she's accomplished as a way of focusing her. Marvin may be asked to arrange the furniture for committee work at the beginning of each social studies period as a way of settling him down (and getting him to class on time).

Following are some examples of procedural routines that serve different purposes. Some serve efficiency and effectiveness—a worthy goal. These are related to momentum; that's the kind of efficiency meant here—an efficient flow of events without delays. For example, one such routine is:

Finished work goes in my "in" tote tray; workbooks are left open to first page needing correction. This eliminates the problem of "What do I do with this paper?"

Other routines are aimed at increasing the effectiveness of cognitive learning. They are routines oriented toward academics. For example:

Word Bank and Word File are ongoing collections of words the children have found hard to spell. The student finds the correct spelling of a word, writes the word on a card, and then tapes the card to the "word bank," which is a set of twenty-six pockets—one for each letter of the alphabet—mounted on the wall. Cards are later filed in a permanent "word file" for future use in spelling.

A third group of routines shows how much additional mileage can be gotten out of routines if they are used thoughtfully and deliberately. These routines reveal what many would call the "hidden curriculum": the indirect *personal and social learning* students receive just from being present in a particular classroom. "Personal learning" refers to students' learning something about themselves or some ability that might be described in terms of character development rather than skill. "Social learning" refers to students' learning something about others, about groups, about people together (cooperation, sharing). An example of such a routine is:

> ## *Additional mileage can be gotten out of routines—the "hidden curriculum."*

After I call on the first student to read, he in turn calls on the next reader. This keeps a larger percentage of the students involved. It also raises questions of fairness (boys shouldn't only call on other boys) and consideration of differential reading abilities.

We believe that teachers should be as aware and explicit as possible about their hidden curriculum, and it is through this parameter that they can see much of it. If teachers want, they can make their routines serve multiple purposes. 🐦

Checking on Routines

1. Check any aspects of the communication of routines that apply, and see if you can cite an occasion to back up your claim with something that was said or done.

    ___ direct

    ___ specific

    ___ repeated

    ___ with positive expectancy

    ___ modeled

    ___ tenacious

    ___ consistent

2. Circle the one that applies. The standards embedded in the routines are:

    none

        few consistent

           low

              too high

                average

                  inspirational—vague

                    high but reasonable

3. Matching: Circle the performance level that applies.

    no routines

        few erratic routines

          stable routines

            stable and highly efficient routines

              varied routines, alternatives

                routines match group

                  routines match individuals

Routines Summary

Routines Quiz

To illustrate the array of purposeful routines that can comprise a teacher's repertoire, we have provided a sampling of routines in the following quiz. Label each routine by the general purpose you believe it serves: momentum; academic; or personal and social learning. This exercise will help reinforce for you the intentions that may underlie different routines.

After you label the routines, think about your own classroom routines. What routines do you use that are momentum related? that have cognitive learnings built in? that foster particular personal or social learnings? Is there any way you could milk your routines for more, develop them for bigger payoffs?

The following are actual routines as reported by the teachers who use them. (We have commented within brackets upon some of them.) For each of the routines, label one or more of the following in the margin:

▶ *Momentum*

▶ *Academics*

▶ *Personal and social learning (abbreviate this PS).*

To help make your choice, ask yourself what the routine is for—what it seems to accomplish. Then decide which of the three categories that purpose seems to fit best. Some may overlap two categories. Review the examples provided earlier in the text if needed. Answers are given at the end of this section.

1. "Extra credit on enrichment papers: If a student finishes a math or reading assignment early, I have a set of follow-up 'fun' sheets that give extra practice in or extension of the concept we are studying. I give the set of papers to the first student finished, and I then direct other early finishers to get their extra credit papers from that first student. This gives the first student finished early some extra responsibility, and it frees me from breaking up another group to get enrichment materials."

2. "When we go somewhere, I ask the first child in line to hold the door. He then goes to the end of the line. This has helped eliminate some of the rush to be first since he who is first shall be last. There is often no rush for second because usually we go through several doors."

3. "The children are given a new pencil at the beginning of each month. Except on rare occasions, they will not be given another one until the following month (they must borrow one or bring one from home). This discourages misplacing pencils."

4. "Story folders contain all second drafts of a student's writings. They give each child the ability to reread a past story, to note improvement, and to simply enjoy his or her own stories. Also nice to have during conferences."

5. "Children who come to work with me as a specialist each have a folder in which they keep work papers completed and others still to be done or in process. These folders are kept in a plastic milk carton crate with oaktag dividers for each group. When the children come to their session, they get their materials from the box. On the outside of the folders lists can be kept that indicate books read, materials being used, schedule of sessions and other pertinent information."

6. "Each Friday morning, I sit down with a predesignated student [presumably different each week]. Together we mark out a dummy copy of the weekly [class] newspaper. I guide the story, and the student writes it correctly. Then the student copies it over on a master. This provides a positive writing experience for the student. There is little technical risk, and the feedback helps to encourage other types of writing."

[This also provides guaranteed one-to-one time with each student periodically for an extended period of time. Although around an academic/fun activity, it gives the opportunity for teacher-student relationship building, important to good teaching. As an activity it also affords opportunity for community building in the classroom; the articles may be directly about the class, its members, and things they did or things that happened to them together over the past week. Thus, the newspaper creates a kind of class history and can be compiled over the year. Everybody's interested in reading it when it comes out that afternoon. After all—it's about them!]

7. "Another technique I have learned aids in math boardwork. If we are working on unlined math papers, I guide the class in folding the paper before we begin. This creates boxes for the problems and helps organize the paper. It is also a lesson in the exponential powers of 2."

[Some teachers insist math be done on large-box graph paper only to aid in the organization and alignment of columns. They then reduce the size of the boxes and gradually fade out the use of graph paper, demanding that students keep work aligned and organized.]

8. Posting long-term assignments on the board, with deadlines and expecting students to work on them with free class time, helps the children take the responsibility of organizing their time to do the assignments, and by checking the list frequently it helps them to learn to meet deadlines."

[This routine is concerned with students' learning to manage their time—to plan projects that have parts and apportion tasks to time periods so that they meet a deadline. Children may not, however, be very good at this, and the procedures should accommodate some teaching or some strategies to help them learn time management. The first part of the strategy is to give the assignment with the deadline. This gives students the opportunity to succeed and also to fail. Thus the questions can be asked: "How did you/what did you learn from this experience? How can you fix that next time?" Provisions have to be made for asking those questions to individuals. Some teachers provide check-in points along the way where students have to report how far they've gotten in a long-term assignment. They may reserve certain free periods or regular class periods for meeting briefly with every student to check progress. These brief check-ins, in addition to providing feedback on how work is going and motivating some laggards to get in gear, may be opportunities for a needed bit of tutoring or explaining or redirecting. In teaching students time management and organization, the question is, what aspect of your procedures helps them learn that, beyond just giving them responsibility for long-term assignments?]

9. "Three times a week the class has a period of silent reading, at which time the children may read books, magazines, articles, and other materials of their choice. At the end of the period they add to a list, which is kept in their folder, the title of the reading material they read that day and also they indicate the date. I have the children keep this record and collect the sheets about once a month. This helps me keep tabs on what they are reading and to see if they are selecting books at their reading level. I feel it helps the children also to be conscious about how much they are reading. It seems to give some of them a really supportive boost!"

10. "Today's Work Chart lists the work to be done each day [large piece of paper, two axes, students' names up the side, kinds of work across the top; thus, a matrix. Students can look across opposite their name and see which tasks have been marked for them to do]. This chart provides a means of individualizing daily assignments and holds children accountable for knowing what they should be doing each day. Children check off assignments as they are completed, giving them a sense of control."

[Often for a couple of children in the class it is very effective to make a personal work chart or have the student make it. The student keeps it nearby and checks off things as they are accomplished. The student also builds in, through negotiation with the teacher, activities she or he especially likes to do. The chart can cover a period from one day to one week.]

11. "When students are singled out to do something special in class, such as coming up to play a rhythm instrument, I vary the routine of choosing who participates in these ways: (1) Number off down the row. (2) Begin at either the top or the bottom of the class list. (3) Have the children who have already played give their instrument to a 'quiet' person who hasn't played."

12. "Weekly clean-up. On Friday afternoon, I assign students to clean or straighten certain areas of the classroom. I alternate the jobs, and on some weeks kids may have no assignment. Then they can straighten their own desks or notebooks. This gets a clean, neat classroom and cooperation on the job."

    [It's not clear here, but perhaps teams of students are assigned to the areas of the room. Some teachers do that to encourage cooperation; the group is responsible for getting its job done. This raises questions such as, "What if one member of the team doesn't carry his own weight? How will the team work out such conflicts?" This is an opportunity to teach conflict resolution strategies. It also creates situations where students may accommodate one another by letting a fellow student in a jam finish an assignment and cover for him or her in cleanup.]

13. "Give students options of any one of three ways for l e a r n i n g new vocabulary words: flash cards, write the word three times with meaning, or make a 'flip-sheet' for studying and saying the word with its meaning. This helps students learn alternative ways of memorizing and, hopefully, discover the one which works best for them."

14. "I have often prepared visuals to organize the time when students are arriving at and settling in for class activities. At various times the transparencies may contain quizzes to review skills, directions for an activity that might involve special preparation of a paper (i.e., margins, numbering, etc.) for work that will follow, a list of words to be copied into notebooks, or instructions for specific group work. In the upper right-hand corner of the transparency I indicate the time at which the overhead will be turned off. Students understand that I expect work directed on the transparency to be completed by that time.

    "I've found that this technique encourages prompt arrival at class, provides a focus for student attention from the time they arrive, and gives me a chance to take care of routine matters without having students slip into conversations or other involvements that must be cut off in order for class to begin."

15. "I have a decorative tin can sitting on my desk with a sign 'Notes from Home.' The children are to put notes that they bring in the morning in the can. This way I'm not interrupted each time a child comes in with a note, and it enables the children to have a place to put them if I am busy at the time."

[Some teachers use a similar device for receiving notes from the children in the class who are finding it hard to get the teacher's ear or who have a private message they would rather write than say directly. In both this and the above case, the teacher has to remember to look in the note can or box periodically. That proves to be no obstacle, however, if it is regularly used.]

16. "The art cart always carries half the boxes of crayons, pastels, and marker sets needed to give each child a set. Sharing and mutual responsibility are the goals."

[Here we have planned scarcity to make children learn how to deal with it. This kind of planned scarcity also requires good mediating skills from the teacher. Active listening is appropriate here, as is Glasser's "what are you going to do about it then" approach. (See Discipline chapter.)]

17. "As one or two children approach a finished product (this is a manipulative, project-oriented class), the new lesson is then introduced [to everybody; presumably the teacher calls for everybody's attention and introduces the new project]. The new materials are left on the table so the children can start their new projects by themselves when they finish the old one. Finished products are put in the cabinet. Then I take children who are finished and show them a next logical step with the project they've just finished (enrichment). I give them the option of starting the new project or going one step further with the one they've just completed. Nine out of ten times they are motivated enough to continue the old project."

[In project or lab-oriented courses, the procedure tends to keep the class together, even if students work at widely different rates, offers enrichment to those who will benefit from it, and minimizes confusing transitions.]

18. "Papers are passed in from two certain people moving in opposite directions. This I do to facilitate paper collection, avoiding wasting of time." [Two people are probably opposite the teacher in a circle and sitting next to each other. They start the passing in opposite directions.]

19. "Assignments are designed to permit students to help each other at the same time that each is required to give individual answers. This supports students' learning from each other and legitimizes talk among peers in class by making it work related. It makes copying obvious and unacceptable."

[This introduces the subject of cooperative learning and how to structure assignments and working environments so that it takes place productively, a topic explored in Chapter 15.]

20. "Instruments in the musicmobile are distributed in an assembly fire-brigade fashion, when each child is to have an instrument. The teacher can remain at the front of the group as the instruments move and not lose momentum."

[This also gives each student something to do, but probably requires practice with a group, especially younger students, so a child who drops an instrument doesn't cause a traffic jam.]

21. "Students will bring the correct books to class according to the 'book chart' in my classroom. The reason is to avoid excuses."

[It could be that this book chart is posted on the door or in some other highly visible spot so that students see as they go out or come in what books are required for the next class.]

22. "As a motivation to speed up and ensure student completion of revision activities for writing projects, use masking tape or colorful tapes to divide a large bulletin or chalk board into a series of frames, each large enough to display a student's final draft and each labeled with an individual student's name. As students complete work and have it checked, they are permitted to display it in their personal frames. P.S. The idea works! Students are very anxious to fill in their frames."

23. "Two girls or boys are responsible, on an alternating basis, for taking the morning attendance and delivering it to the office. This develops responsibility and cooperation and allows me to talk with students informally in the morning when I can often catch an important fact about what has happened recently in the student's life."

[The important thing here is the teacher's goal: to have the first five to ten minutes of the day free of any management tasks so that the teacher can make personal contact with some students. The point of this contact may be relationship building, getting information, or filling full the cup of an attention-demanding child early on so she or he doesn't have quite the need to get attention later and fracture class momentum in doing so.]

24. "Every week or two I hold a lottery and parcel out jobs to my class. The whole process of choosing deals with arithmetic, chance, choice, reading, and so forth."

25. "When presenting a musical play to the school or to parents, these rules are followed: (1) Participants arrive one hour early and meet in the music room for makeup and final touches on costumes. (2) Only the stage manager, lighting people, and stage hands are allowed in the auditorium before the performance. (3) When everyone is ready, songs from the play are sung for a warm-up and solo songs are begun but not finished. (4) During the performance, everyone not on stage at the moment remains in the room—not behind stage or milling about in the halls. (5) An attempt is made to keep everyone in a calm state, rather than

allowing loud, boisterous behavior before the performance. (6) All the leads are responsible for their own props. (7) Each student is responsible for his or her own costume before and after the performance.

"Following these criteria guarantees the best possible performance."

26. "Bulletin board: Any articles from local papers that might interest the students or include their name(s) are put up on the bulletin board. I also put up the weekly lunch menu, various cartoons that the kids would like, pictures, or poems. The kids also can bring in clips to display. Kids take pride in seeing their names in print. I can also follow up class topics."

[The last phrase, "follow up class topics," puts this procedure in the cognitive category. But there are other things going on here, too. The whole thing might be seen in terms of its role in community building in the classroom. The board happens to be located by the door, is often seen, and is the topic of conversation while students are lining up or just coming into the room. It seems intended to be a conversation stimulator. This raises the question of displays in general and challenges us to get as much mileage out of them as we can, besides reinforcing skills and looking attractive.]

27. "When children are involved in a variety of activities, I take a moment to glance quickly about the room and note [on paper] where each child is and with whom. This gives me concrete information regarding children's choices of materials and friends. I can see activity patterns forming. It also gives me insight to make constructive suggestions or introduce another concept to some activity and/or children."

[Anecdotal notebooks can be used for note taking and record keeping throughout the grade levels. When used in this way the teacher does not have to reserve time at the end of the day to sit down and record anecdotal notes for each child. Instead, a class roster in a looseleaf notebook is dated with the current date and left open on top of a cabinet, shelf, or desk. Teachers write words or phrases next to students' names as things come up, or when they happen to be passing the shelf where the notebook is kept. The notes might be about activities, behavior, skill needs, or virtually any kind of performance. If the blank back of yesterday's roster is used to write or block out today's plans, the notebook may double as a plan book. The notes beside students' names may indicate things to get to with them today—reminders for the teacher. They also constitute an ongoing and cumulative record of student performance with dates. This is a rich database difficult to get any other way and very useful at conferences.]

28. "When square dancing or any kind of dance involves a partner of the opposite sex, I make it clear that: (1) As boys are chosen they are asked to fill in the first, second, third, or fourth place in each square. (2) Girls are then numbered off and asked to go to a certain square and stand by whatever boy has the corresponding number. (3) After each dance, the girls switch to another square but keep their same number positions. (4) No one is allowed to make derogatory comments about his/her own partner or anyone else's partner. (5) No one is forced to dance if he or she doesn't want to. (6) Those students not participating are assured they can come up next and either form a new square themselves or choose a partner by taking someone's place who has already danced. These procedures encourage consideration of each other, especially in a situation that at first feels a little uncomfortable because of the closeness of the opposite sex."

Quiz Answers

 1: Momentum and Academics

 2: Momentum

 3: PS

 4: Academics

 5: Momentum

 6: PS and Academics

 7: Academics

 8: PS

 9: Academics

10: PS

11: Momentum

12: PS

13: Academics

14: Momentum

15: Momentum

16: PS

17: Momentum

18: Momentum

19: PS

20: Momentum

21: Momentum

22: Academics and PS

23: PS and Momentum

24: Academics

25: Momentum

26: Academics and PS

27: Momentum

28: PS and Momentum

Source Materials on Routines

Randolph, N., and W. Howe. *Self-Enhancing Education*. Palo Alto, Calif.: Stanford Press, 1966.

Taylor, J. *Organizing the Open Classroom—A Teachers' Guide to the Integrated Day*. New York: Schocken Books, 1972.

Special Note

We appreciate the contributions of the following teachers, who were kind enough to share some of their routines with us: Nadine Bishop, Steve Bober, Peggy Bowlby, Jeff Levin, Ann Lindsay, Barbara Lipstadt, Betty Murray, David Negrin, Loren Robbins, Sally Springer, Gene Stamell, Bill Tate, Alan Ticotsky, and Joe Walsh.

7

Discipline

How do I deal with very resistant students?

Causes

Expectations and Consequences

Giving Students Control
and Responsibility

Six Models of Discipline

Matching

Responses to Illegitimate Behavior

Section I
Introduction and Overview

"What do I have to do to get students to apply themselves to their work and stop fooling around and being disruptive?" That is the bottom line question of the Discipline parameter. Many teachers spend a disproportionate amount of energy dealing with it; some leave teaching because they find they rarely deal with anything else. There is no question that good discipline is a prerequisite for good education; we must bring all of our best knowledge to bear on it so we can stop the needless hemorrhaging of both teacher and student energy that it causes. We have the knowledge and the capability to retire this issue and to move on to the question most teachers are more interested in, namely, "How do I build self-discipline and responsibility in students?"

In this chapter we will address both questions, but first things first. If students are inattentive and disruptive, there may be one or more of the following causes at work:

1. Poor general management (Attention, Momentum, Space, Time, Routines, Personal Relationship Building)

2. Inappropriate work that is too hard, too easy, or a glaring mismatch to students' learning styles (Objectives, Learning Experiences)

3. Boring instruction (Learning Experiences)

4. Confusing instruction (Clarity)

5. Unclear expectations and consequences (Expectations)

6. Student sense of powerlessness

7. Physical causes

8. Ignorance of how to do the expected behaviors

9. Value clashes

10. Heavy emotional baggage students bring with them (e.g., being convinced one is a failure)

Figure **7.1** represents these causes and some indicators. Let's take a quick look at the 10 causes and go into a few of the more important ones in depth.

The first four causes all have to do with other parameters, some of which we've treated earlier in this book. If these basic classroom management parameters (Attention, Momentum, Space, Time, Routines, Personal Relationship Building) are not in good shape, discipline problems will result. When there are discipline problems, these are the first places to look, especially if the problems are endemic to a whole class, because, for example, kids with time on their hands will find an outlet somewhere for their energy and creativity—and that outlet may well be disruptive. (With prolonged boredom, disruptions are probably a sign of mental health and physical vitality in normal kids.) Thus, competent handling of Space, Time, Momentum, and Personal Relationship Building forms a foundation for good behavior. Conversely, absence of their skillful handling creates distraction, fragmentation, downtime, and resentment.

Even if these parameters are well managed, we need to make sure the work is appropriate for the kids (Objectives). If it is too hard or too easy, then we risk frustration or boredom—either of which may induce disruptive behavior.

The environment of the class itself may be a mismatch for certain students, and a simple change of the environment can reduce or eliminate problems for them. The most obvious variable is the degree of structure in the class (Colarruso 1972). High-structure environments leave students less choice in what activities to do when, with whom, and where in the room. Low-structure environments (which may, nevertheless, be highly planned and highly organized) have more student movement and more flexibility in who does what, when, since students are making more choices and are more in charge of their personal schedules. Similarly, teachers can manipulate the degree of auditory and visual stimulation. In *Teacher Effectiveness Training*, Thomas Gordon (1974) has some very useful checklists for other ways to modify the environment (under the categories of "enriching," "impoverishing," "restricting," "enlarging," "rearranging," "simplifying," and "systematizing"). When looking for ways to improve students' behavior, we should therefore look also at the appropriateness of the environments we have created for them. We need to weigh how much these environments may be contributing to (rather than reducing) problems. The goal is obviously to arrange them so that we do not play to kids' weaknesses and trigger disruptive behaviors.

Finally, using the same format or activity structures day after day (too much lecturing, too many worksheets) may also induce boredom and acting out behavior in some classes. But even if we are satisfied that basic management is handled well and instruction is of reasonable difficulty, there may still be problems.

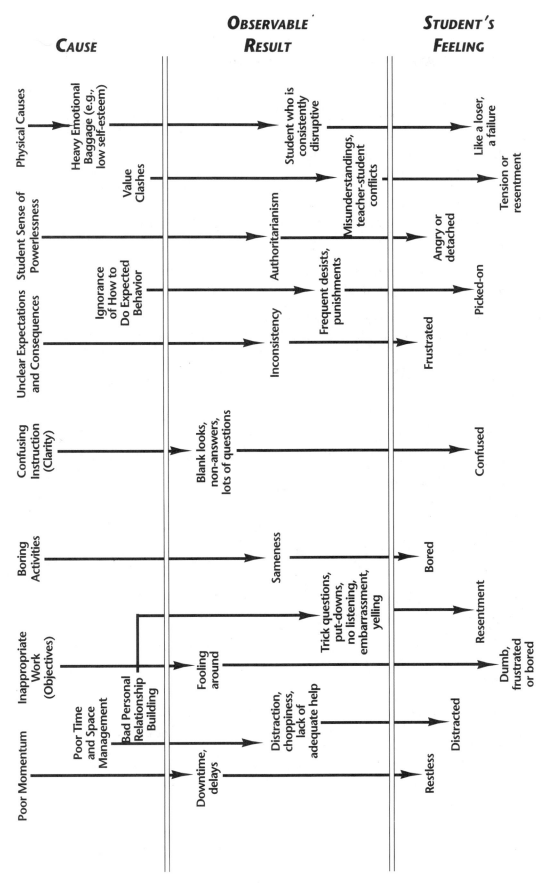

FIGURE 7.1: CAUSES OF MISBEHAVIOR
Note that the first four causes deal with other parameters treated in previous chapters.

A more serious, and more common, cause is unclear expectations and consequences; the intricate web of mutual understandings that goes with them may not be clearly established between teacher and students. We have yet to find a teacher with widespread discipline problems (rather than just one resistant child) who didn't need help here. In Section II we will go into considerable detail to specify the essential "how to's" of building this web.

Schools as institutions resemble the army, prisons, and hospitals in the way they can systematically make students feel helpless. Schools can frustrate the basic human need for control of one's own fate by leaving little (in some cases no) room for initiative, decision making, and leadership. While this deprivation does not smart for the passive, for a large part of any population this environment makes children want to push back. And they do! If we use power skillfully, we can control these students—but we will probably also make them hate school and learn less. This is no pitch for free schools; learning is often hard work and requires doing assignments given by others, and that is okay. But without compromising high academic standards one iota, teachers can structure classes so that students feel some ownership and control of what goes on. When we take up students' sense of powerlessness, we will see that every increment of progress in this direction takes pressure off behavior management because kids' energy starts to push with it instead of against it. In Section III of the chapter we will elaborate on how teachers can do this.

> ### Schools as institutions resemble the army, prisons, and hospitals in the way they can systematically make students feel helpless.

Sometimes seemingly inattentive students simply don't hear as well. They fail to carry out directions not because they're daydreaming or willful; they simply mishear key words. We have known "inattentive" students to be diagnosed with hearing loss after 2-1/2 years in primary school, and after much energy went into behavior modification and other focusing strategies for the children. So, the message here is simply to be sure to rule out physical causes when working with kids who appear resistant or spacey. These include vision, organic hyperactivity, thyroid irregularities, and a host of other possible physical problems.

Youngsters bring to school both the manners and the cognitive habits they have learned elsewhere. Failure to meet our expectations for lining up without running, for listening to directions, for lining up their work neatly on paper, or for putting materials away in an orderly way may simply come from the fact that they don't know how to do so! It is a fact that some kindergartners don't know how to walk rather than run in certain situations (which is to say they don't know how to predict consequences, control impulses, or plan physical movements). It is a fact that some older students simply don't know how to categorize objects to expedite a cleanup, much less plan their time and movements during it. In these cases, teaching the behaviors step by step, is the antidote to the disruptive behavior, not clever consequences or contracts. There's no use trying to motivate youngsters to do something for which they lack the tools. It is our assumption here that can cause us to overlook these possibilities. It may simply never occur to a teacher that the deepening cycle of threats and punishments has its origin in simple ignorance. We urge teachers facing disruptive behavior to examine the students carefully. More often than is realized, we assume capacities that are not there in students' behavioral repertoires. In these cases, putting the behaviors into their repertoires is what's needed. A question not to overlook when trying to figure out a resistant class or individual is, "Do they know how to do what I am asking them to do?"

Cultural clashes between teachers and students may underlie resistant behavior. This cause is rare, but real, and should be considered in classes where students' home life has strong ethnic roots in another culture.

Hardest of all—despite all the best efforts in responding to the issues above—there may be a few students who resist learning and, for one reason or another, do not function in school. They may be passive and withdrawn, or act out severely and consistently. The final section of this chapter will address these students—the few, not the many; the troubled, not the norm. There are at least six major strategies for dealing with resistant students, each cohesive and each different, and they are all effective—if used with the right students. Our job shall be to learn what they are, how to use them, and how to match them appropriately to individual kids. Here, you will be challenged to broaden your range for responding to resistant students; you can acquire a repertoire from which to draw. You will be asked to look carefully at students and become a practical diagnostician so you can draw appropriately from your repertoire. There are no surefire formulas for matching students to strategies, but we are not reliant upon trial and error either. A good deal is known about what is likely to work with whom. You will have that knowledge to use here and apply in case studies of your students; but you will have to work hard to be able to use it. We will take up each of the six strategies and explore how-to-do-it and how-to-match.

The six strategies are: Behavior Modification, Self-Awareness Training, Personal Influence, Logical Consequences, Reality Therapy, and Teacher Effectiveness Training. Each strategy has an intellectual parent, a central figure who has pulled it together and written extensively about it (except Behavior Modification which has so many parents, aunts, uncles and cousins it is hard to single one out). Each strategy is distinctly different from the others. Each strategy has a particular series of steps to go through and a way for teachers to respond to disruptive students.

It will be our point of view that these six strategies are all good when used appropriately—that no one of the six is inherently better than any other. Furthermore, there are good grounds for believing that we can choose appropriately from the six—that we can match particularly resistant students with what we do, and that we do not have to rely upon—in fact, should not rely upon—just trial and error, eclectic sampling from available strategies. In

Section IV we will first analyze the nature of each of the six strategies. Then, we will elaborate the components of each in detail and provide primary source references for further study. Finally, we will describe a rationale for choosing among them to match a particular student.

We now take some of the 10 causes of misbehavior for more in-depth treatment. Section II will deal with how to set up an effective system of expectations and consequences. Section III will deal with how to give students a feeling of control and influence in classroom life, thereby reducing discipline problems because kids have more of a stake in the school as a community. Section IV will describe the six Models of Discipline for severely resistant students and how to match them appropriately to which kids.

Section II
The Web of Expectations and Consequences

Are the rules and consequences clear and specific enough, both to me and to the students?

The prerequisite for strength in this whole area is that students have a clear and unambivalent picture of what the expectations for their behavior really are. Something must happen to get that information across. There are numerous ways this may be done: tell them directly, make up a chart, brainstorm, or negotiate the class rules at a class meeting. Expectations are sometimes not codified as formal rules or laid out all at once, but they become known to students through what a teacher reacts to consistently. At any rate, the students must be clear about what they are, and thus expectations must be *specific* so there is no misunderstanding (or room for argument). It may not be enough to call for "silent reading time." The class may need clarification on what silence means. Does it mean absolute silence, or whispering, or quiet talking? Can the students discriminate the difference and modulate in a controlled way between those levels? If "silence" really means "quiet," then perhaps it really should not be called "silence" and vice versa. If students are supposed to arrive on time for class, does that mean being no more than two minutes late, being in the room when the bell rings, being in their seats, or being in their seats with notebooks open and ready to go? *Where* these boundaries are drawn is less important than that they are established clearly. There must be no doubt as to when a rule has been broken.

Mendler and Curwin (1983) describe a comprehensive strategy for involving students in rule-making (called the "social contract") so that there is no doubt about what the rules are. After the teacher specifies certain nonnegotiable rules and establishes consequences, students work in small groups to propose rules for the *teacher's* behavior, including consequences. (For example, "Rule: The teacher must call on students by their names.

Consequences for violation: a) Remind teacher of rule, b) Teacher will apologize." "Rule: Teacher should check our papers in private. Consequence for violation: Teacher will read to the class two chapters from the current book she is reading.") Mendler and Curwin explain:

> All of the rules and consequences are reviewed by the class to insure proper understanding of what they mean. Role play is often a useful strategy to illustrate the exact meaning of a rule or consequence. For example some students want the teacher not to yell. It is important for the teacher to speak louder and louder until agreement is reached as to what constitutes yelling. (Mendler and Curwin 1983, p. 73)

Then, a careful process of decisionmaking occurs in which the teacher and students decide which of the proposed rules and consequences will be incorporated into the contract. (For details see Mendler and Curwin, pp. 73-74). Finally, students take an exam that tests their knowledge of the contract. Classroom privileges can be earned by passing the test with a 100 percent score! This novel social contract procedure accomplishes several things: first, students' developing rules for teachers gives them an added investment in making the process work; second, the test for comprehension and the link to classroom privileges sends the message that this contract is important and underlines the content of what the rules really are.

Do I convey positive expectancy?

Expectations need to be repeated, and often. One finds teachers, especially in the beginning of the year, restating and reminding students about expectations, eliciting expectations from students just prior to events that may strain the behavior. For instance: "We're going to the auditorium now, kids. What might it be like there as we walk in? What will we need to do? What should we keep in mind for our behavior as a good audience?" Or: "Okay, we're ready to go to gym now. What do we think about when we are in the halls? Why?"

An attitude of *positive expectancy* may be embedded in the utterances with which a teacher restates expectations. This positive expectancy has two aspects. The first has the flavor of "why of course you're going to do it." This is not something the teacher says outright, but it is the assumption conveyed by body language and attitude. The other aspect of positive expectancy is encouragement, confidence, the "I know you can do it" attitude. It is often associated with positive statements of specific behaviors or questions ("Can you remember to raise your hand?") rather than direct desists ("Stop calling out!").

Another way to convey positive expectancy is to be assertive in the way we request appropriate behavior. Lee Canter calls for combining four attention moves—eye contact, hand gesture, the student's name, and touch—for an assertive effect:

The teacher observed Steve roughly pushing and shoving the children standing beside him in line. The teacher walked up to Steve, looked him in the eyes, placed her hand on his shoulder, and stated, "Steve, keep your hands to yourself." (while gesturing with her free hand). (Canter 1977, p. 75)*

If students counter with excuses or other diverting moves, Canter recommends the "broken record" technique:

Teacher: "Sue, I want you to raise your hand and wait to be called on before you speak." (Statement of want)

Sue: "None of the other children do."

Teacher: "That's not the point. I want you to raise your hand." (Broken record)

Sue: "You never call on me."

Teacher: "That's not the point. I want you to raise your hand." (Broken record)

Sue: "Okay, I will."

In this interchange, the teacher simply kept repeating (broken record) what she wanted from the child and would not become sidetracked by Sue's responses. The teacher maintained control of the interaction with the child.

In utilizing a broken record, you first need to determine what you want from the interaction with the student (i.e., "I want Sue to raise her hand." This becomes your statement of want and the gist of your interactions. You can preface your statement of want with, "That's not the point, but I want you to raise your hand", or "I understand, but I want you to raise your hand.") No matter what manipulative response the student presents, if you respond with your statement of want—"that's not the point, I want you to...", or "I understand, but I want you to..."—your statement will be more effective. (Canter, pp. 79-80)*

This technique can be surprisingly effective, especially with students who are verbal. Remember though that when you use it, you must know what consequences (or range of consequences) you are prepared to deliver if the behavior persists. Without that clear image, one's assertiveness will be hollow. Furthermore, after reasserting the expectation three times, a teacher had better be ready to implement the consequence.

Are the consequences logical rather than punitive?

Rudolph Dreikurs understood that punishment breeds resentment whereas logical consequences begin to teach students the reality of the social order. Punishment is any aversive stimulus (like being paddled or writing "I will not throw paper on the floor" one hundred times) intended to discourage the recurrence of the behavior. You will be less likely to do the behavior next time because this unpleasant thing may happen to you again. Logical

*Reprinted with permission. Canter, L. (with M. Canter). *Assertive Discipline*. Santa Monica, Calif.: Canter and Associates, 1977.

consequences, on the other hand, are connected to the behavior in such a way as to feel like fair retribution for the violation. If you have broken a rule against copying another's homework, it is a logical consequence to have to do it all over again under supervision (rather than stay after school as punishment). If you have littered the floor, it is a logical consequence to clean it up during recess (rather than write "I will not litter" one hundred times). If you have hurt someone's feelings with rude remarks, it is a logical consequence to do something nice for him or her (rather than sit detention). (More on logical consequences can be found later in this chapter in the section devoted to Dreikurs' model.)[1]

Do I have a range of consequences rather than one rigid response for every transgression?

If each rule has an automatic consequence tied to it, you can get boxed into a corner. One consequence only for each rule is a mistake. Mendler and Curwin cite the case of a teacher whose consequence for undone homework is staying after school to finish it. One day one of her best students says, "I'm sorry, Miss Martin, but my father was very sick last night. I had to babysit while he was taken to the hospital, and in the confusion, I didn't have time to get my homework done." The teacher is now in the dilemma of either being unfeeling and rigid ("I'm sorry, but you have to stay after school anyway") or letting the kid off and teaching the rest of the class that "good" excuses can pardon undone work. This could have been avoided if the teacher could pick from an appropriate *range* of consequences for each rule. For undone homework, the range might be:

> Reminder
>
> Warning
>
> Hand in work before the close of school that day
>
> Stay after school to finish it
>
> Conference with the teacher, student, and parent to develop a plan.
>
> With this range of alternatives, Miss Martin could gently remind Susan that homework is due on time, and then discuss how her father is doing, etc. In this way she is implementing one of the prescribed consequences, yet she is not being overly rigid with Susan. With another student who had been late six times that month, she might make him stay after and finish it. (Mendler and Curwin 1983, p. 119)

Fair need not always be equal.

---

[1] It is interesting to examine how "detention" is used in one's school in light of logical consequence theory. Sometimes detention can indeed be logical when a student has not done work and detention is used to get it done. But it is also quite possible for detention to be punitive and counterproductive when used as a consequence for, say, defacing a desk or talking back to a teacher.

Do I deliver consequences in a way that is tenacious, consistent, prompt, matter-of-fact, and indicates student choice?

Every time an expectation is not met, the teacher must consistently react (not meaning "react the same way," but "react every time"). That is not to say punish. The reaction may be anything from a reminder to a consequence; but something has to happen. The teacher must *do* something; otherwise the students—especially resistant students—come to disregard the expectation (or else become confused over where it applies). The transgression usually cannot be ignored. (Sometimes the teacher may choose to ignore certain behaviors when they are minor and calling attention to them would just reinforce them, or the teacher may recognize them "economically" and briefly). The general mission here is to communicate to students that one's expectations are really one's expectations. You mean them. They get this message when they find the teacher reliably calls them on certain behaviors—reliably and consistently *does something* about it. This "does something about it" is often cited as the most important of the attributes under communication of expectations (Rogers 1972; Canter 1977; Mendler and Curwin 1983), and it will usually mean arranging some sort of consequence for the behavior. Mere admonishing and reprimanding without action that goes beyond words usually sends the message that expectations are weak.

> *Teachers must be tenacious. Classes will test teachers to the limits.*

Teachers must be *tenacious* about the business of restating expectations and consistently reacting. Individuals and sometimes whole classes will test teachers to the limits on this. The thing is not to give up, even though misbehavior continues in the face of specific expectations consistently upheld. Some very difficult students will push teachers this far to see if they really care (meaning care about them). If the reactions to the misbehavior are reasonable, appropriate, and fair, tenacity will carry the day.

Lee Canter (1977) tells the story of a very aggressive third grader, Carl, who consistently abuses other children, both verbally and physically. On several occasions he has also extorted money from his classmates! At a meeting with the child's parents, the principal, and the teacher, a contract is signed that Carl will be excluded from school if he does any of the following things: threatens children, cusses them, extorts money, or physically assaults them. The parents agree to follow through with the exclusion at home.

> The next day, on the way into the classroom, Carl got into an argument with another student and roughly shoved him. Ms. S. immediately went up to Carl and simply told him, "You pushed Sol. You've chosen to go home for the rest of the day!" Ms. S. contacted the office: the principal called Carl's mother, who came to get him. Carl went home and spent the rest of the school day in his room doing the work he would have done had he stayed in school.

The following day, during a spelling assignment, another student refused to let Carl copy his work and Carl became angry. He threatened to beat the student up. Ms. S., hearing this, told Carl what he had done and that he would be going home again. His mother picked him up, and he spent the rest of the day at home in his room. Carl behaved appropriately for the next two days. On the third day, during free choice, Ms. S. observed him angrily cursing and screaming at a girl who would not give him the puzzle that she was playing with. Ms. S. repeated the same procedure of informing him of what he had done and that by behaving inappropriately he had chosen to go home. For the first time Carl became upset. He began to cry and say that he did not want to go home. Ms. S. simply told him that "he made a choice" and that he would be going home.

As was typical, the "third time was the charm." Ms. S.'s ability to deal assertively with Carl's behaviors let him know that his disruptions would not be tolerated. Carl thus chose to control his temper and behave in an appropriate manner with his fellow students.

Of all the sections in this chapter, this is probably the most important. It takes determination and tenacity to keep delivering consequences when the behavior persists. But without that tenacity students will not believe teachers are serious about their expectations. Follow-through at the beginning of the year on plans such as the one Canter describes (assuming you have a student who needs such a strong plan) will be keenly observed by the rest of your class and let them know you mean what you say. Inconsistency and lack of follow-through early in the school year is a common cause of school discipline problems.

Children may not care if you keep them after school once, suspend them every now and then, or send them to the corner infrequently. But there are few children who would not care if they knew that they would have to stay after school every day they chose to, even if it meant five days straight. There are few children who would not care if they knew they would be suspended every time they acted out, even if it meant three straight days of suspension. There are few children who would not care if they knew you would send them to a corner for their inappropriate behavior every time they chose to go, even if it meant five times a day.

What we are trying to say is this: if you really care, the children will really care. If you are prepared to use any means necessary and appropriate to influence the children to eliminate their inappropriate behavior they will sense your determination and quickly care about the consequences which they will have to face consistently if they choose to act inappropriately. (Canter 1977, pp. 109-110)

Almost any behavior we really want to get, we can get if we have the determination, because we do have the power.

Does this mean that if one keeps delivering consequences persistently, the behavior is sure to change? First, it is possible to deliver a consequence over and over again consistently and have no effect. That can happen if the consequence is not strong enough, or if it somehow turns out to be a reward for the child. It can also happen if the behavior comes from a physical cause, ignorance, or a value clash. Second, the way in which the consequence was delivered in Canter's scenario had a lot to do with its success. The teacher did not blame, criticize or humiliate the student; she simply (but promptly) went up to him, noted the behavior ("You pushed Sol"), and delivered the consequence ("You have chosen to go home for the rest of the day"). She pointed out that going home was the child's choice in this case since he knew that pushing Sol would lead to that. Thus, the teacher reacts with matter-of-fact emotion rather than anger. It is, in fact, easier to react that way when you know precisely what you are going to do. That knowledge (versus the helpless feeling of a child who seems outside your control) gives a teacher both confidence and calm, which in turn allow for better judgments. So, being persistent with consequences can also fail if the consequence is not delivered in the right way.

The specific technique described in Canter's scenario is a strong one—systematic exclusion of a student to eliminate particularly disruptive and persistent behavior. But it can be very effective. Seymour Sarason describes another powerful exclusion technique that works without parents or contracts. It relies on the cooperation of another teacher into whose room the child is sent for exclusion. The host teacher has a special place the student goes that is not fun and where the student does work. For details see Sarason (1971), pp. 136–139.

Do I recognize and reward responsible behavior effectively?

No discussion of consequences would be complete without examining positive consequences—how we respond to students who are meeting expectations. There is a case to be made that good behavior should not be rewarded; it is expected; it should be the norm; no reward system should be necessary to maintain it. Nevertheless, with certain classes where discipline problems are an issue, explicit reward systems can play a useful role (and we're not just talking about elementary classes either).

Ingenious reward systems such as Canter's marbles-in-a-jar,[2] or numerous others such as those described in CLAIM (see Section IV), have been devised to acknowledge positive behavior in students. Mendler and Curwin's (1983) approach relies more on social praise delivered in private. He likes to catch students being good, and goes out of his way to deliver both positive and negative consequences quietly so only the receiving student can hear. Thus, when he is bending over a student to say something privately, the rest of the class doesn't know whether it's something like, "You have continued talking to neighbors despite two warnings. The consequence is you'll have to stay after class with me and work out a plan to avoid this behavior…" or, "You've been focusing on your work and written two balanced sonnets this afternoon. That's what I call being productive!"

---

[2] Lee Canter (1977, p. 140) advocates dropping marbles in a jar as a reward. The sound of the marble landing serves as an immediate audible signal to all that they are behaving appropriately. A full jar earns the class some predetermined reward such as a popcorn party or extra recess.

Do I take sufficient time and care at the beginning of the year to establish expectations?

One elementary teacher we know will not send her kids to specials for the first two weeks in September so she can ensure solid learning of her expectations, establish routines, and begin to build class cohesion. Suspending specials may not be necessary, but the focus on expectations certainly is. It is useful to think of this period as one of teaching or training for the students. Training requires practice; thus, if students are noisy and disruptive in the hallway, one can say, "I can see we need more practice in hall walking from the way we just came back from gym." And you can, indeed, take the class out for some "practice" with you right then and there. This is not punitive, but logical as a consequence. (Mendler and Curwin 1983 cite a school that has an after-school class in cafeteria behavior, including practice and an exam for those kids who have been disruptive at lunch. Students must get 100 percent on the exam to "graduate.")

Do I have high enough expectations for behavior no matter what the kids' backgrounds?

A teacher can control students, even if the expectations are inappropriate, by sheer power and fear. The presence of control, however, does not tell us anything about the appropriateness of the teacher's expectations. Making judgments about these standards for behavior takes us into a fuzzy but important area. If the demands we make on students are inappropriate, that will go a long way toward explaining discipline problems. We might create a scale for teacher standards going up the following ladder:

- *No expectations evident*: pretty much a laissez-faire treatment.

- *Few consistent expectations evident.*

- *One uniform set of expectations that appears low*: that is, too easy, permissive, undemanding for what students seem capable of when judged by age and performance.

- *Uniform set of expectations that are unreasonably high or age inappropriate* (or in some other way inappropriate).

- *Uniform and average expectations.*

- *Uniform and high expectations*: demanding but still reasonable.

We could try to place ourselves on this ladder, but there would still be an important aspect of standards to examine. Once we have a general sense for our expectations-as-standards, we can look beyond and ask how we differentiate for groups or for individuals within these standards. Four separate and logical levels of performance have been identified which discriminate among teachers in how they apply their standards to different pupils. We can represent these levels in the following statements:

1. I have the same expectations for everyone.

2. I have different expectations for different kids, meaning I expect some to misbehave more than others, display self-control less. This may or may not mean I am more tolerant or understanding or accepting of this misbehavior from them; but anyway I don't demand that they meet the standards I do demand and expect of others.

3. I have different expectations for individual kids' ability to behave in different tempting or otherwise high-risk situations for them. I know their weaknesses and know the situations that can trigger them. I try to provide for them in advance of these situations.

4. I understand kids' differential abilities to behave in high-risk triggering situations that are hard for them (as in the above entry), and I make some adjustments and allowances for them, but my ultimate expectations for their behavior remain as high as they are for the other kids, and I let them know that. I am striving with them toward ever closer approximations of those high standards. I am not surprised by their misbehavior when it occurs, so in a sense I 'expect' it from time to time; but I do not accept it. In fact, I work actively to change it.

When we look analytically at ourselves and try to get better control of behavior in our classes, it is useful to compare ourselves to these four statements. The third and fourth are distinctly different from the first two; they show up in teacher behavior that is also different and will have a marked effect of general discipline.

A distinction has been made between what teachers *think* a student will do (they may have "varying expectations") and what they *want* a student to do or measure up to (they may have different "standards").

Every year we work with at least one or two teachers, excellent teachers, talented and caring people whose effectiveness is reduced by their ambivalence about expectations. They are unsure how reasonable it is for them to expect—to push—kids toward more responsible and attentive behavior in class. They see the irresponsible "wacko" behavior of students who appear out of control, who have family and other problems, and feel they must make allowances. They thus undersell the kids and undershoot with their goals for student behavior. Who says first graders can't sit still in a circle and listen to each other for a 15-minute meeting? Who says ninth graders can't learn to function in self-organized task groups to plan and organize a project?

Again and again, we have seen it demonstrated that you can get what behavior you want if you work hard enough at it, are tenacious and determined enough, are committed to the idea that it is right and attainable behavior for your students, and are willing to teach them the skills they may need to function at that level. (What you decide to "want," of course, can be unreasonable and age-inappropriate, in which case what you get is what you deserve!) This is true even for some disturbed students, though they tax you much more, your setting may need adjustment, and it will take considerably longer. Anything less is ultimately a disservice to our students.

If you have a clear notion of what you want and keep expecting, expecting, expecting *out loud* to students, with consequences when they don't measure up, with explanations of "why" over and over again, and with as much kindness and rationality as you can muster, you will get there; and that's no pipe dream. But first you must decide to do so.

Section III
Building Self-Discipline and Responsibility

Do I give kids a real and legitimate sense of control, influence, responsibility, and power in class life?

In the introduction to this chapter, we argued that teachers could structure classes so students felt some ownership and control of what goes on, and that doing so could reduce discipline problems. Bear in mind, however, that this is no substitute for clear expectations and consequences. They should come first. Interestingly, we know a first-year teacher who never really did get expectations and consequences sorted out in her own head, but who nevertheless salvaged the year by starting an individualized contract learning system. The students invested in it, and much energy that would have gone into fighting the teacher went into meeting their learning goals instead. But it was still a rocky year with less than optimal learning. If expectations had been established right from the beginning, her contract system would not just have salvaged this particular class; it would have put it into orbit.

Three excellent approaches for giving students ownership in classroom life are: negotiating Mendler and Curwin's "social contract," using the principle of learning called "Goal Setting" (see Principles of Learning, Chapter 9), and teaching through one of the five cooperative Models of Teaching (see Learning Experiences, Chapter 15).

While studying the Clarity parameter, an English teacher in one of our courses realized he often played guess-what's-on-the-teacher's-mind in his question asking. He confessed this to his class the next day and asked if they concurred. They did. He then asked them what they could do about it, specifically what action class members might take if he victimized them with such a question or if they observed him doing it to someone else. After collecting ideas in a general class discussion, they settled on the following procedure: when students feel that they have been asked such a question, they can call the teacher on it directly and ask him to restate the question. Alternately, students who cannot answer a question can redirect it to another student in the class by name. At other times the teacher will go around the class, in order, asking review questions about the text read for homework. If the student cannot answer a question or answers incorrectly, the next student gets the same question. If three students in a row fail to get the answer, the teacher acknowledges that it was somehow a poor question and rephrases it. The net result for these students, previously a low-performing class, was higher class participation and higher achievement. It is our belief, however, that there was a lot more going on here than simply eliminating guess-what's-on-the-teacher's-mind questions. First of all, the teacher was showing fairness and realness (Personal Relationship Building) in admitting that he could be the cause of a problem for students and looking in an open way for a solution. Second, what these techniques accomplished was giving the students some say in determining the rules of the classroom game and controlling the flow of events.

Another teacher we know tried to increase students' motivation for doing homework assignments well. It had been his practice to give students daily quizzes based on homework readings. One day he told them that if they got four 100's in a row, they could earn a free 100 points which they might then "spend" on future quizzes at any time and in any way they pleased. They could skip some future quiz and take 100 on it, they could take 30 points of it and elevate a 70 to 100 sometime in the future, or just save the points. He found that students' efforts on homework assignments and quizzes dramatically improved, even those students who had already been doing well. Our hypothesis is that what was powerful about this technique was the way in which it gave students something to control: namely, a bank account of earned points. Whether they earned them, and if earned how they would spend them, was entirely within their control. (For the students already scoring well, perhaps it was an insurance policy against future mishaps.)

Other teachers have replicated that technique, but have eliminated the requirement that the four 100's be in a row; simply attaining four 100's earns the 100 point bonus. These ingenious experiments by the two teachers we have just cited suggest to us that there are many places in classroom life where we can look for ways to give students more legitimate control including, as these two people taught us, the way we handle recitation lessons and the way we do grading.

Do I explicitly build community in the class (knowledge about, appreciation of, and cooperation with one another)?

William Glasser's classroom meetings (Glasser 1969), Gene Stanford's cycle of activities for *Developing Effective Classroom Groups* (Stanford 1977), relationship building activities (Wilt and Watson 1978), cooperative learning (Dishon and O'Leary 1984): these are all specific (but not simple) strategies for building the kind of affiliation and harmony in a class that prevents discipline problems.

Even without concerns about discipline, all four would be inherently worth doing. But when relationships among class members are stressful or fractious (or both), these strategies can lower the pressure and productively rechannel energy that is going into fighting with one another.

Before describing the strategies, it is important to note that, as with a Model of Teaching, one cannot read an article and then launch the strategy successfully. These are not Attention moves or Clarity moves, which are easily grasped and tried. They are more complex patterns of moves and it is important to understand the beliefs and the spirit behind them to make them work. Thus, people should: (1) take their time in learning the strategies; (2) be willing to stick with them through the rough ground of initial tries; and (3) perhaps most important, *not do them alone.* You need someone else who's trying it also to check in with, to get feedback from, and to troubleshoot with. Also invaluable would be a coach or an on-site person knowledgeable in the strategy. Best of all would be both.

Over the past 15 years we have used classroom meetings with many of our own classes, and as staff developers have helped others to make them a regular feature of classroom life. We have rarely seen another practice so powerful for building a general sense of community in a class or so directly useful for handling problems such as scapegoating, bullying, and cliques.

Schools Without Failure is the book in which William Glasser describes in detail how to conduct "Classroom Meetings." He reports, "I haven't met a child incapable of thinking and participating to some degree in school if we let him know we value what he can contribute" (p. 97). That belief is essential for a teacher who wants to make classroom meetings work, because being nonjudgmental and accepting of student contributions is a key skill in leading meetings. The meetings are the vehicle through which students experience both the participation, the sense of being valued, and a sense of being part of something real. Class meetings are held regularly (at least weekly and preferably several times a week), with students and teacher seated in a tight circle. Teachers lead the whole class in nonjudgmental discussions about topics that are important and relevant to them. The three types are open-ended meetings, social problem-solving meetings, and educational-diagnostic meetings.

In open-ended meetings, either teacher or students introduce a topic for discussion. One of the teacher's roles is to build a focusing question for the students around the topic, which can be anything of current interest to the students. In citing a meeting where the students wanted to talk about Disneyland, the teacher asked, "Who would like to go to Disneyland?" Almost every child responded affirmatively. "Suppose someone gave me two tickets to Disneyland and said I should give these tickets to two children in my class. To whom should I give the tickets?" In addition to translating open topics into focused discussions, teachers use skills of active listening and summarizing.

Open-ended meetings begin building a sense of involvement with each other, and lay the foundations for using the meetings for generating significant investment in academic work and the more difficult area of social problem solving. Chapters 10, 11, and 12 of Glasser's book are a good manual for learning and implementing these meetings, so we will not go into more detail here. We would, however, like to quote a literal description of a social problem-solving meeting so as to create a more vivid image of how classroom meetings can be used to improve some of the more intractable (and usually untreated) sources of disruptive behavior in classes.

> At another meeting, Mike was introduced as the topic. Physically overweight and not too clean-looking in appearance, with hair in his eyes and a very loud, offensive voice, and holes in all his tee shirts caused from biting and twisting and chewing on them, he was not pleasant to behold! Mike said he didn't like the class because they didn't like him. When asked why they didn't like him, he said it was because he was fat. The children eagerly disagreed. They said that had nothing to do with it. Mike wanted to know why, then. He was given the opportunity to call on those children he wanted to explain to him what they found offensive about him. Someone said it was because he wears funny hats to school, like the pilot's helmet he wore the day before. (Incidentally, he never wore it again.) Some said he dressed sloppily. Martin said it was because he said things that hurt people. For example, when Martin came home from Europe and showed the class several treasures that he brought to share, Mike said he didn't believe they were from Paris and that he bought the same things here. Martin said that hurt his feelings. David said that when he shared things with the class, Mike blurted out similar derogatory remarks. (Mike still has not cured himself of this, by the way.) John, who had become much more introspective and perceptive, said it was because Mike always made funny faces and looked up at the ceiling with a disgusted look on his face when people tried to talk to him. While he was saying this, Mike was doing just that. John said, "See, Mike, you're doing it right now, and you don't even know it." Mike was asked if anyone, in his opinion, went out of his way to be nice to him. He said, only Alice, whom he liked. Everyone giggled. Alice said she didn't care if everyone did laugh at her, she liked Mike and was not ashamed to be his friend. She liked being nice to him. We talked as a group about the importance of having one friend at least. The others found that no one really tried to go out of his way to be his friend, but each person would try to make some gesture to show they would try in the next week. They really rose to the occasion, but soon forgot about it and were their usual apathetic selves. However, no one seemed to go out of his way to be nasty, which was a change. Alice continued being nice to Mike, and the children stopped teasing her about it. Harriet, who was one of the girls who was teasing Alice, apologized in a class meeting for doing so and she said she had once been teased for befriending someone without other friends, and that it took more courage to be his friend and yet she wanted to. She told Alice that even though it had hurt her feelings when the others teased her, she had forgotten and teased Alice and that she was sorry, and she could really understand how Alice felt. There has been a tremendous change in Mike this semester. He is not lackadaisical about his work or appearance, speaks more quietly, uses more self-control, plays a fairer game in the yard, gets along much better with others, and has more (or some) friends. (Glasser 1968, pp. 152-153)*

We have had teachers read this account and get scared off by it. It seems to some like opening wounds or beginning a process that can get out of control. Yet two teachers with difficult classes with whom we worked last year, teachers who took six months to work up their courage to bring up comparable issues in their own classes, now view their own series of meetings as among the most significant accomplishments of their careers. We are glad they took time to work up their courage, because they were also working up their skills at leading meetings on safer topics. They also used many of Gene Stanford's strategies to build community in the class over that period (to be described shortly). But the point is that these kinds of issues fester and hurt and drain students' energy even if we don't address them; and bringing them out into the open with skillful leadership can make dramatic differences in class climate. Neither the teacher in Glasser's account or those with whom we have worked were specially trained in counseling techniques. They were regular classroom teachers who had the courage and the commitment to want to help students build strong community within their classes, and who knew that there were large dividends for the effort in academic learning as well.

A few notes on the Glasser excerpt above: phrases like "He was given the opportunity to call on those children who…" mask key decisions by the teacher-leader. What really happened was that at that point the teacher decided that Mike could benefit from specific examples of how his behavior put others off and called for them. Furthermore, the teacher decided that it would involve Mike more (and make it safer for him) if he (Mike) did the calling on kids. Later: "Mike was asked if anyone went out of his way to be nice to him." The *teacher* asked Mike that question, sensing an appropriate moment to turn the discussion around and focus on the positive. Then: "We talked as a group about the importance of having one friend at least." The teacher asked a few key questions to *guide* the discussion that way. It didn't just happen on its own. (The first two examples, especially, illustrate the misleading nature of the passive voice in effective communication.)

Learning to recognize such key junctures and opportunities is part of the skill learning we go through when we undertake social problem-solving classroom meetings. It is, indeed, not the sort of thing one rushes into on the first day. But these skills are within the grasp of most teachers. Overall, classroom meetings regularly practiced are one of the most significant climate builders for successful learning.

While teaching high school English, Gene Stanford came to the same conclusion and developed a carefully sequenced series of activities to build class cohesion over a year. In *Developing Effective Classroom Groups* (1975), he organizes the activities according to the stage of growth the class is in in its movement toward mature functioning. Students have to know something about one another before they can appreciate or become involved with one another, so Stage I is Orientation. In Stage II activities explicitly develop norms of Group Responsibility (through teaching awareness of others), Responsiveness to Others (meaning good listening skills), Cooperative Skills, Consensus Decision-Making Skills, and Social Problem Solving Skills.

Stage III is Coping with Conflict; Stage IV is about Productivity; and Stage V is about Termination, that is, dealing with the end of the year, the end of the life of the group, and people's feelings about that. All this is integrated with an academic program and an emphasis on writing.

A number of specific Models of Cooperative Learning have been developed which structure academic tasks themselves in such a way that students build affiliation, mutual understanding, and class cohesion. (There is overwhelming evidence, by the way, that they are at least equally effective for academic learning as well. Many, such as Slavin, Johnson and Johnson, and Sharam, argue they are better.) Cooperative Models of Teaching usually have students work in groups. Contrary to most "group" work observed in schools, however, the activity is structured so that either task completion or reward (or both) depends on everyone's participation. Yet groups are not penalized for having slow students or rewarded for having the "best" students in them. For an excellent summary of how to implement these techniques see Dishon and O'Leary (1984). A further range of cooperative models is outlined in the Learning Experiences chapter of this book.

This section of the Discipline parameter has attempted to connect good discipline, meaning more narrowly an absence of disruptive and resistant behavior, with building a sense of community in the class. From our point of view, building community would be worthwhile in and of itself; but there is no denying it is also a powerful preventive force against discipline problems. Simultaneously, it is a wonderful source of strength for building environments that support the best kind of academic learning.

Now it is time to turn to the most resistant students, the group whom we have saved for last, the group who continue to resist and disrupt despite clear expectations and consequences, and despite our best efforts at creating ownership and building community in the class. These are the very needy kids who bring heavy emotional baggage through the door with them every morning and act out their needs in disruptive behavior that is resistant to standard measures. Fortunately, there are not too many of them. Most of the students who initially appear in this category just need more clarity, conviction, and tenacity from us about expectations and consequences.

> **Building community is a powerful preventive force against discipline problems.**

If you are pondering such a student now, be sure you have really gone the limit with standard measures before plunging onward. Yet these days it is not unusual to have at least one such student in a grade; and one is all it takes to create class-wide distractions and make us pine for June. The following section explores six comprehensive models for dealing with such students.

Section IV
Six Models of Discipline

In this section we will describe the how-to's of the six models in some detail. First, here is a brief description of the six strategies.

Behavior Modification is a very orderly approach based on the assumption that unproductive behaviors can be eliminated and productive ones can be substituted by analyzing and controlling one's environment and its rewards. Behavior Modification systematically: (1) clips (cuts off) rewards for unproductive behavior; (2) identifies substitute and more productive behaviors; (3) targets these new behaviors explicitly with the student; and (4) begins rewarding them on a schedule that starts out consistent and high in frequency, and gradually becomes variable and lower in frequency. Behavior Modification aims to work itself out of business as the new learned behaviors become inherently rewarding.

Self-Awareness Training teaches students to read their own signals so that they know when they're getting angry, afraid, frustrated, or whatever else leads to outbursts or other unproductive behaviors. Students can learn a set of coping strategies they can plug in when these things are starting to happen, coping mechanisms they eventually do on their own. At the beginning, the teacher plays a very active, verbal, and supportive role to the student, which gradually diminishes as the student is helped toward greater autonomy with the system.

Personal Influence is based on strong mutual relations between the teacher and student. The teacher works hard to build this relationship in certain specific ways. Teachers bring in enough of their outside-school life and accomplishments so as to earn some respect as a figure in the world, a person of some interest and significance beyond the immediate classroom environment. Teachers then draw on this relationship like money in the bank and are quite firm with students when disruption occurs. They act quickly and decisively with consequences for disruptive behavior and let students know they are upset. They show their affect strongly without losing control.

Logical Consequences maintains a low level of teacher affect and draws upon creative thinking to have students experience not simple punishment, but consequences that are logically connected to what they did. Power struggles with teachers as authority figures are avoided. Teachers analyze student motivations and use these analyses to help students understand themselves. Students learn about the reality of the social order through logical consequences consistently applied and do not get moral lectures. They are also not let off the hook. There is a strong orientation toward democratic thought and the involvement of the group in establishing students' understanding of the social contract.

Reality Therapy gets students to face, to acknowledge, what they are actually doing. A nonjudgmental but involved teacher gets students to evaluate what they have done in light of their basic needs. Students explore alternatives and are asked to make commitments to courses of action. This strategy is based on teacher involvement, follow-up, and tenacity. Students learn to face the reality of what they are doing and what that behavior in turn is doing to their relations with others. This is a strategy for developing responsibility and self-worth through the involvement of someone who won't give up on you.

In *Teacher Effectiveness Training* teachers and students clarify who really owns the problem, use appropriate skills, and if it's a mutual problem negotiate a no-lose solution using a set of sequenced moves. These solutions meet the needs of both the teacher and the student. It requires good "active listening" skills to find out a student's real need or real problem sometimes. And teachers need skill at sending "I messages" so students perceive the teacher's need. Good communication skills are required, and mutual respect grows from the problem-solving process.

To be able to implement these strategies is not terribly hard, but each does take real study and practice and each is distinctly different from the others in the teacher moves it calls for. The behaviors and skills one needs are probably not outside the existing repertoire of most readers—you probably have made every move somewhere in your life. It is their order and application that takes time to learn; and believe us, they make a difference.

No one should think that by merely reading the balance of this chapter one is equipped to go out and do a strategy well. We issue this warning because we want the strategies to get a fair chance before someone who didn't really know how to do, say, Reality Therapy, comes back with no results after one try and says, "Oh, that didn't work for me." It can work for anybody if you know how to do it and apply it *in the right cases*. And that brings us to that matter of knowing when and who is the right case. Matching is the crux of this chapter—the crux of teaching itself. But before we go into what's known about matching with the six strategies, we feel it necessary to develop each one in more depth so you have more of a context in which to read about matching. So, there follow now six subsections elaborating each of the strategies; then will come the final and most important section on matching, Section V, with brief profiles of students for whom a given strategy is appropriate.

Our objective in the following six subsections is to make the descriptions of the six strategies more vivid and more complete, to show how they differ and how they are designed to work. Upon completing these subsections interested readers can go to Wolfgang and Glickman's excellent *Solving Discipline Problems* (1980), where four of our six models are presented in full chapters, including scripts of the strategy in operation. Beyond that, readers should move to the primary sources cited at the end of the chapter to start more rigorous skill building. (Some readers may wish to skip directly to the Section V on "matching" at this point, and then return to the subsections on the six separate strategies.)

Let us start by looking at the most structured of the six strategies, Behavior Modification. We will describe for you a particularly well-constructed packaging of it for teachers called Classroom and Instructional Management—CLAIM. To analyze it and the other strategies, we will use a framework modifying and expanding categories that Joyce and Weil (1972) use to analyze a model of teaching. The categories are: (1) definitions; (2) assumptions; (3) values; (4) goals; (5) rationale; (6) syntax (or steps); (7) principles of teacher response; (8) support system; (9) social system; (10) transcript; and (11) effects.

Behavior Modification Using CLAIM

Discipline as Behavior Engineering

There are many who have applied the principles of Behavior Modification to classroom management. As an exemplar of this school of thought we have picked *CLAIM*, a timeless book from CEMREL, written specifically for teachers on how to practically apply these principles in classrooms. Some of *CLAIM's* values, assumptions, and goals may not be shared by all those who advocate Behavior Modification in the classroom. We point this out at the beginning so there will be no misunderstanding by adherents of this school. What follows is an analysis of one particular interpretation of Behavior Modification principles in a particular applied system. Other interpreters might differ in certain respects. What distinguishes *CLAIM* from many of the writings on Behavior Modification is that it is more fully a "model" than what is found elsewhere or, as teachers have been heard to say, "It is more practical" which is another way of saying, "It is good theory").

Definitions

The following definitions are derived from the application of the terms within *CLAIM*, and are not necessarily consonant with definitions of the same terms elsewhere in the literature of Behavior Modification (see especially modeling).

1. *Reinforcement*: anything which increases the frequency of a given behavior.

2. *Punishment*: anything which reduces the frequency of a given behavior.

3. *Schedule*: the relation of reinforcement to emitted behavior over time. Continuous reinforcement is reinforcement for every occurrence of the desired behavior. Intermittent reinforcement is reinforcement on an unpredictable basis for the occurrence of the desired behavior.

4. *Extinction*: elimination of a behavior, usually through elimination of the reinforcement, sometimes through pairing with punishment (negative reinforcement, aversive consequences).

5. *Response cost*: fines, usually in the form of removal of tokens or other forms of scrip redeemable for reinforcements.

6. *Baseline*: a record of the frequency of a given behavior over time before beginning of selective reinforcement and/or extinction procedures.

7. *Reversal*: the restoration of a behavior to its baseline level, or near that level, when the selective reinforcement schedule is cut off.

8. *Shaping*: a gradual change in behavior accomplished through reinforcement of successively closer approximations of the desired behavior.

9. *Prompting*: giving necessary clues, hints, or prompts so that the subject can make the desired response in the presence of the appropriate stimulus.

10. *Target behavior*: the desired behavior to be achieved through application of Behavior Modification principles.

11. *Contingency*: the student response or behavior necessary to produce or earn the reinforcement; the job for which pay is given.

12. *Fading*: the gradual elimination of one reinforcer and its replacement by another reinforcer as the maintainer of the behavior.

13. *Modeling*: imitating the behaviors of others that are producing reinforcements for those others.

Many other terms from the universe of Behavior Modification are not defined here simply because they are not part of the *CLAIM* vocabulary (e.g., *operant conditioning, stimulus generalization, satiation*).

Assumptions

1. All behavior is learned.

2. Teachers cannot deal with the source of a student's problems outside the classroom (e.g., home environment).

3. If unruly behavior exists and persists, the teacher has become responsible.

Values
Efficiency and Effectiveness.

Goals

1. Illegal behavior will decrease in frequency and be replaced by legal behavior.

2. Maximum academic progress possible for each student will be made.

Rationale

Systematic analysis of payoffs and systematic application of reinforcement theory to classroom behavior will yield an engineered environment most suited to maximum progress in learning. All behavior, even deviant behavior, is earning a payoff. If a teacher can identify the payoff and clip it, the behavior will be extinguished. If the payoff can be controlled and given for desirable (legal) behavior instead, the legal behavior will become established.

When misbehavior is reduced, the way is clear to efficient learning. Applying the same principles of reinforcement to learning tasks will effectively motivate individual students.

Steps

1. Pinpoint the target behavior—the behavior which you want to occur.

2. Observe deviancies from the target behavior.

3. Chart a baseline rate for the deviancies systematically over a period of time (often weeks).

4. Analyze what the reinforcement is for the deviancy, what payoff the child is getting.

5. Identify potential reinforcers the teacher can give for performance of the target behavior.

6. Choose a reinforcer likely to appeal to the child.

7. Design a progression and sequence of reinforcement for the child: his schedule of reinforcement, whether or not shaping will be used, specific increments of behavior change that will be reinforced if shaping is used.

8. Tell the student the target behavior.

9. Design a method for observing and recording behavior frequencies.

10. Apply reinforcement.

11. Record behaviors.

Principles of Teacher Response

1. Reinforcement should be immediate.

2. Beginning with schedules of continuous reinforcement, reinforcement should become intermittent to make target behaviors more firmly resistant to extinction.

3. Use ignoring, fines, time-out from reinforcement, and simple aversive punishment to extinguish undesirable behaviors.

4. When your program seems to be failing, reevaluate your reinforcers to see if they are really reinforcing, and look back at your analysis of what payoff the student was (is) getting from the undesirable (deviant) behavior. Maybe the error lies there.

5. Associate social reinforcers with reinforcers in other categories (edible, activity, material).

6. Attempt to fade to social reinforcers.

CLAIM takes the view that inherent satisfaction in performing academic activities like reading cannot accrue to a child until reading becomes a part of his response repertoire. In other words, if a student can't read, he won't know reading can be fun. So Behavior Modification, therefore, should be viewed as a transitional technique, to bring a child to a certain level where inherent reinforcers can take over.

Likewise in the realm of social behavior, a student may not know how to gain attention in socially acceptable ways. Behavior Modification can bring him to a level of performance where he sees for the first time that other forms of interaction give him the attention he wants. If acceptable social behavior is simply not part of a student's learned repertoire of behaviors, he has no inkling that they can be reinforcing.

Thus the strategic goal embedded in *CLAIM's* syntax is to fade out the material, edible, and activity reinforcers they teach teachers to use, and wind up with the social and inherent reinforcers in effect.

Support System

1. Appropriate reinforcers must be available in the categories chosen (i.e., in either activity, material, edible, or social categories).

2. Time and personnel must be available to make the observations and record data for establishing baselines and compiling progress records once reinforcement is introduced.

Social System

1. The teacher is the identifier, author, and dispenser and withholder of reinforcement. The student is the receiver, the one operated upon, the one to whom "treatment" is given.

2. Authority: it rests clearly with the teacher.

3. Norms: established by the teacher, communicated to the students; conformance to norms is reinforced.

Effects

1. The direct effect of *CLAIM's* interpretation of behavior modification should be attainment of target behaviors by students as chosen by the teacher. Classroom deviancy becomes reduced; on-task, learning time becomes maximized. Learning carries on in an efficient and effective manner.

2. Implicit effects are to make for a passive student, accustomed to reacting in engineered ways to engineered reinforcements. An external orientation tends to develop a "payoff" mentality, though *CLAIM* tries to move against this tendency by fading to social and inherent reinforcers.

Others have raised questions about the effect of life in the environment of systematic behavior management upon creativity and upon initiative.

Self-Awareness

Discipline as Self-Control

The Self-Awareness model has several forms which we will present in this section. Therapists, teachers, and parents have used these strategies successfully with children of all ages, and in treating adult control problems. An understanding of the values of self-induced relaxation training and of self-control through inner speech may finally make us realize that people who talk to themselves aren't so crazy after all!

Assumptions

1. Students may have no perception of the type, severity, or frequency of their behaviors.

2. Students may have no perception, or inaccurate perceptions, of their own feelings, their own interior states.

Values

This model values the mental health of students. What is important is that students become aware of their feelings and actions so that they can come to terms with them; thus they learn to anticipate and control impulsivity, outbursts, withdrawal, and other erratic behaviors that are symptomatic of their lack of awareness of themselves.

Goals

The goal of this model is to teach students to read their own signals and to engage coping strategies when the signals cue them that they are about to "blow" or follow some other dysfunctional pattern common to them.

Rationale

Students who are disconnected from their own inner selves need help in simply perceiving what their actions really are. An impulsive youngster may have no awareness that he jumped to his feet, knocked a book off the table, bumped two children while running to the door, and stepped on a painting as he went by the easel. All that he's aware of consciously is that "it's time to go." An older student may not be aware that he is getting increasingly frustrated at not being called on in an instructional group, that he is drumming his fingers and clenching his fists precedent to an outburst where he will lash out impatiently. Both of these students need to recognize these situations and read inner cues about how they're thinking and feeling. They need to be aware that these are triggering situations, and that something is happening inside them, before they can do anything about it. This model directly addresses with students what the triggering situations are for them, and then it teaches them to become aware of their reactions as these triggering situations develop. When they learn to read these reactions as cues to trouble, they need to know what to do. The Self-Awareness strategies offer a variety of techniques which students can learn, practice, and then use under stress to cool off, to control themselves, and to continue functioning effectively in school. The strategies include: (1) simple counting or graphing of behavior; (2) relaxation; (3) self-coaching through inner speech (cognitive behavior modification).

Steps

Simple Counting

Anna-Marie is always calling out and interrupting in class. It is impulsive on her part, and the teacher decides to use simple counting to highlight the behavior, to call Anna-Marie's attention to it. After a group one day, the teacher says, "Anna-Marie, do you know that you call out an awful lot without raising your hand? It's really distracting to me and unfair to the rest of the kids who want to speak." "I'm sorry. I'll stop. I promise." (They have had these conversations before.) "Are you really willing to work on it? Well, I'd like to help you. How many times do you think you call out in a lesson?" "I don't know—maybe five?" (It's more like 25.) "Well, let's see tomorrow. I'll put a piece of masking tape on my wrist and every time you call out I'll put a mark on it without saying anything or stopping the lesson, but you'll be able to see me doing it and you'll know what it means. OK?" "OK."

This technique can be extremely effective in reducing habitual or impulsive annoyance behaviors when no more serious issues are involved than attention-getting and impulsivity. Simply seeing the teacher make a stroke on the tape reminds the student of the goal—to reduce calling out. "Oops," says Anna-Marie as she sees another stroke going down. Pretty soon she learns to anticipate a stroke before a call-out and starts inhibiting the call-outs herself. Afterwards, the teacher and Anna-Marie can add up the total call-outs and set a goal to reduce the total tomorrow. A week of this may be quite sufficient to teach the self-inhibition Anna-Marie needs to control calling out.

This technique and other forms of specific counting or record keeping about behaviors make students more aware of what they're doing, and make the reduction of unwanted behavior a mutual teacher-student goal. The counting is the feedback to students about their progress and needs to be prompt, complete, and frequent (Van Houton). Students have to be willing to try for the technique to work. Sometimes a teacher count of a behavior before discussing it with students produces data with which to confront them. They may be so surprised by how often they behave inappropriately that the shock value will motivate them. Teachers can use the technique on a whole class as well as on individuals. Here the goal becomes lowering the *class* total of call-outs or whatever is the inappropriate behavior being brought to awareness.

Relaxation

Bruno-Golden (1976) and Koeppen (1974) have produced scripts for teachers (or anyone) to use with students to achieve progressive muscle relaxation. These exercises involve students' assuming a comfortable position and alternately tightening and relaxing various muscle groups in a systematic sequence. It's a good technique for any teacher to know. Which of us hasn't wished for some device to calm down a hyperactive class at one point or another?

For certain students, however, knowing how to relax can be a coping strategy against stress that might otherwise make them crack. In private or small group sessions, the teacher can instruct the student in the technique, and gradually fade out the coaching until the student can self-instruct through a set of exercises with minimal teacher guidance. A point can be reached where only a cue to start from the teacher is necessary and the student can carry out the exercise alone. "Robbie, you and I know you've been having a tough time controlling your temper these days, right? Well, I'd like to teach you something that will help. Are you game?"

Along with the training, teacher and student must discuss triggering situations, try to identify the settings and the conditions that set up the student for an outburst, and try to predict them. They need, further, to talk about the student's inner feelings, and the overt symptoms the student and teacher may observe, as pressure builds up on the student. For students who are out of touch with their inner selves and have a great deal of difficulty talking about their inner feelings, the two of them may do better by focusing on objective, observable qualities of events: "It's usually when you're in small groups. You start to clench your fists and your knuckles turn white." The point is, ultimately, for students to be able to read their own signals and turn on their coping mechanisms *before* they lose control. Along the way, they may need help from the teacher to recognize these cues. A code word can be set up between them. Or, the teacher may have to intervene beyond cue giving in any one of the following ways that Wolfgang presents (Wolfgang 1977), getting more and more intrusive depending upon how much control the student has:

- proximity—looking on
- "I see you starting to get out of control."
- "You're getting out of control. I will help."
- Physical interposing—verbalizing what the student is doing—holding student: "I won't let you hurt yourself or hurt others." (for young children)

For less disturbed children, coping strategies simpler than relaxation can be employed. Students can take a walk in the halls to cool off, or go to a private corner of the room. In both strategies, however, the teacher and students are confederates. They alone may be privy to the cuing system and the coping strategy. Students see the teacher as someone helping them to gain self-mastery. Teachers work to fade their active role to the minimum required to keep the student functional, delivering as much support as necessary but looking to reduce students' dependence on them.

Explosive youngsters badly out of touch with their feelings can be greatly helped by strategies such as this one, but may need therapy in addition.

Self-Instruction through Inner Speech (Cognitive Behavior Modification)

In Self-Instructional Training, students are taught to use their own inner speech to talk themselves through difficult situations, difficult because they are struggling to contain impulses, to remain in control, and to employ alternate strategies. Teaching a student to alter his internal dialogue "will have directive effects on: (a) what the individual attends to in the environment; (b) how he appraises various stimulus events; (c) to what he attributes his behavior; and (d) his expectations about his own capacities to handle a stressful event" (Meichenbaum 1977, p. 206).

One such approach is the Think Aloud technique. Meichenbaum describes a program conducted by Bash and Camp in which twelve aggressive second-grade boys were seen in small groups:

> The program began with a 'copycat' game, which introduced the child to asking himself the following four basic questions: What is my problem? What is my plan? Am I using my plan? How did I do? While the 'copycat' was being faded, cue cards similar to Palkes et al.'s were introduced to signal the child to self-verbalize. Over the course of training there was a shift from cognitively demanding tasks to interpersonal tasks à la Shure and Spivak. Initial results from this Camp et al. study were quite promising. The results generalized to the classroom. The results of the Think Aloud training program take on particular significance when we consider Camp's findings that aggressive boys had verbal facilities that were comparable to normal boys on various performance tasks, but that the aggressive boys failed to use their abilities to think through and plan solutions to problems. Bash and Camp state:
>
> 'Even when the rules of the game call for blocking the first stimulated response, aggressive children have more difficulty performing this inhibition (e.g., playing Simon Says game). Their natural inclination is to respond rapidly, but when specifically instructed to verbalize overtly before responding, they may achieve response inhibition more readily than normal.'
>
> The self-instructional training program, Think Aloud, successfully taught such self-verbalization skills. (Meichenbaum 1977, p. 42)*

In teaching these self-instructional strategies to students, teachers need to work with them alone or in small groups. Instruction starts with a situation that is often hard for the student to handle, for example, a transition where the job is getting from a class meeting or an instructional group to the door, lined up and ready to go to lunch. At the outset of this chapter we described

*Reprinted with permission. Meichenbaum, D. *Cognitive Behavior Modification*. New York: Plenum Press, 1977.

a child who jumped to his feet, knocked a book off a table, bumped two children running to the door, and stepped on a painting as he ran by the easel. The internal dialogue we eventually want the student to carry on with himself might go like this:

Defining the problem	"Let's see, what's my job? To get to the line without bumping anyone."
Focus attention on what to do.	"What do I have to do to get there? Start walking slowly—look where I'm going." "That's it; not too fast now."
Self-evaluation, monitoring	"Watch out for that easel rack." "How's it going? Pretty well."
Self-reinforcement	"Hooray! I made it!"

How does one teach a student to do that? Gradually. First the teacher has the student watch the teacher act out the motions and verbalize out loud the dialogue above. Then the teacher asks the student to walk through the motions of getting to the door while the teacher again verbalizes the dialogue out loud. The sequence then proceeds as follows through six phases:

TEACHER	STUDENT
1. out loud self-instructions, performs motions	watches
2. out loud self-instructions	performs motions
3. whispers instructions	says self-instructions out loud, performs motions
4. moves lips only	whispers self-instructions, performs motions
5. watches	moves lips only, performs motions
6. watches	inner speech for self-instruction; performs motions

Variations of this strategy, under different names (e.g., "stress inoculation"), are used with older students and with adults. But the principles remain the same. Students are taught to identify stressful situations for them so that they can prepare coping strategies (relaxation, self-instruction) in advance. They are also taught to recognize their own signals of stress, so that when caught unprepared, they can realize that they are on the edge of trouble and can spontaneously engage one of their coping strategies.

Social System

The teacher is a helping person in this model. Ultimate decision making power on whether to use, and when to use, the coping strategies rests with the student, although the teacher is a trusted confederate and has the job of sending cues and prompts when the student is beginning to lose control.

Principles of Teacher Response

When the student loses control, the teacher steps in as strongly as necessary to restore it, but no more strongly than necessary; after all, the object is to build the students' own capacity for self-control. Alertness, cue giving, and minimal response consistent with safety are the watchwords here.

Support System

Teachers need time and access to students outside normal class time—or the flexibility to get students alone in a private setting during class time. Teachers need to have identified in advance some triggering situations to work on with the student.

Effects

Successful practice of this model reduces outbursts and disruptive conflicts for students who are impulsive and out of control. It also builds their self-confidence and sense of accomplishment: this is, after all, a kind of mastery they are achieving. As a result, doors open for them to more productive relationships with other students who are less likely to regard them as "crazy" or be resentful and hostile toward them.

A related model is called "Interpersonal Cognitive Problem Solving." This model teaches youngsters "alternative-consequences" thinking. It is aimed primarily at young children and teaches them problem solving strategies they can use to replace fighting, bickering, and resolution of conflicts by power alone. The following script from Shure and Spivack (1978) is illustrative. The teacher leads children to review their actions and the consequences of those actions, then to generate alternate actions that might get the child's need met.

Teacher: Dorothy, were you working with these puzzles?

Child: Brian did, too.

Teacher: Did you and Brian work together? (Teacher gathering facts of situation.)

Child: Yes.

Teacher: Is it fair for Brian to pick them up by himself and for you not to pick them up?

Child: No.

Teacher: Is it fair for you to pick them up and not Brian?

Child: No.

Teacher:	What is fair? (Teacher guides child to see problem from point of view of both children.)
Child:	Brian won't help me.
Teacher:	Can you think of a way to get Brian to help you pick up the puzzles? (Child guided to think of solution to problem.)
Child:	I could ask him.
Teacher:	That's one idea. What might happen if you did that? (Teacher guides consequential thinking.)
Child:	He won't help.
Teacher:	That might happen. What else could you think of to do if he says no?
Child:	Hit him.
Teacher:	You could hit him. What might happen then?
Child:	We'll fight.
Teacher:	Maybe you'd fight. Can you think of a third, different idea?
Child:	You tell him.
Teacher:	I could tell him. How will that help you when I'm not here? (Teacher continues to guide child to think of solutions to problem.)
Child:	I could say I won't play with him anymore.
Teacher:	Is that a good idea?
Child:	Yeah.
Teacher:	Why?
Child:	'Cause then he'll help me.
Teacher:	Maybe. See what you can do to get him to help.

(Shure and Spivack 1978, pp. 146–147)*

The syntax that is embedded in the above dialogue is summarized by the authors in the following way:

1. Elicit from the child his or her view of the problem in a non-accusatory way; for example: "What happened?" "What did the other child do or say?" "Why did he do that?" "What is it you want him to do?" "How do you know he won't do that?"

2. Ask the child, in a matter-of-fact fashion, why he acted as he did. "Why did you call him a dummy?" "Why did you feel like hitting him first?"

3. Guide the child to think about how he felt (feels) and how he thinks others felt (or might feel). You might ask, for instance, "How do you think he felt when you did that?" "How did you feel when he did that?"

4. Raise the question of how one can find out how another child thinks or feels. "How can you find out if he likes your idea?" "How can you tell if he is happy or sad?"

5. Ask the child to give his idea about how to solve the problem. "What can you do if you want him to let you do that (have that, let you play with him, stop hitting you)?"

6. Ask the child to think about what might happen next. "If you do that, what might your sister do or say?" "If you keep bothering him, what might happen next?"

7. Guide the child to evaluate whether he thinks his idea—regardless of its content—is or is not a good one, on the basis of his idea about what might happen next. "Is hitting back a good idea?" "Is trading a good idea?"

8. Encourage the child to think of different solutions to a problem, when relevant. "Can you think of a second different way to get him to give you a turn (let you play with them)?" "If they do not want to play now, can you think of something different to do that will make you happy?" (Shure and Spivack 1978, pp. 157, 229–230)

The responses of children indicate that they are more likely to take action when an idea is their own than when it is suggested or demanded by an adult. Although children do at times need to take adult advice, experience indicates that when the child comes up with a solution he likes, he tends to move to action with a spontaneous motivation that stems from the natural connection between his thinking and his action. If his idea fails, he thinks again and may try another solution before reacting with impulsiveness, frustration, or withdrawal. He has learned a problem-solving style of thinking.

Personal Influence

Discipline Through Personal Regard

In the Personal Influence model, teachers build strong relations with students and use these relationships to motivate students toward more responsible behavior. Teachers make deliberate moves to enhance their personal significance to students, and use their position of respect and regard and closeness to induce behavior change. Teachers show high affect and high commitment; students find their relationship with the significant teacher is a two-way street. While this may sound obvious and connect with what many of you believe you do already, a careful reading of this model may produce some surprises.

Assumptions
Students are more motivated to behave and to do good work if they respect and like the teacher.

Values

The things that are important in this model are student self-image and class order. The syntax reflects a conscious value that students build confidence in themselves as worthwhile people through a close relationship with a significant adult. It also has a clear commitment to class order and taking steps to stop disruption firmly when it occurs.

Goals

The first goal of the model is to build relationships between the teacher and resistant students in order to increase the personal influence of the teacher on students. The second goal is to establish clear expectations for behavior, with swift and consistent consequences for misbehavior.

Rationale

The relationship between teacher and student is like a bank account: it makes a student feel more comfortable, safe, and secure to have it. It enables a student to invest and grow, operating from a safe base to reach out tentatively to try new experiences. And it is something for both teacher and student to draw upon in times of need. A good relationship with a liked and respected teacher will motivate students to try harder both in their work and in their efforts toward better behavior. It will also make a reproof from that teacher more telling—and reproofs there should be! In this model teachers show students when they are upset with them: not losing control and ranting and raving, but showing anger, frustration, disappointment. And that means something to a student because of who the teacher is by that time to the student—a significant person. Students are less inclined to risk this relationship with a teacher through irresponsible behavior when the relationship is important to them. The teacher never uses the relationship

> *The relationship between teacher and student is like a bank account.*

as a threat, or the denial of closeness as a punishment. In fact, after reprimands or episodes where students must be removed from the room, the teacher looks for the earliest possible opportunity to relate to the student positively in another context, to reassure and rebuild the relationship. Nevertheless, though the teacher does not use loss of love threateningly as a club, the very presence of the relationship acts as a healthy inhibitor of disruptive behavior from the student. It is healthy because wanting to please those who are important to us by acting responsibly is a healthy thing. It is not the most advanced form of moral reasoning in the world, but for lonely and confused students it can be a definite step up.

Through this relationship students can gain confidence, try harder, and succeed more in their work. From the stable base with the teacher they can reach out and be brought into contact with other students in controlled settings, sometimes cooperative projects, so that they begin to extend their circle of successful relationships and begin to feel more worthwhile. As they can be accepted by more and more students, as they can see themselves as successful with others, so their capacity and desire to act in ways that will preserve these relationships grows.

Steps

1. Build a friendly relationship with an individual student aimed at closeness and open communication by looking for, and capitalizing on, moments for positive, friendly, one-to-one interaction:

   a. few minutes before class

   b. few minutes after class

   c. inviting student to have lunch together in the room once in a while

   d. after-school projects

2. Practice "Active Listening" and other behaviors detailed under the Personal Relationship Building parameter.

3. Share with the class things about yourself that are interesting: travels, experiences, especially any accomplishment or proficiencies you have (like playing an instrument or some craft ability) that make you real and significant in their eyes without appearing boastful. In general, this means showing them these abilities rather than telling about them. Bringing them in to show and share is more likely to be interpreted as "interesting" than boastful if not overdone.

4. Connect the student with other students in safe and structured ways. For example, teach a young student a game and then set him up for the first ten minutes of the day—typically a hard time for these children—to teach it to two other designated students. With older students, have them pass out materials, or play designated roles in group projects.

5. In one-to-one interactions with the resistant students, let them know exactly what your expectations are explicitly (see Expectations parameter). If appropriate, make behavior contracts and record keeping charts to help focus on what needs to improve and to keep track of progress.

6. When the student acts disruptively, react swiftly with consequences (which will frequently involve removal or isolation of some kind).

7. Always talk to the student afterward, calmly, but expressing some emotion. Get the student to analyze what went wrong and what needs to be done.

8. Look for an early opportunity after a disciplinary episode with a resistant student to have a positive exchange about something. "Gee, that's a nice piece of work, Jim"—especially if you've been very tough about the discipline. The purpose is to reopen communication and establish that your relationship is still alive. The caution is not to overdo it so the student learns a reward (e.g., after-school project) will follow most serious disruptions. Keep the relationship rebuilding low-key, just enough to reopen and reassure.

9. Maintain frequent and direct contact with parents to involve them in the plan as much as possible.

Principles of Teacher Reaction

1. Active Listening during relationship building.

2. Go out of your way to find or make opportunities to build relationships.

3. Show affect when disciplining.

4. Be calmer and more analytical in postmortems with students.

5. Rebuild relationships in low-key fashion after toughest episodes.

Support System

To carry out this model, a teacher needs sufficient access and frequency of contact with students to build relationships. Teachers need to be consistent with consequences and follow-up. Where this is limited by modular scheduling, the school should consider a more self-contained class setting, or at least fewer teacher changes for this student. The teacher needs to have a set of consequences figured out in advance for the student (and perhaps rewards, too, if this Personal Influence strategy is paired with behavioral contracting). These arrangements may require cooperation and agreement with other teachers or administrators (see Seymour Sarason's form of consequences in the following section). But the message is, "Have your ducks lined up." Know what you're going to *do* when the student's behavior crosses acceptable boundaries and gets too disruptive to continue instruction. Usually this will mean some form of removal to a mutual cooling-off room or other site. You have to know *where*.

Social System

The teacher is the authority figure and the norms for behavior come primarily from the teacher. The class may be intimately involved in the setting of rules in general. But even when democracy is part of the class's life, and when it may be the way behavior norms are determined, Personal Influence does not intend to be a democratic model. If a student needs this model, democracy is not the cure to his ills.

Effects

Direct: Deviant behavior is reduced.

Nurturant: 1. The teacher provides a role model of caring and of responsibility, to which the student begins to attach.

2. The student begins to build positive relationships with other students.

Before leaving this model we wished to include one more specific strategy that fits in with it: an unusual, well thought out, and highly effective form of exclusion for disruptive students developed by Seymour Sarason and his associates. It appears in a book far removed from discipline: *The Culture of the School and the Problem of Change* (Sarason 1971). It is a form of response to disruption that you may well find occasion to use and that is also consistent with the Logical Consequences model coming up.

Sarason's strategy is a carefully sequenced set of steps to produce dramatic suppression of hostile defiance. The essence of it is pairing two teachers and removing the defiant student from one teacher's room to the other's. The success of the exclusion depends upon the preparation of the personnel, their pairing, and the support of the principal.

When a student is excluded from the sending teacher's room, that student must stay in the receiving teacher's room for one-half hour, be given a seat at the back, and excluded from any form of participation in that class's activities or interaction with the students there. If the student refuses to leave the sending teacher's room, the pair of teachers carry the child out (for children up to second grade). Older students who refuse to leave are informed that their parents will be phoned immediately if they do not go. Sarason reports that he has never witnessed a child refusing to respond to that pressure and that the excluded child under these conditions is never the slightest problem in the receiving classroom.

Sarason attributes the effectiveness of the strategy to its ability to immediately terminate defiant outbursts, and to its ability to underline with dramatic action the limits beyond which the student may no longer go.

The procedure must be introduced to the whole class at once, not as a punishment procedure but as a way of helping children remember to follow rules that allow them to enjoy learning. "It should be explained to the children repeatedly that a child will not be excluded because he is unwanted or disliked but because he needs the brief opportunity in another classroom to reflect on the rules he has been disobeying" (Sarason 1971, p. 137).

Teachers are to give disruptive students one private warning that specifies what behavior must cease (and what replaces it) if exclusion is to be avoided. At the same time, the teacher must attempt to explain to the student how the class is being disrupted. If the child has to be excluded, the teacher explains to the entire class in the presence of the child being excluded why the step is necessary.

On returning to the classroom, the teacher should review the situation with the class covering reasons behind the relevant rules, alternative ways the excluded child might have behaved, and whenever possible having a brief discussion of how the class can help the excluded child in future.

After school, the teacher should have a short interview with the excluded child, explaining how the exclusion was to help the child remember class rules, not to cause embarrassment. Sarason places emphasis on the importance of this after-school interview and its power to point out "how it is the child himself and not the teacher who decided whether he is to be excluded from the room" (Sarason1971, p. 138).

Sarason has used this strategy with students through fourth grade. We see no reason why it cannot be applied successfully in higher grades as well.

The following will summarize the major steps in this strategy:

1. Introduction
   a. Introduce exclusion move to whole class with its causes and consequences.
   b. As a way of helping students, remember and follow rules that allow them to enjoy learning.

2. Implementation
   a. Give one private warning with specification of behavior.
   b. Give public explanation of why child is being removed.
   c. Remove child, voluntarily or physically if necessary, or call parent.
   d. Maintain for one-half hour.
   e. Child is excluded from participation or interaction with second class.
   f. Review situation with class including:

      —alternative ways the excluded child might have acted

      —reasons for the rule

      —how to help him/her follow the rules.

3. After-School Interview
   a. To help, not to embarrass, is the motive.
   b. Teacher hopes warning will be sufficient in future.
   c. Teacher explains how it is the child who decided, by behavior, when to be excluded.
   d. Show affection and respect.

Rudolf Dreikurs' Logical Consequences

Discipline as Social Contract

Rudolf Dreikurs seeks to eliminate the authoritarian use of power by parents and teachers, which he sees as inappropriate in a democratic age, and harmful to relationships between youngsters and adults. He blends Adlerian psychology with a new technique for responding to misbehavior called Logical Consequences. Reacting with logical consequences will take the acrimony—the child-adult power struggle—out of discipline and enable mutual respect to grow.

Definitions

1. Natural consequence: an aversive result to a child's behavior that occurs by itself, naturally, without any human engineering or intervention (e.g., tipping back in chair, child finally falls over).

2. Logical consequence: an engineered aversive result to a child's behavior that is logically connected to the behavior.

Assumptions

1. Equality is the only basis on which we'll ever be able to solve discipline problems.

2. The fundamental human need is to belong, and it develops into a striving to function in and with a group in order to feel worthwhile.

3. All behavior is purposive. The goal of self-determined direction motivates children's behavior.

Goals

Apply these values in dealings with children so as to:

1. Eliminate the "outright warfare" Dreikurs sees between delinquents and society, between rebellious youngsters and parents and teachers.

2. Apply Adler's first social law—the law of equality, the logic of social living which "demands recognition of every human being as an equal" (Dreikurs and Grey 1968, p. 8).

3. Provide the means by which the student can function properly in an atmosphere of freedom ("properly" here meaning with responsibility rather than license).

4. Eliminate autocratic methods of discipline.

5. To eliminate the obnoxious behavior of the average American child who "fights with his brothers and sisters, refuses to put things away or to do homework or help around the house" (Dreikurs and Grey 1968, p. 10).

6. Cultivate relations based on mutual respect between children and adults.

Rationale

The goals can be accomplished if we understand the causes of students' behaviors, and stop trying to deal with them by autocratic methods. Our responses to behavior must manifest the reality of the social order by allowing students to take responsibility (and logical consequences) for their actions. When teachers/parents start generating responses to misbehavior from this framework of social reality, students will no longer resent, rebel, or feel oppressed because adult responses will no longer appear to be emanating from personal authority.

Furthermore, when the causes of misbehavior in individual students are understood, positive paths of action can be followed that relate to meeting the needs of the child. Thus, new responses to misbehavior based on democratic theory and positive programs of action to meet the needs of children who regularly misbehave will be the two prongs of the Dreikurs attack.

Students develop concepts, through learning, of what behavior will help them develop a place in the group. They may have the concept that cooperation will do so, or that being the center of attention will do so. We can find immediate goals behind every misbehavior. All misbehavior is the result of a discouraged student's mistaken assumption about the way he can find a place and gain status (see Glasser's view of deviant behavior as bad choices).

> **All misbehavior is the result of a discouraged student's mistaken assumption how to find a place and gain status.**

Logical Consequences has the student be impressed with the needs of reality and not the power of an adult. The principle of dealing with each other as equals yields a relationship based on mutual respect. Students are our equals now, not in power or size, but in their right and ability to decide for themselves instead of yielding to a superior force. Whereas punishment represents the power of personal authority, Logical Consequences, as the expression of the reality of the social order, operate at the impersonal level. Punishment says, "You are bad"; Logical Consequences say, "Your behavior yields this result." No judgment is made about "you" as a person.

Syntax

1. Observe the student's behavior in detail.

2. Be sensitive to your own reaction to the student's behavior.

If your reaction is:	*The student's goal may be:*
annoyance	attention
threatened	power
hurt	revenge
helpless	display of inadequacy

3. Give the student "corrective feedback." You stop the student, reprimand him, and see how he reacts. If he simply stops, the behavior may be simply a bid for attention. If the misbehavior increases, its goal may have been to express power. If the student seems hurt, the goal may be revenge.

4. Confront the student with the four goals asking one or more of these four questions, in order—but after a cooling-off period from the moment of conflict.

   a. "Could it be you want me to notice you?" (Attention)

   b. "Could it be that you want to show me that you can do what you want to do and no one can stop you?" (Power)

   c. "Could it be you want to hurt me and the pupils in the class—to get even?" (Revenge)

   d. "Could it be that you want to be left alone?" (Inadequacy)

5. Note the recognition reflex, that is, which one of the four questions the student seems to respond to verbally or with body language.

6. Apply appropriate corrective procedures depending on the student's goal as summarized in FIGURE 7.2.

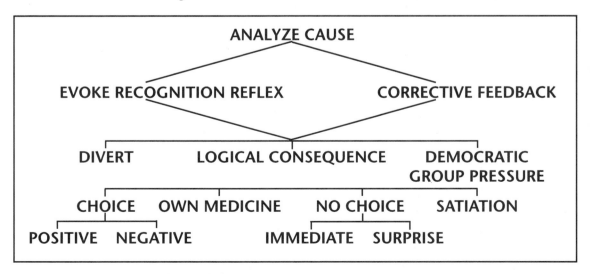

FIGURE 7.2: TYPES OF LOGICAL CONSEQUENCE
Subcategories of Logical Consequence are not delineated by Dreikurs but are derived from an examination of his examples.

When using a Logical Consequence, pick an appropriate type. There are a variety of types of Logical Consequence from which to choose, as the chart in FIGURE **7.2** reveals.

In the CHOICE type of logical consequence, the student can avoid the logical consequence right away by choosing to alter his behavior. The positive choice is akin to Thomas Gordon's "owning the problem." (See the following subsection on Teacher Effectiveness Training.) If dallying with dressing and eating breakfast is making the student late for school, you simply let him handle the problem, own the problem. You may point out his choice to the student, but let him have positive control over handling the outcome. The adult's action is nil.

In a NEGATIVE CHOICE, the teacher/parent points out what logical consequence will accrue to the student through the instrumentality of the teacher if he doesn't perform in a certain way. Not doing assigned work in school will result in his having to stay afterwards to finish it. Having to finish it later is a logical consequence of not finishing it now. That's the way it is; staying after school is not viewed or presented as a punishment, it's just the way things are for people who don't finish their work. The teacher has to stay after too to finish up her work and can't go until it's done. This is the "social reality." This kind of logical consequence is considered NEGATIVE CHOICE here because the child is confronted with, "If you do X, then Y will happen." And Y is an aversive consequence for the child.

OWN MEDICINE type of logical consequence means giving it back to the student. Interrupt the interrupter; make an unlivable supermess around the sloppy student. In effect, hold a mirror of his behavior up to the student. There ought to be a certain amount of humor and appreciation of rational limits when employing this technique, certainly not vindictiveness.

In NO CHOICE logical consequences, the teacher levies the consequence upon the student right after the misbehavior occurs. What separates this from punishment is the logical connection the teacher must establish, at least in the student's mind says Dreikurs, between the behavior and the consequence. (The statement makes it sound as if, for Dreikurs, the distinction between punishment and NO CHOICE logical consequences is not really so great, but that the trick is to convince the student there is a logical connection, whether there really is or not, and thus that the adult is not really dispensing punishment.) NO CHOICE logical consequences can be simply IMMEDIATE (removing two fighting children from a recess baseball game to sit out the recess) or SURPRISE, containing some element of novelty and originality (e.g., the teacher has rock throwers on the playground start rounding up all the rocks they can find, and then has them throw the rocks into a vacant lot to make the playground more safe). Other examples given of original reactions sometimes smack of embarrassment. One morning the seventh grader who continually taps his pencil in an annoying way is given a crayon instead of a pencil; the teacher states, "If you cannot use a pencil correctly, you will have to write with this."

SATIATION means the same to Dreikurs as it does to Behavior Modification people. Make the student do the illegal behavior over and over again until he is sick of it. Have the spitball thrower chuck spitballs into a box all morning; have the wanderer walk around the room all afternoon.

In Dreikurs' last work, we hear that logical consequences are most useful in a goal one situation—attention getting. With power or revenge, logical consequences may backfire and should not be used. Natural consequences are all right anytime, however, except against goal four—feeling of inadequacy..

Principles of Teacher Response

1. Make sure the consequence is logically related to the misbehavior.

2. Present the consequence matter-of-factly, as an expression of the reality of the social order, not personal authority.

3. Make no moral judgments about the behavior or the student.

4. Be kind, and use a friendly voice; never act in anger.

5. Be firm. In a NO CHOICE logical consequence, there really is no choice. This is what's going to happen to the student, and it must be carried through. Don't change your mind; don't give in; don't deviate from your announced procedure.

6. Act; don't talk. Too much talk (threats, warnings, explanations, exhortations) is the downfall of good discipline.

7. Be concerned with the "now," not with the past. There must be no element of "sin" in the teacher's view of the misbehavior, or any element of retribution for past offenses in the consequence used.

8. Never get involved in a power struggle with a student. You will always lose. No contests of wills. ("I won't." "Yes you will, Jimmy Preston, and RIGHT NOW!") Simply refuse to be engaged in this kind of conflict. Sidestep it.

The *positive program:*

While refusing combat, be aware of the cause of the conflict. If the teacher diagnoses "need to show and assert power" as the cause, look for opportunities

> ### *Act; don't talk. Too much talk is the downfall of good discipline.*

for the child to show pride in accomplishment. Try to channel that need to show power into positive paths. If the cause is need for attention, look for opportunities to praise accomplishments, ignoring deviant behavior that is attention-seeking. If the misbehavior stems from assumed disability, treat it with encouragement; ensure success in the classroom; give responsibility, carefully chosen, but publicly visible. If the cause is revenge, then haul out your stamina and dig in for the long pull. Make the student feel liked. Dreikurs talks about group discussion and acceptance in this context, but leaves us with a direction rather than a syntax.

Use sociograms to gather data on popular and unpopular students, extroverts and introverts, he urges. Use this data in seating arrangements and class groupings to have isolates experience new skills of socialization, to put compatible students together.

Have regular class discussions once weekly to consider class problems. Stimulate students to learn to listen, to understand each other, and to help each other.

The positive program has four thrusts, each responding to one of the four causes of misbehavior that Dreikurs cites. But unlike the syntax of direct response to misbehavior, the positive program consists of general principles of teacher response to be applied in a prescriptive manner rather than specific actions. Another way Dreikurs has of talking about the causes of misbehavior is to consider the four causes as goals of the student. The positive program, then, seeks ways to meet these goals for the student without his having to misbehave.

Encouragement is the utility-infielder of this positive program, being applied to three of the four causes. Dreikurs has written a whole book on the subject.

Support System
The Dreikurs model is claimed as most successful with children of elementary age. Beyond that age, more complicated and far-reaching motives add to the basic four with the onset of adolescence.

Effecting a logical consequence requires decisiveness on the part of the teacher, and, in some instances, an ability for novel or original thinking (the SURPRISE type of logical consequence). To levy a NO CHOICE, IMMEDIATE type of logical consequence, the teacher needs the self-confidence and quick response seen in experienced teachers who have developed a large repertoire of responses over the years. Failing the experience and the repertoire, the beginning teacher presumably must be able to think quickly on her feet and apply principles of teacher response to the situation, and develop a logical consequence for the misbehavior.

The teacher must keep her ego off the line, maintain a detachment, a separateness that enables her to avoid power conflicts with children—another difficult challenge, especially for the beginning teacher who is inevitably involved to some degree with proving herself. It is this same kind of ego-detachment on the part of the teacher which will permit the student to own his own problem in the CHOICE, POSITIVE category. Furthermore, to try and convince a vicious-acting student that he is liked means liking an unlikable child—this demands a most secure and giving, empathetic teacher.

Dreikurs' method demands firm, calm, nonjudgmental ways of talking to students when handling misbehavior and the techniques of sounding out and structuring the expression of the group's feeling about the misbehavior.

The space and time required for specific consequences may be considered. (Will there be someone around after school to supervise finishing work? Will shooting paper clips into a box in the corner of the room be too visibly distracting to the rest of the class in the setup of this room, or too noisy?)

Social System

The teacher's role as autocrat is the target of the model. Get the teacher off the power pedestal, says Dreikurs; don't take the position of rule maker and enforcer as a personal role. Yet the teacher is the rule enforcer in his system; it's just that the rules are seen as not stemming from the teacher, but rather from the nature of things, from the social reality. It is the teacher who devises the logical consequence for a misbehavior, and it is the teacher who makes sure that the logical consequence is applied. If the consequence would apply all by itself, it would be a "natural" consequence. Logical consequences require human intervention to be affected.

Rule making is more democratic. Students are included in the constitutional process.

But when all is said and done, the teacher holds and openly uses power in the Logical Consequences system. This use of power is masked and blunted; resentment it might otherwise generate is reduced by having teachers avoid direct power struggles with children, and by clothing the consequence in an attitude of detachment on the part of the teacher, and logic in its relation to the misbehavior. It is not that power is used in a deceptive way, but rather that it is deceptive to think of the system as one that avoids the use of power. Logical Consequences cultivates an attitude about power in teachers and children that seeks to associate it with social reality rather than personal confrontation; but it does not reduce or eliminate its use.

In Dreikurs' last work (with Pearl Cassel, *Discipline Without Tears*, 1974), there is a qualification to the use of Logical Consequences that meliorate the above conclusions. Logical Consequences are sanctioned in this book against goal 1, attention getting, and only there, whereas in previous books there was no such limitation. One does not use Logical Consequences when the student's goal is power or revenge, or display of inadequacy. This, it seems to us, represents a shift of position from Dreikurs' earlier views. Taken at face value, this new position makes the Dreikurs model less reliant upon power and more reliant upon encouragement and such things as use of sociometric data. The new book has a chapter on the evils of competition in school situations, a new theme for Dreikurs, and a chapter on how to conduct democratic class discussions, not a new theme for him. Several quotes from William Glasser suggest that these new emphases may come from a reading of Glasser's *Schools Without Failure* (1968), where the competition theme is found with similar arguments to those used by Dreikurs, and where the syntax of a class meeting is discussed in considerable detail.

Effects

Direct: Deviant behavior is reduced.

Nurturant: Teachers and students can relate to each other without the barrier of power struggles. Mutual respect is cultivated and democratic practices are supposed to become more a part of classroom life. Students become more realistic in their view of the world, more appreciative of the social value of cooperation.

Now let us examine a model of classroom discipline where exercise of sanctions by teachers is eschewed. We will start with the man who seems to have influenced Dreikurs at the end of his life—William Glasser.

William Glasser's Reality Therapy and Schools Without Failure

Discipline as Involvement

William Glasser translates the principles of Reality Therapy into a series of steps (syntax) for teachers to use in responding to misbehavior. By using these steps teachers can get students to take responsibility for their own behavior, and for altering their behavior if it is not meeting their own needs for self-worth, or respecting the rights of others to meet their needs. The result is a school climate of mutual respect, caring, and cooperative problem solving.

Definitions

Glasser establishes his basic definitions in *Reality Therapy* (1965). Some are translated into different vocabulary for *Schools Without Failure* (1968), but the meanings remain the same. RT will designate a definition from *Reality Therapy*; SWF will designate a definition from *Schools Without Failure*.

1. *Respect*: self-respect, a feeling of self-worth. (SWF)

2. *Self-worth*: a feeling of value to oneself and to others; feeling that one is a worthwhile person. (RT and SWF)

3. *Relatedness*: being connected or involved with other people in a relation of caring. (RT)

4. *Involvement*: relationship with a person or persons you care for and whom you know care for you in return. (RT and SWF)

5. *Love*: involvement. (SWF)

6. *Responsibility*: the ability to fulfill one's needs in a way that does not deprive others of the ability to fulfill their needs. A responsible person does what gives him a feeling of self-worth and a feeling he is worthwhile to others. (RT)

7. *Realistic*: action can be called realistic only when its remote as well as immediate consequences are taken into consideration, weighed, and compared. (RT)

8. *Identity*: state that results, is achieved, when one feels love and self-worth. In SWF, Glasser sees self-worth as necessitating confidence in one's knowledge and abilities in school. Love, in a school context, means social responsibility, caring for each other, helping each other. Love is seen as the opposite of and the eliminator of feelings of loneliness and failure. (SWF)

9. *Success*: an established identity; a state of having one's basic needs of relatedness and respect (or of involvement and self-worth) met. (SWF)

10. *Failure*: a state where one's basic needs are not met. To understand Glasser's model it is important to keep in mind the full and special meaning of his definitions of involvement, responsibility, realistic, success, and failure. (SWF)

Assumptions

1. The basic human needs of all people are:

   a. relatedness (involvement)

   b. respect (self-worth)

2. All people are responsible for their actions.

3. All people are capable of acting responsibly, regardless of their background, past experience, or current environment.

4. A change in behavior will lead to a change in attitude.

5. The first five years of school are critical to the development of responsibility and to the development of the ability to succeed.

Values

1. Caring for one another, affection.

2. Courage to attempt solution of one's problems in life.

3. Thinking versus rote learning in education.

4. Relevance to the issues children face in their lives built into curriculum content.

Goals

1. Achievement of personal success by individuals (defined as meeting the two basic needs of involvement and self-worth).

2. Achieving a social climate that manifests mutual respect, caring, and rational, honest, cooperative problem solving.

3. Structuring the expression of affection in schools; creating a form for it, and institutionalizing the expression of it. Making it a recognized part of the purpose, and building it into the activities, of school life.

Rationale

Success, as previously defined, comes through being realistic (as previously defined), responsible (as previously defined), and right (which means acting in accordance with accepted moral standards).

This can be restated: Meeting one's basic needs of involvement and self-worth can be accomplished by considering the long-range consequences of one's acts, by acting to meet the needs of others, and by acting in accord with moral standards.

To achieve this kind of success, one needs involvement as a starting point; one needs a "significant other" in one's life about whom one cares, and from whom affection is returned. When we have that, we can then begin to relinquish action based on the pleasure principle, that is, immediate gratification. But involvement alone is not enough. After involvement exists, something must be done to raise the feeling of self-worth. We can feel worthwhile only if we maintain a satisfactory standard of behavior.

To maintain satisfactory behavior, we must become capable of, and practice, self-evaluation; we must look at our behavior and judge whether it is responsible (whether it meets our two needs) without depriving others of the ability to fulfill their needs.

Deviant behavior is unrealistic and irresponsible. Deviant behavior shows children have made bad choices about how to meet their needs. They can't make better choices unless they are involved with those who can.

Discipline, which is what those who love give us, points out unrealistic and irresponsible behavior and helps the child become realistic and responsible.

Steps

1. "Make Friends," says Glasser to teachers. "Become involved," he says to the therapist. "Establish a relationship," he says to both, "with mutual confidence in and expression of affection."

2. Ask, "What are you doing?" when a student misbehaves. This is identifying, verbalizing, facing the reality of the behavior. This is a real step for some students, and not something they realize, much less ask on their own.

3. Ask, "Is it helping you?" Evaluate. Judge the behavior. Behind the question is the thought that the behavior is not helping the child meet his two basic needs. But one does not talk explicitly about the two needs with students. One simply asks for an evaluation of the behavior: "Is it helping you?"

Questions 2 and 3 may not be addressed by the students if the involvement is not previously established and if they do not know that there will be no punishment.

4. No punishment.

5. Make a plan. The teacher asks the student to make a plan to avoid the behavior, or how to cope with the situation in an acceptable way the next time it crops up. It is okay for the teacher to give suggestions and advice here (see versus Thomas Gordon's view). But the plan must be enough for the student so he can make a commitment to it.

6. Get a commitment from the student to carry out the plan. This can be verbal or written.

7. No excuses: "When will you do it?" And the teacher holds the student to the answer. No excuses are acceptable for not meeting the commitment. Though there is no punishment, the teacher holds the student to his commitment, and if the student does not meet it, asks the student to reevaluate his plan, make a new one, or renew his commitment. The process may need repeating over and over again. The teacher who is involved is willing to start all over again repeatedly. But always there is the expectation and the trust that the student will finally meet it. One expects and one expects and one expects. One never, however, excuses or condones or makes allowances, or fails to hold students to commitments.

8. Class Meetings. These form a regular part of the response system of the teacher to misbehavior (as well as a format for establishing the requisite involvement). For a complete discussion of class meetings see Principles of Teacher Response which follow.

Principles of Teacher Response

1. Point out the reality of the situation—of the behavior.

2. Never condone irresponsibility.

3. Focus on the present, not the past.

4. No punishment, no sarcasm, no ridicule. Sarcasm and ridicule are destroyers of affection, of closeness, of relationships, of involvement.

5. Don't avoid speaking in the first person. Say, "I want you to..." not "we should," or "you should."

6. The environment should never be manipulated so the child does not suffer reasonable consequences of his behavior.

7. Handle class problems in Class Meetings.

There are three kinds of Class Meetings: Social Problem-Solving Meetings, Open-Ended Meetings, and Educational Diagnostic Meetings. Social Problem-Solving Meetings are used to work out solutions to problems pertinent to the group or to any individual in the group. They are the kind of meetings that fit into the syntax of response to misbehavior. Open-Ended Meetings discuss questions of interest and relevance to the children's lives. In addition to making at least part of the day focus on issues of relevance to the students, however, these meetings perform a vital function in establishing involvement between the teacher and students, and among the students themselves. Educational Diagnostic Meetings are used to assess how well children are grasping aspects of curriculum and to plan future steps.

The leadership of Social Problem Solving Meetings by teachers is handled in accordance with certain principles also:

    a. Solution to the problem is the focus of the discussion, never fault finding or punishment.

    b. The teacher remains nonjudgmental in his or her comments, though the students are not expected to do so. (Experiencing the feedback of his peers is one of the "reasonable consequences" a child suffers for an irresponsible behavior.)

    c. Conduct the meetings in a tight circle.

    d. Keep them short.

    e. Don't overdwell on a single problem student (three times in a row on a class bully would be overdwelling).

    f. Make the majority of class meetings in the other two categories (Open Ended and Educational Diagnostic).

    g. Use Class Meetings as a vehicle for as much teaching of regular curriculum as possible.

Support System

1. Heterogeneous, homeroom-based classes. The class must spend most of the day together as a social unit for the feelings of involvement with each other and with their teacher to develop.

2. No "ABCDF" type of grading. (No labeling as "failure.")

3. Curriculum must have a "thinking" emphasis, so that...

4. Curriculum is relevant to issues in the students' lives.

5. Success in reading. Glasser sees this achievement as so much a part of social expectation about school and, in fact, so necessary for achieving feelings of success in school, that special attention must be paid to its accomplishment in the design of school curriculum. To achieve it, he is even willing to dissolve the homeroom class unit for a portion of the day.

6. Probably most important, the teacher must be the kind of person willing to make the personal commitment and investment of self to become "involved" with her students.

Social System

1. Nonpunitive.

2. Students participate in rulemaking.

3. Trusts and tryouts. The constant willingness of the teacher to start again with a student who has not met a commitment expresses a confidence, a trust, in the student to eventually succeed. (It also expresses a depth of involvement on the teacher's part.)

4. The teacher's role is as a model of responsibility.

5. The teacher also has a role as a benevolent despot, not through punishment, but through rule enforcement and the holding of children to commitments they have made.

6. Reasonable rules. Participation of students in the constitutional process tends toward making the rules more reasonable. But Glasser realizes and approves of the fact that adults serve as a major source for principles from which rules come. This is the practical reality. The statement that rules "should be reasonable" is something Glasser says to teachers and administrators knowing they will have and should have major say in what they will be. (Glasser is not a Summerhillian.)

7. The students are responsible for their own behavior and free to choose at all times what their behavior will be like. Their responsibility extends not only to themselves, or even to the teacher, but also to all the other members of the class.

Effects

Direct: Social problems are worked on openly with an orientation toward solution, not blame.

Relevance is stressed in curriculum.

Nurturant: Warmth and affection grows among students and between teacher and students.

Respect for each other's needs and rights is cultivated.

Empathy develops as students' needs are met and their responsibility grows.

The next model, Thomas Gordon's Teacher Effectiveness Training (T.E.T.), builds on the principles of the similar Parent Effectiveness Training and has been translated into an in-service course offered nationwide to schools and school districts.

Thomas Gordon's Teacher Effectiveness Training

Discipline as Communication

In the T.E.T. model, Gordon seeks to eliminate the conflicts and misunderstandings that cause poor relations between teachers and students by teaching them communication skills. The T.E.T. communication skills give students and teachers an alternative to power in resolving conflicts of needs. No longer does the teacher have to win at the expense of the student's needs (Method I), or the student win at the expense of the teacher (Method II). The "no-lose" Method III, taught in T.E.T., enables both students and teachers to meet their needs.

Definitions

1. *Active Listening*: listening for the feeling content (the encoded message) in a speaker's remark, and feeding this back to the speaker.

2. *"I" message*: a nonjudgmental description of another's behavior, a statement of the behavior's tangible effects upon you, and a statement of the feelings generated in you by this behavior. These three elements in any order comprise an "I" message.

3. *Gear Shifting*: switching into active listening after sending an "I" message.

Assumptions

1. Acceptance enables change and growth. When a person feels he is "OK" as a person, accepted for what he is in the eyes of another, he will be receptive to changing his behavior. In addition to enabling change, acceptance is a near sine qua non for it. When one feels nonacceptance from a change agent, one resists the change. Gordon's base in Maslow and Rogers is evident here.

2. The Gordon system presumes relatively mentally healthy children; it is not designed for dealing with emotionally disturbed children.

3. A valued relationship exists between teacher and the student. The system applies only when the teacher has "bought into the relationship," that is, cares about the relationship, values it. (No wonder Gordon and Glasser are now giving training sessions together.) One won't be motivated to go through the steps of active listening and the others in the syntax if one does not care about the other party.

4. Students can take responsibility for, and solve, their own problems.

Values

Gordon values honesty and openness in communication. He values forthrightness in the recognition of, and respect, of one's own needs and those of others. He values nonjudgmental communication as an expression of that acceptance. He values the mutual respect of meaningful relationships where people, in caring about each other, try to meet each other's needs. He lastly values behavior which facilitates the personal growth of others. These values translate directly into Gordon's goals.

Goals

1. Build a relationship between student and teacher whose result will be to make all teaching more effective.

2. Get students to take responsibility for their own behavior.

3. Increase the no-problem area (see Rationale below), and thus make more time available for teaching-learning.

Rationale

All classroom pupil behavior is either acceptable or unacceptable to the teacher. "The Rectangle" below illustrates this universe of behavior. Everything above the line is acceptable; everything below the line is unacceptable. The placement of the line (and thus the size of the areas) varies with personality, and within persons varies with time, mood, conditions, and environment. Whispering to a classmate may be acceptable one day and unacceptable another, depending on other factors in the teacher's life (if the principal has just given her a tough grilling, for example).

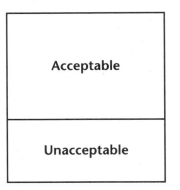

Another way of looking at the universe of classroom pupil behavior is "Problem Ownership." Either a pupil behavior is giving the teacher a problem, giving the student a problem, (sometimes both), or is no problem for anyone (like working on math problems, or going to sharpen a pencil in an acceptable way). This no-problem area is called the teaching-learning area.

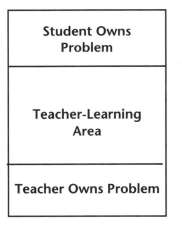

The causes of misbehavior (behavior in the problem area) are unmet needs of children and teachers. Instead of trying to identify and deal with these needs, teachers often use power, which results in poor relations with students; poor relations aggravate poor communication, and the circle goes around and around. Using communication skills to identify and meet teacher and student needs without the use of power is Gordon's strategy for reducing misbehavior.

Steps

1. Determine if a problem exists.

2. Own the problem. This one is harder than it sounds. You, the teacher, really own the problem only if it is having a tangible effect on you. We (adults, parents, teachers) often "own," take responsibility for problems that are not really ours. For example, Margie is dillydallying in the morning, is slow getting down to breakfast. Mother, who always has to harass her to get her to school on time, is a nervous wreck by the time the school bus finally leaves. Whose problem is this? Mother has made it hers. But who really owns the problem? Margie does. Right now Mother always solves it for her. If Mother lets Margie own her own problem, then Margie will have to deal with the consequences (walking to school, being late, waiting until Dad leaves for work and hitching a ride, also being late). If we choose to take responsibility for a problem that is not really ours, it may begin to have some tangible effects on us (Mother is a tangible nervous wreck). But if we let the problem rest with its real owner, then only the owner feels the effects.

   If the second-grade teacher is recapping open paint jars every night and mumbling about the irresponsibility of her class, whose problem is the paint jars? If the teacher lets the children own their problem of leaving paint jars uncapped and having only dried cake to paint with the next day, whose problem is it?

   If the students are working productively but noisily, and the class is next to the principal's office and the teacher is afraid the principal will get the wrong idea and give her a bad evaluation, whose problem is it?

3. Active Listening. Active listening, as defined before, is listening for the feeling content (encoded message) in the speaker's remarks and feeding that feeling back to the speaker. ("What do you like in a girl, Dad?"—really meaning, "You're wondering what to do to get boys to like you.") Active listening tends to get at the real root of the problem, which may be buried under several layers of feeling, only the topmost of which is showing at first. Good active listening extracts facts, meaning, and feeling content from heard remarks. While we are accustomed to listening for facts and meaning, we are not accustomed to listening for the important feeling content going on behind the remarks. If we are in the problem area, it may be this encoded feeling that is the cause of the problem, reflecting some unmet need. If we are dealing with a problem the student owns, "active listening" may help the student work his way through to a solution.

3a. The teacher owns the problem. "I" messages are brought to bear. For example:

Say the room is too noisy for her tolerance and her conception of a level conducive to learning, but the students are happy with it, aren't finding the noise offensive anyway. The teacher sends an "I" message with the elements previously described (non-judgmental, description of the behavior, tangible effects on her, feelings generated in her). "The noise level in this room is giving me a headache!" (Description—effect.) "I ache for some peace and quiet." (Feeling.)

4. Gear shifting. The "I" message may take care of the problem by itself. If the students have regard for the teacher and a satisfactory relationship with her, they may be motivated to change their behavior. But if they have a need of their own that is not being met, we have a conflict of needs situation. In this case the teacher, after sending an "I" message, must gear shift into active listening to identify the needs of the students. After a period of this, she may restate her "I" message. If both teacher and students own the problem, a Method III solution may be called for.

5. Method III. Method I is teacher power: teacher wins, students lose. Method II is children power: students win, teacher loses. Method III is the no-lose solution consisting of the following steps:

   a. Define the problem in terms of needs.

   b. Students and teacher mutually brainstorm solutions.

   c. They mutually evaluate solutions.

   d. They mutually pick one acceptable to both.

   e. They determine how and when to implement.

   f. They appoint a later date for reassessment of the solution and meet on the date.

   Method III is used only when it has been previously explained and "bought," at least for a trial, by the students.

6. Modifying the environment. Here the teacher takes the initiative to enrich, impoverish, restrict, enlarge, rearrange, simplify, systematize, or plan the environment, but not at the expense of the students (not making them "lose").

Social System

Students and teachers are both conceived as individuals with needs to be respected and met. Whoever has the problem takes the initiative to send "I" messages to the person or persons whose behavior is having a tangible effect on them. If the students are not skilled enough in sending "I" messages, the teacher is sensitive to their needs and uses active listening to bring them out. Conflict of needs is handled through the modified negotiation techniques of Method III or by having the teacher take initiative to modify the environment so that the behavior goes into the no-problem area. *Decisions are negotiated only when there is a conflict of needs.* When acting in the no-problem area, there is nothing to prevent the teacher from taking initiative and making instructional decisions based on other models of teaching.

Principles of Teacher Response

In the no-problem area the teacher can respond out of whatever framework she or he likes. Even the dirty dozen[3] can be okay! But when there is a problem, the syntax provides clear steps to take, starting with defining and owning the problem. At the basis of all the steps are mutual respect and a desire to meet the other's needs.

Principles of teacher response are empathy, separateness, facilitation, self-respect, and negotiation.

- Empathy is manifested in active listening.

- Separateness means allowing others to own their problems, not identifying with or assuming unto oneself the problems of others—letting people take responsibility for themselves.

- Facilitation means that, though separate, one helps others find their own way to reach solutions to problems; one facilitates their progress.

- Self-respect here means standing up for yourself too, not repressing your own needs, but recognizing, articulating, and seeking to meet them openly, at the same time as one is a helping person to others.

- Negotiation is the principle at the root of Method III solutions, the method called into play when there is a conflict of needs.

Support System

1. Active listening requires of the listener:

   a. A trust in the ability of the student to solve his own problem.

   b. Genuine acceptance of the other's feelings.

   c. An understanding that feelings are transitory. ("I hate you!" Maybe he really does, at this moment, but not deeply, and probably not in five minutes.)

   d. A real desire to want to help the student.

   e. Separateness—an ability to psychologically separate yourself from another's problem, from identifying and assuming responsibility for the other, but not preventing you from helping.

   f. An understanding that students seldom start by sharing the real problem, that the real problem may be buried beneath several layers of feeling.

   g. Respect for the privacy of others, who may not want to reveal certain feelings to you, or intend them only for your ears when they do.

[3] Advising, ordering, sympathizing, threatening, moralizing, lecturing, judging, ridiculing, analyzing, interrogating, distracting, and praising.

h. Time—enough time to go through the process (which you don't have in a crowded hallway with 30 kids on the way to lunch).

2. "I" messages require of the sender:

   a. honesty in expressing feelings.

   b. risk: You are, after all, revealing a feeling to another person.

3. Gear shifting from "I" messages back to active listening requires significant ego control. With a strong need of your own, just expressed in the "I" message, suddenly you have to tune in to the other person's need and actively listen to it. (This I view as the most underrated and demanding aspect of Gordon's system.)

4. Method III requires that:

   a. Students understand what it's all about and "buy" it.

   b. Students believe you will do your part and not resort to power in the end.

   c. You have time to go through all the steps.

As you can see, the elements of the support system pertain to attitudes and beliefs on the part of the teacher, rather than physical supports. One must be a certain type of person, with certain understandings and beliefs, and have the time to carry out the system in a given situation, in order to make Teacher Effectiveness Training work. Thus, we may classify these support elements as belonging almost entirely to the "presage" category.

Effects

Direct: The direct effects of the system, according to Gordon, are that "teachers like kids and kids like teachers"—that is, improved relationships. These improved relationships result from improved communication skills. Thus, the no-problem area expands in the "Rectangle" (see Rationale) and more time is available for teaching-learning. More teaching-learning takes place; teaching becomes more effective.

It is interesting to see that the result of this humanistic approach is related to more effective teaching, but Gordon has a special understanding of "effectiveness."

Nurturant: Remembering his base in Maslow and Rogers, and carefully reading his comments on the benefits of such things as active listening, reveals that "effectiveness" to Gordon means facilitating personal growth; that is what one becomes "effective" at doing. The new T.E.T. communication skills create better teacher-child relations, which manifest themselves in a changed learning environment of warmth, responsibility, mutual respect, and acceptance. The new learning environment facilitates personal growth and, therefore, simultaneously enhances academic learning.

Other nurturant effects are student modeling of active listening, "I" messages, and Method III techniques.

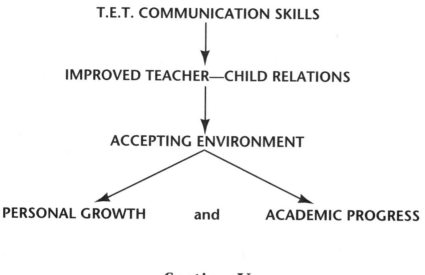

T.E.T. COMMUNICATION SKILLS

↓

IMPROVED TEACHER—CHILD RELATIONS

↓

ACCEPTING ENVIRONMENT

↙ ↘

PERSONAL GROWTH and **ACADEMIC PROGRESS**

Section V
Matching

One of Dreikurs' statements has always struck us as significant: "All behavior is purposive." While his four "purposes" (attention, power, helplessness, revenge) don't seem nearly to cover the waterfront of motives behind misbehavior, the basic notion is a powerful one—people do what they do for a reason—always. They may not know the reason consciously, but it's always there. From this idea, we can recognize that behind all previous patterns of student misbehavior are needs, felt psychological needs that the student is trying to meet through the behavior. This doesn't make us sappy, too "understanding," or permissive; it simply tells us: "figure out what the student is really trying to get through this behavior, and that will tell us a lot about how to respond." What the student may be trying to get, the unmet need that might be working actively inside him, may be:

Safety/Security	"I have enough trust. Things are at least minimally safe for me. I know what's going to happen next."
Self-Control	"I can control myself. I'm not afraid I'll hurt myself or others."
Affection	Somebody significant cares about me."
Inclusion	"I'm accepted in this group."
Control as Power	"I have some control over my fate, over what happens to me."
Self-Esteem	"I'm a worthwhile person."
Recognition	"Other people have esteem for what I've done, for who I am."
Self-Actualization	"I'm realizing my potential."

Remember, now, that *most* misbehavior need not be traced to unmet psychological needs. Students who test a teacher by calling out, passing notes, or doing a thousand other things may be doing nothing more complicated, in fact, than simply *testing the teacher*. They're trying to see how much they can get away with. We're not talking about that here. We're talking about the one or two very resistant students who persistently misbehave despite appropriate treatment through Expectations and the other Management Parameters.

The psychological needs listed above are arranged in sequence starting with the most fundamental. We will develop the hypothesis that there is a relation between the psychological needs driving a student's behavior and the most appropriate response strategy, along the lines shown in this chart:

Psychological Needs That May Be Driving Resistant Students	Response Strategies
Self-Actualization	
	Teacher Effectiveness Training
Recognition	
Self-Esteem	Reality Therapy
Control	Logical Consequences
Inclusion	
	Personal Influence
Affection	
	Self-Awareness Training
Safety/Security/Trust	
	Behavior Modification

The six strategies are arranged, bottom to top, from least mature to most mature, from those that demand the least maturity and competence of the student to those that demand the most. Students with unresolved needs in the early (lower) part of the sequence seem to be less mature emotionally and require strategies from the less mature part of the continuum (Behavior Modification, Self-Awareness Training). Students driven by later needs (e.g., control) seem better able to respond to more mature strategies (Logical Consequences, Reality Therapy).

Over a long period of time with a particular student, we should try to move up the chart. That is, we should start with strategies appropriate to the student's current needs, but help the student grow by moving into more mature strategies. In this way, we are moving students toward more self-discipline, even if we have to start off doing all the discipline for them

(Behavior Modification). Their growth toward improved mental health and emotional maturity is not just paralleled but fostered by our ability to modulate our strategies upwards over time. If this seems like a big demand to be making on teachers—to master and practice appropriately six different strategies of discipline—we agree. Teachers aren't trained to do that in college. But one doesn't have to be an expert to start using this framework for understanding behaviors and trying to tailor responses. The fact is, we already have these students in our classes and we have to start somewhere. Getting to know and try the different strategies takes time and practice, and proceeds much better if at least two teachers work on it together. But learning them is eminently doable, and an immense service to students who have no other stable anchors in their lives than their school and their teacher. But let's backtrack. Where did we get that list of psychological needs to begin with?

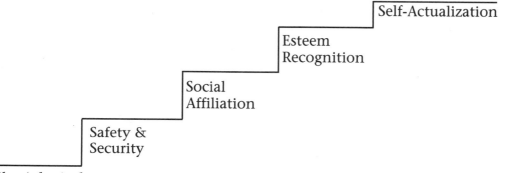

Many authors, such as Maslow (1962), have brought to their work the notion of certain universal psychological needs shared by all humans. Some authors arrange them hierarchically:

"Hierarchically" to Maslow means that lower needs have the greatest strength (e.g., physiological) until satisfied. For instance, if you're hungry you don't worry much about social acceptance. If physiological and safety needs are met, social affiliation needs come to the fore. One tries to meet that need and it could account for much behavior we see. This same person, however, would not be driven strongly by needs for esteem and recognition; at least, that would not be the dominant force behind behavior until social affiliation needs were satisfied.

Maslow and others do *not* view these needs as developmental steps which, once traversed, do not need to be reworked. People move up and down the ladder according to current circumstances: If I lose my job, I am suddenly thrown two or three steps down the stairs and begin operating out of my need for safety and security. If a student's parents get divorced, the same thing may happen.

In **Figure 7.3**, we have spread out the basic psychological needs as described by a number of authors. While each author uses different terms and highlights a different number of needs, there is considerable overlap amongst them, boiling down to eight basic needs that seem to be included by all the writers.

Maslow	Dreikurs	Schutz	Glasser	Erikson	SUMMARY
Self-Actualization				Integrity vs. Despair Generativity vs. Sterility Intimacy vs. Isolation Identity vs. Identity Confusion	SELF-ACTUALIZATION RECOGNITION
Esteem Recognition	(Helplessness)/ Competence		Respect	Industry vs. Inferiority	SELF-ESTEEM
	Power	Control		Initiative vs. Guilt	CONTROL
Social Affiliation	Attention	Inclusion Affection	Relatedness		INCLUSION AFFECTION
				Autonomy vs. Shame	SELF-CONTROL
Safety/ Security/Trust				Trust vs. Mistrust	SAFETY/ SECURITY/TRUST

FIGURE 7.3: BASIC PSYCHOLOGICAL NEEDS

Note that we have included Erikson's eight psychological stages, or psychological crises, on our list, too. Erikson is a developmentalist; in other words, he does see these crises as stages which must be traversed before addressing later issues up the scale. And the crises usually do not reoccur once resolved, yet people (and children) can get stalled with unresolved crises at a lower level, which prevents their moving to healthy later stages of emotional development. What is relevant here is the connection between any one of Erikson's stages successfully navigated and the psychological need that gets met by that successful passage. There seem to be parallels between what Erikson sees happening—for example, during the crises of "initiative versus guilt"—and what Schutz sees as meeting the basic need for control.

Taken together these writers seem to be sending some clear messages: (1) All humans have certain psychological needs in common; (2) The needs are related in regular ways (maybe hierarchical); (3) Needs drive behavior. When a basic need isn't met, it motivates observable behavior and enables us to account in some way for what we see.

How can we use those ideas to match resistant students with the six strategies? What is the relationship between a strategy a teacher may choose and the need that may appear to be driving the student's behavior?

In this section we offer some guidelines in answer to those questions, but the following caveat is necessary. We are not psychologists, and we are not trying to make teachers into psychologists. The last thing we want to do is to get teachers to label a student with a psychological need and begin "treatment." The whole business is much too 'iffy' for that. Even mental health professionals, we feel, diagnose too often and too early. We can't really know what's going on inside another person's head and why they're acting as they do; but we can have conviction that *there is a reason,* even if it remains obscure to us (and to them). And there is no other way to pick appropriate response strategies except to try to make some logical match-up between what *might* be the student's need and a strategy that's in line with that need. Don't diagnose; be very, very tentative—but try to use behavior to get clues to needs and make connections to strategies. That will be better than using one strategy with everyone as if it were the method of Discipline, and it will be better than random, eclectic bouncing around with different strategies.

Six Typical Profiles
Behavior Modification is the most controlling of the strategies; and one thing we know about it is that it really works. If you do it well enough, you can get a student to do almost anything, even high school students. Why would a teacher want to be so controlling? One reason might be desperation: the class (or the student) is so disruptive you can't think of anything else to do! Or, students may simply not have in their repertoires the behaviors they need to function properly: *not know how* to pick up and put away, *not know how to* do assignments in order; *not know how to* meet deadlines; *not know how to* resolve a dispute without fists. Behavior Modification can allow students to experience behaviors they would never try on their own and thus discover

that there are other ways of doing things. Students in extreme inner states of insecurity or anxiety can be helped to function, to get through the demands of the day, by leaning on the strong structures of a Behavior Modification program. It actually supports them, helps them function as opposed to flop around, during times when they are weak and confused. Rather than controlling in these circumstances, Behavior Modification is supportive, even protective. It stops the negative cycle of behavior that is destroying a student's relations with others and confirming a self-image that is probably already poor. It gives students a lifeline to hang onto until they can gain some control over themselves. And that is what we want to work for ultimately—self-control, self-discipline.

We are always trying to move students up the list toward the more mature strategies because a person who can respond to the Reality Therapy approach, for example, is more emotionally mature than a person who needs Behavior Modification all the time. In any given year, you may find yourself starting off with Personal Influence for Jimmy, but able to move to Reality Therapy by the end of the year. Many connections and transitions between the strategies are possible, but one always tries to move up the list with a student. Over a period of several years in a public school, we have seen skilled teachers move a student along from Behavior Modification in grades K and 1, to T.E.T. by grade 5. Other things outside the teacher's control must support a student's personal growth to enable dramatic progressions like that, but we are also quite certain it could not have happened without a team of teachers who shared this point of view and planned with each other to help the student grow.

The *Self-Awareness* strategies are also suitable for students in tenuous emotional states. These students may intellectually know the difference between productive and unproductive behavior but be unable to control themselves. Their tempers often flare out of control; they don't trust themselves and have difficulty forming friendships. They may withdraw, spend a lot of time drawing, reading, or wrapped up in some objective activity. If they have a bent for science or art, they may produce fabulous projects, and in fact only through these projects do they build the superficial relationships they do have with others. They hate to talk about their feelings, in fact, are unable to, afraid to, and may refuse to if pressed. When they do speak about themselves, it is in connection with events and objects, not people or feelings. For young children in this plight, the strategies of Wolfgang (1977) and Lederman (1969) are right on target. For older students, the self-instructional strategies of Meichenbaum are more appropriate, though forms of these are also useful with young children (e.g., the "Turtle Technique").

Students who are suited to the *Personal Influence* model often generate love-hate feelings in you. They have likable, charming, even lovable qualities. One moment you feel like hugging them, and the next you want to throw them through the wall. One-on-one they tend to be great; in a group they can be poison, inciters, show-offs. Curiously, they are often quiet in large groups where there is more anonymity, but incorrigible in small groups where the social tensions of establishing themselves with the others are too much for them. When they come in in the morning they may drift around the room, checking out what everyone is doing, moving from thing to thing, settling in nowhere. They have a real need for affection and inclusion and those are often missing in their lives. In those morning meanderings they are looking for their place, wondering where they can plug in, and they don't quite know how to connect. Their reputations, their relations with the other students, don't make entry easy for them in unstructured situations. They long for friends, for closeness with other students and with the teacher, but they repeatedly behave in ways guaranteed to antagonize. The structure, the demands, the warmth, and the relationship building of the Personal Influence model help them bridge a difficult period in their lives.

With younger children, one may borrow from Behavior Modification to help these students gain more awareness and control over their most disruptive behaviors. With older students, contingency contracting can help supplement the "tough" half of the Personal Influence model.

Sometimes we meet students who say "no," who defy and are openly challenging of authority at every turn. These students may be candidates for the *Logical Consequences* model. They refuse to do their work or do it only when they "feel like it." They *look* for power conflicts with authority figures, actually invite them. Of course, there are some students who get into frequent arguments with peers and with teachers but who do not appear to deliberately set them up; the students we're taking about here, however, *do* set up challenges to authority, and the argument is usually about "doing it my way." Such students can be tyrants in games with others, and may do a considerable amount of bullying and outrageous pushing around of other students and of teachers, too, up to the limit they can get away with. Their psychological need for control is driving the behavior—only the need has gone haywire, gone out of perspective, and is damaging these students and those with whom they come in contact. They have come to believe, as Dreikurs would say, that the only way they count in the world is by showing their power, by controlling others. That is how they think they must act in order to be significant and worthwhile people. This mistaken belief must be changed if their behavior is to change in any way other than a temporary one.

Dreikurs' method avoids the power conflicts the student seeks and tries to teach the reality of the social order through logical consequences. These consequences do not represent the imposed power of the teacher, but rather the way things really work in the world. Thus, students can't get mad at the teacher and back into their old unproductive power game. They begin to see their behavior as having consequences for themselves because the behavior is incompatible with how the social order works, not because the adults "won't let me." They begin to learn something about the social contract. They are put in a position of seeing their behaviors in relation to what a society, a group, needs to function, and the group itself is used in classroom meetings to reinforce that message, which brings us to Glasser's Reality Therapy and Classroom Meeting model, where the use of the group is more developed.

Candidates for *Reality Therapy* are students who are acting irresponsibly—students who are always forgetting books, showing up late, not doing work, missing appointments and obligations, blaming others and not perceiving or at least acknowledging their own role in conflicts. These students may act quite disruptively, knocking over others' books, punching students they pass in the hallway, slamming lockers. But they are not premeditated or deliberate about these acts in the same way as an attention-seeker would be. They just seem to fall into these behaviors. They're like emotional drifters who are easily led into bad practices and bad company. When asked why they bumped into a student they'll likely say, "I don't know," and shrug. Given punishment and reprimands, they won't argue, won't comply, and won't change.

In Reality Therapy, students are brought up against the consequences of their behavior for their relations with *other people*. It is a more personal focus than the Dreikurs model, where the intended learning is: "This behavior doesn't work in the world." Glasser's learning is more like: "It isn't working for *me*. Now what am I going to do about it?" This is toward the top of the scale of maturity among the six models because the responsibility for seeing, evaluating, and changing the behavior lies with the student, even though an involved teacher is necessary to get them into each step. Glasser, who doesn't focus much on the causes of misbehavior, likes to deal with the here and now. Many people, he believes, who act crazy, can decide *not* to act crazy. They have the inner control to do that if they can go through the Reality Therapy steps and decide that it is worth their while to do so—if they have someone who's involved enough to walk the road with them and not give up on them. So Glasser might be inclined to use Reality Therapy with students operating at quite a low level.

Classroom Meetings broaden the sense of "involvement" from between teacher and student to include students with each other. Eventually through these meetings, students gain a place to talk to each other about what's really on their minds. Resistant students get to hear how others are perceiving them, and the others are enabled to share those perceptions in a problem-solving environment.

A good candidate for *Teacher Effectiveness Training* (T.E.T.) is a student who appears resentful, maybe sitting out his school time like a prison term, occasionally rebellious or wise, but usually functional. Work may be satisfactory or inferior. These students may feel the teacher never listens to them, and the teacher may feel they have no respect for or understanding of what school is all about. There is poor communication between teacher and student and both feel their needs are unmet. Both are unsatisfied with their relationship in class even though overt conflict may not be frequent between them.

Such a student usually has a cumulative history of increasing hostility and seems ready to manifest it toward *all* teachers, unless they prove themselves otherwise. With other students relationships are often fine. It is to adults that the student has begun to generalize the notion that "all they ever do is give orders, tell me what to do. They never listen." And the student has given up sending messages about his beefs.

T.E.T. can also be right on target for a student with a problem where, through active listening, a skillful teacher can help the student reach his own solution.

T.E.T. isn't a model that lines up with a particular psychological need like some of the others. It is the most mature of the models, because it calls on the student to have sufficient empathy or at least understanding to read a teacher's "I" message and be willing to respond through "no-lose" (or "win-win") negotiation. Method III solutions themselves require listening and sending skills on the part of both parties that are difficult for very troubled students. Gordon himself says that T.E.T. is not designed for disturbed students. However, it is our experience that active listening and "I" messages are skills that are immensely valuable on their own, even when one is not using the whole T.E.T. model. Active listening is very helpful, almost necessary, in the Self-Awareness model, and "I" messages complement the Personal Influence model nicely. And, of course, active listening is the key skill for unlocking the longer-term resentment of the student profiled above.

To summarize, then, each of these six strategies seems most appropriate for a particular kind of student. We have offered a typical profile for each of the six as general guidelines for matching, and referred to psychological needs that may be behind the profile. To pick a strategy, a teacher must start with the student's behaviors themselves. They should be written down—the what, when, with whom, how often, and where of these behaviors. Simply listing behaviors and circumstances, however, will not be enough. *How* a behavior is done (as reported by an observer) is important, too, for from that "how" we will try to infer the motive behind it: Did Charlie knock over the books casually as he passed them, a kind of afterthought in his meanderings (Reality Therapy candidate)? Did he swagger down the aisle and knock them over with a cocky flick and insolent glare back (Logical Consequences candidate)? Did he let out some pent-up resentment simmering all morning and knock them over in exasperation (T.E.T. candidate)? Did he knock them over in an impulsive pell-mell rush to get to his seat (Self-Awareness candidate)? What are the other behaviors that make up Charlie's profile? As we develop that profile, we may get closer to where Charlie is in life and see more clearly what strategy is most likely to help *him* function successfully and grow emotionally.

It is interesting to reflect on how the teacher's role changes in different models (see FIGURE 7.4). In T.E.T. the teacher is conceived as an equal to the student: both have their needs and their rights, and both participate in looking for no-lose solutions that will consider both their points of view. In Reality Therapy the teacher functions as therapist; though involved with and supportive of the student, they are no longer equals: the teacher is now a helping person who regularly and directly brings the student back to earth and makes him or her face facts. In Logical Consequences there is more detachment yet, with the teacher now representing society. Teachers who use Personal Influence become admired authority figures to students. Self-Awareness Training turns teachers into coaches and systems designers, and is not far removed from Behavior Modification, within which teachers are not only systems designers, but operators of the machine.

As one goes down the list, the student's role diminishes and the teacher swells in authority, responsibility, control, and status. Conversely, as one goes up the list, the teacher diminishes in importance and the student grows as a fully functioning, socially aware person who can deal with life successfully. Through understanding teacher and student roles in the various models, we can broaden our perspective on the relations of the models to each other, and underline the value of seeing them in a developmental progression. That perspective says to us simply: take students where they are, and help them grow in maturity.

BEHAVIORAL CHARACTERISTICS	MODEL	TEACHER'S ROLE
resentment	T.E.T.	an equal person
irresponsibility	Reality Therapy	therapist
defiance & attention seeking	Logical Consequences	representative of society
loneliness & attention seeking	Personal Influence	significant other
impulsiveness	Self-Awareness	coach & confederate
ignorance or lack of control	Behavior Modification	operating the system

FIGURE 7.4: VARIATIONS IN A TEACHER'S ROLE USING DIFFERENT MODELS
The student's role increases and the teacher assumes less authority, status, and control as the list progresses upward.

The arrows in **FIGURE 7.4** indicate some of the common progressions one can observe when students are able to respond to increasingly mature strategies. Behavior Modification can help a student get in control enough (calmed down enough) to enter Self-Awareness Training, or to respond directly to a teacher using Personal Influence. Both Personal Influence and Logical Consequences can be a springboard to Reality Therapy and Classroom Meetings. It is neither necessary nor appropriate to move through all six strategies with any one student. For a certain student, for example, the most natural step after Personal Influence may be Reality Therapy. At a certain point, the student may not need a teacher to act as his conscience, but may be able to move directly to evaluating his own behavior.

REPLACING AND TEACHING NEW BEHAVIORS

behavior modification
identify target behavior
tell child/goal set
clip reinforcers
keep count
reinforce approximations
note progress to child
(Buckholt et al.)

teaching to think of
of alternatives,
consequences of
behavior, impulse
control

(Shure and Spivack)

SELF-AWARENESS
(Cognitive Behavior Modification)

looking on
"I see you're starting to
get out of control."
"You're getting out of
control. I will help."
intervening/describing
what you are doing
hold
teaching children to read
their own signals, be
aware of their actions
and feelings

(Meichenbaum)
(Wolfgang)

TAKING RESPONSIBILITY
(Reality Therapy)

What are you doing?
Is it helping?
(What are you doing to
do about it?)
involvement
humor, no excuses,
tenacity; seeing oneself
as worthwhile and
connected to others

(Glasser)

CONSEQUENCES

teacher pairings
limits
warnings
removal
enlisting the class

creative and relevant
logical consequences
no "battles"
reality of the social order,
not punishment
(Dreikurs)

PROBLEM SOLVING
(T.E.T.)

teaching children
to see their messages
clearly, listen to others'
messages accurately,
and negotiate
solutions.
active listening
"I" messages
gear shifting
Method III

(Gordon)

PERSONAL INFLUENCE

personal relationship
building
clear expectations of a
significant other
direct
specific
repeated
positive expectancy
"You can do it"
tenacity
consistent reactions
noticing
high teacher affect

(Hymes)
(Wallen and Wallen)

FIGURE 7.5: SIX FAMILIES OF RESPONSE TO RESISTANT CHILDREN'S BEHAVIOR

Section VI
Responses to Illegitimate Behavior

To respond to a behavior one must see it (or hear it, or "feel it") or in some other way perceive it. Kounin has given us the term "withitness" for teachers who are particularly good at this: They seem to have eyes in the back of their heads, and not only know when illegitimate behavior occurs, but make some move so the students *know* they know. "Boy, you can't get away with anything on Miss Dooley!"

Once the behavior is perceived the question becomes: How does the teacher respond? We distinguish four levels of response:

- ▶ *No withitness (no response).*
- ▶ *One general pattern of response.*
- ▶ *More than one general pattern of response (variety); different patterns (strategies) at different times.*
- ▶ *Patterns of response chosen in light of the individual student's characteristics (matched).*

Between variety and matching to individuals, we may be able to discriminate patterns matched to situations and to groups.

We know a teacher who displays basically one pattern of Discipline in her class: direct desists and logical consequences. However, she uses another pattern on the playground when children get into fights with each other (and are not challenging her or her classroom expectations directly). Out there, she uses the Glasser model. In other settings not directly confronting her clear classroom expectations, she will usually use methods not based on her own power (e.g., cafeteria disputes between children and lunch room aides when she is called in).

If we were to focus only on the classroom, we would judge her as using only one pattern. Broadening our consideration to the whole school environment, we would judge her as using "variety." If we focus on the playground only, we might see power moves against certain illegitimate behavior (e.g., dawdling in lining up to come in) and Glasser-type moves when she intervenes in fights. What we are facing is the subdivision of "illegitimate behavior" into subclasses: (a) those that could be interpreted as challenging the teacher, those which children might consider as something to "get away with"; and (b) those that do not challenge the teacher (fights, misbehavior in the lunchroom, in another teacher's class).

If a teacher has only one way of operating in each setting, but acts differently in each setting, that is a kind of variety sure enough, but not the same kind as for a teacher who demonstrates variety in both settings. We may thus revise and finalize the judging for "response to illegitimate behavior" in the following way:

- No withitness.

- Withitness and one pattern of response.

- At least one pattern each
  in two different settings   OR   ♦ more than one pattern
  in each setting.

- Patterns matched to children.

The Positive Program

Omitted from this discussion has been any detailed consideration of the positive side of Discipline; that is, notions such as self-discipline as the "purpose of it all"; building community and regard among students through deliberate activities; teaching students to work together cooperatively and effectively as group members; teaching students to listen to one another; making curriculum involving, interesting and relevant; making classroom life democratic so that students have a stake and a say in the order and civility of how they behave toward one another and toward the teacher. We treat these issues in some detail in Chapter 13, Classroom Climate.

Following, in the form of a Quiz, are some profiles of real students we have known. We invite you to read them and see which of the six models of Discipline you think would be most appropriate. What is your rationale for your choice? (This exercise is particularly beneficial when done with colleagues as a group.) ஐ

Figuring Out Discipline Problems:
21 Questions

1. Is the work too hard or too easy?

2. Do I build good personal relationships with students

3. Do I maintain good momentum in lessons?

4. Do I manage time and space well?

5. Do I make appropriate attention moves and make them promptly enough?

6. Is my instruction confusing to some students?

7. Do I vary instructional format and materials enough to avoid students being bored?

8. Are the rules and consequences clear and specific enough both to me and to the students?

9. Do I communicate expectations in a way that is:

   ◢ direct

   ◢ specific

   ◢ repeated

   ◢ shows positive expectancy (both "you can" and "you will")

10. Are the consequences logical rather than punitive?

11. Do I have a range of consequences rather than one rigid response for every transgression?

12. Do I deliver consequences in a way that is:

    ◢ consistent and tenacious

    ◢ prompt

    ◢ matter-of-fact

    ◢ indicates student choice

13. Do I take sufficient time and care at the beginning of the year to establish all of the above?

14. Do I have high enough expectations for behavior no matter what the students' backgrounds?

15. Do I refuse to accept excuses?

16. Do I give students a real and legitimate sense of control, influence, responsibility, power in class life?

17. Do I recognize and reward responsible behavior effectively?

18. Do I explicitly build community in the class (knowledge about, appreciation of, cooperation with one another)?

19. Are there physical reasons (hearing/vision loss, organic hyperactivity) for this behavior?

20. Is there a value or culture clash between teacher and students (or among students) that is behind the behavior?

21. Do the students know how to do what I'm expecting of them?

Planning for Very Resistant Students

1. Have I gathered enough objective data on the student's behavior?

2. Have I presented it to a team to get additional input and questions?

3. Have we come up with the best guesses as to the "psychological need"?

4. Have we picked a matched response model?

5. Have we worked out a coordinated plan for all teachers who contact this youngster?

6. Have we included the youngster's family in the plan?

7. Have we provided for periodic review and modification of the plan?

Discipline Quiz

For each of these student profiles, which of the six models of Discipline would be most appropriate? Write the model in the margin next to each profile.

Jimmy

Jimmy seems on the edge of life. He's quite unpredictable. Sometimes he behaves like a lamb, looking at you with those beautiful brown doe eyes. He likes to cuddle, responds to warmth and physical affection. He will try his work for a while, some days (not often) get quite involved in it. More often he does a little (or none) and is off around the room.

He'll grab things from other kids, push and shove, yell, be combative. In class meetings or instructional groups he may yell; when singing with a group he'll be the first to degenerate into shouting or meaningless yells. Occasional periods of passive immobility, anger and striking out, and out-of-control craziness (throwing things, messing things) speak of deep inner sadness.

Jimmy is six and from a single-parent home. His mother is often, however, not there when he returns in the afternoon, but he's not always sure which afternoons these will be. He has a key. He walks home with his sister who is five. His mother is loving, but unstable and troubled herself.

In large and small groups, whether for a class meeting or for instruction, he often bursts out of control—yelling, shouting, tugging or pinching kids near him. He often smiles as he does this, as if it's a form of showing off, but he also responds quickly to teacher reprimands for a few seconds. The expression that flashes across his face when reprimanded shows acknowledgment that he's done something wrong, but then there he goes again. He is often removed from groups to a corner of the room or the hallway.

He doesn't get much work done, has a short attention span, but is a bright child. He responds to warmth and cuddling, seeks out adult laps. He does considerable running in the room, lots of grabbing, fighting, bumping. When removed from the group he may sob deeply and genuinely for considerable periods of time. These periods of wrenching sadness and crying are not uncommon. Often he will burst into tears for no apparent reason.

You never know how he'll come in through the door. But what you see the first few minutes usually sets the tone for the day. A frequent scene is Jimmy standing at the door, not coming all the way in, peering anxiously around looking at what is going on, being defensive about his space, probably getting bumped by a child behind him going in, and responding with a punch and angry face.

He will space out for short periods, looking sad and immobile; at other times he may get quite involved with a story or with a science activity. He can work cooperatively with other children, but these times will often degenerate into fights over sharing or over real or imagined slights. He is easily set out of control, especially at transition times.

If you call for cleanup and lineup for lunch, he'll throw things in the general direction of where they're supposed to go (or just leave them where they lie) and run to the door. Frequent bumpings and fights result at these times. Running seems the only response he knows for a call to go from one place to another.

At times, of course, he won't come at all, seeming not even to hear, being totally absorbed in blocks or clay. These periods of total absorption are less frequent than abuse of materials like sitting at the clay table making small balls and throwing them at nearby students or pretending a large block is a bulldozer and crashing another child's building.

The only thing that seems to settle him down is physical restraint and cuddling. Sometimes you have to go through 5-10 minutes of restraint.

Ken

Ken is a ninth grader, though he looks a little young. He's always in hot water, rarely in class. Last week he got into a wrestling match—basically playful—with a buddy and destroyed a bed of spring flowers under the principal's office window by rolling all over them.

In private, teachers call him a "wild-ass kid." He seems to live from moment to moment, and to have no roots anywhere, home or school. Others can get him involved into almost any kind of mischief—and often do—stealing, vandalism (painting the dome of the new gym with silver spray-painted obscenities); it's getting so he occasionally thinks up a few things like that to do on his own.

He seems to act with no internal guidance system, an unguided missile; has no goals, nothing to shoot for, nothing to get out of school. Beneath the rollicking prankster seems a fearful young man who, when caught and confronted with his deeds, shrinks visibly. When being addressed by the vice-principal for discipline he will not talk much, shrug his shoulders, look very depressed and alone. He accepts punishment and it does absolutely no good. He makes promises and disregards them entirely.

Freddie

Freddie seems out of contact with his body, ungainly and awkward, almost disconnected from his limbs. He looks as if he might bump into something at any moment without knowing it, and sometimes he does.

Freddie is 11, tall for his age, and has a high-pitched voice.

He will come into the cafeteria, usually toward the end of the line. He walks with a lurching, shuffling gait, head bobbing. He will look around, head almost swiveling. By the time he's gotten through the line and to a table he will be talking very loudly, a little wildly. Squeezing into a seat at a table he may be abusive to adjacent children: "Hey, you slobbo, let me in!" Minutes later there may be wild laughter, grabbing or throwing of food, and very hyper, out-of-control behavior. The cafeteria overstimulates him, as do other large group settings.

Freddie is not hyperactive though. In fact, in class he is most often completely absorbed in his work—his own work, that is, not the teacher's. He likes to draw fantastic machines, to read about anything scientific, and will immerse himself in these activities at every opportunity, withdrawing from class participation.

In total class instruction and small group work he calls out, does a lot of things seemingly to be center stage, and is often silly. If he can withdraw, however, he will just as soon pass these times covertly drawing or studying something that interests him.

He can get very angry at other students and has hurt a few with hard punches or by pushing them into desks this year. He will lose his temper, have outbursts, and really get out of control.

He won't talk about his feelings, can't seem to respond to anything that asks him to talk from inside. He talks about things.

He knows a great deal about a number of scientific and technical topics and loves to repeat this knowledge to adults. As a younger child he was one of those fanatical and knowledgeable dinosaur experts. In general, his mind is very absorbent of facts and general information, but his lack of concentration seems to block him from making connections, from developing concepts you might expect from so verbally advanced a boy.

In skill work, like determining if a given word would be on a given dictionary page or learning the algorithm for long division, he has very little patience, tends to rip up papers if he doesn't get it right away. He won't ask questions, and when it's reexplained for him he'll leap into applying what he's absorbed before the explanation is even complete, almost with panic. Once he's got it, though, he can do it competently and generalize to new situations. He will race through work, however, and make many mistakes.

He doesn't have any real friends, but does play with other children in such activities as fort building outside. He will not enter organized games readily if at all. His play will be something that allows him to do his own thing, play his own part, focus his eyes and body on, say, the fort. His talk at these times will be about the fort or about some dramatic fantasy the children develop as they build the fort: "Hey, look at this cool slide here [that he's just made]. They'll be able to go ZOOM over the wall there." He will seldom look at another child as he speaks.

Source Materials on Discipline

Adler, A. *The Problem Child*. New York: G. B. Putnam & Sons, 1963.

Aronson, E. *The Jigsaw Classroom*. Beverly Hills, Calif.: Sage Publications, 1978.

Buckholt, D. R., D. E. Berritor, H. Sloane, G. M. Della-Piana, K. S. Rogers, and I. F. Coor. *CLAIM—Classroom and Instructional Management Program*. New York: Walker Publishing Co., 1975.

Canter, L. (with M. Canter). *Assertive Discipline*. Santa Monica, Calif.: Canter and Associates, 1977.

Colarusso, C. *Diagnostic Educational Grouping: Strategies for Teaching*. Bucks County (Pennsylvania) Public Schools, 1972.

Dishon, D., and P. W. O'Leary. *A Guidebook for Cooperative Learning*. Holmes Beach, Fla.: Learning Publications, Inc., 1984.

Dreikurs, R. *Psychology in the Classroom*. New York: Harper and Row, 1957.

Dreikurs, R., and P. Cassel. *Discipline Without Tears*. New York: Hawthorne Books, 1974.

Dreikurs, R., and L. A. Grey. *A New Approach to Classroom Discipline: Logical Consequences*. New York: Harper and Row, 1968.

Erikson, E. H. *Childhood and Society*. 2d ed. New York: W. W. Norton, 1963.

Ginott, Dr. H. *Between Parent and Child*. New York: Macmillan, 1965.

Glasser, W. *Reality Therapy*. New York: Harper and Row, 1965.

——. *Schools Without Failure*. New York: Harper and Row, 1969.

Gordon, T. *Parent Effectiveness Training*. New York: Peter Wyden, 1970.

——. *Teacher Effectiveness Training*. New York: Peter Wyden, 1974.

Hersey, P., and H. Blanchard. *The Family Game*. Reading, Mass.: Addision-Wesley, 1978.

House, E. R., and S. D. Lapan. *Survival in the Classroom*. Boston: Allyn and Bacon, 1978.

Hymes, L. Jr. *Behavior and Misbehavior*. Englewood Cliffs, N.J.: Prentice-Hall, 1955.

Johnson, D. W., and R. T. Johnson. *Learning Together and Alone*. Englewood Cliffs, N.J.: Prentice Hall, 1975, 1987.

Jones, F. H. *Positive Classroom Discipline*. New York: McGraw-Hill, 1987.

Joyce, Bruce, and Marsha Weil. *Models of Teaching*. Englewood Cliffs, N.J.: Prentice-Hall, 1972.

Lederman, J. *Anger in the Rocking Chair*. New York: McGraw-Hill, 1969.

Martin, G., and J. Pear. *Behavior Modification*. Englewood Cliffs, N.J.: Prentice-Hall, 1978.

Maslow, A. *Toward a Psychology of Being*. Princeton, N.J.: Van Nostrand, 1962.

Meichenbaum, D. *Cognitive Behavior Modification*. New York: Plenum Press, 1977.

Mendler, A. N., and R. L. Curwin. *Taking Charge in the Classroom*. Reston, Va.: Reston Publishing Co., 1983.

Pierson, C. *Resolving Classroom Conflict*. Palo Alto, Calif.: Learning Handbooks, 1974.

Rogers, D. M. *Classroom Discipline: An Idea Handbook for Elementary School Teachers*. New York: Center for Applied Research in Education, 1972.

Sarason, S. *The Culture of Schools and the Problem of Change*. Boston: Allyn and Bacon, 1971.

Sharam, S. "Cooperation Learning in Small Groups." *Review of Educational Research* 50 (Summer 1980): 241–272.

Schutz, W. J. *Expanding Human Awareness*. New York: Grove Press, 1967.

Shure, Myrna. *I Can Problem Solve. (ICPS): An Interpersonal Cognitive Problem-Solving Program*. Champaign, Ill." Research Press, 1992.

———. *Raising a Thinking Child*. (Audiotape). New York: Pocket Books, 1996.

———. *Raising a Thinking Child Workbook*. New York: Henry Holt, 1996.

Shure, M. B., and G. Spivack. *Problem Solving Techniques in Childrearing*. San Francisco: Jossey-Bass, 1978.

Slavin, R. E. "Cooperative Learning." *Review of Educational Research* 50 (Summer 1980): 315–342.

Stanford, Gene. *Developing Effective Classroom Groups*. N.Y.: Hart, 1977.

Swap, S. "Disturbing Classroom Behaviors: A Developmental and Ecological View." *Exceptional Children* (November 1974): 163–172.

Van Houton, R. *Learning Through Feedback*. New York: Human Sciences Press, 1980.

Wallen, C. J., and L. Wallen. *Effective Classroom Management*. Boston: Allyn and Bacon, 1978.

Wilt, J., and B. Watson. *Relationship Building Activities*. Waco, Texas: Educational Products Division, WORD, 1978.

Wolfgang, C. *Helping Aggressive and Passive Pre-Schoolers Through Play*. Columbus, Ohio: Charles E. Merrill, 1977.

Wolfgang, C., and C. Glickman. *Solving Discipline Problems*. Boston: Allyn and Bacon, 1980.

Wood, Samellyn, Roger Bishop, and Davene Cohen. *Parenting: Four Patterns of Child Rearing*. New York: Hart Publishing Co., 1978.

Additional Readings on Relaxation Training compiled by Dr. Barbara Bruno-Golden

Bernstein, D., and T. Borkovec. *Progressive Relaxation Training: A Manual for the Helping Professions*. Champaign, Ill.: Research Press, 1973.

Bruno-Golden, Barbara. "Progressive Relaxation Training for Children: A Guide for Parents and Children." *Special Children* AASE/Box 168, Fryeburg, Maine (Fall 1974) and (Summer/Fall 1975).

Jacobson, J. E. *Teaching and Learning New Methods for Old Arts*. Chicago, Ill.: National Foundation for Progressive Relaxation, 55 East Washington St., 1973.

Koeppen, A. "Relaxation Training for Children." *Elementary School Guidance and Counseling* (October 1974): 14–20.

Northfield, W. "How to Relax" *The Psychologist Magazine Ltd.* Denington Estate, Wellingborough, Northamptonshire, England, 1973.

Commercially prepared cassettes for home training programs in adult relaxation skill development are available through Bio Monitoring Applications, Inc., Suite 1506, 270 Madison Ave., New York, N.Y. 10016.

8

Clarity

What does it take to explain things clearly?

Cognitive Empathy
The Big Picture

Clarity is a variable that is long on research and short on meaning. It has been included in studies many times, even making Rosenshine's "Big Nine," the nine variables most related in correlation studies to student growth on standardized tests (Rosenshine and Furst 1973). But the problem has always been that we have not known what "clarity" meant to those researching it—nor have they (see Hiller et al. 1969, Belgard et al. 1971, and Martin 1979 for attempts at definition). High-inference ratings of teachers' clarity don't inform us what the low-inference components of the concept are. Why is it that some people are better at explaining things than others? What do they do to be clearer than others?

Consider this episode: $2^2 \bullet 2^3 = ?$ is the problem and many in the class have gotten it wrong. "What many of you did," says the teacher, "was to multiply the 2's so you got $2^2 \bullet 2^3 = 4^5$. That's wrong. *It's 2^5.*" He erases '4^5' and writes '2^5' in its place. "The 2 doesn't change." Then he moves on to the next problem.

The teacher has covered the problem, but he certainly hasn't explained it. The episode is notable for its omissions—for what *didn't* happen—more than for what did. The teacher didn't check to see if there was any understanding of the rule at work for doing this sort of problem ($N^a \bullet N^b = N^{a+b}$). He didn't check to see if there was any conceptual understanding of why the rule works. He didn't do any explaining of the process for doing the problem: he just indicated wrong and right answers. Importantly, he didn't elicit any student participation to see how many and who might still be confused. For instance, he didn't check to see if any students could now do a similar problem. There is little about this episode that is clear—to either the teacher or his students.

The behaviors we're concerned with in the Clarity parameter underlie the process of delivering clear instruction. The situations we will be concerned with here include presenting new material, explaining concepts, giving directions or explaining directions when they need to be elaborated, activating prior knowledge, reexplaining old material, dealing with student confusions, and making connections during instruction. Over the course of this chapter, we will examine the repertoires that exist for dealing with these events.

I. Cognitive Empathy

Perhaps central to this parameter and to good teaching in general is something the Teacher of the Year, Mary Clark, said in a 1981 interview. In describing how to teach, she said, "Know what is inside your students' heads, including the information, feelings and goals they bring to the classroom."[1] This implies that Clarity involves a kind of *cognitive empathy* (as well as emotional empathy)[2] that enables teachers to know *when* students don't understand and then to zero in on *what* or what part of the material they don't understand.

Knowing when students don't understand and then determining what they don't understand are two different skills. Knowing *when* students don't understand suggests that teachers have means of *checking for understanding* during instruction. Determining *what* students don't understand implies that teachers have ways of *unscrambling confusions* that identify the specific point(s) of misunderstanding and deal with them. Since both skill areas are important to Clarity, we need to consider separately how teachers perform each.

Checking for Understanding

We use the word *checking* to describe when teachers are trying to determine whether students are confused. When teachers are checking, they are reacting to the class, reaching out to students, getting outside of themselves to make a "yes…no…who?" judgment about whether confusion exists. How *do* teachers detect confusion? We've been able to identify four levels of performance, which we characterize with these headings:

1. presses on
2. reads body language
3. asks checking questions
4. dipsticks

These four levels of performance are not mutually exclusive; a teacher might display several of them at different points during the same lesson.

At the first level, teachers may simply not be responsive to students' lack of understanding. Remaining oblivious to students' confusion during instruction, teachers just *press on* with their explanations. Or, not being aware of the potential for confusion, they fail to give any directions for tasks that require explanation. Not checking and pressing on can occasionally be appropriate in fast-paced reviews of material previously taught if there has been thorough checking in the past and today the teacher's purpose is to highlight key terms or concepts. Even here, however, since checking takes so little time, it would be wise to do it.

---

[1] Parsons, C. "Grading Teachers for Quality." *The Christian Science Monitor* (October 28, 1981): B6.

[2] Knowing what's going on with students' feelings and goals is also very important and is taken up again in the chapters on Classroom Climate and Personal Relationship Building.

At a second level, teachers may check for understanding by *reading body language* (e.g., postures, facial expressions) that signifies confusion. Only when they notice such cues do they pause in their instruction. Relying on whether students appear to understand, however, can be risky. Students may provide no readable cues even though they are not following the instruction. For example, in a study of student thought processes during instruction, Peterson and Swing (1982) describe how students fooled observers who judged them to be attending to the lesson:

> Melissa's responses to the stimulated-recall interview suggested that she was not attending [although observers judged from her behavior that she was] and instead seemed to be spending much of the time worrying about her performance and the possibility of failure. For example, when asked what she was thinking after viewing the first videotape segment, Melissa replied: "...since I was just beginning, I was nervous and I thought maybe I wouldn't know how to do things." After viewing the second segment, Melissa said the following: "I was thinking that Chris would probably have the easiest time because she was in the top math group." After viewing the third segment Melissa responded: "Well, I was mostly thinking about what we talked about before—I was making a fool of myself." Finally, after the fourth segment, Melissa stated: "Well, this might be off the subject. I was thinking about my crocheting meeting 'cause I wanted to have it done." (p. 485)*

Teachers, at a third level, may *check* more directly for general student understanding with periodic questions. They probe to see if students are still with them, successfully comprehending the instruction. This checking may concern general understanding of content, procedures, or directions. It is worth pausing here for a minute to consider the use of recall and comprehension questions in checking for student understanding.

Recall questions call for factual answers that come directly from the material presented. For example, "What is the formula for finding the area of a triangle?" The answer is the direct recall of the formula: one-half the base times the height. On the other hand, comprehension questions can be answered only if students truly understand a lesson's concepts or operations. For example, "What would you multiply to get the area of this triangle [one that has measurements marked, but no terms labeled]?" The answer requires both the recall of the formula and the understanding of how to apply the formula to a specific triangle.

Comprehension questions are those that can be answered only if students understand the concept being checked. Another example, "Why couldn't 'gobble' be on the page?"—where the guide words on the dictionary page are "hunt" and "mound." Students can answer that question only if they understand how guide words bound the range of entries on a dictionary page.

---

*Reprinted with permission. Peterson, P., and S. Swing. "Beyond Time on Task: Students' Reports of Their Thought Processes During Classroom Instruction." *Elementary School Journal* 82, no. 5 (1982): 481–491. © 1982 University of Chicago Press. All rights reserved.

We are not introducing Bloom's taxonomy here and beginning a discussion of the levels of thinking stimulated by teachers' levels of questions. (That, however, is an important topic in itself and will be considered in Chapter 15.) During checking, we sometimes think we are getting a reading on students' comprehension, but in reality are checking only their recall of key words. An example of this appears in the Quiz at the end of this chapter.

A fourth level of checking for understanding involves what Madeline Hunter christened *dipsticking*. Dipsticking is characteristic of a teacher's teaching if he or she is

- monitoring student understanding frequently and
- broadly across many students simultaneously
- on the same topic or concept
- during instruction.

Hunter and her colleagues teach students to use signals—thumbs up, thumbs down, thumbs to one side—to send periodic messages to teachers about how well they're understanding something. There are any number of other forms of dipsticking teachers use to accomplish the same thing—for example, asking students to "nod your head if you're with me so far," or calling for unison responses from the class, both of which can give a general reading according to how many students respond and how emphatic the response is.

These signals call for student self-assessment of whether they understand, but they may think they do when actually they don't. A more developed form of dipsticking gets an actual content answer from each student. In trigonometry a teacher says: " When I call for the signal, hold up 1, 2, 3, or 4 fingers to show in which quadrant the angle will terminate." In an English class each student has cards that say S (for sentence), F (for fragment of a sentence), and RO (for run-on.) The teacher says, "Hold up the appropriate card after I read each of the following."

The forms of dipsticking above all involve students' sending signals with their hands, cards, or another device. But one can accomplish dipsticking without signals. Some teachers pause in the middle of classes and give one-question quizzes—then circulate and look over shoulders as students are writing to see how everyone is doing. This takes only a minute or two and gives an accurate reading of how well the students are understanding the material. Figure **8.1** shows the relationship between signal and nonsignal forms of dipsticking.

Good performance on dipsticking is indicated when there is evidence that a teacher is taking constant readings across all (or at least most) of the students in the class to see if they're still "with it." Frequency and breadth characterize these readings of student understanding. Teachers may get these readings by simply asking a high volume of questions for a large number of students if they are on the same topic.

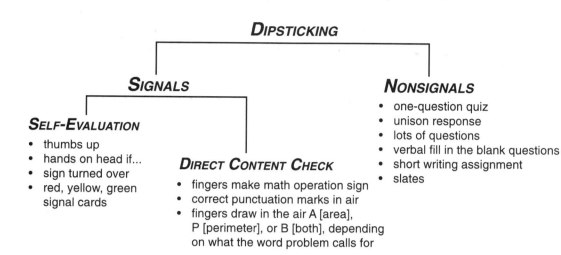

FIGURE 8.1: DIPSTICKING
Dipsticking includes all four attributes.
Dipsticking means asking questions and eliciting answers (1) frequently (2) across a lot of students (3) on the same topic or concept (4) during instruction.

The relationship of dipsticking to recall and comprehension questions is as follows: one can do dipsticking—checking that is frequent and broad across the class—at the recall or the comprehension level, or both. But just because one is asking recall and comprehension questions doesn't necessarily mean dipsticking is taking place. They are overlapping but not necessarily inclusive sets (**FIGURE 8.2**).

One could be asking recall and comprehension question and not be dipsticking. How could that be? The teacher could be asking comprehension questions of individual students and moving on when the right answer was produced, thus not finding out if the rest of the students also understood (a frequent pattern in recitation lessons).

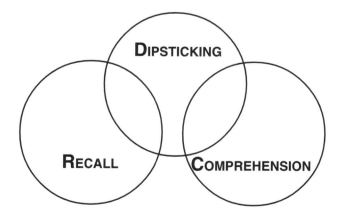

FIGURE 8.2: DIPSTICKING/RECALL/COMPREHENSION
These activities are overlapping but not necessarily inclusive sets.

One might ask, "Does this mean that 'dipsticking' should be a constant feature of every lesson I teach?" Not necessarily. It could be out of place in a true discussion where a line of argument is being developed, or a conceptual change lesson where students are encountering events in conflict with their native theories, constructing new theories to account for what they've observed and testing the new theories. But even here there will be benchmarks when teachers will want to check students' understanding of something everyone should now know. At those times, taking a true dipstick reading will give the teacher much needed information about who does and who doesn't "have it" yet and prevent the lesson from leaving the station without the passengers on board.

Anticipating Confusions and Misconceptions

A cartoon we have shows a little boy standing on his head on a bathroom scale. His friend reads the weight and says, "Your head weighs 43 pounds—same as your feet."

As in the cartoon, students bring many misconceptions to instruction, misconceptions that are very resistant to change and interfere with instruction if they are not recognized and contradicted. One of the three forms of anticipating confusions and misconceptions means finding out what these misconceptions are, surfacing them and dealing with them directly. If we don't, they will linger and distort students' assimilation of instruction. (Eaton, Anderson, and Smith 1984)

A series of investigations by science educators (e.g., Eaton et al. 1984; Eylon and Linn 1988) revealed many misconceptions students have about how the world works: for example, "air is empty space" and "my eyes see by direct perception" (rather than receiving reflected light). They bring these misconceptions to instruction and unless teachers discover them, surface them, and explicitly contradict them, students hold onto them and reconcile them with the instructional information. The resulting "maps" they create in their heads may seem logically consistent, but they're wrong and present serious obstacles to learning. This can happen even when the instruction is ostensibly clear as a bell—because of the failure to account for the misconceptions students bring with them to the instruction. And though the research is best developed for science concepts, there is no reason to believe the same thing does not happen with concepts from any other discipline. The implication for us as teachers is simply to be aware that students do not come to class as blank slates. What's already in their heads has great bearing on how our instruction gets interpreted. In the section of this chapter on "Activates Students' Current Knowledge" we will see a number of devices teachers can use to find out what misconceptions the students are bringing.

> *Students do not come to class as blank slates. What's already in their heads has great bearing on how our instruction gets interpreted.*

Predicting in advance common student misconceptions

– *"All rivers flow north to south"* –

Based on your experience, you are able to spend time explicitly contradicting the misconception and highlighting what the correct idea is. To do so you may draw on a range of explanatory devices.

Predicting in advance that material will be hard to learn,

and drawing upon a range of explanatory devices and frequent checking.
After a demonstatration of the concept of density with two cups of corn flakes, one crushed and one not, the teacher sketches on the board and says, "Raise you left hand if diagram 1 is more dense, right hand if the diagram 2 is more dense. Tina, tell me why you chose this one. OK, everyone, in your notebooks, in 3 lines or less, define density and give one everyday example of something which is more dense than something else."

Noticing or perceiving on the spot that students might not understand

or might interpret differently something just seen or heard.
"Hold it, Todd. Look, everybody, see what happened?
He did two steps at once in his head. First he..."

FIGURE 8.3: THREE FORMS OF ANTICIPATING FOR CONFUSION
Teachers may draw on a repertoire of moves for anticipating for confusion.

In a second form of anticipating confusion (see **FIGURE 8.3**) teachers use what they know about their students and their content to anticipate confusions and probable points of misunderstanding because the material is difficult to understand or easy to misinterpret. We are not talking about prior student misconceptions here but difficult material for which the teacher goes above and beyond the norm to make it clear and prevent ambiguities or misinterpretations. The teacher anticipates, for example, that when explaining free fall in physics, students might associate that term with an object falling on earth, straight down with the force of gravity; "free fall," however, means the free motion of an object in orbit around a central body, like the moon around the earth. The term refers to "falling around"—with circular motion of objects in orbit in space. By anticipating confusions, teachers become aware of when students are likely to have difficulty understanding and can spend time clarifying the material before students become confused.

Sometimes a teacher becomes aware of a possible confusion "on the fly" while teaching and makes a preventive move. A student is correctly solving an algebra equation, but is manipulating terms in his head at a rate the other students might not be able to follow. So with an on-the-fly move to prevent confusion of the other students, the teacher interrupts the student and says to the class, "Wait—see what he's doing here: he's doing two steps at once in his head; he's cross multiplying and taking the square root. OK, go ahead Todd." This teacher has slowed down the action for the benefit of the others and unpacked the two steps that Todd was doing simultaneously in his head, which the teacher anticipates the others might not be able to understand.

Anticipating confusions is often one of the most subtle and difficult performances to observe because students do not, in fact, become confused: teachers head them off at the pass, taking care of the potential lack of understanding before it develops. But for this very reason it also represents a high level of sophistication in clarity.

What does it take for teachers to be able to do all of this checking for understanding? They are able to get inside students' heads. The disposition to and the ability to *get inside students' heads* is the foundation of this entire parameter. Teachers skillful at Clarity want to know how it's going for their students and have a repertoire of ways for finding out. They have a degree of cognitive empathy for the workings of the learners' minds—an ability to put themselves in the learners' shoes—and that guides everything they do.

Unscrambling Confusions

When teachers do detect that students are confused, the next Clarity task involves finding out what the students are confused about and tailoring re-explanations accordingly. We call this *unscrambling confusions*.

When students have signaled (or teachers have discovered) that they don't understand something and teachers are attempting to reexplain or clarify the point of information, we can observe five different levels of teaching performance:

1. No response
2. Reexplains
3. Isolates point of confusion with pinpoint questions
4. Perseveres and returns
5. Has student explain own current thinking

At the first level, teachers make *no response* to the perceived confusion. At a second level, teachers simply launch into a *reexplanation* of the item. It may be slower and/or more detailed than the first explanation, but it is basically the same thing over again without any venture into the students' thinking.

At the next level, teachers question the students with *pinpoint questions* to discover precisely where in the sequence of learning the students went offtrack and became confused. When that point is finally pinpointed, these teachers swing in, economically omitting reexplanation of things the students have already assimilated and moving on with the reexplanation.

At another level, clear teachers *persevere* when they find a student confused over an idea. They will stick with students, perhaps have several exchanges with them if time allows and then, most important, come back to them later in the period to see if they really got it. This return visit may be via review questions or by asking the student to apply the idea in some other context to make sure it is really understood. Sometimes there isn't time in the period for a teacher to unscramble all the confusions of all the students—a reality we all live with in teaching. In that case, what one may see from a persevering teacher is some way of noting or recording who specifically is still foggy on the new concept. Perhaps the teacher will make some provision for a return engagement with those students (arranging for a short small group session right then and there, or asking Bill and Mary to stop by after classes for a few minutes) or some other move aimed at noting who still needs more explanation and creating a setting where they'll get it.

At a final level, teachers ask students to describe their thinking for more than sequence: they probe for *how a student thinks* about the concept or operation. They try to understand the student's frame of reference, the way of conceptualizing the item. They ask such questions as: "How did you get that answer?" "How do you approach this kind of problem? Can you tell me what you did or thought about it?" "What did you try first? Why?" "What do you think this might mean?" "What does 'city government' mean to you?" In this way, sometimes we discover that apparently "wrong" answers aren't really wrong at all if we understand the student's assumptions and logic. Using the student's frame of reference with its meaning orientation enables the teacher to reexplain the concept (or ask a series of questions that will bring the student closer to self-discovering the concept). If the concept turns out to be outside the student's frame of reference, then it's an inappropriate objective altogether. And that is an important thing to find out.

Three authors stand out for their work in raising our consciousness about the importance of understanding students' thinking. Throughout the 1970s, Bill Hull conducted a series of "Children's Thinking Seminars" where teachers met regularly to discuss children's processing.

> ## *Sometimes "wrong" answers aren't really wrong at all if we understand the student's assumptions and logic.*

Through logs, writing, and discussion, teachers were (and are, for these groups continue at many sites) stimulated to reflect on the children's thinking to try to see how and why they were interpreting phenomena and doing problem solving as they were. Hugh Mehan (1974) analyzed classroom discourse between teachers and children and showed that children's "errors" in following directions were really eminently logical interpretations of the adult talk when understood from the standpoint of *students*. Eleanor Duckworth (1981) conducted a series of investigations with teachers into youngsters' thinking, in which the starting point was teachers' studying their *own* thinking and learning processes.

The outcome was that

> to "give a child reason" became the motto, the aim, of much of the teachers' subsequent work. This was the challenge they put to themselves every time a child did or said something whose meaning was not immediately obvious. That is, the teachers sought to understand the way in which what a child says or does could be construed to make sense—they sought to "give him reason." (Duckworth 1987, pp. 86-87)

One of Duckworth's important messages is to point out that Piaget's main contribution to teachers is not his stages of development; it influences teaching little to be able to identify a child's stage in the Piagetian hierarchy once we accept the value of using concrete materials (especially when we realize the value of teaching concretely even for adults). What matters and what improves our teaching is understanding Piaget's clinical interview technique "in which the adult role is to find out as much as possible about what the child himself believes about an issue" (Duckworth 1981, p. 14). In addition:

> To the extent that one carries on a conversation with a child, as a way of trying to understand a child's understanding, the child's understanding increases "in the very process." The questions which the interlocutor asks, in an attempt to clarify for him/herself what the child is thinking, oblige the child to think a little further, also. What do you mean? How did you do that? How does that fit with what she just said? I don't really get that; could you explain it another way? Could you give me an example? How do you figure that? In every case, those questions are primarily a way for the interlocutor to try to understand what the other is understanding. Yet, in every case, also, they engage the other's thoughts and take them a step further. (Duckworth 1987, pp. 96-97)*

(For further discussion of the way in which students' understanding can be deepened by having them reflect on their own thinking, see the Summarizing section at the end of this chapter.)

Explanatory Devices

Checking and unscrambling confusions are essential to good Clarity behavior—probably the heart of it. But there are other things that bear on it too—like a teacher's repertoire of explanatory devices to assist in explaining. Such devices include analogies; highlighting important items; mental imagery; physical models; media/technology; use of charts or the blackboard; translation into fuller or more precise language; modeling thinking aloud; use of simple cues; use of progressive minimal cues and graphic organizers. Most of these terms speak for themselves, but a few deserve additional comment.

Mental Imagery

One of the most powerful and least used explanatory devices is mental imagery. Mental imagery means making pictures in your head; and, when properly guided by teachers, students can use these pictures:

- To understand physical states, events or processes
- As analogies for concepts
- For mood, scene, or context setting
- For improving memory of information or relationships

*Reprinted with permission. Duckworth, E. *"The Having of Wonderful Ideas" and Other Essays on Teaching and Learning.* New York: Teachers College Press, 1987, pp. 83–97.

Imagery has long been used in sports to improve physical performance (Whisler and Marzano 1988). Readers may remember Dwight Stone in the 1980 Olympics prior to his jumps: eyes closed, standing in the sandpit, moving slightly as he imaged himself pelting down the runway and jumping over the bar; or Arthur Ashe during his winning final match at Wimbledon in 1975 sitting with eyes closed during court changes, imaging himself following his serve close to the net and bending to volley the return perfectly. In these and many other instances athletes use mental rehearsal to focus their minds, concentrate, practice, and improve physical performance. In school, these same powers can be brought to bear to focus attention on academic material, to elucidate meaning more clearly, and to activate visual and right brain channels for stronger learning.

A guided imagery trip of a seed pod traveling from mother plant to germination miles away can illustrate the steps and mechanisms of seed migration memorably. A trip inside an imaginary atom can illustrate properties of nuclei and electron orbits in ways that anchor new concepts lastingly just as an imagery trip around a familiar playing field can anchor the concept of "perimeter." Using guided imagery to reconstruct conditions inside the *Mayflower* prior to landing at Plymouth can make the study of the colony's founding more vivid and real for students. Using imagery to have primary children see themselves reentering the room after recess, checking the assignment board for tasks and walking slowly and quietly to their places, can dramatically improve behavior at transitions. The uses of guided imagery are legion and cross all curriculum areas.

The following guidelines are useful for teachers planning imagery exercises with students:

1. Prepare narration ahead of time. Include sufficient description and detail to evoke images, avoid irrelevant details that will distract from main images, and plan pauses.

2. Prepare students. Get them relaxed and comfortable in the seats. Tell them where the image will take them—for example, *"We're going to travel the Mississippi on a raft."*

3. Clarify the purpose. What will the image accomplish? Share this with students (e.g., *"This will help you to understand why Huck Finn…"*).

4. Pause strategically as you speak. Allow time for the images to form.

5. Process with students. What did they see or become aware of? What did they understand through the imagery?

Many teachers like to accompany imagery with music such as compositions by Kitaro or baroque pieces by Vivaldi.

Teachers need to be aware that in any class there may be one or two students who are weak visual learners and cannot image easily. This is no reason to avoid using imagery; strengths can be built through practice. But it is a strong reason to acknowledge the possibility beforehand to prevent such a student's blaming himself or herself (or blaming the teacher) for inadequacy. It is also a reason not to rely exclusively on imagery for teaching a particular piece of content.

Descriptions of successful imagery programs (Pressley 1976; Escondido School District 1979) often include having students speak about and/or share their pictures: "What do you see?" "Tell me about your picture." "What else can you see?" Researchers (see McNeill 1984 for additional references) have demonstrated increased student comprehension, retention, and ability to make inferences from material treated in this way.

Modeling Thinking Aloud

For teachers who like to role-play, this technique is right up their alley. When teachers model thinking aloud for students, they go through the thinking step by step as a student would, role-playing just what one would do. This includes being puzzled, making mistakes, self-correcting, and checking themselves along the way. Modeling thinking aloud is appropriate for any kind of multistep operation where problem solving is involved. By doing the thinking aloud, teachers get a chance to show students where the pitfalls are and how to get through common hang-up points, as well as model the appropriate steps. An example of modeling thinking aloud (partially) for the problem 7,301 divided by 45 might sound like this:

> "Let's see, I have to divide 45 into 7,301. So 45 will go into 7?...no, into 73, how many times? 2. No, 2 times 45 is 90; it must be 1. 1 times 45 is 45. 73 minus 45...borrow 1 from 7, 13 - 5 = 8. 4 from 6 is 2...26. Now I bring down...the zero. Try to put 45 into 260. So that's what?"

Modeling thinking aloud is done by the teacher in front of the class. It is a dialogue with oneself. Beth Davey (1983) shows how the technique can be used to teach students a variety of comprehension strategies. For example, you come upon a word you don't know in the text: "Hmmm, what does that mean?...better reread the sentence...still don't get it. Maybe I'll read ahead to see if it gets clearer...Nope, still doesn't make sense. Let's

> *There is no guarantee that students understand or even notice a strategy and its application just because they witness it.*

see. Do I recognize any of its parts?" In this way, the teacher can take a set of guidelines—reread; read ahead and back to see if the context gives a clue; look for parts you know, particularly stems, prefixes, and suffixes—and show what they look like in operation. At the conclusion of the modeling, it is important to debrief with the students what it is they saw and heard the teacher do; there is no guarantee that students understand or even notice a strategy and its application just because they witness it.

Modeling thinking aloud is one of the least seen and most powerful of the explanatory devices. It is especially useful in teaching any kind of problem-solving or step-wise procedure. It's essential attributes are these:

- Internal dialogue made external
- Asking yourself questions
- Weighing alternatives and using criteria to choose
- False starts and self-correcting
- Persistence
- Debriefing

Cues and Progressive Minimal Cues

In small group or one-to-one tutoring, one can often see a teacher using silent finger-pointing skillfully as a simple cue to call a student's attention to an attribute of a word or a part of a problem he needs to look at again. The *minimal* part of the cue giving is important here, meaning just enough to get students looking at what they need to, but not so much as to deny them an opportunity for thinking out the error. For example, if a student reads "cot" as "cat," the teacher silently points to the "o" in "cot"—a minimal cue. If necessary, the teacher progresses up the scale of cues, making successive cues less and less minimal until the student gets it. The next step would be to spell the word aloud, stressing the "o"—"c-o-t"—but not telling the word.

Graphic Organizers

Graphic organizers are "words on paper, arranged to represent an individual's understanding of the relationship between the words" (Clark 1990). They are diagrams, but a particular kind of diagram: they contain words instead of just pictures, and the form of the diagram represents a particular kind of organizing structure or pattern of thinking which can be generalized: cause and effect, part-whole, comparison and contrast, description, problem and solution.

To extend Clark's definition, a graphic organizer is a *diagram* with *words*, and a diagram whose *form* shapes the *relationship* of the words to one another. The form represents a particular *kind of thinking* and is *generalizable* to use with other content organized by that kind of thinking.

Graphic organizers are powerful devices not only for explaining ideas and their relationships but also for having students summarize what they know. They help students:

- See the relationships of concepts and elements
- Organize information into a coherent structure
- Attend to important items
- Capitalize on visual learning and activate the right brain

When students are taught to use graphic organizers themselves to record or summarize information, they also learn to be active readers and listeners.

There are a great many terms floating around for special-purpose graphic organizers: mind maps, story maps, semantic maps, webs, concept maps, thinking maps, clusters. Some of them (mind maps, clusters, semantic maps) are used for recording a rapid flow of ideas and are taught to students for their own use in recording and organizing their thoughts prior to writing or research. Others (story maps) are used when students are reading literature to record plot line and character development in visual form. Still others (concept maps, a term commonly used in science and social studies) are used to record the relationships between concepts and facts in visual form and to profile the essential attributes and nonattributes of concepts themselves (Bulgren 1991).

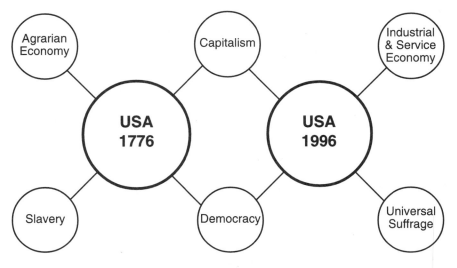

FIGURE **8.4**: CIRCLE GRAPHIC ORGANIZER
This figure is adapted from David Hyerle's "double bubble" design.

Concept maps (Archer 1990) and thinking maps (Hyerle 1990) are both forms of graphic organizers where the form of thinking in the presentation of the material (e.g., comparison and contrast) indicates use of a particular form for the diagram—say a matrix, or Hyerle's "double bubble." For example, if a text is comparing life in America of 1776 with life today, "1776" would go in one bubble and "Today" would go in the other (see FIGURE **8.4**). Circles between "1776" and "Today" with links to both would contain elements they shared in common, like capitalism and a democratic form of government. Circles to the left and linked only to "1776" would contain elements unique to that time and not present today—contrasts to current life like the agrarian base of the economy and acceptance of slavery. Circles connected at the right to "Today" and only to "Today" would contain elements of society present now but not in 1776—elements that are contrasts to 1776 (like an industrial and service economy and universal suffrage). The form or thinking the author brought to the organization of the material would indicate which form of graphic organizer would be best for representing it.

Teachers can use graphic organizers to record class discussions and organize information they are presenting by drawing the organizer on the board as they go. Without ever using the term *graphic organizer* or even naming the kind of thinking it represents, this use of graphic organizers will help students understand concepts and assimilate information. A higher goal, however, is to teach the graphic organizer forms to students themselves so they can eventually use them independently. At the end of this rainbow, then, one might hear a teacher make this assignment: "Take notes on your reading tonight and choose the form of graphic organizer you think most appropriate." This is asking students not only to be active readers, but also to be analysts of the form of thinking used to organize the information. (See FIGURE 8.5.)

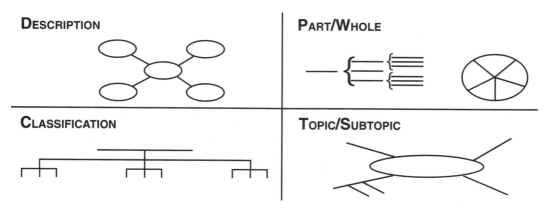

DESCRIPTION

PART/WHOLE

CLASSIFICATION

TOPIC/SUBTOPIC

FIGURE 8.5: FOUR USEFUL GRAPHIC ORGANIZER FORMS
Students may choose the appropriate organizer to understand concepts and assimilate information.

A research tradition in the reading field (see e.g., McGee and Richgels 1986; Heimlich and Pittelman 1986; Armbruster, Anderson, and Ostertag 1989) has demonstrated that graphic organizers improve comprehension when used as adjuncts to good instruction. Students learn that all text is written according to some structure of thinking, each of which has a corresponding graphic form that could be used to represent it.

Teachers can move students at appropriate rates toward independence with graphic organizers and toward being active thinkers and readers by phasing in organizers slowly as in the following sequence over a considerable period of time:

Phase 1: Teacher makes presentation or leads discussion and records information into graphic organizer as class discussion develops.

Phase 2: Teacher chooses form and fills in main entries and subordinate entries as discussion proceeds. Teacher identifies the form of organizer being used and names the kind of thinking it represents.

Phase 3: Teacher chooses form, fills in the main elements for the students, but has them fill in the rest.

> Phase 4: Teacher chooses the form of the graphic organizer, but students make all entries.
>
> Phase 5: Students choose the form and make the entries.

Graphic organizers are very popular with teachers who are interested in teaching thinking skills, because identifying and naming the form of thinking behind the organization of the material under study automatically happens when one is at mature stages with this device. Even students in the primary grades can understand ideas more clearly when represented through graphic organizers.

As we end this section on Explanatory Devices, we would like to raise a caution flag. Explanatory devices are powerful in their place, but they need to be matched to content, situations, and students. It is not the more the better.

To analyze their own (or observe another's) use of explanatory devices, teachers can make a simple count of how many and which they use in explaining and clarifying information. But for any individual lesson, the watchword is appropriateness, not quantity. There is no evidence that any one of these devices is better than another; but there is considerable support for variety in teacher presentation as correlated with effectiveness. Using a number of devices in lessons is one form of variety certainly. And common sense argues that by using a repertoire of these devices, a teacher can increase the likelihood of retaining students' attention and engaging their learning style.

Speech

Another area obviously involved in clear communication is the speech of the teacher. It must meet certain minimum criteria for diction, pronunciation, enunciation, grammar, syntax and then choice of words (appropriate vocabulary) in order for students to understand what is said. Smith and Land (1981) have analyzed speech patterns of effective and ineffective teachers. Their studies and those of others consistently show negative effects on students' achievement when teachers use "vagueness terms" and "mazes" in their speech. Following are some examples they cite.

> Vagueness terms (*italics*):
>
> This mathematics lesson *might* enable you to understand a *little* more *about some things* we usually call number patterns. Maybe before we get to *probably* the main idea of the lesson, you should review *a few* prerequisite concepts. *Actually,* the first concept you need to review is positive integers. *As you know,* a positive integer is any number greater than zero.

> Mazes (*italics*):
>
> This mathematics lesson *will enab...*will get you to understand *number, uh,* number patterns. Before we get to *the main idea* of the lesson, you need to review *four conc...*four prerequisite concepts. The first *idea, I mean, uh,* concept you need to review is positive integers. A positive *number...*integer is any whole integer, *uh,* number greater than zero.

CATEGORIES OF VAGUENESS TERMS

CATEGORY	EXAMPLES
1. Ambiguous designation	Conditions, other, somehow, somewhere, someplace, thing
2. Approximation	About, almost, approximately, fairly, just about, kind of, most, mostly, almost, nearly, pretty [much], somewhat, sort of
3. "Bluffing" and recovery	Actually, and so forth, and so on, anyway, as anyone can see, as you know, basically, clearly, in a nutshell, in essence, in fact, in other words, obviously, of course, so to speak, to make a long story short, to tell the truth, you know, you see
4. Error admission	Excuse me, I'm sorry, I guess, I'm not sure
5. Indeterminate quantification	A bunch, a couple, a few, a little, a lot, several, some various
6. Multiplicity	Aspect(s), kind(s) of, sort(s) of, type(s) of
7. Negated intensifiers	Not all, not many, not very
8. Possibility	Chances are, could be, maybe, might, perhaps, possibly, seem(s)
9. Probability	Frequently, generally, in general, normally, often, ordinarily, probably, sometimes, usually

FIGURE 8.6: CATEGORIES OF VAGUENESS TERMS*
These categories drawn from Smith and Land (1981) are based on Hiller et al. (1968).

Mazes are false starts or halts in speech, redundant words and tangles of words. Vagueness terms take many forms (see FIGURE 8.6). Hiller et al. (1968) "presented evidence that vagueness occurs as a speaker commits himself or herself to deliver information that he or she can't remember or never really knew" (Smith and Land 1981). It can also occur when a teacher does not wish to appear authoritative about information and allows a confused sense of personal relationship building to obscure Clarity. Such confusion can occur when a teacher goes overboard on a desire to be seen as open to student ideas and as a facilitator rather than an information giver. What results is a tentative teacher who uses many vagueness terms.

---

*Reprinted with permission. "Low-Inference Verbal Behaviors Related to Teacher Clarity" by L. R. Smith and M. L. Land, published by the *Journal of Classroom Interaction*, 1981, 17/1, 37–42.

Beyond acceptable speech, there are some things that are not so obvious. We can discriminate between teachers who speak in different ways to different students, perhaps varying their way of speaking by type of occasion too. They have, in short, a variety of ways of speaking. The difference may be in the range of vocabulary used; in the accent; in the use of slang; in the cadence, speed, or rhythm of the speech; in the formality or informality of the language (Joos 1967). We are led to wonder if the teacher can speak to the students in their own language in language forms that are likely to be effective for explaining, clarifying, elucidating—that is better suited to the kind of interaction occurring.

In analyzing teacher behavior, for teachers who speak in different ways at different times to different students, an observer can note "variety" with some objectivity on speech. If, in addition, there is some evidence that a particular way of speaking at a given moment is chosen to match some characteristic of a group or an individual, then matching may be noted.

Explicitness

Explicitness means expressly communicating and not leaving to implication the:

- Intention of cues
- Focus of questions
- Necessary steps in directions
- Meaning of references
- Reasons for activities

These five events are the main places we can observe explicitness in action. Having said that, let us recall that instructors don't always teach by explaining, nor do they intend to. They may teach inductively or Socratically or in many other ways. But when it comes to direct explaining behavior, especially where a student confusion has been detected, then we look for explicitness.

Intentions of Cues

Effective explainers cue students explicitly to make the connections and use the kinds of thinking that will lead to learning the material. They leave no logical gaps. Teachers who are not explicit make assumptions (unfortunately, often faulty) about students' ability to read their cues or read their intentions. These teachers are often guilty of playing "guess what's on the teacher's mind" or "guess why we're doing this," a game that serves no purpose in learning and intimidates and confuses students. When giving explicit cues, teachers build little bridges for students between cues they give and how the students are supposed to use them. Here is an example of an explicit cuing behavior:

"Before defining 'concave,'" Orr asked, "Where do bears sleep?" He thought students would create an image of a cave that would help them remember the definition. Both students noticed this odd question and understood that it was supposed to provide a device for learning the definition. However, neither perceived that this device was an image. (Winne and Marx 1982, p. 510)

Now Mr. Orr didn't have a bad idea here; he was just so inexplicit with his cue that the students couldn't use it. He intended the image of the cave to be a visual mnemonic: when standing in front of a cave the space seems to belly away from you. Likewise a concave surface curves away from you.

Focus of Questions

Sometimes the focus of questions isn't explicit and we wind up in another version of "guess-what's-on-the-teacher's-mind." In the example above there are several good answers to Orr's question: "Where do bears live?" But he only wants one from the possible universe of correct answers. Here is another example: A Latin teacher has a student read a question from an exercise in a text. "What type of question is that?" the teacher asks. The student does not respond. No other students volunteer or appear to know either. What the teacher really means is: "Which of the six types of questions on yesterday's handout—questions with 'quid,' 'cur,' 'quis,' 'quem,' 'ubi,' or 'quo'—is this?" He assumes the student realizes this—but the student doesn't. The teacher doesn't realize that "what type" is not a cue to the student to scan the six "types" on yesterday's worksheet and pick one. The universe of possible answers the student is scanning is not six choices, it is infinite and so he is at a loss.

The episode continues: The teacher directs the student to turn to yesterday's handout and read the first item. The student obliges. In a tired voice the teacher says, "OK, read the next item." The student obliges. This second item is an example of the type of question from the exercise that confounded the student. The student finishes reading it. There is a pause. The teacher gives the student a wide-eyed look, "Well?" "Oh," says the student and goes on to identify the text line as a 'quid' question.

This confusion would have been avoided if the teacher had been explicit about the mental operation he wanted the student to do: "...and by 'what type,' Jimmy, I mean which of the six types we discussed yesterday. Check your handout compared to the text line you just read. Everybody else check, too, to see if you'll agree." (This is an active participation move.)

The above episode is a good example of "guess what's on the teacher's mind." By contrast, teachers who are explicit show students directly how what they're doing now—or next—will help them get to the learning goal.

By looking for explicitness in instruction, we look for clear steps that enable learners to know why questions are asked and how directions or examples relate to learning tasks. "He always asks us questions we can't answer" is a common report that students make on unclear teachers. They can't answer questions because the teacher fails to define or at least reference the domain the question is tapping. Consider this episode: "What is good writing?" asks

Ms. Jones and she has a specified list of attributes in mind which she proposes to get up on the board. But the question is a 'sucker' question, because students are going to volunteer all sorts of plausible answers that don't fit in with her lesson plan. That would be okay if she were to collect them all, discuss them, and then perhaps compare them to the text list she has in mind. But instead she's going to say, "No," and "That's not quite what I'm looking for," and invalidate much good student thinking as she 'develops' (that's how her lesson plan puts it) her list. She doesn't really mean, "What do you think good writing is?" She means, "What do I think good writing is?"—in other words, "Read my mind."

Another easy trap for teachers to fall into regarding explicitness is asking questions in series. Good and Brophy (1978), citing Grossier, describe a teacher who in discussing the War of 1812 asks in one continuous statement, "Why did we go to war? As a merchant how would you feel? How was our trade hurt by the Napoleonic War?" The teacher is trying to clarify his first question and to focus thinking upon an economic cause of the war. In his attempt, he actually confuses.

> **Explicitness moves build a series of bridges back to objectives from individual activities and between activities themselves.**

Questions in series are a temptation whenever we ask a question and get silence back from the whole class. We want to give a clue, so we ask another question that is intended to lead the students toward our focus. What we may accidentally do, as above, is jerk students' train of thought around and leave them confused as to what we are really after.

Necessary Steps in Directions

Teachers may direct students to commence tasks but inadvertently leave out necessary steps in the directions. This can happen when we make unwarranted assumptions that students understand the conventions for how certain tasks are done. "Get together in groups of 4 or 5 and brainstorm as many endings as you can for this short story." This teacher has neglected to instruct groups to choose a recorder and they have all started brainstorming without one.

Another example: "Fix these sentences and then move on to the next assignment." Some students have interpreted "fix" as cross out and write over the words that are wrong (which the teacher, in fact, intends). Others are recopying the entire sentences with the corrections, which is taking four times as long. As a result, they won't have time to finish the second assignment.

The injunction of this area is simply to spell out completely what we mean in directions and not assume steps are inherently obvious to students.

Meaning of References

Sometimes teachers make references to famous people, ideas, events, or works which are intended to elucidate current instruction; yet the students may not know the references and therefore they confuse rather than clarify. They may, in fact, subtract from instructional effectiveness in this way: while students are being puzzled about the reference and asking themselves what it means, they may miss the next one or two points that are made.

"Reading James Michener's *Hawaii* can make one feel like Sisyphus, which becomes apparent by about Chapter 25." That sentence won't mean anything to students who don't already know that Sisyphus was a cruel Greek king who was condemned to be forever rolling a huge stone up a hill in Hades, only to have it roll down again every time he neared the top. Therefore to feel like Sisyphus means to feel hopeless about ever finishing.

Being explicit at times like these would not foreclose our using arcane references, but would cue us to explain them on the spot so students could benefit from them.

Reasons for Activities

Surprisingly, students often have no notion about the purpose of activities they are asked to do and make no link between activities and instruction they have just received (Tasker 1981). This form of Explicitness simply means telling students why they are asked to do a particular activity. More particularly, it means explaining why the activity will help them learn something or contribute to a larger learning or task performance. "The reason we're doing this experiment is to show how hard it is to take data and record information simultaneously. You just can't do it. So, like all scientists, we're going to have to 'extrapolate' our readings. Remember that term from the graphs we worked on in the chapter?"

THE OBJECTIVE

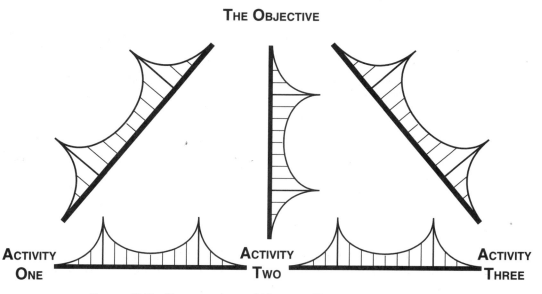

ACTIVITY ONE   ACTIVITY TWO   ACTIVITY THREE

FIGURE 8.7: EXPLICITNESS IN WORKING TOWARD AN OBJECTIVE
Each activity must bridge the relationship to the overall activity objective.

Another example: "The reason we're doing these sentence-combining worksheets is so you can use these same techniques to make your own writing more interesting in the adventure stories we're writing."

Explicitness moves of the kind illustrated in Figure **8.7** build a series of bridges back to objectives from individual activities and between activities themselves.

Sometimes the move shows students how the current activity fits into patterns of other experiences they've been having or are about to have. "The reason I'm asking you to locate these references in the library reference computer is to build up your speed and check your accuracy. You'll have to use this database a lot next month when you start your research papers and I won't be around to help much of the time. So you've got to be able to use it independently to find books you want."

Without these explanations, many students do assignments mechanically, with minimal care and investment. They do them because they're "work" and you're supposed to do your work. But the work isn't leading in a meaningful way toward anything they understand. Readers who have worked with learning styles and studied the intriguing work of Bernice McCarthy (1981) and Anthony Gregorc (1979) know that "quadrant one" learners especially need to understand these connections.[3]

We have been discussing moves teachers make to show students how current activities or assignments relate to intended learnings (objectives). That, indeed, is a form of explicitness. For it to occur, however, students have to know what the objectives are in the first place; otherwise, there's nothing to relate the activity to. Before considering how well and how often we are giving students reasons for activities, we need to ask whether we're communicating the learning objectives themselves. This question will be early on our agenda in the following section, The Big Picture.

II. The Big Picture

The last group of Clarity behaviors cluster together around a common mission we have christened "The Big Picture"; it is composed of behaviors thought to help students place current information or operations in a larger framework of meaning. These teaching behaviors can be considered in a simple presence/absence, yes/no way. They are:

- ▶ *Giving students the itinerary,* the list of activities they'll be doing

- ▶ *Communicating what the students will know or be able to do at the end of the upcoming instruction (the objective)*

- ▶ *Activating current student knowledge about a new concept or curriculum item*

[3] McCarthy has synthesized several significant theorists on learning style into a model that categorizes learners into four main types. These are represented on a visual pie diagram as four quadrants. One of the learning styles, quadrant one (also called "Innovative Learners"), has a particular need to know why a given learning is taking place. To serve those students well, teachers need to explain why.

> ◆ *Making connections that show resemblance of the old and the new, integrating information into the context of previous work or previous knowledge*—"demonstrating to students how the things you are talking about resemble what they already know" (Friedrich, Galvin, and Book 1976, p. 78)
>   - makes transitions between ideas within the same lesson
>   - signals shift in activity, pace, level
>   - foreshadows ideas to come
>
> ◆ Summarizing

These behaviors have been included because we or others think they might play a part in a future science of teaching, a future set of laws explaining teaching outcomes. Current research does show a correlation between them and improved student learning; but we cannot definitively claim cause and effect for them yet. One thing we do know, however, is that there are a variety of ways to accomplish each of them and the repertoire for doing so has been developed by practitioners. That is where we have gone to discover the repertoires developed below and indeed, in this whole book. Thus, this effort to assemble the professional knowledge base of our craft, teaching, is clearly dependent on continued partnership between two communities that should be one: teachers and researchers.

Giving Students an Itinerary

An itinerary is a listing or delineation of the steps that will occur over the course of an activity or period. An itinerary is like an agenda or road map. It tells where things are going and in what order. For example, it is common to hear a teacher say, "This morning we'll be going over your homework answers and then looking at the material in the new chapter. Then we'll do some group work on your projects." This is useful for students to know. It gives them a mental sequence to follow and lets them know what to expect. Learners with sequential learning styles are particularly responsive to the practice of posting itineraries in a visible place.

Communicating What Students Will Know or Be Able to Do (Objective)

Giving students an itinerary for the activities they'll do today is not the same as stating the objective of that work. There is nothing wrong with giving kids itineraries; its just that an itinerary is not an objective. Likewise, giving clear directions and outlining what procedures students are going to follow also is not the same as stating an objective (giving clear directions and outlining procedures are covered in the "Structuring Learning Experiences" section of Chapter 15). Following is a clear statement of an objective in which the teacher lets students know what they'll be able to do when the instruction is over: "Today we're going to learn how to write on paper what you've been telling me out loud in math groups—that you have one-half or one-fourth or three-fourths of a whole something. Well, there is a special way of writing numbers that stand for those things and when we're done today you'll be able to use it."

Most teachers have been taught how to say and write behavioral objectives. That language serves a purpose, but it need not be used all the time. The objective may not be a detailed behavioral one at all. The example happens to be a behavioral objective stated in language to match eight-year-olds (give this teacher a pat on the back for "matching" on speech). But other language patterns can serve as well—for instance: "We're going to look at this filmstrip and see what we can learn about the personality characteristics of Hemingway the man." Once again, students are oriented toward what they're supposed to know at the end of the lesson. Such statements frame the "big picture," giving an overall orientation to what is to follow, a frame that helps the students make sense of subsequent activities. To note "yes" here, an observer wants to see a teacher appropriately introduce lesson activities with something that casts them within a bigger frame, purpose, or objective, so that the students know what they're going to learn.

Before leaving this discussion of communicating objectives, there is a related but separate area we should consider: communicating to students *why the objective is worthwhile*. This is the "Who cares?" question. As a result of our skill at communicating objectives, students may know exactly what it is about the Vietnam War that we want them to understand at the conclusion of the lesson; they just may not think it matters. For some students, understanding the usefulness or relevance to them of a learning objective makes a big difference in their investment. Writing about "quadrant one learners," McCarthy (1987) says:

> Students need reasons to proceed with learning. All students do. But for the Innovative Learners "Why?" is an absolute necessity. It seems simplistic to mention that students need reasons, but they are rarely given. Teachers assume students know that what is taught to them is necessary. Teachers assume their reasons are sufficient, that students will value what experts say they should learn. Not so. Students need reasons of their own…Every teaching or training enterprise should begin by creating a desire. Even in adult education, where highly motivated students come for their own personal needs, teachers must give reasons why the program is important. The teacher must take the time to discuss what s/he hopes to do and why. Giving them a reason, a need of their own for proceeding, is so simple and fundamental that one can only marvel that it is not done. (McCarthy 1987, pp. 92, 94)*

Thus it would be particularly important for some learners (and useful to all) to know our reasons for wanting them to know the principal causes of the Vietnam War and U.S. involvement. "The reason this is important to us is that the Vietnam War has causes in common with many other wars in history. If this country enters another war, it's very likely that many of you will be drafted into the armed services and have to fight. Therefore it will be important to you as citizens to be able to follow current events and the decisions of your leaders in government to see where we're headed. As citizens, you can make informed choices in voting for leaders who stand for policies you want. Our study here will help you decide in the future what you think we should fight for as a country—and at some point that choice is sure to be yours."

While not so dramatic as topics, we might be equally clear about why it is worthwhile to learn geometric proofs; to study myth as a literary genre; or to identify by their attributes igneous, sedimentary, and metamorphic rocks.

Giving reasons for learning something isn't an event that should happen with every lesson. Most lessons are taking students one increment further or developing skill one degree higher on a particular objective. At the beginning of new units or topics, however, giving reasons for objectives can be very appropriate.

Preparing to deliver these reasons to students can be a useful exercise for teachers too. If we can't give a good reason for learning something, maybe we shouldn't be teaching it.

Activating Students' Current Knowledge About a Concept

The most important single factor influencing learning is what the learner already knows. Ascertain this and teach him accordingly.

David Ausubel, *Educational Psychology: A Cognitive View*

Techniques that activate students' current knowledge about a concept or topic not only tune them in to what's coming but prevent the dreaded "Charlie Brown Syndrome":

> Recall what Charlie Brown does when he gets a new book. Before he even looks at the book, he counts pages—625 pages—"I'll never learn all that!" He is defeated before he starts, before he has not had a chance to realize that he does not have to learn all that. It is not all new. He already knows something about it. He has not given himself the chance to learn what he already knows about what he is supposed to know. (McNeill 1984, p. 34)*

What we want to do, in one way or another, is ask students this question—"What do you already know about X?"—and record (or get them individually to record) what they come up with. As the concept or topic is developed, the teachers can go back to these initial lists or charts to compare what students learned with their original ideas. Sometimes students find themselves fitting new learning into old charts; sometimes they find parts of their old conceptions contradicted. But in any event, having created an image of what they already know about a topic places before them a map against which they bounce (and into which they put) new information. It is in this way that we are serving the big picture.

Numerous techniques have been developed to accomplish activation of current knowledge. One is *semantic mapping*. McNeill (1984) provides the following description:

> Begin by asking pupils what they think of when they hear the word X (X is the topic they are about to read about). Free association is desirable. As pupils offer their associations, list the responses on the chalkboard. Try to put the associations into categories.

*Reprinted by permission. McNeill, J.D. *Reading Comprehension: New Directions for Classroom Practice.* Glenview, Ill.: Scott, Foresman and Company, 1984. © 1984 Harper Collins College Publishers. All rights reserved.

For example, responses to money might be categorized into uses of money, kinds of money, denominations, consequences of having money, ways of earning and other associations. Help the pupils label the categories and then ask them to read the selection to learn more about X. It is fine to encourage pupils to pose their own questions about what they want to learn about X from the text. Next, after reading the selection, the class gives attention to the set of categories and prereading questions related to X. Pupils at this time add new ideas acquired from their reading, correcting and augmenting the original map. (McNeill 1984, p. 10)

McNeill's description is of a semantic mapping exercise prior to reading a selection of text. But it could be used equally well before doing an experiment, viewing a film, or interviewing a guest. The point is that the teachers are getting students ready for new information by calling up their own maps (or "schemata" as the researchers would say) of what they already know about the topic. The effect is to make students more active listeners, watchers, and readers.

Other techniques like Wordsplash or KWL (Know—Want to Know—Learned) have been developed by practitioners and researchers in the reading and language fields and are well worth study by teachers from all disciplines. They have in common the effect of getting students cognitively active in relation to new incoming information.

A Wordsplash (Hammond 1985) takes 10 to 20 key words or terms from an article, story, or text chapter and "splashes" them at random angles and positions on a chart or chalkboard under the title of the text. Prior to reading, students are asked to follow the rules of brainstorming in groups with a recorder as they respond to the following direction: "Say sentences that show what you think the relationship is or will be between these key words and terms and _____ (supply the title or the article or text)." This technique produces wide student participation, higher-level thinking, focused reading, and better comprehension.

A version of KWL we like exposes students in a large group to a stimulus on a topic (like a picture on a book cover with the title) and asks them to share aloud their reactions. The teacher has students assign their remarks to one of three columns: Know, Think I Know, or Want to Know. No discussion or question answering occurs during the building of the chart. This activity, similar to Wordsplash, produces active participation, reveals student preconceptions, and generates student-owned agendas for reading.

The charts are worth saving for a return visit after reading the piece (or studying the topic). Some "knows" may turn out to be untrue; some "think I knows" are validated and others are overturned; and all the "want to knows" should have been answered.

Makes Connections

Shows Resemblance to Something Students Already Know

It is useful when teachers show how new learnings resemble previous work or students' previous knowledge, "demonstrating to students how things you are talking about resemble what they already know" (Freidrich 1976). Following are some examples:

> [Comments in parentheses are student responses.] The teacher says, "When we first worked on multiplying you learned that it was related to addition—how?" (Repeated addition.) "Right! Meaning what?" (Multiplying is like adding the same number over and over again—as many times as you're multiplying it by.) "Okay, very good. Now this division operation we've been working on today is really a lot like multiplication, except what it's doing in short-cut fashion isn't adding a number over and over again, it's what?" (Subtracting it.) "Right! Everybody see that? Jimmy?" [Score yes on 'Checking' for this teacher!] "Can you explain in your own words how division is like multiplication?" [Score yes on 'Comprehension Questions'!] (It's the backwards of multiplying.) "An interesting way to put it; I think you understand. Margie, what do you think Jimmy means by backwards? [Score *yes* on 'Comprehension Questions'!]

Here's another example from a beginning chemistry course.

> The teacher says, "So we've proven this welding torch burns hotter than the straight propane burner. Do you remember what we did at the beginning of the year, heating sodium chlorate in the test tube? What happened when we held a glowing ember over the tube?" (It burst into flame.) "How did we explain that?" (Heating the sodium chlorate drove off oxygen and the oxygen made the ember burn faster and hotter.) "Right! And a welding torch is like that. We've got these two tanks." [Teacher goes on to show how a welding rig mixes two gases, acetylene and oxygen and that the presence of the extra oxygen vastly increases combustion temperatures].

The integrating of the old with the new builds intellectual links between items of information in such a way as to deliberately keep the picture of the whole emerging chain visible too. As students learn the new item, the new link, they simultaneously see the whole chain that is now one link longer. The link and chain analogy may break down for bodies of information that relate in other ways—like a web, for example—but the Clarity move serves the same purpose—linking the new item with the larger picture of established knowns (Ausubel 1968; Gagne 1974).

Janis Bulgren and others from the Institute for Research on Learning Disabilities at the University of Kansas use anchoring tables to show in a visual and a precise way exactly what the similarities and differences are between new and old concepts. An anchoring table is a graphic organizer—in this case a special-purpose one—to compare and contrast new information to previously learned information (Figure **8.8**). The steps for phasing in their use with students are the same as those for phasing in Graphic Organizers.

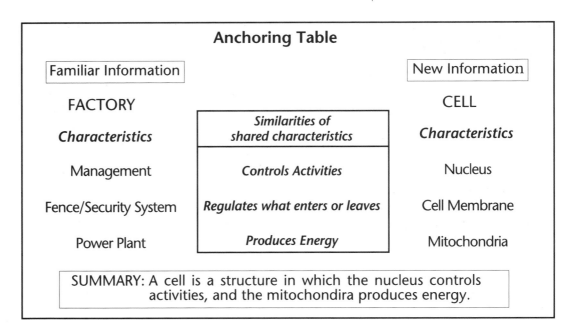

FIGURE 8.8: ANCHORING TABLE
An Anchoring Table is a special-purpose Graphic Organizer used to compare and contrast new information to previously learned information.

The difference between this kind of integrating and "Activating Students' Current Knowledge" is this: "Activating" looks forward. It gets up on screen, as it were, students' present conceptions. Thus, their minds are warmed up and they have something to compare and contrast with the new learning when it comes along. What they already have "on-line" may or may not be accurate, may be complete or incomplete. The purpose of bringing it up is to get them in gear and give them a reference point to test against the new learning. They may ask themselves: Is what we learn about chemistry what we thought chemistry to be?

The purpose of "Showing Resemblance to Something Students Already Know, " on the other hand, is to look backward. The teacher wants students to see that the new learning coming up isn't really so new or different (or so hard); and the teacher wants them to see that the new learning fits in with something they already know, that there already exists a structure or a continuum in their heads to accommodate it.

Makes Transitions Between Ideas
These are brief, within-lesson transitions like segues made by an announcer and mostly applicable where direct instruction is taking place. (The teacher doesn't have the opportunity to guide transitions between items of information unless the teacher is leading the instructional activity.) In terms of Clarity, these moves are verbal markers that help the student follow the road map as the teacher makes a left turn here, a right turn there, or circles back to the point of origin—for instance: "Okay, that word problem required us to multiply. Now let's move on to the next one and see if it is the same."

Notice the difference between that remark and a teacher who simply says, "Okay, let's move on to the next problem." Telling the students to move on gets them from one place to the next sure enough, but does not provide a transition. A Clarity transition move takes something about what has just been done and relates it to what's coming up immediately. It provides intellectual links like integrating moves do, but instead of linking to the learner's past experience, or to learning from other disciplines or other times, this link is to what has come immediately before the lesson itself.

Here's a good example: "So that's how the commercial banking system multiplies money deposited in checking accounts and creates new money. Now another way new money gets created is through consumer credit. Let's look at how all those plastic credit cards add to the banking sytem to create even more money."

Signals Shift in Activity, Pace, or Level

These moves are simple statements at transition points to prepare students for a change in the nature of cognitive work.

Shift in Activity	"OK, that's all we're going to do with the lab reports today. Now let's take a look at the next chapter so we can preview the new material."
Shift in Pace	"We're going to pick up the pace now, so get ready for a little more action!"
Shift in Level:	"Now we're moving on to three-step problems instead of two-step, but still with the same operations."

Foreshadows

Consider these two teacher statements:

"Well, you couldn't *have* two hydrochloric acid molecules on that side of the equation because it wouldn't balance. You don't have to worry about that now, but soon we will get to this notion that chemical equations must balance. When we talk about balancing equations, we'll be experimenting with the proportions of different chemicals that get used up in chemical reaction."

"And if you think Laura worked hard helping Ma around the house, wait till you see what she did with Pa Ingalls around hay making time. ('What's that mean?' a student asks.) Well, that's harvesting the hay and that was a very important part of farm life then—now too. Anyway, hay making is coming up in a couple of chapters. I think you'll enjoy that section."

These examples of foreshadowing take a term or an idea that crops up and create a brief image of what it will be like or what it will be about. This is done so that when the students get to that point, it's not totally strange territory. "Oh, I remember we talked about that last week," a student may say to himself and start assimilating the ideas into his cognitive framework. Foreshadowing moves may crop up as moments of opportunity during instruction and are often unplanned. For instance, in the second example, the students had commented on how hard Laura works around the house, and their remarks made the teacher think of the days of hard labor she spent with her father making hay, so she brought it up for comparative purposes, knowing it's coming up in a few chapters.

When teachers end a lesson with a forecast of what the students will be doing next, that is foreshadowing of a kind, but we tend to see that kind of move as a cognitive transition. The difference is that a cognitive transition makes direct links between what has just been completed and what is immediately to come in the flow of instruction—even if 'immediately' is interrupted by overnight. Foreshadowing puts intellectual markers or hooks in place for items that are down the road and will not be dealt with the very next time the students work on this subject.

Summarizing

Teachers don't always summarize themselves; sometimes they ask a student to do it. It doesn't matter how it gets done; if someone explicitly pulls everything together at the end of a lesson for all to see or hear, then summarizing has taken place and "yes" can be noted for the teacher on this tenth area of clarity.[4]

When students do the summarizing themselves and when all of the students are involved in doing so simultaneously, two other powerful factors are added. First, the principle of learning called active participation is engaged (see Chapter 9). Second, students must get cognitively active with the material; they have to reorganize the information and concepts they have received personally so that they can state them in their own words. Asking students to do the summarizing inherently means asking them to say what they have learned in their own words. (It also means having to check their summarizing to see that it is accurate and complete.) The "in your own words" feature is critical because it forces the learners to sift, reorder, and organize the information themselves. They can't just let the new learning lie on the library shelf of their minds as a memory trace. They have to pick up the pieces and put them together; and the very act of doing so strengthens the learning.

There are many ways to accomplish this summarizing so that all of the students get involved. Keeping a learning log (Pradl and Mayher 1985) is one way.

> Typically, students make entries during the last five minutes of each period, responding to the following types of questions:
>
> > What did I learn today? What puzzled me?
> >
> > What did I enjoy, hate, accomplish in class today?
> >
> > How did I learn from the discussion or lesson?
> >
> > How was my performance in class? (Sanders 1985)

---

[4] Asking students to make up a quiz on the important points covered in the class gets them all involved in summarizing nicely.

Teachers can also ask students to do this orally, in pairs at the end of class, or at appropriate stopping points within class. Mary Budd Rowe has demonstrated that students' retention increases when 2 minutes is provided for students to summarize and clarify for each other in small groups after every 10 minutes of teacher-led instruction. This "10-2" rule provides students the same kind of opportunity to get active with the material *in their own words*. Tobin (1985) comments, "The results [of this technique] are consistent with our interpretation that students need time to process lesson content in information-dense subjects such as science."

Summarizing questions can be made specific and tailored to any content: "Based on our discussion so far, tell your partner the principal causes of the Civil War. Then have your partner tell them back to you." If the class has reached consensus on the causes, this is a summarizing of the information. (If the class has not resolved the question, having pairs dialogue like this is more than summarizing—especially if they are asked to back up their respective positions.) Additionally, a teacher may ask students to summarize in writing (perhaps in notebooks) the main idea of each section in textbook chapters. Having to stop and summarize periodically as one reads forces active cognitive processing; you have to put it in your own words to write a summary—Voilà, better learning! Studies have shown improved comprehension of text (not just stories) with convincing consistency (e.g., D'Angelo 1983) when students do this kind of summarizing. And a number of writers have offered useful models for *teaching* students how to do this summarizing-in-writing as they read (Hahn and Gardner 1985).

In this chapter we described three behaviors that had to do with a teacher's cognitive empathy for students; we called them "Anticipates Confusions or Mis-Conceptions," "Checking" (for finding out when students lose the thread of meaning), and "Unscrambling Confusions" (for finding out where and fixing it). We were able to discriminate several different qualitative kinds of performance on those behaviors. Then we added an index of how many and which Explanatory Devices a teacher uses and analyses of teacher Speech patterns and Explicitness behaviors. Finally, we described five teacher moves that help to clarify the Big Picture for students: Giving Itineraries; Communicating Objectives; Activating Students' Current Knowledge; and Making Connections (four kinds). Each of these is a functional aspect of the Clarity parameter.

We've just summarized the chapter. And that's the final Big Picture move: Summarizing. Can you now summarize what has been new learning for you in this chapter?

On the next pages we have provided a Quiz as a means for you to review, by yourself or with a colleague, the moves of the Clarity parameter. ❧

Checking on Clarity

Examine your own teaching, or that of a colleague and see which of the following apply. For each behavior or level of performance that you credit, see if you can cite an example to back it up.

COGNITIVE EMPATHY

1. Anticipates Confusions and Misconceptions

2. Explanatory Devices:

charts or chalkboard	*translation into fuller or*	***mental imagery***
analogies	*more complete language*	*simple cues*
media/technology	*physical models*	*diagrams*
modeling thinking aloud	*progressive minimal cues*	***graphic organizers***
	highlights important information	

3. Speech

unacceptable	*matched to group*
acceptable	*matched to individual*
variety	

4. Explicitness. Expressly communicating, not leaving to implication:

intention of cue	
meaning of reference	*necessary steps in directions*
focus of questions	*reasons for activities*

5. Checking:

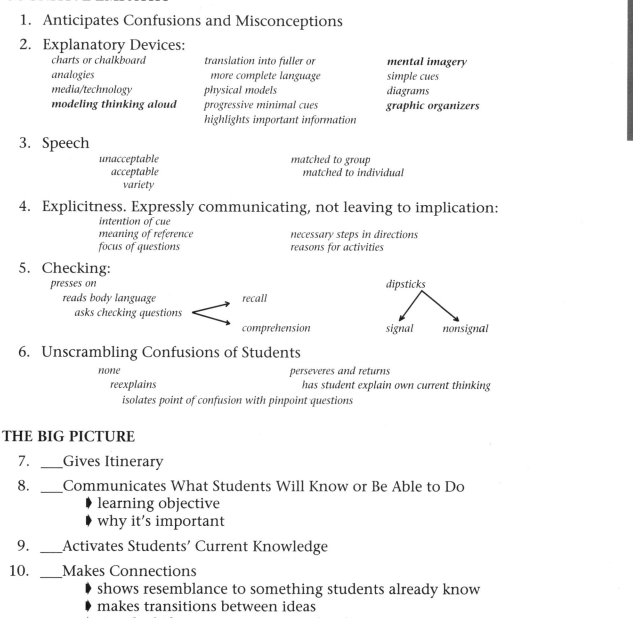

   presses on
   reads body language → *recall*
   asks checking questions → *comprehension*

   dipsticks → *signal* / *nonsignal*

6. Unscrambling Confusions of Students

none	*perseveres and returns*
reexplains	*has student explain own current thinking*
isolates point of confusion with pinpoint questions	

THE BIG PICTURE

7. ___Gives Itinerary

8. ___Communicates What Students Will Know or Be Able to Do
   - learning objective
   - why it's important

9. ___Activates Students' Current Knowledge

10. ___Makes Connections
    - shows resemblance to something students already know
    - makes transitions between ideas
    - signals shift in activity, pace, or level
    - foreshadows

11. ___Summarizes

Clarity Quiz

Read the following excerpts from classroom lessons. In the margin, name the Clarity move represented by each episode or quote.

1. A student has bombed all the questions on her biology test that involved categories of plant life. The teacher is chatting with her before class: "So Marie, explain to me what you understand about the relationship between angiosperms, gymnosperms, and the others types on the list we've been working with this week."

2. Physical education teacher to volleyball class (15 minutes into class): "We've been drilling on tosses and bumps to get better at receiving serves and not being afraid of the ball. Now in this exercise we're going to concentrate on bumps and make it more realistic. This will get you ready for real game play where the back row should often bump toward the front rather than try to hit it all the way over."

3. Teacher to class: "First, this period you are going to have a chance to work on your reading logs; then we are going to work with more problems that require careful reading. At the end of the period you'll have a chance to write your own careful reading problem."

4. A student is working on dissolving substances in a liquid in a chemistry lab experiment. The teacher comes by and asks, "Is this partially or totally dissolved?" The student responds, "Partially." Teacher then says, "Now what does that mean?"

5. Teacher to class: "Before we begin our study of the United States during the Great Depression, let's brainstorm all the things we already know about the depression, plus the things we think we know and the things we need to know. When you contribute a piece of information, just let us know which category it fits into."

6. Teacher to class: "Raise your hands when you get the answer to this problem on the board." (Teacher circulates while students are working.)

7. A student's brow is furrowed while pausing over his work. The teacher walks over to him and asks, "Is something puzzling you?"

8. "And so Mrs. Ward sent her two black friends on their way via the Underground Railroad. Now the Underground Railroad was not a subway from Mississippi to Canada. It was something quite different."

9. Teacher to class at end of defining "transcendence": "So that, in brief, is what it means. We haven't seen it a lot in the literature so far, but we're going to be talking about it when we get to poets. So be on the lookout for that term; we'll be returning to it."

10. Teacher, standing by seedling box, to class: "We've been measuring our seedlings and will have to come up with a class average eventually. So this morning our math worksheet will help us get ready for that. This morning in math we're going to spend some time on averaging to give you some practice in doing it."

11. Teacher to class: "So there was a real turning point in the American Revolution. What's the date we're looking for?" (Teacher waves in general direction of the blackboard on which the date is written.) (No student response.) "David just said it." (No response.) "Look at the board." (Students reply.)

12. A student has been a bit overwhelmed by what seems like so many steps in math word problems. The teacher sits down with her to go over some problems: "Here's how I solved this problem; follow along and see if you did the same thing: Let's see—it says, 'Ten full boxes of detergent weigh 100 lbs. The detergent alone weighs 90 lbs. How much does each box weigh alone?' Okay. That's without the detergent...what can I figure out here...hmm...if the total weight is 100 lbs. and the detergent alone is 90 lbs.,...hmm...I can subtract 90 from 100 and get the total box weight. Okay, that would be 10. Now...what does the problem want? Oh, the weight of each box. Well, if 10 is the total box weight and there are 10 boxes...I can divide 10 by 10. I get one. So that's it...one pound per box."

13. Teacher to class: "We've worked on a large number of problems during this unit and learned a number of different tips for solving them. Let's come up with a class list of all the problem-solving strategies that we've found to be effective during this unit."

14. A student has gotten a math problem wrong on a homework paper. The teacher, working with him, asks, "Let's see where you went wrong here. How many cubes did you count?" ("Six.") "That's okay. How many sides does each cube have?" ("Six...Oh!") "What number did you use for the number of sides?" ("Three.") "So that's where you broke down. Remember each cube has six sides, so six cubes would have six times six sides or 36 sides altogether. Do you see where you went wrong?"

15. Teacher to class: "Remember when we developed criteria for judging presidents and then you each chose a president to evaluate using those criteria? Well, today we're going to do something similar. We're going to be developing criteria for judging legislation and then you'll evaluate a specific bill based on those criteria."

16. A student had consistently cross-divided instead of cross-multiplied on his algebra homework assignment the night before. Before the period began, the teacher went over the work with the student who appeared to understand what he had done wrong. Even though the class was focusing on another algebra concept that day, the teacher called on this student twice during the period when the process involved cross-multiplying.

The following two items are examples of mistakes in two different areas of Clarity:

17. Teacher to class: "I'm going to be giving you a fable for you to read and do some work on. Something will be missing from the fable; what do you suppose is missing?" ("Dialogue?") "No. Some element in a fable that's always in a fable and is missing." ("Setting?") "No." ("Plot?") "No." ("Moral?") "Right. You are going to have to figure out the moral."

18. Teacher to class: "I want to see if you really understand how photo-synthesis works. What's the name of the substance in plants that makes them green?" ("Chlorophyll.") "Good. What does the prefix 'photo' mean?" ("Light.") "Great. In order to grow, plants need to be exposed to what?" ("Carbon dioxide.") "Super! You do under-stand. Let's move on."

Source Materials on Clarity

Abel, R. Robert, and Raymond W. Kulhavy. "Maps, Mode of Text Presentation and Children's Prose Learning." *American Educational Research Journal* 23, no. 2 (Summer 1986): 263–274.

Anderson, L. M., C. M. Evertson, and J. E. Brophy. "An Examination of Classroom Context: Effects of Lesson Format and Teacher Training on Patterns of Teacher Student Contacts during Small-group Instruction." *Journal of Classroom Interaction* 15, no. 2 (Summer 1980): 21–26.

Anderson, Linda M. et al. "Classroom Task Environments and Students' Task-related Beliefs." *Elementary School Journal* 88, no. 3 (1988): 281–295.

Anderson, Valerie, and Suzanne Hidi. "Teaching Students to Summarize." *Educational Leadership* (December 1988/January 1989): 26–28.

Armbruster, Bonnie, Thomas H. Anderson, and Joyce Ostertag. "Teaching Text Structure to Improve Reading and Writing." *Reading Teacher* (November 1989): 130–137.

Ault, Charles R. Jr. "Intelligently Wrong. Some Comments on Children's Misconceptions." *Science and Children* (May 1984): 22–24.

Ausubel, D. P. *Educational Psychology: A Cognitive View*. New York: Holt, Rinehart & Winston, 1968.

Bagley, Michael T., and Karin Hess. *200 Ways of Using Imagery in the Classroom*. Monroe, N.Y.: Trillium Press, 1987.

Barell, John. "'You Ask the Wrong Questions!'" *Educational Leadership* (May 1985): 18–23.

Baroody, Arthur, and Herbert Ginsburg. "The Effects of Instruction on Children's Understanding of the 'Equals' Sign." *Elementary School Journal* 84, no. 2 (November 1983): 199–212.

Belgard, M., B. Rosenshine, and N. L. Gage. "The Teacher's Effectiveness in Explaining: Evidence on Its Generality and Correlation with Pupils Ratings and Attention Score." In *Research into Classroom Processes*. Edited by A. Bellack. New York: Teachers College Press, 1971: 182–191.

Bennett, Neville, and Charles Desforges. "Matching Classroom Tasks to Students' Attainments." *Elementary School Journal* 88, no. 3 (January 1988): 221–234.

Black, H., and S. Black. *Organizing Thinking, Book II. Graphic Organizers*. Pacific Grove, Calif.: Midwest Publications, 1990.

Bragstad, Bernice Jensen, and Sharyn M. Stumpf, "How a Map Is Born." In *A Guidebook for Teaching Study Skills and Motivation*. Boston: Allyn and Bacon, 1982.

Brophy, Jere E. "How Teachers Influence What Is Taught and Learned in Classrooms." *Elementary School Journal* 83, no. 1 (1982): 1–13.

Brophy, Jere. "Teacher Effects Research and Teacher Quality." *Journal of Classroom Interaction* 22, no. 1 (December 1986/January 1987): 14–23.

Brophy, J. "Teacher Praise: A Functional Analysis." *Review of Educational Research* 51, no. 1 (Spring 1981): 5–32.

Bulgren, Janis. "Teaching Concepts: Concept Diagramming and the Concept of Teaching Routine." Institute for Research in Learning Disabilities, University of Kansas, Lawrence, Kansas, August 1991.

Burton, Grace M. "Writing as a Way of Knowing in a Mathematics Education Class." *Arithmetic Teacher* (December 1985): 40–44.

Bush, A. J., J. J. Kennedy, and D. R. Cruickshank, "An Empirical Investigation of Teacher Clarity." *Journal of Teacher Education* 28, no. 2 (1977): 53–58.

Carnine, Douglas "New Research on the Brain: Implications for Instruction." *Phi Delta Kappan* (January 1990): 372–377.

Carpenter, T. P., et al, "Using Knowledge of Children's Mathematics Thinking in Classroom Teaching: An Experimental Study." *American Educational Research Journal* 26, no. 4 (Winter 1989): 499–431.

Clarke, John H. *Patterns of Thinking.* Boston: Allyn & Bacon, 1990.

Coffman, Joy, and David O. Tanis, "Don't Say Particle, Say People." *Science Teacher* (November 1990): 27–29.

Cooper, C. "Different Ways of Being a Teacher: An Ethnographic Study of College Instructors Academic, and Social Roles in the Classroom." *Journal of Classroom Interaction* 16, no. 2 (1980): 27–36.

Costa, A. *Teaching for Intelligent Behavior.* Orangevale, Calif.: Search Models Unlimited, 1985.

D'Angelo, K. "Precise Writing: Promoting Vocabulary Development and Comprehension." *Journal of Reading* (March 1983): 534–539.

Dank, Milton. *Albert Einstein.* New York: Franklin Watts, 1983.

Davey, B. "Think Aloud—Modeling the Cognitive Processes of Reading Comprehension." *Journal of Reading* (October 1983): 44–47.

Dishner, E. K. et al. "Attending to Text Structure: A Comprehension Strategy." In *Reading in the Content Areas: Improving Classroom Instruction,* 234–245. Dubuque, Iowa: Kendall/Hunt.

Donald, Stanley J. Jencks, and Louis J. Chatterley. "How Can You Tell?" *Elementary School Journal* 80, no. 4 (March 1980): 178–89.

Doyle, Walter. "Stalking the Mythical Student." *Elementary School Journal* 82, no. 5 (1982): 529–538.

Driver, Rosalind, Edith Guesne, and A. Tiberghien. *Children's Ideas in Science.* Milton Keyes, England and Philadelphia: Open University Press, 1985.

Duckworth, E. *"The Having of Wonderful Ideas" and Other Essays on Teaching and Learning*. New York: Teachers College Press, 1987.

Duffy, Gerald, Laura R. Roehler, and Gary Rackliffe. "How Teachers' Instructional Talk Influences Students' Understanding of Lesson Content." *Elementary School Journal* 87, no. 1 (1986): 3–16.

Dunkin, M. J., and B. J. Biddle. *The Study of Teaching*. New York: Holt, Rinehart & Winston, 1974.

Eaton, Janet. "Research on Teaching." *Educational Leadership* (October 1982): 75–76.

Eaton, J. F., C. W. Anderson, and E. L. Smith, "Students' Misconceptions Interfere with Science Learning: Case Studies of Fifth-Grade Students." *Elementary School Journal* 84, no. 4 (1984): 65–379.

Edwards, John, and P. Marland. "Student Thinking in a Secondary Biology Classroom." *Research in Science Education* 12 (1982): 32–41.

Escondido School District. *Minds Eye*. Escondido, Calif.: Board of Education, 1979.

Eylon, B., and M. C. Linn, "Learning and Instruction: An Examination of Four Research Perspectives in Science Education." *Review of Educational Research* 58, no. 3 (Fall 1988).

Fogarty, Robin, and James Bellanca. *Patterns for Thinking: Patterns for Transfer*. Palatine, Ill.: IRI Group, 1987.

Fortune, J. C., N. L. Gage, and R. E. Shute. "The Generality of the Ability to Explain." Paper presented at the A.E.R.A. Convention, Chicago, 1966.

Friedrich, G. W., K. M. Galvin, and C. L. Book. *Growing Together: Classroom Communication*. Columbus, Ohio: Charles Merrill, 1976.

Gage, N. L. "Exploration of Teachers' Effectiveness in Explaining." Tech. Report No. 4. Stanford: Stanford University Center for Research and Development in Teaching, 1961. EDO28 147.

Gagne, R. M. *The Essentials of Learning for Instruction*. Hinsdale, Ill.: Dryden Press, 1974.

Galyean, Beverly-Colleene. "Guided Imagery in the Curriculum." *Educational Leadership* (March 1983): 54–58.

———. *Mind Sight, Learning Through Imaging*. Berkeley, Calif.: Zephyr Press, 1988.

Garmston, Robert, and Diane Zimmerman. "Beyond Recipe: Teaching for Taste." *California Catalyst* (Spring 1993): 4–8.

Geller, Linda Gibson. "Conversations in Kindergarten." *Science and Children* (April 1985): 30–32.

Ghatala, Elizabeth S., et al. "Training Cognitive Strategy-Monitoring in Children." *American Educational Research Journal* 22, no. 2 (Summer 1985): 199–215.

Goleman, Daniel. " Cues Are Easy to Misinterpret." *New York Times,* September 17, 1991.

Good, T. H., and J. E. Brophy, *Looking in Classrooms.* New York: Harper and Row, 1978.

Graham, S. "Teacher Feelings and Student Thoughts: An Attributional Approach to Affect in the Classroom." *Elementary School Journal* 85, no. 1): 91–104.

Gregg, Charles I. "Teachers Also Must Learn." *Harvard Educational Review* 10 (1940): 30–47.

Gregorc, A. "Learning/Teaching Styles: Potent Faces Behind Them." *Educational Leadership* (January 1979).

Hahn, A. L., and R. Gardner. "Synthesis of Research on Students' Ability to Summarize Text." *Educational Leadership* (February 1985): 52–55.

Harris, Paulette, and Kevin Swick. "Improving Teacher Communications." *Clearing House* 59 (September 1985): 13–15.

Heimlich, Joan E., and Susan D. Pittelman. "Semantic Mapping: Classroom Applications." *IRA Service Bulletin, Reading Aids Series.* Newark, Del., 1986.

Harron, J. Dudley. "Piaget for Chemists." *Journal of Chemical Education* (1952): 146–150.

Hess, Karin K. *Enhancing Writing Through Imagery.* New York: Trillium Press, 1987.

Hesse, Joseph. "From Naive to Knowledgeable." *Science Teacher* (September 1989): 55–58.

Hyerle, David. *Designs for Thinking Connectively.* Lyme, N.H.: Designs for Thinking, 1990.

Hiller, J. H., G. A. Fisher, and W. A. Kaess. "A Computer Investigation of Verbal Characteristics of Effective Classroom Lecturing." *American Educational Research Journal* 6 (1969): 661–675.

Hines, Constance V., Donald R. Cruickshank, and John J. Kennedy. "Teacher Clarity and Its Relationship to Student Achievement and Satisfaction." *American Educational Research Journal* 22, no. 1 (Spring 1985): 87–99.

Hunter, Madeline. *Master Teaching.* El Segundo, Calif.: TIP Publications, 1982.

Institute for Research on Teaching. "Kids Have Misconceptions." *Communication Quarterly* (Fall 1981).

Institute for Research on Teaching. "Explicitness is Key to Reading Instruction." *Communication Quarterly (*Winter/Spring 1984).

Johnson, David R. *Every Minute Counts: Making Your Math Class Work.* Palo Alto, Calif.: Dale Seymour Publications, 1986.

Johnston, Peter. "Teaching Students to Apply Strategies That Improve Reading Comprehension." *Elementary School Journal* 85, no. 5 (1985): 635–645.

Joos, M. *The Five Clocks.* New York: Harcourt Brace, 1967.

Kallison, James M. Jr. "Effects of Lesson Organization on Achievement." *American Educational Research Journal* 23, no. 2 (Summer 1986): 337–347.

Land, M. L., and L. R. Smith. "The Effect of Low Inference Teacher Clarity Inhibitors on Student Achievement." *Journal of Teacher Education* 30, no. 3 (May/June 1979): 55–57.

Liedtke, Werner. "Diagnosis in Mathematics: The Advantages of an Interview." *Arithmetic Teacher* (November 1988): 26–29.

Lopez, José A., and Arthur B. Powell. "Writing as a Vehicle to Learn Mathematics: A Case Study." Presented at the Seventy-first Annual Meeting of the Mathematical Association of America, January 1988.

Margulies, Nancy. *Mapping Inner Space: Learning and Teaching Mind Mapping.* Tucson, Ariz.: Zephyr Press, 1991.

Marino, Jacqueline L., Sandra Gould, and Lester W. Haas. "The Effects of Writing as a Prereading Activity on Delayed Recall of Narrative Text." *Elementary School Journal* 86, no. 2 (1985): 199–205.

Martin, J. *Explaining, Understanding and Teaching.* New York: McGraw-Hill, 1970.

Marx, Ronald W., and John Walsh. "Learning from Academic Tasks." *Elementary School Journal* 88, no. 3 (1988): 207–219.

McCaleb, J. L., and J. A. White. "Critical Dimensions in Evaluating Teacher Clarity." *Journal of Classroom Interaction,* 15, no. 2 (1980): 27–30.

McCarthy, B. *The 4MAT System.* Barrington, Ill.: Excel, 1981.

McLean, Thomas J. "U. of Arizona 'Humanizes' Classes with Computers." *Dollars and Sense* (September 1991).

McNeill, J. D. *Reading Comprehension: New Directions for Classroom Practice.* Glenview, Ill.: Scott, Foresman and Company, 1984.

Mehan, H. "Accomplishing Classroom Lessons." In *Language Use and School Performance.* Edited by S.V. Cicouril. New York: Academic Press, 1974.

Mett, Coreen L. "Writing as a Learning Device in Calculus." *Mathematics Teacher* (October 1987): 534–537.

Murdock, Maureen. *Spinning Inward.* Boston and London: Shambhala, 1987.

Novak, Joseph D., and D. Bob Gowin. *Learning How to Learn.* New York: Cambridge University Press, 1984.

Ogle, Donna M. "K-W-L: A Teaching Model That Develops Active Reading of Expository Text." *Reading Teacher* (February 1986): 564–570.

Osborne, Roger, and Peter Freyberg. *Learning in Science: The Implications of Children's Science.* Portsmouth, N.H.: Heineman, 1984.

Parsons, Cynthia. "Grading Teachers for Quality." *Christian Science Monitor* (October 26, 1981): B1.

Peterson, P., and S. Swing. "Beyond Time on Task: Students' Reports of their Thought Processes during Classroom Instruction." *Elementary School Journal* 82, no. 5 (1982): 481–491.

Peterson, P., et al. "Students' Cognitions and Time on Task During Mathematics Instruction." *American Educational Research Journal* 21, no. 3 (Fall 1984): 487–515.

Pradl, G. M., and J. S. Mayher. "Reinvigorating Learning Through Writing." *Educational Leadership* (February 1985): 2–8.

Pressley, G. M. "Imagery and Children's Learning: Putting the Picture in Developmental Perspective. *Review of Educational Research* 47 (1977): 585–622.

———. "Mental Imagery Helps Eight-Year Olds Remember What They Read." *Journal of Educational Psychology* 68 (1976): 355–59.

Raths, James. "Enhancing Understanding Through Debriefing." *Educational Leadership* (October 1987): 22–27.

Rohrkemper, Mary M., and Barbara Bershon. "Elementary School Students' Report of the Causes and Effects of Problem Difficulty in Mathematics." *Elementary School Journal* 85, no. 1 (1984): 127–147.

Rose, Laura. *Picture This, Teaching Reading Through Visualization.* Tucson, Ariz.: Zephyr Press, 1989.

Rosenshine, B., and N. Furst, "The Use of Direct Observation to Study Teaching." *Second Handbook of Research on Teaching.* Edited by R. M. Travers. Chicago: Rand McNally, 1973.

Roth, Kathleen J., Charles W. Anderson, and Edward L. Smith. "Curriculum Materials, Teacher Talk and Student Learning: Case Studies in Fifth Grade Science Teaching." Paper presented at the annual meeting of the National Reading Conference, Symposium on Teacher Explanatory Talk, Austin, Texas, December 1983.

Roth, Wolff-Michael. "Map Your Way to a Better Lab." *Science Teacher* (April 1990): 31–34.

Rowe, M. B. "Getting Chemistry off the Killer Course List." *Journal of Chemical Education* 60, no. 1 (1983): 954–956.

Sagan, Carl. *Cosmos.* New York: Random House, 1980.

Sanders, A. "Learning Logs: A Communication Strategy for All Subject Areas." *Educational Leadership* (February 1985): 7.

Sinatra, Richard. "Semantic Mapping: A Thinking Strategy for Improved Reading and Writing Development: Parts I & II." *Teaching Thinking and Problem Solving* 12, no. 1 (1990).

Singer, Harry. "Active Comprehension from Answering to Asking Questions." *Reading Teacher* 31, no. 8 (May 1978): 901–908.

Smith, Lyle, and Michael Land. "Low-Inference Verbal Behaviors Related to Teacher Clarity." *Journal of Classroom Interactions* 17, no. 1 (1981): 37–42.

Tasker, R. "Children's Views and Classroom Experience." *Australian Science Teachers' Journal* 27, no. 3 (1980): 33–37.

Tobin, K. "Wait-time in Science—Necessary But Insufficient." Paper presented at the annual meeting of the National Association for Research in Science Teaching, French Lick Springs, Ind., April 1985.

Whisler, Jo Sue, and Robert J. Marzano. *Dare to Imagine: An Olympian's Technology*. Aurora, Colo.: Mid-continent Regional Educational Laboratory, 1988.

White, R., and R. Gunstone. *Probing Understanding*. London: Falmer Press, 1992.

Winne, Philip H. "Steps Toward Promoting Cognitive Achievements." *Elementary School Journal* 85, no. 5 (1985): 673–693.

Winne, P.H., and R.W. Marx. "Students' and Teachers' Views of Thinking Processes for Classroom Learning." *Elementary School Journal* 82, no. 5 (1982): 492–518.

Special Note

Thanks to Hal Manley of Concord-Carlisle Regional High School and to Richard Deppe of the Carlisle Public Schools for assistance in generating examples of Clarity behaviors.

9

Principles of Learning

How do I make lessons more
efficient and effective?

This chapter describes twenty-four little packages of power, each one self-contained and ready for use by itself, each a possible addition to any teacher's repertoire, and each certain to increase the rate and durability of students' learning. A strong claim? Perhaps, but for once in education, a certain one.

What do these names mean to you: Pavlov, Thorndike, Hull, Watson, Guthrie, Mowrer, Spence, Tolman, Skinner? We don't hear much about them these days, yet these are men who approached learning as a phenomenon about which universal laws might be deduced and operating principles discovered—and they discovered quite a few of them. The tradition of their research goes back to 1885 (Ebbinghaus) and is the strongest, longest, and soundest base we have in education for how-to recommendations. Taken together, their principles do not add up to a cohesive theory

> **Twenty-four little packages of power certain to increase the rate and durability of students' learning**

or approach to how to teach as we get from some of their modern counterparts (Bruner, Ausubel, Piaget). Instead, each of these principles was shown in its own way to make a contribution to learning effectiveness, and they lie scattered about the literature like so many precious stones waiting to be picked up. Many of them were collected in the 1970s and put into accessible form for teachers by Madeline Hunter and her associates (*Teach More, Faster* is an exemplary title of one of her books for teachers). But somehow these principles have not become part of the currency of in-service teacher training or college teacher education.

As you read this chapter, you will recognize some of these principles from your own teaching. We find that most teachers routinely use six or seven of them intuitively, without knowing the labels you will learn for them as you read here. Some teachers use more, some fewer. We have yet to find a teacher who uses them all, however, and so believe that there is something new in this chapter for everyone.

We have identified twenty-four of these principles in the literature (see such sources as Hilgard and Bower 1966; Bugelski 1971; and Hudgins 1977 for useful summaries and extensions of the principles). By studying them and looking for opportunities to use one or two new ones, you can expand your repertoire and improve student learning.

Later in this book we will study different models of teaching and explore both how to do them and what their different aims and theoretical bases are. When we get to models, we will be looking at teaching as a playwright looks at a script. We'll look at the design and sequence of the whole lesson and what discrete teacher moves have to do with the overall design of a particular kind of learning. We won't refer to any of these principles of learning then, but we won't be invalidating them either. They're always there and always relevant.

Meaning

The more meaningful and relevant the task or application of information is to the students' world, the easier it is to learn. Teachers using this principle may make explicit references to students' personal experiences as a tie or a hook for connecting content with students' lives, or they may simulate the experiences in the learning activity or in some other way embed the new content in the students' meaning framework. One teacher using the principle gave us the following example: "The goal is to understand the difference between chronology and history. I do a two-part assignment. For one day, students are asked to keep a time line of their activities. The next day they are to write a narrative history of the one day for which they kept the time line, showing, where possible, a cause-and-effect relationship." This assignment makes a nice distinction between chronology and history around a context that has intimate personal meaning for the students: their own day's activities.

> *The more meaningful and relevant the task or application of information is to the students' world, the easier it is to learn.*

Similarity of Environment

Similarity of environment (actions, feelings, formats, routines) elicits the learner's "set to perform." This principle holds that certain features of the environment, when regularly associated with a particular type of learning or a period in which a particular type of attention or work is expected, trigger a mind-set in learners that "plugs them in" and turns on their operators for that particular kind of lesson or activity.

Therefore, teachers can regularly use repetitive formats for certain kinds of learning—when the environment assumes certain space, time, and routine features—to create expectational mind-sets in their pupils for that kind of work. For example, a science teacher we know has thirty lab coats hung on a row of pegs inside his classroom door. When students enter, they are expected to put on a lab coat and proceed to their seats. The lab coats signal a change of mind-set into being scientists.[1]

In addition, teachers may warm up students for a lesson by doing an activity that starts them thinking the way they'll be asked to think in the lesson. For instance, suppose a teacher is going to do a lesson on outlining, which requires students to categorize their ideas into topical groups. The teacher may warm up the class by playing Guess My Category. The teacher slowly develops the lists below on the board, writing the terms one at a time in the order indicated, under "yes" for positive examples of the category and "no" for negative examples. The students must guess the category to which the "yes" examples belong ("southern states").

YES	NO
Mississippi	New York
Virginia	Wyoming
Georgia	California
Kentucky	Iowa
Florida	Arizona

When the game is over, the teacher says, "Now, the kind of thinking we were doing here is similar to what our minds have to do with facts in this outlining activity for today. Take out your note cards and…"

Doug Russell (1980) points out that this activity is also an excellent sponge for students arriving in class (see the Momentum parameter in Chapter 3). It gets them involved immediately with a meaningful activity yet does not penalize those who haven't arrived yet. Thus it eliminates downtime and waiting.

Contiguity

"First impressions stick" is one way of thinking about this principle. Events, objects, operations, and emotions close to each other in time and space tend to become associated in the mind of the learner. A first association, once learned, is hard to unlearn—whether it's calling Mary Ann, "Mary Lou" the first time you meet her and finding yourself doing so every time thereafter or adding the tens column first and then the ones, and finding that a hard habit to break.

[1] Thanks to Bruce Oliver of Fairfax County, Va., for passing on this idea.

Learners should not be allowed to practice errors and build an incorrect association. Students who practice footnotes in the wrong format the first time find that the wrong model interferes with the right one when they finally learn it. (Twenty years later one of the authors is still getting confused over the order of elements in a footnote, because he hasn't completely expunged the wrong model he was allowed to practice one night in homework with no corrective feedback.) This principle pertains mainly to paired-associate memory and procedural learning like vocabulary words and math algorithms, not higher-level thought questions. For memory learning, the implication for teachers is to anticipate errors where they are likely to occur and prevent these errors, even by giving the right answer where appropriate (e.g., a new sight word) *before* a student has a chance to make a wrong guess (and thus learn a wrong association that must later be unlearned). Teachers should never allow a student to leave a paired-associate learning situation with a wrong answer; the last response that occurs should be correct.

Teachers should also be on the watch for potential negative emotional associations students may form. For example, students coming in to class after a recess full of fighting and negative emotions, who are then introduced to a new topic, may form negative associations with the topic that will interfere with future learning. This is not the time to introduce poetry for the first time. The teacher might preface the introduction to the topic with a brief activity that raises positive feelings in students.

Close Confusers

Ensure an adequate degree of original learning before "close confusers" are introduced. Teachers following this principle are careful not to confuse or weaken recently learned items—say, the letter "d"—by introducing new items easily confused with it—the letter "b." In this example, the primary teacher will go on to "t," then maybe "f," then some other letters, all the while reviewing "d" in the expanding set of letters recognized and then finally introduce "b" as a new letter when "d" has been thoroughly learned and practiced. To generalize the statement of this principle in other terms, teachers should not sequence new material so as to require fine discriminations between two contiguous terms when grosser discriminations can be used first. The making of fine discriminations can be demanded when at least one item of the content pair has had an adequate opportunity to be thoroughly learned. (Note that textbooks unfortunately often introduce close confusers at the same time, such as rotation and revolution of the earth or weathering and erosion.)

Similarly, exceptions to rules are not to be introduced until original rules are practiced and established sufficiently. Mindful of this principle, a secondary teacher writes:

Constitutional law is a central part of any middle school social studies curricula. Instruction frequently involves explanations of the Bill of Rights, including illustrations of case law. For example, "freedom of speech" is usually tackled by considering yelling "fire" in a crowded theater. Before a teacher can realistically ask students to distinguish between acceptable and unacceptable forms of "free speech," he must be sure that they have a grounding in the basic concepts, including the important case law. Once they have this, they can examine a more complex situation.

Isolation of Critical Attributes

Teachers who practice this principle identify explicitly the critical unvarying attributes or elements of the item under study and label them. Particularly with regard to definitions of new concepts, they isolate the qualities or attributes essential to the concept, attributes "without which it is not" (without which the object is not the object but something else). For example, "What are the critical attributes that define an estuary?" Answer: delta or fan shaped; at the bottom of a river; brackish water (part salt, part fresh) and sedimentary deposits at the bottom. Without any one of these four elements, we don't have an estuary.

Another example, when preparing students to write myths in their study of literary genres, it is very useful to develop the following list:

- Heroic figures
- Magic
- Explains the origin of a natural phenomenon

These are the essential attributes—the defining attributes of "myth." If any one of them is missing in a story, it's not a myth. One can develop the list of attributes in any number of ways—for example, have students read a variety of myths and extract what they have in common, consult reference books for definitions of myth, or tell students the attributes in direct instruction with examples. However it happens, *that* it happens can make a positive difference to learning.

A second way to use the principle has to do with concepts that are similar but different—perhaps concepts that are close relatives. For example, in comparing tattling and reporting, one may see the teacher develop two parallel lists of attributes and compare them. For tattling and reporting, the lists will be identical except for one item: intent. Intent (to get someone in trouble as opposed to giving needed information) is the critical attribute that discriminates tattling from reporting. What is the critical attribute that discriminates prejudice from discrimination?

So far we have discussed two slightly different ways to use the principle: (1) listing the definitional attributes that make something what it is ("myth" as example) and (2) comparing two parallel lists of similar concepts to distinguish the critical attributes that separate the target concept (tattling) from its close relative (reporting). A third use helps us see which from among the many attributes that may characterize an entity are the critical ones—the ones it must have to separate it from the pack. For example, many mammals have hair and bear their young alive (rather than in eggs). But there occur mammals without those characteristics too. All mammals, however, nurse their young. That is the critical attribute without which a mammal is not a mammal.

Through any of these three variations—isolation of definitional, essential, and critical attributes—this principle can strengthen learning.

When teachers highlight items as important, that is not isolation of critical attributes. Highlighting is highlighting! Things can be important without being critical attributes—for example, "These four formulas may be the most important things to know in the chapter: or "These three events may be the most important things to know about the month preceding the Civil War." Neither set of important things, however, is the critical attribute of anything. Highlighting important items is something teachers do deliberately and usefully to focus students' attention on more important items, but that is quite different from identifying the definitional attributes of a concept.

In exploring the difference between a developed and an underdeveloped country, the teacher may highlight certain critical attributes that define developed: for example, mechanized planting and harvesting, efficient national market distribution system, and infrastructure of highways and transportation networks. It is not enough, however, for this list of attributes simply to be presented in the text or on the board. The teacher must see to it that the critical attributes are generated, call the students' attention to them (or elicit them from the students), and then have students apply the attributes in deciding which cases (here, what countries) do or do not contain those critical attributes. When students can discriminate developed from underdeveloped countries through analysis of critical attributes in new settings, or in studies of countries where they're not specifically asked to look at them as developed versus underdeveloped, then we know this learning has transferred.

Teach for Transfer (from Setting to Setting)

This principle is at work when teachers create a series of assignments or tasks in which the call for using a skill is progressively distanced from direct instructional settings. Here is a good example of teaching for transfer: After defining fact ("that which is immediately verifiable by the senses, or that upon which most experts in the field would agree") versus opinion ("a belief; evidence exists to support differing beliefs"), the teacher has students label examples as fact or opinion: for example, "Mary is wearing a sweater" and "Mary is the prettiest girl in the class." Examples get more and more difficult over time ("Some people believe in reincarnation") until students are asked to generate the examples themselves. Then, they are asked to bring in newspaper articles (a new setting), which they are expected to analyze for fact and opinion. Finally, students are given cues to transfer their skill to settings where it isn't an assignment to distinguish fact from opinion, as in text readings.[2]

Sometimes we don't need to do anything extra for transfer to occur; it happens by itself. If we have taught children to borrow in subtraction and they know how to do it, they will probably transfer that skill to the supermarket that very afternoon when buying supplies for a class party. But for many skills, transfer will not happen spontaneously. We need to engineer a series of events that will induce it. The final event in the chain, the actual transfer of the skill to a new context, is one students take by themselves. That is what makes understanding this principle a bit tricky. We take students along a planned series of steps up to the edge of the water, but they have to jump in themselves for there to be evidence that transfer has actually occurred.

Mrs. Crane, for example, is teaching her junior high students about characterization. They look at pieces of dialogue and physical actions of characters in stories to see what these pieces of behavior reveal about the characters. The objective is to learn to recognize how authors develop readers' images and understandings of characters through dialogue and physical actions. In the long term, Mrs. Crane wants her students to be able to use characterization in everyday life, that is, to "read" people they encounter, to make inferences about what they are feeling and thinking from bits of dialogue and physical actions the students observe. She wants them, in other words, to transfer their ability to recognize characterization as a literary device to their own ability to use it in understanding people they meet. After analyzing the text in novels for characterization, she assigns students to watch one of their favorite TV programs; they are to take down bits of dialogue or describe physical actions they see that are in some way indicative of the character's personality. Later in the week her students are asked to bring in examples of characterization from their observations of people in their neighborhoods or their family. She is thus progressively distancing their use of characterization from the academic context of novels they are reading and pressing them to use the skill in ever closer approximations of real life.

If students have learned to read novels and plays for authors' biases, transfer has occurred if they then read nonfiction and magazine articles in the same way. Teachers encourage this kind of transfer by proper sequencing of assignments and by pressing students to be aware of the multiple applications of their learning (Brown 1989; Fogarty, Perkins, and Barell 1991). This principle is easily confused with (but different from) Application in Setting, where a skill taught in an abstract setting is put to use right away in a realistic setting.

---

[2] This example is based on Madeline Hunter's *Teach for Transfer* (1971).

Application in Setting (from Skill to Setting)

Students should practice new behaviors or skills in the settings and in the way those learnings will be used in life. Thus, spelling will more likely transfer to composition if spelling tests embed new words in sentences (perhaps from dictation). The ability to listen to others will transfer to real discussions and to conflict resolutions if practiced in class meetings and real or simulated disagreements. Notice that we used the word *transfer* in both of these examples. Application in Setting is a principle that, when applied, makes it more likely that transfer will occur. As part of Teaching for Transfer, one is likely to see several instances of Application in Setting. Application in Setting is something we see and give as a label to single-instance activities that are having students use a skill in some real-life context, such as identifying and labeling logical fallacies (e.g., the straw man fallacy) in arguments of current political candidates. But to claim Teaching for Transfer itself, we would have to see a series of such activities deliberately orchestrated so as progressively to distance the skill from abstract academic contexts. Each one of them singly may have been by itself an example of Application in Setting.

> *Students should practice new behaviors or skills in the settings and in the way those learnings will be used in life.*

Vividness

The vividness, liveliness, energy, novelty, or striking imagery of a learning experience is thought to impress new learning on students more deeply perhaps through mediation of the attentional mechanisms. One can claim this principle to be in operation by virtue of observed student reaction to learning experiences, the "ooh aah" reactions, the high level of arousal or emotion (surprise, fascination) we attribute to observed student behaviors (wide eyes, open mouths, rapt gazes, unusual stillness). In trying to practice what he preaches, one of the authors once introduced a group of teachers to the principles of learning by pulling a series of small gift-wrapped packages out of a case labeled "Idea Bag," to highlight that each principle is discrete and valuable, self-contained and important.

Active Participation

In classes of teachers who use this principle, students are operating, responding, moving, and talking during the course of the learning experiences. Sitting passively and listening is not characteristic of learning experiences embodying this principle. Active participation of all students might not require small or large muscle movement or manipulation; it could conceivably involve written participation, with each student responding to each question; or it could be all verbal participation, with the setting structured in such a way that many students can talk at once (divided into pairs or small groups to reach consensus on something or debate some issue).

There are many techniques for structuring this kind of participation from students. For example, after finishing a presentation of the structure of an atomic nucleus and the meaning of atomic number versus atomic mass, the teacher says, "OK. Now explain to your neighbor the difference between atomic number and atomic mass." Teachers aware of this principle look for opportunities to make that kind of move.

Feeling Tone

Feeling tone propels learning in proportion to degree. This principle posits that students learn more and faster in proportion to the level of feeling provoked during the learning—positive or negative feeling. The rule is held to apply, however, only up to a point. On one side, the more pleasurable the learning experience is, the more the learning will take place—up to the point where the pleasure takes over and begins crowding out the learning. There is, in other words, a point of diminishing returns for efforts to make learning pleasurable. When teachers raise the level of concern of students ("I'm going to check you all individually on this material this period") learning is potentiated, but only up to a point. Too much concern turns into anxiety, quickly interferes with learning, and blocks it. Again, a point of diminishing returns is quickly reached.

Application of this principle sees teachers either making moves to make learning experiences enjoyable (without becoming hedonistic) and/or raising levels of concern ("We'll be having a quiz on this material sometime this week"), but neither to extreme. Judging the extreme, or the point of diminishing returns, is not a judgment for which rules can be cited. To credit this principle as operative, however, an observer would have to cite evidence of teacher moves to raise positive or negative feeling tone and be subjectively convinced (by watching student reactions) that extremes had not been violated.

Mnemonics

Teachers using this principle help students use mediational devices for remembering new learning—devices such as imagery, anagrams, or jingles ("30 days hath September"). Here is a familiar one:

> *"30 days hath September."*

Desert—one "s," all alone in the desert.

Dessert—you get bigger in the middle if you eat too much of it.

There are many mnemonic devices and a growing body of research comparing their effectiveness. For example, one particularly effective technique, the key word technique, is used for learning new vocabulary words (in any language) and new terms. Students are asked to learn a key word (word clue) for the new term that sounds acoustically similar to it (e.g., "purse" for "persuade"; "he's a date" for "hesitate"). Then students are asked to remember the content of a cartoon (plain line drawing) that contains the key word interacting in some way with the definition of the new term. Levin et al. (1982) show a cartoon for the new vocabulary word *persuade*. One woman points to a purse in a store and says, "Oh, Martha, you should buy that PURSE!" Martha replies, "I think you can PERSUADE me to buy it." At the bottom of the cartoon is written, "Persuade (Purse): When you talk someone into doing something."

In these cartoons, one character's utterance contains the key word, and the other contains the new term to be learned. Studies have been highly positive and uniform in demonstrating the effectiveness of this technique for learning new words (Levin 1993.)

Here are the steps in using mnemonic key words:

1. Think of a sound-alike or rhyming word you know that resembles the new word you're trying to learn. This word is the key word.

2. Make up a visual cartoon in which both the key word and the word to be learned are represented in the action or the objects.

3. Have dialogue between two characters in the cartoon, one using the key word and the other the word to be learned.

4. Make the dialogue meaningful, and arrange it so that the context of the dialogue and the cartoon illustrates the meaning of the word to be learned.

Sequence and Backward Chaining

It turns out that the first and last items in a series are the easiest to learn; the one just past the middle is the hardest. Learning can be accelerated by chaining a sequence backward from the last item and sequences can be broken into small parts to avoid interference. This set of principles is applicable to rote learning and is easily observed when practiced in math fact and spelling drills or any other body of items in some sequence that students are expected to memorize (such as poems). Teachers can use this knowledge to improve the learning of items in the difficult positions. The sequence (or list) can be shortened or split in half so the difficult item becomes first on the shortened list. The order of items can be changed; the hard parts can be given extra practice; the hard items can be made more vivid (darker print, use of colors). A high school Latin teacher writes:

Students are expected to learn ten new Latin vocabulary words each week. (1) They quiz each other from the list at the beginning of each class period for five minutes. (2) Then they drill alone on the ones they missed in the partner quiz. (3) They write the list in their notebooks along with the meanings, putting the ones they missed first and last in the reordered list (and second and ninth if need be). Words they know best are put in the just-past-the-middle position. They cover the answers with their hand and go down the list several times quizzing themselves. This procedure is repeated each day with missed words in first and last positions. The whole thing takes about ten minutes, which I use to circulate and talk to individual students.

This principle of sequence and the importance of the first and last positions is also applicable to the use of time. What happens at the beginning and end of a class period (or day or term) is most easily remembered; thus these spots should be milked to maximum advantage for learning. (See Chapter 5.)

Knowledge of Results

Knowledge of results should be specific and timely. Practitioners of this principle give explicit feedback to students on their work as rapidly as possible after completion. The rationale is that this feedback has optimum corrective impact when most proximal to the student's engaging the materials and that it has maximum communicative effect when it is both full and specific. (Under the Personal Relationship Building parameter, in Chapter 12, it is argued that full and complete feedback is a form of respect by which teachers show students they value students' work enough to look at it closely.)

Here are two examples of knowledge of results:

> Upon completing a worksheet on social changes as a result of the Industrial Revolution, students see answers displayed on an overhead (or revealed from behind a rolled-up map). They correct their own papers and then ask clarifying questions of the teacher.

> Students correct all their own workbook and worksheet pages from answer books, fixing all individual mistakes and explaining their errors.

Students' getting feedback from a teacher does not mean this principle is in operation. Finding out how they did on a test is not the principle. Students find out how they did at some point in every class, but there's nothing special about that. What is special (and what empowers learning) is feedback that is rapid, specific, and complete. Computer games give instantaneous knowledge of results, though not always with specific information about how to improve.

Teachers can claim they're using knowledge of results if they're giving students feedback about how they did very soon after they perform, along with an opportunity to self-correct or at least see what would have to be done to improve (Butler and Winne 1995).

Reinforcement

A reinforcer is anything that strengthens a behavior and can range all the way from edibles and tokens to teacher statements of recognition like, "You stuck with that hard one until you got it and you didn't give up!" Verbal reinforcement is the focus here because it is so overworked in the literature, so common a part of teachers' vocabulary, yet it is astonishing how little it is used skillfully. Many opportunities pass for applying this powerful stimulus to learning. The knowledge base tells us that verbal reinforcement should be precise, appropriate, and, when appropriate, scheduled from regular to intermittent.

Precise means that the statement should specify what it is specifically that the learner has done that is good. "You didn't rush today, and you got them almost all right" is better than "Good work." The student is much more likely to reproduce the high accuracy rate, which is due to not rushing, if not rushing is explicitly reinforced. When a teacher says, "You finished those problems and then you put your stuff away without me giving you any reminders, and you started on your writing. That's great," the student knows what is great.

Appropriate reinforcement is important. If a student doesn't want it, it's not reinforcing. Being praised in front of someone else may be embarrassing. Being told his handwriting is "so nice" may turn off a sixth-grade athlete and get him kidded by his pals; more appropriate feedback for him might be, "John, you're one of our best ball players and I see your fine motor coordination is just as good as your coordination on the ball field" (Hunter 1977). Thinking about this makes it easy to see why studies of praise and reinforcement that count frequency of the behavior and look for correlations to student achievement can never get anywhere. Only appropriate use of reinforcement works.

Scheduling is the third important feature of reinforcement. B. F. Skinner discovered that behaviors established through operant conditioning become more stable and more durable if reinforcement is delivered with every occurrence of the behavior *at first*. But then reinforcement should skip occasional occurrences at random, and the span of unreinforced occurrences between reinforcers should gradually be lengthened. Such a schedule could be charted as follows:

Delivery of reinforcers   o o o   o o   o o   o   o   o

Occurrences of the behavior   x x x x x x x x x x x x x x x

Use of intermittent scheduling to establish behaviors is more in line with a systematic plan for behavior modification a teacher might use to develop, say, hand raising versus calling out or promptness versus tardiness to class.

Although researchers agree universally on the positive effects of intrinsic reinforcement, a debate has raged for years over whether extrinsic reinforcers ought to be used. Paul Chance (1992) has put the matter in perspective by pointing out the conditions under which extrinsic reinforcers are not only okay (meaning they do not damage students' motivation to do the activity when there are no reinforcers around) but are very helpful to learning. Chance points out that extrinsic reinforcers include teachers' smiles, praise, congratulations, saying "thank you" or "right," shaking hands, hugging, a pat on the back, applauding, providing a certificate of achievement, or other behaviors that "in any way provide a positive consequence (a reward) for student behavior." Extrinsic rewards can decrease motivation to engage in a behavior (reading) if it is given as a task contingency, that is, for merely participating in an activity without regard to how well one does at it. But when rewards are success contingent, that is, delivered when students perform well or meet goals, there is no negative effect on engagement with the activity later when rewards are no longer given. Indeed, success contingent rewards tend to increase interest in the activity.

Intrinsic rewards are available to students only if they can perform sufficiently well in an area to get the reward, for example, if they can read well enough to get the pleasure of a good story. "While intrinsic rewards are important, they are insufficient for effective learning for all students" (Chance 1992, p. 206) if one has to rely on them exclusively.

Degree of Guidance

How much guidance will students need to get the most out of (or just to get through) the task? Guidance should be high with new tasks and withdrawn gradually with demonstrated student proficiency. Evidence for this principle cannot be simply to observe teachers delivering different degrees of guidance to different students. Evidence must cite different degrees of guidance offered to the same student or group of students over time as they progressively show increased proficiency with the new material. This is sometimes difficult to see in short observations. Nevertheless, a teacher may introduce a new skill to a class and immediately provide adequate guidance in practicing it. This may mean working with just one group after introducing haiku to the whole class, while giving the rest of the class something else they still need to practice but without so much teacher guidance, and then rotating through the class with groups that focus on the new skill. Or it may mean the teacher puts on track shoes and gets around to everybody, giving guidance and help where needed. The latter is more time efficient if the teacher can pull it off (pulling it off is not so much a function of teacher skill as good judgment—what new material will or will not require more intensive individual guidance for students to be able to use it proficiently).

Breaking Complex Tasks into Simpler Parts

One often sees evidence of this principle when teachers are attempting to explain or clarify operations students have failed to grasp. The task is broken down into smaller parts, and one part, now isolated, is focused on for learning. For example, if students are having trouble with word problems, the teacher may have the students identify the central question and the operation called for without doing any computing. Or students may be asked to draw a picture of what happens in the problem as a way of conceptualizing it, again without any computing. This principle manifests as task analysis and ensures that sequential prerequisites for present learning tasks are established.

Practice

Practice should be massed at the beginning of learning a new skill or operation (meaning frequent practice sessions, close together in time), then distributed over increasing intervals of time. The smallest unit of new information that retains meaning should be practiced at any one session and worked on for the shortest unit of time to allow the students to feel they have accomplished something. After they have achieved proficiency, they should practice learned items two or three more times to make the learning more permanent (*overlearning*). Unlike athletics and motor skills, where practice makes perfect and the more the better (up to a point), long practice sessions with academic skills quickly reach a point of diminishing returns.

For areas like the times tables, each fact is a unit of meaning on its own, separate from the others, and only one or two of them should be introduced at a time, embedded in groups of already known facts for drill. (Certain tables and groups of facts, however, such as the 10-times table, group all at once as a single unit of meaning.) In teaching students to analyze a story, which is a complex task, only one part would be assigned at first, say, identifying the setting; later would come describing the plot. In practicing a difficult piece of music, one would practice not a page or a bar (which might be too small a unit to have meaning) but a measure.

Practice sessions should be short (2 to 5 minutes, not 20) and frequent (twice a day rather than twice a week). This is quite at odds with the schedules we often see when students labor over workbooks in classrooms.

If a teacher wants students to practice writing news stories in a journalism course, the "leader" (the opening sentence or paragraph that contains all the critical information of who, when, where, and what) is a meaningful unit. Students may be asked to practice writing just leaders for frequent short practice periods before being asked to write entire stories.

Goal Setting

The point here is goal setting by students. When students get involved in goal setting for their own learning, they learn more. As well as being common sense, this conclusion is strongly supported by a line of research (Schunk and Gaa 1981). When students take ownership for goals (either self-set, teacher set, or jointly negotiated), their motivation to accomplish them and their ability to self-evaluate (and self-regulate) increase.

Student goal setting will not happen by itself except for very motivated students. Teachers have to do something to facilitate the process—perhaps taking a few minutes of class time for students to write their goal for the period (or the unit) on a piece of paper or having periodic goal-setting conferences with individual students at timely intervals (like the beginning of new units or projects). These conferences can be quite short, but the goals chosen should be recorded, and later students should be asked to evaluate how they did.

> **When students get involved in goal setting for their own learning, they learn more.**

Student goal setting does not automatically lead to increased student performance. Certain properties of effective goals need to be present; they need to be *specific*, *challenging* but attainable, and able to be accomplished *soon*.

Specific goals contain items that can be measured, counted, or perceived directly as criteria for accomplishment. "Try my best" doesn't fit this mold; "Master the twenty spelling demons" does.

The more difficult the goal is, the more effort the student will expend, providing the goal is viewed as attainable. In guiding students to set goals, teachers have to help them walk the tightrope between what is "duck soup" and what is unrealistic.

Finally, goals that can be accomplished in the short term work better than long-term goals. This does not mean long-term goals should not be set, only that long-term goals need to be broken down into short-term goals or subgoals with their own plans of action, if one is to be maximally effective in reaching them. (Divide and conquer.) Learning or work accomplishment goals for students seem to work best around specified skills and products and for time spans of one period to several days rather than over several weeks or months.

A common misinterpretation of this principle is that it means students are picking what they will study (that is, the content). Not so. Much more often (and usually more productively), they are setting goals about speed, quantity, or quality. Here is an example of a speed goal: The student makes a commitment to how fast he will do some amount of work:

Teacher:	Glen, how many of these do you think you'll get done in the next half-hour?
Glen:	I think this whole page.
Teacher:	Really? Do you really think that's a reasonable amount?
Glen:	Yes, I'll do it.
Teacher:	OK. Show them to me when you're done.

And here is a quantity goal:

Teacher:	How many references will you use in researching that, Brenda?
Brenda:	About six.
Teacher:	OK. If you think that's enough, put it down in your outline sheet.

There is no particular rate at which the researching must be done (except ultimately the deadline of the paper). It is a commitment Brenda makes to do a specified amount. The same kind of goal applies to how many books students will read for free reading, for example, or how many extra credit or supplementary exercises they'll do.

Quality goals are particularly interesting. In these goals, students make a commitment to how well they'll do something. This can take the form of targeting what aspect of their work they'll focus on improving. Teachers can give them the assignment to explain what they're working to improve (and maybe even ask for it in writing):

Teacher:	So, Jamie, what's your quality goal going to be on this paper?
Jamie:	I'm going to work on improving spelling and punctuation.
Teacher:	How about you, Tara?
Tara:	My goal's going to be to use fewer tired words.

By getting students to set goals, teachers do not relinquish their ability to make assignments. They enlist the students in making personal commitments to speed, quantity, or quality. It is possible to have students choose content in some cases—"I want to learn everything I can about frogs," says Freddy. There are places where it will fit in with curriculum requirements and time available to help Freddy do so (especially if one of the teacher's goals is to stimulate and support an inquiring attitude). But it may be equally powerful to get students to set quality goals, thus involving them inevitably in self-evaluation to come up with a target for improvement.

In our experience, this principle of learning, so plain sounding and simple to understand, is one of the least practiced in education. If we devoted just a little time and energy to it, we might see big payoffs in student performance and in students' learning directly about self-regulation and self-evaluation.

Concrete-Semiabstract-Abstract Progression

Teachers using this principle use tangible or manipulative materials at one stage of instruction, move to pictorial representation of the same material, and at still later stages of instruction deal with the same materials with the students in purely abstract ways. This progression is effective not only with young children who are at Piaget's stage of concrete operation but also with adult learners. Dealing with concrete materials anchors images and experiences, which later connect with and are summoned by the abstractions that refer to them. One doesn't have to learn everything by experience (you don't have to be bitten by a rabid dog to learn they're dangerous), but experience anchors learning in a powerful way. Herron's 1975 study using models in chemistry instruction showed that using concrete materials was startlingly effective for developing concepts in college chemistry courses.

Modeling

Learning can be enhanced by modeling new skills or operations and preserving these models for student reference during early stages of learning. After explaining and demonstrating the algorithm for two-digit multiplication (or the format for writing a book report, or anything else with procedures and steps), the teacher leaves a model showing the separate steps on the board as students go to work practicing examples.

Conceptual models that have visual representations of what concepts mean and how they work improve student recall of the concept and performance on problems that ask them to extrapolate from what they have learned (Mayer 1989). For example, a lesson on radar included a five-step diagram that showed a sequence in which a radar pulse moves out from the source, strikes an object, and bounces back, with the distance determined as a function of the total travel time. Perkins and Unger (1989) posit that powerful conceptual models have four characteristics: they are analogs, constructed, stripped, and concrete.

1. *Analogs*. They provide some kind of analogy for the real phenomenon of interest (e.g., the Thinkertools computer program, which models the paths of rockets with dots) (White and Horwitz 1987).

2. *Constructed*. They are fabricated for the purpose at hand.

3. *Stripped*. Extraneous clutter is eliminated to highlight critical features.

4. *Concrete*. The phenomenon is reduced to concrete examples and visual images.

253

Say-Do

The more perceptual modes one engages for students—seeing, hearing, moving, touching—the better the learning will be. But in striving to increase the range of perceptual channels made active during learning, be particularly aware of the power of having learners say their learning out loud, and get involved in using it to do something. The title of this principle, Say-Do, is meant to highlight the powerful effects achieved when these two channels for expressing learning are engaged.

What do we know about the relative power of various perceptual channels for acquiring information? How much do students retain over time if the only way they acquire information is to read it versus hearing it versus seeing it? What if they both see and hear the information? What if students were to read the information and then summarize their learning out loud to someone (read-say?) What would be the learning retention effects if students read information to acquire it, then had to summarize it out loud to someone, and then finally put the information to work by actually using it to do something? The graph in Figure **9.1** summarizes the relative effectiveness of different perceptual modes.

At first glance, the most surprising assertion in the graph is the magnitude of the boost in learning retention when "say" is added to the simple input channel of reading. The effect would probably be similar for see-say and hear-say, though there are no studies found to verify this claim. Studies of the effect of learning logs and dialogue journals confirm positive learning effects for hear-write and read-write (Pradl and Mayher 1985; Fulwiler 1987; Connolly and Vilardi 1989).

To summarize in your own words, either verbally or in writing, what you have learned in a given experience is a complex cognitive act; it causes search and retrieval of memory, organization of ideas, and summoning of language to recast the meaning in your own terms. It is logical that this complex set of cognitive acts would create neural networks and deepen memory traces.

The implications for teaching and learning are large. Foremost is the call to have students stop and summarize, either singly in journals or together out loud in pairs, what is important in a recent episode of learning. The need to create such pauses means that a teacher will build periodic summarizing into teaching as a regular practice.

The "do" part of this principle means getting students active as soon as possible using the materials in some realistic way.

A note on the research behind this principle: figures like those in Figure **9.1** show up regularly in popular articles (Boardroom Report 1989) and workshop presentations (Betty Wagner at A.S.C.D. 1990.) They occur in the literature as well (National Training Labs, Bethel Maine undated; Edgar Dale's "Cone of Learning," University of Ohio). But as far as we have been able to determine after fourteen years of inquiry, no single study ever actually

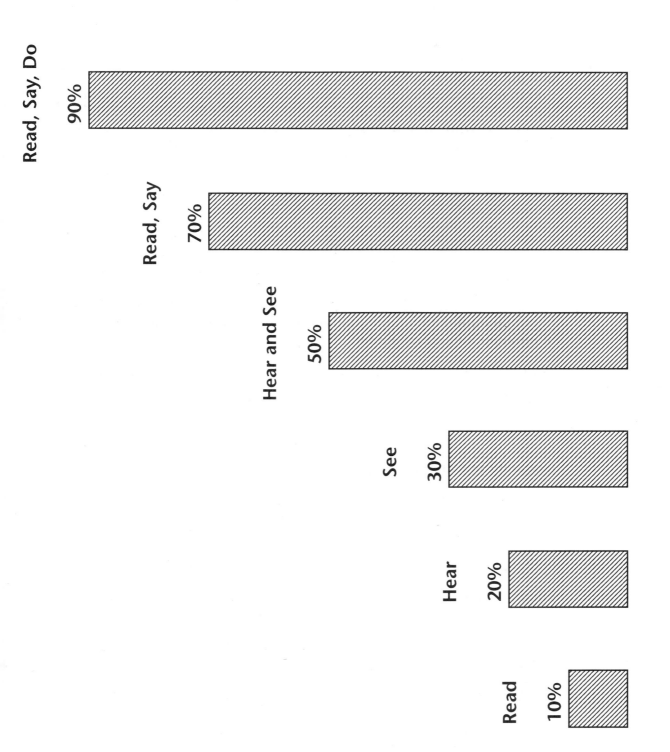

FIGURE 9.1: SUMMARY OF THE RELATIVE EFFECTIVENESS OF DIFFERENT PERCEPTUAL MODES
This chart represents an amalgam of many individual studies.

investigated the relative effects of all the perceptual channels in Figure **9.1**. (For years we heard from various sources of the mythic "Mobil Oil Company Study" in the late 1950s, presumably done by their training department. No hard copy has ever surfaced.)

Research however has compared the relative effectiveness of perceptual channels, and there is a considerable literature on the effects of student verbalizations of their learning (Pauk 1974; Webb 1982; Morrow 1985; King 1990). One particularly well-designed study by MacKenzie and White (1982) comes close to including all the conditions in Figure **9.1**. In their study of eighth and ninth graders' learning and retention of geographical facts, they involved learners in three different conditions to learn facts and skills in the geography of coasts, including information about landforms and plants. All three treatment groups studied a carefully designed programmed learning package of materials containing thirty-five pages and thirty-seven questions to encourage processing. *(Read)*. The program was supported by sixty photographs on 35-mm slides *(See)*. "Other characteristics of the program were statements of expected performance, worked examples and test items, practice at working new data, prompts to stimulate recall of relevant information and subordinate skills, indications of relevance of information to subsequent application, and transfer of verbal propositions to maps, diagrams and slides."

Treatment group 1 received the package described above. Treatment group 2 went through the programmed package too and went on a field trip to a beach, two sets of cliffs, and two mangrove flats where the pictures in the program had been taken. The students were given an explanatory field guide designed to reinforce the information in the program they had done at school. A teacher guided them around the five sites, pointing out items in the guide. In the middle of the trip, students had to complete one set of questions. So in addition to the classroom-based instruction of treatment group 1, this group had a great deal more of seeing and hearing built in to their experience, as well as more calls to answer questions about the information.

Treatment group 3 also went on the field trip, but with some powerful additions. "At each site students received a worksheet, a map of the area, and a tide table. The teacher supervised while the students, individually and in groups, completed the tasks on the worksheets. Group discussions *(Say)* were held frequently. Students were continually required to do things *(Do)*: observe, sketch, record, answer questions. Several unusual events were arranged, such as walking through the mud of the mangrove shore, tasting foliage for salinity, scrambling over cliff platforms, wading in the sea. It is emphasized that the students in [treatment group 2] saw the same things...and spent the same time at each site. They had information repeated to them more often, but did far less."

The achievement results in this experiment were striking. In the initial achievement tests, both field trip groups outperformed the classroom-only group by a wide margin, but the two field trip groups were about equal to each other in student achievement means. After 12 weeks, however, the retention with respect to initial mean scores was 51 percent for the classroom-only group, 58 percent for the treatment 2 field trip group, and 90 percent for the treatment 3 field trip group. The addition of Say and Do together in this condition had a huge impact on long-term retention.

Cumulative Review

Any information or skill one doesn't actively use tends to be forgotten. Therefore old learnings should be included in practice and drills of new material so that these old learnings are periodically exercised. As students move on in a skill sequence, the range and number of skills demanded in the practice exercises grow cumulatively to include all the old skills. To prevent practice tasks from becoming unwieldy when the range of skills is big, only a representative sample of them is included in exercises focusing on new material.

Certain skill sequences automatically cumulate old skills in new products without any design steps required by the teacher—for example, report writing. As students learn new punctuation and grammar skills, these are automatically practiced each time writing takes place and are expected to be done correctly. And as students use more elaborate language forms and learn to organize ideas better, these also are automatically expected to be continued in future writing. But other skill sequences require more deliberate design for cumulative review to take place effectively.

In drilling on flash cards to learn times tables, each new pack should contain a representative sample of all previously learned facts and occasional packs should be entirely review to solidify old learnings. In learning geographical features of a country in South America, the features should come up again and again in the context of the questions about the country's elections, political system, and economy. A violation of this principle would see students studying the geographical features of *all* the South American countries in sequence, then going back and studying *all* their political systems, then *all* their cultural highlights, and so on.

End Without Closure

Consider the impact of this teacher statement: "Think about three ways you might get out of this dilemma and be ready to share them with us tomorrow when you come in" (Russell 1980). Leaving students without an answer and with something percolating overnight may be more effective in some cases than coming to a neat ending of each class with all issues resolved.

Keep Students Open and Thinking through Teacher Responses to Student Answers

Art Costa (1985) has pointed out that the way that teachers respond to student answers is probably more important than the questions themselves. Every time a student answers a question, a teacher *does* something. Similarly, if a student responds with silence because he or she can't answer the question or is slow to think it through, teachers still *do* something—give a cue, or refer it to another student, or offer to help. It is through these acts— repeated hundreds of times over a day—that teachers set a climate about whether it's safe to open one's mouth in this class. It is through teachers' patterns of actions at these moments that they exert a force either to keep students open and thinking or become a force to restrict thinking and risk taking.

This arena of classroom life—responses to student answers—is also an arena through which teachers send the three critical expectation messages:

- ▶ "This is important."
- ▶ "You can do it."
- ▶ "I won't give up on you."

We defer elaboration of this repertoire to a section in the Expectations chapter.

Reviewing Principles of Learning

Within the chapter, we have described twenty-four "little packages of power"—techniques teachers can use to increase the rate and permanence of students' learning. Following is a summary of these "double dozen" principles of learning:

1. **Application in Setting**: Practicing new behaviors in settings where they'll be used.

2. **Meaning**: Connecting to students' personal experience.

3. **Teach for Transfer**: Engineering a planned sequence of activities that progressively distance the skill from abstract academic contexts.

4. **Isolation of Critical Attributes**: Highlighting and labeling the attributes.

5. **Concrete-Semiabstract-Abstract Progression**: Following as a progression with the introduction of new material.

6. **Modeling**: Step-wise products, procedures, and processes preserved for student reference.

7. **Similarity of Environment**: An activity that gets minds in gear for upcoming events.

8. **Active Participation**: Encouraging through unison, checking with a partner, signals, and so on.

9. **Vividness**: And varying of practice formats.

10. **Feeling Tone**: Fun, but not too much; worry, but not too much; raising level of concern.

11. **End Without Closure**: But with follow-up at a later time, to invite percolation.

12. **Breaking Complex Tasks into Simpler Parts**: Down into simpler, smaller pieces; isolating trouble spots for focused work and practice; higher-frequency practice and repetition of new items.

13. **Degree of Guidance**: High with new tasks; withdrawn gradually with familiarity.

14. **Close Confusers**: Ensuring an adequate degree of original learning before introducing close confusers.

15. **Say-Do**: Using all perceptual channels but emphasizing particularly saying and doing.

16. **Mnemonics**: Devices to aid in memory (key words, images in sequence, jingles, etc.).

17. **Sequence and Backward Chaining**: First and last are easiest; just past the middle is hardest.

18. **Practice**: Massed at beginning, then distributed; smallest meaningful units; short practices; overlearning.

19. **Contiguity**: Don't allow practice of errors with paired-associate learning.

20. **Cumulative Review**: In practice, periodically including representative sample of previously learned material.

21. **Knowledge of Results**: Promptly through monitoring.

22. **Reinforcement**: Precise, regular, and intermittent.

23. **Goal Setting**: By students; ownership, specific, challenging; able to be accomplished soon, then over the longer term.

24. **Keep Students Open and Thinking**: For example, supply questions for which answers are right, deliver prompt, and hold accountable.

Principles of Learning Quiz

For each vignette below:

1. *Determine what is important about what the teacher did. Why is it likely to support effective learning?*

2. *In the margin, write the name of the principle of learning in operation.*

Note that some vignettes may exemplify more than one principle, though one will be dominant.

1. Each spelling test covers this week's words, three words from last week, and the two most frequently missed words from previous weeks' lists.

2. The teacher is illustrating the permeability of membranes by pushing various-sized balls between the bars of a metal milk crate. "We'd call this semipermeable because the marble will go through, but, as you can see [pushes, it finally goes] it goes through with difficulty, not just gliding through like the peas did." Later in the period students draw diagrams to illustrate the permeability of membranes they have been experimenting with. On their unit tests and in the review session before it, they will be asked to explain the meaning of permeable, semipermeable, and impermeable in sentences.

3. A Spanish teacher said: "In drilling on your sixteen vocabulary words for tonight, divide them into two groups with eight cards in each group. Put the words on the front of the card and the meaning on the back. When arranging your packs, put the words that are hardest in the first and last positions and the one that is easiest for you in the fifth position."

4. The teacher told his group of eleventh graders that he wanted them to understand clearly the concepts of prejudice and discrimination and be able to explain them. He defined prejudice, writing on the board: "Social prejudice is a hostile feeling toward a person or persons because of their membership in a particular group." He underlined the words *feeling*, *membership*, and *particular group*. He then went on to define discrimination as "preferential treatment" of a person or persons because of their membership in a given group. After writing this on the board, he underlined the words *treatment*, *membership*, and *particular group*. He emphasized that the discriminating attribute in each concept was feelings versus treatment or actions. Probing students further on these concepts, he asked what the difference was between disliking someone and being prejudiced against the person. A student suggested that the key was whether the dislike was based

on the person's membership in a particular group. The teacher asked if someone could provide an example of prejudice. A student said, "If an adult doesn't like a kid because he's a teenager." The teacher asked the class, "Is this prejudice? Why?"

5. In a third-grade physical education lesson on jump roping skills, the teacher took a few minutes at the beginning of class to let the children express what they had successfully accomplished by the end of the last class (e.g., jump ten or more times) and to decide individually what they were going to work toward (e.g., jumping more times without missing; jumping into the rope while it was turning; two people jumping at the same time). He checked with individual children from time to time, talking with them about what they'd said they'd try for and helping them make modifications when appropriate.

6. In that same physical education class, the teacher put the students in groups and made sure each was involved all the time; for example, two children were turning the rope, one (or two) were jumping, and one was counting. The children in a group would switch tasks after the jumper(s) had a few turns.

7. In the same physical education class, the teacher said most children could jump rope only a few times and were not at all skilled when he started this series of lessons. Therefore, he wanted to focus on this activity for a few classes, organizing tasks so that they would have enough practice to improve. They were now jumping ten or more times, and most were increasing the variety of conditions they were working under (e.g., jumping in; jumping with different children turning the rope; two children jumping at the same time).

8. In the same physical education class, the teacher stayed with a student who was having trouble for about 4 minutes at the beginning of class. During this time, the teacher isolated the variables that the student needed to attend to in order to jump rope successfully (keep your eye on the rope; start jumping when the rope goes over your head; stay in the middle of the rope; jump to the rhythm set by the rope and the "counter"). He also provided the student with specific feedback about his performance and asked the student to tell him what he was going to try to remember. When the student started to jump successfully ten times without missing, the teacher moved away to other children and other groups. However, he returned to this one student several times during the class, providing as much help as necessary (e.g., taking the rope from one of the turners who was having trouble keeping a regular rhythm and turning the rope himself; asking the student to look where he was standing).

9. The teacher began class by asking who could explain the story: "Now this is a difficult story. Could any of you explain to a younger student why the author wrote the story?" To the five or six students who raised their hands, the teacher said, "Write your reasons on the board." As the students were writing, the teacher told the rest of the class to get in pairs and discuss which of the answers on the board was best. She added that they might be called on to defend their choice.

10. Suddenly the teacher yelled at a student who had just dropped a book (the whole event was staged). Students looked shocked at the teacher's overreaction. Then the teacher smiled and explained, "You all looked very worried. Why?" Students responded with obvious reasons, generally saying they had never before seen the teacher lose her temper. She then went on to make a connection to the character in the story who begins to act in unexpected and unaccustomed ways.

11. The goal is to understand the difference between chronology and history. On the first day, students are asked to keep a time line of their activities. On the next day, they write a narrative history of the day for which they kept the time line, showing, where possible, cause-and-effect relationships.

12. A child read *quit* for *quite*. The teacher says, "That would be right if the word didn't have an 'e' at the end. What does the 'e' do to the vowel in the middle? Right. So what is the word?"

13. When students drill each other on the symbols in the periodic table (names and symbols for elements learned in chemistry courses), they introduce one or two new symbols at a time to each other in flash card packs. They do it in this way: "This is a new one. 'Fe' is iron. You say that." ["'Fe' iron."] "Right. Now, what's 'Fe'?" They're not to let their partners guess or try to figure it out, if they get a hint the partner is going to guess and get it wrong. The teacher doesn't want them to practice any wrong associations. As she flips through the pack, she makes sure the ones they're missing come up more often than the others too. As they learn them, she is more willing to let them hesitate when they see one.

14. The kindergarten teacher draws individual numerals or letters on large sheets of paper. As the children watch, she draws the first part of the numeral or letter with the side of a broken purple crayon and the second part with a green crayon. Baretta-Lorton (1976) claims that "this really helps eliminate reversals and gives the children a sequential pattern to follow when writing numerals or letters." The teacher-drawn letter or numeral sequence cards are then hung in the room so that they can be easily seen by the children throughout the school year.

15. Students have had instruction on reading and writing large numbers (tens of thousands, hundreds of thousands, millions, tens of millions, etc.) but they are having trouble. They are getting confused with the place value and tend to start at the left with a guess about millions or hundreds of thousands, disregarding the commas. To get them to remember to count places from the right and observe the commas, the teacher gives a lesson where all the examples have blank places such as: _ _ _ , _ _ _ .

On the board is a model:

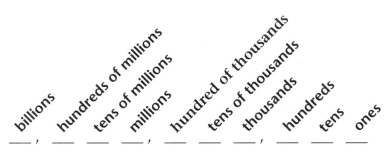

There are also a number of problems on the board with no numbers, in these forms:

_ _ , _ _ _   _ _ , _ _ _ , _ _ _

_ , _ _ _ , _ _ _   _ , _ _ _

_ _ _ , _ _ _   _ , _ _ _ , _ _ _

When called on, students start from the right and count out to the last place. They are expected to respond in the form, "ones, tens, hundreds, thousands, tens of thousands, hundreds of thousands." After doing a number of examples like this in unison and then calling on various individuals, the teacher has the students do a practice sheet by themselves in the same form while she circulates giving help. Later they will move on to reading big numbers with the numerals back in but no medial zeros. When they show competence there, the teacher will add medial zeros to the examples she expects them to read and write.

Acknowledgments

We are grateful to the following teachers for sharing examples of their applications of the principles of learning with us: Nadine Bishop, Carol Callahan, Nancy Dennison, E. G. Downes, Joan Grossman, Matt King, Dave Mayall, Ellen Epstein Maxwell, Heather Robinson, Alan Ticotsky, Sal Trento, Jim Treweiler, Joe Walsh, and Mary Wilinsky.

Source Materials on Principles of Learning

Baretta-Lorton, Mary. *Math Their Way*. Reading, Mass.: Addison Wesley, 1976.

Barringer, C., and B. Gholson. "Effects of Type and Combination of Feedback upon Conceptual Learning by Children: Implications for Research in Academic Learning." *Review of Educational Research* 49 (Summer 1979): 459–478.

Beeson, G. W. "Influence of Knowledge Context on the Learning of Intellectual Skills." *American Educational Research Journal* 18 (Fall 1981): 363–379.

Bellezza, F. S. "Mnemonic Devices: Classification, Characteristics, and Criteria." *Review of Educational Research* 51 (Summer 1981): 247–275.

Blank, M. *Teaching Learning in the Preschool: A Dialogue Approach*. Columbus, Ohio: Merrill, 1973.

Brophy, J. "Praise: A Functional Analysis." *Review of Educational Research* 51 (Spring 1981): 5–32.

Brown, Ann L. "Analogical Learning and Transfer: What Develops?" In S. Vosniadou and A. A. Ortony, eds., *Similarity and Analogical Reasoning*, pp. 369–412. New York: Cambridge University Press, 1989.

Bugelski, B. R. *The Psychology of Learning Applied to Teaching*. Indianapolis: Bobbs-Merrill, 1971.

Butler Deborah L., and Philip H. Winne. "Feedback and Self-Regulated Learning." *Review of Educational Research* 65 (Fall 1995): 245–281.

Chance, Paul. "The Rewards of Learning." *Kappan* (November 1992): 200–207.

Connolly, Paul, and Teresa Viladri. *Writing to Learn Mathematics and Science*. New York: Teachers College Press, 1989

Costa, Arthur. *Teaching for Intelligent Behaviors*. Orangevale, Calif.: Search Models Unlimited, 1985

Dunkin, M. J., and B. J. Biddle. *The Study of Teaching*. New York: Holt, Rinehart and Winston, 1974.

Ebbinghaus, H. *1885. Memory*. Trans. H.A. Ruger and C. E. Bussenius. New York: Teachers College, Columbia University, 1913.

Fogarty, Robin, David Perkins, and John Barell. *How to Teach for Transfer*. Palatine, Ill.: Skylight Publishing, 1991.

Fulwiler, Toby, ed. *The Journal Book*. Portsmouth, N.H.: Heineman, 1987. Good, T. J., and J. E. Brophy. *Looking in Classrooms*. New York: Harper & Row, 1978.

Graham, S. "Teacher Feelings and Student Thoughts: An Attributional Approach to Affect in the Classroom." *Elementary School Journal* 85 (1985): 91–104

Haughton, E. "Aims—Growing and Sharing." In J. B. Jordan and L. S. Robbins, eds., *Let's Try Doing Something Else Kind of Thing*. Arlington, Virg.: C.E.C., 1972.

Herron, J. Dudley. "Piaget for Chemists." *Journal of Chemical Education* (1975).

Hess, R. D. et al. "Some Contrasts Between Mothers and Preschool Teachers in Interaction with 4-Year-Old Children." *American Educational Research Journal* 16 (Summer 1979): 307–316.

Higbee, K. L. "Recent Research on Visual Mnemonics: Historical Roots and Educational Fruits." *Review of Educational Research* 49 (Fall 1979): 611–629.

Hilgard, E. R. and G. H. Bower. *Theories of Learning*. New York: Appleton Century Crofts, 1966.

Hudgins, B. B. *Learning and Thinking: A Primer for Teachers*. Itasca, Ill.: F. E. Peacock Publishers, 1977.

Hunter, M. *Motivation*. El Segundo, Calif.: T.I.P. Publications, 1967.

———. *Reinforcement*. El Segundo, Calif.: T.I.P. Publications, 1967.

———. *Retention*. El Segundo, Calif.: T.I.P. Publications, 1967.

———. *Teach More—Faster*. El Segundo, Calif.: T.I.P. Publications, 1967.

———. *Teach For Transfer*. El Segundo, Calif.: T.I.P. Publications, 1971.

Hunter, M. "Improving the Quality of Instruction." Paper presented at the A.S.C.D. Conference, Fifth General Session, Houston, March 1977.

King, Alison. "Enhancing Peer Interaction and Learning in the Classroom Through Reciprocal Questioning." *American Educational Research Journal* 27 (Winter 1990).

Levin, J. R. "Mnemonic Strategies and Classroom Learning: A Twenty Year Report Card." *Elementary School Journal* 94 (November 1993): 235–244.

———, et al. "Mnemonic versus Nonmnemonic Vocabulary—Learning Strategies for Children." *American Educational Research Journal* 19 (Spring 1982): 121–136.

Mackenzie, Andrew A., and Richard T. White. "Fieldwork in Geography and Long-term Memory Structures." *American Educational Research Journal* 19 (Winter 1982).

Mayer, R. E. "Models for Understanding." *Review of Educational Research* 59 (1989): 43–64.

Morrow, Lesley M. "Retelling Stories: A Strategy for Improving Young Children's Concept of Story Structure, and Oral Language Complexity." *Elementary School Journal* 85, no. 5 (1985).

Pauk, Walter. *How to Study in College.* Boston: Houghton Mifflin, 1974.

Perkins, David N., and C. Unger. "The New Look in Representations for Mathematics and Science Learning. " Paper presented at the Social Science Research Council Conference, "Computers and Learning," Tortola, British Virgin Islands, June 26–July 2, 1989.

Pradl, Gordon, and John S. Mayher. "Reinvigorating Learning Through Writing." *Educational Leadership* (February 1985).

Pressley, M., J. R. Levin, and H. D. Delaney. "The Mnemonic Keyword Method." *Review of Educational Research* 52 (Spring 1982): 61–91.

Rosswork, S. "Goal Setting: The Effects on an Academic Task with Varying Magnitudes of Incentive." *Journal of Educational Psychology* 69 (1977): 710–715.

Russell, Doug. "Teaching Decisions and Behaviors for Instructional Improvement." Talk given at the Association for Supervision and Curriculum Development Convention, 1980.

Schunk, D. H., and J. P. Gaa. "Goal-Setting Influence on Learning and Self-Evaluation." *Journal of Classroom Interaction* 16 (1981): 38–44.

Sefkow, S. B. and J. L. Myers. "Review Effects of Inserted Questions on Learning from Prose." *American Educational Research Journal* 17 (Winter 1980): 435–448.

Trabasso, T. "Pay Attention." In J. P. DeCecco, ed. *Readings in Educational Psychology Today.* Del Mar, Calif.: CRM Books, 1970.

Webb, Noreen M. "Student Interaction and Learning in Small Groups." *Review of Educational Research* 52 (Fall 1982).

White B., and Paul Horwitz. *Thinkertools: Enabling Children to Understand Physical Laws.* BBN Report No. 6470. Cambridge, Mass.: BBN Laboratories, 1987.

10

Models of Teaching

How can I vary my teaching style?

For students of teaching, few other efforts are as rewarding and as challenging as learning new models of teaching. Even the most mature and sophisticated of professionals can add to their repertoires and to their power to reach a broader range of students.

A model of teaching is a particular pattern of instruction that is recognizable and consistent; you can recognize it and label it when you see it, yet it is distinctly different from patterns in other models of teaching. A model has particular values, goals, a rationale, and an orientation to how learning shall take place (e.g., by induction, by discovery, through heightened personal awareness, by wrestling with puzzling data, or by organizing information hierarchically). And that orientation is developed into a specific set of phases teachers and students go through, in order, with specific kinds of events in each phase. Each model of teaching is a particular entity with specific components, well worked out, and with markedly different appearances and effects.

Each of the dozens of models is a design for planning lessons so as to achieve two outcomes: the teaching of content and the teaching of a particular kind of thinking. Almost any model can be used to teach a given piece of content; although the information learned may be the same, the intellectual experience for students will be different. For example, if Mr. Jones uses Taba's Inductive Model for a lesson on Hemingway, he wants students to learn not only about Hemingway but also to think inductively. The model is carefully sequenced to get them into that kind of thinking. If he teaches through the Jurisprudential Model, he may want the same learnings about Hemingway, but he also wants his students to think like lawyers, taking positions and arguing them with evidence. If he uses the Group Investigation Model, he may still want students to learn the same core information about Hemingway, but in addition he wants them to learn about group process, leadership, and coordinated plans of inquiry. If he uses the Advance Organizer Model, he wants them to learn about hierarchical thinking and subordination of ideas. Models of teaching provide a way for teachers to be more articulate and precise about implicit learnings students take from instruction. They enable us to broaden the ways we instruct and thus broaden the range of students' intellectual experience in school.

Research over several decades has shown no one model superior to the others for achieving learning as measured by test scores. That stands only to reason, since that was not their intention. Models of teaching were not created to be more efficient hypodermics to inject knowledge into students' heads. They were intended to teach students how to learn and think in different ways. Educators can use a variety of models to match students' preferred learning styles and to broaden students' capacity as thinkers and learners beyond their favored style.

Teachers who have multiple models in their repertoires may use several different ones in a day or even within a class period. Teachers who master additional models find themselves able to modulate across them like connoisseurs, thus giving professionalism a new dimension. But lest we wax poetic too early in the game, let us examine the models themselves, first with a more detailed description of what a model is, and then with a look at a number of specific models.

The Inductive Teaching Model: An Example

The Inductive Teaching Model has nine logical steps:

1. Enumerating.

2. Grouping.

3. Labeling.

4. Discriminating.

5. Comparing.

6. Inferring.

7. Hypothesizing.

8. Evidencing.

9. Generalizing.

This model, introduced by Hilda Taba, prizes developing students' ability to make inferences from data. Like all other models, it has a series of phases that unfold over time like acts in a play. Each phase looks and sounds different from the previous one; but like scenes in a play each is carefully articulated with the previous and the succeeding phases to achieve a cumulative effect.

If we wished to use the Inductive Teaching Model to present a lesson on Ernest Hemingway, we might start by showing a filmstrip biography of Hemingway's life. This is phase 1: gathering data. After the filmstrip, we would ask students to tell us items of information they remembered, and we would record the information on the board or on charts. The items might appear disconnected and random: "Had a fishing boat named the Pilar." "He went to Spain three times during the Spanish Civil War." "He had a house in Key West." "He liked to write early in the morning while sitting on a balcony overlooking the streets of Paris." Perhaps we might collect two dozen such items, which students would remember and contribute to the database.

In phase 2, we would ask students to group the items from the database that belonged together. Students would look at the sentences on the board and put certain items together because they bear some relationship with one another.

In phase 3, we would ask students to give a title or a label to the groupings they were creating—for example, "Hemingway's work habits as a writer" or "Hemingway the outdoorsman" in which information about hunting on the Serengeti and fishing in Michigan would appear. Students around the class might group items in similar clusters, but there would also be some differences in the categories students created.

In phase 4, we would see to it that the students' groupings of the items about Hemingway were displayed in some fashion for all to see (charts, overheads). In this phase, discriminating, we ask students to explain the thinking behind their categories. What really makes this grouping hang together? The categories and the thinking behind them are compared and contrasted as we guide the students through a discussion of the different ways the information could be grouped and why.

In phase 5, we ask the students if there are any ideas occurring to them about Hemingway as a result of what they have done so far. Are there any inferences they would be willing to make about Ernest Hemingway as a man? In a recent demonstration lesson we did with adults, one person said at this point, "I think Hemingway was really a very lonely man." At no point in it does Hemingway's biographer ever make that point explicitly, so no single item of information in it would ever lead a viewer to that conclusion. Yet as a result of having been through these phases and manipulating the data in the way those phases require, inferences such as this and others become available to students.

There are several other phases to this model, but we will not develop them in any detail. Our objective is only to show that the steps or phases in a model of teaching unfold in a planful way so as to lead students toward developing a particular way of thinking. We could summarize the first five phases of Taba's model by listing the key question of each phase:

Phase 1: What are the data?

Phase 2: How would you group the data?

Phase 3: What name would you give to your categories or groups?

Phase 4: What makes your groups hold together?

Phase 5: What inferences would you be willing to make about the topic?

Eight Models of Teaching

The notion of models of teaching was introduced by Bruce R. Joyce in 1968 through Teacher Innovator: A Program to Prepare Teachers, funded by the Department of Health, Education and Welfare. In 1972, Joyce and Marsha Weil published *Models of Teaching*, which described a large number of models in detail. These descriptions have been updated in four subsequent editions (1980, 1986, 1992, 1996) which have added models and elaborated prior descriptions until we now have over two dozen models of teaching well described with anecdotes, examples, and outlines of steps. These books have been an important contribution to the literature on teaching because they made operational the theoretical approaches to learning developed by such luminaries as Jerome Bruner, David Ausubel, B. F. Skinner, William Glasser, Richard Suchman, Jean Piaget, and others.

To analyze each model of teaching, Joyce and Weil asked and answered the following questions for each theorist:

1. What is the orientation to knowing and learning to know in this Model? Does the teaching appear to be aimed at specific kinds of thinking and means for achieving it?

2. What sequence of events occurs during the process of instruction? What do teachers and students do first, second, third?

3. How does the teacher regard the student and respond to what he or she does?

4. What teacher/student roles, relationships, and norms are encouraged?

5. What additional provisions and materials (materials and support systems) are needed to make the Model work?

6. What is the purpose of the teaching? What are the likely instructional and nurturant effects of this approach to teaching?

The descriptions of these models display the range of teaching alternatives and allow comparison of their unique features. The language of models enables us to visualize clear patterns of action in teaching. Thus, we can talk more precisely about what we might do if we taught a lesson through a different model; also we can talk more precisely about why we might do so and what the expected effects of using a particular model might be.

We have provided a review of eight models of teaching. Each is described in only the briefest details, and we need to remind ourselves that in-depth study is required for the teacher to gain skill in them. We hope to illustrate the range of models that have been developed and the wonderful menu for learning that lies before us as teachers. Most teachers already use one or two of these models, but very few of us have been exposed to the full range, much less trained in the subtleties of implementing them and matching them to different students and curricula.

Because we have the Joyce and Weil book available, there is no need for us to elaborate the steps or phases of each model in detail here. To do so would take an entire book anyway. Our intention is to give a flavor for the different qualities of mind models develop in students. Readers can focus further reading and learning on models that best meet their current priorities.

At the end of the chapter, we provide a bibliography of original source works on the models that will allow those readers interested in doing so to go beyond the chapter on a given model provided by Joyce and Weil.

To make the models more vivid, we use a specific content in our survey: beginning geometry.

Advanced Organizer Model

Advanced organizers are concepts derived from well-defined bodies of knowledge: mathematics, grammar, sociology, and so forth. The following set of geometry concepts illustrates a well-defined, integrated, and progressively differentiated set of organizers:

P			
r		Point	
o			
g		Space	**Integrative Reconciliation**
r			
e		Line segment	
s			
s		Line Ray	
i			
v		Angle	
e	**D**		
	i	Vertex	
	f		
	f	Side of angle	
	e		
	r	Congruent	
	e		
	n	Right angle	
	t		
	i	Acute angle	
	a		
	t	Obtuse angle	
	i		
	o		
	n	Straight Angle	

In the Advanced Organizer Model, these concepts are introduced by the teacher progressively, one by one, through lectures, films, demonstrations, or readings. The student then applies the organizer and demonstrates mastery of the geometry concept. For example, the teacher might define an acute angle as any angle that is less than a right angle (less than 90 degrees) and then might clarify specifics through examples. In phase 2, the student might be asked "to make a drawing that represents an acute angle and to label it ABC." From exercises such as this one, the teacher can determine student mastery, step by step, and integrate new ideas with previously learned content, which Bruner calls "integrative reconciliation." Then the teacher moves on to subsequent organizers.

A teacher using this model primarily seeks to advance the conceptual organizers of a body of knowledge and to promote a meaningful assimilation of information. "Meaningful" means within the context of a hierarchical arrangement of knowledge. Students are expected to learn these organizers because they are basic and fundamental to academic knowledge. Some consider these conceptual organizers the bread and butter of school learning.

Concept Attainment

Closely related to the Advanced Organizer Model is concept attainment: learning by logic, analysis, comparison and contrast. Instead of advancing the concept, the teacher presents the data in the form of positive exemplars, and the students search for attributes to identify the concept. The teacher also uses nonexemplars that do not contain attributes of the concept to assist students in determining relevant attributes.

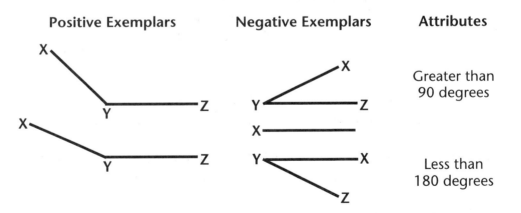

FIGURE 10.1: EXEMPLARS IN CONCEPT ATTAINMENT
This figure illustrates the concept: "any angle that is greater than a right angle and less than a straight angle."

The student is expected to arrive at the concept inductively—to learn by identifying the salient features and formulating an abstract statement. The concept illustrated in FIGURE 10.1 is: "any angle that is greater than a right angle and less than a straight angle." The mathematical label is less important than the student's awareness of these defining attributes.

The value of using the Concept Attainment Model is that students learn not only the concepts themselves but the awareness of how concepts are formed from attributes, sensitivity to logical reasoning, and a deepening regard for alternative points of view. These instructional and nurturant effects are learned through practice with concept attainment; the student in effect reconstructs knowledge through guided learning.

Inductive Thinking Model

The Inductive Thinking Model enables students to generate knowledge as if they themselves were scholars responsible for producing insights into factual reality.

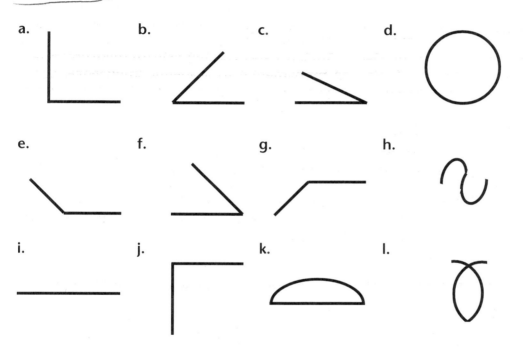

FIGURE 10.2: INDUCTIVE THINKING MODEL
This model enables students to generate knowledge on their own.

Consider the array of data in **FIGURE 10.2**. Then ask a series of questions to lead students through a systematic sorting of the basic angles:

What do you see?

Which ones belong together? Why?

What would you call them? Why?

What do you notice about one of the groups?

What similarities and differences do you see?

What do these tell you about geometry?

What do you think would happen if...?

What evidence would you use to support your guess?

What can we say is generally true?

The likely concepts from such a logical process might more or less approximate formal knowledge of geometry, but there is no guarantee, nor does it matter to the teacher that she doesn't know the concepts in advance. The teacher values student thinking: attention to logic, sensitivity to language, awareness of building knowledge, and concept formation. The students work cooperatively toward building ideas about these shapes.

Inquiry Training

In inquiry training the student is expected to put his or her knowledge to work to solve a problem. In the process there is more knowledge to be gained, in both substance (mathematical knowledge) and process (inquiry training).

Let us say that the problem is to make two squares and four equal triangles out of a rectangle measuring 5 inches by 1 inch. To solve the problem, the student needs to construct a solution consisting of geometry concepts—a process of verifying relevant facts about objects, properties, conditions, and events—and simultaneously hypothesize possible configurations of space, shape, and size. For example, the student might think through the solution shown in FIGURE 10.3.

Step 1

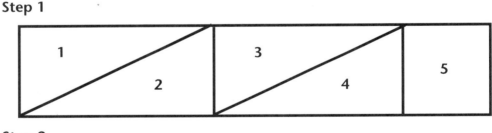

Step 2

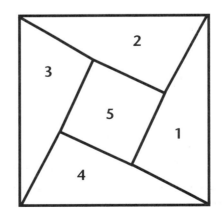

FIGURE 10.3: INQUIRY TRAINING SOLUTIONS

After being presented with the problem, students are encouraged to inquire together as a group while the teacher answers yes-no questions, seeks clarification, encourages student verifying, hypothesizing, and explaining behavior, and guides the group dynamics.

The Inquiry Training Model introduces a more tentative knowledge in which organized knowledge from the disciplines is synthesized and employed in the formulation of a solution. Mastery of knowledge is not the goal of instruction; rather, the student is expected to test out his or her own knowledge. In addition, students learn strategies for inquiry by witnessing their own inquiry behavior and learning to ask questions about objects, events, properties, and conditions. This happens when teachers and students go over their problem-solving behavior following the cooperative exercise. There is an interdependence in inquiry learning too. Students learn to listen well and use the insights of others for solving a problem. It also provides learners with experiences that prepare them for the uses of knowledge in actual situations.

Awareness Training Model

The preceding models of teaching were developed from information-processing theory and represent traditional approaches to teaching. However, knowledge of space and points in space can be a personal experience as well. Awareness training seeks to bridge the individual's own experiences with experiences of other people—in this case, those of a mathematician. Imagine students with a rope who are able to experience geometric configurations equivalent to line segments and triangles (see FIGURE 10.4).

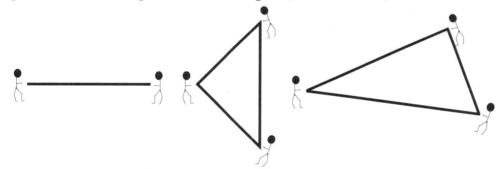

FIGURE 10.4: AWARENESS TRAINING MODEL
This model allows the student to "experience" geometry.

After experiencing "geometry" in this way, students should be encouraged to discuss their feelings and thoughts—that is, to give form to them in language within the social context of the classroom.

These experiences may appear elementary, but they are in fact extremely rich in personal relevance and serve to integrate knowledge and self. The teacher values the students' world and the students' ability to express themselves. Awareness is often thought to be a first type of knowing that can undergird subsequent learning; however, it is a very special personal ability that marks the individual's maturity. We all like to be around people who can express their personal realities as well as those more commonly held by communities of scholars.

Synectics Model

The Synectics Model has been derived from a set of assumptions about creativity and analogies. Creativity means seeing connections between the familiar and the strange and exploring new solutions to old problems. It means experiencing psychological states such as detachment, involvement, autonomy, speculation, and deferment. We attain these psychological states through analogies, which lead toward the attainment and mastery of new and difficult material and novel vantage points for reconsidering problems. Both the means and ends of teaching are influenced by these assumptions.

In "Making the Strange Familiar," a title Gordon (1970) gives to certain phases of synectics, the teacher introduces the new material or content through lecture, film, or demonstration. Without comment, the teacher then solicits a possible analogy and asks students to describe it. To personify the analogy, the students act it out. Describing and acting out the analogy provide the particulars for the fourth and fifth steps—listing the similarities and differences between the analogy and the new material. Finally, the students return to the original material to examine and review it, and to discuss details that might have been omitted from previous activity during the analogic thinking. Consider the following example:

Step 1:   The teacher presents material on geometry.

Step 2:   The students select an analogy—in this case, a tree.

Step 3:   The students describe the tree in detail.

Step 4:   The students act out being parts of a tree.

Step 5:   The students point out similarities between the tree and geometry—for example, the "angle of the branches to the tree trunk" or "the points from where the branch begins to end."

Step 6:   The students point out differences—for example, that the crooked branches are not straight lines.

Step 7:   Teacher and students consider what aspects of geometry were not covered in the discussion of similarities and differences.

The synectics process induces creative thinking and mastery learning of content. It is both a personal experience that integrates geometry and personal knowledge and an analogic one that capitalizes on students' ability to make connections. In addition, it is a wonderful group experience. We diversify our efforts to learn through the synectics model and achieve several goals: mastery of subject matter, analogic thinking, personal integration, fun, and group productivity.

Nondirective Teaching

Learning is a personal experience. The individual experiences planning, responsibility, and a teacher who values the student's perspective. Acquiring responsibility for one's own learning and the skill to plan and to develop those plans is no small matter. A teacher who wants students to become independent learners can use nondirective teaching to establish the interpersonal relationships that can facilitate personal productivity. The following transcript shows how this works:

> "John, we're going to study geometry for the next three weeks, and I'm hoping each person will plan a personal project."
>
> "What do you mean, Mr. Rogers?"
>
> "Well, what would you like to learn about geometry?"
>
> "I'll be honest: I never thought about geometry. To me it's just another school subject."
>
> "I understand. We plan so much of your activity in school that it just doesn't seem right to have to think about it for yourself. However, it is important to me that you have this opportunity to set your own goals, to develop the project, and to share with me in assessing your progress."
>
> "I wouldn't know where to begin."
>
> "I'd like to help you. As a teacher I've learned a great many planning skills. I guess that's what makes this project so important to me."
>
> "What do you mean?"
>
> "Well, I want you to learn to organize your own learning, to feel a sense of responsibility for where you're going and how you get there—more important, that you feel progress. I know you can do it, and I want to help you."

This type of experience for the student is not casual or mindless teaching. In its own way it is a rigorous experience for both the teacher and the student. The teacher who normally plans and organizes instruction uses that knowledge and skill to facilitate the student's own efforts. It is necessary to share the student's anxiety and anger, yet remain firm in efforts to support him or her. The student lacks the know-how to move along, but with courage, experience, and a sense of making progress, structuring learning becomes easier and more productive.

There are some very persuasive reasons for using the Nondirective Teaching Model. Students learn to take charge of their own school lives, not in the sense of excluding teachers and other students but in the sense that some part of what goes on is from the individual: it belongs to the student. Personal development is a real goal. Students also become aware of their feelings and thoughts about themselves and others, and they are required to deal with them. Finally, students learn to plan and organize, carry out, and evaluate their own learning.

Group Investigation

When a teacher thinks about teaching geometry, he or she is not often likely to consider social-oriented models of teaching because the traditions of mathematics education have been centered on the individual and mathematics content. Nevertheless, there are many opportunities for group activities that promote affiliation and interpersonal skills and also provide opportunities for collective inquiry and other problem-solving experiences. The individual gains mutual support during the time spent learning problem-solving behaviors. These are relevant to students not only during schooling, but after graduation when the application of mathematics is done in the workplace as members of teams.

Group investigation, a problem-solving model for groups of students, consists of the following events:

1. Students experience a puzzling situation.
2. Students discuss their reactions.
3. Students identify the problem.
4. Students make a plan and discuss roles.
5. Students carry out the plan.
6. Students reflect on their experiences.

In these events, the teacher guides the group dynamics and acts as a resource person. The social climate is cooperative.

An example of the application of group investigation to teaching geometry is how to measure heights. Such objects as flag poles, buildings, and trees, are difficult to measure with devices, and getting students to plan and carry out original strategies for problem solving has both the effect of practical problem solving plus enhancing the more mathematical solution to the problem. The students need to explore aspects of the problem in practical ways, and attempts to resolve these practical problems provide varied experiences, which help students to appreciate a more generalizable solution.

In order to teach geometry through the Group Investigation Model, a teacher has to appreciate both the instructional and nurturant effects of instruction. The experience involves respect for different people's points of view and knowledge construction, learner independence from the teacher, effective group process, a commitment to group inquiry and social dynamics, and disciplined inquiry. Group investigation synthesizes these value orientations. From an observer's vantage point, we need a polyfocal perspective to appreciate the richness of this model of teaching.

Patterns of Instruction

Besides the models of teaching, there are three other common patterns of instruction in classrooms today: lecturing, recitation, and direct instruction (which probably between them account for the majority of what one might see).

Lecture

A good lecture is systematic and sequential and conveys information in an orderly and interesting way. Effective lecturers draw skills from the Attention, Clarity, and Learning Experiences parameters, as well as from the Objectives and Curriculum Organization parameters. The pattern of teacher behavior in lecturing, however, draws nothing from any internal theory of good lecturing or cohesive theory of learning. A lecture is a composite animal with no secondary goal about learning how to learn. (When the lecture is a step in the Advance Organizer Model, then the story is different.) Nevertheless, a good lecture is a worthwhile educational experience and certainly has a place in schooling.

A lecture is poor when the performance on one or more of the five parameters listed above is poor, not because of poor performance of a model called lecturing. A poor lecture may qualify as no teaching at all. Even an interesting speaker who holds our attention or keeps us amused with clever anecdotes may be doing no teaching if the content is not organized around the course objectives and is not designed with the principles of organization in mind. Students can look forward to class and be well entertained, but leave without having learned a thing.

Recitation

A recitation is an oral test. The teacher asks questions, students respond, and the teacher makes value judgments on the responses. Its goal is to cover the material, go over it, ask questions, and see who knows what. By the time it's over, all the important material should be out (or have been said by someone and heard by all). Reviews for tests are often recitations. A recitation doesn't have a series of steps, but we could construct a checklist of events and qualities that might discriminate a good recitation:

- ◗ Covered all the material.
- ◗ Highlighted important items.
- ◗ Identified student confusions.
- ◗ Got maximum student participation.
- ◗ Took opportunities to stimulate higher-level thinking.

For the rest, if we wanted to judge the quality of a recitation lesson, we'd have to go back to the Management parameters of Attention, Momentum, and Clarity. Recitations have a place in school, but not as large a one as they seem to occupy. When one is over, students and teachers are aware of who knows what, who has read the assignment, and who gets A's. As an educational experience used for more than occasional review, it has no guiding principles or point of view behind it, and little chance that the students will get better at learning in some particular way.

Direct Instruction

Direct instruction is usually used for skill work and does have a syntax:

1. The teacher states the aims of the lesson.

2. The teacher presents concepts or an operation.

3. The teacher gives examples or demonstrates.

4. The teacher asks questions to check student understanding.

5. Students practice with direct monitoring, feedback, help, and hints from the teacher, usually in the group.

6. Students practice alone (seatwork or homework).

7. The teacher corrects and decides whether to reteach, regroup, or move on.

8. The teacher gives frequent tests.

Direct instruction lacks model status because it has no theoretical basis, teacher-student response pattern, or social-technical environmental conditions tailored to optimize a specified learning behavior. But we know that good direct instruction in groups with high time on task produces mastery of skills. Direct instruction reflects the current trends toward training, task analysis, and biofeedback. These preferences for instruction, which have evolved from the business community, reflect values of efficiency and effectiveness.

Lecturing, recitation, and direct instruction are all prominent patterns of classroom instruction, and most teachers view them as models of teaching. But in theory and practice, they are not models at all. Models of teaching have elaborate theoretical statements and descriptions of patterns of behavior that teachers can be trained to perform. There are discrete teacher-student interactions that characterize one model and distinguish it from another. Models are similar to theatrical plays, though not so closely scripted; if teachers know the model, they can visualize the classroom activity before it occurs and use that image to monitor and regulate the flow of activity. The content and goals of models are equally distinctive. In one model the content is derived from an academic discipline, such as mathematics; in another it may draw from recent student experiences for the content. A model will be chosen not only to convey content but to stretch the way students think and learn about learning.

Models of teaching allow us to ask of good teaching, "Good for what?" and to answer out of the things a particular model is designed to be good for (e.g., logical thinking, inductive reasoning, personal self-organization, cooperation and group skill).

How many models of teaching do you use? Which ones? How could you better match some of your students with different models? ❧

Checking on Models of Teaching

1. The teacher's repertoire of models includes:

    no patterns

      recitation

        direct instruction

          a complete model _____

            a complete model and segments of another

              several complete models

              _____

              _____

              _____

              _____

2. Models of Teaching used are:

    inappropriate for students and/or material

      appropriate to material

        matched to group

          matched to individuals

Source Materials on Models of Teaching

Joyce, B. R., and M. Weil. *Models of Teaching*. Englewood Cliffs, N.J.: Prentice-Hall, 1972, 1980, 1986, 1992; Reading, Mass.: Addison-Wesley, 1996.

Social Models

Group Investigation Model

Major theorists: Herbert Thelen, John Dewey

Mission: Development of skills for participation in democratic social processes through combined emphasis on interpersonal and social (group) skills and academic inquiry. Aspects of personal development are important outgrowths of this model.

References:

Dewey, J. *Democracy and Education*. New York: Macmillan, 1916.

Thelen, H. *Education and the Human Quest*. New York: Harper & Row, 1960.

Thelen, H. *Dynamics of Groups at Work*. Chicago: University of Chicago Press, 1954.

The Jurisprudential Model

Major theorists: Donald Oliver, James P. Shaver

Mission: Designed primarily to teach the jurisprudential frame of reference as a way of processing information, but also a way of thinking about and resolving social issues.

Reference:

Oliver, D., and J. P. Shaver, *Teaching Public Issues in High School*. Boston: Houghton Mifflin, 1966.

Social Inquiry Model

Major theorists: Benjamin Cox, Byron Massialas

Mission: Social problem solving, primarily through academic inquiry and logical reasoning.

Reference:

Massialas, B., and B. Cox. *Inquiry in Social Studies*. New York: McGraw-Hill, 1966.

Laboratory Method Model (T-Group)

Major theorist: National Training Laboratory, Bethel, Maine; Leland P. Bradford

Mission: Development of interpersonal group skills and, through this, personal awareness and flexibility.

References:

Bany, M., and L. V. Johnson. *Classroom Group Behavior: Group Dynamics in Education*. New York: Macmillan, 1964.

Bennis, W. G., K. D. Benne, and R. Chin (eds.). *The Planning of Change: Readings in the Applied Behavioral Sciences*. New York: Holt, Rinehart and Winston, 1964.

Bradford, L. P. (ed.). *Human Forces in Teaching and Learning*. Washington, D.C.: National Training Laboratory, National Association, 1961.

Bradford, L. P., J. R. Gibb, and K. D. Benne. *T-Group Theory and Laboratory Method*. New York: John Wiley, 1964.

Human Relations Laboratory Training Student Notebook. Washington, D.C.: U.S. Office of Education, 1961.

Information Processing Models

Concept Attainment Model

Major theorist: Jerome Bruner

Mission: Designed primarily to develop inductive reasoning.

Reference:

Bruner, J., J. J. Goodnow, and G. A. Austin. *A Study of Thinking*. New York: Science Editions, 1957.

An Inductive Model

Major theorist: Hilda Taba

Mission: Designed primarily for the development of inductive mental processes and academic reasoning or theory building, but these capacities are useful for personal and social goals as well. The model was developed from a specific kind of thinking that underlies scientific inquiry.

References:

Taba, H. *Teaching Strategies and Cognitive Functioning in Elementary School Children*. Cooperative Research Project 2404. San Francisco: San Francisco State College.

———. *Teacher's Handbook for Elementary Social Studies*. Reading, Mass.: Addison-Wesley, 1967.

Inquiry Training Model

Major theorist: Richard Suchman

Mission: Designed primarily for the development of inductive mental processes and academic reasoning or theory building. The generalized model of inquiry was developed from a general analysis of the methods employed by creative research personnel.

References:

Suchman, J. R. *The Elementary School Training Program in Scientific Inquiry.* Report of the U.S. Office of Education. Project Title VIII, Project 216. Urbana: University of Illinois, 1962.

———. "A Model for the Analysis of Inquiry." In H. J. Klausmeier and C. W. Harris (eds.), *Analysis of Concept Learning.* New York: Academic Press, 1966.

———. *Inquiry Box: Teacher's Handbook.* Chicago: Science Research Associates, 1967.

———. *Inquiry Development Program: Developing Inquiry.* Chicago: Science Research Associates, 1966.

Biological Science Inquiry Model

Major theorists:Joseph J. Schwab, Jerome Bruner (curriculum reform movement)

Mission: Designed to teach the research system of the discipline but also expected to have effects in other domains; for example, sociological methods may be taught in order to increase social understanding and social problem solving.

Reference:

Schwab, J. J. *Biological Sciences Curriculum Study, Supervisor. Biology Teachers' Handbook.* New York: John Wiley, 1965.

Advanced Organizer Model

Major theorist: David Ausubel

Mission: Designed to increase the efficiency of information-processing capacities to absorb and relate bodies of knowledge.

References:

Ausubel, D. P. *The Psychology of Meaningful Verbal Learning.* New York: Grune and Stratton, 1963.

———. *Learning Theory and Classroom Practice.* Bulletin 1. Toronto: Ontario Institute for Studies in Education, 1967.

Developmental Model

Major theorists:Jean Piaget, Irving Sigel, Edmund Sullivan

| Mission: | Designed to increase general intellectual development, especially logical reasoning, but can be applied to social and moral development as well. |

References:

Furth, H. G. *Piaget and Knowledge*. Englewood Cliffs, N.J.: Prentice-Hall, 1969.

Kohlberg, L. "Moral Education in the School." *School Review* 74 (1966).

Piaget, J. *The Origins of Intelligence in Children*. New York: International University Press, 1952.

Sigel, I. E. "The Piagetian System and the World of Education." In D. Elkind and J. Flavell (eds.), *Studies in Cognitive Development*. New York: Oxford University Press, 1969.

Personal Models

Nondirective Teaching Model

Major theorist: Carl Rogers

| Mission: | Emphasis on building capacity for self-instruction and through this, personal development in terms of self-understanding, self-discovery, and self-concept. |

References:

Rogers, C. R. *Client Centered Therapy*. Boston: Houghton Mifflin, 1951.

———. *Freedom to Learn*. Columbus, Ohio: Charles E. Merrill, 1969.

Classroom Meeting Model

Major theorist: William Glasser

| Mission: | Development of self-understanding and self-responsibility. This has latent benefits to other kinds of functioning (e.g., social). |

References:

Glasser, W. *Reality Therapy*. New York: Harper & Row, 1965.

———. *Schools Without Failure*. New York: Harper & Row, 1969.

Synectics Model

Major theorist: William Gordon

| Mission: | Personal development of creativity and creative problem-solving. |

References:

Gordon, W. J. *Synectics*. New York: Harper & Row, 1961.

———. *The Metaphorical Way of Learning and Knowing*. Cambridge, Mass.: Synectics Educational Press, 1970.

Awareness Training Model

Major theorists: William Schutz, Fritz Perls

Mission: Increasing personal capacity for self-exploration and self-awareness. Much emphasis is placed on the development of interpersonal awareness and understanding.

References:

Brown, G. *Human Teaching for Human Learning*. New York: Viking Press, 1971.

Schutz, W. J. *FIRO: A Three Dimensional Theory of Interpersonal Behavior*. New York: Holt, Rinehart, and Winston, 1958.

———. *Expanding Human Awareness*. New York: Grove Press, 1967.

Behavior Modification Models

Operant Conditioning

Major theorist: B. F. Skinner

Mission: General applicability. A domain-free approach, though probably it is applicable to the information processing function.

References:

Schramm, W. *Programmed Instruction: Today and Tomorrow*. New York: Fund for the Advancement of Education, 1962.

Skinner, B. F. *The Science of Human Behavior*. New York: Macmillan, 1956.

———. *Verbal Behavior*. New York: Appleton-Century-Crofts, 1957.

Taber, J., R. Glaser, and H. S. Halmuth. *Learning and Programmed Instruction*. Reading, Mass.: Addison-Wesley, 1965.

11
Expectations

How do I communicate to students what I expect of them, and are my expectations appropriate?

Three Key Messages
Four Kinds of Expectations
Standards
Pygmalion Effects
Ten Arenas of Classroom Life

*Nothing influences behavior so strongly
as the clear expectations
of a significant other.*

Jim Steffen
Management Consultant

Classrooms are dynamic and complex societies that are rife with expectations: expectations that teachers have for students and that students have for teachers and for each other. These expectations explain a good deal of what we see in classrooms—the good and the bad, the productive and the wasteful. But the expectations themselves can't be seen. They hang in the air almost like an atmosphere; they exist only between people and comprise a part of their relationship.

In this chapter we discuss the Expectations parameter of teaching. Of course, we will not be satisfied to talk merely about atmosphere. We are interested in behavior: controllable behavior, things teachers say and do to produce atmospheres. So within this parameter we explore what teachers say and do to create and communicate expectations to students clearly. We also take up the issue of standards: Are they high enough, reasonable, and appropriate as we look at a teacher dealing with different groups and different individuals? If they are, what does it take from a teacher to get these expectations met? Then we shift gears and take up the ten arenas of everyday classroom life through which teachers send (or don't send) confidence messages to students about teacher beliefs in the children's capacity, the value of hard work over being "smart," and the value of effort in school success.

The opening quotation to this chapter contains two key elements pertaining to Expectations. The first is the word *clear*. Students have to know with certainty what a teacher expects. The second is the phrase *significant other*. Teachers, like parents, are automatically significant others to students, if for no other reason than that they have power over them. If the relationship contains respect and regard too (and perhaps affection), the teacher becomes even more

> ✳ *What you expect is what you get.*

significant. How such relationships get built is the subject of another important parameter, Personal Relationship Building, discussed in Chapter 12. In this chapter, we look at the expectations themselves and the process for communicating them. The assumption of the opening quotation is that within limits, *what you expect is what you get* and that teachers can raise (or lower) students' performance by expecting more (or less) of them—quite a responsibility.

Three Key Messages

The bottom line of this parameter is sending the following three messages to students:

1. THIS IS IMPORTANT.
2. YOU CAN DO IT.
3. I WON'T GIVE UP ON YOU.

People of widely different personalities and various teaching styles can and do succeed in sending these messages to students. Success here is not a matter of style. From the lighthearted to the stern, from the free-flowing creative to the analytical, the best teachers find ways to convince students that they, the teachers, are believers—believers in the students and in the subject. Such teachers do not do so by magic or osmosis. Their words and actions, some quite subtle but nonetheless observable, send these messages and thereby make a huge difference in learning, especially to low-performing students.

We can be just as behavioral in studying this parameter of teaching as we were with Attention and Clarity. The approach will be the same: What is the repertoire of ways to send the three messages and match the ways to individual students?

Four Kinds of Expectations

There are four basic kinds of student performance for which teachers have expectations:

1. Quality and quantity of work. — *Individual output & production rates*
2. Work habits and work procedures.
3. Business and housekeeping routines. — *Attendance lunch count*
4. Interpersonal behavior.

Expectations for the *quality and quantity of students' work* have to do with individual output and production rates for items of work. For example: How good is the work Jason is doing? When the teacher responds, "Well, he could be a lot more thorough" or, "He's really sloughing off. I think he could do a lot better if he tried," the teacher reveals a negative evaluation of the work Jason was expected to produce. The teacher has higher expectations for Jason than he is meeting.

Depending on the teacher's expectations for Jason's work, there are other ways in which his evaluation may be expressed. Here are two other versions that reveal that the teacher's expectation has been met: "Just fine. That's really the quality I expect from Jason " and "Well, that's about all you can expect from Jason."

These expectations for students' current performance are different from those for students' performance growth over time. It's quite a different thing to ask from the teacher's point of view whether the increments of difficulty for new objectives or new lessons are appropriate for the students. Here, the subject is not so much the stretch that new work demands of the students with regard to what they have mastered recently; it is the current products and the teacher's expectations for how well the work, and how much work, will be produced.

The expectations for *work habits and work procedures* pertain to how students go about their work, not the products of work themselves. Some of these expectations may focus on such matters as getting assignments, following directions, getting help, handing in work, and doing research. For example, a teacher may say, "Every time you do a paper, I expect you to make an appointment with me to go over your first draft at least one week before the final draft is due." Or students may be expected to keep a log of books read with dates and comments, keep it accurately and up to date, and do so on their own without teacher reminders.

We are talking here about ongoing habits and procedures that students are routinely expected to do in their work, not directions on how to do individual assignments. As an observer, one may hear a teacher reminding students of these ongoing procedures from time to time. At the beginning of the year, there may be repeated and direct attention to teaching them to students, but during most of the year (if they're working well) they won't be talked about at all. They just function, underlying the academic work students are doing. These expectations may be for following routine managerial procedures in preparation for teacher-led groups (where to go, when, with what materials, what the order of events shall be) or may pertain to personal work habits, such as writing posture, organization of math problems on a page, order of operations.

The third kind of expectations, for *business and housekeeping routines,* pertain to nonacademic work–related procedures such as attendance, lunch count, clean-up, and other operations. For example, ninth-grade students may be expected to organize and carry out their own lab clean-up at the end of each period. Third graders may be expected to move counters to register their attendance and use them to indicate their choice of free-time activity when they arrive at class each morning.

Finally, expectations for *interpersonal behavior* pertain to how students should treat each other and cooperate with the teacher. We examine these under the Discipline parameter (Chapter 7).

Here we will be dealing with the first of the four kinds of expectations: *quality and quantity of work.* Each of these four kinds of expectations has been considered separately because it is possible that a teacher with high expectations for quality and quantity of work may have few or unclear expectations for work habits and procedures. There seems to be no necessary correlation between a teacher's behavior on one kind of expectation and the same teacher's handling of another. Though one might not expect it logically, we have observed inconsistencies in numerous teachers on this parameter. There is a strong correlation between the behaviors that serve to communicate all four kinds of expectations, whatever the standards behind them, and it is with these behaviors that we begin.

Over the course of this chapter the following important aspects of the Expectations parameter will be considered:

- Do students know what the teacher's expectations are? How are these expectations communicated to students?

- What is the nature of the expectations themselves? What can be said about the standards embodied in them?

- How appropriate are those standards for groups and for individuals? How are they varied or adjusted (matched)?

Communication of Expectations

There are six important qualities to look for in the communication of expectations:

1. *Direct*. The expectation is explicitly brought to students' attention, usually verbally.

2. *Specific*: The details of the expectation for students' performance are clearly stated or otherwise specified in the communication (which may be written and not verbal).

3. *Repeated*. The expectation is repeated often to make sure students absorb it.

4. *Positive expectancy*: The statement of expectation has a "you can do it" flavor: the communication of the expectation is not seen as an order to the student but as an expression of confidence (sometimes challenge) on the part of the teacher that the student can and will meet it (Tanner 1978). Another version of positive expectancy has a more imperative quality: "Of course, you'll meet this expectation!" "It's what's done!" is the implication conveyed by tone and body language.

5. *Modeled*: This has two meanings. The first is to "show" or "demonstrate." A teacher may clarify to students what is expected by performing the behavior as a model of what to do. The purpose of this form of modeling is clear communication. The second meaning of modeling is to "practice what you preach." In regular practice and behavior, the teacher is a model of thoroughness, or self-evaluation, or courtesy, or whatever else is expected of students. Whether it's expectations for procedures, interpersonal behaviors, work habits, or application of skills, students take powerful messages from observing how faithfully teachers follow their own dicta.

6. _Tenacity_: This quality surfaces in response to resistance, and it subsumes repetition and consistency. One would not see tenacity without repetition, but repetition does not necessarily imply tenacity. When students resist teacher expectations and getting them met seems hopeless, teachers who struggle on nevertheless display tenacity (presuming that the expectations are realistic; if they aren't, "foolish" would replace "tenacious"). For example, we have observed teachers displaying tenacity in the following ways: teacher goes to study hall to get a student; teacher reminds a student she's expected at 1:15 to go over some work; teacher nabs students before and after class and makes appointments; teacher calls parents at home. All of these are ways of reinforcing an expectation.

> **_Students take powerful messages from observing how faithfully teachers follow their own dicta._**

This quality or behavior we've called tenacity raises an issue for some teachers. "It isn't my job to chase them around if they don't do their work; it's their responsibility. And if they don't understand something, I expect them to come and ask me!" There is a certain "come-and-get-it—or else!" message in this attitude. That message can intimidate certain students and prevent them from learning what they might because it cuts them off from the person from whom they might learn—the teacher. On the other hand, the responsibility for ensuring that learning takes place cannot rest solely with the teacher. Students must do their part. As observers of ourselves and others we have the duty to ask, "Are we doing enough, being tenacious enough without creating dependence, chasing students enough so that they get the message that we really care about their investment in their work?" The message that tenacity sends is we care.

These six qualities are important elements of the messages teachers send to students about what is expected. In addition, when it comes to work, the feedback students get about their products seems particularly important in communicating expectations. The following important attributes of this feedback show up again and again in interviews with teachers and students:

▶ _Prompt and complete._ Products are returned to students within a very few days of submission—sometimes the same day—and there is evidence to the student that the teacher has given thorough attention to what the student has done.

▶ _Detailed_. Feedback contains detailed remarks, suggestions, or questions from the teacher to the student. These can be notes in the margin, responses in a student journal, or verbal comments.

▶ *Personal contact.* There are frequent occasions of face-to-face feedback to students—during class, before and after class, even in the hallway. Perhaps they'll be jocular: "Hey, Jimmy! Before you get locked up in your shoulder pads this afternoon, you're going to see me with those corrections, right?"

▶ *No excuses.* Teachers go after students, personally and with tenacity. Teachers hold students accountable, putting them on the spot when work is not turned in, is late, or is inadequately done and not letting them off the hook by accepting inadequate explanations. Teachers give the work to students to correct or to do over again, set deadlines, offer help when necessary, or make provisions for students to get what they need to do the work (materials, peer tutoring, etc.). "No excuses" means giving consequences for poor performance, without rancor or anger.

▶ *Recognizes superior performance.* When students do well, there is some special form of recognition that highlights their accomplishment: posting especially good papers on a bulletin board, displaying a product in a public place, or complimenting in front of the class. (The issue this behavior raises is how a teacher provides for the student who might never produce a "superior" product and whether a teacher can adequately define "superior" for a student in terms of progress from past work.)

▶ *Logical consequences for poor performance.* Equally important are consequences for nonperformance or poor performance. If something happens as a result of not doing homework or classwork or as a result of doing shoddy work (or as a result of tardiness or sloppy clean-up or the many other areas of performance for which teachers have expectations), then students become convinced the teacher means it.

Effective consequences have the following characteristics: (a) they are clear in advance to students; (b) there is a range of consequences rather than just one rigid one for each expectation; (c) they are logical rather than punitive; (d) they are delivered with appropriate affect; (e) teachers make clear to students that they—the students—have made a choice. These attributes are developed in more detail in the Discipline chapter (Chapter 7).

Standards

After examining the communication of expectations, the next aspect to look at is the relative standards embodied in the expectations. We find that a teacher's standards for expectations can be viewed along a continuum:

1. *None.*

2. *Few consistent.*

3. *Low.* Teachers demand less of the students than they might.

4. *Too high.* Standards are inappropriately demanding for most students.

5. *Average.* Standards reflect a midlevel of demand attainable by most students.

6. *Inspirational-vague.* Teachers who use this standard are often charismatic, stimulating performers, and students may work hard to please them. These teachers may instill in students a feeling that the subject is important, worthy, and dignified. The problem is that the teacher's standards may never be clear, and each student's learning may ricochet down the track in a somewhat uncontrolled manner, since they are never quite sure what the definition of good performance is. For a few students this lack of definition may antagonize them and neutralize the inspirational effect.

7. *High and demanding but reasonable.* Standards are quite demanding; expectations are pushy on the part of the teacher but attainable by most students.

From an observer's point of view, figuring out where a teacher is on standards requires some knowledge of age-appropriate norms for the students and some specialized knowledge of the population of the class in order to make valid judgments. But teachers can certainly analyze their own performance and strive to make the standards inherent in their expectations appropriate to their students.

A Note on Standards and Expectations

We make a distinction between what a teacher thinks students will do (expectations) and what a teacher wants students to do (standards). Often, however, *expectation* is used in both senses (and until recently, one rarely heard the word *standards* at all). Yet both are important ideas. Unless these two ideas are separated and conceptualized clearly by practitioners, it is possible that teachers will have expectations in the sense that they have forecasts of what students will do but no notion of standards at all—no goals or heights for which to reach (or have students reach)—in their behavior in the four areas of expectations discussed here. Having expectations without standards may color much of teaching today.

Matching with Standards

Consider the following four statements and their implication for both the teacher's standards and how those standards are applied to students of different ability:

1. "I have the same expectations for everyone. There's a certain amount of work to be done in this course, and I expect everybody to do it."

2. "I have different expectations for different kids. I know some of them can't be expected to perform as well as others; this is the way it is in any large group. There are certain demands I just don't make on the lower-ability students."

3. "I have different expectations for different kids. I know some of them have better backgrounds for getting this material, and maybe they're just quicker. I make special provisions for the slower students to try to bring them along as far and as fast as they can go."

4. "I understand that kids in here have different abilities and speeds of learning, but I also know what a quality performance is like from a student, and I know what it means to really know this subject. I press them all toward that standard of excellence. I provide extra boosts and help those who need it, and I know they'll still move along at different rates and with different degrees of success. But the standard is there, and I push them all toward ever closer approximations of it. If they never get there, at least they learn about excellence and get rewarded mightily for their incremental steps toward it."

These statements represent real people and real attitudes in our profession. The beliefs and intentions behind the positions these people hold are worth spelling out in some detail because they translate into action that has a powerful and sometimes decisive effect on student achievement. So we would like to describe more fully what these four people mean. Though they are, we grant, stereotypes, they are nonetheless real—that is, there are people like these, and understanding what they mean by their statements will help us examine our own expectations and how we communicate them.

Teacher 1 makes no discriminations between students. What is expected seems conceived more in terms of coverage or amount of work done rather than quality of performance. The same standards for productivity are rigidly applied to everyone. Due dates are enforced, and students are expected to learn the material or take the consequences. These teachers can let low-performing students be invisible as long as they are passing. The students are invisible because they hunker down and the teacher teaches past them.

Teacher 2 is differential and accepting. This teacher forecasts that students have different abilities and will perform according to those abilities. Those performances are accepted as representing what the students are capable of, and no effort is detected to press them to new heights. They all get pretty much the same material, and they do what they can do.

Teacher 3 is differential and provisioning. The teacher provides for students who may have difficulty with the material—maybe by tailoring their assignments down within their range or supplementing them through extra help, peer tutoring, or extra instructional materials.

Teacher 4 is clear about an image of excellence in the subject area. That standard is held out for all students as a challenge and as a purpose of the instruction. When students say the teacher "really makes me feel this stuff is important," it reflects this kind of teacher commitment. This teacher also knows students have different capacities for learning and different rates, and makes allowances (provisions) for these differences, not by tailoring assignments down but by providing extra help for those who need it. The teacher rewards whatever incremental steps students make toward the standard of excellence but never forgets that standard or lets students forget it.

Teacher 1 does no matching. Teacher 2 has different expectations for students that turn into self-fulfilling prophesies. Teachers 3 and 4 are both individualizing in the sense of adjusting instruction within the class to students performing at different levels; but there is more of a confidence about Teacher 4 that they all can do it, or at least get near it. Teacher 4 behaves a lot like the Mastery Learning paradigm. For students who are struggling, the teacher breaks down tasks into however many small steps each student needs to succeed. The tasks are sequenced toward the eventual mastery that's intended for all the students, and the time individuals spend on various tasks or subtasks is adjusted for what

> **Expectations for students turn into self-fulfilling prophesies.**

they need. But the same mastery is the target for them as for everybody else, and the teacher will not give up on them. Teacher 4 believes that all students can learn and shows it. This teacher is uncomfortable with grades because grades interfere with the messages he or she is trying to convey to the students. The teacher gives much genuine praise for real progress that may still be far short of excellence and is always pressing students to outperform their stereotypes of themselves. Teacher 4 may bend C's to B's for students who are knocking themselves out, but not B's to A's. These teachers believe they can really make a difference, despite some students' difficult home environments (Dembo and Gibson 1985).

A Teacher 4 who "goes haywire" focuses on the standard of excellence without giving students adequate opportunity or help in meeting it. The teacher may avoid the pitfalls of stereotyping students as "bright" or "slow," and may press everyone toward excellence but without providing the wherewithal to get there. Instruction is at fault. Such 4's who lose perspective may also lose sight of individuals in their passion for excellence. They may press special education students and low performers too far and too fast and into failure. If Teacher 3 loses perspective, he or she may individualize like crazy, with all kinds of different materials and techniques available, but will not demand enough of the students. This teacher unconsciously forms stereotypes of what the students can accomplish and stops pushing or borrows from a Teacher 2 and starts accepting whatever students produce as representative of what they can do, without consciously classifying students.

Teacher 3 continues to work very hard and match (or attempt to match) students' learning styles, but in the zeal to provide for all, is susceptible to overfocusing on affect and going soft on content. Thus, the teacher may subtly sabotage his or her own rescue missions.

In sum, we wind up with four qualitatively different levels of teacher performance on matching expectations to different students:

1. No discrimination.
2. Differential and accepting.
3. Differential and provisioning.
4. Working for high standards (excellence) with allowances.

Some might argue that working for high standards with allowances risks damaging the self-image of students who can never reach the teacher's standard of excellence and that good teaching is being differential and provisioning. This position, however, runs the risk of pressing students to do less than they might achieve. Others would argue that working for high standards with allowances is more appropriate at higher grade levels and that "standards of excellence" does not apply so clearly in the primary grades, where mastery of basic skills is the big agenda and we would do better to think in terms of segmental mastery learning rather than excellence. Still others would argue that excellence is excellence, and everyone should be made to reach for it. The fact that students are not all equally prepared to meet a standard is a fact of life. And the fact that not everybody does the same quality of work should not be concealed from students as long as they are not made to feel crummy about what they *do* do with effort. What is important is conveying to all students the belief that they can meet the standard given adequate time, good strategies, and persistent effort.

As teachers we should examine which attitude we hold and how that affects our teaching performance: How do we match our expectations and standards to different students?

Pygmalion Revisited

Our comments on expectations are noticeably different from the literature that has unfolded since *Pygmalion in the Classroom* (Rosenthal and Jacobson 1968). We have aimed to focus attention on teachers' standards for an individual student's performance at the item level—that is, for specific tasks—and have invited teachers to discriminate their standards between students, and within an individual student, for different tasks and different kinds of tasks. Further, we have invited teachers to be explicit and up front with themselves and with the students about what their standards are, so that by virtue of being explicit, the standards may assume the character of shared learning goals between teachers and students.

The literature has been on a different tack, shedding a different kind of light on the subject of expectations. First, these other authors and researchers have not distinguished standards at the task level within students and between students. They have not asked about a teacher's expectations for whether Jimmy could write better sentences, or Mary could do her math faster, and what it would take to get them there. Rather, by "expectations," they have meant a teacher's gestalt impression of a student's general competence or aptitude. In their work, these authors have demonstrated that teachers create categories of students—the "brights" and the "slows."

Second, these investigators have shown that teachers then communicate their impressions to students by subtle and indirect messages that students nevertheless read and that influence their academic performance (and probably self-image). Understanding specifically how teachers send these subtle messages to students turns out to be an important lens on teaching. In the next section we elaborate what is known about the communication of these gestalt messages through ten specific arenas of classroom life that teachers perform in daily and control. These are arenas in which we all need to develop large and purposive repertoires.

Ten Arenas of Classroom Life

These ten arenas are settings in which regularly recurring events happen and can be observed:

1. Calling on students—the Pygmalion behaviors.

2. Response to student answers.

3. When students don't answer.

4. When students ask for help.

5. Feedback on student performance.

   ◆ unmet expectations

   ◆ students doing well

   ◆ significant change in performance

6. Dealing with errors.

7. Grading.

8. Students who don't "get it" yet.

9. Grouping.

10. Giving and negotiating assignments and tasks.

Calling on Students—the Pygmalion Behaviors

Cooper (1979) pulled together these subtle teacher communication behaviors into five categories:*

1. *Climate*: "It was found that teachers who believed they were interacting with bright students smiled and nodded their heads more often than teachers interacting with slow students. Teachers also leaned towards bright students and looked brights in the eyes more frequently" (p. 393).

2. *Demands*: "Students labeled as slow have been found to have fewer opportunities to learn new material than students labeled as bright" (p. 393).

3. *Persistence*: "Teachers tend to stay with the highs longer after they have failed to answer a question. This persistence following failure takes the form of more clue giving, more repetition, and/or more rephrasing. Teachers have been found to pay closer attention to responses of students described as gifted. Teachers allowed bright students longer to respond before redirecting unanswered questions" (p. 394).

4. *Frequency of interaction*: "Teachers more often engage in academic contact with the high than low-expectation students" (p. 394).

5. *Feedback*: "Teachers tend to praise high-expectation students more and proportionately more per correct response, while lows are criticized more and proportionately more per incorrect response" (p. 395).

There are thirteen distinct behavioral items in these five categories, and they provide empirical evidence that many teachers do classify students as "brights" and "slows" and act differently toward them, thus creating self-fulfilling prophecies. The following checklist can be used as a self-assessment or a peer observation protocol:

- Do I smile and nod more toward "highs"?
- Do I lean more toward "brights"?
- Do I look "brights" more in the eyes?
- Do I give "slows" fewer opportunities to learn new material?
- Do I give "highs" more clues when they fail to get an answer—more repetition or more rephrasing?
- Do I pay closer attention to the responses of "the gifted"?
- Do I allow "brights" longer to respond?
- Do I have more frequent academic contact with "highs"?
- Do I give "highs" more praise per correct response?

*Reprinted by permission of the publisher. Cooper, H. M. "Pygmalion Grows Up: A Model for Teacher Expectations, Communication and Performance Influence." *Review of Educational Research* 49 (Summer 1979): 389–410. © 1979 by the American Education Research Association.

‣ Do I give "lows" more criticism per incorrect response?

‣ Do I do any of the above more with girls than
with boys, or vice versa?

Response to Students' Answers

Another arena through which expectations are communicated is what teachers do right after a student has been asked a question: that is, what response does the teacher make to the student?

The student may not make an overt response; the student may be stumped and remain silent. Still, after asking a question, whatever the student does or doesn't do, there follows an action of some sort from the teacher. That is the arena, and a powerful one, where teacher actions have embedded messages about their belief in the student's capacity.

There exists a repertoire of responses one may observe from a teacher at moments like these—and it is a moment that happens hundreds of times a day. What teachers say and do at these moments sends messages to individuals and cumulatively to the whole class about whether it is safe to open your mouth in here, whether one can risk trying something that's hard, and whether the climate is supportive of thinking and effort or punitive for not having the right answer.

Students get powerful messages from the teacher's responses to their answers.

Art Costa, co-director of the Institute for Intelligent Behavior in Sacramento, California, has pointed out that the way that teachers respond to student answers is probably more important than the questions themselves. Students get powerful messages from the teacher's responses to their answers, and it is these messages that influence the way they participate in lessons from that point on. Depending on how the teacher responds, a student may get one or more of the following messages:

"I'm dumb."

"Well, I muffed that one!"

"My job is to guess the answer in the teacher's head and say it in precisely the way he's thinking it."

"I muffed that one, and I should get back in gear. I know this stuff."

"The teacher thinks I can think this one through and get it."

"What I said was worthwhile, but there's more."

"My teacher really listens to what I say."

"My teacher really wants to know what I mean. There must be something worthwhile in what I said."

"My idea wasn't as good as that one. Boy, I'm glad I didn't get called on."

"Wow, I guess I did pretty well on that one."

"It's not safe to risk an answer in here unless you're really sure."

"It is safe to risk an answer in here. If I don't get it, I won't be put down."

"I can say what I think and be respected and accepted for that."

"If I can't get it, I'll be helped to remember or figure it out."

Clearly the effects of these messages can be powerful. We have all received them at one time or another in our own experience as students. The effects are either to open students up or close them down; to make them feel more confident, curious, and encouraged to participate, or more afraid, timid, protective, quiet, and defensive. Simultaneously, the effect is either to stimulate students to search, scan, wonder about, reflect, and in general think, or instead to try to get it right and shine, impress, and win (and/or protect themselves from getting wounded).

Look at the following list of ways teachers respond to student answers to the question, "How do you find the area of a circle?"

- ▶ *Criticize*: "That's not even close. Come on, wake up!"

- ▶ *Give the correct answer*: "No, it's pi r^2."

- ▶ *Redirect to another student after the first student's answer*: "Judy, can you tell us?"

- ▶ *Redirect to get more, build, extend*: "Okay. You're on the right track. Judy, would you add anything to that?"

- ▶ *"Wrong" with the reason*: "Not quite, because you left out the exponent." Then the teacher waits while the student tries again.

- ▶ *Supply question for which answer is right, cue, hold accountable*: "That would be right if I asked for the formula for the circumference. Now, do you remember anything about the use of exponents in that formula? [Now the student gets it right.] Right! And I bet you'll remember that after lunch if I check you too. I'll ask you then, and I bet you'll get it!"

- ▶ *Wait-time*: Silence.

- ▶ *Follow-up question to double-check or extend*: The student answers correctly with "pi r^2."] "Okay. And what precisely does r^2 mean?"

- ▶ *Acknowledge*: "Um hmmmm."

- ▶ *Restate in fuller language*: "Okay. So you get the area by multiplying pi times the radius of the circle squared."

> ◗ *Ask student to elaborate*: "Can you tell me more about what
> you meant by that?"
>
> ◗ *Praise*: "Way to go!"

These responses form a repertoire. (See Figure **11.1**.) No one of them is inherently best; matching is the name of the game. One could create the context in which each of them, even criticizing (but not put-downs), could be appropriate. Several of them, however, are particularly effective for specific purposes and should be considered for inclusion into any teacher's repertoire. Wait-time is one such behavior.

Mary Budd Rowe discovered almost thirty years ago that if teachers waited 3 seconds or more after asking a question (that is, they were willing to endure at least 3 seconds of silence) some very desirable things happened. (She also discovered that almost no teachers do so. The average wait-time after asking a question before the teacher jumps in with cuing, redirection, telling the answer or restating the question is 0.5 second!) When teachers were willing

> ### *Responses form a repertoire. Matching is the name of the game.*

to wait the 3 seconds, many students who ordinarily did not answer did so, the answers tended to be in full sentences rather than single words or phrases, the answers were at a higher level of thinking, and students were more likely to start responding to each other and to comment on each other's answers.

Similar findings have been obtained when a student has answered, and the teacher waits 3 seconds again before commenting on the answer. Waiting after a student has responded is called "wait-time II." (Waiting after asking the question but before the student has answered is called "wait-time I.") This response behavior achieves similar desirable outcomes to wait-time I: teachers tend to increase the cognitive level of their questions, students increase the cognitive level of their answers, students speak in more complete and more elaborate sentences, and students who would otherwise not elaborate do so.

Supplying the question for which the answer is right, cuing, and holding the student accountable accomplish several things. First, they salvage a little student self-esteem. A student does not see or hear as much if he or she is smarting with humiliation. As Hunter says, "When someone is humiliated or feeling unworthy, their perception narrows. Our job is to help learners be right, not catch them being wrong." This strategy also strengthens a connection between the answer and the question it does go with by supplying that question. To use this strategy with every wrong answer would not be practical. It is an excellent strategy to use frequently, however, and especially when there's a question to link up the wrong answer with, often an item of recent learning.

TEACHER RESPONSES TO STUDENT ANSWERS

Ways of moving on to another student	Criticizes. "Come on. That answer shows no thought at all."
	"No," and redirect to another student.
	"No, then give correct answer.
	"No," with reason why—which may serve as a cue.
	Cue but move on to another student.
	Move to another student if first student doesn't answer.
	Redirect to another student to add more, build, extend. "Would you add anything to that, Jim?"
	Student authorized to call on another student to answer in his or her place.
Ways of sticking with a student	"No, but it's good you brought it up because others probably thought that too."
	"Try again."
	Validate what is right or good about an answer, then cue, sticking with the student.
	Ignore answer and cue student.
	Wait-time II.
	Follow up with expression of confidence or encouragement. "I think you know."
	Follow up with expression of confidence or extend.
	Ask student to elaborate.
	Call for self-evaluation of answer.
	Follow up question to clarify. "Are you saying that..."
Ways of acknowledging, affirming	Acknowledge, "Um hmmmmm."
	Repeat student's answer
	Restate answer in fuller or more precise language.
	"Right."
	"Right," with reason why.
	Praise or praise and extend.

FIGURE 11.1: TEACHER RESPONSES TO STUDENT ANSWERS
Teachers who convey positive expectations practice moves from the middle of this continuum.

We do not mean to imply that a teacher is never again allowed to say a simple "no" or "wrong," in fear of damaging student learning. Quite the contrary, it often doesn't do any harm at all to say "nope" pleasantly. But giving the student a cue and lingering sends quite a different message from saying "no" and immediately calling on another student. Sticking with students (the middle part of the continuum) sends messages that the teacher has confidence in their ability to think through to an appropriate response. Moving on or, worse, cuing the student but then calling immediately on another says you don't really think they have the capacity (or sufficient speed) to use the cue.

Whereas any response from this continuum can be appropriate in a given situation (and we will be continuing to point out appropriate applications below), the main point of this section is that teachers who convey positive expectations, teachers who build confidence and risk taking in students, do a lot of "sticking" with students, that is, practice many moves from the middle of the continuum.

Sometimes teachers in our workshops wonder aloud how an instructor has enough time to do such "sticking" and cuing with students and still get through all the material they wish to cover. The fact is that it takes hardly any more time at all to do so—seconds more at best. Sticking does not slow down the rate of "coverage" (though for other reasons, such slowing down might be a very good idea). And think of the cost of not sticking with students who don't answer or answer incorrectly the first time: it is so easy to feel inept at a moment like this—and consequently shut down cognitively— that it is too great a risk not to "stick." Finally, by not sticking, the teacher forfeits the chance to support a student's thinking and explicitly build confidence in the capacity to perform with academic material. Every long wait or period of silence when a student feels intimidated or unsure about a question is an opportunity to build confidence and capacity.

There are other responses as well to student answers. A follow-up question to double-check or extend (called a "probe" in research literature) is a way of checking to see if the student really understands the meaning of an answer or is just parroting. For example, a student might be able to recite "pi r^2" without knowing that r stands for the radius of the circle.

Acknowledging a student's answer nonjudgmentally leaves the door open for further comment from other students or for adding to the original answer by the same student.

Restating in fuller language is a move a teacher would do for the benefit of the other students—to make sure they understood what the answer meant.

Asking students to elaborate on their responses helps the teacher know what they really meant: "Could you explain that a little further?" "I'm not sure what you meant by that, Jerry. Can you say a little more?" "You need to be more specific, Jane. How far exactly are you saying the fulcrum has to be from this end?"

Praise can be an effective response to a student answer, but only if used well. Jere Brophy's (1981) definitive review of the research on praise summarized how to praise well. To be effective, teacher praise must be:*

- *Specific*. It specifies exactly what is praiseworthy about the student's performance: "John, I'm impressed with the variety of verbs and sentence patterns you used in this composition. This is your best work so far."

- *Contingent*. The praise is dependent on successful student performance and not given randomly or for encouragement. Noncontingent praise (given randomly and sometimes for incorrect answers) is frequent and found "most often among teachers who have low expectations for student learning. Within any given class, it is most likely to be directed toward the lowest achievers. No doubt such praise is given in an attempt to encourage the student. However, it seems likely that to the extent that the students recognize what the teacher is doing, the result will be embarrassment, discouragement, and other undesirable outcomes" (Brophy 1981, p. 13).

- *Genuine*. The teacher means it. The praise is not manipulative, or given to "reinforce" (translation: engineer) a specific behavior but reflects real appreciation on the teacher's part.

- *Congruent*. Gesture, tone of voice, stance, and posture send the same message as the words. If the teacher leans back, looks away, and says in a bored tone of voice, "I can see you really worked hard on these problems, Freddy," Freddy is not likely to be convinced.

- *Appropriate*. The choice of words, setting, and style is matched to the particular student. Public praise to individual middle school students can embarrass them. Public praise for certain behaviors can make them want to crawl under the table: "Oh, John, your handwriting is so tidy and neat" (said to a macho eighth grader).

Brophy also points out that effective praise uses students' own prior accomplishments as the context for describing present accomplishments, is given in recognition of noteworthy effort or success at difficult (for this student) tasks, attributes success to effort and ability, implying similar successes can be expected in the future, and fosters endogenous attributions (students believe that they expend effort on the task because they enjoy the task and/or want to develop task-relevant skills).

Each of the behaviors just described—wait-time, follow-up questions, acknowledgment, restating in fuller language, asking students to elaborate, and praise—has research to support it as an effective teacher behavior (Costa 1985; Dunkin and Biddle 1974). In addition, there is similar support for redirecting in the literature, and even a case for the appropriateness of criticism with certain students as long as the criticism is not a putdown (Graham 1985).

*Reprinted with permission of the publisher. Brophy, Jere. "Teacher Praise: A Functional Analysis." *Review of Education Research* 51 (Spring 1981): 5–32. © 1981 by the American Educational Research Association.

Since many of these response techniques are inherently worthwhile in and of themselves for stimulating thinking and attaining clarity, they are worth adding to all teachers' repertoires. And it is a good bet that among the list cited, there are several new ones for any teacher. (Least frequently seen, in our observations, are wait-time, asking students to elaborate, and effective praise.) But beyond incorporating them into one's repertoire is the issue of matching. Are the response techniques being used appropriately in the right situation and with the right students? Wait-time, for example, is inappropriate when asking low-level questions or doing drill. Giving students time to think and process is most effective when higher-level thinking is called for. Redirecting prematurely can deny a student the opportunity to think through an answer or refine one already given. Restating in fuller language can aid the understanding of the rest of the class, but if done unnecessarily or to excess can teach students not to listen to one another. The bottom line here, as elsewhere in the quest to understand teaching, is to work first to expand repertoires to respond more appropriately to more students in different situations, and then improve the effectiveness of matching. The third guideline is to skew responses to the middle "sticking" part of the repertoire so as to take every opportunity to build confidence and capacity in students.

When Students Don't Answer

The previous arena assumed that students answer teachers' questions, but, of course, they often do not have the answer at their fingertips and there is that loaded second or two in which to decide what to do. Are we embarrassed for the student and want to get the spotlight off that child? Do we stick with the student, giving cues? Do we ask the question over again? Do we redirect the question to another student?

What are the options when students don't answer questions? What is known about their effects? How do we pick which one to use with Jerry, who is looking at the ceiling and grimacing as he gropes for the answer?

We can identify a progressive continuum of responses teachers may make to keep students open and thinking when they don't answer:

♦ Use wait-time I.

  ♦ Repeat the question.

    ♦ Cue.

      ♦ Ask a simpler question.

        ♦ Ask a fact-only question.

          ♦ Give choices for the answer.

            ♦ Ask for a yes or no response.

              ♦ Ask the student to repeat or imitate an answer.

                ♦ Ask for a nonverbal response, such as shaking the head or pointing.

                ♦ Instruct the student to say, "I don't know."

The benefits of wait-time have been described. Simply enduring a little silence while Jerry grimaces may give him the time he needs to come up with the answer. Modeling this behavior can have a powerful influence too.

One of us once attended a session where David Perkins, co-director of Project Zero at Harvard University, was asked a question. He turned his head, looked sideways, then up at the ceiling, and continued in silence for a full 10 seconds. By this time I was getting nervous for David as a presenter and looking for something to say, some way to jump in and rescue him from what seemed like a paralytic attack. But just at that moment, David looked the questioner calmly in the eye and delivered a brilliant reply. He didn't appear in the least ruffled. He had simply been comfortably thinking out his answer. It was I who had been uncomfortable with the pause, not Dr. Perkins!

Several other times in that session similar pauses for reflection followed complicated questions from the audience. After the first time, I was not worried about David any more and spent the time thinking about the question too. In fact, Perkins's modeling of wait-time for himself to think through an answer had an immediate effect on the class. The whole discussion became more reflective and thoughtful. And by having our instructor model his willingness to think before he spoke, we in turn became more comfortable doing so. The result was to elevate the level of the entire discussion.

Wait-time is a behavior where coaching or some form of peer feedback is particularly helpful. We are so used to filling silences with talk that unless we specifically commit ourselves to try wait-time and get someone in to watch us trying it, we will likely fail to learn this valuable behavior. The very presence of an observer will remind us of our commitment and increase the likelihood of successful practice.

Turning to the other behaviors on the continuum, we see a progression where less and less is required of the student, until finally only imitation or headshaking is requested. This continuum was developed by Good and Brophy (1978) for nonresponsive students. Their point is that students should not be allowed to "practice" nonresponsiveness but instead should be expected to participate. Referring to Blank's work (1973) with inner-city children, they write:

> If they fail the initial question, the follow-up question should be a simpler one that they can handle. In general, questions that require them to explain something in detail will be the most difficult. Progessively simpler demands include factual questions requiring short answers, choice questions requiring them only to choose among presented alternatives, and questions that require only a yes or no response. If the students do not respond to any level of questioning, they can be asked to repeat things or to imitate actions. Once they begin to respond correctly, the teacher can move to more demanding levels as confidence grows. Inhibited students need careful treatment when they are not responding. As long as they appear to be trying to answer the question, the teacher should wait

them out. If they begin to look anxious, as if worrying about being in the spotlight instead of thinking about the question, the teacher should intervene by repeating the question or giving a clue. He or she should not call on another student or allow others to call out the answer. (Good and Brophy 1978, p. 226)

When Students Ask for Help

Another arena of significance occurs when individual students ask teachers for help. It happens dozens of times a day or sometimes more. Read the following two scripts. In one the teacher conveys positive expectations for the student. In the other the teacher conveys negative expectations (Good and Brophy 1978). Can you tell which is which? Analyze which words or phrases in the actual dialogue send the positive and negative messages.

Script I

Student: I can't do number 4.

Teacher: What part don't you understand?

Student: I just can't do it.

Teacher: Well, I know you can do part of it, because you've done the first three problems correctly. The fourth problem is similar but just a little harder. You start out the same, but then you have to do one extra step. Review the first three problems, and then start number 4 again and see if you can figure it out. I'll come by your desk in a few minutes to see how you're doing.

Script II

Student: I can't do number 4.

Teacher: You can't? Why not?

Student: I just can't do it.

Teacher: Don't say you can't do it. We never say we can't do it. Did you try hard?

Student: Yes, but I can't do it.

Teacher: Well, you did the first three problems. Maybe if you went back and worked a little longer you could do the fourth problem too. Why don't you work at it a little more and see what happens?

In the second script, the teacher asks, "Why not?" when the student say, "I can't do number 4." That's a set-up question. If students know why they can't do it, they're able to move forward and ask for more specific help.

The teacher responds to "I just can't do it" with an injunction, "Don't say you can't do it ," and then a bit of moralizing: "We never say we can't do it." Now the teacher may mean that as an encouraging gesture to buck up and get right in there, kiddo, but whatever hope of being encouraging that is possible is crushed by the no-win question: "Did you try hard?"

If the student has already been trying hard, then there is only one conclusion possible: "I must be dumb." And if the student hasn't been trying hard, then she or he must admit sloth.

The last paragraph implies without much hope that maybe *longer* and *harder* will somehow put the student over the top. But no specific strategic help is given. "See what happens" is the parting shot, and we and the student are left feeling that not much more will happen.

In the first script the teacher's first question—"What part don't you understand?"—credits the student with understanding most parts and asks him or her to zero in on the stumbling block. When the student stalls, the teacher explicitly expresses confidence in the student's capacity: "Well, I know you can do part of it, because you've done the first three problems correctly." Then the teacher goes on to give explicit coaching help and promises to return in a few minutes "to see how you're doing." The teacher will help but believes the student can do it. Nevertheless, the student won't be left hanging; the teacher will return as a safety net if there is still difficulty.

The point of studying these two scripts is to increase awareness of word choice and approach when students ask for help. With only subtle changes in what we actually say, we can convey confidence, point out how students can use what they already know, give strategies or cues as help, and check back at appropriate intervals—or we can moralize, simplify, or dumb down the task, suggest inadequacies, hint blame, and convey—sometimes masked behind polite words—that we really don't think the student is capable of doing the task.

One outcome we desire for readers of this section is that they will find themselves carrying a third eye and a third ear into their own classrooms. The third eye and ear is your own! And it is monitoring and giving feedback to you as you speak when you find yourself being asked for help. What messages are you conveying as you interact with students to give help?

Feedback on Student Performance

We have discussed the importance of feedback to students being prompt, detailed, and sometimes delivered through personal contact rather than just in writing if expectations are to be communicated clearly. Now we move away from clarity of communication to the implicit messages contained within the communication. We take up the way in which feedback on student work can send "I believe in you" messages in three circumstances: unmet expectations, students doing well, and significant change in performance.

Unmet Expectations

When students do poor work, it is important they hear about it from teachers in a way that conveys belief that they can do better. Students can easily interpret low affect, neutral, noncommital response to low-quality work as an expression of their teacher's lack of interest or lack of belief in them. It often is.

On the other hand, if a teacher gets excited about poor work and spends time and energy telling a student what's wrong with it and how to make it better, that expenditure of energy signals desire for more student investment. It also signals the teacher's belief that student effort will pay off. Students may display reluctance or resistance when a teacher acts in this direct and sometimes high-energy way. There will be no thanks forthcoming for the tenacity and friendly nagging such people display (at least perhaps not until many years later). But without it, a large segment of students will not believe sufficiently in themselves to work hard or well.

The danger is particularly present for students who hold an "entity" theory of intelligence (Dweck 1989). Such students believe that intelligence or "ability" is something they have or don't have, and if they are doing poorly, it is confirmation of not having enough ability. These same students, according to attribution theory (Weiner 1972, 1974), believe that when they do poorly, it is because of task difficulty—and underneath that belief, the damning suspicion that they are not bright enough.

Attribution theory says that we all have ways of accounting for our successes and our failures. There are four basic reasons to which we might attribute these performances: ability, task difficulty, luck, and effort. Weiner arranges them in the grid shown in FIGURE 11.2.

	Internal	External
Constant (Stable)	Ability	Task Difficulty
Variable (Unstable)	Effort	Luck

FIGURE 11.2: ATTRIBUTION THEORY GRID
Source: Weiner 1972, 1974.

It turns out that successful people tend to attribute success to internal factors that they can control: effort, for example. Unsuccessful people tend to attribute failure to task difficulty and to bad luck (with a secret inner fear that they really just don't have enough ability). When they succeed, they attribute their success to task difficulty and luck. "Must have been an easy test." "I guess I just luckily studied the right chapters!"

Attribution retraining means helping students change their attributions of success and failure away from external factors (luck and easy or hard work) to internal factors (effort and a belief that the student has more than enough mental capacity to do high-quality work). That is easier said than done, but attribution theory research shows that these attributions, which represent a mental model of how the world works and how one functions in it, make a tremendous difference in how much effort students are willing to put out in school.

When students do poorly, going after them with high energy and affect becomes a form of attribution retraining. It is an implicit statement of belief in their ability and a call for more effort.

Doing Well

When students do well, another opportunity for attribution retraining occurs. It is important that the praise given to them attributes their success specifically to effort (and perhaps secondarily, by implication, to their having sufficient ability). "You came in for extra help, studied before the test, and took your time checking your answers before handing it in. And it really paid off!"

Change in Performance

A significant change in performance, either dramatically better or worse, is another opportunity for attribution retraining. "This is nowhere near the standard you're capable of." A remark like that from a respected teacher can be a powerful spur to a flagging student. But what about the reverse?

Suppose a student with a D average gets an 83 on a test. On the way out the door, the teacher stops the student and says, "Say, you did really well on this test. Why do you think you did so well?" The student pauses, looks down, and mumbles, "Must have been an easy test." (Note the connection to external attribution—luck or task difficulty.) The teacher replies, "Easy test! I don't give easy tests; everybody knows that. And you got number 14 right. That was the hardest one. Now come on, what do you think. How come you did so well?"

This teacher is trying to get the student to consider that he has the ability to do well, and perhaps also put in enough effort studying for this test to produce the results. But more than likely the student will be silent at this point in the dialogue. The suggestion behind the teacher's question can be threatening in several ways. ("What if I am capable of good work? Will she expect it of me all the time? What if I tried and couldn't do this well again?") Another student may want to keep expectations low just to avoid working hard.

Still another possibility is that by challenging the student to think about why he succeeded, one may be throwing him or her into social jeopardy. Segments of peer culture in schools are built around not doing academic work and dumping on school. To become a student and be seen to be trying hard could be interpreted as a rejection of one's peer group. This syndrome recurs often for students of color where striving in school settings gets interpreted as "acting white" (Fordham and Ogbu 1986).

When we seize opportunities for attribution retraining like the one above (a student doing unexpectedly well on a test), we need to be ready to support the student through the thinking and the possible perceived risks. "Well, you think about it, and when you come in tomorrow I'm going to ask you again why you think you did so well." And though silence may be the response tomorrow, we may have cracked the door and begun to get the student thinking about the risks and rewards of trying hard, because he believes for the first time he might have the ability to do well.

Dealing with Errors

If I believe errors are signs of weakness, I will avoid them at all costs. In fact, I will avoid topics and types of work where I think I may make errors so I don't have to face the "truth" about my stupidity (or my low aptitude in that area). And I will get impatient with "hard" work that does not come easily or quickly, because I will interpret the "hardness" as a sign of my low ability. On the other hand, if I interpret errors as feedback, that is, data to be used to indicate gaps I can fill or alternate approaches I must seek out, then I do not shy away from material I do not grasp quickly. This view requires an underlying belief in one's capacity to be able to get it ultimately if one works at it (and if it's worth the effort).

These two reactions to error are highlighted in the work of Carol Dweck. She finds that children (and adults) tend to be either entity theorists about intelligence or incrementalists. Entity theorists believe that intelligence is a "thing"—an entity that is fixed and responsible for any success; conversely, having low intelligence results in poor academic performance. Entity theorists take every assignment, every test, every task as an evaluation of their innate ability in a direct causative way. These students form what Dweck calls a "performance goal orientation" toward academic work. Low performance (errors) indicates low ability. High performance indicates high ability. "I only like to do the things I already do well," says a girl who is an entity theorist.

Incrementalists believe that ability is built incrementally through effort and use of feedback from the environment. They form a "learning goal orientation" according to Dweck, where their goal is to learn something new rather than to prove themselves able, as is the goal of the entity theorists. The consequences of these two internal theories of intelligence and the goal orientations that go with them are huge. Imagine the pressure a student feels who is constantly on trial, who experiences every academic challenge as a measure of self on a dimension so highly prized in our society: intelligence.

Not all students (or adults) are at the poles of the entity versus incrementalist continuum, but large numbers are. The closer we are to the entity pole, the harder it is to mobilize energy and strategies when we are experiencing difficulty. The closer we are to the incrementalist pole, the easier it is to treat the difficulty and the errors as data. Teachers have the opportunity every time they help students deal with error to help them interpret it as data rather than as a low-ability message—for example:

- "You can do this if you have the right strategy, Carl, so you must need a different strategy. Let's see, which ones have you tried and which ones haven't you tried yet? "

- "You're able to understand stories when you have the right background knowledge, Julie. So there must be something the author is assuming about experiences you've had that isn't true. Let's see, what could it be? Show me one of the places you got confused."

- "Well, you do can do fine experiments when you understand what the task really is. So there must be something in the directions that didn't communicate. Take me through the lab set-up, and show me where it's unclear."

In the chapter on Classroom Climate we will examine how teachers build a climate proactively for risk taking and confidence so that students learn to treat errors as opportunities for learning. In this section we have introduced the significance of students' attitude toward error and indicated how teachers can respond when they occur in such a way as to support the incrementalist view of intelligence and the learning goal orientation.

Grading

Grading practices send strong implicit messages about teachers' beliefs in students' capacity. Consider the practice of allowing students to retake tests. Many teachers allow students to retake a test if they do poorly. Then the teacher will commonly average the second (usually better) score with the first for the final grade. But look what message this sends. Averaging retakes with original scores rewards those who did well the first time around and says that mastery or ultimately reaching high performance is not what we care about. What we care about is speed, for that is what we reward.

Some will argue that giving the highest score as the final score will encourage students to skip studying the first time, because they can always have another crack at it. We think, however, that very few students will be more inclined to put off study because they see retakes as a safety net. This has been borne out anecdotally with every teacher we know who has adopted the practice. Students who adopt procrastination as a policy soon find themselves so far behind that the safety net doesn't help much.

Now look at the consequences of the opposite practice: averaging. Students who manifest genuine effort and reach equal proficiency with others get lower grades. Thus speed is rewarded, not effort, and all that may have gone with it (goal setting, seeking appropriate help, consulting others, extra hours on the job, soliciting feedback and critique from others).

We would propose that the only grades that make sense are A, B, and "not yet." One high school we know has adopted this scheme. "B" means "meets the standard," and the standard is set at a high level. "A" means "above and beyond the standard" and can be obtained by doing an extra project using the material of the course but beyond the requirements of the course. Any student who has not met the standards of proficiency defined for the course or demonstrated mastery of the knowledge called for is not finished with the work of the course yet. Their grade is incomplete.

To adopt this grading policy, a teacher (and a school) has to take seriously its efforts to get all students to meet the standard (which requires being clear about what the standard looks and sounds like). And opportunities must be available—after school, on weekends, in the evenings—wherever they can be found or created to offer students reteaching and additional help. At one high school we know, faculty members and community volunteers are in the school on Tuesday and Thursday evenings and on Saturday mornings to help students finish their "not yets."

If schools are intended to be sorting mechanisms, then traditional letter grading A through F serves the purpose. Students can be labeled by their grades and selected out for various levels in society and various roles. And it can be argued that sorting was indeed the reason grades were invented. This was the ethos behind the creation of the modern American graded classroom at the turn of the century (Cremin 1965) as we evolved beyond the community schoolhouse with mixed-age grouping into the classroom with fixed-age students and uniform curriculum.

Letter grading also contains within it the assumption that many students will not meet a high standard of performance and will be graded along a scale that indicates partial attainment of the standard or attainment of some of the standards but not others (though one can't tell which standards have and haven't been met by the "grade").

But what if we believed that all students could meet the standard given adequate prior knowledge, sufficient motivation, and good instruction? What if we believed that society needs all students to meet the standards of the courses they take because the nature of the workplace and of the world requires all its citizens to be able to do problem solving, work with others, and use language effectively? Then the only grading system possible would be one based on mastery (A,B, not yet), not on sorting.

The grading system currently in use in America is based on a belief that the purpose of schools is sorting and that many, if not most, students are too dull to reach high standards with rigorous academic material. If we believe all students can learn to high standards, we must radically change our grading system to one compatible with that belief. The chapter on Assessment will elaborate further on what it takes to replace grading with more informative reporting systems.

> *The belief that all students can achieve high standards transforms nearly everything about the way we approach schooling.*

The belief that all students can achieve high standards with rigorous academic material transforms nearly everything about the way we approach schooling, for grading is only the tip of the iceberg. The practice of giving "A,B, not yet" grades opens a positive Pandora's box of implied changes in instructional practices, staff development for expansion of teacher repertoires, and community support for quality schooling for all children.

Students Who Don't "Get It" Yet

It is a common event for a class to end and for a teacher to perceive that several students don't "get it" yet. And those students, as well as the rest of the class, probably know who they are. What, if anything, is going to happen so they have another chance and can "get it"?

For a teacher who assumes some students won't ever get it really, or will get it only partially, the teacher feels obligated to move on to new material. "After all, they get what they can get. I can give them slightly different assignments [translation: less demanding] so they can feel success [what they really feel is shame]. I have to move on with the curriculum. After all, I have to get these kids ready for Regents/APs/finals! I can't hold the others back!"

This teacher doesn't think the slower students could ever get the material and believes that the implication of getting all students to pass is slowing down the whole class and dumbing down the standards. But what if we really believed that all students can reach a high standard given hard work, effective effort, and adequate prior knowledge? What instructional practices would we see?

For students who didn't get it fast or the first time around, a "reteaching loop" can be set up as a regular classroom practice (**FIGURE 11.3**). A reteaching loop—a better name might be "booster group" or "scholars' loop"—is a time and place where a concept or idea previously introduced is taught again or made available again to students with additional explanations, different examples, or different perceptual modes. It may or may not be teacher led. Other students or other adults may lead it. Self-directed learning experiences or computer simulations may be in the loop. But something happens for students who didn't get it the first time around to ensure they do get it, at the original level of rigor and at the original standard, not a watered-down one. The loop has these components:

1. Students should be asked to self-select for the reteaching loop. To do so means one has to self-evaluate: "Do I really get this?"

2. Students need the clarity and aid of a criterion test or task given to them in advance so they can accurately self-assess. The learning target or the performance they are shooting for should be no secret.

3. The teacher creates and continually reinforces a psychological climate of safety and, in fact, esteem for students who nominate themselves for reteaching. One hears from such teachers constant remarks acknowledging the difficulty of material. "This is really quite difficult, because you have to get used to thinking about two things at once: identifying the relevant information and the relevant operation." In addition to legitimizing difficulty, such teachers praise the thoughtfulness of self-evaluation and the risk it takes to say one doesn't know something: "Good going, Jason. You looked hard at your writing and decided to get a boost in this skill before moving on. You're going to know it very thoroughly when you're through, and probably incorporate this skill into your writing for life."

4. The teacher encourages the students who have entered reteaching while they're there. "Keep struggling—you've almost got it. I know you're going to get there. Try to put it in your own words now."

5. The teacher acknowledges difficulty and makes the reteaching loop a team effort. "I must not be saying it right. Julie, can you take a crack at putting it in your own words and explaining it to Marsha?"

The most important part of the reteaching loop is the tenacity and expressed confidence of the teacher to each student that sticking with it will bring success. That means frequent assessments and follow-up with the students until they do.

Creating reteaching loops often requires breaking the class into groups and giving the other members of the class an enrichment or extension activity to apply their knowledge in new contexts. It takes extra time and effort to come up with those activities. There is no doubt that carrying out the belief that "all children can learn to a high level" calls for more work from teachers than if we allow those who don't get it first and fast to settle to the bottom of the tank. Sorting students has always been easier than teaching them.

One way to make the workload rational in managing reteaching loops is to team-teach. Two teachers with a double-size class can divide up the preparation chores when they decide they need to have reteaching and extension activities.

To summarize, reteaching loops are effective when they have the following attributes:

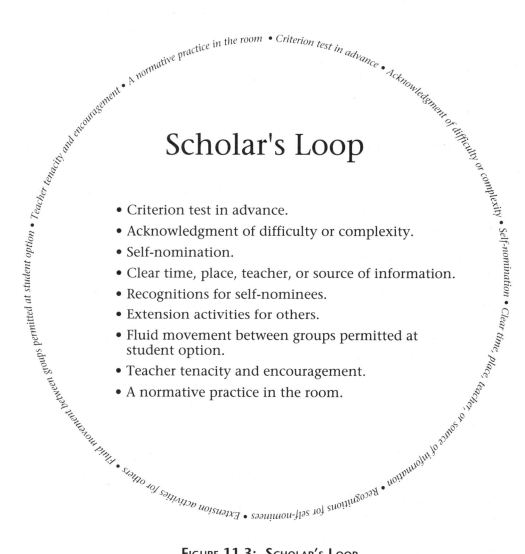

Scholar's Loop

- Criterion test in advance.
- Acknowledgment of difficulty or complexity.
- Self-nomination.
- Clear time, place, teacher, or source of information.
- Recognitions for self-nominees.
- Extension activities for others.
- Fluid movement between groups permitted at student option.
- Teacher tenacity and encouragement.
- A normative practice in the room.

FIGURE 11.3: SCHOLAR'S LOOP
The key elements of the loop are teacher tenacity and the confidence that students who stick with it are successful.

Grouping

The grouping of students for instruction is an arena that *can* send powerful messages about belief in students' capacity—but it need not. It is our belief that the grouping of students is not nearly so important as the standards students are pressed to reach once they are in a group, the flexibility of entry and exit from the group, the quality of instruction, the tenacity of the teacher and his or her expressed belief in the students' capacity to learn, and the understanding the students themselves have of why they are in a particular group.

Many years ago, one of the trainers in our group at Research for Better Teaching was tracked with the lowest-performing eighth graders in his junior high school. This was true tracking in that the students stayed together for all their subjects and were put together on the criterion of prior academic performance—the classic low track. This placement might have condemned him to low performance and low expectations for the rest of his school career, but it didn't. The difference was that his teachers started the year saying to his whole group: "You've fooled people long enough. We know you have good brains and can do well in school. And we believe it's too important for your future to continue to allow you to do so poorly. So this year you're going to work as you never worked before, and learn more and do better than you ever have before."

The students' pace was accelerated, and the assignments and demands escalated significantly, as was the intensity of the instruction they received. By the end of the year most of them had mastered two year's worth of academic content.

This practice of raising standards and expectations for low-performing students and accelerating instruction has been called "academic redshirting" and has reappeared in the philosophy of Henry Levin's "accelerated schools" (Hopfenberg et al. 1993). The reason we cite this practice is to put forth a salient example of the preeminence of practices, attitudes, and beliefs of teachers and students within groups over the fact of grouping itself, no matter what the criterion is for forming the group.

Well-documented examinations of tracking in the United States (Oakes 1985) show conclusively that low-track students are systematically disadvantaged by low expectations, less opportunity to learn, less interesting material, and less interesting teaching. The studies show further that children of color,

> *Raising standards and expectations for low-performing students has been called "academic redshirting."*

especially in urban areas, are particularly disadvantaged. Yet the inferred recommendation to eliminate tracking and do heterogeneous grouping in secondary schools appears to help matters little. No wonder! Changing the structure won't help without changing the teaching and the beliefs and attitudes of teachers and students as well. (The one exception to this generalization may be the practice of summarily eliminating the lowest track in multitrack schools, and just applying the standards and expectations of the next higher track to the lower-track students who are incorporated into the next track up.)

The research on heterogeneous grouping, synthesized from a number of original studies as well as the two best research syntheses we could find (Slavin 1988 and Gamoran 1992), finds that the overall average achievement of students in tracked and untracked schools is about the same and is called "productivity" in the literature. Tracked schools are not any more "productive" than untracked schools—or vice versa. But tracked schools produce a bigger spread of student achievement than untracked schools. The highest-performing students do better in some tracked schools, probably because they are offered accelerated curricula (and boosted by the confidence of adults who expect them to do well). The low-track students do much worse in tracked schools than the lowest-performing students in untracked schools. On the surface this seems to imply that untracking is good for low-performing students, but cheats the most capable high-performing students of reaching their full potential.

Yet we know from individual studies that low-performing students in tracked schools can do well if grouped and given accelerated programs with high expectations for their success. And we also know that the most capable students in untracked settings can be suitably challenged if their teachers diversify instruction.

The inferences seem clear:

- Eliminate the bottom tracks where multiple tracking is present.

- Help all teachers to internalize the beliefs and behaviors in this chapter for communicating high positive expectations to all students.

- Help teachers diversify their teaching repertoires so that top tracks can be collapsed and include a wider range of students without denying the highest-performing individuals their chance to be fully challenged.

Now let's look at the data from the elementary studies. Tracking in elementary schools doesn't seem to affect the achievement of either the high- or low- performing students much. Slavin (1992) argues that the reason for this low effect is that elementary tracking probably does not reduce real heterogeneity very much. Thus the elementary tracks are still quite heterogeneous. Many authors speculate, though, that the damage to self-esteem and motivation that befalls elementary children labeled as "low track" is deep and permanent and shows up later in secondary school performance. Therefore tracking children in elementary schools seems all loss, no gain. The one exception is that certain studies show "gifted" students may be advantaged by homogeneous grouping in the elementary school. Their needs, however, can be met by differentiated instruction in the regular classroom by teachers who have appropriate repertoires.

"Tracking" and "between-class grouping" both mean that groups of students are sorted by ability or prior performance. Tracking tends to mean students are sorted by general ability and grouped together for all their courses in secondary schools. In less rigid school structures, students can take high-track courses in some subjects and lower-track courses in other subjects. "Between-class grouping" is a term most often used in reference to elementary schools and means students are assigned to grade-level classes by ability.

Within-class grouping means grouping students temporarily for instruction in some skill, concept, or operation where they all need exactly that instruction; they are homogeneous in their readiness for and need of what the group is going to work on. The research on this kind of temporary grouping is strongly positive when the following four conditions are present:

1. The students are heterogeneously grouped most of the day.

2. The grouping truly reduces heterogeneity for a specific skill being taught.

3. Grouping is flexible.

4. Teachers adapt the pace and level of instruction to the readiness and learning rates of the students.

The Joplin plan, though rarely implemented, has particularly strong positive findings in numerous studies. This plan is an elementary grouping model where students regroup throughout the whole school for periods to receive instruction with mates who need similar instruction, regardless of class or grade. Since strong positive research findings have never led to wide adoption of proven practices, this story should not be a surprise. But it can be inferred that to implement a Joplin plan requires a high level of organization, leadership, and teacher communication, conditions absent in far too many schools.

What implications can we draw from the research on grouping? First, we should do within-class grouping from time to time, even in high school classes, for instruction in specific items where ad hoc groups need more instruction or more practice, as long as we follow the four caveats in the previous section. In order to do this within-class grouping, we need to have activities prepared for the other students that are worthwhile, be able to manage student engagement, and give feedback on progress to those not in the instructional group. Thus the teacher must bring to bear well-developed repertoires of management skills in Space, Time, Routines, and Momentum and of planning skills to include selection of Objectives, Learning Experiences, and Assessment. (Ninety-minute periods or some other configuration of extended class periods prove especially useful because they give the flexibility to do small group instruction within classes and still have time for whole group activities and discussions.) The bottom line seems to be that good instruction for a wide range of students may require that teachers have the capacity to do small group instruction, and good small group instruction requires well-developed repertoires on a wide range of parameters in this book.

Second, the greatest danger of tracking or of grouping of any kind is that students get dull, skill-drill oriented, remedial, dumb-downed instruction. The cost is not only their self-esteem but also their interest and motivation. Low-skill, low-performing students, whether grouped together for instruction or not, must still be involved in learning experiences about interesting or relevant topics. Above all, these students must be involved with higher-level thinking and discussions. Instead they often get passive worksheet activities that call for little more than identification and recall.

The teaching approaches that make interesting discussions possible with low-skill readers in a ninth-grade social studies class involve explicitly teaching these students reading strategies (like reciprocal teaching, a powerful interactive reading strategy, developed by Palinscar and Brown 1984) and study skills like notetaking and note studying within the regular curriculum. And often it also means teaching them discussion skills and social skills as well. We systematically build into students the capacity to use the good brains they have to interact successfully with higher-level thinking. Doing this teaching requires for many secondary teachers a reconceptualization of their role as teachers. It means one isn't a teacher of a subject and a content specialist only; it means one is a teacher of students, and that role includes teaching students to use strategies and skills for more effective learning. Teachers need to draw on all the other material in this book on learning style, variety in learning experiences, clarity devices, principles of learning and so forth to search for strategies and skills to teach to students explicitly so as to magnify their school competence as effective learners.

Giving and Negotiating Tasks andAssignments

When we give students assignments we often convey other messages as well: whether we think the task is hard or easy, whether we think they'll struggle as individuals, whether we believe they'll succeed, whether we think their success will depend on ability, effort, or luck.

In Chapter 8 on Clarity, we discussed other aspects of giving assignments and tasks: whether the students really knew what to do (the directions); whether they understood why they were doing the assignment—or what connection it had to a particular learning objective. But in this section we are tackling the confidence messages students get through the way we give assignments.

A teacher says to her sixth graders: "This weekend your assignment is to read the last three chapters of *Tituba* and be prepared to give the factors that you think contributed to a climate in Salem for the witch hysteria." So far that's pretty straightforward. The students may have some confusions about what "climate" or maybe even "factors"means in this context, but let's suppose the students know what's expected. No messages have been sent to individuals yet. How do they get communicated?

As the students go out the door, Ms. Hunt stops several of them for a private word.

- "Kaneisha, you should do really well on this. You've been reading carefully and taking good notes on each of the last two assignments. I think you're ready to put it all together."
- "John, how much time are you going to put in on this tonight?"
- "Marie, you're taking your book home, aren't you? [Marie smiles and says, "Sure."] Un huh. Right!" [Ms. Hunt purses her lips.]
- "Do the best you can, George. At least read all three chapters."

Ms. Hunt has sent Kaneisha a high, positive-expectation message. She thinks Kaneisha is ready for a good performance that puts it all together.

It's hard to tell what message she has sent to John. If John is a slacker and she has communicated before that she thinks he is, then John may interpret her question to mean, "I don't think you're going to really do this, John." And John may be inclined to conform with that preconception. On the other hand, maybe she has had a series of conferences with John and done goal setting with him around planning his time use for homework. Perhaps she is reminding him of the agreements he made and getting him to commit to a real number of minutes right now that she'll hold him accountable for the next day. Then the message is quite different from the "slacker" inference.

It sounds as if Ms. Hunt doubts Marie is really going to take her book home. Her "Uh huh. Right!" may give Marie license to skip the work—because her teacher expects her to.

George is getting a low-expectation message. The teacher will be content if he at least plows his way through the words in the book but doesn't expect him to be able to think through the question. At best, George will plow but not likely think. The expectation is no higher than getting through the three chapters. The expectation is actually less, since the teacher has said, "At least try," which implies that he won't be able to do it but that "trying" a little is expected.)

The examples illustrate how the choice of words combined with body language communicates inner beliefs about what students can do and about what they will do on a given assignment. In addition to individual comments at the door and elsewhere, teachers sometimes communicate to a whole class at once about an assignment. When Ms. Hunt said, "Now this will be hard; it requires thinking back to all the other chapters we read too. But I know you can do it if you take your time and use your notes from our previous discussions," she is sending a high, positive-expectation message to the whole class at once. Acknowledging the difficulty of the task validates students' exerting effort. It's not supposed to be easy. (Calling a task easy is a no-win message. If it turns out to be easy, the student has no sense of accomplishment. Anyone could have done it. If children struggle and it was supposed to be easy, they may conclude they are stupid or not good enough at it; otherwise it would be easy.)

In addition to verbal messages to individuals and whole class groups, there are whole class messages that may be embedded in written directions sheets to students about assignments: "This problem set is important and is a good chance to raise your grade. Use this opportunity well."

We hope readers will listen to themselves during these daily and repeated moments when we actually communicate assignments and tasks to students—and especially attend to the side comments we make to individuals right after giving the task and the directions. In addition we urge readers to seize these opportunities to send deliberately positive and encouraging messages to individuals who may be low-performing, low-motivation, and low-confidence. "Charlene, this is a good one for you to show your stuff on. Now come on, dig in tonight. You've got a great brain and I want to see you use it as a leader in tomorrow's discussion!"

Summary

An observer (or a teacher monitoring himself or herself) could adopt either of the two approaches described in this parameter for profiling a teacher's behavior: (1) examine the explicit nature of a teacher's communication of expectations in terms of its being direct, specific, repeated, positive, and tenacious for different tasks in different cases—and then look at the standards implicit in those expectations; or (2) examine the implicit nature of a teacher's communication of expectations in terms of the ten arenas as indicators of class prejudice between the "brights" and the "slows." Certainly it is well worth looking carefully at ourselves to be sure we're not falling into the bright-slow stereotype trap.

The important implication is that these patterns of behavior on the Expectations parameter should be consistent with the belief that all students can learn rigorous academic material at high standards. What we say explicitly regarding "all students can learn" should be congruent with what we do. If we seek to overcome the constricting grip of bright-slow class prejudice, which researchers are telling us is an unfair restriction on the equality of educational opportunity offered to students, then we will not do the unholy thirteen Cooper has collected and we will be explicit with expectations in each of the arenas and attempt to press all students toward excellence. And we will give students a lot of opportunities to exceed our expectations.

Having completed three strife-torn decades of desegregation in schools with a moderate degree of success we are faced nonetheless with dramatic underachievement among blacks, Hispanics, and other people of color in our society. Communicating positive expectations and dissolving our stereotypes—perhaps even *their* stereotypes of themselves (Howard and Hammond 1985)—is especially important. The roots of what people will do are planted firmly in their beliefs about what they can do. What are we as educators doing to help students, especially students of color, become believers in themselves as achievers? Avoiding the Pygmalion behaviors is a good start, but what's next?

A steady stream of authors and researchers are telling us that new curricula and new tougher standards are not enough. "First, without a doubt, the indispensable characteristic of successful teachers in low-income-area schools is a positive attitude. It is not enough for a teacher to use the right words. The critical question is, what implicit and explicit messages are students getting from the teacher about their ability to learn?" (Frick 1987).

Young children believe success comes from effort; in fact, effort and ability are synonymous to them (Nicholls 1978). But as they get older, children start attributing academic success more and more to native ability rather than effort. This creates a bind, because if one is not doing well, the only possible conclusion is that one must be dumb. Thus, many low-performing students opt out of school and quit trying by middle school because it's better to be considered lazy than dumb. The more we can press for and attribute success to ability and effort as students go through school (rather than luck or easy work), the better our success will be with students of color—in fact, with all students. "If you have a C average or below, you should spend three hours studying for this test" means, "That's what it will take to get an A, and you can do it."

Jeff Howard[1] has made the case repeatedly (Howard 1985, 1990, 1995) that the deeply ingrained American paradigm of "intelligence → achievement" is both wrong and simultaneously the governing principle behind the design of our schools. No less than Lauren Resnick, who is guiding the nationwide assessment project to create national standards, agrees:

> What is the relationship between aptitude and effort? Early in this century we built an education system around the assumption that aptitude is paramount in learning and that it is largely hereditary. The system was oriented toward selection, distinguishing the naturally able from the less able and providing students with programs thought suitable to their talents. In other periods, most notably during the Great Society reforms, we worked on the compensatory principle, arguing that special effort, by an individual or an institution, could make up for low aptitude. The third possibility—that effort actually *creates* ability, that people can become smart by working hard at the right kinds of learning tasks—has never been taken seriously in America or indeed in any European society, although it is the guiding assumption of education in societies with a Confucian tradition.[2]

[1] We are indebted to Jeff Howard of the Efficacy Institute, Lexington, Massachusetts for his pioneering work in emphasizing the primacy of effort in determining student achievement. His ideas are prominent in the next two pages.

[2] An exception to this generalization may be Alfred Binet, the inventor in 1908 of the first cognitively based IQ test, who said, "Intelligence is susceptible to development; with practice and training and especially with appropriate methods of teaching we can augment a child's attention, his memory, his judgment—helping him literally to become more intelligent than he was before." Intelligence was not a fixed amount, or a constant, or some Platonic, bounded essence. Intelligence was "educable." He advocated a "mental orthopedics" that "teaches children to observe better, to listen better, to retain and to judge better; they gain self-confidence, emulation, perseverance, the desire to succeed and all the excellent feelings that accompany action; they should especially be taught to will with more intensity; to will, this is indeed the key to all education."

[In such an ability-bound view] students do not try to break through the barrier of low expectations because they, like their teachers and parents, accept the judgment that aptitude matters most and that they do not have the right kinds of aptitude. Not surprisingly, their performance remains low. Children who have not been taught a demanding, challenging, *thinking curriculum* do not do well on tests of reasoning or problem solving, confirming our original suspicions that they did not have the talent for that kind of thinking. The system is a self-sustaining one in which hidden assumptions are continually reinforced by the inevitable results of practices that are based on those assumptions.

It is not necessary to continue this way. Aptitude is not the only possible basis for organizing schools. Educational institutions could be built around the alternative assumption that effort actually *creates* ability. Our education system could be designed primarily to foster effort. (Resnick 1995)

The implication of the work of the authors cited is that it is a teacher's belief, deep within, that almost all students really *can do* rigorous academic work at high standards that is fundamental to communicating high positive-expectation messages to all students. Different though we may be in our genetic endowment, if we could all do the incredibly complicated analytical task of learning to speak by age three, then we all have at least enough intelligence to do academic material well—that is, if we exert enough effective effort. The key word here is *effective*. Just exerting more effort—harder or longer—is no guarantee of success for a struggling student.

> ## *Effort actually creates ability.*

This conviction about student capacity makes it incumbent on teachers to teach students how to exert effective effort; many don't come already knowing how to do so. That adds a new dimension to the role of teaching. Effective effort has four attributes:

1. Time.

   Students put in enough minutes and hours to get the job done. Although this is far from sufficient to accomplish difficult academic tasks, it is a sine qua non. And it is true that some students truly don't realize that several hours of outlining, drafting, and editing may be required to make an essay meet a high standard. As teachers it is worth discussing with students and coming to agreements about how much time they should expect to put in on academic assignments to meet high standards.

2. Focus.

   Work time should be efficient and low in distraction. Some students don't find music distracting while they work, even loud music. There is plenty of latitude for individual style in defining focus. But talking to friends about the upcoming weekend or watching TV while doing academic work is not compatible with the concept of focus.

3. Resourcefulness.

   Students are willing to reach beyond themselves for help and know how to do so and where to go. Sources of help may be other people (study buddies, homework help centers, relatives) or other sources (reference books, on-line services, reference librarians). Preparing students to be resourceful means teaching them directly what such resources are and how to use them. In a fourth-grade class one of us visited, groups of children were giving reports on Native American tribes. It could have been any fourth grade in America—models of hogans, teepees, longhouses—except for one thing. Every group started its report with a child's recounting where they had gotten their information, what the obstacles were, and how they had overcome them. This was a teacher who had taught the students how to use outside help to get information, and who expected them to do so at every opportunity.

4. Strategies

   Students know and use appropriate strategies to deal with academic tasks. A voluminous literature confirms that students do significantly better in academic work when their teachers explicitly teach them strategies for improving reading comprehension, organizing and revising writing, and reviewing, remembering, and summarizing. (Paris, Wasik, and Turner 1991; Pressley, Borkowski, and Schneider 1987). Parallel literature is available for teaching strategies in math. Readers may be familiar with the names of some of these strategies like reciprocal teaching, SQ3-R, and mnemonic keyword technique.

All teachers, regardless of content area or specialty, can improve students' performance by broadening the concept of the teaching role. We must all be teachers of metacognitive strategies for extracting meaning from text and for organizing and representing thoughts well in writing. This includes math, science, and foreign language teachers as well as health, physical education, music, and art teachers. We must all be teachers of reading and writing, because those are proxies for being able to study and think well.

This point of view has a long history of advocacy, and even a name of its own—Reading and Writing in the Content Areas—and a literature that includes textbooks for teachers (Vacca and Vacca 1989). This position now receives added impetutus from the research in this chapter. If we are to build students' confidence in the value of effective effort and change their attributions about innate intelligence, then we must be prepared to teach them the strategies they need.

A Few Final Thoughts

Maybe every school needs a person in charge of "exceeding expectations,"

> *Maybe every school needs a person in charge of "exceeding expectations."*

someone who shakes up teachers, who goes around periodically reminding them to reexamine what they are expecting and demanding of students in the way of performance. Perhaps that will be one effect of this chapter on readers. In the end, the hope and the promise of this parameter is that it will give better performance from students and give them fairer and more equal treatment from us.

The Expectations parameter is an example of the way in which teaching is more a calling than a job. If successful teaching involves getting students to be believers in themselves, then that is a way in which this business resembles the clergy more than a craft. ❧

Checking on Expectations

1. Do I know clearly and with conviction what my expectations are?

   Have I communicated them clearly to the students in ways that manifest these characteristics?

   - direct
   - specific
   - repeated
   - positive expectancy
   - modeled
   - tenacious
   - prompt feedback on work
   - detailed feedback on work
   - personal contact for feedback
   - no excuses
   - recognition of superior performance
   - logical consequences for poor performance

2. Do I communicate these general messages to all students:

   "THIS IS IMPORTANT."

   "YOU CAN DO IT."

   "I WON'T GIVE UP ON YOU."

3. Are my overall standards appropriate?

   - None.
   - Few consistent.
   - Too low.
   - Too high.
   - Average.
   - Inspirational-vague.
   - High but reasonable.

4. How do I match my expectations to different students?

- ◗ No discrimination.
- ◗ Differential and accepting.
- ◗ Differential and provisioning.
- ◗ Working for excellence with allowances.

5. Pygmalion Effects. Do I do any of the following:

Smile and nod more toward "highs"?

Lean more toward "brights"?

Look "brights" more in the eyes?

Give "slows" fewer opportunities to learn new material?

Give "highs" more clues when they fail to get an answer (more repetition and more rephrasing)?

Pay closer attention to responses of "gifted"?

Allow "brights" longer to respond?

Have more frequent academic contact with "highs"?

Give "highs" more praise per correct response?

Give "lows" more criticism per incorrect response?

Do I do any of the above more with girls than with boys, or vice versa?

Expectations Quiz

Our repertoires on Expectations stem from our beliefs about our roles as teachers and our beliefs about students' capacity. The purpose of this quiz is to check for understanding of the relation between beliefs and the implied practices that would proceed from those beliefs.

Communicating Expectations

1. Give an example of an expectation in each of the following four areas:

   Quality and quantity of work

   Study habits and work procedures

   Business and housekeeping routines

   Interpersonal behavior

2. What are the consequences of being clear about expectations in some of the four categories above but not in others? Create examples, and be specific.

3. Instead of saying, "Your editing needs to improve," I might communicate my expectations specifically by saying….

4. Give an example of what it means to communicate expectations in ways that are repeated.

5. Teachers can explicitly communicate positive expectancy that a student "can do it." Use a quotation to show what that might sound like in some real context.

6. What are the two meanings of the word "modeled" in expectations?

7. Describe at least five different ways tenacity might show up in teacher behavior.

8. Describe the factors to weigh when deciding how tenacious to be with a student.

9. A student has a legitimate reason for not handing in a paper on time. How will you handle this and still be consistent with the principle of "no excuses"?

10. Give two examples of giving feedback that recognizes superior performance.

11. Give two good examples of logical consequences for poor performance.

Attribution Theory

Attribution theory is concerned with our explanations to ourselves of our successes and our failures. One's perceptions of the reasons behind one's performance are critical to one's self-concept, expectations for future performance, feelings of power and subsequent motivation. The following questions review Attribution Theory.

1. Young children attribute their degree of success to _____ and _____.

2. Older children and adults tend to attribute their degree of success to _____.

3. The reason a teacher would be loathe to say, "Don't worry, this is an easy test," is _____.

4. The reason teachers should be careful about saying, "Good luck on this assignment," is _____.

5. The reason we might avoid saying, "You guys are really smart," after students do well is: _____.

6. The reason we would not tell a student who was stymied to just "work harder," is _____.

7. If a student says she got a good grade on the test because it was easy, to initiate attribution retraining we might say _____ _____.

Ten Arenas: Communicating the Three Key Expectations Messages

1. What guidelines would one use for calling on students to send the three messages to all pupils?

2. Any response from the repertoire in Figure 11.1 can be an appropriate response to a student answer, and any of them can be inappropriate. Explain how praise can be inappropriate and how criticism can be appropriate.

3. If we want to send the three messages, how do we deal with withdrawn and sometimes silent students who don't answer when we call on them in class? What is this approach intending to do?

4. When students ask for help, what principles should guide our language choices?

5. Give an example of praise that includes the attributes of being specific, contingent and genuine, and appropriate.

6. Give an example of praise that attributes success to effort and ability together.

7. Why does averaging tests with retakes send a negative expectation message?

8. What are the key elements of a successful reteaching loop?

8. Give an example of an assignment you might communicate verbally in such a way as to acknowledge its difficulty but signal confidence in students' capacity.

9. Teachers almost invariably send expectations when they identify student error and work with students to correct errors. Write a dialogue with a student who has made errors in which the teacher does some attribution retraining, that is, works to effect the student's belief that effective effort is the main variable in success.

Global Belief Systems About "My Role as a Teacher."

The following questions refer to the four teacher types profiled in Figure **11.2.**

1. How are special education or low-performing students treated in the class of a teacher with a type 1 belief system and a type 4 belief system?

2. What does it take to get an A in the class of a teacher of:

   Type 1:

   Type 2:

   Type 3:

   Type 4:

3. Give several examples of what can happen to a teacher with a type 4 belief system who loses perspective.

4. There are many similarities between a type 3 and a type 4 belief system. What are the differences?

5. Which of the four belief types is most likely to lead to discipline problems, and why?

6. Which type tends to burn out first, and why?

7. What is the difference between teachers with a type 2 belief system and teachers with a type 4 belief system?

8. Why is it important to study these four types of belief systems?

9. What teaching practices would be most called for from a high school teacher implementing a type 4 belief system?

Source Materials on Expectations

Bennett, N. "Research on Teaching: A Dream, a Belief and a Model." *Journal of Education* 160 (August 1978): 5–37.

Blank, Marion. *Teaching Learning in the Preschool: A Dialogue Approach.* Columbus, Ohio: Merrill, 1973. In Good, Thomas L., and Jere E. Brophy. *Looking in Classrooms.* 2d ed. New York: Harper & Row, 1978, p. 255.

Brophy, Jere. "Teacher Praise: A Functional Analysis." *Review of Education Research* 51 (Spring 1981): 5–32.

Brookover, W. B., J. Schweitzy, J. Schneider, C. Beady, P. Flood., and J. Wisenbaker. "Elementary School Social Climate and School Advancement." *AERA Journal* 15 (Spring 1978): 301–318.

Cooper, H. M. "Pygmalion Grows Up: A Model for Teacher Expectations, Communication and Performance Influence." *Review of Educational Research* 49 (Summer 1979): 389–410.

Costa, Arthur L. *Developing Minds.* Alexandria, Va.: Association for Supervision and Curriculum Development, 1985.

Covington, M. V. "The Self-Worth Theory of Achievement Motivation: Findings and Implications." *Elementary School Journal* 85 (September 1984): 5–20.

Cremin, Lawrence A. *The Transformation of the School.* New York: Vintage Books, 1964.

Dembo, M. H., and S. Gibson. "Teachers' Sense of Efficacy: An Important Factor in School Improvement." *Elementary School Journal* 86 (November 1985): 173–184.

Dunkin, Michael J., and Bruce J. Biddle. *The Study of Teaching.* New York: Holt, Rinehart and Winston, 1974.

Dweck, C. S. "The Role of Expectations and Attributions in the Alleviation of Learned Helplessness." *Journal of Personality and Social Psychology* 31 (1975): 674–685.

———. "Self-Theories and Goals: Their Role in Motivation, Personality, and Development." In R. Dienstlier (ed.), *Nebraska Symposium on Motivation.* Lincoln: University of Nebraska Press, 1991.

Fordham, Signithia, and John U. Ogbu. "Black Students' School Success: Coping with the 'Burden of 'Acting White.'" *The Urban Review* 18 (1986): 176–206.

Frick, R. "Academic Redshirting Two Years Later: The Lessons Learned." *Education Week,* January 28, 1987, p. 20.

Gamoran, Adam, "Is Ability Grouping Equitable?" *Educational Leadership* 50 (October 1992): 11–17.

Good, T. "Classroom Expectations in Pupil-Teacher Interactions." In *The Social Psychology of School Learning.* New York: Academic Press, 1980.

Good, Thomas L., and Jere E. Brophy. *Looking in Classrooms*. 2d ed. New York: Harper & Row, 1978.

Graham, S. "Teacher Feelings and Student Thoughts: An Attributional Approach to Affect in the Classroom." *Elementary School Journal* 85 (1985): 91–104.

Hentoff, N. "Teachers: Accomplices in Failure." *Learning Magazine* (July–August 1980): 68–74.

Hopfenberg, Wendy S., et al. *The Accelerated Schools Resource Guide*. San Francisco: Jossey-Bass, 1993.

Howard, J. *The Social Construction of Intelligence*. Lexington, Mass.: Efficacy Institute, 1990.

———. "You Can't Get There from Here: The Need for a New Logic in Education Reform." *Daedelus* (Fall 1995).

Howard, J., and R. Hammond. "Rumors of Inferiority." *New Republic,* September 9, 1985, pp. 17–21.

Hunter, Madeline. "Improving the Quality of Instruction." Presentation at Association for Supervision and Curriculum Development Conference, 1977.

Hunter, Madeline. *Mastery Teaching*. El Segundo, Calif.: TIP Publications, 1982.

Means, V., J. W. Moore, E. Gagne, and W. E. Hauck. "The Interactive Effects of Consonant and Dissonant Teacher Expectancy and Feedback Communication on Student Performance in a Natural School Setting." *AERA Journal* 16 (Fall 1979): 367–374.

Nicholls, J. G. "The Development of the Concepts of Effort and Ability, Perception of Academic Attainment, and the Understanding That Difficult Tasks Require More Ability." *Child Development* 49 (1978): 800–814.

Nicholls, J. G. and J. T. Burton. "Motivation and Equality." *Elementary School Journal* 82 (March 1982): 367–378.

Oakes, Jeannie. *Keeping Track: How Schools Structure Inequality*. New Haven: Yale University Press, 1985.

Palincsar, A. S., and A. L. Brown. "Reciprocal Teaching of Comprehension-Fostering and Comprehension-Monitoring Activities." *Cognition and Instruction* 1 (1984): 117–175.

Paris, S., B. Wasik, and J. Turner. "The Development of Strategic Readers." In R. Barr, M. Kamil, P. Modenthal, and P. D. Pearson (eds.), *Handbook of Reading Research,* 2: 609–640. New York: Longman, 1991.

Pressley, M., J. Borkowski, and W. Schneider. "Cognitive Strategies: Good Strategy Users Coordinate Metacognition and Knowledge." In R. Vasta and G. Whitehurst (eds.), *Annals of Child Development*, 5: 89–129. New York: JAI, 1987.

Resnick, L. "From Aptitude to Effort: A New Foundation for Our Schools." *Daedelus* (Fall 1995).

Rist, R. C. "Student Social Class and Teacher Expectations: A Self-Fulfilling Prophecy in Ghetto Education." *Harvard Educational Review* 40 (August 1970): 411–451.

Rosenholtz, S. J., and C. Simpson. "The Formation of Ability Conceptions: Developmental Trend of Social Construction." *Review of Educational Research* 54 (Spring 1984): 31–63.

Rosenthal, R., and L. Jacobson. *Pygmalion in the Classroom*. New York: Holt, Rinehart and Winston, 1968.

Slavin, Robert. "Synthesis of Research on Grouping in Elementary and Secondary Schools." *Educational Leadership* 46 (September 1988): 67–77.

Tanner, Laurel N. *Classroom Discipline for Effective Teaching and Learning*. New York: Holt, Rinehart and Winston, 1978.

Vacca, Richard T., and Joanne L. Vacca. *Content Area Reading*. 3d ed. Glenview, Ill.: Scott Foresman: 1989.

Van Houton, R. *Learning Through Feedback*. New York: Human Services Press, 1980.

Weiner, B. *Achievement Motivation and Attribution Theory*. Morristown, N. J.: General Learning Press, 1974.

Weiner, B. *Theories of Motivation: From Mechanism to Cognition*. Chicago: Markham, 1972.

12

Personal Relationship Building

How do I build good personal relationships with students?

Ways of Relating
Eight Key Teacher Traits

The parameter of Personal Relationship Building concerns the relationships that teachers forge between themselves and their students and the elements that go into making those relationships productive. Teachers have many good reasons for building relationships with students, and one of them is good classroom management. Students who like and respect their teachers are less likely to buck the program, less likely to be discipline problems, more likely to accept instruction and focusing moves. Students who dislike or have affectively neutral relationships with their teachers are less inhibited from misbehavior and more likely to resist instructional focusing moves. But there are other reasons teachers build relationships, such as making students feel as if they are worthwhile people, making the human environment of the classroom safe, pleasant, and healthy, and making teaching fun. All teachers build relationships of one sort or another with their students, and those relationships are an important variable in understanding what goes on in the complex society of a classroom and how students perform within it.

There are two ways to look qualitatively at the Personal Relationship Building that goes on between teachers and students: the variety of ways teachers have of contacting students' personal worlds and the traits of teachers that seem to engender affection and regard in a relationship.

Ways of Relating

In order to relate to you as a person, I have to attend to you, focusing on you as an individual. If I am teaching math, I may be focusing on the math and not on you, but if I am able also to focus on you, then I am alert to your responses and make moves to enable you, particularly you, to assimilate the concepts. I am then relating to you personally and in a particular way: as an information processor. If I relate to you as a feeling being with hopes, fears, dreams, and goals, then I am attending to those aspects of you, listening for cues to those states, thinking about you and your interior states—yet another way of relating to people at a personal, one-to-one level. If I play sports with you, I interact with you as a teammate or a competitor and relate to you around the game. Maybe I talk to you about current events, do craft projects with you, help you plan your work, talk over interesting personal experiences at home or outside school that are important to you. There are many possible ways in which I can relate to you.

There are also many possible ways in which teachers may relate to students: as information processors, as feeling beings, over current events, over shared interests in some activity or topic, and so on. Further, teachers may relate in different ways to different students, and in different ways at different times to any one student. It is useful to examine our own repertoires here and look for opportunities to match how we relate to the needs of students and the circumstances of classrooms. In this area of the Personal Relationship Building parameter, we can distinguish four levels of performance a teacher may exhibit:

1. *Does not relate to students as individuals at all.*
2. *Relates to students as individuals primarily in one way* (e.g., as information processors, around sports, or chats during breaks).
3. *Relates to students in a variety of ways.*
4. *Matches the way of relating to the student.*

The fourth level describes teachers who seek points of contact with students as individuals beyond what may be obvious or easy. They may go out of their way to identify, or create, opportunities or events during or outside the school day to contact particular students. Some teachers arrange conferences with each student each month (say, one a day). Others occasionally have lunch with individual students back in the classroom. Perhaps, for example, the first way to build a relationship with Chris will be around the piano where the teacher can play a duet with him, or just play a song he may want to learn.

Clearly the better a teacher can match ways of relating to individual students and to particular circumstances, the stronger and more productive relationships will be with all students.

Eight Key Teacher Traits

Considering teacher characteristics or traits brings in a viewpoint generally foreign to our work and obsolete in the field of studies on teaching. However, we believe that it is necessary to highlight certain classes of teacher behavior that are repeatedly mentioned as important by students in interview studies when they are asked about their teachers (Johnson 1976). The traits and behaviors that seem most important are fairness, appearance, humor, courtesy, respect, realness, reestablishing contact, and active listening. It is reasonable to connect these traits with Personal Relationship Building because they foster more personal regard for a teacher, which can be a basis of good personal relationships.

Fairness *— Most inept trait*

This seems to be the sine qua non for personal regard. Unless students perceive teachers as being fair in making decisions that bear on them (e.g., making assignments, arbitrating disputes, giving help, choosing teams) they cannot begin to like them.

Appearance

Appearance is mentioned more than one might have expected when students describe teachers for whom they have regard. Perhaps students take good grooming and neat, clean clothes as signs of respect or regard from the teacher—that the adult considers them important enough to look good for them.

Humor

William Glasser, creator of "Reality Therapy," says humor is a form of caring. Teachers need not be joke tellers, but those who respond openly to humorous moments or who can kid with students seem to strike particularly responsive chords.

Courtesy

A courteous move, even though it might be quite formal and almost ritualistic, is still a direct gesture in recognition of, and often in behalf of, an individual. As such, it is a personal gesture, however remote, and connected with this parameter of Personal Relationship Building. Students tend to respond to courtesy in kind. No case needs to be made for courtesy as a desirable teacher behavior. It is included here as a trait related to Personal Relationship Building because students mention it and because it seems reasonable as a basis for relationships in the same way fairness is: a sine qua non for personal regard. A lack of courtesy blocks relationships and creates resentment. It would seem that an acceptable minimum of courteous consideration would be discernible in a yes-no sense. Discriminations beyond that would be very difficult.

Respect

Teachers show respect to students as people in many ways (Moustakas 1966). They may honor student interests by making a place in the day for students to pursue them or attempt to integrate these interests into the meeting of standard curriculum objectives through learning activities. They may show respect for student ideas by allowing or encouraging students to express them without criticism (though not necessarily without correction). They show respect for students by correcting errors without using putdowns, or without making students feel dumb or as if they've walked into an ambush (Randolf and Howe 1966), or they may join corrective feedback with recognition of strengths. They may show they value students' products by treating them with care, providing for their display, and giving feedback that shows the teacher has truly examined the product, whether the feedback is positive or corrective (for instance, saying, "You really captured all the tiny parts of the spider in your drawing," rather than just saying, "Beautiful" or "Good work").

We don't argue that praise such as "good work" or "beautiful" is bad or meaningless, or even necessarily less good in certain circumstances than praise that specifies the attributes that are praiseworthy (Ginott 1965). It's just that to tie feedback to respect rather than just praise, the statement must show some real attention to the product. Conceivably, the teacher could show this attention and respect for the student's product nonverbally by looking long and carefully at the piece, and then perhaps sincerely saying, "Good work, Julia."

Realness

Authority acts as a screen that obscures seeing the "boss" as a person—that is, as a thinking, feeling being with a life history of experience. Instead, we tend to see the boss as the boss, the teacher as the teacher—the authority role figure. Young children who address their teacher as "teacher" rather than by name are clearly in this mode. Children begin to see their teacher as real, as a person, only if the teacher lets them.

There are behaviors by which teachers reveal aspects of themselves that allow this image of authority figure to be tempered by images of teacher-as-real-person. Teachers share anecdotes with students from their own lives, integrating personal experiences into explanations and presentations. "I" messages as described by Thomas Gordon (1974) are direct verbal behaviors by which teachers explicitly state their feelings and the behavior or circumstance made them feel that way. (See Attention chapter.) Effectiveness Training Associates reports numerous cases of children who, when confronted by "I" messages, change disruptive behavior: children who had no idea their behavior was affecting their teacher adversely. When these statements are used, it is sometimes the first time students have been asked to see their teacher as a person with feelings.

Reestablishing Contact

When a teacher strongly reprimands a student (e.g., sends the student out of the room) or shows anger by carrying out some high-voltage disciplinary move ("Stop that right now! You cannot destroy someone else's work. Then if you can't help him rebuild it, this area is closed to you for the day. Goodbye!"), their relationship may be under a cloud of tension (as it should be). After such incidents, the teacher who keeps good relationships looks to interact in a positive, personal way with the student around some other context. This is reestablishing contact: conveying the message that the teacher is not carrying a grudge, that the relationship is still intact. It removes the tension between the teacher and student and gives the student an emotional entry back into the flow of activities. There is no apology in the teacher move or any implied backing down from the firmness of the previous move or from the anger. It's simply a way of saying, "Okay, let's get in touch again"—a return to normalcy.

To observe this type of behavior, one would simply have to see a personal move with a student close on the heels of a discipline or desist incident. We need not guess how far the teacher went out of the way to create the positive interaction; we just have to see the move in reasonable time proximity to the incident.

Active Listening

Reflective listening feeds back to speakers the content of their remarks and thus confirms to them that they have been heard. Active listening adds a feeling component to the feedback, and the listener restates or infers the feeling state of the speaker aloud. For example, an active listener might say, "You're stuck on these problems [content] and getting really frustrated [feeling]." Teachers who use active listening are communicating concern for students' personal feeling states directly. Although it can be used manipulatively and insincerely, it is reasonable to argue that on-target and genuine active listening is a relationship-building behavior. It is the verbal behavioral embodiment of empathy. When combined with accuracy and respect (Egan 1975), active listening makes children feel understood and cared about (Aspy and Roebuck 1977). "She really listens to me" is a common statement students make about teachers they like and respect.

The quality of relationships between teachers and students is a deep and constant backdrop to all that is transpiring in classrooms, and one well worth examining. In analyzing your own teaching behavior (or observing another's teaching) for these traits, bear in mind that the appropriateness of moves from any trait may vary with the form of instruction or learning environment in operation at any given moment. For instance, moves that show respect for students as individuals may not surface when students are in a period of programmed instruction and interacting with the system rather than with the teacher as person. It might take the course of a whole day, or even many days, to see a teacher display the full range of his repertoire for the traits described in this section. Thus, checking on these behaviors requires an extended observation, or perhaps even several repeated observations, in order to see the full range of behavior. ❧

Checking on
Personal Relationship Building

Examine your own teaching, or that of another, and see which of the following apply. For each behavior or trait that you credit, see if you can cite an event or an exchange to back it up. For those you wish to develop, note a time or an opportunity for trying them out. Be as specific as you can.

1. Ways of relating to students: Circle the level of performance.

   no way

       one way

           variety of ways

              matches the way to individuals

2. Traits: Check any that apply.

   ___   fairness

   ___   appearance

   ___   humor

   ___   courtesy

   ___   respect

   ___   realness

   ___   reestablishing contact

   ___   active listening

Personal Relationship Building Quiz

1. Respect and fairness are two of the six traits in personal
    relationship building. Generate a list of events, arenas, or
    situations where students make up their minds about teachers
    regarding fairness and respect.

2. Pick two events, arenas, or situations in respect and two in
    fairness. Give three specific examples in each arena of how a
    teacher might act in order to be perceived by students as having
    respect or being fair.

Source Materials on
Personal Relationship Building

Allender, J. S., M. Seitchik, and D. Goldstein. "Student Involvement and Patterns of Teaching." *Journal of Classroom Interaction* 16 (Summer 1981): 11–20.

Aspy, D., and F. N. Roebuck. *Kids Don't Learn From People They Don't Like.* Amherst, Mass.: Human Resource Development Press, 1977.

Brophy, J. "Teacher Praise: A Functional Analysis." *Review of Educational Research* 51 (Spring 1981): 5–32.

Brown, L., and R. C. Goodall. "Enhancing Group Climate through Systematic Utilization of Feedback." *Journal of Classroom Interaction* 16 (Summer 1981): 21–25.

Egan, G. *The Skilled Helper.* Monterey, Calif.: Brooks/Cole Publishing Co., 1975.

Fraser, B. J., and P. O'Brien. "Student and Teacher Perceptions of the Environment of Elementary School Classrooms." *Elementary School Journal* 85 (May 1985): 567–580.

Ginott, H. G. *Between Parent and Child.* New York: Macmillan, 1965.

Gordon, T. *Teacher Effectiveness Training.* New York: Wyden Press, 1974.

Johnson, M. S. "I Think My Teacher Is." *Learning* (February 1976): 36–38.

Joos, M. *The Five Clocks.* New York: Harcourt, Brace & World, 1967.

Mergendoller, J. R., and M. J. Packer. "Seventh Graders' Conceptions of Teachers: An Interpretive Analysis." *Elementary School Journal* 85 (May 1985): 581–600.

Moustakas, C. *The Authentic Teacher.* Cambridge, Mass.: Howard A. Doyle Publishing Co., 1966.

Randolf, N., and William Howe. *Self Enhancing Education.* Palo Alto, Calif.: Sanford Press, 1966.

Rogers, V. R. "Laughing with Children." *Educational Leadership* (April 1984): 44–50.

13

Classroom Climate

Community and Mutual Support
Risk Taking and Confidence
Influence

The research on classroom climate is thin but clear: thin because the volume of studies is much smaller than in the cognitive areas, clear because the findings are consistent across populations, ages of students, and subjects. Whenever students feel empowerment, acceptance, and safety to take risks and try things that are hard for them, they like school better and learn more (Moos and Moos 1978; Haertel, Walberg, and Haertel 1981; Fraser and Fisher 1983; Fraser 1986, 1989; Nunnery, Butler, and Bhaireddy 1993).

That sounds like common sense, and it is, but the research in this area is approximately where research on clarity was thirty years ago. At that time we knew that teachers who were rated as clear on a Likert scale got better results with students. We did not know, however, what they did in their practice to earn those ratings. We did not have a construct for the elements of clarity and how they were related to one another, an operational model for how they worked in interrelationship, or a sense of whether some of the elements were more important than others. We know a great deal more about clarity now. We can at least profile essential elements and have data to support their individual contribution to successful teaching and learning. The same is not true for classroom climate. Here we are at the Likert scale stage.

Although the tradition of research on classroom climate has roots in the 1920s, Withall (1949) was the first to formulate a definition of the group phenomenon known as social-emotional climate. He noted

> a general emotional factor which appears to be present in interactions occurring between individuals in face to face groups. It seems to have some relationship to the degree of acceptance expressed by members of a group regarding each other's needs or goals. Operationally defined, it is considered to influence: (1) the inner private world of each individual; (2) the *esprit de corps* of the group; (3) the sense of meaningfulness of group and individual goals and activities; (4) the objectivity with which a problem is tackled; (5) the kind and extent of interpersonal interaction in the group.

Studies since then have examined "high-inference" variables and found better student achievement when the class is rated high on measures such as cohesiveness and satisfaction and low on measures such as friction, difficulty, and competitiveness (Fraser and O'Brien 1985).

Overall, these studies show that "students' cognitive, affective, and behavioral outcomes are related to students' perceptions of psychosocial characteristics in classrooms" (Chavez 1984; Battistich et al. 1995).[1]

The following four propositions speak to the importance of classroom climate:

1. The basic psychological needs of all humans make up an acknowledged and universal list: safety, self-control, affection, inclusion, self-esteem, recognition, self-actualization and freedom and fun (see Maslow 1962; Dreikurs and Gray 1968; Schutz 1967; Glasser 1965, 1994).

2. The degree to which one's psychological needs are met determines how much of one's energy and attention is available for learning. If an individual is hurt and severely wanting on any of these needs, learning slows to a crawl or a halt. If these needs are adequately met, learning proceeds normally. And if they are met at a high level and nourished, learning flourishes.

3. Classroom climate directly influences how students do in school. It influences individually how their thermometers read on each of the basic psychological needs. It is not the only variable, but it is a major variable shaping the degree to which each student's psychological needs are met during class time.

4. When the climate goes beyond meeting safety and security needs and develops strength on the important dimensions of climate—community, risk taking, and influence—learning accelerates.

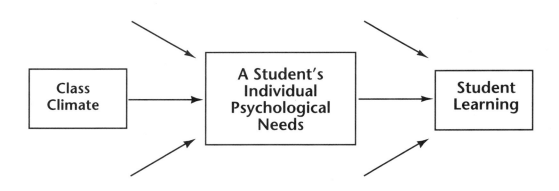

[1] In recognition of the importance of these characteristics, major staff development programs such as Dimensions of Learning (Marzano and Pickering 1992) have begun to include components on students' feelings of acceptance, ability, and safety. Educators for Social Responsibility, a nonprofit corporation, offers workshops throughout the country for teachers on conflict-resolution strategies and community building. It is located at 23 Garden Street, Cambridge, MA 02138; 800-370-2515. The Northeast Foundation for Children offers similar high-quality workshops. It is located at 71 Montague City Road, Greenfield MA 01301; 800-360-6332.

Classroom Climate: What Is It?

Our operational definition of classroom climate will be "the feelings and beliefs students have and the cumulative patterns of behavior that result from those feelings and beliefs regarding community and mutual support, risk taking and confidence, and influence and control." *Community and mutual support* are defined as an individual's feelings in relation to a group—feelings of acceptance, inclusion, membership, and maybe beyond into friendship and affection. *Risk taking and confidence* represent an internal, personal dimension that is influenced significantly by the reactions of others to one's behaviors. Put-downs and sarcasm, however subtle they may be, reduce one's confidence that it is safe to risk thinking and trying. A classroom climate that rewards effort and persistence will deemphasize speed and help students learn that errors are merely opportunities for learning, not signs of personal deficiency. *Influence and control* represent the dimension of class climate that pertains to personal efficacy, defined as one's power to produce effects. It answers the following questions: To what degree do I as an individual get to make my presence felt legitimately in helping things function in here? How am I empowered to be a player, an influencer, someone who matters as opposed to a silent cipher whose existence makes no observable difference in the flow of life in the room, to say nothing of making choices about how I spend my own time? All three of these dimensions of class climate matter for student learning.

These three major strands of classroom climate are summarized in Figure **13.1**, which treats each as a developmental aspect of climate—developmental in that there are stages of sophistication and maturity for each of the three strands, so a teacher planning to strengthen any of them would do well to plan activities and new practices with the stages in mind. The stages for the first strand, community and mutual support, are well treated in the developmental literature (Aspy 1977; Wood 1994; Johnson and Johnson (1995). The stages in the other two strands are more hypothetical, though their elements are supported individually by research.

The sections that follow examine each strand separately and describe the meaning of each element in it (e.g., what does "knowing others" in the community strand mean, and why is it important to classroom climate?). Before leaving each element, we will describe specific strategies and practices teachers can use to develop it.

Community and Mutual Support

This dimension of climate describes the degree of inclusion, affiliation, and mutual support students feel with one another. When it is well developed, the student can say, "I feel accepted and included here. People are on my side. I can help others, and they will help me. "

Within this dimension are five levels of development, each paired with a characteristic statement:

Climate for High Achievement for All Students

COMMUNITY AND
MUTUAL SUPPORT

CONFIDENCE AND
RISK TAKING

INFLUENCE AND
CONTROL

"I feel accepted and included in
this group. People are on my side
and want me to do well. I can help
others and they will help me."

"It's safe to take a risk. If I try hard,
learn from errors, and persist, I can
succeed here."

"I can have some influence on
the way things go here. I can
have some say. I matter."

Inclusion and Affiliation	5 Student Beliefs That Liberate or Limit Learning		Personal Efficacy
Knowing others	Mistakes help one learn. vs	Mistakes are a sign of weakness.	Empowering students to influence the pace of class
Greeting, acknowledging, listening, responding and affirming	You are not supposed to understand everything the first time around. Care, perseverance and quality are what count. vs	Speed is what counts. Faster is smarter.	Negotiating the rules of the classroom game
Group Identity, responsibility and interdependence	Good students solicit help and lots of feedback on their work. vs	Good students can do it by themselves.	Teaching kids to use the principles of learning and other strategies
Cooperative learning, social skills, class meetings group dynamics	Consistent effort and effective strategies are the main determinants of success. vs	Inborn intelligence is the main determinant of success.	Students' using knowledge of learning style and making choices
Problem solving and conflict resolution	Everyone is capable of high achievement, not just the fastest. vs	Only the few who are bright can achieve at a high level.	Students and their communities as sources of knowledge

FIGURE 13.1: THREE MAJOR STRANDS OF CLASSROOM CLIMATE
Each strand can be broken down into discrete stages of development.

1. *Knowing others:* "I know these people and they know me."

2. *Greeting, acknowledging, listening, responding, acknowledging, and affirming:* "I feel accepted and included. People respect me, and I respect them."

3. *Group identity, responsibility, and interdependence:* "I'm a member of this group. We need each other and want each other to succeed."

4. *Cooperative learning, social skills, group meetings, and group dynamics:* "I can help others and they will help me."

5. *Problem solving and conflict resolution:* "We can solve problems that arise between us."

These relationships of warmth and inclusion don't get built by accident or by themselves. Teachers contribute to the strength and texture of the climate of inclusion and affiliation that students experience through their behaviors (Cabello and Terrell 1993): their verbal interaction patterns with individual students, their means of handling conflicts between students, the cooperative structures they introduce for interaction among students, and their explicit teaching of social skills.

Knowing Others

Gene Stanford, a high school English teacher, identified this strand of classroom climate as a developmental continuum in his 1977 book, *Developing Effective Classroom Groups*. He realized that the foundation of being a group member was knowing something about the others in the group. As a result, he regularly did brief get-acquainted activities (twenty-one listed in his book) in the early months of the school year with students in his classes.

Teachers who periodically take a few minutes several times each week to do these activities do not report time problems keeping up

> *Modest front-end investments in building community increase efficiency and time on task in the long run.*

with the curriculum or studying what is required. These modest front-end investments in building community increase efficiency and time on task in the long run. (The same can be said for the other levels of community building in this strand.)

Dozens of books are available with excellent get-acquainted activities (Stanford 1977; Shaw 1992; Seigle and Macklem 1993; Bennett and Smilanich 1994) that are active and enjoyable. In People Bingo or the version called Find a Person Who, students mingle and try to get signatures in boxes of a grid where facts are listed about unknown people in the group, for example,

"Spent a year in France." Each student has to find the person matched to that fact and get his or her signature in that box. Some activities are more lengthy, like structured interviews of partners. After the interview, each partner introduces the other to the class or to a small group based on the interview.

One of our favorites has always been Artifact Bags, which is just as popular among groups of adults as it is among fifth graders. Participants bring in unlabeled shopping bags containing five items that represent something about their lives or their interests. At each session, one participant chooses a bag at random and displays the items in it one at a time to the other participants, who are sitting in a circle. Participants try to guess who the owner is. After the fifth item is shown and described by the person who has been picking from the bag (some items may be too small for all to see thoroughly when just held up), the group makes a collective guess. Then the real owner reveals himself or herself and explains the significance of each item. There may be time to do two or three people at each session.

The popularity of this activity with adults signals how little opportunity there is in schools and school districts as workplaces to come to know one's colleagues. One doesn't have to take the whole faculty away on a retreat to pay attention to group building and relationship building.

Community-building strategies gain importance in the overall picture of classroom climate building for students as the forces of scheduling and course structures assume more importance starting in grade 6. These forces depersonalize and fractionate the sense of community for students.

Greeting, Listening, Responding, Acknowledging, and Affirming

Have you ever noticed that in some settings (sometimes in whole towns) people look you in the eye, smile, and greet you when you walk by or enter their space? Beyond simply getting students information about each other, we might work on creating the conditions and teaching the skills of acknowledging and responding to one another. People who are greeted and acknowledged regularly feel affirmed and tend to be more available for learning. In the Morning Meeting structure at the Greenfield Center School in Greenfield, Massachusetts, the first activity uses one of the dozens of formats available for having the children greet one other around the circle. This is not a practice confined to the primary grades. Positive greeting is a form of acknowledgment worth fostering at any age. Wood (1994) writes, "It is important for students [of grades 4, 5, 6] to not only greet each other in the morning, but to learn to greet any member of the class in a friendly and interested way. Issues of gender, cliques, and best friends are developmental milestones for 9–13 year olds. Greetings help students to work on these issues in a safe structure every morning. It is the entry point for the teacher in her social curriculum each morning."

A sample greeting activity appropriate for the elementary grades is a ball toss greeting, which can be varied so that it will be challenging and build cooperation for older children. It begins with the children standing in a circle and greeting each other one at a time by tossing a ball. For example,

Leslie starts the greeting by saying, "Good morning, John!" and then tosses the ball to John. He returns Leslie's greeting, then chooses another child in the circle to greet and toss the ball to. When the ball has been tossed to everyone except Leslie, it finishes by returning to her with a greeting. In a variation, the ball goes around one more time silently (with no greeting or talking) repeating the pattern it just made. Children will enjoy doing it several times this way and competing against the clock (Stephenson and Watrous 1994).

Acknowledging and affirming one another can be structured into group meeting times. The Social Competency Curriculum (Seigle and Macklem 1993) uses Spotlight as an activity to affirm positive attributes and behaviors. One child is picked by the teacher (a different one each time) to be in the spotlight. The others then take turns giving the selected child compliments with specific examples: "Tim, it's nice the way you are considerate of other kids, like when you made room for me to get into the circle." Each child may speak only once and must address the child selected, not the teacher. The child in the Spotlight just listens.

Good listening can be taught explicitly. Students can be warmed up to the qualities of good listening by doing a mirroring exercise. Two partners stand and decide who will be the leader (person A) and who the follower (person B). Partner A puts his or her hands up and moves them around, palms facing partner B, who has to make his or her hands exactly mirror A's hands. After about 45 seconds the facilitator calls "time," and partners switch roles. A becomes the follower and B the leader. To do this activity well, both partners need to focus intently on each other. That sets the stage for direct teaching and practice of social skills, especially listening.

Direct teaching of children to listen involves role playing and practice. It can begin by asking students, "Think of someone who really listens to you. Why do you think that person does it?" Role-play listening attentively with the class, and have them tell you what they saw and heard. Record their answers. Next have students describe someone they know who doesn't listen. Do a role-play with someone, and record what students say about these behaviors they heard and saw. Students are now ready to practice listening in trios: one listener, one speaker, and one observer.

Many teachers embed practice in listening in classroom routines—for example, by asking a student who wants to speak to summarize what the previous students said in a discussion. This request is thrown out randomly so students can't predict when they'll have to summarize the previous student.

Group Identity, Responsibility, and Interdependence

Cooperative learning structures (see Kagan 1992) and cooperative models (Johnson and Johnson 1987; Slavin 1986) encourage team building because they form natural groups where individuals are allied with one another. Thus, creating a team name, a logo, or a banner becomes a natural way for getting the kids involved with one another. On a higher level, students start depending on one another and see how they need one another. Jigsaw structures (Aronson 1978) force interdependence because students must rely on their peers to learn certain material so they can present it to the others on the team. (See the section on competition in the Learning Experiences Chapter.)

Broken Squares is an activity often used to introduce students to interdependence. Five perfect squares, each 6 inches on a side, are cut into pieces, mixed up into five piles, and put in five envelopes (see FIGURE 13.2). Each team of five gets one envelope each. Their job, *without talking or signaling,* is to make five perfect squares. Individuals may not take pieces from anyone else; they can only give pieces away. When they give a piece to a team member, individuals may not put the piece in place in the person's puzzle: they can just give it to the person. Debriefing this activity with the questions listed in FIGURE 13.2 provides a fine entry point for discussing what happens if a person is ignored or withdraws or if a person tries to dominate the task.

Regular academic tasks can be adapted to the Broken Squares structure. An oaktag sheet with spelling words (or technical words or foreign language or English vocabulary words) can be cut up into a pile of individual letters. The letters are sorted randomly into five envelopes. Each of five team members gets one envelope. Their job as a group, *without talking or taking pieces from another,* is to build the words, spelled correctly. A poster of the words spelled correctly should be available for the group to consult while doing the task.

Social Skills and Group Dynamics

The fourth level of community building focuses more explicitly on developing the skills to work effectively in groups. Social skills are taught in the manner of the Listening example already described. Class meetings become a common framework for teaching and exercising these social skills, which are often posted by name around the classroom. (Three excellent sources on how to run classroom meetings for social skill development are Glasser 1969, Seigle and Macklem 1993, and Wood 1994.)

Consensus-seeking exercises with an analysis of behavior and results afterward are useful. Tasks such as Lost in Space and Arctic Survival (Lafferty 1987) give problems to teams from fifth grade on up that require prioritizing a list of items; for example, which ten of twenty potential items should be taken from a crashed plane if the group has to survive in subarctic conditions until rescued? Individuals do the task alone first, then redo it with team members by sharing information and the rationales they used. The group choices almost always turn out to be closer to the expert's best answer than any individual's answer alone. Thus, the point is made about the benefits of pooling expertise and using consensus. After the activity, groups follow directions to examine the roles various members of

> *Class meetings become a common framework for teaching and exercising social skills.*

Broken Squares

Directions

Each of you has an envelope which contains pieces of oaktag for forming squares. When the signal is given, the task of your group is to form five squares of equal size. Each square will measure 6" X 6". The task will not be completed until five perfect squares have been completed.

Rules

1. No member may speak.

2. No member may ask another member for a piece or in any way signal that another person is to give him or her a piece. (Members may voluntarily give pieces to other members.)

(The letters on the pieces are irrelevant to the task; they are just for getting pieces back into the right envelope at the end of the exercise.)

Processing "Broken Squares"

1. What happened first? What strategies were in use at the beginning?

2. What were you (each individual) thinking about the first few minutes?

3. What happened next? Did strategies shift? Were there different phases to how you functioned as a group?

4. Did someone make a move that shifted the group's approach or in some way broke a long jam?

5. Did anyone feel left out or appear to be left out?

6. What role did each individual play in the group?

7. What did you become aware of about yourself about cooperation and competition?

8. What insight/awareness did you get about groups in cooperative tasks?

DIRECTIONS FOR MAKING A SET OF BROKEN SQUARES

A set consists of five envelopes containing pieces of cardboard cut into different patterns which, when properly arranged, will form five squares of equal size. One set should be provided for each group of five persons.

To prepare a set, cut out five cardboard squares, each exactly 6" X 6". Place the squares in a row and mark them as below, penciling the letters lightly so they can be erased.

The lines should be so drawn that, when the pieces are cut out, those marked A will be exactly the same size, those marked C the same size, etc. Several combinations are possible that will form one or two squares, but only one combination will form all five squares, each 6" X 6". After drawing the lines on the squares and labeling the sections with letters, cut each square along the lines into smaller pieces to make the parts of the puzzle.

Label the five envelopes 1,2,3, 4, and 5. Distribute the cardboard pieces into the five envelopes as follows: envelope 1 has pieces I, H, E; 2 has A, A, A, C; 3 has A, J; 4 has D, F; and 5 has G, B, F, C.

Erase the penciled letter from each piece and write, instead, the number of the envelope it is in. This makes it easy to return the pieces to the proper envelope, for subsequent use, after a group has completed the task.

Each set may be made from a different color or cardboard.

FIGURE 13.2: BROKEN SQUARES ACTIVITY
This activity is often used to introduce students to interdependence.
Reproduced from *A Handbook of Structured Experiences for Human Relations Training, Volume I*
J. William Pfeiffer and John E. Jones, Editors. La Jolla: University Associates Publishers, Inc., 1974.

the group played when they were working together. Valuable learning emerges about what behaviors individuals can do to make groups effective. Information emerges about blocking behaviors and what each individual could do to be a more potent group contributor next time.

Mysteries (Stanford 1977) is another such structure. The clues necessary to solve a mystery are put on 3 x 5 index cards and one clue is given to each student. The task is to identify the culprit with deductive logic by a process of elimination if all the information from all the clues is available. The students who sit in a circle can read their card aloud but cannot give it to anyone else, nor can any student read another student's card. This structure forces students to share information, organize it, and develop organization and leadership skills. As with all such tasks, the analytical discussion afterward (called *processing*) is the most important part of the activity. It is here that students reflect on what helped and what obstructed the group's progress, and they make commitments about what they'll try to do better next time.

In Mysteries, the class is asked to make an accusation only when they all agree. If they are wrong, the teacher doesn't give the right answer but sends them back into the group to reexamine the evidence. In any event, after 20 minutes, the activity ends if the guilty party hasn't been identified, and the class returns to the task on another day.

The things students learn about successful group processes and about individual social and task skills from these activities do not necessarily transfer into their everyday behavior unless teachers specifically plan for that transfer. Successful teaching of social skills requires (1) naming the skill, (2) creating an understanding of the utility of the skill in life, (3) modeling it, (4) having students practice it, and (5) giving students direct feedback on how they're doing. In addition to feedback from their teacher, having students process their own level of functioning in a group (that is, discuss it and self-assess) consistently correlates with better skill development and better academic learning (Yager et al. 1986). The explicit teaching of social skills and the frequent debriefing or processing by students of how they did builds an expectation through repetition that the skills will be used generally in the classroom. Transfer to settings outside school is more likely to happen if we follow the guidelines of the principle of learning Teach for Transfer found in Chapter 9.

Conflict Resolution

The final stage of development for a healthy classroom (or school) community is building the capacity of its members to solve their own conflicts. This work includes acknowledgment that conflicts are normal and that controversy, which is not the same as conflict, is actually good for learning.

Conflict is defined as a situation where the needs of two people are at odds, and the current course of behavior or action appears to make one the winner at the expense of the other. *Conflict resolution* means coming up with a solution that meets the needs of both parties or a compromise that both can live with.

Most conflict-resolution models have similar steps and teach similar skills. For example, Thomas Gordon's (1974) model includes the skills of active listening and "I" messages, which are vital communication skills for enabling people to work through classic conflict-resolution steps.

The following steps occur in variations in most programs:

1. Recognize your anger, calm down, and collect yourself. Some programs teach relaxation or self-imposed time-out techniques for this stage.

2. Identify the real problem. Johnson and Johnson (1995, pp. 5–6) break down the second step into valuable components:

    • Jointly define the problem as small and specific.
    • Determine what each person wants.
    • Determine how each person feels.
    • Exchange reasons and rationale for positions.
    • Reverse perspectives.

This stage can take some time. Many models advocate teaching students to identify their *needs*, not to speak in terms of actions or the solutions they want. Probing questions, clarifying questions, and considerable active listening are often required here. That is why a neutral mediator is often introduced into the process.

3. Decide on a positive goal. State a desired outcome in positive terms—for example, "We will both get enough time at the computer to rewrite our drafts."

4. Think of several solutions. Brainstorming techniques are often taught to students in this stage.

5. Evaluate the solutions, and pick one to try.

6. Make a plan. Often just picking a solution—"Share the computer time after lunch fifty-fifty"—isn't enough. A specific plan is needed designating who will do what, when, and where. The plan may need to be written and agreed to in writing.

7. Evaluate the plan to see if both parties are keeping their part of the bargain, if the plan is good, or if it needs to be revised. (For details and elaboration of these steps see Johnson and Johnson 1995, pp. 5:1–5:30.)

We are convinced that Johnson and Johnson (1995) are right: *every* student, not just some, should be trained as a mediator. It is in being a mediator that students learn and internalize the skills of conflict resolution. Only then will they have the skills available for their own autonomous use when they get into conflicts themselves. The implication is that mediation training for *all* students is the most powerful model for teaching effective conflict-resolution skills and getting students to transfer them into daily practice.

Social Problem Solving meetings as described in William Glasser's *Schools Without Failure* (1969) are an ideal forum for developing these steps and the skills to go with them.

In the only classroom climate study to investigate differential effects of climate variables by gender and race, Deng (1992) found that the achievement gap between blacks, Hispanics, and whites in mathematics and the achievement gap between boys and girls in mathematics widened when community was weak and tension was high. This finding underlines the importance of community as a variable in academic achievement for girls in math and perhaps for students of color in all subjects when classes are integrated.

Risk Taking and Confidence

As we move from community building to the domain of risk taking, we examine what teachers can do to promote confidence and a safe atmosphere to "go for it." The five levels of this dimension of classroom climate are not as clearly developmental as they were in community because each level here is really a belief rather than a set of steps. We believe that the foundation of intellectual risk taking in classrooms is built on internal beliefs about errors and what they mean, about speed of learning and what it signifies, about the need to "get it" on your own as opposed to working with others and getting help.[2] Productive beliefs about errors, speed, and getting help may be derived from one's basic belief about intelligence (namely, that intelligence can be developed, and everyone can do well if they put in the time and use good strategies to learn). Whatever the relationships between these beliefs turn out to be, it is clear that we can identify a repertoire of teacher behaviors associated with strengthening each belief.

FIGURE **13.3** shows the five beliefs that underline risk taking in their negative and positive forms. The positive beliefs are life liberating, the negative ones life limiting.

---

[2] Thanks to John D'Auria for his creative thinking in helping to work out this framework.

POSITIVE BELIEFS	NEGATIVE BELIEFS
On errors:	*On errors:*
Mistakes help one learn.	Mistakes are a sign of weakness.
On speed:	*On speed:*
You are not supposed to understand everything the first time around. Care, quality, and perseverance are what count.	Speed is what counts. Faster is smarter.
On getting help:	*On getting help:*
Good students solicit help and lots of feedback on their work.	Good students can do it by themselves.
On effort and ability:	*On effort and ability:*
Consistent effort and effective strategies are the main determinants of success.	Inborn intelligence is the main determinant of success.
On effort and ability:	*On effort and ability:*
Everyone is capable of high achievement, not just the fastest.	Only the few who are bright can achieve at a high level.

FIGURE 13.3: FIVE BELIEFS THAT UNDERLIE RISK TAKING
Positive beliefs are life liberating, the negative ones life limiting.

This risk-taking dimension of climate has to do with the amount of confidence a student has and the amount of social and academic risk taking the student will do. If it is well developed, a student might be able to say, "It's safe to take a risk here. If I try hard, learn from errors, and persist, I can succeed."

There is a need to collect specific strategies and approaches for nourishing student risk taking, a need that has been suggested but thus far unfulfilled. Others often acknowledge the importance of risk taking but seldom explain how to cultivate it. For example, one author writes, "A big piece of teaching for understanding is setting up social norms that promote respect for other people's ideas. You don't get that to happen by telling. You have to change the social norms—which takes time and consistency" (Lampert 1994).

But how to do this, one wonders.

Here is another example. In a wonderful exposition on the practices of exemplary teachers who use cognitive strategies to move students from novice to expert in their problem solving in various disciplines, Bruer (1993) writes:

The benchmark lesson on gravity begins 6 weeks into the course. By this time Minstrell [the teacher] has established a rapport with his class. He has created an environment conducive to developing understanding, a climate where questioning and respect for diverse opinions prevail, a climate where the process of scientific reasoning can be made explicit and self-conscious. Even veteran teachers marvel at how uninhibited Minstrell's students are in expressing ideas, suggesting hypotheses, and arguing positions. (p. 42)

How does Mr. Minstrell get his students to be so uninhibited?

A few days later, Minstrell and the class analyze their reasoning about the time it would take a 1-kilogram and a 5-kilogram object to fall the same distance. They run the crucial experiment—a miniature replay of Galileo's apocryphal experiment at Pisa. After both balls hit the floor simultaneously, Minstrell returns to the board where he had written the quiz answers. "Some of you were probably feeling pretty dumb with these kind of answers. Don't feel dumb," he counsels. "Let's see what's valuable about each of these answers, because each one's valuable. Why would you think heavier things fall faster?"* (pp. 43–44)

Now we are beginning to get clues about creating this uninhibited atmosphere.

Here is a final example acknowledging the importance of risk taking:

Inquiry teaching is difficult for teachers and requires skills that must be developed through intensive staff development. If a student whose answer is challenged does not trust the teacher, or the other students, the follow-up question, intended to cause the student to think more deeply about the subject, may have the opposite effect. The student may interpret the follow-up question as a clue that the initial response was wrong and that he or she is about to be made to feel foolish in front of the rest of the class. Threat seems to reduce our ability to think at higher levels, and what could be more threatening than public failure and ridicule?

For this type of instruction to be effective, a teacher must create a classroom environment where students *feel safe to express their thinking*, where they trust their teacher and fellow students, and where they understand the difference between criticizing ideas and criticizing people. (italics added) (Ellsworth and Sindt 1994)†

> *Most children learn early in school that mistakes are signs of weakness instead of data to use.*

This interpretation of the effect of removing threat—the threat of being laughed at, of feeling foolish, or of being wrong—is resoundingly confirmed by current trends in research on brain function (Sylvester 1994). What then can we say about specific ways to strengthen a climate for risk taking?

*Reprinted with permission from the Summer 1993 issue of the *American Educator*, the quarterly journal of the American Federation of Teachers. Bruer, John T. "The Mind's Journey from Novice to Expert." *American Educator* 38 (Summer 1993): 6–15.

†Ellsworth, P. C., and V. G. Sindt. "Helping 'Aha' to Happen: the Contributions of Irving Sigel." *Educational Leadership* 51 (May 1994): 40–44. Copyright © 1994 by ASCD. Reprinted by permission. All rights reserved.

Errors

In this country we tend to believe in the fixed, innate, and unalterable nature of intelligence. Most children learn early in school that mistakes are signs of weakness instead of data to use and an opportunity for learning. Cultivating the latter belief about mistakes is the very foundation for confidence and risk taking in the classroom. Thirty years ago Jerome Bruner represented this idea when he said that our goal should be to help students "experience success and failure not as reward and punishment, but as information." People who succeed in building this element of climate do so explicitly. Beverly Hollis, a seventh-grade English teacher in Lincoln, Massachusetts, writes:

> At the beginning of the year, when students are reticent to answer and wait time has been exhausted, I ask, "Is this a life-or-death situation? No, well, so what if you're wrong then? This is one answer out of the trillion you will give in your life, so what if it's wrong? If it is wrong, I guarantee I won't let you leave until you've heard the right answer, and you'll probably remember it longer for having missed it. But most importantly, you will have risked giving the answer. So many insightful answers and comments are never made because you, as students, are afraid to be wrong. I don't want that to be the case in this room."

> I talk about risks in my personal life—my month-long wilderness canoeing trip—and risks I'm taking by teaching a unit in a particular way. I'll say, "I want to try something new I've learned in my class, and I need your feedback." I do ask for their feedback after every unit. I tell them they can say they disliked a particular approach I used on the material covered as long as they offer positive criticism in pointing out what they didn't like and why, and if they offer alternatives or suggestions of what else I could have done to make it better. [Notice that in letting students critique her units, Ms. Hollis is giving them power.] I also give them choices about how they want to learn a particular unit and ask them to tell me why this would be the best approach to take. They love having the power; they have been incredibly perceptive, and as a consequence, they have been very accepting of my high expectations and my criticism when they fall short of the mark. I have students earn extra credit points to improve their grades on tests by listing what they were mixed up about or how they "messed up" on a test answer. And I openly and readily admit my own mistakes. Hopefully, this climate of honesty and risk taking allows me to correct students and myself without any of us feeling guilty or stupid for having made a mistake.

Anna Shine of the New England School of English in Boston says:

> One of the behaviors I encourage is making mistakes or guessing. I tell my students that I don't care if they are wrong, but I do care if they don't try, that there is no shame in trying and making a mistake or in falling short of their goals, but there is shame in not trying. And worse than shame, a learning opportunity is not maximized. Again and again, I say to them, "Mistakes are not important; understanding is."

Obviously students will not take risks unless it is safe to do so. So, in my classroom, I try to create this environment, to make it safe to make mistakes because students can learn from mistakes. In fact, I reward students with big (2 inches in diameter) gold stars in two situations. One is if they produce great work, and the other is if they produce great mistakes.

On the first day of class, when I show them my gold stars, they look at me as if I'm crazy. "A gold star for a mistake?" they think. "She doesn't know what she's doing." However, they soon learn that a gold star mistake is a mistake from which every student in the class can learn something. By making this great mistake, the student has provided everyone with a new learning opportunity, and the student himself has learned that it is safe to take a risk. By taking that risk, he grew (his knowledge and his confidence), the class learned, and he received one of the coveted gold stars.

In a similar vein, Terry McCarthy of the North Pole Elementary School in Fairbanks, Alaska, gives "Bravery Points" to kids who have the courage to try hard questions or problems even if they're not sure they can get them. In these and other ways invented by thoughtful teachers, climates of risk taking and safety to make errors are deliberately created and nurtured.

Speed

A second belief about learning that children bring to school in this country is that faster is better instead of believing that care, quality, and perseverance are what matter. What do teachers do to disabuse students of the life-limiting belief in the virtue of speed versus care and perseverance?

In Chapter 11, we described a policy on retakes of tests that would grant students as a final grade the highest score they got on a test or its retake no matter how many tries they took (assuming alternate forms of tests are available). This practice would replace averaging the test and its retake. Beyond that practice, giving only A, B, and Not Yet as grades signals that ultimate performance at high standards is what we're after, and nothing less will do. Getting there after suffering through a period of "Not Yet" does not make one's A any less valuable—just longer in coming.[3]

Use of wait time, with an explanation of it to the class, is an everyday practice that reinforces thoughtfulness and perseverance rather than quickness. Mary Ann Pilat of the Wellesley Middle School uses a related practice, called the Level Playing Field:

I explain to students that linear thinkers can come up with prompt answers to class discussion questions, but that gestalt, divergent thinkers, an equally legitimate learning style, often are stimulated onto side connections and thoughts by questions in class. So while following those interesting thoughts, the speedster linear thinkers have answered the question and appear to be getting all the answers. Divergent thinkers tend to participate less in class. So to make the playing field level for them in getting ready for a class discussion, I

---

[3] Innovative school schedules can support this grading policy. Trimesters can be scheduled instead of two semesters. In between each trimester, a week can be reserved for two purposes: students who have completed all course requirements at a high level can take enrichment or extension courses; students who have not yet completed course requirements at a high level can have one extra focused week with teacher support to finish their "Not Yets."

put the major questions we're going to discuss on the board and give everyone five minutes to think about them first before starting the discussion. I've been getting much greater participation from lots more kids, including some who never spoke in class before.

The final strategy for valuing care and perseverance above speed is the routine practice of Reteaching Loops described in Chapter 11. To make Reteaching Loops do what they can for classroom climate, nominating oneself for inclusion in a loop must be a behavior of high esteem and status in the class.

Getting Feedback and Help

Another factor that obstructs learning and contaminates most classroom climates is the belief that "good students do it by themselves," instead of the belief that what makes good students is that they solicit help and lots of feedback on their work.

Teachers support the development of this belief by explicitly modeling and encouraging it and by creating structures that manifest it. For example, the peer editing process in place in many writing programs can be applied to reports in other

> *What makes good students is that they solicit help and lots of feedback on their work.*

subjects; students would be expected to have peers critique their drafts according to commonly understood criteria and to do final drafts with their input in mind.

Other structures for mutual help can be structured into classroom routines:

- Students can take turns taking notes for the "absentee folder," which sits on a desk in the back of the room as a resource for absent students. When students come back after an absence, the notes help them catch up on what they missed, and the student who took the notes is available for personal help to the student who was absent.

- Teachers can organize students in groups or pairs of "study buddies" who are expected to help each other interpret assignments and prepare for tests.

- Various models of cooperative learning build in incentives for all team members that each member does well. Improvement of any individual's score on a quiz over that person's previous average earns points for the whole team. Team study time is provided so the members can help each other out. (See Slavin 1986.)

Many other activity structures, such as Teammates Consult, Four Corners, Pairs Check, and Learning Buddies (Kagan 1992), are available for helping students get committed to asking for appropriate help.

Effort and Ability

To the degree that students believe intelligence is innate, fixed, measurable, and unevenly distributed, they will probably also believe that whatever quantity of intelligence they have is the main determinant of how they will do in school and elsewhere in life (Howard 1993). It is difficult to be brought up in this country believing anything else, for the concept of intelligence as an entity that regulates our possibilities is more developed and more influential in the United States than in any other nation. In fact, the concept of intelligence as a fixed and measurable entity was created on our very own shores at a particular time in history, between approximately 1890 and 1920 (Gould 1982; Oakes 1985).

In this section we move on to the consequence of this belief, to the sweet fruits of its opposite, and how to transform students' belief into that opposite image. The opposite belief—the life-liberating one that fuels motivation and accelerates learning when it replaces the belief that innate intelligence is the main determinant of success—is this: Consistent effort and effective strategies are the main determinants of success (Howard 1993). With these two things in place, everyone is capable of high achievement, not just the fastest and most confident.

Attribution theory explains the dynamics at work in the two different belief systems (Weiner 1970). The theory posits that the reasons we give to ourselves (the attributions we make) for our success when we succeed and for our failure when we fail have a dramatic impact on our future behavior. In fact, these internal explanations account for our future behavior. Teachers who want to help students change their beliefs about the value of effort and the importance of good strategies versus innate intelligence pursue positive behaviors in the ten arenas of classroom life described in Chapter 11. For example, they stick with students who don't answer quickly; they give cues and use wait time. Here the chapter on Classroom Climate overlaps with Chapter 11 (the study of teaching behaviors that convince students they are able and that effort is what matters). The arenas through which the three messages—"This is important," "You can do it," "I won't give up on you"— are sent are also the vehicles on hand for convincing students they already have enough intelligence to do rigorous material well. What they need to do is work long enough, be resourceful, and learn strategies that will help them. Teachers' responsibility is to teach them strategies explicitly.

Influence

"Effective teachers know that to become engaged, students must have some feelings of ownership—of the class or the task—and personal power—a belief that what they do will make a difference" (Dodd 1995). This belief is echoed in two bodies of literature of the 1980s and 1990s. First, many frameworks for understanding thinking and personality style (e.g., Myers and McCaulley 1985; Harrison and Bramson 1982) find large percentages of people who have the need to be in charge or in control of at least certain aspects of their environment in order to function well. Second, the literature on constructivist learning and teaching posits that learning for true understanding requires students to construct their own meaning (Brooks and Brooks 1993). This involves owning their own questions and pursuing their own lines of inquiry with teacher guidance. These two literatures support the same proposition: Successful teachers find ways for students to have some ownership and influence over the flow of events and the intellectual life of the classroom.

There are many ways to offer students choice and influence over their lives in school. One pertains to the social system of the classroom—the rules of the classroom game as opposed to the rules for interpersonal behavior one often sees posted on walls. The rules of the classroom game pertain to social norms and procedures for conducting class discourse. They are often undiscussed and unwritten, though that is something we would recommend changing. The teacher asks a question, the student responds, and the teacher evaluates is a typical cycle of discourse reflecting the "rule" that the teacher will control the talk in the room. Without losing control of the class or the curriculum, a teacher can permit students to participate in shaping and operating these procedural systems for discourse and business.

Another route to ownership and influence goes through learning style and choices. Many authors (e.g., Mamchur 1990) urge giving students choices whenever possible about how to work on learning new concepts or carry out assignments. Student choice making can be improved and empowered by knowledge about their own learning styles.

Finally, in addition to having some control over the rules of the classroom game and the shape of the learning activities they pursue, students can have some joint ownership of the intellectual life of the classroom through the way in which questions are posed and meaning is generated.

The five sections that follow might be thought of as levels of depth and sophistication in our strategic approach to giving students authentic influence in classroom life. Whereas you could work on them in any order or even simultaneously, it is useful to understand which ones are more complex and why. Then you can avoid biting off more than you can chew in developing this strand of classroom climate. You need not address the five issues sequentially and wait for a certain level of "development" before beginning practices aimed at another level. For example, there is no need to wait until students are stopping a class to ask for clarification before teaching students about their own learning style and how to use that knowledge to influence assignments. But it might be worth bearing in mind that the five approaches described below do increase progressively in complexity. Therefore, if you are interested in developing student ownership and influence you might start with the simpler and then move slowly to the more complex forms of student ownership.

Stop My Teaching

"Stop my teaching" refers to empowering the students to use signals to tell a teacher when the instruction is leaving them behind. Lilian Katz (1992) talks about giving her son, a beginning teacher, some basic principles of practice for successful teaching:

> One of the things you always want to do as a teacher...teaching children old or young, doesn't matter who, you always want to teach the children to say to you things like: "Hold it; I'm lost." "Can you go over this one more time?" "Is this what you mean?" "Can you show me again?" "Have I got it right?"...ways in which you empower the learner to keep you posted on where they need help. If the children are very young you just say, "Pull my sleeve." whatever, as long as the child has the strategy to say to you "I don't get it." "I'm lost." "You're going too fast. "Hold it" and so on. (ASCD Conference 1992)

Teachers who take this injunction seriously develop signal systems where students can indicate on their own initiative that they are lost and want the teacher to stop and explain again. Hand signals like thumbs down held tight against one's chest could be such a signal. Or students could put red, yellow, or green cards on the corner of their desks like traffic light signals. Thus, teachers could get a quick visual read on how well students were understanding a discussion.

When the idea of stopping the teaching becomes part of classroom culture, other symbols or phrases come to represent the practice. One teacher told her class the story of a family vacation where she and her husband and six children stopped at McDonalds for lunch. Loading up hurriedly in the tightly packed van after their quick meal, they didn't do a head count and were four miles down the road before Mom said, "Where's Bobby?!?" Bobby was back at McDonalds.

The teacher now uses that phrase frequently in class as a coded signal: "Have I left you at Macdonalds?" and the children also use the code to signal when they're getting lost. "Ms. Swift, I think I'm back at MacDonalds!" The humorous shared code serves to authorize the practice of stopping the teacher's teaching, and the teacher's affirming reaction shows the practice to be a valued one that earns kudos for the child rather than a frown or a veiled accusation of inadequacy.

Negotiating the Rules of the Classroom Game

Negotiating the rules of the classroom game means involving students in creating the routines and procedures of classroom discourse and class business. These rules are different from the rules of behavior that teachers and students commonly work out at the beginning of the year. The rules we are talking about here are usually tacit, underground, and unstated. They pertain to teacher-student and student-student interaction around such issues as questions and answers, class dialogue, and procedures and protocols for taking turns. Recitation lessons of teacher questions and student answers do indeed often turn out to be a game, where students try to win by getting the right answers and avoid losing by shrinking into invisibility when they don't know the answers.

Once in one of our courses, Dick Adams, a housemaster at Newton North High School in Newton, Massachusetts, asked his students if he had ever played Guess-What's-on-the-Teacher's-Mind with them. The concept had come up when we studied questioning techniques under clarity. Recall that teachers who play Guess-What's-On-the-Teacher's-Mind (GWOTM) ask inexplicit questions when they have a particular answer in mind but the way they ask the question allows for a universe of possible answers. "I don't ever do that, do I?" asked Dick. A number of slow, knowing affirmative nods came back at him from the students. "No…Really? Give me some examples."

They did. And from that opening there proceeded a class discussion of how to conduct class discourse in such a way as to eliminate student pet peeves and increase productive participation. For example, they decided together that a student who couldn't answer a question could refer it to another student, whom they named. If three students in a row couldn't answer the question, Dick would conclude he had asked a bad question; then he had to ask it in a different way or ask students where the gap was.

His students became so excited over the way the class was going that they asked one of us to videotape the class. We realized that the students were not just happy over the new dynamics and improved clarity of class discussions, but elated over having been a force that influenced the shape of the class itself. Students had changed the rules of the classroom game in collaboration with their teacher and emerged from the traditional nether region of passive ciphers to active and authorized players in determining how things go.

The point of this story is to raise the question: What opportunities do students have to influence the rules of the classroom game, to shape the form and dynamics of interaction and operation? How can we give them ownership in these rules?

Teaching Students to Use Principles of Learning and Other Strategies

A third way to give students influence in classroom life is to share with them teaching and learning strategies we use ourselves. By including them in the secret knowledge of teaching and learning strategies, we give students choices, power, and license to control their learning.

Many of the Principles of Learning set out in Chapter 9 should be taught to students directly so they can use them themselves to be more powerful learners. The same is true for a number of techniques in Chapter 8. This is a good moment to review those principles to decide which ones you think would be most beneficial to turn over to your students as tools for learning. The more we are interested in empowering students and giving them choices, the more we will explicitly put learning tools at their disposal and urge them to use them autonomously.

Here are some of our nominees for principles to teach to students:

- *Sequence:* Students can use this principle to sequence their own lists when studying vocabulary words (or anything else that is sequential in nature) so the items hardest for them are in the optimal first and last positions.

- *Practice:* Students can use knowledge of this principle to optimize their personal practice schedules.

- *Goal setting:* Students can use this principle to set realistic academic and behavioral targets for improvement and make effective plans of action to meet them.

- *Explanatory devices:* Visual imagery and especially graphic organizers can become regular tools for students. Imagery can be used to pause during study and construct meaning in a visual way. Graphic organizers can become a habit as a note-taking technology through which students assimilate information as they read, hear, or see it. Teachers can integrate the use of these devices into assignments and work toward having students choose when and how to use them. (See Chapter 8.)

While passing these strategies on to students, teachers who are aware of attribution theory and who are committed to conveying the three expectations messages—"This is important," "You can do it," and "I won't give up on you"—will see they have a special opening. They will seize frequent opportunities to connect the use of these strategies with student success rather than let students attribute successful performance to intelligence. "Well, José, did you use any graphic organizers when you reviewed that chapter? No? Well, look—you're a strong visual learner. You and I both know that. Let's go over how to use that strategy with material like this. I know you can make it work for you!"

Learning Style and Choices

"Students using knowledge of learning style" means teachers are not just using their knowledge of learning style to adapt lessons for the styles of their students; they are teaching the students about their own learning styles and the implications of those styles for what kinds of assignments will be difficult and what will be easier. Furthermore, they encourage students to use knowledge of their own styles to guide their study routines and even to ask for modifications in assignments that allow them to use their strengths. These steps set the stage for a more complex level of empowerment, that is, giving students explicit choices over assignments, forms of tests, and forms of projects. The "Nonreport Report" is a practice that invites these choices.

Many readers will have been to a workshop on learning style in their careers, and some may be thoroughly trained in one or more of the learning style frameworks. These frameworks help us understand the similarities and differences in the ways humans take in, process, and express their learning. They also help us understand the features of the learning environment and the different kinds of activities that work best for individuals. For example, some people learn best when they can talk and interact with others as they deal with new concepts. Others like to read, listen, view, and assimilate alone before interacting with other people. This body of knowledge about learning style preferences can be a powerful vehicle for giving students ownership in classroom life.

Helping students understand their own learning style sets the stage for some important forms of empowerment. First, students can predict (and teachers can help them predict and prepare for) the difficulty of certain assignments or tasks that do not match their preferred learning style. If we have set the stage properly and taught about learning style, the value system associated with learning style frameworks enables students to see their difficulty in certain tasks as attributable to differences, not deficiencies. Second, the capacity to predict learning style match or mismatch to tasks enables students to mobilize extra effort and to seek help when appropriate. When we encourage students to use knowledge of their own learning style to do either of these two things, we are empowering them in significant ways.

The simplest place to start teaching students about learning style is with modality preference: visual, auditory, kinesthetic, or combinations of them. Simple modality preference tests (see Barbe and Milone 1980) can be used to have students identify their preferences. Then we must look for (and share out loud with students that we are looking for) ways to vary our teaching to address different modalities.[4]

Another framework for learning style differences that students can use in the same way is the left-brain–right brain or global-analytic framework. Rita Dunn's (1990) provides another useful set for students to know about and for them to use to empower their learning effectiveness. Anthony Gregorc's (1985) framework provides a fourth and more complicated but highly useful cut at style difference. Bernice McCarthy's 4MAT System (1987) is a fifth, and Gardner's Multiple Intelligences (1983) frameworks provides a sixth. Finally the sophisticated Myers-Briggs provides a seventh.

All of these frameworks are worthy of study, and we believe they are an important part of teachers' professional knowledge. But for the sake of classroom climate and this particular dimension of influence, the point is to choose one of them and work overtly on giving the framework to students, that is, teaching them to use it not to label themselves but to modulate their effort, seek help when appropriate, and sometimes take initiative to alter assignments based on their self-knowledge from a learning style perspective.

---

[4] Useful resources for thinking about including multiple modalities in instruction are David Lazear, *Multiple Intelligence Approaches to Assessment* and *Seven Pathways to Learning*, published by Zephyr Press.

Giving students license and encouragement to speak up in this way to ask for modifications of assignments brings us to the topic of choices.

What kinds of choices do students get to make about their academic work and how they do it? Carolyn Mamchur (1990) writes: "Giving students choices may seem like a complex issue. But actually, it is dead simple. The rule is this: whenever you can give a student a choice of any kind, do it."

A Nonreport is a good example of students' influencing assignments and the shape of products. There is nothing particularly unique about Nonreports. They are simply outside assignments—but with several major differences. A Nonreport is anything that does not fall into the category of straight written information. The task is to convince students accustomed to the way school is supposed to be that their teacher will accept and value their ideas. Their first question is usually "What do you want?" since they know that pleasing the teacher is the quickest way to a good grade. Here is how a Nonreport works:

1. Impress on them that a standard written report will receive no credit, since it does not meet the requirements of the assignment.

2. Make the assignment worth enough points so that not doing it will result in a substantial drop in grade. At first, there is a great risk in doing something not completely spelled out, so the risk of losing credit must be greater.

3. Create a grading scale that gives equal merit to content and to creativity (more loosely, to the effort the student has to make to personalize the knowledge he or she conveys).

4. Keep the topic very general, giving the students ample opportunity to select from among a wide variety of ideas. For example, if you are studying a unit on measurement, allow them to select anything at all dealing with measurement. Point out to them that there are few occupations (hobbies, sports, etc.) that do not contain measurement of some kind. Give them examples. Challenge them to name something that apparently has nothing to do with measurement—but be quick enough on your feet to find the measurement involved.

5. If they insist, and they may at first, give them a couple of examples of Nonreport-type formats (they are endless and limited only by imagination). For example, they could create a game, write a song, role-play a game show, do a slide or tape presentation, make a scrapbook, or build a model. But warn them that they will receive more credit for doing something you haven't thought of than copying something you have. And stick by that statement!

6. Perhaps most important, don't do this assignment unless you are willing to truly value the students' ideas. If you can't suspend your own idea of what is right or good and try to see the product from their point of view, they will never believe you again. But neither should you give credit for hastily conceived and executed junk. I once received a shoebox with a hole punched in one end that was labeled "Working model of a black hole." Hah!

I have found that giving 10 points for the idea, 10 points for the execution, and 10 points for the content, plus 5 for effort, works out well—a total of 35 points. The effort points come in when a person has had three weeks to do a project that might be reasonably well done but obviously took only 15 minutes compared to someone else who spent several hours. You can tell by looking.

The first time you do this, you will probably receive the usual assortment of collages, collections, and posters copied from books. But when these students see the more adventurous, creative, and "fun" projects getting all the praise, they will be more willing to let go a little the next time.

By the end of the first year that I had students do these projects, I turned them loose on a topic we had not covered in class: solar energy. They researched the topic, did their Nonreports—including a working parabolic solar cooker and a miniature solar greenhouse complete with Trombe walls made of plastic soft drink bottles—and presented them to the class, thus covering almost all the important aspects of solar energy—with no effort on the part of the teacher. One of the most rewarding aspects of these assignments is that, frequently, the students who usually get C's or D's in regular assignments really come into their own on Nonreports.

Nonreports allow students to plan, research, and execute. It evokes their creative potential and forces interaction with the content. Many students sought "experts" to help them and learned the intricacies of carpentry, photography, sound and art—because they wanted. And it is tremendously exciting to see projects come into the classroom that are far beyond anything the teacher would have assigned or expected. (Anonymous, *Mindsight*, New Lenox, Ill., 1989)

We would add specific criteria for success that make clear to students exactly what the attributes of quality work in the Nonreport will be. For example, in the Nonreport on solar energy, the criteria could be: (1) explains three different ways of converting solar energy, (2) discusses costs and efficiencies of various forms of solar energy, and (3) uses data to compare the efficiency of solar, fossil fuel, and nuclear energy. Students using these criteria could create dozens of different kinds of products to represent their learning, from radio shows to models to hypercard assemblies.

Randolf and Evertson (1995) give a simple example of student choice that suggests how plentiful are the opportunities for giving them:

Ms. Cooper often delegated tasks that would typically be assigned [by her] to students. We have already described students as providing the text for writing class through Sharing Models/Generating Characteristics. In this activity, students also took on the task of controlling the floor, which would traditionally be a teacher task. Areas of student control include deciding how to participate, getting the class's attention and leading the discussion by calling on peers...student readers usually stood in the front of the room, but Ms. Cooper gave students the option of reading from their desks.

Students were given the same choice when they shared their rough drafts with the class. The fact that Ms. Cooper did not define this aspect of appropriate participation gave students choice in how to manage this aspect of controlling the floor.

The ability of students to make choices and control the activity flow and the discourse within the group is partially responsible for the success of cooperative learning. In all cooperative learning models, students work in groups in which they control the dialogue, who speaks, when, and for how long.

Students and Their Communities as Sources of Knowledge

Constructivist Teaching

Constructivist pedagogy brings student influence to the intellectual life of the classroom and may be the most advanced level of student ownership. It is also the most complex and requires the largest paradigm shift for teachers; most of us, after all, were educated in schools where other people's constructions of knowledge were handed to us for consumption and digestion. Brooks and Brooks (1993) provide five overarching principles of constructivist pedagogy:

1. Posing problems of emerging relevance to learners.
2. Structuring learning around "big ideas" or primary concepts.
3. Seeking and valuing students' points of view.
4. Adapting curriculum to address students' suppositions.
5. Assessing student learning in the context of teaching. (p. 33)

There is still a place in good education for "active reception learning" as Ausubel (1963) puts it. But there is also a large place for carefully designed teaching that allows students to construct meaning for themselves.

Randolf and Evertson (1995) in their analysis of interactive discourse in a writing class describe this kind of pedagogy: "The construction of knowledge, which takes place through negotiation, depends on the redistribution of power from teachers to students. The fact that knowledge is presumed to come from students defines students as knowledge-holders, an identity usually retained by the teacher."

Constructivist teaching puts students in the legitimate role of knowledge generators and knowledge editors, whether in science, social studies, language arts, or any other academic discipline (Brooks and Brooks 1993). The examples in the Randolf and Evertson study describe a series of lessons on literary genre. They show how teachers' conscious regulation of dialogue and interaction with students can make students genuinely empowered knowledge generators. For example, one teacher, Ms. Cooper, asked students to bring in examples of fables to share and discuss in class so they could extract the characteristics of fables from analyzing these examples. At one point she asked the class to look for generalizations they could make about the morals of fables:

Teacher:	What can we say about the characteristics of morals? [Students offer some suggestions.]
	Maybe we need to explain what a lesson or moral is—how to be a better person. I'm going to put that up, unless you have objections.
Laurie:	They're trying to prevent you from making mistakes. [Teacher writes, "Stories are used to help you become a better person and not make mistakes."]
Tim:	I disagree. Sometimes some of the things are wrong.
Hillary:	Can be [used to help you]. [Teacher changes "are" to "can be" in the sentence on the board: "Stories can be used to help you become a better person and not make mistakes."]
Onika:	But everybody makes mistakes.
Teacher:	You're right [Adds to the sentence on the board: "or learn from characters' mistakes in the story."], but the purpose of the fable is to help you not to make so many mistakes.

In analyzing this episode Randolf and Evertson (1995) comment:*

The discussion begins with Ms. Cooper's question. The answers she receives do not give her the information she wants, so Ms. Cooper supplies her own answer: a moral teaches how to be a better person. In stating her answer, Ms. Cooper clarifies her question: she is asking about the purpose of a moral. With this new information, Laurie is able to supply a response that Ms. Cooper validates by incorporating it into the characteristic she is writing on the chalkboard. So far Ms. Cooper is in the position of authority in the classroom, initiates the topic, students respond with possible answers, and she evaluates them, rejecting all responses until she hears one that fits her expectations.

The nature of the interaction changes, however, as Tim questions the characteristic that is the joint construction of Ms. Cooper and Laurie. In effect, Tim takes on the role of evaluator of the response, moving Ms. Cooper into the role of co-collaborator with Laurie. Ms. Cooper's response is thus demonstrated to be as open to evaluation as any other participant's response.

Onika and Susan then join the deliberation, questioning the need for morals as they have defined them in class more than they are questioning the definition itself. Why, they argue, should morals try to keep you from making mistakes, when you're going to make them anyway, and they help you learn? These contributions are initiations of a new topic, which Ms. Cooper responds to and evaluates by treating them as negotiations of meaning, signaling

*Reprinted with permission. Randolf, Catherine H., and Carolyn M. Evertson. "Managing for Learning: Rules, Roles, and Meanings in a Writing Class." *Journal of Classroom Interaction* 30 (Summer 1995): 17–25.

her acceptance by incorporating the new contribution into the statement on the board. Thus, the characteristic as it is finally stated is the joint construction of Ms. Cooper, Laurie, Tim, Hillary, Onika, and Susan.

Similar scenarios can be found in the literature for helping students construct knowledge in science and mathematics. This kind of teaching requires a role shift for some teachers of significant proportions away from being dispensers of knowledge to facilitating negotiation of meaning by students.

The role of the teacher in constructivist science teaching is often to involve students in predicting phenomena, then reacting to observed phenomena and constructing hypotheses, which they then test to account for their observations. For example, most students predict that heavy objects fall faster then lighter ones—which is incorrect. The hypothesis making and dialogue about subsequent experiments and explanations that constructivist teachers facilitate have similar qualities to the dialogue in the Randolf and Evertson example.

The changes that take place when teachers move to include more constructivist teaching in their repertoire are subtle but significant. The classroom does not look any different, and the assignments and topics may not seem much different. Where the changes show up is in dialogue with students and in the roles teachers and students are playing in the conversations they have in class. Though surface changes may appear small, the role shift is large, and the evidence is strong that the effect is large in student motivation, effort, and understanding (Newmann and Wehlage 1995).

Culturally Relevant Teaching

As we move toward the year 2020, when fully half of all children in the United States will be people of color,[5] it is especially important to be creating schools that acknowledge and value the culture of all students. Excluding these children's cultures from school artifacts, customs, arts, and curriculum not only demotivates but alienates significant numbers of students (Cummins 1986). Ladson-Billings (1995) brings this argument into the more immediate domain of curriculum by pointing out that using the community as a source of curriculum experiences makes learning meaningful and active and also culturally relevant:

> Early in the school year, one teacher asked the students to identify one area in which they believed they had expertise. She then compiled a list of "classroom experts" for distribution to the class. Later, she developed a calendar and asked students to select a date that they would like to make a presentation in their area of expertise. When students made their presentations, their knowledge and expertise was a given. Their classmates were expected to be an attentive audience and to take seriously the knowledge that was being shared by taking notes and/or asking relevant questions. The variety of topics the students offered included rap-music, basketball, gospel singing, cooking, hair braiding, and baby sitting. Other students listed more school-like areas of expertise such as reading, writing, and mathematics. However, all students were required to share their expertise. (Ladson-Billings 1995)

[5] Hodgkinson, H. Presentation to Phi Delta Kappan Annual Conference, 1993.

Some may wonder how such open-ended assignments can be congruent with a school curriculum that contains specific skills the students are supposed to be mastering. By using practices described in Chapter 16 of this book, teachers can weave skill objectives for research, organization, and reading, writing, and speaking skills (or any other skills that are in the curriculum) into the criteria for good presentations by student experts. The point that Ladson-Billings makes is that the students own the knowledge they present, and the knowledge is acknowledged to have value. The "classroom experts" assignment is a practice that is congruent with augmenting student ownership and influence because the knowledge of students and the culture from which that knowledge comes—namely, the students' own culture—is explicitly validated by a school learning activity.

"Culturally relevant teaching" is the topic of the article from which the Ladson-Billings excerpt comes. Culturally relevant teaching does not mean teaching about other cultures, though that can have value. It means validating the culture of students by including in-school learning experiences topics, scenes, and knowledge that derive from the culture of the students themselves. It looks not only to individual students but also to the community from which the students come as a source of curriculum experiences.

> One teacher used the community as a basis of her curriculum. Her students searched the county historical archives, interviewed long-term residents, constructed and administered surveys and a questionnaire, and invited and listened to guest speakers to get a sense of the historical development of their community. Their ultimate goal was to develop a land use proposal for an abandoned shopping center that was a magnet for illegal drug use and other dangerous activities. The project ended with the students making a presentation before the City Council and Urban Planning Commission. One of the students remarked to me, "This [community] is not such a bad place. There are a lot of good things that happened here, and some of that is still going on." The teacher told me that she was concerned that too many of the students believed that the only option for success involved moving out of the community, rather than participating in its reclamation. (Ladson-Billings, 1995, p. 479)[6]

---

[6] In other parts of her report, Ladson-Billings (1995) argues extensively for building class community and an atmosphere of mutual support and help.

Classroom Climate Survey

This is a good point for readers to assess where they are in their thinking and practices with regard to classroom climate. We encourage readers to fill in the following survey for each of the three strands and compare answers in groups with colleagues.

Community and Mutual Support

How are students encouraged to get to know one another and to get to know other people?

When are students listened to, acknowledged, and affirmed as worthwhile, important, and cared-for people?

When do students learn group responsibility and interdependence?

What opportunities are there for learning social skills and cooperative learning?

How are conflict-resolution strategies being learned and practiced in the classroom and around the school?

Risk Taking and Confidence

What are the times when students are encouraged to take risks and find out it's okay to do so?

What do I do to disabuse students of the life-limiting belief in the virtue of speed versus care and perseverance?

When does the belief "good students solicit help and lots of feedback on their work" get communicated in the classroom?

In what ways do students learn that effort makes the difference?

Influence

What are the times when students are in a controlling or influencing role?

What principles of learning are students knowledgeable about and encouraged to use?

What are the opportunities for giving control to students within the models of teaching being used?

What opportunities are there to have students be authentic knowledge producers and structure classroom discourse from the constructivist perspective?

What opportunities are there for students to be experts?

What are the ways in which the local community culture is viewed as a source of "authorized" curriculum and thus as a worthwhile source of knowledge?

Source Materials on Classroom Climate

Anonymous. *Mindsight*. New Lenox, Ill., 1989.

Aronson, E. *The Jigsaw Classroom*. Beverly Hills, Calif.: Sage Publications, 1978.

Aspy, David, and F. N. Roebuck. *Kids Don't Learn from People They Don't Like*. Amherst, Mass.: Human Resource Development Press, 1977.

Ausubel, D. P. *The Psychology of Meaningful Verbal Learning*. New York: Grune & Stratton, 1963.

Barbe, Walter B., and Michael N. Milone, Jr. "Modality." *Instructor Magazine* (January 1980).

Battistich, Victor, Daniel Solomon, Dong-il Kim, Marilyn Watson, and Eric Schaps. "Schools as Communities, Poverty Levels of Student Populations, and Students' Attitudes, Motives, and Performance: A Multilevel Analysis." *American Educational Research Journal* 32 (Fall 1995).

Battistich, Victor, Solomon, Marilyn Watson, Judith Solomon, and Eric Schaps. "Effects of an Elementary School Program to Enhance Prosocial Behavior on Children's Cognitive-Social Problem-Solving Skills and Strategies. *Journal of Applied Developmental Psychology* 10 (1989): 147–169.

Bennett, Barrie, and Peter Smilanich. *Classroom Management*. Ontario, Canada: VISUTRONIX, Bookation, 1994.

Berger, Ron. "Building a School Culture of High Standards." Unpublished paper. Shutesbury, Mass.: Shutesbury Schools, 1990.

Berman, Sheldon. "Educating for Social Responsibility." *Educational Leadership* (November 1990): 75–80.

Brooks, Jacqueline Grennon, and Martin G. Brooks. *The Case for Constructivist Classrooms*. Alexandria, Va.: ASCD, 1993.

Bruer, John T. "The Mind's Journey from Novice to Expert." *American Educator* 38 (Summer 1993): 6–15.

Cabello, Beverly, and Raymond Terell. "Making Students Feel Like Family: How Teachers Create Warm and Caring Classroom Climates." *Journal of Classroom Interaction* 29 (1993): 17–23.

Charney, Ruth Sidney. *Teaching to Care: Management in the Responsive Classroom*. Greenfield, Mass.: Northeast Foundation for Children, 1992.

Chavez Chavez, Rudolpho. "The Use of High-Inference Measures to Study Classroom Climates: A Review. *Review of Educational Research* 54 (Summer 1984): 237–261.

Crocker, Robert K., and Gwen M. Brooker. "Classroom Control and Student Outcomes in Grades 2 and 5." *American Educational Research Journal* 23 (Spring 1986): 1–11.

Cummins, James. Empowering Minority Students: A Framework for Intervention. *Harvard Educational Review* 56 (February 1986): 18–36.

Curran, Lorna. *Cooperative Lessons for Little Ones*. San Juan Capistrano, Calif.: Resources for Teachers, 1991.

Deng, Bing. *A Multilevel Analysis of Classroom Climate Effects on Mathematics Achievement of Fourth-Grade Students*. Paper based on Ed.D. dissertation at Memphis State University, February 1992. ED 348 222.

Dodd, Anne Wescott. "Engaging Students: What I Learned Along the Way." *Educational Leadership* (September 1995).

Dreikurs, R. *Psychology in the Classroom*. New York: Harper & Row, 1957.

Dreikurs, R., and L. A. Grey. *A New Approach to Classroom Discipline: Logical Consequences*. New York: Harper & Row, 1968.

Dunn, Rita, and Kenneth Dunn. *Teaching Students Through Their Individual Learning Styles: A Practical Approach*. Reston, Va.: Prentice-Hall, 1978.

Ellsworth, P. C., and Vincent G. Sindt. "Helping 'Aha' to Happen: The Contributions of Irving Sigel." *Educational Leadership* (February 1994).

Fraser, B. J. "Two Decades of Research on Perceptions of Classroom Environment." In B. J. Fraser (ed.), *The Study of Learning Environments* (pp. 1-33). Salem, Oreg.: Assessment Research, 1986.

Fraser, B. J., and D. L. Fisher. "Student Achievement as a Function of Person-Environment Fit: A Regression Surface Analysis." *British Journal of Educational Psychology* 53 (1983): 89–99.

Fraser, Barry J., John A. Malone, and Jillian M. Neale. "Assessing and Improving the Psychosocial Environment of Mathematics Classrooms." *Journal of Research in Mathematics Education* 20 (1989): 191–201.

Fraser, Barry J., and Peter O'Brien. "Student and Teacher Perceptions of the Environment of Elementary School Classrooms." *Elementary School Journal* 20 (1985): 567–580.

Gardner, Howard. *Frames of Mind: The Theory of Multiple Intelligences*. New York: Basic Books, 1983.

Gibbs, Jeanne. *Tribes: A Process for Social Development and Cooperative Learning*. 2d ed. Santa Rosa, Calif.: Center Source Publications, 1989.

Glasser, W. *Reality Therapy*. New York: Harper & Row, 1965.

———. *Schools without Failure*. New York: Harper Colophon Books, 1969.

———. *The Total Quality School*. 1994.

Gordon, Thomas. *T.E.T.: Teacher Effectiveness Training*. New York: Peter H. Wyden, 1974.

Gould, Stephen J. *The Mismeasure of Man*. New York: W. W. Norton, 1982.

Gregorc, Anthony F. *Inside Styles: Beyond the Basics*. Maynard, Mass.: Gabriel Systems, Inc., 1985.

Haertel, G. D., H. J. Walberg, and E. H. Haertel. "Socio-psychological Environments and Learning: A Quantitative Synthesis." *British Educational Research Journal* 7 (1981): 27–36.

Harrison, Allen F., and Robert M. Bramson. *The Art of Thinking*. New York: Berkeley Books, 1982.

Hodgkinson, H. Presentation to Phi Delta Kappan Annual Conference, 1993.

Howard, Jeffrey. *The Social Construction of Intelligence*. Lexington, Mass.: Efficacy Inc., 1993.

Johnson, David W., and Roger T. Johnson. *Learning Together and Alone: Cooperative, Competitive, and Individualistic Learning*. 2d ed. Englewood Cliffs, N.J.: Prentice-Hall, 1987.

Johnson, David W., and Roger T. Johnson. *Teaching Students to Be Peacemakers*. Edina, Minn.: Interaction Book Co., 1995.

———. "Why Violence Prevention Programs Don't Work—What Does." *Educational Leadership* (February 1995): 63–68.

———. *Learning Together and Alone*. 2d ed. Englewood Cliffs, N.J.: Prentice-Hall, 1987.

Kagan, S. *Cooperative Learning*. San Juan Capistrano, Calif.: Kagan Cooperative Learning, 1992.

Katz, Lilian. "Five Keys to Successful Implementation of the Whole." Presentation to Association for Supervision and Curriculum Development 1992. Audiotape 612-92123.

Kreidler, William J. *Creative Conflict Resolution*. Glenview, Ill.: Scott Foresman, 1984.

Ladson-Billings, G. "Toward a Theory of Culturally Relevant Pedagogy." *American Educational Research Journal* 32 (Fall 1995).

Lampert, Magdalena. "When the Problem is Not the Question and the Solution Not the Answer: Mathematical Knowing and Teaching." *American Educational Research Journal* 27, no. 1 (1990): 29–63.

Lafferty, J. Clayton. *The Subarctic Survival Situation*. Plymouth, Mich.: Human Synergistics, 1974, 1992.

Lazear, David. *Multiple Intelligence Approaches to Assessment: Solving the Assessment Conundrum*. Tucson: Zephyr Press, 1994.

———. *Seven Pathways of Learning: Teaching Students and Parents about Multiple Intelligences*. Tucson: Zephyr Press, 1994.

Mamchur, Caroline. "But the Curriculum." *Phi Delta Kappan* (April 1990).

Maslow, A. *Toward a Psychology of Being*. Princeton, N.J.: Van Nostrand, 1962.

McCabe, Margaret E., and Jaquelline Rhoades. *The Nurturing Classroom.* Willits, Calif.: ITA Publications, 1989.

McCarthy, Bernice. The *4MAT System: Teaching to Learning Styles with Right/ Left Mode Techniques.* Barrington, Ill., 1987.

Moos, R. H., and B. S. Moos. "Classroom Social Climate and Students' Absences and Grades." *Journal of Educational Psychology* 70 (1978): 263–269.

Myers, Isabel B., and Mary H. McCaulley. *Manual: A Guide to the Development and Use of the Myers-Briggs Type Indicator.* Palo Alto, Calif.: Consulting Psychologists Press, 1985.

Nelson, Jane, Lynn Lott, and H. Stephen Glenn. *Positive Discipline in the Classroom.* Rocklin, Calif.: Prima Publishing, 1993.

Newmann, Fred M., and Gary G. Wehlage. *Successful School Restructuring.* Madison, Wisc.: University of Wisconsin, 1995.

Nunnery, John A., E. Dean Butler, and Venkata N. Bhaireddy. "Relationships between Classroom Climate, Student Characteristics, and Language Achievement in the Elementary Classroom: An Exploratory Investigation." Paper presented at the Annual Meeting of the American Educational Research Association, Atlanta, April 1993.

Oakes, Jeananie. *Keeping Track.* New Haven, Conn.: Yale University Press, 1985.

Pfeiffer, J. William, and John E. Jones. *A Handbook of Structured Experiences for Human Relations Training.* Vol. 1–8. La Jolla, Calif.: University Associates, 1974.

Poplin, Mary, and Joseph Weeres. *Voices from the Inside.* Claremont, CA: Institute for Education in Transformation, Claremont Graduate School, 1992.

Randolf, Catherine H., and Carolyn M. Evertson. "Managing for Learning: Rules, Roles, and Meanings in a Writing Class." *Journal of Classroom Interaction* 30 (Summer 1995): 17–25.

Scearce, Carol. *100 Ways to Build Teams.* Palatine, Ill.: IRI/Skylight Publishing, 1992.

Schutz, W. J. *Expanding Human Awareness.* New York: Grove Press, 1967.

Seigle, Pamela, and Gayle Macklem. *Social Competency Program.* Wellesley, Mass.: Stone Center, 1993.

Sharan, Yael, and Shlomo Sharan. *Expanding Cooperative Learning through Group Investigation.* New York: Teachers College Press, 1992.

Shaw, Vanston. *Community Building in the Classroom.* San Juan Capistrano, Calif.: Kagan Cooperative Learning, 1992.

Slavin, R. *Using Student Team Learning.* Baltimore: Center for Research on Elementary and Middle Schools, John Hopkins University, 1986.

Solomon, D., M. Watson, K. Delucchi, E. Schaps, and V. Battistich. "Enhancing Children's Prosocial Behavior in the Classroom." *American Educational Research Journal* 25 (1988): 527–554.

Stanford, Gene. *Developing Effective Classroom Groups.* New York: Hart Publishing Co., 1977.

Stephenson, James, and Beth Watrous. "The Morning Meeting Repertoire: A Collection of Ideas That Work." *The Responsive Classroom* 5, no. 2 (Fall/Winter 1993): 8.

Sylvester, Robert. *A Celebration of Neurons: An Educator's Guide to the Human Brain.* Alexandria, Va.: Association for Supervision and Curriculum Development, 1994.

Vernon, D. Sue, Jean B. Schumaker, and Donald D. Deshler. *The SCORE Skills: Social Skills for Cooperative Groups.* Lawrence, Kansas: Edge Enterprises, 1993.

Wade, Rahima C. "Encouraging Student Initiative in a Fourth Grade Classroom." *Elementary School Journal* 95 (March 1995): 339–354.

Weiner, B. *Theories of Motivation: From Mechanism to Cognition.* Chicago: Markham, 1972.

Wentzel, Kathryn R. "Social Competence at School: Relation Between Social Responsibility and Academic Achievement." *Review of Educational Research* 61 (Spring 1991): 1–24.

Withall, John. "The Development of a Technique for Measuring the Social-Emotional Climate of the Classroom." *Journal of Experimental Education* 17 (1949): 347–361.

Wood, Chip. *Yardsticks.* Greenfield, Mass.: Northeast Foundation for Children, 1994.

Wood, Chip. *The Responsive Classroom.* Greenfield, Mass.: Northeast Foundation for Children, 1994.

Yager, Stuart, Roger Johnson, David Johnson, and Bill Snider. "The Impact of Group Processing on Achievement in Cooperative Learning Groups." *Journal of Social Psychology* 125 (1986): 389–397.

14

Objectives

What should I teach, and how should I frame my objectives?

Five Kinds of Teacher Thinking

Teacher Thinking and
Lesson Planning

Level of Difficulty

Primary Sources of Objectives

Secondary Sources of Objectives

Eighty percent of those polled in an early validation study of the parameters thought the most important parameter of teaching was objectives (Saphier 1980). In explanation, they said, for example, "If you don't know where you're going, you can't get there," "Objectives have to be the point of departure," and "Everything you do is built on knowing what you want to accomplish."

All of their answers seemed quite logical and convincing. (Eventually we stopped asking the question. We came to see that all the parameters are reciprocally important. Good objectives clearly don't go anywhere without good instruction, or good assessment.) What was interesting about the responses was the contrast between stated values and known behavior. We know that most teachers don't think in terms of objectives for student learning when they do their planning (Peterson, Marx, and Clark 1978; Joyce, Clark, and Peck 1981). They think in terms of activities. They plan what they will do and in what order, and also what activities students will do and in what order. Joyce, Clark, and Peck (1981) explain this format in terms of decisions made at the beginning of the year, for example, which text and what materials will be used.

> *If you don't know where you're going, you can't get there.*

The danger here is that it becomes easy to lose track of where you're going when you don't think or write in terms of student learning objectives. A teacher can get tied to materials and activities, have students involved and liking their classes, but be achieving uncertain, erratic, and unpredictable results. Student involvement and enjoyment of school are a fine goal, but they do not by themselves make for effective teaching and learning.

Madeline Hunter, former director of the UCLA Lab elementary school, tells a story that illuminates how fuzzy thinking about objectives can dilute learning. She finds a kindergarten teacher holding her head amidst a room that's a mess of paper and glue. There are mimeographed turkeys all around on which children have been pasting squares of colored tissue paper to make Thanksgiving collages. Madeline asks what's been going on. "Well, it was an art experience for the kids," is the reply. The exchange then continued:

Madeline: Why did you go to the trouble of mimeographing the turkeys? Why not just give them a piece of paper and the tissue and let them be creative, express themselves?

Teacher: It really wasn't that. It was really a lesson in eye-hand coordination.

Madeline: Well, then why didn't you have them outline the turkey? You can't tell whether they stayed within the line or not when they've got them pasted all over the turkey.

Teacher: Well, it really wasn't that. It was a lesson in conservation.

Madeline: Conservation!

Teacher: Yes. The kids have really been very wasteful of paste. So I was trying to teach them to put just a tiny piece of paste on.

Madeline: Then why didn't you give them a piece of paste, or a paper of paste, and see how much of their turkey they could finish before they ran out of paste? You can't tell if there's a cup of paste under some of these turkeys.

Teacher: Oh, for cryin' out loud, can't kids just have fun?

Madeline: Sure they can have fun. What do your kids like to do?

Teacher: The thing they like to do best is just chase out on the school grounds.

Madeline: Why didn't you take the last half-hour and go around, supervise them while they chased, and you wouldn't have this mess to clean up? (Hunter 1977)*

Many of the differences we see in people's teaching can be traced back to their thinking about objectives. The quality of that thinking is what makes the difference. When some teachers think objectives, they are really thinking about what they want to cover: "My objective tomorrow is to get through the material on gas attacks in World War I." A teacher thinking in terms of coverage focuses on getting through everything, and what is important is that the information gets said and that the class finishes. This outlook will influence the teaching. The teacher tends to become wed to an agenda and a timetable and tends to do less checking, less intellectual exploration, and less integration with other learning. Instruction tends toward recitation.

Five Kinds of Teacher Thinking

There are five kinds of thinking about objectives we have observed teachers using. Each has a place in planning; but if any one becomes an exclusive mind-set, the instruction that results can have significant gaps for students. In the sections that follow we profile these five kinds of thinking.

---

*Reprinted with permission. Hunter, M. Presentation at ASCD, 1977.

Coverage Objectives

A coverage objective means a teacher is thinking in terms of herself or himself, not the students. She is going to present, describe, explain, demonstrate, or cover identified information, events, procedures, or processes. When she's through the agenda, the lesson is done. She has "covered" it, taking it out of her head and putting it "out there." She is not necessarily doing it in a way that is guided by what is in the students' heads before she starts. And she doesn't know if it passed through the nether regions of "out there" into students' heads.

Activity Objectives

At other times when teachers think about objectives, they mean what they want the students to do—activities that students will get through: completing workbook pages, answering questions, solving problems, doing an experiment, discussing a chapter, and so forth. The objective then is really that they get the activity done. With such a focus, it is possible that the activity is not teaching what should be taught or that it can be done without students' learning anything

"Write a story," for example, may be the activity objective for after lunch in a primary grade room. To get the children involved (make the activity more fun, more attractive, more motivating) the teacher has textured wallpaper pieces they can use to make covers for their "books" and is going to help them bind their books. The quality of stories ranges from complete plots with beginnings, middles, and ends to random pictures with no text at all. While binding each book, the teacher asks the children about their stories: some make comments; some don't. The teacher is focusing on the binding

> *When teachers' objectives are to get the activities done, they miss opportunities to underline the critical learnings.*

and keeping the flow of students moving. An observer in the class sees no evidence that there is any particular feature the teacher is looking for in the stories. She is making an effort to be positive about some aspect of each child's work, but appears to be looking for nothing in particular. The real objective is just that they produce stories—of any quality. Clearly this is an activity objective. The teacher might not admit that if asked, but no other statement of the objective-in-action is supportable.

When teachers' objectives are to get the activities done, they miss opportunities to underline the critical learnings, make connections between learnings for students, and check and evaluate student learning. A teacher thinking in terms of activities is concerned with management. The focus is on giving directions and having everyone engaged. There may also be an emphasis on excitement, involvement, and debate—in which case there is also an involvement objective.

Involvement Objectives

When teachers think about objectives in terms of student involvement, what they're really after is that students "get into it." A teacher might say, "My objective tomorrow is to get all students to react personally—say, what they'd do if they invented a horrible weapon. Would they turn it over to the government?"

Studies of teacher planning (conducted by having teachers think aloud) have shown that activity objectives and involvement objectives dominate planning (Clark and Yinger 1979). Involvement objectives are met if students appear to engage in the activity with some absorption, enthusiasm, or intensity. The objective of involving the students is that the students like the activity and stick with it. There is nothing wrong with that state of affairs. In fact, it's wonderful. But it is possible to be absorbed in an activity that isn't teaching anything. Students like to do it perhaps, but fun does not necessarily equal learning. It doubtless enhances learning, but such activities may not be productive in and of themselves.

Let us say that students love to do word searches, so I make up one with their spelling words in it and they do it for seatwork. I notice they are having fun. "Boy, they really got into that word search today!" I think. But did it help them learn their spelling words? Did I, in fact, assign it because I thought it would help them learn to spell the words? No. I assigned it because I thought they'd like to do it, and they do. But as it turns out, there is no evidence that word searches improve students' ability to spell the words they find. It may improve their ability to scan complex data fields for visual information; they may (some of them) develop systematic searching strategies for finding the words more efficiently. But this was not my objective, and students who learn "systematic search" are learning it at random and incidentally, not through any deliberate approach of mine.

Mastery (or Student Learning) Objectives

If the objective is mastery of the spelling words, then the teacher will do something that should increase the likelihood that the students will spell the words right: perhaps quiz each other in pairs and then make a list of the words they missed and go through a practice routine of seeing, saying, writing in the air, and retesting, over a 10-minute period. Clearly the objective is a mastery objective for the students.

Perhaps a teacher says, "My objective for tomorrow is for students to be able to distinguish between rational, amoral, and moral reasons for decisions from the list of positions we will generate in class." If he focuses on student learning, there will be lots of checking to see what students' know, perceive, or can do. Timetables are flexible, and what's important is that students learn well, even if less is covered.

To summarize so far, here are the four kinds of thinking about objectives we have described:

1. *Mastery (student learning) objective*: "When we're done they'll be able to…"

2. *Involvement objective*: "I want them to get involved in…"

3. *Activity objective*: "First they will…then they'll/we'll…then I want them to…"

4. *Coverage objective*: "What I'm going to do first is to give them…then I'll describe then I'll ask them to…"

These four kinds of thinking are not mutually exclusive and tend to be cumulative. A teacher planning in terms of student learning has to consider activities, involvement, and what will be covered. But it is possible to think in terms of either coverage or activities and not consciously about student learning.

> *The quality of thinking about objectives accounts for much of what we see (or don't see) in classrooms.*

This is an interesting lens for supervisors to use in reviewing events with teachers. Inquiring into the nature of thinking about objectives will often help solve puzzles about why certain pieces of teaching are going awry or not living up fully to their promise. The quality of thinking about objectives accounts for much of what we see (or don't see) in classrooms.

Generic Thinking Objectives

Let's go back to the word search. Suppose I want students to learn something about systematic search as a strategy. That's the kind of skill we use to look through a collection of nuts and bolts for a particular size, or scan a map for Maple Street and only know that it's somewhere on the page.

A teacher who wants students to learn strategies for systematic search would certainly talk about how different children were going about looking for the words: comparing approaches and strategies, giving names to the different strategies, listing them on the board, asking students where else they could use these strategies or what other kinds of tasks would be good places to try them out (transfer), and so forth. This teacher has a generic thinking objective—that is, an objective to develop a thinking skill apart from any particular content knowledge.

Consider a seventh-grade social studies class working on a chapter about Bedouins of the Arabian desert. There's a lot of information in the chapter—facts and concepts galore. But not only does their teacher want them to learn the facts . She wants them to learn about hierarchical relationships—not just relationships in Bedouin life, but the nature of hierarchical relationships in general, how to find them and represent them. So she adds something to the

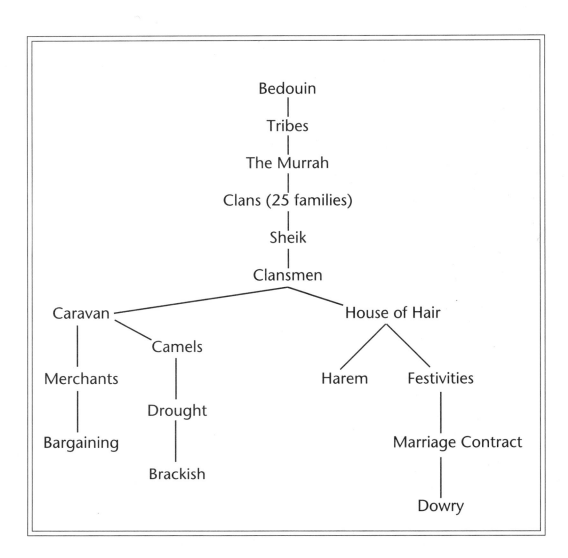

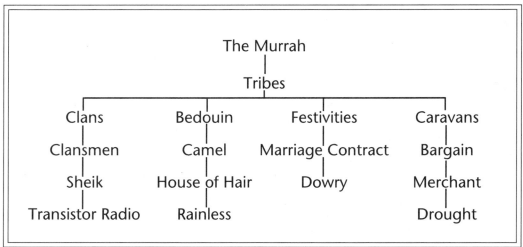

FIGURE 14.1: HIERARCHICAL RELATIONSHIPS IN BEDOUIN LIFE

assignment, asking them to identify key terms from the chapter and make a diagram that shows their relationships to one another. Now something more is required. FIGURE **14.1** shows two different diagrams that students might draw up.

Note the different kinds of thinking behind these two diagrams. The first has terms arranged subordinately according to size. The Murrah is one of many tribes. Each tribe (Murrah included) is composed of clans of about twenty-five families, and each clan is headed by a sheik. Each family is organized around a patriarch and inhabits a "house of hair" (a Bedouin dwelling) with a harem. Then the relationships shift to category groupings.

The second diagram shows relationships that are random and nonlinear. The diagram seems to have been created by free association rather than consistent application of some particular kind of relationship.

Now students compare their diagrams in small groups and explain the kind of relationships their connecting lines represent. They talk to each other about their thinking and later in a total class discussion will develop in particular what hierarchical or subordinated relationships mean, using their examples. The teacher will use those words (*hierarchical*, *subordinated*) because the objective for this and for the upcoming series of lessons is that they become able to do that kind of thinking, whether it's around Bedouins, sports, or computer programming. The objective here goes beyond mastery of content (though it includes that) to developing a particular thinking skill.

There are literally dozens of thinking skills that may be targeted and taught simultaneously with and through academic content. The point to note is if and when such an objective is present and how it alters the nature of assignments and of instruction.

Distinguishing Thinking Skill Objectives and Mastery Objectives

There is an important distinction between "thinking skill" objectives and "mastery" objectives. They are both, to be sure, a form of mastery. In the latter the goal is for students to master knowledge (e.g., be able to explain the causes of the Civil War) and operational skills (e.g., write with good grammar; solve three-step word problems; locate points on the globe with latitude and longitude). In the case of "thinking skill" objectives, the goal is for students to master a generic form of thinking skill, like comparison and contrast, or understanding one's assumptions, or defining the real problem before listing solutions. Put another way, the goal is for students to learn or get better at a particular thinking skill and be able to transfer it to material other than today's content.

But merely giving assignments whose fulfillment *calls for* certain thinking skills is not *teaching* the thinking skill, just as round-robin reading, which calls for students to perform reading, is not necessarily teaching them anything about how to get better at reading (Duffy and Roehler 1986).

Almost everything teachers ask students to do requires them to think in some way. But only when they are deliberately and explicitly teaching a particular kind of thinking skill that can be named can it be said that there is a thinking skill objective.

If I desire that the students learn thinking skill X, I may repeatedly give them tasks that call for it, that is, do a task that requires the thinking skill to do it correctly. But I may not have clarity about what it takes to get them there, and I may not have the true commitment to go the extra step of teaching it explicitly.

When teaching a particular thinking skill is a real objective of mine, I name the thinking skill, teach it, coach it, and arrange for the children to get feedback on how they're doing with it—all this in addition to having them practice it. To claim a teacher had a thinking skill objective for children (rather than just a thinking assignment or a task that calls for thinking), one would need to see the teacher:

1. Naming the skill.
2. Dealing explicitly with how to do it (e.g., modeling aloud with the steps or having students share strategies for doing it).
3. Highlighting steps.
4. Giving tips and coaching pointers.
5. Having students practice with feedback.
6. Evaluating how the students are doing with it.

Unfortunately, we usually only see step 6. That's not teaching a thinking skill; that's testing for it and hoping the students will learn the skill from the test or the task. Merely giving assignments whose fulfillment calls for certain thinking skills is not teaching the thinking skill, just as round-robin reading, which calls for students to perform reading, is not necessarily teaching them anything about how to get better at reading (Duffy and Roehler 1986). Almost everything we ask students to do requires them to think in some way. But only when we are deliberately and explicitly teaching a particular kind of thinking skill we could name can it be said we have a "thinking skill" objective.

FIGURE **14.2** summarizes the five kinds of thinking about objectives described so far and FIGURE **14.3** shows them in a graphic organizer.

NAME	LANGUAGE USED	THE OBJECTIVE
Generic thinking skills: Student centered—centered on ways children function intellectually.	"Diagram the relationship between key terms describing Bedouin life."	For students to express or develop a certain kind of thinking skill
Mastery of academic knowledge or skills: Student centered—centered on what children will learn in the way of information or skills.	"Be able to describe to each other the principal causes of World War I." "Measure distance using scale on the map."	For students to know or be able to do something specific
Involvement: Student centered—on how children will react.	"After giving a dramatic reading of the story, I'll solicit their opinions and get them involved in a discussion."	For students to be visibly involved—at least to participate actively and at best to be excited and have fun
Activity: Student centered—on what children will do.	"They'll look at the filmstrip, then make a map of the South, then answer the questions at the end of the chapter."	For students to finish certain tasks
Coverage: Teacher centered—on what the teacher will do, what agenda to get through	"First I'll discuss the heat of reaction; then I'll go over endothermic reactions, entropy, enthalpy, and then review valences."	To mention or get students to mention answers or ideas

FIGURE 14.2: FIVE KINDS OF THINKING ABOUT OBJECTIVES

The Five Objective Circles

No one can teach a thinking skill objective without having some content for the students to apply it to, so a teacher who is teaching to a thinking objective almost always has a mastery-of-knowledge or skills objective too. That is why the "thinking" circle in the diagram in FIGURE 14.3 includes the "mastery of knowledge and skills" circle. But the reverse is not necessarily true: A teacher can be teaching for mastery of knowledge without necessarily aiming to teach a particular thinking skill.

Similarly, the way in which the other circles in FIGURE 14.3 contain one another shows the overlapping relationship of different kinds of teacher cognition about objectives. For example, one can think "coverage" without having any activities for the students to do, but there cannot be activities without having some content the students are dealing with. To give another example, a teacher can have activities without any clear notion of what she

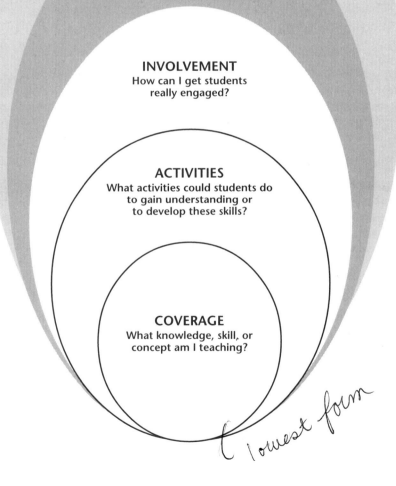

THINKING SKILLS
What thinking skills do I want students
to practice and develop?

MASTERY OBJECTIVES
What do I want students to know or
be able to do when the lesson is over?
How will I know if they know it or can do it?

INVOLVEMENT
How can I get students
really engaged?

ACTIVITIES
What activities could students do
to gain understanding or
to develop these skills?

COVERAGE
What knowledge, skill, or
concept am I teaching?

lowest form

FIGURE 14.3: THINKING ABOUT OBJECTIVES: KEY QUESTIONS IN LESSON PLANNING
This graphic organizer maps five kinds of thinking about objectives.

wants students to learn. (We fear this is all too common.) But she cannot have a true mastery objective without having both something for the students to do (activity) and some content on which to do it. Thus the "mastery of knowledge and skills" circle contains the other two.

Teacher Thinking and Lesson Planning

Up until now we have been making the case that teachers tend to fall into categories in terms of their thinking about objectives. Some teachers are coverage thinkers. Since their real goal is to get through material, their teaching is predictably characterized by certain phenomena: more teacher talk, more lecture, less checking for understanding.

Activity thinkers tend to have classes where students are often busy, sometimes working in groups. There may be good record keeping systems on student completion of tasks and assignments, but activity thinking, when it dominates, tends to produce classes where students are clear neither on what is to be learned nor on the criteria for quality work.

Involvement thinkers add higher energy and more fun, but their classes may look essentially the same as those of activity thinkers.

In previous chapters we have presented repertoires and argued that all behaviors in a repertoire can be "good" if they are an appropriate match to the student, situation or curriculum. The "repertoire" argument needs to be modified, however, to be valid for the five kinds of thinking about objectives. Being an activity thinker or a coverage thinker is not good enough if one never gets as far as mastery thinking in preparing for lessons.

On the other hand, fully developed planners—teachers who have clear images of what they want students to know and be able to do—still do have to identify content to deal with coverage. They still have to invent or find activities for the students that could logically lead students to master the intended learnings. Good planners, in fact, ask the key questions involved in all five kinds of thinking in FIGURE **14.3**; and they may, depending on personal style, ask them in any order as long as they ask and answer the mastery question thoroughly at some point. That question is, "What do I want students to know or be able to do? How will I know they know it or can do it?" (See FIGURE **14.3**.)

Some teachers are logical, linear, and analytic. They like to start with a statement of the mastery objective and proceed deliberately to develop assessment criteria and criterion tasks. Then they identify activities and materials that fit in with this objective.

Other teachers have "neat" activities or materials they love to use or that they think will be highly engaging for students. A teacher can start with activities in her own planning process, but must ask and answer comprehensively the mastery question before too long in the planning process.

Each of us in teaching, in looking back at a class we taught or observed, ought to be able to infer a clear statement of what students were supposed to be able to do at the end.

A clear objective is one that creates an image of specifically what a student will know or be able to do when the instruction is over: a picture in your mind, a sentence of inner speech you say to yourself, or a written statement. What's important is that the image is framed from the students' point of view. The objective is a clear picture of a students' performance that the teacher has.

We would argue that there are no objectives that cannot be framed as a clear image of student performance—even objectives pertaining to "attitude" or "appreciation." Second, we argue that objectives that are not thought through in this way typically wind up as coverage objectives, activity objectives, or involvement objectives, and all three of these are weaker than mastery objectives. Third, we argue that thinking in terms of mastery objectives tends to improve teaching by leading teachers to do more goal stating with students, more checking, more feedback according to criteria, better record keeping, and more diagnosis of individual student needs.

Let's return to the first point: There are no objectives that cannot be framed as student learning objectives (creating a specific image of what a student will know or be able to do). How about attitude objectives?

Mr. Caswell wants students to develop a positive attitude toward classical music. How would we know if he'd accomplished that? What does he mean when he says, "I want my students to appreciate Beethoven"? He might mean that he expects knowledge of the intricacy and subtlety of the design of a Beethoven symphony to generate respect. Further, he may believe that for some people, having to listen in a focused way to the symphony as they analyze its parts will lead to aesthetic enjoyment. All of that may be his concept of "appreciation": respect through knowledge and liking through repeated experience. If that is his concept, it will lead him to do certain activities in class aimed at generating specific student performances: performances like being able to analyze parts of the symphony and label a score; describing in words the principles by which Beethoven developed and restated themes; or identifying the different symphonies. All of these student performances he can picture because he has thought about what "appreciation" means. But if he doesn't translate "appreciation" into some sort of student performance in his head, then what Mr. Caswell does with students in class may be random in its effect; he will not be looking inside their heads to create anything in a planful way. He will be operating outside their heads with activities and presentations that may or may not contact anything inside students. Who can tell? Without that image of the student performance he's aiming for, Mr. Caswell may do activities that lead to no performance or to an opposite student performance.

Objectives that say "students will be exposed to" make us very nervous. If you're going to "introduce" students to an idea or "expose" them to an experience, do you expect anything to stick? If you do, you can say what it is and go for it specifically. If you don't, why are you exposing them to the idea to begin with? ("All you get from exposure is a cold," quipped Jim Kilroy of Tulane University.)

Here is another way of looking at this: A teacher without an image of the student performance sought is likely to pick activities that inadvertently get another performance—or no performance. If I don't specifically know where I'm going, why would you expect me to get there? If I do get there, it will be by accident, by luck, and certainly will take a lot longer. If we look at the students who are along for the ride in such a class of twenty-five students, some may peel off and get to the destination on their own, despite the instruction. Others never arrive.

So again, the big question: Was there a clear objective? When you reflect on the period, can you infer a clear statement of what students were supposed to know or be able to do at the end?

Maybe the teacher stated the objective, and the job of identifying it is easy; or maybe the objective is written down somewhere in the book, on the worksheet, or in the packet. That is nice when it happens (and valuable for student learning), but often that is not the case. The observer (or self-observer) must be able to go back over the lesson from an outsider's point of view and say, "Well, clearly from what I saw and heard, the objective must have been for students to identify the six parts of a story (protagonist, antagonist, conflict, plot, climax, theme) and be able to find examples of them in the story read for homework." Maybe the teacher never said that in so many words, but clearly that is what students were supposed to learn how to do. The students too should know what the objective is. They should be able to make some such statement of objectives if asked at the end of the period.

Note also that the objectives we infer from observations may not be just cognitive. Pairs of students are coaching individuals on a certain bookkeeping procedure, and we infer that there is an objective about cooperation and helping others in the room. Deirdre is excluded from the class meeting (first grade) and sitting near (though facing away from) a pile of blocks. We hear a few remarks and see some body language from the teacher that lead us to conclude she has an objective in mind for Deirdre: cleanup; you can't get out of your responsibilities to others by pouting and stalling.

In our work, we have found that the question "Was there a clear objective?" can be answered by "yes," "no," or "yes, but fuzzy." The type of class most likely to look like a "no" or a "fuzzy" on objectives is a rambling discussion that touches assigned material in an erratic way or not at all or that covers course material without making relevant connections between items or making links to other course material. Another "no objectives" class has some students doing busywork, often on worksheets, about material they already know or have mastered. Calling this "reinforcement" won't wash. Practice has its place, of course, but the practice must be strengthening a learning that needs it.

How About the Level of Difficulty?

"'Not too hot, not too cold, but ju-u-u-u-st right,' said Goldilocks. And she ate it all up." Even before J. McVicker Hunt (1961) named it the "problem of the match," educators were striving to make the work given to students not too hard and not too easy, but just hard enough to stretch them toward optimum rate of learning. The problem of the match makes teachers look at where students are now and ask, "How big a bite can I give them for the next increment of learning?" For example, judging the size of the bite for six second graders may lead their teacher to teach fractional notation and adding of fractions with common denominators in the same lesson. They can grasp that. The students in an eleventh-grade German history class may not only assimilate the background and content of Bismarck's "Blood and Iron" speech but also in the same class explain it in terms of Bismarck's character.

If you think this sounds like individualizing, you're right. It is individualizing the number of learnings tackled at once and their pace—the size of the bites of learning—to individuals and to groups. There are many other variables that the term *individualizing* may include (see Chapter 15). Most of those variables are about how the learning shall proceed. Here we are talking about what, and how much, shall be aimed at for learning, regardless of the how.

What evidence might there be that the size of the bite was a good match for a group of students? Perhaps there was some initial struggling but then grasping of new ideas; perhaps moments of silence followed by student questions and clarification of difficult concepts; perhaps episodes of puzzlement culminating in "aha!" reactions; perhaps diligent note taking. Negative evidence is easier to spot: confusion, dismay, frustration, or mute silence for work that's too hard (or inadequately presented); boredom as pencil tapping, looking around, chatting, or sloppiness for work that is too easy. (Easy work is far from the only cause of this litany, but it should be checked out when the behaviors occur.)

It is possible as well that none of those overt behaviors may be present, yet the objectives might still be mismatched to the students. In that case, only a knowledge of the students' capacities in relation to the demands the teacher is making could help us make a judgment. Of all the attributes of teaching, this one—matching the size of the bite—requires the most specific knowledge of the students and the context in order to make an accurate judgment.

Where Did the Objectives Come From?

The classic question of the curriculum field is, "What shall be taught?" The question overlays two critical issues: (1) Who will decide what shall be taught and learned? and (2) What kind of things are important and therefore will be allowed on the menu? We must look at the sources of the objectives in classrooms to answer those questions. The primary sources (the student, the teacher, an authority, or the group) tell who is doing the deciding. The secondary sources tell what the program designers think it is important to learn.

Primary Sources

All objectives can be attributed to one of four primary sources:

- *The student.* A student is fascinated by frogs and toads and wants to learn everything about them. An eighth-grade student is curious about movie special effects and wants to know how they're done. The teacher who legitimizes these learning objectives (maybe seeking ways to work in other ones from, say, math and language arts with what the student plans to do) makes available time and resources for the student to pursue them.

- *The teacher.* Things the teacher values may become objectives for no other reason than one's own idiosyncrasies, background, talents, experiences, or preferences. A teacher with particular knowledge and interest in whales may make that available to students through curriculum. A teacher with a musical background may choose objectives relating to instruments in an orchestra. A teacher who values critical thinking as an important attribute of the educated person may make that a direct objective that students work on often.

- *An authority.* Many objectives come from outside authorities: a text, a district curriculum guide, a system, a learning activity packet, or a teacher's manual. Suppose the teacher chose the text. In this case, who is the source of the objective: the teacher or the text? If the text is used regularly or methodically, text is the source regardless of who chose it. If the teacher uses many texts and moves back and forth among them in some deliberate or purposeful way or in a way that shows she is doing some thematic discrimination, then the source of the objective is the teacher.

- *The group.* The whole class as a group, or a subgroup of it, can be the source of an objective. Coalescing around some common interest, and usually in negotiation with the teacher, a learning objective may be developed by and for a particular group. "Let's make a movie!" The idea captivates six seventh graders, and they organize a project, under the teacher's general supervision and guidance, to produce a film about their class. In the process a series of learning objectives about film production emerges (type of film: this will be a documentary that students can discriminate and describe, as distinct from other types; planning a film: use of storyboards and formats, interviews of students, use of various techniques, and editing).

We can discriminate teachers whose objectives come from only one source, or from two, three, or four sources in an overview of their teaching. Knowing the primary sources different teachers use accounts for important differences between teachers and the experiences they offer students. Teachers who allow the group or the individual to choose some objectives have a very different climate and outcome from teachers who draw objectives exclusively from an authority. Teachers who allow (or are allowed to have) themselves as a source may have different amounts of energy and commitment to those objectives. It would be untenable to assert that any one of these four sources is any better than the others. Clearly all four have a place in schooling. To understand the experience students are having, however, and to be in a position to bring our own values to shaping those experiences, we all—parents, teachers, administrators, and school boards—need to know what stands behind the objectives in curriculum. That goes also for the secondary sources.

Secondary Sources

Regardless of the primary source, any one or more of the following could be secondary or origins of objectives (many of these were developed by Tyler 1949):

- *Contemporary life.* Good examples recently have been ecology and pollution; the causes of inflation and how to protect oneself against it; and marriage and divorce and the family. Objectives pertaining to these issues may or may not have been relevant in the past, and may not be in a future age, but are seen as important now. Curricula dealing with racial awareness and cultivating awareness and appreciation of differences in people, while universal in application and importance, may be particularly appropriate in integrated schools experiencing racial tensions and thus have their secondary source in issues of contemporary life.

- *The culture.* Certain objectives may tacitly be mandated by local culture for consideration in the schools—for example, correctly used terminology of weather in coastal fishing communities where weather affects livelihood directly day by day or a country's history for its inhabitants or understanding the cycle of plant growth for children in farm communities (though by no means limited to there).

- *The community.* Local resources may invite objectives that exploit these resources as objects of study—for example, the ecology of pond life, the operation of the postal service (if a post office is nearby); or the life and thought of local author Henry David Thoreau (for residents in Concord, Massachusetts).

- *The academic disciplines.* Each discipline—mathematics, literature, biology, history, geography, art—has a hierarchical structure to its knowledge, and when students enter this world, seeking to acquire the knowledge in a hierarchical way or to learn to think in the way of the discipline, then the secondary source of the objective is rooted in the discipline. We find many objectives in schools with a tie to the disciplines.

▶ *Needs of the learners.* Certain groups of students may have particular need for instruction in hygiene, for example. Curriculum will be designed or chosen for them around health, cleanliness, and perhaps nutrition because the school (or the teacher) sees these students as lacking in these areas. Another group of students may fight a lot, not listen to each other, and need work on social problem solving. Objectives with a source in the needs of the learners develop when someone judges that a deficiency exists: perhaps the teacher's judgment, or perhaps the administrators or the board of education. The deficiency may be with regard to present functioning (health and hygiene) or in anticipation of future needs. Most broadly construed, all objectives are in anticipation of future needs, including instruction in basic skills, but the needs of all learners will not be admitted as part of the meaning of this source of objective since that would include practically all objectives. By "needs of the learners," we therefore mean a particular group of learners who, by virtue of a perceived deficiency or a special future need that is not general to all learners, are judged to need a particular piece of learning.

▶ *Subject matter as bodies of information.* Some objectives have as their secondary source the communication of a body of information related to a subject. Knowing the main products of the South American countries is information not from a discipline of hierarchical concepts but a body of knowledge on a subject. We find objectives around such bodies of information throughout school at all levels. Who were the principal poets of eighteenth-century England? What are the math facts to 10? What is the profile of a patient going into shock?

▶ *Philosophy.* Ideas about what should be—conceptions of the ideal—stand in back of some objectives. A vision of the "educated person" as one who thinks critically, listens to and reacts to others' positions while evaluating them objectively, stands up for his or her own positions: All these and many other conceptions of the "good" may be found behind certain objectives. Certain classroom programs stress independence, decision making, and creativity because they reflect values of the program designers or, put another way, the program designers' visions of desirable characteristics to develop in learners. Objectives related to a vision of the good may be said to derive from "philosophy" as a secondary source.*

*Reprinted with permission. Tyler, R. W. *Basic Principles of Curriculum and Instruction.* Chicago: University of Chicago Press, 1949. © 1949 University of Chicago Press. All rights reserved.

The origin of objectives tells what is important to those in control of the educational program. Primary sources give information about who should choose the objectives. Should the student have a role in the process? Should the teacher be allowed to bring some of himself directly and formally into the curriculum? How much shall the expertise of outside authorities influence the curriculum?

Secondary sources tell what the program directors think is important to know. What things should be known or learned by the students? What is important? What issues are related to contemporary life, local culture, the community? How much importance do the program designers place on the concepts from the disciplines? How much do they examine the learners and tailor objectives to their particular needs? How much and which ideas from philosophy enter the program through objectives? Answers to these questions give important information about what is being taught and why. When we gather data about the sources of objectives, we collect useful information for answering all these vital questions and can thus characterize a teacher's teaching in important and interesting ways.

Detailed Behavioral Mastery Objectives

In the 1960s Popham (1970) and Mager (1962) popularized the writing of detailed behavioral objectives in which criterion levels for performance were specified as well as the conditions under which students would perform them. For example:

> Given ten multi-step word problems involving multiplication and division, students will complete them in one-half hour at 90 percent accuracy.

This movement, which eventually became the butt of jokes and a target of scorn, had aimed to sharpen thinking about student outcomes and to improve accountability for student results.

Particular kinds of content do lend themselves well to very detailed behavioral objectives, typically operational skills that can be observed at criterion levels of mastery (mathematical manipulations, decoding in reading, technical writing skills, etc.), but this same kind of objective may not serve instruction so well when one attempts to apply it to an area like cooperation. How can a teacher meaningfully specify a criterion level for mastery with respect to cooperation? He could have a student discriminate cooperative from noncooperative behavior at a criterion level in stories read or videoclips viewed, but how useful would that be?

Different levels of specificity in language serve best with different types of content. Thus, we expect teachers to use different kinds of objectives and to use the language most suited to the content at hand. Two levels of performance can be discriminated here: teachers either do, or do not, match the language in objectives they formulate to appropriate content. The use of detailed behavioral objectives for an art curriculum or an oil painting course might well trivialize that content.

On the other hand, what about the teacher who uses general language in objectives for material that would lend itself nicely to detailed behavioral objectives? Here's an example: "Children will add three-digit numbers with medial zeros competently." What is competently? Here Popham and Baker (1970) would argue that a criterion level for mastery is essential if one wants to sharpen the delivery of skills and the evaluation of who knows what.

Summary

Taken all together, this chapter offers five questions to ask about objectives:

1. Is there a clear objective that creates an image of specifically what students will know or be able to do?

2. Does the teacher use the key questions from all five objective circles in planning?

3. Is the level of difficulty appropriate?

4. Where do the objectives come from (sources)?

5. Is the language of the objective a good fit for the content? &

Checking on Objectives

1. Is there a clear objective that creates an image of specifically what students will know or be able to do?

   yes   no   fuzzy

2. Is the level of difficulty appropriate?

   too hard

   too easy

   appropriate

   stretches students with optimum match

3. Where do the objectives come from?

   student   community

   teacher   disciplines

   group   needs of learners

   authority   bodies of information

   contemporary life   philosophy

   culture

4. What types of teacher thinking are evident?

   generic thinking

   student learning (mastery)

   involvement

   activity

   coverage

Objectives Quiz

Thinking About Objectives

Identify the kind of thinking (coverage, activity, involvement, mastery, generic thinking) behind each of these key questions in lesson planning.

1. How can I get students really engaged?

2. What thinking skills do I want students to practice and develop?

3. What knowledge, skill, or concept am I teaching?

4. What activities could students do to gain understanding or develop these skills?

5. What do I want students to know or be able to do when the lesson is over? How will I know if they know it or can do it?

Identify the kind of thinking behind these objectives. There could be more than one type in each answer.

1. Students will read *The Red Pony*, share the parts they liked best, and write a one-page paper recommending the book to a friend.

2. "Today we're going to move on to quadratic equations. I'll be presenting the definition with samples of one way to solve quadratic equations, and then you will do five problems in your cooperative groups."

3. "OK. I think you're really going to be excited about what we're going to do today. There are five new centers set up for you to practice your reading and writing. Some you'll be doing alone and some with a partner. In some you'll be writing, in others listening to tapes, and in others sharing and reaching agreement with a partner."

4. Students will give the attributes of a one-celled animal, draw an example of three different one-celled animals, and predict what the next stage of development will be and why.

5. "Read the article I have given you on fruit bats, answer the study questions on the worksheet, and then we'll have a discussion."

6. "Using the techniques you learned last week on how to analyze and evaluate the critical junctures in John F. Kennedy's campaign, analyze and evaluate the critical junctures in the current presidential campaign."

7. "For the next week we're going to be doing a series of activities on the genre of mysteries—whodunits. You're going to focus on mysteries through reading stories, simulations, and role playing. I really had fun planning this unit for you."

8. "You are going to use a graphic organizer of your choice to identify the events that led to the war in Vietnam starting in 1945. When you have had a chance to check your choices with a partner, you will select one event that, if changed, might have significantly affected the outcome. You will prepare a 4-minute speech to present and defend your choice. Use the skills of analysis and evaluation we have been practicing to help you."

9. "We're going on a field trip to the zoo. When we return, you will draw a picture and write a story about your favorite animal."

10. "Today in band practice we'll play all of the selections for our spring concert in order. Look sharp."

Assignments

Much of our thinking about objectives shows up in the assignments we give. Assignments can help students achieve mastery and generic thinking objectives, or they can be activities the students will do. Identify the kind of thinking represented in the following assignments.

1. Read Chapter 14 on the origins of the universe.

2. Read the fable "The Fox and the Hen," and use a graphic organizer to identify and give evidence of the five attributes of a fable.

3. By tomorrow be ready to show that you can define, spell, and use correctly in a sentence five new vocabulary words from the chapter on butterflies.

4. Read the chapter on the midwestern states, and correctly fill in the names of the states on the outline map.

5. Read the second act of *Romeo and Juliet*. If you are a boy, be prepared to read Juliet's part tomorrow; if you are a girl, be prepared to read Romeo's part.

6. Read the chapter on creation, and be prepared to compare and contrast Darwin's theory of evolution with the biblical theory of creation.

7. Do the odd-numbered problems on subtracting negative and positive numbers.

8. By tomorrow I want you to identify the product you will use in your advertisement, your choice of lettering and why, your choice of color range and why, and the medium you have chosen and why.

9. Tomorrow we're going to be baking bread. Review the steps in the recipe and be ready to go.

10. Today I presented the steps in how to use the drill press correctly. Come in tomorrow with any questions you have.

Evaluation

Another place where there is evidence of thinking behind objectives is in the ways we evaluate student learning. Identify the kind of thinking behind objectives involved in the following ways to evaluate student learning:

1. Were the students actively participating in the discussion?

2. Did the students behave on the field trip to the museum?

3. Were the students correctly able to define the elements of a fairy tale?

4. Could the students categorize and name the categories of the information they studied on Edna Ferber?

5. Could the students compare and contrast the leadership of Martin Luther King with Mahatma Gandhi?

You Make It a Mastery Objective

The following examples of objectives are NOT written at the mastery level. Rewrite them so they represent thinking at the mastery or generic thinking level.

1. Students will participate in a discussion on mammals.

2. Students will state how Roman civilization was like Greek civilization.

3. Students will demonstrate their enthusiasm for painting.

4. Students will play basketball.

5. Students will read the chapter on the West and talk about what it was like to be a cowboy.

6. Students will participate in a discussion on the breakup of the Soviet Union.

7. Students will go to the Museum of Fine Arts and write a paper on their favorite painting.

8. Students will use a circular saw, drill press, band saw, and table saw.

9. Students will participate in the winter concert.

10. Students will know all the books of Laura Ingalls Wilder.

Source Materials on Objectives

Bussis, A. M., E. A. Chittenden, and M. Amarel. *Beyond Surface Curriculum: An Interview Study of Teachers' Understandings.* Boulder, Colo.: Westview Press, 1966.

Clark, C. M., and R. J. Yinger. "Teachers Thinking." In P.L. Peterson and H.J. Wahlberg (eds.). *Research on Teaching.* Berkeley: McCutcheon, 1979.

Duffy, G., L. Roehler, and G. Rockliffe. "How Teachers' Instructional Talk Influences Students' Understandings of Lesson Content." *Elementary School Journal* 87, no. 1 (September 1986).

Hunt, J. McV. *Intelligence and Experience.* New York: Ronald Press, 1961.

Hunter, M. Presentation at ASCD, 1977.

Joyce, B. R., C. Clark, and L. Peck. *Flexibility in Teaching.* New York: Longmans, 1981.

Mager, R. R. *Preparing Instructional Objectives.* Palo Alto: Fearson Publications, 1962.

Peterson, P. L., C. W. Marx, and C. Clark. "Teacher Planning, Teacher Behavior, and Student Achievement." *American Educational Research Journal* 15 (Summer 1978): 417–432.

Popham, W. J., and E.L. Baker. *Systematic Instruction.* Englewood Cliffs, N.J.: Prentice Hall, 1970.

Saphier, J. D. "The Parameters of Teaching: An Empirical Study Using Observations and Interviews to Validate a Theory of Teaching by Linking Levels of Analysis, Levels of Knowing and Levels of Performance." Ph.D. diss., Boston University, 1980.

Tyler, R. W. *Basic Principles of Curriculum and Instruction.* Chicago: University of Chicago Press, 1949.

Zahorik, J. A. "Learning Activities: Nature, Function, and Practice." *Elementary School Journal* 82 (1982): 309–317.

15

Learning Experiences

How can I adjust for students' learning styles?

The term "learning experience" is not the same as the content with which a course deals nor the activities performed by the teacher. The term "learning experience" refers to the interaction between the learner and the external conditions of the environment to which he can react. Learning takes place through the active behavior of the student; it is what he does that he learns, not what the teacher does.

R. Tyler, *Basic Principles of Curriculum and Instruction*

The main point of this parameter is to enable you to survey the activities you offer to students so that you can describe them in a new way. This new way may give you a fuller picture than you have had before of what students are experiencing in your class—or it may give you a picture of what they are *not* experiencing, that is, the characteristics your learning experiences do not have. This information could lead you to make one of the following statements:

▶ "That's fine. It's okay not to have these features. What I'm doing is really on target for this curriculum, and those wouldn't be."

▶ "Well, there are some things I'm not doing that would be good to do. I'd like to do them, but there's just so much time. I think I'll put them on the back burner for now and look into adding them when things slow up a bit."

▶ "Well, there are a few things I hadn't thought about much before. They'd be really good, and I'd like to try them now."

The point is that you should be able to look at your teaching, or that of someone else, and see more than you have before and then make some decisions based on new understanding. You may come away from this chapter newly aware, or perhaps reminded, of some important things that you can design into students' experiences.

This parameter is constructed from the students' point of view. We ask first, "What are students experiencing in their environment? What are the attributes of the activity? What is it like from the students' angle to be doing this?" Then, we ask, "So what? What difference does it make? Of what importance is what students are experiencing on this particular attribute? What does it mean about their overall school learning?" This enables us to make choices, because the shape of the learning experience is, after all, something we control as teachers.

We analyze a student's learning experience almost as if it were a real, tangible thing, like a rock. It *isn't* tangible, but it is *real* and has describable features like a rock does. A rock has attributes (e.g., shape) and possible values on each attribute (e.g., spherical, egg, cylindrical, cube; for the attribute of color the values might be brown, grey, blue, reddish, silver). So does a learning experience. Supervision, for example, is an attribute with three possible values (or options): independent, facilitated, or directly supervised. Which are students experiencing right now? They may be closely and directly supervised right now, and independent later in the day. Their learning experience may change based on this attribute, and when it does, it's a different learning experience.

A learning experience takes place over a time span with a beginning, middle, and end. It can be quite short—a matter of minutes—or extend to hours. When it changes on significant attributes, it's a different learning experience.

This kind of analysis yields a full and accurate picture of what the student is experiencing in a planned activity. We can look at activities over a period of time and see what patterns and ranges are built into these experiences. Then we can decide if the range is appropriate. Are we ever giving students a chance to work cooperatively, for example, or is it always competitive or individualistic? Which sensory input channels are stimulated? Do we ever use the kinesthetic channel? What is the balance between concrete and abstract in our teaching? This parameter provides a set of questions with which to survey our teaching periodically and see if we are offering what we want to offer. Finally, the parameter gives some sharp-focus lenses for looking at matching and adjusting learning experiences for individual students or groups.

In the following sections, we describe the attributes of learning experiences one by one and lay out the possible forms each may take. You may choose to profile yourself as you go, noticing which of the options characterizes learning experiences you offer and then deciding if those choices are broad enough and appropriately matched to your students.

Sources of Information

Definitions

We can examine learning experiences to determine whether the information the students are working with is *conventional*—from conventional sources, such as a text, a reference book, the teacher, or some other source that gives the information to them—or *constructed*—meaning that the students constructed the knowledge through some process of their own, such as observation, experiment, interview, deduction, induction, application of logic, discussion, debate, or questioning.

Looking something up is always a conventional source of information. The student's own initiative, objective, and choice of learning experience may be behind the act of looking up, for instance, design features of airplanes, but the source of the information is still conventional.

Significance

It is significant to know whether students are ever challenged or put in positions where they are able to use their own resources as active agents for the generation of knowledge new to them, as opposed to receiving information that has been assembled, organized or predigested for them. Neither source of information is better than the other, but they are clearly different in their effects on the learner. If teaching uses either source to the exclusion of the other, we are led to ask whether learners have sufficient balance in their educational program.

Resources

Definitions

Students may use any one or more of the following resources in the course of their work:

- A text
- The teacher
- Peers
- Parents
- Interviews with outside people (not parents, teachers, or peers)
- Observation
- Audiovisual material
- On-line services or electronic sources
- Reference books
- Their own imaginations or experiences

We use this attribute as an index to the breadth of resources brought to bear on the student's learning experience and can tally a simple count of how many are used.

Significance

Over the course of a student's education, we would expect all of the resources listed to be used. In any one course, grade, or class, we would ask which resources and how broad a range were appropriate and desirable, and compare that with the reality. In examining an individual student's educational experience, we could usefully ask how many of these resources were brought to bear across different courses and evaluate the fit of the operating range of resources to the intentions of the program.

Personal Relevance

Definitions

On this attribute, learning experiences are found to be contrived, simulated, or real. The degree to which the learning experience relates to aspects of life that have personal meaning to the students is indexed here. Does it connect to their real world outside school?

Doing a workbook page that contains problems of adding money in the form $124.35 + 3.50 = ?$ would be judged as contrived since calculating the answer on a workbook page is not connected to the students' world of experience outside school. But if the class has set up a model store selling grocery items (or anything they might find in a real store), and the students are buying items using play money (or even real money), then this activity simulates real experiences from the students' lives. If the class takes a trip to a supermarket and spends money it has made through some project to buy supplies for a party, and they collect, purchase, and pay for the items, and get change, then the activity is judged real; it is integrated, connected, and related directly to the real world.

"Contrived" in this sense does not have a negative connotation. Much of learning and knowledge construction is contrived in that it does not simulate or reproduce the reality outside school, nor could it. It is impractical for almost all of us to learn about the history of India by visiting historic Indian sites (though that would be nice). And aspects of historical study necessarily require reading books and other contrived (versus real) experiences to proceed effectively with the learning. There is no general value implied in this attribute that real learning experiences are superior to contrived ones.

> ***Many educators believe learning experiences should connect to real world meaning.***

Students do not have to leave school on a field trip to enter the realm of real learning experiences either. The act of painting is real no matter where one does it. Painting is painting and not a simulation of painting, whether or not one does it in school or in an art studio. The same applies to creative writing or other aesthetic work of any kind. Having a debate is a real experience between the debaters and not simulated just because it is not taking place in a court of law or a legislative chamber. Many experiences in the school are inherently real for students. Settling a dispute with another student over how to share materials is a real experience in which students play a deliberate role and act as mediators according to certain designs.

Significance

Many educators believe it is important that as many learning experiences as possible connect to students' real world of meaning—their world of experience outside of school. One school of learning theory holds that such learning experiences are more effective, more powerful, and more lasting in effect (Dale n.d.). The student, it is said, has a context in which to embed the new information and because of its relevance to his personal life is more impelled to attend to and participate in what's going on. This then guarantees a level of involvement on the part of the student with the learning experience that will maximize learning. To people of this persuasion, it is important to know how much realness is characteristic of learning experiences being offered. Early childhood educators and open classroom educators are especially interested in this attribute of learning experiences (Bussis, Chittenden, and Amarel 1976).

Regardless of one's beliefs about the learning theory of personal relevance, it is a distinction we can make among learning experiences. It produces data to bring to an analysis of teaching-in-action in comparison with teaching's intentions. We can look at curriculum designs to see where and how often opportunities for realness exist and how appropriate such experiences might be to the content and to the learners. We can evaluate the efficiency of a curriculum in terms of the balance among contrived, simulated, and real experiences that is best for accomplishing the objectives of the instruction in the time allowed.

Competition

Definitions

Johnson and Johnson (1975, 1987) set out a three-point typology for learning experiences: cooperative, competitive, and individualized. (They don't use the term *learning experiences*; they say *goal structures*.) A learning experience specifies the type of interdependence existing among students—the way in which students will relate to each other and to the teacher. One might say they have taken a specific aspect of the social climate—that aspect related to competition and its presence, absence, or opposite—and defined it in detail:

> When students are working together to find what factors make a difference in how long a candle burns in a quart jar, they are in a cooperative goal structure. A cooperative goal structure exists when students perceive that they can obtain their goal if and only if the other students with whom they are linked can obtain their goal. Since the goal of all the students is to make a list of factors that influence the time the candle burns, the goal of all the students has been reached when they generate a list. A cooperative goal structure requires the coordination of behavior necessary to achieve their mutual goal. If one student achieves the goal, all students with whom the student is linked achieve the goal. When students are working to see who can build the best list of factors influencing the time a candle will burn in a quart jar, they are in a competitive goal

structure. A competitive goal structure exists when students perceive that they can obtain their goal if and only if the other students with whom they are linked fail to obtain their goal. If one student turns in a better list than anyone else, all the students have failed to achieve their goal. Competitive interaction is the striving to achieve one's goal in a way that blocks all others from achieving the goal. Finally, if all students are working independently to master an operation in mathematics, they are in an individualistic goal structure. An individualistic goal structure exists when the achievement of the goal by one student is unrelated to the achievement of the goal by other students; whether or not a student achieves her goal has no bearing upon whether or not other students achieve their goals. If one student masters the mathematics principle, it has no bearing upon whether other students successfully master the mathematics principle. Usually there is no student interaction in an individualistic situation since each student seeks the outcome that is best for himself regardless of whether or not other students achieve their goals. (Johnson and Johnson 1975, p. 7)*

Johnson and Johnson have an observation checklist with a series of yes-no questions for classroom organization, student-student interaction, and teacher-student interaction. The outcome scores of the checklist are three percentage figures for the three possible goal structures. There is a recognition that a learning experience will rarely be exclusively cooperative. From the percentage figures of Johnson and Johnson's observation checklist, one could make a statement about the dominant quality of the learning experience along the attribute of competition.

An important body of research literature has emerged on the effectiveness of cooperative learning for cognitive as well as affective ends. This is accompanied by an emerging technical literature on how to do cooperative learning. At least five different forms of cooperative learning are developed and available for teachers to try (**Figure 15.1**). They are arranged in the figure in the order of the demands they place on students for interaction and communication skills (from least demanding on the left to most demanding on the right).

If you want to rate yourself on this attribute, you will want to be able to look at a single learning experience and characterize its dominant quality: cooperative, competitive, or individualistic. For example, in certain science lab courses we have observed, groups of students worked together sharing apparatus, ideas, and information as they performed a common experiment. This we considered significant cooperation. At the same time, these students were recording experimental results in individual notebooks the teacher graded separately. Different groups of students were at different places in the sequential programmed curriculum. Some were working alone, either because no one else was at the same place as they or because they wanted to work alone (which the teacher allowed). Students took tests individually when they felt ready. Individual pretest feedback was given by the teacher to students, and tests were graded individually. This was significant evidence for calling the learning experience individualistic. In this lab course there were no observed instances of students' comparing test scores in a competitive way, though in interviews teachers cited cases where that happened. Indeed,

*Reprinted with permission. Johnson, D. W., and R.T. Johnson. *Learning Together and Alone.* Englewood Cliffs, N.J.: Prentice Hall, 1975, 1987.

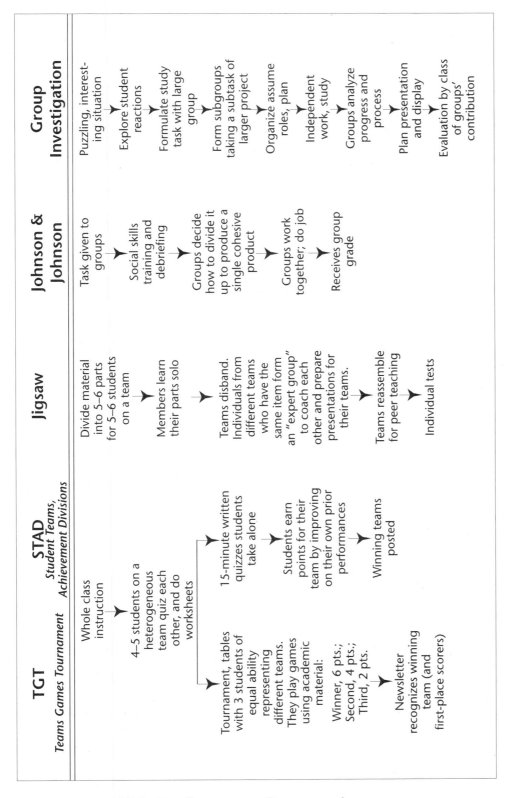

15.1: FIVE FORMATS FOR COOPERATIVE LEARNING
Options range from left to right in order of increasing demands placed on students for interaction and communication skills.

even if we had observed students' comparing scores it wouldn't necessarily merit a judgment of competition as a value of the learning experience on this attribute. It could be argued that comparing test scores reflects competitive qualities inherent in children, in humans, in the culture, or in the process of testing itself ("Whadjaget?").

The kind of competition we looked for was one designed into the learning experience by the teacher and/or the curriculum—something like a team game, or a contest for speed or accuracy involving a group of students, or a recitation period where a student gives right answers in competition with peers. Many competitive forces emanating from students themselves, from peers, from parents, or from the culture and community may affect student behavior. These forces are not examined here. This attribute looks at aspects of the design of the learning experience that set up, by virtue of that design, interactions that are competitive, cooperative, or individualistic in nature. Only students' behavior of these three types that is encouraged or arranged by the design of the learning experience will enable us to make a judgment on this attribute. Competitive, cooperative, or individualistic behavior of children that cannot be attributed to the design of the learning experience that comes from some other source is deemed irrelevant to the judging of this attribute.

In the case of the science lab course, competition would not be scored as a significant quality of the learning experience because whatever of it there was couldn't be traced to the teacher or the design of the learning experience.

Significance

It is not hard to get a discussion started among educators, or parents, or even passers-by on the street, about the merits or evils of competition. It is a condition of life we have all experienced and about which we all have formed some values. This attribute of teaching calls attention to teachers' ability to control in aware and deliberate ways *how* competitive, cooperative, or individualistic are the experiences of students in our schools. Educational decision makers bring different values and different histories to their settings, as has always been the case. But whatever their decisions about the shape of learning experiences, these decisions can be informed and deliberate if made by professionals who know the full implications of their acts. This attribute provides tools for surveying your own teaching to see how much cooperation or competition you are putting into students' experiences. It also offers resources for getting the balance you want.

In this attribute, as in all the other attributes of learning experiences we have touched, there is an analyzable nature, an emergent reality to the experience students have on each attribute. That experience is in the form it is because an educational decision maker has made it that way—either deliberately or in ignorance. Each attribute is controllable, alterable, and subject to change by educators who seek to be knowledgeable and deliberate about the environments they create for learners.

Matching

There is matching if the teacher differentiates deliberately among groups or individuals as to the competitive, cooperative, or individualistic quality of learning experiences.

Supervision

Definitions

Students may be directly supervised by a teacher who checks on what and how everybody is doing, may be independent and responsible for their own work, or the teacher may facilitate their work, by being available as a resource person and occasionally intervening with suggestions, recommendations, or stimulating questions (Dunn and Dunn 1978). During observations, the number of these three possible conditions present in a teacher's teaching—supervised, facilitated or independent—can be counted.

Significance

A limited range on this attribute—for example, a teacher who always supervises all learning activities—excludes certain kinds of learning in a classroom. The breadth or narrowness of a teacher's range on this attribute is something we can look at for its nurturant effects on students, that is, the effects on them of living in an environment of that kind. We (or the teacher) can then ask if that is what is wanted. And we can, of course, compare this range of supervisory modes and the nurturant effects attached with the goals of the curriculum and the teacher.

Matching

Teachers who discriminate among students on how much supervision they require or can tolerate so as to maximize their performance match the amount and kind of supervision they provide to the characteristics of students. Jane flourishes if left to work independently much of the time, checking in occasionally for conferences with the teacher. Working under direct supervision for the bulk of the day unnecessarily limits her learning experiences. But Martha can't seem to get herself organized; she'll have several false starts and then may socialize away her morning if she is not directly supervised in her work. Her teacher provides much direct supervision for her and much independence for Jane. The same kind of distinction can be made for subgroups of the class and would enable us to conclude "yes" for the matching on supervision.

Expressing the Self

Definitions

Students may or may not be given the opportunity to express something of themselves in a learning experience . If they are given such an opportunity, the self-expression may be delivered through drawing, creative writing, performing, speaking, or building or construction of some sort. Merely to respond or recite is not to express one's self as meant here. Expressing one's self means expressing something that is unique to the individual or expressing some standard information in a way that encourages students to bring something of themselves to the expression. An assignment to diagram mitosis for biology (though different students will embellish the product to different degrees) is a prescribed product that has the student express mitosis, not himself or herself. An assignment to represent the "1812 Overture" in paint is also prescribed but frees the student to express things unique to him or her that are stimulated by the music. A recitation question asking a student to summarize Turner's frontier thesis does not allow for self-expression as would a question asking a student to say how he would have responded to the offer of free western land had he been alive 100 years ago.

Significance

The significance of this attribute relates to the value placed on self-expression by those responsible for the educational program. Data on the attribute tell us what we have and enable us to raise the attribute as an important and perhaps overlooked aspect of learning experiences over which program designers and teachers have control. And as before, we can compare realities with intentions, where intentions about self-expression have been considered by program designers and made explicit.

Matching

We may look to see if teachers who allow for or encourage expression of the self allow for differences in ways students can best do that expressing. If matching were present, one would see not only a range on this attribute but also negotiation or direct planning of students' activities where they were asked to or permitted to express themselves in ways different from other students.

Degree of Abstraction

Definitions

Learning experiences can be scored as concrete, representational (iconic), or abstract (Bruner 1966). *Concrete* means manipulative: students are touching or seeing real objects that are integral to the learning experience. *Iconic* means representational: a picture, image, or other facsimile of real objects is embedded in the materials with which the learner is interacting. *Abstract* means symbolic: words or thoughts are the stuff of which the learning experience is made without support from facsimiles or concrete objects.

Significance

We can compare the range of levels of abstraction offered to the nature of the content and make judgments concerning appropriateness. Similar comparisons can be made in consideration of the age and learning style of the students. With young children, for example, we might expect to see more concrete experiences than at other grade levels.

Matching

Because students of the same age are often at different levels with regard to their ability to process abstract information, we might expect a teacher to discriminate among students and adjust the level of abstraction of the learning experiences offered to characteristics of individual students. Conrad Toepfer (1981) and others have applied these insights to the typical middle school curriculum and found that much of it demands formal operational thinking of students, a kind of thinking that, according to their statistics, only 12 percent of American youngsters are capable of at age 12. Toepfer makes a strong case that teachers who match the level of thinking to the students' capacity for abstract thinking, especially in the plateau period of 12 to 14 years of age, make a huge difference in school failure rates. He and his colleagues recommend testing students for their level of thinking (onset of concrete operations, concrete operations, initial formal operations, established formal operations) and accommodating instruction to the stage. Intelligence, he points out, is different and uncorrelated to stage thinking. Super-bright youngsters go through the same Piagetian stages of growth and in about the same proportions per given age as students of normal and below-normal IQ.

This attribute of learning experiences bears a hard look. Research may help us use it to serve students much more effectively by tailoring instruction to accurate assessment of a student's stage of intellectual development.

Cognitive Level

Definitions

Bloom's taxonomy (1956) sets out six cognitive levels to consider: recall, comprehension, analysis, application, synthesis, and evaluation. We can examine learning experiences to see what cognitive level of performance they ask of students. We can also look across learning experiences that teachers offer to identify the range of thinking embedded in them. We can count the number of levels for which evidence can be produced.

Significance

Researchers have long investigated the number of higher-level questions teachers ask students in verbal interaction. The research implies that the more higher-level questions there are the better, and studies have attempted to correlate the proportion of higher-level questions with student achievement (Winne 1979a). However, large doses of high cognitive levels may be quite inappropriate for students who have not worked through lower levels with the same material. When we considered the Models of Teaching parameter in Chapter 10, we saw that for certain models (like Taba's), it is the order in which cognitive operations are demanded of students that is important, not the raw amount at any level.

Focusing on the cognitive level embedded in learning experiences offered by a teacher enables us to collect data on the range offered. Any predominance of one or two particular levels will prompt us to ask, "Why?" If a teacher or a curriculum has some specific thinking objectives in mind, we can compare intentions with reality.

> *In differentiation teachers may deny to low-skill students the opportunity for higher-level thinking, deepening their cycle of failure and their subsequent rejection of school itself.*

Matching

If we see a teacher tailoring or adjusting learning experiences on the same or similar material so that the cognitive level demanded is different for different students, then we have evidence the teacher is differentiating cognitive level across students. The danger in such differentiation is that teachers may deny to low-skill students the opportunity for higher-level thinking. This pattern appears when teachers have low expectations for students derived from impressions of their lower innate ability. Thus instruction can be more drill-oriented and less interesting for these students, deepening their cycle of failure and their subsequent rejection of school itself.

The point here is to wave a potential danger flag if a teacher limits the involvement of certain students with experiences from the higher levels of Bloom's taxonomy. Teachers can differentiate learning experiences appropriately for different students in many ways, including pace. But teachers should look for ways to offer the full range of cognitive levels to both high- and low-skill students.

Structuring

We have all heard people refer to students who need a high degree of structure. We have often wondered exactly what is meant by that word and discovered, not too surprisingly, that people mean different things: that the student has to be closely supervised or that the task has to be broken down into small pieces and the student told exactly what to do, when, and how. We find out how structuring is being handled when teachers give directions. We would have called this section "giving directions" except that giving directions is only one way that activities get set up. Sometimes students are asked to set procedures, and sometimes teachers and students negotiate what to do and how. One way to analyze differences in teachers' instruction is to examine how much and where these different kinds of structuring are occurring: by teachers (high structure), by negotiation (moderate structure), or by students (low structure). Another question to ask is if teachers differentiate among students along this attribute of who structures activities. That is matching.

When teachers give directions, they often structure (that is, make decisions and give instructions about) the content to be worked on, the procedures to follow, the behavior to do (e.g., "write," "discuss," "compare," "listen"), the form of student products, and the point of closure (signaling when it's over). Content, behavior, procedures, products, and closure are the five components of structuring:

WHO DECIDES

	No one decides	Student decides	Negotiation	Teacher decides
	(Low structure ——▶ *High structure)*			
1. Content				
2. Behavior				
3. Procedures				
4. Products				
5. Closure				

A similar breakout appears in Berlak et al. 1975.

Content

Content means information or objects dealt with at the item level. Who decided, introduced, or is responsible for the presence of the particular items students are working with? To make reliable assignments of responsibility here, we must be clear on the unit of analysis. Just how big or small is an item? Some examples will help.

ACTIVITY	ITEM	RESPONSIBLE PARTY
Recitation or review of Civil War battles with teacher leading questioning in chronological order, seeking identification and sequence.	Pieces of information elicited from students	Teacher
Teacher says, "Read this book, and answer the questions at the back."	The book The questions	Teacher
Teacher says, "Pick a book you'd like to read, and summarize it verbally for me."	The book	Student

(Although the use of time is structured by the teacher, and the behavior and writing are also structured, the content—what is operated upon, written about—comes from the student.)

Teacher suggests, "Use the blocks to make a model of the store we visited."	Model of store	Teacher

(Although the student controls the shape of the product, what the store will look like, the item on which he is operating—blocks—and the model of a stores were directed by the teacher. If the student was free to represent the store in any medium he chose (e.g., paint, clay), then the behavior would have been attributed to the student as the shape of the product; but the content would still be the teacher's decision about what to represent.)

Class discussion about the pros and cons of busing to integrate public schools; teacher serving as facilitator and clarifier, not taking a stand, trying to get students to show their positions.	Arguments, positions, and evidence for positions	Students
Following a discussion of movies, students form interest groups to study selected aspects of movie production: special effects, casting, scriptwriting, shooting schedules. Students nominate themselves into groups, and teacher mediates which groups may form and the membership.	Special effects Casting Shooting schedules Script writing	Negotiated

At the most general level, the teacher is almost always responsible for content. In the example where students debate the pros and cons of busing, the teacher probably (though not necessarily) introduced the subject. The teacher is responsible for the topic—the area being treated—but clearly that is above the item level. If teachers are responsible for the responses the students are producing in that they ask factual or leading questions, then we can also say they are responsible for the content. But if the students are bringing in information not directly tied to the teacher's questions, items, or objects that could not be the only reply to the question or the lead-in of the teacher, then the students are responsible for the content at the item level (though perhaps not the general topic).

What can be said about a discussion where the teacher starts off being responsible for the content, say, a recitation, and then switches to more open-ended exploration of the same material, and all within the same discussion: "And now what would you have done in General Lee's position? Do you think he did the right thing? Can you justify your position?" Here the responsibility for content has shifted from teacher to students, and an important attribute to the learning experience has changed. We will be interested in knowing what other attributes of the learning experience have changed.

For individual learning experiences, we can note who is responsible for the content at the item level. Across learning experiences we can note which of these parties are responsible if we survey a number of lessons: teacher, student, or negotiation.

Behavior

To determine who has structured the student behavior within the learning experience, the question is to ask what verb describes what the student is doing. Who is responsible for that operation (verb) being the operation: the teacher, the student, or negotiation? The student is reading, writing, summarizing, responding verbally, building, or painting. Who chose that? These are questions we ask of individual learning experiences. Then when we look across learning experiences and note a teacher's range on the structuring of behavior, we ask how many of the three possibilities were exercised. (Or perhaps none was exercised.) It may be that the teacher has a behavior in mind for the learning experience but fails to state it. This is of no consequence if the behavior is obvious or understood by the students. ("Doing" a page in a workbook is understood to mean, "Follow the directions on the page," which almost always calls for a written response in a blank or on a line.) But if the behavior is not clear to the students or was not fully thought out by the teacher ("What do we do, Mr. Jones?"), then we could conclude "none" here. For example, "Do the next chapter in your book" may mean, "Read and answer the questions at the end," "Read only," "Read for the general idea." Unless some routine has been established for what "reading a chapter" means, we could conclude this is "none" on structuring behavior.

Procedures

Procedural moves set the details of who and how—for example, dividing a class into teams for a spelling bee, giving directions for a worksheet exercise, and describing the procedure in a concept attainment game. Included in this category are the negotiations, which may go on at some length, when students are given the opportunity to decide how they want to go about studying a given content area. Procedures may come from the teacher or from the students, or they may be negotiated. Which are the following?

"We are going to divide the class into three groups. John, Gary, and George will be in group 1."

"First we're going to do worksheets. Then I want you to write down the items that were difficult, and when you've done that, we'll discuss those items."

"We're going to go around the circle here, and each of you will tell us something you read about Hemingway and I'll write it on the board."

"How shall we do this? Shall everybody participate?"

"John has suggested that we invite the editor of the newspaper to speak. Do you agree that this is a good way to begin our study of journalism?" (Joyce 1969)

It may be that the teacher has some procedures in mind for the learning experience, but fails to state them. In that case, there is no structuring of procedures. If a teacher says, "Work on your folders, boys and girls," and within each folder there is a structuring of procedures for each child in the form of a note ("Charlie, do the first two worksheets and then bring them to me for checking"), then the procedures are structured by the teacher. But if it is unclear what the procedures are to be because the teacher has failed to state them or failed to think them out, and she doesn't explicitly ask students to make decisions about procedures, then one might conclude "none."

Closure

How will the student know when the learning experience is over? The end point can be defined in terms of time, quantity of material completed, or certain kind of product being produced. Who determines these limits: teacher, student, or both together?

For certain experiences closure is inherently determined by the student (e.g., a painting or creative writing—except where the teacher says, "Write a four-page story"). For others it is clearly teacher determined. ("Do the first three lines of problems.") But if closure is not inherently or explicitly delegated to the student, then failure to state it may lead us to conclude "none" on structuring of closure. The key questions are, "Which ways does the teacher have for structuring closure to learning experiences?" and, "Are they used appropriately?"

Teachers who hand out folders containing pages of new worksheets and expect students to begin working are evidencing "none" for structuring of procedures and closure—and they often experience the consequences of that lack of structuring.

Products

Who determines the form of the tangible products: teacher, student, or both together?

◗ *Teacher* "I'll tally votes here on how many thought the Civil War represented progress versus setbacks." The tally is the product.

◗ *Student* Any creative or expressive activity (painting, creative writing) makes a student responsible for the form of the product.

◗ *Negotiated* "How shall we represent the data from our poll?" Students and teacher negotiate a form, perhaps deciding on bar graphs.

Matching

One reason teachers treat students differently with regard to structure is learning effectiveness (see Colarusso 1972). Jimmy may be capable of designing his own procedures for collecting data from his science experiment, whereas Fred needs the teacher to structure procedures to maximize the benefit he gets from the experience. A certain group of students may be quite capable of picking their own reading material, whereas another is not (content).

But another reason might have to do with long-range goals. Some teachers have as a goal helping students to become more independent, self-motivated learners. This means moving gradually from high to progressively lower structure. Such a teacher takes students where they are and provides the degree of structure necessary for learning to proceed efficiently. If this happens to be high structure, so be it. Over time, the teacher introduces negotiation of certain attributes, say, procedures and closure, with some students. Over the course of the year, more and more students become involved in more and more decision making about their learning as they show they are ready.

We feel that understanding structuring (and accountability) is the key to understanding the erratic record of open classrooms in the 1960s and 1970s. Those that worked were in control of structuring and matched it to the students in the class. Those that didn't offered too little structure to students who were unprepared to deal with it. The physical look and arrangement of the room, open versus traditional, is usually no clue about the level of structure and the degree of appropriateness for different students. Whole populations of students may be matched to a level of structure, or structure may be differentiated across different individuals and groups within the same class. Few American visitors to British infant schools in the early 1960s perceived the high degree of structure and accountability built into students' working routines, despite the open, child-centered, and apparently effortless flow of constructive activity (Berlak et al. 1975).

A continuous line of research developed by David Hunt and his associates since 1966 has established the better learning that results when students experience a degree of imposed structure matched to their level of development. Numerous instruments are available for determining whether a student is suited to a high- or low-structure treatment (Hunt 1971; Hunt and Sullivan 1974; Rich and Bush 1978). The possibilities we have sketched for who does the structuring—teacher, negotiated, or student—correspond to Hunt's ratings of high, moderate, and low degrees of imposed structure.

Grouping and Interpersonal Complexity

Definitions

Students may work alone, with a single peer, with a group of peers, with the total class, in a dyad with the teacher, with other adults (the principal, a visitor, a parent), or in a small group with the teacher. Any one or more of these six possible combinations may characterize learning experiences over the course of a day or week. Each individual learning experience may have its own grouping. First, one can simply count the number of groupings evidenced to index a teacher's range.

Significance

Characterizing the groupings in a teacher's teaching allows us to ask of the curriculum, What kinds of interpersonal complexity are consistent with the objectives of the curriculum? It also allows us to see how much congruence there is between intentions and reality. Notice we have replaced the word *grouping* with *interpersonal complexity*. This is because there is more to say about a group than how many people are in it. It is also important to know what kind of interaction they are having with one another. Six students and a teacher may be answering recitation questions in a small group; these students have no interaction with each other and only simple interactions with the teacher as they give direct factual answers. Thus the interpersonal complexity is low. In that same group, however, the teacher may invite students to respond to or extend, interpret, or refute other students' answers. Students may begin speaking directly to one another without the teacher as intermediary between every student utterance. The teacher may still moderate the discussion and call on people, but the interpersonal complexity is now moderately complex and no longer simple. If the students are freely interacting with each other and create their own conversational rules and agendas as they go, the interpersonal complexity is high.

In a curriculum stressing social objectives—say, cooperation, listening to each other, or mutual respect—we would expect to see learning experiences with groups of students, dyads, and other combinations that brought students together without exclusive teacher direction. Whatever the themes of the curriculum, the types of interpersonal complexity displayed enable us to describe an important and real part of the learning environment and ask questions about the effect of those patterns on students' learning. Taken from the perspective of curriculum as planning, interpersonal complexity is a design feature of learning experiences that a teacher can tailor to the nature of the objectives and the needs of the learners.

Matching

In studying a teacher's teaching, we can determine whether the teacher discriminates among students in the kind of interpersonal complexity designed or allowed for in learning experiences (Colarusso 1972). Jim works well in large groups but tends to act out or be silly in small group instruction. He does have a few peers with whom he seems able to work effectively. He allows these students to help him and can work cooperatively with them when he has to deal with them only one at a time. So the teacher engineers teacher-Jimmy and peer-Jimmy learning situations as often as possible (while also working on his difficulties with being in groups) to maximize his productive learning time in the class. She has matched the interpersonal complexity in his learning experiences to observed characteristics of Jimmy.

A teacher observes that this class attends very poorly in a large group. So while making attention an objective for them, the teacher makes sure they have as many individual and small group work situations as possible. That is a decision to match the needs of this particular class.

Ms. James notices her English class does not handle the high level of interpersonal complexity she encourages; they seem alternately to flounder or to attack each other when discussing the readings. She reduces the interpersonal complexity to moderate and increases her role as mediator. They prove quite capable of handling high-level literary analysis but require less interpersonal complexity than last year's class.

Where teachers show different patterns of grouping and interpersonal complexity for different children, we can note matching on this attribute.

How about the possibility of a mismatch? What would it look like so that we could defend such a judgment? Probably the learning experience wouldn't be going very well. A mismatch means that something is wrong, and when something is wrong, we expect to see symptoms: usually disruptive behavior or inattention. Students are experiencing difficulty under these conditions, and we must be able to attribute this difficulty to inappropriate grouping or interpersonal complexity rather than to other causes (students' emotional baggage, inappropriate work, poor transition). How can we distinguish such causes in an observation?

Repeated observations over a long period of time might enable an observer to see groupings that were consistently successful for a certain student and others that were consistently unsuccessful. If the students were frequently placed in these failure settings, the observer could attribute mismatch to the grouping or interpersonal complexity. This would put the observer in the position of knowing, through repeated observation, something the teacher did not. Although such a situation is conceivable, a single observation is rarely enough to produce it. More likely the observer would be in a position to problem-solve with the teacher, exploring what the cause of the problem might be.

Information Complexity

"Students who are low in conceptual level (CL) are less capable of processing information in a complex way and less capable of dealing with information in a responsible fashion; students higher in CL are more capable of processing information in a complex way" (Hunt 1971). It sounds simplistic, but it is not.

> *The conceptual level of students is not the same as their intelligence or ability.*

The conceptual level of students, however, is not the same as their intelligence or ability. We can often find two youngsters who are both quite bright but different in CL. What does it mean to process information in a complex way? We will define three levels of information complexity: high, moderate, and low.

At level 1, low complexity, information is linear and direct. One thing leads to another. Qualities of the learning tend to include remembering, sequence, performance, concepts, and skills. Learners are not asked to consider alternatives or make distinctions between points of view or such things as people's feelings or orientations. They have difficulty developing concepts on their own but can learn them receptively without difficulty.

At level 2, the notion of alternatives appears. Students are asked to make distinctions and to differentiate sources, points of view, courses of action, and possible explanations. They can assimilate the idea that there is more than one possible explanation for a phenomenon. Comparison and contrast enter the picture. Students can develop their own concepts from data.

At level 3, high complexity, students can consider several alternatives. Their ability to differentiate and distinguish increases and develops into the ability to see the relationships between different points of view or different explanations.

Significance

Clearly there is a developmental quality to these three levels. (Five year olds are usually not ready to describe the relationships between different points of view.) Thus, this attribute reminds us to look at students and to check if we are challenging them appropriately with the complexity of their tasks. It further challenges us to ask if they are ready to move toward the next level. And finally it challenges us to differentiate among students within a class and adjust their work appropriately.

Hunt's developmental model (1971) considers what we have called separately structuring, grouping/interpersonal complexity, and information complexity all at once. These are three facets of conceptual level, and they correlate with one another. That is, a student who is low in CL (as measured by Hunt's paragraph completion test) will function best with a high degree of imposed structure, simple dynamics in groupings, and low information complexity. Conversely, a high-CL student learns best with low structure, more complex grouping interactions, and more complex information processing. The research supporting the effectiveness of this matching has been quite striking and quite consistent. It has proved applicable for adults as well as children and has been used successfully as a way to form classroom and instructional groupings (Gower and Resnick 1979; Rich and Bush 1978).

Sensory Channels

Definitions

This attribute of learning experiences is about the perceptual modalities and motor expressions students are called upon to use as they engage new information or ideas and then make a product or express what they know. Sensory input channels may include one or more of the following: visual, auditory, or tactile kinesthetic. Motor expressions that students exercise in the context of the learning experience may be large motor muscles, small motor, their voice, or nothing at all. Finally, the design of the learning experience may call for student output in the form of talk, writing, or performance of an observable skill.

Significance and Matching

Matching students' optimum input and output channels is often cited as one way to individualize learning experiences for different students. Dunn and Dunn (1978) make a strong case for it. To the degree to which this is taking place, we would expect to see similar or identical objectives being worked on by students through input and output channels adjusted for their characteristics.

A count can be made of how many channels are used for input of information to students in learning experiences: visual, auditory, and tactile/kinesthetic. Regarding how students act in learning experiences (student output), the number of channels from among the following can be counted: talk, writing, or performance of some kind (such as drawing, building, manipulating, acting out motorically). Regarding motor use, one can record how many of the following muscle groups are used by students: large motor, small motor, voice, or passive (no motor).

One might use data about these three attributes of learning experiences to evaluate how active the learning was and how that level of physical activity fit goals for the learning program or for the needs of the students. But more likely the greatest significance of this data will be raising teachers' awareness of the range they can create and the potential for matching that the range will offer.

Simply seeing a variety of perceptual channels operating differentially across students does not prove matching. To support a yes judgment on matching, there must be evidence that a particular mode is being used with a particular student or group of students and that there is not just random variety. Such evidence might be provided by a teacher remark or by a systematic assignment system for directing certain students to a learning experience with a dominant perceptual mode different from other learning experiences being offered around the same objective to other students.

Scale

Definitions

Sometimes the scale of objects, print, or models used in learning experiences has been adjusted in some way—enlarged or reduced. The scale of materials used can be either of these two, or it can be normal, that is, as normally found. This attribute begins by a simple count of how many of these three possibilities are present.

Significance

Like all the other attributes, scale is an attribute of a learning experience that affects the interaction of the learner with the environment, and that environment is under the control of the curriculum designer and the teacher. It can be controlled to effect. Examining this attribute of teaching brings it to consciousness and provokes questions about whether all the opportunities for scale manipulation in learning experiences have been taken. For example, by miniaturizing into models, we can bring concepts from the abstract to the iconic level to good effect for students who don't function well abstractly. Whole outdoor physical environments (a stream, a town, a valley) can be captured in paint on giant sheets of cardboard (3 feet by 4 feet) and unfolded around the periphery of a classroom to simulate the environment of the stream. By enlarging worksheets or other standard school tasks onto giant plastic-covered boards or using giant felt or plastic numbers, a teacher can provide variety to the conduct of otherwise standard learning experiences.

Matching

When we see the scale of an object adjusted for use with a particular student or students, we can conclude "yes" on matching for scale. This can be particularly important for primary children for whom size of print and number of items on a page can be confusing. 🙿

Checking on Learning Experiences

This summary exercise can be used to profile a given learning experience from the student's point of view. It can also be used to profile a day or a unit of instruction to see how much variety and opportunity for matching students are experiencing.

1. *Source of information*: conventional   constructed

2. *Resources used*:
text	observation
teacher	audiovisual
peers	on-line services
parents	electronic devices
interviews	reference books
	imagination
	experience

3. *Personal relevance*: contrived   simulated   real

4. *Competition*: competitive   individualized   cooperative

5. *Supervision*:
supervised	facilitated
independent	matched

6. *Expressing the self*: no   yes   matched

7. *Degree of abstraction*: concrete   representational   abstract

8. *Cognitive level*:
   recall
   comprehension
   analysis
   application
   synthesis
   evaluation

9. *Structuring*:

	none	teacher	student	negotiated
content				
behavior				
procedures				
products				
closure				

10. *Grouping and interpersonal complexity*:
low	moderate
high	matching

11. *Information complexity*:

	low	moderate
	high	matching

12. *Sensory Channels*:

Student input	visual	tactile/kinesthetic
	auditory	matched
Student motor use	large motor	small motor
	voice	passive
Student output	talk	writing
	performance	matched

13. *Scale*:

	normal	miniaturized
	enlarged	matched

Learning Experiences Quiz

The thirteen attributes of learning experiences are:

Sources of information
Personal relevance
Supervision
Degree of abstraction
Structuring
Information complexity
Scale

Resources used
Competition
Expressing the self
Cognitive level
Grouping and interpersonal complexity
Sensory channels

Each of these attributes has several values or choices we make or don't make in planning what our students will experience. Circle the value that is represented by the quote or description above it.

Sources of Information

1. "We'll be using the dictionary today for our lesson on guide words."

   conventional   constructed   both

2. "When you finish reading the chapter on the American Revolution, you will each choose to be one of the important historical figures of that time and interview your partner on why that character took a particular position. Make sure you pick a partner who chose a historical figure different from yours."

   conventional   constructed   both

3. "After watching the movie on Van Gogh, you will apply the inductive model of thinking to draw conclusions about Van Gogh as a painter. Begin by using the material you hear and see in the movie."

   conventional   constructed   both

4. "Today's lecture will be on the importance of recognizing and responding to a global economy."

   conventional   constructed   both

Personal Relevance

1. Students in business law are participating in a moot court competition.

   contrived   simulated   real

2. Students in sixth grade are constructing King Tut's tomb in a basement room in their school.

   contrived   simulated   real

3. Secondary students are elected to be members of the schoolwide town meeting form of governance. Faculty, secretaries, custodians, cafeteria workers, and bus drivers are also represented in the town meeting.

    contrived   simulated   real

4. At the end of the school year, kindergarten students write and illustrate a book telling entering kindergartners what they will experience and learn in their first year in school.

    contrived   simulated   real

5. Students in a secondary design class design and illustrate the posters and programs for the school plays.

    contrived   simulated   real

6. Students in middle school chorus perform three concerts a year.

    contrived   simulated   real

7. High school accounting students keep the books for each school-related club and activity.

    contrived   simulated   real

8. Sixth graders write and illustrate books to read and give to first graders.

    contrived   simulated   real

9. Geometry students do ten problems for homework.

    contrived   simulated   real

10. Chemistry students experiment with gas laws.

    contrived   simulated   real

Goal Stuctures

1. In groups of four, students write their analysis of an article, read their analysis to each other, and choose the best paper, which is displayed in a "best paper" area of the room.

    competitive   individual   cooperative

2. Students are asked to read a chapter of a novel, write a summary of the chapter, and predict what will happen in the next chapter. These papers are handed in to the teacher.

    competitive   individual   cooperative

3. Students work in groups of four to reach consensus on their math homework. They give the teacher a list of the problems the group was unable to agree on. The teacher will solve these problems for the whole class. During this time, they also practice a group skill chosen to be important by the class. If everyone in the group has completed his or her homework, the group gets bonus points toward a prize agreed on by the group and the teacher. All of the groups are eligible to receive the points and the prize.

    competitive   individual   cooperative

4. In a recitation period, students are called on individually to answer questions asked by the teacher.

    competitive   individual   cooperative

5. In third grade, students work at the learning center of their choice for additional skill practice when they finish their assignments.

    competitive   individual   cooperative

6. In a fourth-grade study of a novel, all students complete a worksheet on the summary of the chapter and their predictions for the next chapter. Students meet in groups of four the next day. One of the four students has prepared a list of new vocabulary words and their definitions from the chapter. A second student has prepared discussion questions for the group. A third has selected examples of simile, metaphor, and comparisons. The fourth is the secretary-checker. At the end of their discussion, they hand in their individual sheets to be graded and the group's evaluation of how well they did today and what they will work to improve the next time the group meets.

    competitive   individual   cooperative

Supervision

In each of the previous six examples, choose whether the teacher is supervising directly, whether the teacher is facilitating the learning, or whether the students are working independently. You may have more than one choice in an example.

1.	supervised	independent	facilitated
2.	supervised	independent	facilitated
3.	supervised	independent	facilitated
4.	supervised	independent	facilitated
5.	supervised	independent	facilitated
6.	supervised	independent	facilitated

Expressing the Self

In the following examples, are the students expressing something of their unique selves?

1. Second-grade students take a field trip to a farm. When they return, they are asked to write and illustrate their reaction to the trip.

            yes   no

2. High school students in an auto mechanics class are asked to design and construct a carburetor given a teacher-supplied minimum selection of materials.

            yes   no

3. Fourth-grade students are asked to construct a model of the solar system.

            yes   no

4. Students research the cultures that existed in North America prior to Columbus's voyage in 1492 and write, draw, and/or speak their reaction to the impact of Columbus on these cultures.

            yes   no

Degree of Abstraction

1. Students are asked to form a molecule of water by forming the bonds between hydrogen and oxygen. They are then asked to draw a diagram of the molecule and write it as a chemical equation.

            concrete   representational   abstract

2. Students write their reaction to a paper they have read.

            concrete   representational   abstract

3. Students make models of two-digit numbers with plastic rods and cubes. They draw the rods and cubes and add them. They put the numbers under their drawing and add them.

            concrete   representational   abstract

4. Students go to a science museum and are able to feel the density of the fur of a stuffed beaver, bear, and deer.

            concrete   representational   abstract

Structuring

1. "Choose a biography you are most interested in and prepare a canned book report on your biography."[1]

    none   student   negotiation   teacher

2. "Today you will finish your reading. Complete the questions at the end of the chapter, and compare your answers with a learning buddy."

    none   student   negotiation   teacher

3. "From our unit on exploration, you will pick an explorer or a period of time you want to study further. Arrange to have a conference with me, so we can discuss your topic, how you will research it, and how you will present your results to the class and/ or to me."

    none   student   negotiation   teacher

[1] In a "canned" book report, students put into a can objects that represent something important from the book. Then they pull the objects out one at a time and explain their relevance to the story.

Source Materials on Learning Experiences

Anter, J., and J. Jenkins. "Differential Diagnosis—Prescription Teaching: A Critical Appraisal." *Review of Educational Research* 49 (Fall 1979): 517–555.

Aronson, E. *The Jigsaw Classroom.* Beverly Hills: Sage Publications, 1978.

Bates, J. "Extrinsic Reward and Intrinsic Motivation: A Review with Implications for the Classroom." *Review of Educational Research* 49 (Fall 1979): 557–576.

Berlak, A., et al. "Teaching and Learning in English Primary Schools." *School Review* (February 1975): 215–243.

Bloom, B. *Taxonomy of Educational Objectives, Handbook I.* New York: David McKay, 1956.

Bruner, J. *Toward a Theory of Instruction.* Cambridge: Harvard University Press, 1966.

Bussis, A. M., E. A. Chittenden, and M. Amarel. *Beyond Surface Curriculum: An Interview Study of Teachers' Understandings.* Boulder, Colo.: Westview Press, 1976.

Colarusso, C. *Diagnostic Educational Grouping: Strategies for Teaching.* Bucks County (Pennsylvania) Public Schools, March 1972.

Dale, E. "Cone of Learning." Unpublished paper, University of Ohio.

Davis, O. L. (ed.). *Perspectives on Curriculum Development.* Washington, D.C.: Association for Supervision and Curriculum Development, 1976.

Deutsch, M. "An Experimental Study of the Effects of Cooperation and Competition upon Group Process." *Human Relations* 2 (1949): 199–231.

Dunn, R., and K. Dunn. *Teaching Students Through Their Individualized Learning Styles: A Practical Approach.* Reston, Va.: Reston Publishing Co., 1978.

Gehlbach, R. D. "Individual Differences: Implications for Instructional Theory, Research and Innovation." *Educational Researcher* 8 (April 1979): 8–14.

Gower, R. R., and H. Resnick. "Theory and Research: Evaluation Results." Project funded by Office of Career Education, U.S. Office of Education, August 1979.

Gregorc, A. F., and H. B. Ward,, "A New Definition for Individual." *MASSP Bulletin* (February 1977).

Hunt, D. E. *Matching Models in Education.* Monograph No. 10. Ontario, Canada: Ontario Institute for Studies in Education, 1971.

Hunt, D. E., and E. V. Sullivan. *Between Psychology and Education.* Hinsdale, Ill.: Dryden Press, 1974.

Johnson, D. W., and R. T. Johnson. *Learning Together and Alone.* Englewood Cliffs, N.J.: Prentice Hall, 1975, 1987.

Johnson, D. W., L. Skon, and R. Johnson. "Effects of Cooperative, Competitive, and Individualistic Conditions on Children's Problem-Solving Performance." *American Educational Research Journal* 17 (Spring 1980): 83–94.

Johnson, D. W., R. T. Johnson, E. J. Holubec. *Advanced Cooperative Learning.* Edina, Minn.: Interaction Book Company, 1988.

Joyce, B. R. *A Guide to the Teacher-Innovator: A Program to Prepare Teachers.* Washington, D.C.: American Association of Colleges for Teacher Education, 1969.

———. *Selecting Learning Experiences.* Washington, D.C.: Association for Supervision and Curriculum Development, 1978.

Rich, H. L., and A. J. Bush, "The Effect of Congruent Teacher-Student Characteristics on Instructional Outcomes." *American Educational Research Journal* 15 (Summer 1978): 451–458.

Rosenholtz, S. J., and B. Wilson. "The Effect of Classroom Structure on Shared Perceptions of Ability." *American Educational Research Journal* 17 (Spring 1980): 75–82.

Sharam, S. "Cooperation Learning in Small Groups." *Review of Educational Research* 50 (Summer 1980): 241–272.

Slavin, R. E. "Cooperative Learning." *Review of Educational Research* 50 (Summer 1980): 315–342.

Toepfer, C. F., Jr. *Brain Growth Periodization Research.* Washington, D.C.: Association for Supervision and Curriculum Development, 1981.

Tyler, R. *Basic Principles of Curriculum and Instruction.* Chicago: University of Chicago Press, 1949.

Winne, P. H. "Experiments in Relating Teachers' Use of Higher-Level Cognitive Questions to Students' Achievement." *Review of Educational Research* 49 (Winter 1979a).

———. "Aptitude-Treatment Interactions in an Experiment on Teacher Effectiveness." *American Educational Research Journal* 14 (Fall 1979b): 389–410.

16

Assessment

Authentic assessment is the Trojan horse of school reform.

Grant Wiggins

L et us start by sharing a surprising set of data. There is almost no correlation between grades in school and success in life on any known indicator: salary, position, status, influence, happiness, or any other (Samson et al. 1984). Given that startling finding, what is the point of any grading system? The things that somehow do matter for success are apparently unmeasured by tests and not reported by our grading systems (which leads to the alarming inference that they may also be untaught).

It is the concern with measuring *significant* learnings, plus dissatisfaction with the effects of current assessment methodologies, that has spawned the alternative assessment movement of the 1990s. And it is because assessment is so

> **There is almost no correlation between grades in school and success in life.**

intimately connected with instruction that this movement has such leverage for influencing instruction and focusing it on worthwhile outcomes.

In fact, among current instructional innovations, the assessment movement may be the most powerful lever we have for improving teaching and stretching and modernizing teachers' repertoires. Assessment influences what we teach, how we teach, how much time we spend on topics, and what activities students are asked to do on a daily basis. It reflects and also pushes our clarity of thinking about objectives. It influences how clear students are on what they're doing, why they are doing it, and how focused and motivated they are to do it.

It won't be long before all teachers are going to be expected to implement assessments with the attributes described in this chapter. Performance assessment for students is rolling down the pike as an educational reform because the shortcomings of standardized testing are becoming widely acknowledged. (Performance assessment for *teachers* is coming too. State law in a number of states mandates that licensing, certification, and recertification be tied to performance assessment of demonstrated capacity.) Standardized test makers eliminate any item that does not discriminate between groups; this is because the bell curve is the religion of norm-referenced standardized tests, and so the test *must* recreate the "normal distribution" to be true to its design purpose: sorting and ranking. Thus, choosing good items or good tasks for measuring important learning is secondary in standardized testing to choosing items that sort the population of students. Such a rationale for tests is no longer acceptable in a society that is calling on us to educate all students for the twenty-first-century workplace.

Sometimes called "authentic assessment," "alternative assessment," or "performance assessment," all of these new approaches aim to augment standardized paper-and-pencil tests with additional measures and in the doing, transform instructional practice too. In this chapter we explore how assessment can work to do this and what the implications are for learning and teaching. The purpose of this chapter is to (1) profile the characteristics of good assessment, (2) provide models of good assessment, and (3) help us enlarge our repertoire of ways to do it.

Good assessment systems have the following characteristics:

1. They are based on significant and deliberate learning objectives.
2. They provide crystal-clear criteria for success, with good models of what it looks like, at the beginning of instruction.
3. They use tasks that approach or simulate real-life experiences when possible.
4. They involve students intimately in self-assessment, collaborative critique, and goal setting.
5. They use multiple means of gathering data.
6. Good records are kept.
7. Assessments meet the criteria of technical soundness.
8. Informative reporting systems are in operation.

In addition to discussing these eight characteristics in the chapter, we will weave a number of themes through the text:

1. Teaching teams and assessments in common: Teams of teachers who share either students or content (or both) should work together to produce assessment tasks that they use in common.
2. Effects of assessment on instructional practices: The capacity to assess student learning can have ripple effects everywhere in the school. It can shape curriculum, guide instruction, and powerfully influence student motivation and focus.
3. Standards: Good assessment systems support learning by holding out the same high standards of exemplary performance for all students. They provide feedback to students on developmentally appropriate benchmarks of progress toward the standard. Grading systems should show how individual students are doing with respect to the universal standard.

The Purposes of Assessment

It is important that teachers be clear about the purpose of assessment and that students be clear too. Strange as it may sound, students often will not know the purpose of a particular assessment unless teachers tell them directly—and that rarely happens. We could count on one hand the number of teachers we have observed in any year who differentiate summative tests and diagnostic tests for students. Telling students, "This test is just to see what you've learned so far," does not make the distinction. It does not tell students what you are going to do with the results. (Group them for instruction? Make reports to parents about overall progress? Identify topics to reteach to the whole class?)

Purposes of Assessment

1. To make summative statements	▶ about how well students have done overall in meeting course or unit objectives
2. To certify students	▶ as competent in a field of knowledge
	▶ as competent in a field of practice
	▶ as eligible for promotion
3. To signal clearly	▶ what knowledge is important
	▶ what the criteria and standards are for quality work
4. To make instructional decisions	▶ about where to start students with instruction
	▶ about which skills are mastered
	▶ about which skills or subskills to reteach to which students
5. To give feedback to students	▶ about students' strengths, weaknesses, and interests
6. To give feedback to teachers	▶ about the effectiveness of instruction
	▶ about the effectiveness of curriculum
7. To report progress to parents and communities	▶ about any or all of the above
8. To elevate the curriculum so as to provide meaningful, higher-level thinking tasks for all students	
9. To sort, rank, or compare students	▶ for honors and awards
	▶ for admissions into programs with limited enrollment
10. To norm students or groups of students	▶ for comparative achievement in relation to national groups
	▶ for comparative achievement in relation to other populations
11. For placement	▶ in courses, grades, or levels
12. To predict	▶ success in a course
	▶ success in school
	▶ success in a job performance

FIGURE 16.1: PURPOSES OF ASSESSMENT

There are many legitimate reasons for doing assessment with students. (**Figure 16.1** summarizes twelve of them.) Teachers sometimes try to use tests for two or more purposes at the same time—for example, getting grades to rank students for honor roll and diagnosing student weaknesses for reteaching—but mixed-purpose assessment usually does not work too well, shortchanging one of the purposes because of the different design demands of different kinds of assessment (Bloom et al. 1981). It is because of these differences in design that all teachers need to be particularly clear about which purposes they have in mind. In this chapter we will examine purposes 4 through 8 in the figure, which focus on instructional decisions and feedback to students.

Now let us begin our discussion of the eight characteristics of good assessment. We will begin at the beginning with objectives.

Characteristics of Good Assessment

Significant, Deliberate Learning Objectives

The foundation of good assessment is starting out with a clear statement of what the students should know and be able to do. (This kind of thinking was discussed in detail in Chapter 14.) The objectives should be worth learning, and the students should know why. Communicating what the objectives are and why they are worth learning is part of the job of teaching.

> *Communicating what the objectives are and why they are worth learning is part of the job of teaching.*

Clear identification of objectives, however, is only the beginning of a cycle of thinking and planning that links objectives with learning experiences and assessment tasks. Through the construction of clear criteria for high-quality work and the concomitant assessment tasks teachers generate, teachers (and then students) become clear on what the objective means.

So which comes first: the chicken or the egg? The criteria for success or the assessment task? Sometimes teachers work backward from tasks they have created in order to derive and specify attributes of quality work; then they differentiate levels of performance on each attribute and give examples of what these different levels would look like. This sequence can be very productive when teachers have invented an authentic task that is motivating for students and complex. But it is also true that big-picture outcomes relative to skills and habits of mind should often be specified in advance of the construction of assessment tasks. The effort to do so in a precise and elaborated way can assist in the later construction of good assessment tasks.

Clear Criteria for Success and Models

The center of good assessment is giving students (and teachers and parents) clear images of what students are supposed to be able to do. We mean actual images of good performance, not just lists of characteristics of good performances. Nothing is as clear and useful for focusing the energy of students as seeing an example of the real thing, along with a good explanation of how this model manifests the characteristics they are told they should achieve in their work.

At the macrolevel, students and parents can be given sample products that represent benchmarks of progress for a whole year in, say, reading and writing. Three samples that the Mather Elementary School in Boston uses to communicate standards for good work by the end of particular grade levels are shown in FIGURE 16.2.

The same thinking applies to communicating images of good work for units of study or for projects. The criteria for success in the task—and therefore in the course or the unit—should be

- public
- clear
- available for student examination in models of previous good performances
- given to students early

This set is probably the most violated characteristic in current assessment practice.

These benchmark products, however, while creating good gestalt images of quality work, do not fully inform students and parents about what exactly made them good. That is where rubrics come in.

Rubrics: What They Are and What They Look Like

The term *rubric* or *scoring rubric* refers to the name for an organized presentation, often in matrix form, that specifies qualities on which a piece of work will be assessed and precisely defines what earns a given score on each quality. FIGURE 16.3 shows a rubric.

The qualities to be assessed—that is, the criteria for a good essay—are organization, sentence structure, usage, mechanics, and format. Each is written down the left-hand side of the matrix. Each quality (criterion) has three paragraphs spelling out three different levels of performance. In between are two blank spots for scoring a student's work if it seems to fall between two descriptions. This arrangement yields a five-point scale for each quality.

Writing - The material below is what an average kindergartener should be able to write by the end of the year

Reading and listening - The passage below, from *In a Dark Dark Wood-* by June Meiser and Joy Cowley, is the level that a student at the completion of kindergarten should be able to listen to with good comprehension. Other books that kindergarteners should be able to understand include: *Caps for Sale, Farmer in the Dell, Blueberries for Sal, If You Made a Million, Stone Soup, The Hungry Crocodile,* and *Why Mosquitoes Buzz in People's Ears.*

> In a dark dark wood, there was a dark dark path. And up that dark dark path, there was a dark dark house. And in that dark dark house, there was a dark dark stair. And up that dark dark stair, there was a dark dark room. And in that dark dark room, there was a dark dark cupboard. And in that dark dark cupboard, there was a dark dark box. And in that dark dark box there was a ghost!

FIGURE 16.2: SAMPLE PRODUCTS FOR COMMUNICATING STANDARDS

Reprinted with permission. Excerpted from *Curriculum Exemplars for Writing and Reading.* The Mather Elementary School, Boston, Massachusetts, 1994.

Writing - The piece below is the level expected of an average student at the completion of the second grade

My Pet by Cathal Doherty
I have pet parrot. His
name is Tweety. I like to
chase him around. It is
grey and white. It talks funny
and it tickles you. We play
together. It is fun to have a pet.

Reading - The passage below, taken from *City Mouse and Country Mouse* by Aesop is the level that a student at the completion of second grade should be able to read with accuracy, fluency, and comprehension. Other books that second graders should be able to read include: *Amelia Bedelia, Angel Child, Dragon Child, Blueberries for Sal, If You Made a Million, Stone Soup, The Hungry Crocodile,* and *Why Mosquitoes Buzz in People's Ears*

The rugs were beautiful bright colors. In each room were beautiful chairs and tables and lights. Best of all was the kitchen. Country Mouse ran up and down everywhere. Everything in the kitchen was shining and bright. There, right in front of his eyes, was a mountain of food.

continued on next page

Writing - The piece below is the level expected of an average student at the completion of the fifth grade.

The Wolverine

I wake up screaming. Pain in my head so intense, I can't put a name to it, can't fight it, can't run away from it. I don't even know where I am. I'm in some kind of cave? Images flash through my brain. Memories, a jungle, a girl then a fight that I thought I won. I was wrong. Still fighting with my brain the pain unbearable like a million white hot needles digging into my skull. I'm beyond reason, beyond hope when that happens I turn animal.

The animal in me fights back pushing back at the needles. The strain takes its toll. I feel the darkness closing in. I thought I was dead only I'm not. I hear voices shouting then the lights come on! What I see in the mirror can't be real, but my senses tell me it is. I feel hard-packed dirt at my feet and sweat sliding down my back I hear the buzzing of insects and crackling of fire. I see a beast out of hell, eyes blazing with arms like tree trunks. I still think I'm dreaming then reality sinks in. Boom! Aagh! I'm a wolverine.

Reading - The passage below, taken from *Island of the Blue Dolphins* by Scott O'Dell, is the level that a student at the completion of fifth grade should be able to read with accuracy, fluency, and comprehension. Other books that fifth graders should be able to read include: *Bridge to Terabithia*, *Roll of Thunder, Hear My Cry*, *Sarah, Plain and Tall*, *Stone Fox*, *Vampire Bat Girls' Club*, *Witch of Banneker School*, *Shiloh*, and *The Land I Lost*.

A short distance beyond the dune, near the cliff, I saw the pack of wild dogs. There were many of them and they were moving around in a circle.

In the middle of the circle was Ramo. He was lying on his back, and had a deep wound in his throat. He lay very still.

When I picked him up I knew that he was dead. There were other wounds on his body from the teeth of the wild dogs. He had been dead a long time and from his footsteps on the earth I could see that he had never reached the cliff.

Two dogs lay on the ground not far from him, and in the side of one of them was his broken spear.

I carried Ramo back to the village, reaching it when the sun was far down. The dogs followed me all the way, but when I had laid his down in the hut, and came out with a club in my hand, they trotted off to a low hill. A big gray dog with long curling hair and yellow eyes was their leader an he went last.

It was growing dark, but I followed them up the hill. Slowly they retreated in front of me, not making a sound. I followed them across two hills an a small valley to a third hill whose face was a ledge of rock. At one end of the ledge was a cave. One by one the dogs went into it.

FIGURE **16.2** CONTINUED

	1	**2**	**3**	**4**	**5**	
Organization	Little or nothing is written. The essay is disorganized, incoherent, and poorly developed. The essay does not stay on the topic.		The essay is not complete. It lacks an introduction, well-developed body or conclusion. The coherence and sequence are attempted, but not adequate.		The essay is well-organized. It contains an introductory supporting and concluding paragraph. The essay is coherent, ordered logically, and fully developed.	**X6**
Sent. Str.	The student writes frequent run-ons or fragments.		The student makes occasional errors in sentence structure. Little variety in sentence length or structure exists.		The sentences are complete and varied in length and structure.	**X5**
Usage	The student makes frequent errors in word choice and agreement.		The student makes occasional errors in word choice or agreement.		The usage is correct. Word choice is appropriate.	**X4**
Mechanics	The student makes frequent errors in spelling, punctuation, and capitalization.		The student makes an occasional error in mechanics.		The spelling, capitalization, and punctuation are correct.	**X4**
Format	The format is sloppy. There are no margins or indentations. Handwriting is inconsistent.		The handwriting, margins, and indentation have occasional inconsistencies—no title or inappropriate title.		The format is correct. The title is appropriate. The handwriting, margins, and indentations are consistent.	**X1**

FIGURE 16.3: RUBRIC FOR SCORING AN ESSAY*
Numbers in the right-hand column indicate the weighting scheme.

Students and parents know after examining this matrix exactly what the teacher is looking for and what the standards for good work are. And they will know even better if a sample of a well-done essay is provided with notes pointing out how and where each quality is manifested.

Wiggins points out that adding the quality of "interest" to rubrics for expository writing would give them a dimension beyond the mechanical.

FIGURE 16.4 shows another scoring rubric, this one for a biology task at West Hancock High School.

Biology I: Observation of Unknown

You are employed as a laboratory technician specializing in observation and reporting for Modern Biology Laboratories. A client presents you with an unknown organism and requests that you describe as many structures the unknown possesses as possible. He also asks you to hypothesize the probable function of each of the described structures. Your lab schedule will allow three days for observation and preparation of a report to be delivered to Mr. G, the presenter of the unknown.

*Reprinted with permission. Archbald, D., and F. M. Newmann. *Beyond Standardized Tests: Assessing Authentic Academic Achievement in Secondary School.* Reston, Va.: National Association of Secondary School Principals, 1988, p.11. Source: Adams County School District #12, 11285 Highline Drive, Northglenn, Colo. 80203.

Laboratory materials available for your use include, but are not limited to, boiled yeast with congo red, cotton fibers, microscope, slides and cover slides as well as a the culture.*

	3	**2**	**1**
Observations	Extensive and critical	Moderate	Minimal and incomplete
Hypothesis of functions	Complete, logical and applicable	Complete but not logical or applicable	Incomplete or illogical or not applicable
Use of materials	All materials used	Materials used with one exception	Materials not used
Lab work	Independent	Independent with some help	Dependent
Data presentation	Complete, organized labeled	Complete, organized missing labels	Incomplete unorganized

NAME _____

FIGURE 16.4: SCORING RUBRIC FOR A BIOLOGY TASK

This example makes it clear that there are five qualities on which the lab report will be judged: (1) extensiveness of observation, (2) completeness of hypotheses, (3) use of materials, (4) independence of lab work, and (5) completeness of data presentation. Nevertheless, such rubrics do not stand as completely self-sufficient devices for communicating expectations. For example, in the biology task, what makes data presentation "organized" between level 1 and 2? What discriminates a complete from an incomplete hypothesis? Students still need positive and negative examples of these criteria if they are to be fully prepared to work toward the highest standard. That is not a criticism of this rubric; it merely points out the elaboration it takes to make many well-constructed rubrics into powerful instructional guides. The same can be said of the example from a government class shown in FIGURE 16.5.

In this task students are asked to demonstrate their knowledge of certain amendments to the U. S. Constitution by showing how they would be applied to a number of cases before the Supreme Court.

*Reprinted with permission. Bob Grandgenett, Biology Instructor, West Hancock High School, Britt, Iowa. "Observation of Unknown."

	1	**2**	**3**
Scope of coverage	All aspects adequately covered	All aspects thoroughly covered, some more than others	Excellent, balanced coverage of all aspects of project
Mechanics of expression	Few mechanical errors; ideas clearly expressed	"Error-free"; mechanics support ideas	Excellent support of ideas through mechanics
Quality of expression	Generally effective style, clear focus and description	Style, quality contribute to the impact of ideas	Ideas well developed, excellent use of style to effectively communicate ideas
Depth of information	Adequate investigation of necessary sources	Abundant sources used; concepts, implications explored	Multi-source investigation used to thoroughly exploit concepts and implications of rights
Appropriateness	Cases properly selected and adequately applied to amendments	Appropriate cases, logically applied to selected rights	Excellent choice of cases; logically applied to all or most of the rights in the amendment

Note: This project takes the place of the semester test. Time allotted for testing will be used to exchange information, discuss cases and the project in general, and get your suggestions for improvement.

FIGURE 16.5: RUBRIC FOR A GOVERNMENT ASSESSMENT PROJECT*

Notice that under Scope of Coverage, the lowest score is for the item, "All aspects adequately covered." That implies that the task is not complete until the student has at least covered all specified aspects of the assignment. (We will come back to this point later in the chapter because the implication is that the teacher has quite high standards and that tasks are incomplete until these standards are met.) Higher scores (2 and 3) go for demonstrating "thoroughness" and, beyond that, "excellent balance" in coverage. Models of "adequate" and "thorough" need to be provided to students so that the descriptions within a rubric like this become meaningful. The same is called for in distinguishing "adequate" from "abundant" under Depth of Information.

A fourth example of a scoring rubric (FIGURE 16.6) is taken from a cross-curricular sixth-grade exhibition developed by Penny Knox at Los Naranjos School in Irvine, California.

*Reprinted with permission. Terry Crane, P.O. Box 57, Rockville, Iowa 50469. Government Assessment Project Rubric.

<u>**Goal**</u>

Student will communicate accumulated knowledge through creative and analytical writing.

<u>**Exhibition**</u>

Using class notes, individual research, literature and information from audio-visual presentations, students will write a letter to their parents describing a trip to an assigned culture by including information on the following aspects of this culture:

- art, architecture, literature
- government
- inventions and technology
- social, economic and political systems
- the daily lives of the common people
- religion and ethical beliefs
- importance of geography in the development of this culture
- why this culture fell or declined

<u>**Expectation**</u>

Guidelines:
- Correct grammar, spelling, capitalization and punctuation must be used.
- Letter will be written in class.
- Final copy of the letter will be typed on school computer word processing program.
- Student will use appropriate note-taking skills and be able to organize ideas in proper outline format.
- Student is able to research notes to communicate knowledge creatively, establishing tone, point of view, and setting.

Model: Student letter is attached.

FIGURE 16.6: RUBRIC FOR A CROSS-CURRICULAR SIXTH-GRADE EXHIBITION

Reprinted with permission. Taken from a "Cross Curricular Sixth-Grade Exhibition" developed by Penny Knox at Los Naranjos School, Irvine, California.

Key: 1   Not Yet   Student_____
      2   Sometimes   Teacher_____
      3   Most of the time
      4   Always

Observational category:

Skill	Practice Date	Practice Date	Practice Date	Exhibition
Student uses basic mechanics of writing, grammar, spelling, punctuation and capitalization.	1 2 3 4 Comments:	1 2 3 4 Comments:	1 2 3 4 Comments:	1 2 3 4 Comments:
Student is able to take notes from various sources (text-book, literature, encyclopedia) and effectively use them as a reference.	1 2 3 4 Comments:	1 2 3 4 Comments:	1 2 3 4 Comments:	1 2 3 4 Comments:
Student is able to use research notes to communicate knowledge creatively, establishing tone, point of view and setting.	1 2 3 4 Comments:	1 2 3 4 Comments:	1 2 3 4 Comments:	1 2 3 4 Comments:
Student is able to outline and follow the basic format of an expository essay.	1 2 3 4 Comments:	1 2 3 4 Comments:	1 2 3 4 Comments:	1 2 3 4 Comments:
Student is able to use word processing program.	1 2 3 4 Comments:	1 2 3 4 Comments:	1 2 3 4 Comments:	1 2 3 4 Comments:

Note that this project gets scored four times on each criterion. Three times are labeled "Practice Date," and the final assessment in simply called "Exhibition." This assessment form reflects a design where students actually produce the final product (write the letter) three times and get detailed feedback each time on the quality of their work. They can use this feedback to develop skills that need work and to refine and improve their background knowledge prior to the final exhibition. In this school, the children take the product home for one of the practice trials and work with their parents to apply the scoring rubric to the child's product. This is a particularly effective way to inform and involve parents in the education of their children.

The four student tasks and rubrics we have described escalate in the time it takes students to complete and the degree to which they are interdisciplinary. The essay assignment might be carried out in a night of homework. The biology observation task takes three successive lab periods. Applying the amendments to cases might well take the group two weeks, and the task itself blends language arts, research skills, and analytical knowledge of the social studies content (the amendments themselves) in order to perform the application task. The letter to parents describing a trip to an assigned culture takes a whole semester and blends grammar, form, organization and writing skill, notetaking, social studies, and technology skills. But what all the tasks have in common is a clear framework for defining quality work specified through the scoring rubrics that accompany the tasks.

Developing a Rubric

A good rubric can fit on one piece of paper, but the complement to a good rubric is a set of samples of actual student work that exemplify the different cells of the rubric. A good rubric offers such samples with explanations of why each sample exemplifies the level of quality claimed for it. *Exemplars*, a monthly publication, publishes collections of benchmark mathematical tasks, K–8, designed by teachers, with actual student work produced for each task. (A benchmark task is one that calls for students to display a variety of competencies thought to be important. Such tasks aren't given every day but are saved for assessing student progress at certain key junctures.) The student products are scored as Novice, Apprentice, Practitioner, and Expert. An accompanying narrative explains how and why the samples exemplify one of the four levels of the rubric.

Behind all the mathematical tasks in the *Exemplars* collection are some criteria for good performance. These three analytical criteria—understanding, reasoning, and communication—serve as guidelines for creating good tasks and also embed important outcomes they want for students. Each issue of *Exemplars* sets out the analytic criteria:

Understanding the problem

- Understands the question the problem poses
- Chooses information that is relevant to the problem
- When using graphic or pictorial representation shows accurate interpretation of the problem

♦ Can restate the problem in own terms

Reasoning strategies and mathematics procedures

♦ Chooses appropriate and applicable strategies

♦ Draws from past knowledge and experience

♦ Communicates reasoning process logically and sequentially

♦ Chooses the appropriate and most efficient mathematical procedure to solve the problem

♦ Sees more than one way of looking at the problem

♦ Develops system for checking accuracy and precision

Communication

♦ Results are presented clearly, coherently and accurately

♦ Uses tools of mathematical communication (e.g., graphs and notation)

Each of the three criteria is then broken out into statements that describe what performance on it would look like for a Novice, an Apprentice, a Practitioner, and an Expert. Arranging these statements in cells of a matrix produces the rubric in Figure 16.7.

The Appendix to this chapter shows a typical package that comes with an *Exemplars* task, including four samples of student work with explanations of their ratings. The samples show the kind of thoughtful analysis it takes to apply a rubric properly.

Though the samples are for mathematics content, similar collections can be assembled for any discipline and any skill or concept within the discipline. Making those collections of exemplars is, in fact, exactly what we are advocating that teams of teachers do.

The Process of Linking Rubrics and Authentic Tasks
The ingredients of successful rubrics as we have developed them so far are these:

1. Openly and explicitly shared criteria for good student performance—criteria that represent value choices about what is important, choices that are directly related to what we want students to know or be able to do.

2. Statements that specify levels of student performance on the criteria (statements that are often arranged in a matrix as a rubric).

3. Samples of student work that exemplify the levels in the rubric.

4. An authentic task.

Level	Understanding	Strategies, Reasoning, Procedures	Communication
Novice	• There is no solution or the solution has no relationship to the task. • Inappropriate concepts are applied and/or procedures are used.	• No evidence of a strategy or procedure, or uses a strategy that does not help solve the problem. • No evidence of mathematical reasoning. • There were so many errors in mathematical procedures that the problem could not be solved.	• There is no explanation of the solution, the explanation cannot be understood or it is unrelated to the problem • There is no use or inappropriate use of mathematical representations (e.g. figures diagrams, graphs, tables, etc.). • There is no use, or mostly inappropriate use, of mathematical terminology and notation.
Apprentice	• The solution is not complete indicating that parts of the problem are not understood.	• Uses a strategy that is partially useful, leading some way toward a solution, but not to a full solution of the problem. • Some evidence of mathematical reasoning. • Could not completely carry out mathematical procedures.	• There is an incomplete explanation; it may not be clearly presented. • There is some use of appropriate mathematical representation. • There is some use of mathematical terminology and notation appropriate to the problem.
Practitioner	• The solution shows that the student has a broad understanding of the problem and the major concepts necessary for its solution.	• Uses a strategy that leads to a solution of the problem. • Uses effective mathematical reasoning. • Mathematical procedures used appropriately.	• There is a clear explanation. • There is appropriate use of accurate mathematical representation. • There is effective use of mathematical terminology and notation.
Expert	• The solution shows a deep understanding of the problem including the ability to identify the appropriate mathematical concepts and the information necessary for its solution.	• Uses a very efficient and sophisticated strategy leading directly to a solution. • Employs refined and complex reasoning. • Applies procedures accurately to correctly solve the problem and verify the results.	• There is a clear, effective explanation detailing how the problem is solved. All of the steps are included so that the reader does not need to infer how and why decisions were made. • Mathematical representation is actively used as a means of communicating ideas related to the solution of the problem. • There is precise and appropriate use of mathematical terminology and notation.

FIGURE 16.7: THE RUBRIC IN *EXEMPLARS*

Reprinted with permission. Kallick, Bena, and Ross Brewer. *Exemplars: A Teacher's Solution*. Volume 1, nos. 4-12. Underhill, Vermont: Exemplars, 1994.

The last step in constructing good rubrics for performance assessment tasks is establishing reliability across teachers in scoring student work samples. *Reliability* means that the rubrics are sufficiently clear and the teachers sufficiently in agreement about the meaning of the levels of performance that different teachers would score a given work sample in the same way. This high level of reliability is established when teachers practice scoring students' work samples together, compare results, reconcile differences through discussion, and continue to practice until they are "reliable" in their scoring. To summarize, the sequence goes like this:

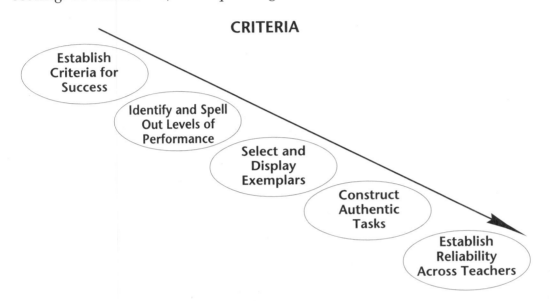

CRITERIA

- Establish Criteria for Success
- Identify and Spell Out Levels of Performance
- Select and Display Exemplars
- Construct Authentic Tasks
- Establish Reliability Across Teachers

The anchor of the process for developing authentic assessments is getting clear on what teachers really want students to know or be able to do. Notice that the analytic criteria set out in *Exemplars* pertain to high-level thinking, problem solving, and communication skills. This does not mean that lower-level skills like mastering calculation skills, times tables, and the like are disregarded, but the value (and thus the assessment) is clearly keyed to reasoning strategies the writers believe are important to using math in life. These choices of higher-level problem-solving skills thus guide the kinds of tasks that will be created.

> *The anchor of authentic assessments is getting clear on what teachers really want students to know or be able to do.*

Teachers who design authentic assessments find it a creative process that benefits from a high level of interaction with peers and often with students too. Once they have discussed what they want students to know or be able to do, teachers then cast around for or create tasks that conform to as many of the the criteria as possible.

Having piloted the assessment tasks, a group of teachers developing rubrics will typically sit down with a large collection of student products. They will quickly sort the student work into four piles representing poor, fair, good, and excellent levels of performance by examining the products with little or no discussion or analysis and grouping ones that seem at about the same level of performance. Placing a sample in a category is done by the sense of how the product strikes one.

Then comes the most important part of the process, which carries the most inherent staff development meat for teachers. Going over student work samples in detail, the teachers describe in writing the characteristics of each category and thus produce the first draft of their rubric. One writer notes that

> The conversation about standards inevitably stumbles over the degree to which standards should be explicitly stated. Is it enough to say student work should demonstrate "attention to detail"? Or should we describe the type and amount of detail we expect? There is little doubt that the latter provides students and teachers better guidance for planning teaching and learning, but capturing and agreeing on the former can be a significant step. (Jamentz 1994, p. 38)

If teachers take the time to work through to consensus on what the items in a rubric really mean and come up with exemplars of each level of performance, they can be very clear with students about intended learnings. Even better, they can produce more precisely designed learning experiences whose activities are more likely to enable students to learn what they want.

"Planning backwards," as Ted Sizer says (1992), means starting with carefully crafted assessments and then asking what learning experiences would likely prepare students to do the performances called for by the assessments. Thus the work that groups of teachers put into designing authentic assessments of important concepts and skills can translate almost immediately into better instruction. This can happen because everyone is so clearly focused on what they want the students to learn that they examine the learning experiences much more critically to see if they are really likely to lead students to these new capacities.

Involving Students in Creating Standards and Rubrics
Once teachers, working in teams, have created the standards, rubrics, and levels of performance within the rubrics, the time has come to involve the students. Students can play a big part in developing criteria for evaluating the products that they are about to create and in the process become clear about the goals and motivated to meet them. Chris Gustafson (1994) got her students involved in defining standards at the beginning of a unit on immigration.

> I handed out a list of topics and asked the students to select one. The next day students who had chosen the same project formed groups that would write a grading standard by which their projects would be evaluated. I explained that a project completed as described on the project sheet [which she had provided] would receive a C. Each group was to decide what they would need to add to my criteria in order to receive a B or an A. As an example, we set a grading standard

together for a writing project. That gave me a chance to discourage responses that were too ambitious: everyone's journal did not have to be typed, but more than a half page of writing on each sheet would be required, and so on.

After writing the journal grading standard as a class, each group decided what [their particular] projects would have to include to receive a B or an A. I took all their suggestions and typed one grading standard for each project. The next day, I handed each person his or her group's grading standard sheet. Now, before students even began the project, they knew how it would be evaluated.

This time, when I took the projects home, each one had a grading standard attached to it. And what a difference that made: because my students didn't have to guess what to do to get a high grade, they were more successful; our high standards resulted in better projects; and although I still made comments, evaluation was easier. Parents could also see exactly how the evaluations had been done. The process was open to all, and the students had had a part in creating it.*

Rubrics and Expectations

Good rubrics and clear criteria in advance are essential for communicating the three messages of expectations: "This is important; you can do it; and I won't give up on you." Without clear criteria for comparing student work, there is no way to make feedback full and informative enough for low-performing students. And without adults who take the time to give this full feedback, along with help to use it, students too easily can conclude they are incapable.

It is not fair to students who do not have a clear image of what quality looks like to ask them to guess. They certainly won't figure it out from being told repetitively that they are not making the grade. Developing clear rubrics built on careful thinking about important standards of performance and involving students in the process can eliminate the student complaint that got Chris Gustafson started on her assessment project. A student said to her after class one day, "I don't understand why I got this grade." It is our belief that the number of students who wonder the same thing when they get back papers and projects form the silent majority of American school children.

Collaborative planning time for groups of teachers is required for the process we have described. In fact, what we are really trying to do is "develop a professional culture in which teacher analysis of student work is expected and valued" (California Assessment Collaborative, in Jamenetz 1993). Principals and department chairs play a key role in communicating that message through what they say, model, and facilitate through scheduling, use of meeting time, and the resources they make available to teachers for this work of building rubrics.

> *It is not fair to students who do not have a clear image of what quality looks like to ask them to guess.*

The administrator as a "school culture builder" (Saphier and King 1985) plays a crucial role in the development of authentic assessments and in building the capacity of teachers to use the assessment process to improve instruction.

In this section we have defined rubrics and discussed how to develop one. We have said that a good development process includes samples of real student work that exemplify cells in the rubric. Now what about designing tasks to assess what students know and can do?

Tasks Approaching or Simulating Real-life Experiences

Marzano, Pickering, and McTighe (1993) say that authentic assessment "conveys the idea that assessments should engage students in applying knowledge and skills in the same way they are used in the 'real world' outside of school." Wiggins (1993) adds, "Assessment is authentic when we directly examine student performances on worthy intellectual tasks." Thus, a test asks a student to do a task that is realistic, complex, and integrated as closely as possible with something the student would have to do in the world outside school and, says Ann Johnson, "replicates or parallels the experiences facing a consumer, citizen, worker, or professional in the field" (workshop handout, 1992).

Authenticity is a key idea in the assessment movement because authentic tasks amalgamate complex performances in the same way real-life problems do, and they are more motivating to students. Thus authentic assessment tasks are a more valid measure of educational effectiveness if we view education as the preparation of young minds for successful living. What will be assessed will not be just subskills like the ability to decode words with

> **Authenticity is a key idea in the assessment movement.**

short *a*, the ability to balance chemical equations given valences and quantities, or knowledge of facts or even comprehension of "the causes of the Civil War," at least as an isolated measurement. Rather, what will be assessed will be the ability to perform complex tasks that require higher-order thinking skills and the integration of knowledge: tasks that are authentic because they are direct models of or simulations of tasks that people have to perform in the real world. In performing these complex tasks, of course, each of us must draw on our knowledge of subskills and facts, but they are put to use in service of a larger task that is realistic.

The following criteria can serve as a checklist for analyzing assessment tasks created for children (from Jamentz 1993):

- Does the task spark students' interest and motivation?
- Does the task require students to construct meaning?
- Does the task encourage demonstration of important habits of mind?
- Does the task encourage multiple modes of expression?

- Is the task free from arbitrary constraints?

- Does the task measure progress over time?

- Does the task require collaboration with others?

- Is the task a representative challenge, emphasizing depth rather than breadth of response?

- Does the task explore and identify hidden strengths?

- Does the task genuinely assess learning and effort, rather than native talent?

- Do the standards for the task cover a wide range of knowledge, skills, and habits of mind considered important to the subject area or, if interdisciplinary, those that transcend a single discipline?

- Are the standards for good performance clear to students before they engage in the task?

- Are the standards for the task appropriately weighted?

- Are the standards for the task in harmony with shared school, district, state, or national goals?

- Does the task match the scoring framework?

- Is the task multidimensional, allowing for a single performance to be strong in some areas and weak in others?

- Is the assessment structured to provide prompt and useful feedback to the teacher and student?

- Does the task provide built-in opportunities for students to practice, rehearse, and retake it?

We think the first three characteristics on the list are particularly essential.

So far in this chapter we have discussed three elements of good assessment systems: (1) significant and deliberate learning objectives, (2) clear criteria for good student performance and (3) authentic tasks that embed the criteria. Along the way we have also discussed the processes through which teachers create these criteria and elaborate them through rubrics. We have also discussed the process by which teachers develop rubrics for scoring and giving feedback through examination of student work samples.

Now, on to the fourth element: student self-assessment.

Student Involvement in Self-Assessment, Collaborative Critique, and Goal Setting

The act of assessment should be an act of learning too; this requires that students be continually self-evaluating and reorienting their efforts as a result of examining their own work, feedback from peers, and feedback from teachers. For assessment to be an act of learning, students must do self-assessment, applying criteria to their own work. This requires that they be clear about the criteria as they go about error analysis and the search for clues on how to correct the errors, and that they reflect on what they have done and chart a route for doing better next time. Such charting of action for the future invites formal goal setting by students, which implies that teachers teach the technology of goal setting directly to students. This technology enables students to integrate it with their feedback from assessment or from self-assessment.

> ## *The act of assessment should be an act of learning too.*

Shavelson and coworkers (1992) point to a "symmetry between teaching and testing. That is, a good assessment makes a good teaching activity, and a good teaching activity makes a good assessment." Many prominent thinkers in the assessment movement (e.g., Wolf unpublished paper, 1992; Zessoules and Gardner 1991) use the phrase "assessment as a moment for learning" to convey this point.[1] The belief behind this position is that errors are opportunities for learning, not confirmations of stupidity. A further implicit belief is that learning is a process—a steady accumulation of knowledge and skill over time—not an event. Therefore achievement should be conceived as a continuum of continuous progress, and assessment helps place a student along that continuum, not on a scale of worthiness or smartness. Assessment tells you where you are in the journey and what you need to do next, not how good a student you are. Those are the beliefs behind "assessment as a moment for learning," and they are reflected in the following statements:

> "Less noticed is that tests routinely fail to inform learning. The efficient collection of data about a sample of student performance for an outside audience has come to dominate over the first audiences and obligations for assessment: to make students and teachers acute critics of the quality of work and able discussants of what should count as excellence....Students infrequently have the opportunity to make use of what they learn from earlier performances to inform a second try. In essence, rarely are school assessments the occasion for making public the standards and strategies for doing good work. Yet all we know regarding the generation of worthwhile work tells us that it requires incubation, revision, collaboration, and the public display of and debate about failure, risk, and excellence.

> The implication for the redesign of current testing is that a major portion of school-based assessment should be conceived as an episode in which students learn how to write or experiment, or do research, using the power of assessment to push them along the "zig-zag path" that Lampert described. In more specific terms, assessment ought to:

> ◆ be live: that is, conducted in the face and threat and promise of serious and on-going work of consequence for the student.

---

[1] Others have made the point that assessment is an occasion for learning. This is because when students are given a challenging problem they are able to see relationships and connections that were not obvious to them before. The learning that takes place is a function of the interaction between the student(s) and the task or the students and each other. It does not take place because the teacher is actively mediating the students' thinking (Baron 1989, p. 315).

- take the form of a series of iterative episodes of work followed by time for personal reflection and the gathering of responses from peers, mentors, and judges.

- allow an individual ways and time for making use of the resulting chorus of opinion so as to make it possible to decide what in the criticism is apt, and what misses the mark.

- permit that individual to plow the fruits of critique and reflection back into his or her final response [or next try]. (Wolfe 1992)

These recommendations imply that teachers must create the time and place in class for students to critique one another's work—and not just writing. They apply as well to dinosaur fact sheets produced by ninth graders, geometry proofs of tenth graders, and science experiments of fifth graders. This collaboration and critique is characteristic of a "portfolio culture, that is, a setting where there is frequent and public discussion about what makes for good work and a clear sense that good work takes a long time to emerge." It thus becomes incumbent on teachers to create frequent opportunities for these public discussions about good work.

In these discussions, "students have access to the criteria that will be used to score their work and those criteria are explained, even debated" (Wolfe 1992). The point is that they learn about the place of qualities like the ability to pose an interesting problem. Modern assessment puts the teacher in charge, not the testing company, because assessment is built systematically into instruction. Since what is assessed is students' evolving and improving *process*, not just one-time simple performances, the data collected are *about* process and strategy as well as product. Student self-assessment is at the core.

In a tenth-grade geometry class, for example, each student is assigned different proofs for homework. Twice a week at the beginning of class, students show their proofs to a partner, who reads the proof and critiques it according to the criteria of logical order, completeness, and readability. (Readability includes neatness and also whether abbreviations and references can be understood.) The teacher periodically models how to do these critiques with proofs at the board; students change partners each day when they critique each other.

In another classroom, the teacher uses self-evaluation to collect data about eighth graders' ability to play different roles in discussion groups (e.g., summarizing, stating issues, breaking tension). She has told the students she is collecting the self-evaluations to see whether they have increased their ability to play multiple roles and so that she can identify students who need more help. Each role has been explained and modeled by the teacher, and students have practiced them in structured exercises. Now students are asked to participate supportively in a new group discussion. In their self-evaluation, they are to record what role or roles they see themselves as having played and the roles played by every other member of their group. They have succeeded when they can claim three or more different roles and the majority of their group supports their claims. One instance of role-appropriate behavior is enough to claim that role. The teacher meets with students who play fewer than three roles and has them pick an additional one to try in the next discussion. Students who claim more roles than their group testifies to are asked to write examples of the unsupported roles, which the teacher may accept as evidence. In her grade book she keeps a checklist of students who meet the criteria. For comparative purposes she has her own observational records of which roles individuals played before instruction.

Self-evaluation can also yield added dividends of more student involvement, more awareness of criteria, and better discrimination of quality. Waters, MacMullen, and Glade (1992) have students periodically isolate their best work from the collections in their writing folders. As they explain, "The making of this collection provides students with an on-going opportunity to review and analyze their best work, choose what best represents him or her, establish a sense of progress, [and] establish a base line from which to move ahead." It also creates the groundwork for individual teacher-student conferences around the collection. Such conferences are unmatched opportunities for involving students in goal setting and helping them generate ownership for their own learning.

Multiple Means of Gathering Data

Fleming and Chambers discovered in 1983 that short-answer paper-and-pencil tests at the fact level dominate assessment in American schools at all levels, K–12. And Goodlad's (1984) data revealed that recitation structures—cycles of teacher questions and student answers, a form of ongoing oral test—account for over 80 percent of all lessons observed. There is a place for recitations in education, just as there is a place for factual tests, but the narrowness of most assessment repertoires (just like the narrowness of teaching repertoires) restricts teachers' capacity to mount effective instruction for all students. Like every other area of teaching examined in this book, there is no one right or best way to do assessment; there exists a repertoire of ways to assess student learning.

Teachers should strive for having command of a wide repertoire of ways to assess student learning—ways that will be good matches for students' learning styles, ways that will be a good match for the curricula of the twenty-first century, when all students must learn to think, problem solve, communicate, and work with others. Obviously more than short-answer tests, essays, and written reports are needed (though these will remain part of our map).

We are going to describe a number of assessment devices and the kind of learning for which they are appropriate. Each device has a place, including old-fashioned short-answer tests, essays, and written reports. But teachers of the future are going to have the capacity to design and use a wide range of these assessment devices because they will be aiming squarely for the kinds of learning the devices measure. FIGURE **16.8** identifies the repertoire of assessment devices and shows their relationships.

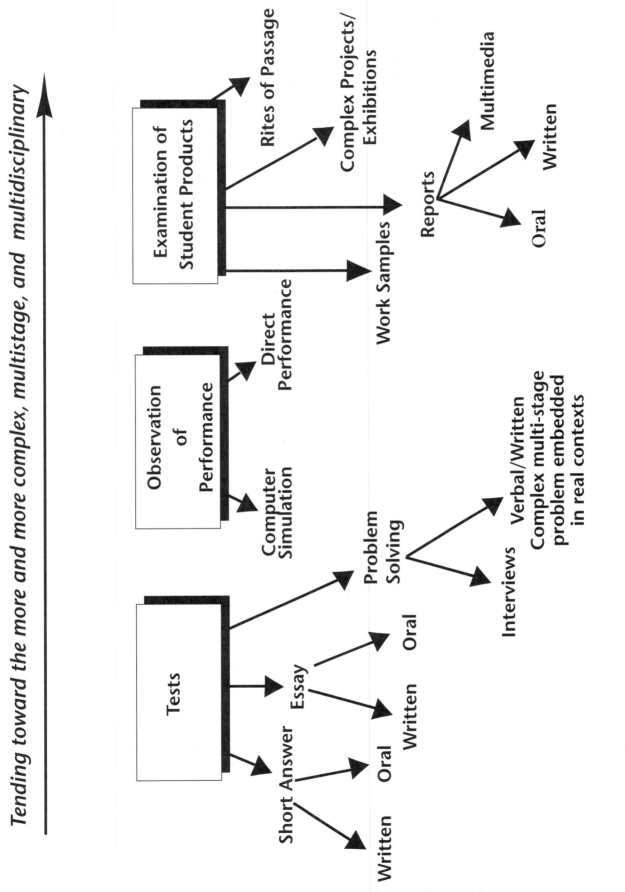

FIGURE 16.8: ASSESSMENT DEVICES FOR GATHERING DATA ON STUDENT LEARNING

Written Tests

Short Answer

There is still a place for short-answer tests in educational practice, but it is much smaller than the place it currently holds. Though they are not "authentic," short-answer quizzes, where students respond to, say, math facts on timed tests, are still important to see whether students have mastered math facts. Short-answer quizzes can be appropriate whenever students need feedback on their factual knowledge to identify what to study.

Short-answer quizzes can also be oral, a much neglected medium. Short-answer oral quizzes can allow students' assessment to be individualized, and they can also be given by students to one another. Then benchmark certification quizzes can be given by the teacher when students declare themselves ready for certification (e.g., ready for the multiplication fact mastery test on tables through 6).

When the characteristics of good assessment are applied to short-answer quizzes, students know what the criteria for success are (e.g., the pack of math flash cards in 60 seconds, knowledge of all the states and capitals without error). Perhaps they keep track of their own progress and use the data on each set of results to plan what and how to study next to reach the criteria.

Essay

An essay test is a highly verbal task, performed orally or in writing, that asks students to do higher-level thinking using information acquired over a period of time. The thinking task may ask students to take and defend a point of view, providing specific evidence, or to show relationships of cause and effect between events or conditions and actions or outcomes.

Essays should continue to play a significant role in assessment, but oral presentations could be used much more frequently, and they could be assessed on the same criteria of organization, evidence to support claims, sentence structure, and so forth. Curry and Samara (1994) present a "product guide" for oral reports:

> *Introduction*—speaker introduced; topic described; impetus for project explained; expected outcomes discussed;

> *Beginning*—topic described in general terms; major points outlined; audience involved;

> *Middle*—major points supported with details; intermittent summarizations; transition statements link major points; audience involved with content;

> *Summary*—major points reviewed; call to action/ask for acceptance of concepts/beliefs/positions;

> *Body language*—sustained eye contact with each member of the audience; formal posture; natural gestures/expressions; clear/well-paced voice;

> *Use of visual aids*—to support major points; intermittent use; limited.

This guide could be used by teachers or students, or both, as criteria for giving feedback to students on their performances. It would also be a formative guide for students in preparing their oral reports.

Problem Solving
Complex problems embedded in real-life situations can be found in many current development efforts at national, state, and district levels. FIGURE **16.9** is an example drawn from the National Assessment of Educational Progress Pilot Study of Higher-Order Thinking Skills Assessment Techniques in Science and Mathematics (NAEP 1987).

Tasks like these tend to be engaging to students because of their personal relevance. But they also go beyond traditional word problems. This one demands that students invent some sort of protocol for converting performances in the three events to individual scores of some kind. No such protocol or guideline is given in the problem; the student has to create it. A student might decide to assign points for first-place finishes, second-place finishes, and so on, and then add up the totals for each competitor (being careful to have most points for first place and not assigning 1 to first—unless the lowest point total would be the winner, another piece of sophisticated thinking). At another level, a student might create a weighting scheme for actual results in the events, regardless of what place someone finished in the event. In either case, explaining the solution is as important as the actual answer.

This sort of item assesses a range of student capacities. In this case, they need the ability to read and interpret a table of data, to analyze the scores and interpret them into rank order for each event, and to invent a scoring rule for comparing overall performance and to explain that rule.

Performances
Assessment of performances gathers data on students in the act of doing something—solving a problem, conducting a science experiment, doing a drawing—and thus avoids the possible mediating effects of language skills called for in traditional tests. The data are thus as much about *how* the student was performing the operation as about the final results.

Direct Observation
A number of states (e.g., Connecticut, New York, and California) have piloted statewide assessments by direct observation of student performance in science. The rationale for direct observation is strong; it is only the cost in time and money that will prevent such assessments from gaining widespread adoption as state-mandated standards spread across the country.

Direct observation of student performance allows teachers to observe exactly what they want to assess without injecting confounding variables into the process as written tests usually do. Suppose I want to know if students understand what variables in science really are; in addition I want to know if they can apply that knowledge to designing and carrying out an experiment that controls the variables and uses consistency and preciseness to reach a conclusion. Then I might design a task like the following.

Triathlon: Interpreting Data

Students are required by this paper and pencil task to examine data about five children competing in three athletic events and decide which of the five children would be the all-around winner. Students must devise their own approach for computing and interpreting the data and explain why they have selected a particular "winner." Students must be careful in their interpretation, because the lower scores are better in the 50-yard dash, while the converse is true in the frisbee and weight lift.

Student Assessment Sheet

Joe, Sarah, Jose, Zabi, and Kim decided to hold their own Olympics after watching the Olympics on TV. They needed to decide what events to have at their Olympics. Joe and Jose wanted a weight lift and frisbee toss event. Sarah, Zabi, and Kim thought running a race would be fun. The children decided to have all three events. They also decided to make each event of the same importance. They held their Olympics one day after school. The children's parents were the judges and kept the children's scores on each of the events.

The children's scores for each of the events are listed below:

Child's Name	Frisbee Toss	Weight Lift	50-Yard Dash
Joe	40 yards	205 pounds	9.5 seconds
Jose	30 yards	170 pounds	8.0 seconds
Kim	45 yards	130 pounds	9.0 seconds
Sarah	28 yards	120 pounds	7.6 seconds
Zabi	48 yards	140 pounds	8.3 seconds

Record Findings

(A) Who will be the all-around winner?

(B) Explain how you decided who would be the all-around winner.
Be sure to show all your work.

Account for Findings

_____

_____

_____

FIGURE 16.9: PROBLEM-SOLVING ASSESSMENT TASK

Reprinted with permission. Archbald, D., and F. M. Newmann. *Beyond Standardized Tests: Assessing Authentic Academic Achievement in Secondary School*. Reston, Va.: National Association of Secondary School Principals, 1988, pp. 15–16. For more information concerning NASSP services and/or programs, please call (703) 860-0200.

Shavelson and Baxter (1992) cite a task where students have to figure out which of three brands of paper towels will hold the most water. To do that task, students take samples from each of the three rolls of paper towel, making sure the samples are the same size; saturate each with water, making sure they are completely saturated; then measure how much water each saturated towel holds, either by weighing or squeezing out the towel and measuring the volume of water squeezed out (a slightly less reliable method since the towels may be unequal in how much water they retain). If there is only one scale to do the weighing, the student has to be sure excess water from the previous weighing is removed before weighing the second towel.

Paper Towels Score Form

Student _____   Observer_____   Score ____

1. Method for getting towel wet
   A. Container   B. Drops   C. Tray (surface)   D. No Method
   Pour water in/put towel in   Towel on tray/pour water on
   Put towel in/pour water in   Pour water on tray/put towel in
   1 pitcher or 3 beakers/glasses

2. Saturation   A. Yes   B. No   C. Controlled (same amount of water–all towels)

3. Determine Result

   A. Weigh towel
   B. Squeeze towel/measure water (weight or volume)
   C. Measure water in/out
   D. Count # drops until saturated
   E. Irrelevant measurement (i.e. time to soak up water, see how far drops
      spread out, feel thickness)
   F. Other

4. Care in saturation and/or measuring   Yes   No   A little sloppy (+/-)

5. Correct result   Most   Least

Grade	Method	Saturate	Determine Result	Care in Measuring	Correct Answers
A	Yes	Yes	Yes	Yes	Both
B	Yes	Yes	Yes	No	One or Both
C	Yes	Controlled	Yes	Yes/No	One or Both
D	Yes	No or Inconsistent		Yes/No	One or Both
F	Inconsistent or	No and Irrelevant		Yes/No	One or Both

FIGURE 16.10: PAPER TOWELS SCORE FORM

Reprinted with permission. Shavelson, Richard J., Gail P. Baxter, and Jerome Pine. "Performance Assessment in Science." In *Applied Measurement in Education* 4, no. 4, Hillsdale, N.J.: Lawrence Erlbaum Associates, 1991, p. 353.

For such tasks it is relatively simple to develop a protocol (that is, a form with places for an observer to record checks or scores) that records how well the student did on various dimensions of the task (e.g., equal size samples, completeness in saturation, care in measuring and weighing, recording of results). (See FIGURE **16.10**.) "Moreover," say Shavelson and Baxter, "the scoring scheme should capture the procedure used and could thereby characterize performance in terms of both processes and outcomes."

Doing large-scale standardized assessments of large numbers of students on activities such as the paper towel task is expensive and time-consuming compared to paper-and-pencil tests. Rooms have to be set up with stations for each task, and a trained observer has to score individual students as they rotate through the stations. Despite the cost, Shavelson and Baxter's own research has made it clear that such performance assessments yield valid and reliable measurement results.[2]

This sort of assessment provides such a direct and realistic measure of the thinking skills students should be learning that it remains valuable for states to sample populations of their students on an annual basis. This sampling will give a reliable statistical report card on how well particular districts are doing in developing the skills and work habits that are valued, even if expense prohibits assessing all children by direct observation in the near future.

Individual teachers can use direct observation of performance much more in assessing their own students, and not only in science. For example, in math, how many times does a teacher have to observe a student doing a complicated long division problem successfully to know the child can do long division? Maybe twice. And then one can record mastery on a checklist. Suppose I have a student who thinks aloud as she does a word problem. How many such problems do I have to witness the student solving to know that she follows orderly steps: identifies the real problem, searches to separate relevant from irrelevant data, and identifies the operation that is called for by the problem? Probably not very many.

Computer Simulation
To simplify and make more economical the observation of student performance, many performances can be converted into computer simulations, which, similar to observation of real performances, avoid the confounding variables of written tests and get straight to what we want to assess. (This remains true as long as students know how to operate the computer adequately.)

Shavelson (1992) has constructed a task where students connect batteries, bulbs, and wires in a circuit to determine the contents of a set of mystery boxes:

---

[2]They also point out, however, that "performance tasks vary on a number of factors, especially knowledge-domain specificity and requirements for students to monitor their own performance as they proceed on a task. Some are inherently more difficult than others. More importantly, some students perform well on one task and others perform well on another task. Consequently, a number of assessment tasks are needed to generalize, with any degree of confidence, from students' performance to the science domain of interest" (p. 358).

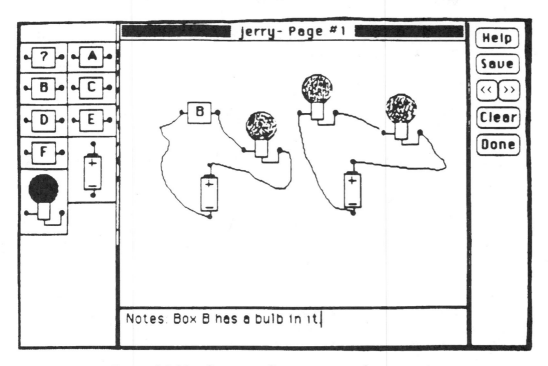

FIGURE 16.11: COMPUTER SIMULATION FOR ASSESSMENT

For the electric circuits investigation, students used a Macintosh computer with a mouse to connect circuits with the mystery boxes to determine their contents [see **FIGURE 16.11**].

The intensity of the luminosity of the bulb in a real external circuit was accurately simulated. Students connected a multitude of circuits if they so desired. Alternatively, they could leave one completed circuit on the screen for comparative purposes. Instructions on how to record answers, erase wires, save their work, or look at a previous page of their work on the screen were given in a teacher-directed tutorial format prior to the test. The computer recorded every move the student made. (p. 355)*

Similar computer simulations have been developed in physics, chemistry, and mathematics and should prove exciting and flexible ways to augment assessment of student performance. Another benefit is that students can schedule taking tests on computers any time agreeable to them and their teachers.

Notebook Surrogates

A final way to get direct data on student performance is through notebooks in which students record their actions and their thinking. Students are asked to use the notebooks while they conduct hand-on investigations. Shavelson (1992, p. 352) praises this methodology because it is inexpensive and "provides an opportunity for students to express themselves in writing, an

*Reprinted with permission. Shavelson, Richard J., Gail P. Baxter, and Jerome Pine. "Performance Assessment in Science." In *Applied Measurement in Education* 4, no. 4, Hillsdale, N.J.: Lawrence Erlbaum Associates, 1991, p. 357.

important skill in doing science and a way of integrating curricular areas." Furthermore, trained teachers can score the notebooks rapidly. The student's capacity to write clearly becomes a confounding variable if the assessment target is purely related to scientific thinking.

Examination of Student Products

Oral, Written, and Multimedia Reports

A report is a vehicle for showcasing language and communication skills. Students who already have these skills will be able to show them off. Students less proficient in language and the organization of ideas will have less to showcase.

Before producing a report, the student must record and organize information and then plan how to present it, which means planning the sequence and deciding on the inferences, conclusions, and hypotheses that will be in it.[3] Thus a teacher who examines and responds to a student's report is examining the student's thinking and communication skills as well as assessing how much understanding there is of the information studied in preparation for the report. One of the reasons a report is a productive assessment device is precisely that it orients both teacher and students toward developing communication skills. A teacher is implicitly stating an objective to improve research, organization, and communication skills when assigning a report.

A report is supposed to be a way for students to show they have internalized a body of knowledge and can do something intellectual with it beyond reciting facts. Thus, reports typically ask students to go beyond information and do any one or several of the following operations: make inferences, give conclusions supported by appropriately selected evidence, make reasoned and supportable predictions or hypotheses, give opinions, surface assumptions, and sometimes make original connections. (These thinking operations can be called for and successfully produced by primary grade children given appropriate experiences and guidance.) Thus the nature of the report assigned makes the report as assessment a potential vehicle for teaching organization and thinking skills. Getting ready to produce the report should therefore be an "episode of learning" (Wolf 1993).

Report writing is not something students are born knowing how to do, or that they learn to do by being assigned the task. Teachers are obligated to teach students how to produce reports, and that means breaking down the task into component parts. The link between assessment and the teaching of report writing is the model of good performance provided at the beginning and the explicit analysis of those good products with the students: "What about this good report we are looking at makes it a good report?"

Similarly, if the report is oral or multimedia, videotapes of former students delivering good reports or a preserved exemplar of an excellent multimedia report need to be presented to students and analyzed for their good points. Analysis means showing exactly where examples of criterion behaviors

---

[3] Studies of writers writing show that the drafting and revision process itself produces some of the steps above. Report writing, like other forms of creative writing, is not the orderly process one might think. "I write what I know to find out what I think" (Henry Glassie in *Passing the Time in Bellymenone*, an anthropological study of Irish village life).

occur—for example: "Now see how this sentence summarizes the main points of the previous four paragraphs? That's what I'm looking for in your reports when I say 'summary sentences' on your criteria sheet. Can anyone find a sentence like that in the second section of the paper?" Here is an example for a multimedia report: "Notice how she uses the music to set a mood at the beginning before saying any words but then brings music back with the jazz piece when the mood she wants is different. Be looking for music that fits with your message in a similar way."

The teacher-student dialogue might go like this:

Teacher: What did you notice about this student's use of visual material?

Student: I noticed that for every main idea there was a different visual—either a chart or a picture—to go with it.

Teacher: Right, and that's something I'll be looking for in your reports too. But the visuals have to be a good fit with the point you're making. How were these a good fit?

Student: Well, when she had a chart with the words, it wasn't really a good fit. It was just having the words printed neatly and using different colors. But when she had the picture of the riot, that was a good fit to show how violent the reaction to the draft really was!

Exhibitions

An exhibition is a complex project that displays the student's capacity to perform a set of higher-level thinking skills that the school thinks are important. The sixth-grade project developed by Penny Knox in which students write a letter describing a culture is an exhibition. It takes the students all year to gather the knowledge and skills required to do it well. All students are expected to do it, and the criteria for success are clearly spelled out in the rubric. In addition, they have several trial runs at the final product before they produce the version that "counts."

In the vision of high school articulated by Ted Sizer's Coalition of Essential Schools, an exhibition is both a gateway to graduation and a target for the student's whole four years of high school. Each student must present an exhibition, and it must meet minimum standards if that student is to graduate.

An exhibition also serves as a powerful stimulus to faculty dialogue about what these skills for graduation should be. The list almost always includes higher-level thinking and communication skills as with the item, "Can state assumptions and argue a point of view with clear evidence." Graduation targets like these push across departmental boundaries and cause teachers to plan within their disciplines for how they can teach for them. They also increase interdepartmental communication and open the door for integration of curriculum. Thus "graduation by exhibition" becomes a genuine force for bringing a school together and shaping practices around certain core outcomes it wants for students (Saphier and D'Auria 1993).

When an exhibition is required for graduation, its magnitude and complexity varies from school to school. Sid Smith and his faculty moved English High School in Boston a significant step forward when they instituted an exhibition requiring all students to write a two-page position paper on a controversial issue of their choice: "It formed the basis of English High School's commitment to decide what its students must know and be able to do to earn their high school diploma. It was the start of the school's effort to require *all* its students to publicly demonstrate their skills and knowledge" (Smith 1993, p. 17). That an exhibition requirement applies to all students for graduation and that it is assessed by competency rather than by grades and numbers makes it a lever for raising standards for all. It also makes schools gauge both the strength of their belief that all students can achieve to a high level and their determination to get them there.

If a position paper is a start on the process of developing graduation by exhibition, the multiple exhibitions collected in a portfolio that are required for graduation from Walden III High School in Racine, Wisconsin, represent maturity. Archbald and Newman, drawing on the student handbook written by Tom Feeney, a teacher at the school, summarize the exhibition requirements in Figure **16.12**.

Requiring a wide-ranging portfolio of this magnitude takes years of faculty collaboration on developing the topics, standards, scoring rubrics, and procedures for students to navigate their way to successful completion. A school that has thought out graduation requirements this far and expressed them in terms of performance knows what it stands for. It is also clear that to prepare students to succeed on these assessments requires substantial integration and coherence between departments. Such is the promise of the authentic assessment movement.

Good Records

Records can take the form of checklists or profiles; logs, journals, or anecdotal records; or portfolios. What is important is that the form of the record be appropriate for the assessment methodology and a good fit for the content or skill being assessed.

Checklists and Profiles

Teachers have traditionally used checklists in the elementary grades to track student skill acquisition, such as mastering multiplication tables, mechanical writing skills, or developmental levels of literacy. The checklist in Figure **16.13** represents a record-keeping device in which a check signals the student's developmental point on a particular behavior.

Checklists represent the idea that important academic behaviors develop over time and can be assessed along a continuum from "emerging" to fully developed. Although most developmental checklists are found in the areas of reading and writing, districts like Bellingham, Washington, have created them for other areas, including mathematics and science competencies.

Exhibition Requirements at

Walden III High School, Racine, Wisconsin

The portfolio. The portfolio, developed during the first semester of the senior year, is intended to be "a reflection and analysis of the graduating senior's own life and times." Its requirements are

1. *A written autobiography*, descriptive, introspective, and analytical. School records and other indicators of participation may be included.

2. *A reflection of work*, including an analysis of the significance of the work experiences for the graduating senior's life. A resume can be included.

3. *Two letters of recommendation* (at minimum) from any sources chosen by the student.

4. *A reading record* including a bibliography, annotated if desired, and two mini-book reports. Reading test scores may be included.

5. *An essay on ethics* exhibiting contemplation of the subject and describing the student's own ethical code.

6. *An artistic product or written report* on art and an *essay on artistic standards* for judging quality in a chosen area of art.

7. *A written report analyzing mass media:* who or what controls mass media, toward what ends, and with what effects. Evidence of experience with mass media may be included.

8. *A written summary and evaluation of the student's coursework in science/technology; a written description of a scientific experiment* illustrating the application of the scientific method; *an analytical essay* (with examples) on social consequences of science and technology; *and, an essay on the nature and use of computers* in modern society.

The Project. Every graduating senior must write a library research-based paper that analyzes an event, set of events, or theme in American history. A national comparative approach can be used in the analysis. The student must be prepared to field questions about the paper in the overview of American history during the presentations, which are given in the second semester of the senior year

The Presentations. Each of the above eight components of the portfolio, plus the project, must be presented orally and in writing to the committee.

FIGURE 16.12: EXHIBITION REQUIREMENTS AT WALDEN III HIGH SCHOOL

(continued on next page)

Reprinted with permission. Archbald, D., and F. M. Newmann. *Beyond Standardized Tests: Assessing Authentic Academic Achievement in Secondary School.* Reston, Va.: National Association of Secondary School Principals, 1988, pp. 24–25.

Six additional oral presentations are also required. However, there are no written reports or new products required by the committee. Supporting documents or other forms of evidence may be used. Assessment of proficiency is based on the demonstration of knowledge and skills during the presentations in each of the following areas

9. *Mathematics knowledge and skills* should be demonstrated by a combination of course evaluations, test results, and worksheets presented before the committee; and by the ability to competently field mathematics questions asked during the demonstration.

10. *Knowledge of American government* should be demonstrated by discussion of the purpose of government; the individual's relationship to the state; the ideals, functions, and problems of American political institutions; and selected contemporary issues and political events. Supporting materials can be used.

11. *The personal proficiency demonstration* requires the student to think about and organize a presentation about the requirements of adult living in our society in terms of personal fulfillment, social skills, and practical competencies; and to discuss his or her own strengths and weaknesses in everyday living skills (health, home economics, mechanics, etc.) and interpersonal relations.

12. *Knowledge of geography* should be demonstrated in a presentation that covers the basic principles and questions of the discipline; identification of basic landforms, places and names; and the scientific and social significance of geographical information.

13. Evidence of the graduating senior's successful *completion of a physical challenge* must be presented to the committee.

14. *A demonstration of competency in English* (written and spoken) is provided in virtually all the portfolio and project requirements. These, and any additional evidence the graduating senior may wish to present to the committee, fulfill the requirements of the presentation in the English competency area.

FIGURE **16.12** CONTINUED

	First Noticed	Developing	Independent
READING			
(Motivational)			
• Expresses a desire to own or borrow books			
• Recommends books or stories to other people			
• Keeps a book close by to be read in spare moments			
• Chooses books at an independent reading level			
• Develops preferences for different genres and for specific authors and illustrators			
(Listening)			
• Listens for increasingly longer times to stories read aloud			
• Listens to stories without interrupting and takes turns in responding			
(Conventions of Print)			
• Understands more complex punctuation during story reading (e.g. quotation marks, period after abbreviation and so on)			
• Continues building on knowledge of sight words			
(Linguistic)			
• Uses all cuing systems in a balanced and integrated way when working out unknown words in a story (e.g. context, picture, and letter/sound cues)			
• Self corrects when reading			
• Uses a variety of strategies when in difficulty (e.g. reads onto the end of the sentence, starts sentence again [the re-run strategy], substitutes a word that makes sense for an unknown word and reads on, and so on			
• Rereads for additional information, clarification, or pleasure			
• Reads familiar material aloud expressively to enhance meaning			

FIGURE 16.13: ASSESSMENT CHECKLIST

Developed by teachers in the Cambridge Public Schools, Cambridge, Massachusetts.

Checklists are useful components in assessment because they allow teachers, students, and parents to summarize in compact form a student's level of skill acquisition and to see on the same form the next target skill. Anyone who shares these checklists with students must be careful not to overwhelm them. Certain children may interpret a sea of empty check boxes as a huge and unattainable roster of things to be learned and throw up their hands in despair.

Logs, Journals, and Anecdotal Records
Observation of student performance is often best recorded in anecdotal records of some sort that are easy to create, access, and interpret. These records may capture observations of anything from student social behavior to comments on their class participation or skill at interpreting books read. Hill and Ruptic (1994) describe systems that use triple-ring binders, folders, file cards, computers, sticky notes, and mailing labels.

The more repetitive the comments become, the more a teacher may be inclined to move to a checklist. It is more efficient to write a behavior once and check off when a student can do it. The more individual or idiosyncratic the comments, however, the more useful an anecdotal record is. Figure **16.14** shows two sheets that allow individual, original entries.

The record forms in Figure **16.15** are designed as check-offs for skills displayed but still allow space for anecdotal comments.

Behind the choice of which record form to use must be clear teacher thinking about what is being assessed. The design of the recording instrument should meet criteria of ease of use, clarity, accessibility, and appropriateness.

Portfolios
A portfolio is a "purposeful collection of student work that tells the story of a student's efforts, progress or achievement in a given area" (Stiggins and Conklin 1992). Portfolios provide the database for teachers to continue exploring and refining successful performance directly with students. They also provide a tangible bank of products over time that reveal (ideally) how far students have come. Thus they become a credible record of progress that can provoke "gee whiz!" responses from parents and students alike in a way grades or compliments never could.

"The feature that defines a portfolio and differentiates it from a folder or collection of work is the selection mechanism. Based on the purpose or purposes, pieces are included to demonstrate progress toward a stated aim. A portfolio is a subset of all work done; something must be rejected for it to be constructed" (Mitchell 1992, p. 107). What makes portfolios an important tool in the framework developed in this chapter is that students do a self-assessment and choose what goes into the portfolio.

A crucial role for the teacher is to pose questions that the students use to select items for inclusion. Ruth Mitchell (1992) supplies one set of questions that might be used in having students reflect on a selection:

1. Why did you select this particular piece of writing. (Why does this piece stand out from the rest of your work?)

2. What do you see as the special strengths of this work?

3. What was especially important to you when you were writing this piece?

4. What have you learned about writing from your work on this piece?

5. If you could go on working on this piece, what would you do?

6. What kind of writing would you like to do in the future?

7. Now that you have looked at your collection of writing and answered these questions, can you identify a particular technique or interest that you would like to try out or investigate in future pieces of writing? If so, what is it? (p. 110)*

These questions show how portfolios set the stage for goal setting as well as self-evaluation. The last question is actually asking the student to set a goal.

Portfolios also enable a powerful form of parent involvement. They can be sent home periodically with students and parents asked to read them thoroughly. Then they are asked to write back (or communicate in some other way) what they noticed, enjoyed, or were concerned about in their child's work. Kathryn Howard uses the form in Figure **16.16** to invite parents to participate in portfolios in her eighth grade writing course.

> *Portfolios enable a powerful form of parent involvement.*

The concept of involving students in self-evaluation and goal setting makes portfolios desirable vehicles for student development in any subject area, including math and science. Knight (1992) and others show how having students save their best tests, best labs, and other best pieces that show forms of their mathematical and scientific knowledge can provoke the kind of self-examination and goal setting that goes with being an effective student.

Developing a climate of self-examination and reflection does not come without its costs. One author writes:

> Portfolios are messy. They demand intimate and often frighteningly subjective talk with students. Portfolios are work. Teachers who ask students to read their own progress in the "footprints" of their works have to coax and bicker with individuals who are used to being assessed [by others]. Halfway through the semester, at least a half dozen recalcitrants will lose every paper or sketch they have ever owned. More important, teachers have to struggle to read and make sense of whole works and patterns of growth. Hence, hard questions arise: 'Why bother? What comes out of portfolio assessment?' The immediate answer lies in integrity and the validity of the information we gain about how and what students learn. (Wolf 1992)

ANECDOTAL RECORDS for *Susan*

12/17 Had to go home w/mom; crying right at 8:45 – called her to take her home – "big fight" Mom/Dad re work	12/18 Home again at 8:45 Back at 9:30 to "help do things for others" after calming down	1/4 Crying again during "Attendance" job... difficult goodbye w/Mo. Stress connected w/ Dad's lay-off and holidays	1/7 Tearless, normal start Even Able to take redirects at writing (off talk) calmly
1/11 Very helpful getting Tory caught up after long illness. Good "teacher" shows how then does own work side-by-side ready to assist "student"	1/21 Having trouble finishing <u>Sacajawea</u> She can read it, but it is a real challenge and seems not to hold her interest. Rdg level/ maturity level issue?	2/1 "I'm not sure I want to do these tubs again" Offered Options: Latin cubes ✶ Estimating ! recording w/ >< = ✶ chose this	2/2 Working on chapter book of her own autobiography – 4 chapters so far
2/12 Good compromising in problem solving activity w/ Theo, Trent and Alanna	3/1 Author's Circle for her autobiography; planning to use comments/questions for revision		

FIGURE 16.14: TWO EXAMPLES OF ANECDOTAL RECORDS

ANECDOTAL RECORDS for **Cindy's Conference Group (teacher)**

Alice	Brad	David	Dylan
1/19 Beginning to read more difficult (Nate the Great) chapter books competently w/ minimal help... hard work, but can do it!	1/11 Talked about getting off the video game words and stretching yourself. Me exasperated about his being stuck in the mire of copying w/ Harry. Took it well - contrite; agreed w/me, made commit-ment to do more.	1/15 Needing to go to the bathroom a lot. He also noticed this - said he would speak to his parents	1/15 Serious about taking responsibility for his own learning. Stayed in at recess to finish. Only took 5 minutes 'til done

Elizabeth	Harry	Jeri	Kathleen
1/12 Off the wall all AM! Popping up and down, interrupting, off-task, noises and other sounds, repeated redirections necessary. "respectful behavior" discussed	1/17 Writing story about "Baseball Diamond Mystery" w/ Andy - Prominent swastikas # all over it and drawing of what looks like Hitler... nothing said yet, but watching this	1/8 w/ Kleenex reading Annie Sullivan "This is sad" "Do any more people die?" Talked about whether to continue — it's okay to cry/feel sad w/ books	1/11 Finished "Kathleen Wore Her..." book. Nudged to correct the few misspelled words - 1st time.

Lawrence	Mandy	Michael	Nancy
	1/12 Really pleased. First day to bring lunch packed at home rather than buying school lunch. "I made it myself!"	1/17 Making a book about fishing trip w/ lift-up flaps showing fish + names of them	

Paul	Randy	Ricky	Susan
1/15 Went to Lawrence's on the bus, but Mom still came by at the end of the day... to check on him?	1/19 On time every day this week... maybe we've licked the tardiness problem?		1/11 Very helpful getting Tory caught up after long illness. Good "teacher", shows how-to, then does own work side-by-side ready to assist "student"

Thomas	Tory	Vince	Zoey
			1/13 Shocked and wanted to share with me what she was reading about. M.L. King jr.

FIGURE 16.14 CONTINUED

Reading Conference Record

Student_____

	Date: 12/8	Date: 12/17	Date:	Date:	Date:	Date:
	Title: Two Little Dogs (G)	Title: Sleeping out (F)	Title:	Title:	Title:	Title:
Level Appropriate	Instructional Frustration ✓	Instructional Independent				
Strategies:						
Whole idea						
Picture clues	✓					
Pattern						
Sight Words	✓	✓				
First letter						
Decodes	✓	✓				
Context clues	✓	✓				
Skip return						
Rereads	✓	✓				
Reads Fluently		✓				
With Inflection		✓				
Literal Comprehension	✓	+				
Interpretive Comprehension	✓	+				
Strategy Taught	contractions context	contractions speech marks				
Comments	door's = door is that's gate's won't = will not don't = do not isn't = is not I noticed you used context to self-correct over (after) the (they)	It's = it is what's = what is she's = she is Ways to show speech: Word bubbles speech marks (quotation marks)				

CODES: + consistently
✓ sometimes

FIGURE 16.15: TWO EXAMPLES OF CHECK-OFF RECORD FORMS

READING CONFERENCE RECORD

Name _____

Date and Title	Miscues & Comments book » said	Skills/Strategies Taught	Fluency	Comprehension	
				Factual	Inferred
10/19 The Witch's Christmas	with → with wreath → w very → every	wr = r Look at pictures	✓	+	✓
10/21 The Enormous Egg	me → my s/c when → than	what makes sense?	—	✓	✓
10/26 Scary Stories	many miscues Read to Demo Dan! Picked book from library · proud	Syllables -oi	—	✓	✓
11/2 The Return of the 3rd Grade Ghostbusters	enough chech → jack discovered how he could "read" periods → expression	gh = ph context	+	+	✓

© 1993   Jan Peacoe.   Bainbridge Island, WA

CODES: + = Very Good
        ✓ = Average
        – = Needs Improvement

FIGURE 16.15 CONTINUED

501

Student ________________________
Reader ________________________
Date ________________________

Please read everything in your child's writing folder, including drafts and commentary. Each piece is set up in back-to-front order, from rough draft to final copy. Further, each piece is accompanied by both student and teacher comments on the piece and writing process. Finally, the folders also include written questionnaires where students write about their strengths and weaknesses as writers.

We believe that the best assessment of student writing begins with the students themselves, but must be broadened to include written questionnaires where students write about their strengths and weaknesses as writers.

When you have read the folders, please talk to your children about their writing. In addition, please take a few minutes to respond to these questions.

- Which piece of writing in the folder tells you most about your child's writing?
- What does it tell you?
- What do you see as the strengths in your child's writing?
- What do you see as needing to be addressed in your child's growth and development as a writer?
- What suggestions do you have that might aid the class's growth as writers?
- Other comments or suggestions?

Thank you so much for investing this time in your child's writing.

Figure 16.16: Parent Portfolio Review and Reflection*

Judith Warren Little once commented in an audiotaped interview (Sparks 1993) that the most powerful form of staff development might be to put a group of teachers in one room with samples of student work. Her point was that in comparing and debating the merits of actual student performances, teachers refine their concepts of standards; in addition, teachers inevitably get hooked into discussions of which learning experiences to use to develop specific student capacities.

It has been our experience that in these situations, teachers go on to invent learning experiences together. Through the examination of student work, teachers are drawn into authentic and productive conversations about teaching that comprise true collegiality. Portfolios of student work provide

*Reprinted with the permission of The Free Press, a division of Simon & Schuster from Kathryn Howard in *Testing For Learning: How New Approaches to Evaluation Can Improve American Schools* by Ruth Mitchell. Copyright © 1992 by Ruth Mitchell. P. 112.

the raw material in organized form for this kind of collegial sharing, refining, and curriculum development. Thus it is reasonable to assume that use of student portfolios can encourage more collaborative work among teachers. It would certainly be a useful practice in schools that are seeking to develop a collaborative culture.

Criteria of Technical Soundness

The topics of technical soundness include validity (is the assessment assessing what we really want to measure?) and reliability (would the assessment give the same result or score if we administered it again to the same subjects?). For complex performance assessments, validity is a particularly important issue as teachers design assessment tasks. Any assessment task requires a range of student behaviors: perhaps reading or listening to directions, or gathering information from sources that require more or less initiative and perseverance, then acting cognitively on the information, then representing the output of that cognition in writing, speaking, or other expressive forms. The more complex the assignment is, the more it resembles a chain where any weak link can cause a break. Complexity is an asset when assessments are used as opportunities for teaching and learning. But a "mastery/not yet" benchmark assessment—that is, an assessment used to signify attainment of some important level of learning for students—must be sure not to contain confounding variables of student performance that are off to the side of what we want to measure. For example, assignments containing a great deal of essay writing to assess science knowledge are good as learning experiences yet may obscure the data on what the student really knows about, say, using microscopes.

The following questions need to be answered satisfactorily if assessments are to be technically sound. The questions include checks (where applicable) on criteria, sample size, objectivity, reliability, and validity:

- Are pre- and post-test measures taken? (Student behavior should be assessed before instruction begins to see if students already know the material or part of the material.)

- Is assessment repeated at some future date after the end of instruction to measure the permanence of the learning?

- Is the sample of items big enough (enough questions on each area) so that chance error doesn't mask what students really know or can do?

- Is the assessment administered objectively, without bias, distractions, or confusion to individuals?

- Are assessments scored or judged accurately?

- Is the assessment reliable?

- Is the assessment device appropriate to students with diverse learning styles, and does it thus represent multiple intelligences? Are assessments culturally responsive?[4]

---

[4] Thanks to Lynn Stuart for this perception.

Informative Reporting Systems

> *One of the purposes of assessment is to report progress to parents and communities.*

One of the purposes of assessment is to report progress to parents and communities. Good assessment systems give parents meaningful information about how their children are doing in school— meaning information about exactly what they have learned and how developed their skills are. Numerical and letter grades do not give such information. They represent nonspecific indicators of their children's performance against some unknown set of criteria. Worse, they represent a ranking of their children in a normal distribution curve; that kind of a grade reports only how well the student has done in relation to others with no reference to actual learning at all.

Reports to parents should be as varied as the examples presented in this book, including portfolios, checklists, rubrics, and anecdotal comments. *This kind of information-rich report can build the support and involvement of parents in their children's education unavailable in any other way.*

It is now part of the conventional wisdom that children do better when their parents are positive partners with the school in their children's education. They cannot do this without information about what their children are supposed to be learning and about what quality work should look like. Similarly, feedback and reporting generated through authentic assessment gives parents specific information and cues about how to help and with what to help their children. No system of letter grades can build this kind of home-school partnership that is now known to be so important for successful schooling.

One of the forces commonly cited as standing in the way of eliminating number and letter grades is that colleges demand grades for their admission process. High schools can't abandon class rank and letter grades, it is argued, because the colleges demand them. Is this really true? Alfie Kohn (1995) reports:

> In researching my most recent book, *Punished By Rewards*, I wrote letters to the Dean of Admission at Harvard and Brown and said, "What would you do if you got an application from a student who went to a school where there were no grades given at all (much less those unbelievably pernicious additive things like Honor Societies and class ranking), where there was only a sheaf of qualitative assessments of the kid? Would you consider such an applicant?" And both Harvard and Brown wrote back and said, "We not only would, we do." In fact, the guy from Brown added that such a student would probably be at a relative advantage because we would have a lot more information about that student than they would with a 3.6 (what the hell does that mean?). Now at state schools it becomes more problematic, to be sure. At least let's pull the plug on this pseudo argument that says, "We have to continue to destroy kids' interest in learning because the colleges demand it." It's more complicated when you look up close. (Kohn 1995)

Another force to preserve letter and number grades is that they are easily manipulated into summative figures that can be used to compare the effectiveness of schools and districts by magazines, newspapers, and political interests.

There is not at the moment a great call from parents for anecdotal reports or for the use of rubrics. Many parents are satisfied by the simplicity of the letter grading system because they are used to it and because it appears to answer their bottom-line question: "How is my child doing?" Letter grades allow short answers like "Doing well" (my kid is getting an A); "Fair" (my kid is getting Bs); "Poor" (my kid is getting Cs or Ds). Those kinds of data also invite quick and easy responses by parents: rewards or praise for doing well and punishments, restrictions, or injunctions to buckle down for not doing well. But this kind of reporting also excludes them from involvement in their child's education in any substantive way. Only through examination of real samples of their child's work in comparison to models of what he or she is supposed to be producing (with specific criteria for what is expected) can they see exactly how to help.

Side by side with this call for authentic reporting is the reality factor of parents' time in a society with many single-parent and two-job families: parents want to be able to digest information about their children's progress quickly. This factor will call for reporting systems that do not overwhelm parents with mounds of rubrics and samples, so teachers should select key products at important benchmarks to share with parents and illustrate the criteria for quality work concisely and compactly. This effort will be rewarded by more support from parents in helping students master what is important.

In describing what reports look like that meet these standards of being informative but time efficient for teachers and for parents, Wiggins (1996) writes:

> Over time what matters is whether Johnny can make discernible progress toward authentic standards, irrespective of the grades teachers are most comfortable giving. But a single score, like a single grade, is inadequate feedback. A more helpful report would disaggregate performance into its many separate elements: Susan is thorough and accurate at laboratory work, though weak on tests; she is very conscientious and accurate in her homework problems. Jamie's labwork is spotty but indicative of understanding; he does extremely well on tests; and his homework, when done, is excellent—but it isn't always turned in on time, and careless mistakes are made in it.

He then goes on to present models of such reports that could disaggregate performances. In the process he distinguishes three kinds of data they would provide for each performance element: achievement levels, work quality, and progress:

> *Achievement levels* refers to exit-level standards of performance sophistication. *Work Quality* refers to the calibre of the products produced, at any level (thus allowing us to make the apt kind of distinction made in diving, figure skating, and music competition:

degree of difficulty vs. quality points). Progress is measured backwards from exit standards. *Progress* would thus be charted along multiyear continuums so that a 3rd grader would know how she was doing against 5th grade and (sometimes) 12th grade standards, just as we find in such performance areas as diving, chess, and band.

He then provides an excellent example from Victoria, Australia; it is shown in FIGURE **16.17**.

Note that the heavier the shading, the more frequently the student performs at that level. This format allows parents and students to see at a glance the upper limits of what a student can produce and the range of performance level he or she usually does produce. Immediately below these shaded bands of level are compact statements of the student's progress relative to the class and overall quality of care and thoroughness in the work. To the right is a summary of the types and number of assignments that were given and a profile of strengths and weaknesses (disaggregating the elements of performance). All of this information is laid out on one page and is visually clear.

As a backup to the report form itself is a page that explains the meaning of the nine bands (levels) of student performance. And there is also a background booklet in parents' hands developed by the district that shows by example what the nine levels mean. It contains performance samples of work at each level, rubrics, and sample teacher comments on the work samples. Thus Wiggins develops a set of criteria for good reporting systems well worth attending to. Good reporting systems:

- Disaggregate performance into its elements (not, for example, calling "Language Arts" one global entity).

- Report separately students' achievement level, work quality, and progress (the sample in FIGURE **16.17** also reports consistency).

- Are based on clear descriptions of what each level of performance means, including booklets for parents that spell out quality performance with examples at different levels.

Creating such reporting systems takes considerable effort and time, especially for such steps as creating the background booklet with good examples of performance at each level plus teacher comments highlighting the way in which each paper or sample illustrates the level. Good reporting systems to parents, however, can create their own market. Until people have experienced something new and useful, they don't know they want it. The better it is, the more they come to feel they can't do without it. Some critics may see this position as naive, believing more cynically that the majority of people will always cling to the easier way: the traditional grading system. It is our belief, however, that parents are likely to want the extra data to help their children perform well and achieve at higher standards. These data will be available only when assessment and reporting systems spring from authentic roots.

> *Good reporting systems to parents can create their own market.*

506

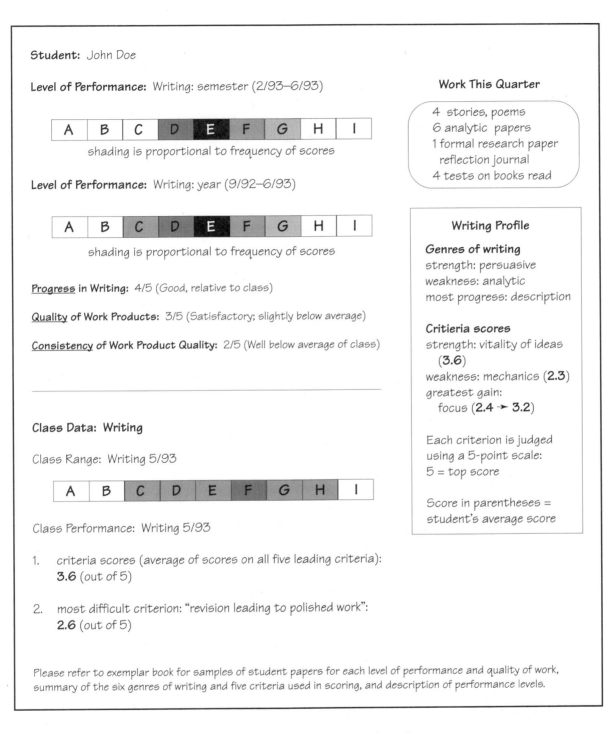

Student: John Doe

Level of Performance: Writing: semester (2/93–6/93)

A | B | C | D | E | F | G | H | I

shading is proportional to frequency of scores

Level of Performance: Writing: year (9/92–6/93)

A | B | C | D | E | F | G | H | I

shading is proportional to frequency of scores

<u>Progress</u> in Writing: 4/5 (Good, relative to class)

<u>Quality</u> of Work Products: 3/5 (Satisfactory; slightly below average)

<u>Consistency</u> of Work Product Quality: 2/5 (Well below average of class)

Work This Quarter

4 stories, poems
6 analytic papers
1 formal research paper
reflection journal
4 tests on books read

Writing Profile

Genres of writing
strength: persuasive
weakness: analytic
most progress: description

Critieria scores
strength: vitality of ideas
(**3.6**)
weakness: mechanics (**2.3**)
greatest gain:
focus (**2.4 ➔ 3.2**)

Each criterion is judged
using a 5-point scale:
5 = top score

Score in parentheses =
student's average score

Class Data: Writing

Class Range: Writing 5/93

A | B | C | D | E | F | G | H | I

Class Performance: Writing 5/93

1. criteria scores (average of scores on all five leading criteria):
   3.6 (out of 5)

2. most difficult criterion: "revision leading to polished work":
   2.6 (out of 5)

Please refer to exemplar book for samples of student papers for each level of performance and quality of work, summary of the six genres of writing and five criteria used in scoring, and description of performance levels.

FIGURE 16.17: DEWEY LANGUAGE ARTS REPORT

ENGLISH PROFILES IN WRITING

Writing Band A

Uses implements to make marks on paper.
Copies "words" from signs in immediate environment.

Explains the meaning of marks.
Writing shows understanding of difference between print and picture...

Writing Band B

Holds pencil/pen using satisfactory grip.
Writes own name.

Writing shows use of vocabulary of print.
Use of letters and other conventional symbols...

Writing Band F

Narratives contain introduction, complication, and resolution in logical order.
Complex sentences—principal and subordinate clauses: use of both active and passive voice.
Corrects most spelling, punctuation, grammatical errors in editing other's written work

A range of vocabulary and grammatical structures.

Understanding of the difference between narrative and other forms of writing.
Consults available sources to improve or enhance writing.

Writing Band H

Vocabulary shows awareness of ambiguities and shades of meaning.
Meaning is expressed precisely.
Edits and revises own work to enhance effect of vocabulary, text organization, and layout.

Organization and layout or written text is accurate and appropriate for purpose, situation, and audience.
Figurative language, such as metaphor, is used to convey meaning.
Edits and revises others' writing, improving presentation and structure without losing meaning or message.

Wiring Band I

Writes with ease in both short passages and extended writing on most familiar topics.
Extension beyond the conventions of standard English writing in a skillful and effective way.

Uses analogies, symbolism, and irony.

Structures a convincing argument in writing.

Source: Victoria, Australia, K–12 "English Profiles." Adapted by permission.

FIGURE 16.17 CONTINUED: DEWEY LANGUAGE ARTS REPORT

Parting Thoughts

Teaching Teams and Assessments

It is rare in teacher training for candidates to study the design of assessment instruments and yet we are arguing here that the kind of thinking that goes into the design and creation of assessment instruments (whatever their form—written tests, performances, exhibitions, essays, etc.) is the foundation of good instruction. Put another way, the detailed conceptualization, design of assessment criteria, and assessment tasks enable teachers to "plan backward" (Sizer 1992, p. 102). The design of effective learning experiences flows from thinking that starts with the students' point of view and flows from clarity about what teachers want the students to know and be able to do at the end of the experience. Thus, *the clearest articulation of the objective appears in the assessment task and its criteria for success.* In fact, the objective is not fully conceptualized until its assessment is defined.

From this perspective, then, expanding the ability to design different kinds of high-quality assessment tasks is essential to the professional teacher. If teaching is not a profession but rather a trade that any competent person can do with a year of basic training, then we can let others make the decisions and do the design work on assessments. But if we are a profession, we must develop the capacity to design and continually refine our own assessments based on changing students and changing curricula.

Don't Overdo It

Alfie Kohn (1995) gives an interesting coda for our consideration as we launch into making our assessments more varied and more authentic:

> The first consideration under authentic assessment is Don't Overdo It! The more students are focused on how they are doing, the less interest they have in what they are doing. Even rich, meaningful, even student-devised approaches for assessing work should not, should not be overdone. For a long stretch of time, arguably for most of the time that a student sits in a classroom, that student should be protected from the constant pressure to think, "How am I doing?" Even if the measure for how the student is doing is denied, you still have a potential problem in terms of kids trying to do the easiest possible thing so that they do well or of kids having their self esteem being on the line and wondering what does this[assessment] say about how smart or stupid I am? We have to beware of an overemphasis on any kind of assessment. It is not just that assessment fails to reflect students' true performance but that an emphasis on assessment fixes their attention on performance and that can be a problem at the expense of intrinsic motivation.*

---

*Reprinted with permission. Kohn, Alfie. "From DeGrading to DeGrading: Basic Questions About Assessment and Learning." Audiotape 95-3213. Alexandria, Va.: Association for Supervision and Curriculum Development, 1995.

Assessment, Power, and the Professionalization of Teaching

Whoever controls assessment controls the process of education. An enormous amount of that control now rests in the commercial testing establishment to which communities have delegated the power to report on how schools, teachers, and children are doing. But in their quest for objectivity and neutrality, public school communities have also ceded to the testing establishment the right to define what is worth teaching and learning.

> *Assessment is the strongest medium there is for telling students, parents, and the community what teachers care about in education.*

Assessment is the strongest medium there is for telling students, parents, and the community what teachers care about in education—stronger than course syllabi, stronger than opening-of-the-year statements, stronger than speeches. What we evaluate and what we report informs everyone what we really value. Assessments are not the first but soon become the more potent conveyers of expectations. Thus, the design of assessments should be in the hands of professional educators, responsible for identifying what children should learn and working in close concert with parents and community.

Teachers will see their status shift from being that of managed employees to that of professionals when they are able to work with colleagues to design in detail the criteria and the models of quality student performance. This is a major recommendation of the Task Group on Assessment and Testing in Britain (Hein in Perrone 1991, p. 127). It has proposed a process of

> moderation by which groups of teachers at various levels—the grade, the school, or the district—get together and discuss results and compare grading standards, especially on the more complex, open-ended questions and performance measures. The proposed 'moderation' scheme assures that grading will converge on a uniform set of standards, and it serves as a continuing inservice activity for teachers. Practicing professionals would do more than compare student achievement from school to school; they would also compare their own understandings and standards with those of colleagues. (Zessoules and Gardner in Perrone 1991, p. 69)

As teaching becomes more and more of a profession, teachers who work with common groups of children will take more and more responsibility for their learning. This may take the form of refining instructional objectives and developing their own assessment tasks and rubrics for student performance. Standardized tests will recede into the background because they only partially correspond to the curriculum as taught and are incapable of assessing all the higher-level thinking and problem-solving capacities children need for the twenty-first century. This is a very positive although demanding development. The design of authentic assessment tasks, scoring rubrics, models of good performance, and feedback systems to students, parents, and community requires a lot. It requires formulation of higher-level, worthwhile objectives (e.g., "students will be able to interpret data and make inferences") and the further ability to spell out in considerable detail the nuances of what that means in behavior. By inventing or choosing authentic assessment tasks and developing the rubrics for them, teachers are moving into new ground. For the first time, they are staking their claim to full professional responsibility, exercising judgment, and being called on to produce accountable results as in any true profession.

As teachers work together to design and refine assessment tasks and scoring criteria, this development work causes thinking, questioning, and stretching among those who do it: it is a premier staff development experience. It also makes for better assessments. And finally it provides a baseline of continuity in the experience of students, no matter whom they have as a teacher. Without sacrificing individual teacher style and autonomy, it enables educators to say to the public and to the community that their curriculum delivers certain important learnings in common to all students.

In future years, the technology of computer networks and CD-ROMs will make it possible for teachers to compile and share an enormous bank of performance tasks for all subjects and all levels. It is not fanciful to imagine that they will become part of our common professional knowledge base and available through a central electronic clearinghouse (Saphier 1994).

Effects of Assessment

Assessment is the strongest medium educators have for telling students, parents, and community what they care about in education. At a more specific level, students, teachers, and families get very clear from the outset about what the criteria for success are in a given course or module. That clarity enables students (and teachers and parents too) to focus their efforts on exactly those learnings that will help them meet the performance criteria and with that focus and direction they do better. This is the opposite of testing by mystery, where the test items are secret and students hope they study the right items (meaning those that will be on the test).

The act of creating authentic assessments can have a tremendous effect on what teachers do and on the way students view school. First, student motivation can rise. If students are assessed on meaningful tasks like gathering data on the costs and benefits of recycling at the town landfill and then taking and defending a position, they immediately get to use skills and knowledge they are being taught (like note taking, using multiple sources of information, understanding the ecological effect of landfills and incinerators) in a meaningful context.

Overall, teachers are induced to plan more sophisticated and integrated instruction. When beginning to implement complex performance exercises, many teachers find themselves asking the empowering question, "What changes should I make in my curriculum and instructional strategies to enable my students to be successful on these performance exercises?" If children are going to be tested on their ability to describe, analyze, and design an investigation to solve a problem, then their teacher feels an inevitable press to give them experiences in describing, analyzing, and designing investigations to solve problems. When assessment is done through the construction of a reflective portfolio over four months, the teachers have to help students create a reflective portfolio where they are doing self-evaluation explicitly, and that drastically alters what the teacher might otherwise have done with instructional time. If a teacher works under the expectation that students' final project report and all its artifacts will be their assessment in social studies, then all instruction is oriented toward helping them prepare comprehensive projects that meet the criteria.

> ### *Assessment of complex tasks presses us toward more integrated curricula.*

Assessment of complex tasks also presses us toward more integrated curricula. Real-world tasks or tasks that simulate real-world situations inevitably cross disciplinary lines. For example, writing a position paper to convince the town assembly to fund a new police station blends economics, social studies, sociology, and English.

Finally, authentic assessment should improve learning itself, as Baron (1991) writes:

> Consistent with the focus on big ideas and essential understandings, the purpose of effective tasks is to allow students to foster and display a depth of understanding rather than a breadth of understanding, permitting them to make connections among previously fragmented knowledge and skills. Effective tasks allow students to be able to tell a whole story. Today, so much of what students learn is highly fragmented and disjointed. Because they lack rich conceptual networks to organize their knowledge, they quickly forget what they learn. When students are encouraged to think about a whole problem, as they would be when designing and carrying out a complete investigation, their knowledge is more unified and more likely to be retained over time. (p. 310)

Standards

On observing the proliferation of the use of standardized tests in 1920, Walter Lippmann, the noted journalist, wrote: "We will breed generations of students and educators who don't believe that those who begin weak can ever become strong." He was right.

Standardized tests are designed to produce normal distributions, not to represent "standards" that all students could reach for. Normal distributions, by definition, must always have a lower half, and within the lower half there must always be a bottom stanine. Lippmann accurately foresaw that the design of standardized testing inevitably led to sorting, and that sorting would produce losers (bottom-scoring students), who would form permanent low opinions of their own intellectual capacity. The structure of the assessment system and the view of unevenly distributed intellectual gifts behind it was inherently incompatible with success for all and in fact damned many to a permanent intellectual underclass.

Authentic assessment might have given Lippmann heart, for here he would have seen a form of testing where everyone can be winners. The location and the look of the finish line—standards clearly laid out for all to see—and periodic feedback and self-evaluation can allow all students to self-correct and chart a course to success.

Authentic assessment provides the map for children to identify the learning targets and track their progress toward the standard. They will take advantage of such a map, however, only if they believe errors are opportunities for learning as opposed to confirmation of their inadequacy (Dweck 1991). Authentic assessment is philosophically aligned with mastery learning because it encourages sustained effort to reach criterion levels of performance. Coupled with teachers who send high and positive expectations to students, one would now have designed an environment where the structures of the school are consistent with a belief in all students' capacity to learn to a high level. If we really want to prepare all students for the demands of the next century, nothing less than this marriage will do.

What's Next?

The gap between the practices advocated in this chapter and the practices found in most schools is about the size of the Grand Canyon, and to close it takes extensive teacher planning time, usually in grade or department groups, that few schools have available. Our advice is to start slowly as individuals with natural partners (say, the two teachers in a high school who teach biology) and to work simultaneously with administrators to devote allocated meeting time to instructional topics—for example, comparing student work samples for quality. Here are some other useful steps that can be begun immediately:

1.   Make a special effort to present students with clear criteria for success and models of good performance for each important topic and assignment. Take the time to help the students understand exactly what about the models of good performance makes them good.

2.   Get students involved regularly in self-evaluation and peer feedback using the criteria for good performance.

3.   Review which methods of assessment and record-keeping devices you are using. Stretch for diversifying and expanding the repertoire. Do you use one-minute interviews or oral presentations as a way of finding out if students have mastered objectives? Do you use direct observation and checklists as a way to record student progress where appropriate?

4.   Explore the possibilities of exhibitions across grades or for graduation as ways of bringing it all together for students.

5.   Develop and refine portfolios as comprehensive collections of authentic student performance including self-evaluation.

The liberator for authentic assessment will arrive when teachers and administrators create planning time to compare samples of student work and develop clear rubrics that define what they believe to be the most important student learnings. 🕊

Appendix

Reprinted with permission. Kallick, Bena, and Ross Brewer. *Exemplars: A Teacher's Solution*. Volume 1, nos. 4–12. Underhill, Vermont: Exemplars, 1994

The Missing Key Dilemma

Grade Level 3–5

Task

Woe is me!!!!! My calculator does not have a 3 key that works!!!! How can I use this broken calculator to do this problem? Explain your reasoning carefully and clearly.

$$23$$
$$X \quad 45$$

Context

We had been studying multiplication and doing some mental math and talking about different strategies. I wanted to know if my students knew the theory behind multiplication, not just how accurate they were with the algorithm.

What this task accomplishes

This task will tell me what students really know about what multiplication does, how it works and how flexible their thinking is.

What the student will do

Most students solved the problem using the algorithm first. Then they began to try different strategies. Some students had to test out their theories to be sure they worked. Other students were confident that their strategy would work.

Time required for task

This taks takes about 15 or 20 minutes.

Interdisciplinary links

This task is purely mathematical; there are not interdisciplinary links.

Teaching Tips

You might want to include this task as part of a test on mulplication. It reinforces the fact that algorithms need to be understood, not just memorized.

Concepts to be assessed and skills to be developed
Problem solving
Reasoning
Communication
Connections
Number theory
Computation

The Missing Key Dilemma

Suggested Materials

None

Possible Solutions

There are so many ways to approach this problem. Some possible solutions are:

22 X 45 + 45   24 X 45 – 45
11.5 X 90   22.5 X 46
(use two numbers whose sum is 23) X 45
45 added 23 times or 23 added 45 times

Rubrics and Benchmarks

<u>Novice</u>

Inappropriate concepts are applied. The student thinks that the strategy for addition (move one number up on the number line and the other number down on the number line) will also work with multiplication. Her mathematical reasoning is faulty.

<u>Apprentice</u>

The solution is not complete. The student found an estimate, not the exact answer. The student's solution is partially useful, leading some way to the solution, but not a full solution.

<u>Practitioner</u>

This student has a broad understanding of the problem. S/he uses a strategy that leads to a solution of the problem and uses effective reasoning in a clear explanation.

<u>Expert</u>

This student has multiple solutions showing a deep understanding of the problem. S/he has the ability to identify the appropriate mathematical concepts.

AUTHOR

Clare Forseth developed this task which was done by students at the Marion Cross School in Norwich, Vermont. Clare is a member of the Vermont Mathematics Portfolio Committee. She has consulted and worked with many school districts. She is a member of the Mathematics Advisory Committee of the New Standards Project as well as its mathematics portfolio working group.

NOVICE

$$\begin{array}{r} 23 \\ \times\ 45 \\ \hline \end{array}$$

Move one dubel diget down three
on the number line so you wont have
to use three, and you'll get the same
ansore as 3 × 45

* and one up thre on the nomber
line.

APPRENTICE

$$
\begin{array}{r}
23 \approx 20 \\
\times\ 45 \\
\hline
115 \\
+920 \\
\hline
1035
\end{array}
\qquad
\begin{array}{r}
\times 45 \\
\hline
100 \\
+800 \\
\hline
900
\end{array}
$$

Estimate 23 to 20. Then multiply 20×45 on your caculator. You can still use your caculator.

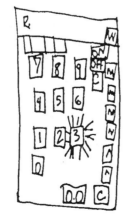

PRACTITIONER

$$\begin{array}{r} 23 \\ \times\ 45 \end{array}$$

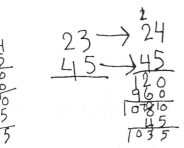

If your Calculator does not have
a three button and you want to
multiply 23×45 you obviously can't
do 23. So you make 23 to 24
and you multiply 24×45. I got
1080 but I knew that since the
you added 45 to the problem
you would have to subtract the
divisor (45) from the problem to
get the answer. My Answer is

1,035

Rule

For any problem like this (that you
can't use a number for example 3)
you just raise the number higher
(23→24) and when you get your
answer subtract the divisor. This tot'd you
makes it possible to something to any
problem. I just raised 43→ to 44 and got
2244 but I had to subtract 51
and not 2192 ——————— over

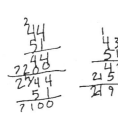

EXPERT

$$
\begin{array}{r}
23 \\
\times\ 45 \\
\hline
1,035
\end{array}
$$

Look at #4

$$
\begin{array}{r}
22 \\
\times 45 \\
\hline
110 \\
880 \\
\hline
990 \\
+\ 45 \\
\hline
1035
\end{array}
$$

① First you do 22×45 because it is very close to 23×45. Your answere will be 990. But you still have 1 more 45 to add on. So you do 990+45. That equals 1,035. You got the is answere without using the three button.

② You could do 45+45 23 times and get your answere without using the three button.

③ You could do the same thin us #1 except do 24×45. Then you'd have to subtract 45 instead of adding it

④ you could do 46×40 and divide by 2

☆ ☆ ☆ ☆ ☆ ☆

Wrapping Mom's Lamp

Grade Level   6–8

Task

> Sarah's mom needs to wrap a lamp she bought for Sarah's birthday. The lamp is 26 inches tall, including the shade, and 8 inches across the circular base. What are the dimensions of the <u>smallest</u> sheet of wrapping paper she will need to wrap the lamp? (Hint: the lamp is fragile, so you might want to put it in a box before wrapping.)

Context

This problem can be given to students with a knowledge of perimeter and area, but this is not necessary to find a solution. It is open ended in that some students will make allowance for the size of the lamp shade and whether or not to use a box with the same dimensions as the lamp.

What this task accomplishes

This task will show whether the student has a basic understanding of area and perimeter and can apply it in a practical situation. On a higher level, it will show reasoning, which goes beyond computation with the dimensions that are given.

What the student will do

The student will need to decide what size box to use and consider that the top and bottom must be covered. They may allow for some overlap for neatness or may take literally the directions to find the smallest piece of wrapping paper which will cover the box. They may consider the width of the shade.

Time required for task

45 minutes to allow time to actually wrap a package before or after recording the solution.

Interdisciplinary links

Links can be made to the many practical situations which involve surface area and perimeter of a three dimensional figure.

Teaching Tips

This task could be done hands-on with wrapping paper and a box followed by a written explanation with pictures or diagrams of how the students arrived at their solution, or the actual wrapping could be done <u>after</u> the solution and explanation have been written to test the accuracy of the solution and make corrections as needed.

Wrapping Mom's Lamp

Concepts to be assessed and skills to be developed

Problem solving skills
Reasoning and decision making
Spatial visualization
Multiplication in context
Understanding the term "dimensions"
Understanding of area and perimeter
Communication

Suggested Materials

You could make available rectangular boxes and wrapping paper.

Possible Solutions

The basic solution is to add 8 inches to the height to allow 4 inches to cover the top from the front and 4 from the back and likewise for the bottom. The length of the paper would thus be 34 inches. The width would be found by multiplying 4 times 8 which is the width of each side of the box. Thus the dimensions are 34" X 32". Other solutions would be to allow for some overlap in the width or to use a larger box in order to pack the lamp securely. Finally, some students might consider that the shade would probably be wider than the base and could even be packed in a separate box.

Rubrics and Benchmarks

Novice

The solution shows experience with computing area, but a lack of understanding of when to use it. S/he does not take into consideration that the top and bottom have different dimensions from the sides.

Apprentice

The solution is not clearly explained in written communication or by the picture. While the 42 inches is probably the result of adding 8 inches to cover the top and bottom to the height of 26", the student does not explain this reasoning for this or the 32" width.

Practitioner

The practitioner shows a broad understanding of the task. The communication is clear and the second picture adds to the understanding of the solution

Wrapping Mom's Lamp

Expert

The expert shows the student has a clear understanding of the task and has taken into consideration the size of the shade. The written communication explains each step clearly, and an alternative solution is given. The student uses mathematical language and pictures. The explanation and pictures are easy to read and understand. A real world application is included.

AUTHOR

Deena Serafin is an eighth grade teacher at Snellville Middle School in Snellville, Georgia.

NOVICE

11-26-93

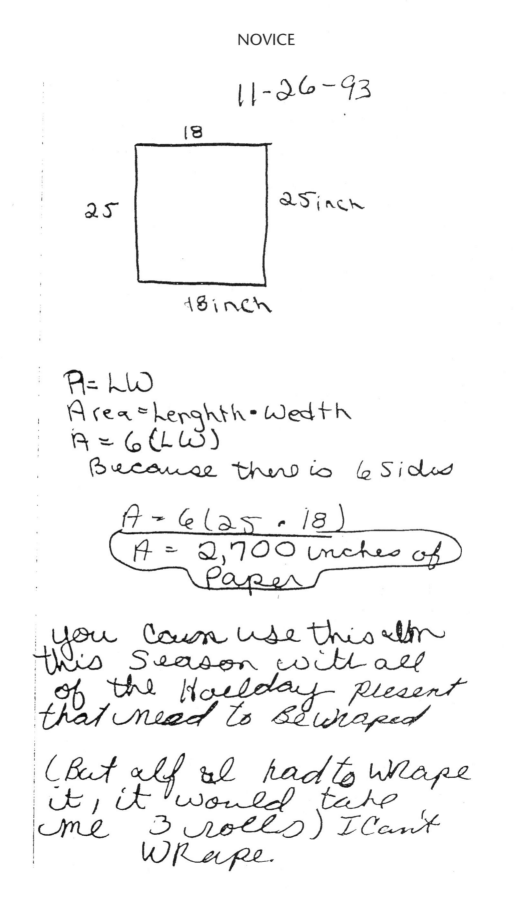

$A = LW$

Area = Lenghth · Wedth

$A = 6(LW)$

   Because there is 6 sides

$A = 6(25 · 18)$

$A = 2,700$ inches of Paper

you caun use this eltr this Season with all of the Hailday present that need to Be wraped

(But alf al had to wRape it, it would take me 3 rolls) I Can't WRape.

APPRENTICE

the answer to this question would
be a box 26 inches tall and 8 inches
wid on all sides and top and bottom
becouse the lamp is 26 inches
tall and 8 inches wide in a
circuler base

graph

The box

↓

lamp

26 inches ↓

8 inches

The sheet of wrapping paper would
be 32 inches long and 42 inches wide

PRACTITIONER

November 28, 1993

Non-Routine Problem

problem: Sarah's mom needs to wrap a lamp
she bought for Sarah's birthday. The
lamp is 26 inches tall, including
the shade, and 8 inches across the
circular base. What are the demensions
of the smallest sheet of wrapping
paper she will need to wrap the
lamp? (Hint: The lamp is fragile,
so you might want to put it in a
box before wrapping.)

Solution: I got 32 × 34 inches for my final
answer. I got this by first imagining
the size of a box that the lamp
would fit in. (26 × 8) I drew a picture
of a box.....

8 inches

26 inches

To find the width of the box, I took 8 inches and multiplied it by 4 to get 32 inches, (because there are ~~3~~ 4 sides).
To find the height of the box I had 26 inches and added 8. Because for the top and bottom of the box you would need to add 4 for the bottom and 4 to the top.

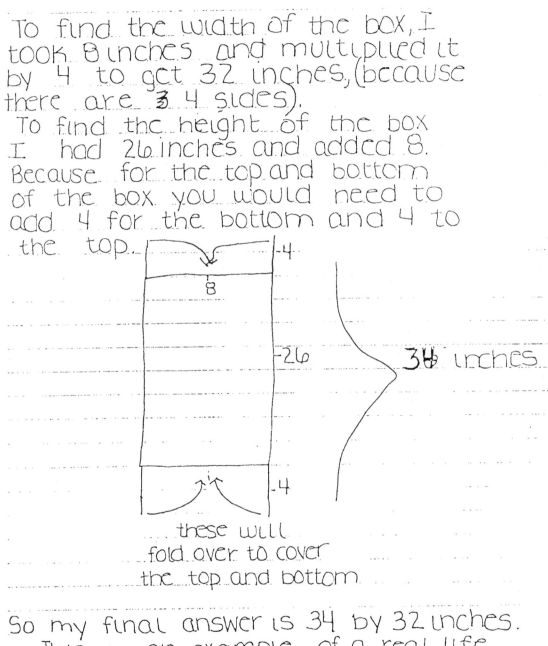

these will fold over to cover the top and bottom.

So my final answer is 34 by 32 inches.
This is an example of a real life situation, If you really did want to know the dimensions of the wrapping paper.

EXPERT

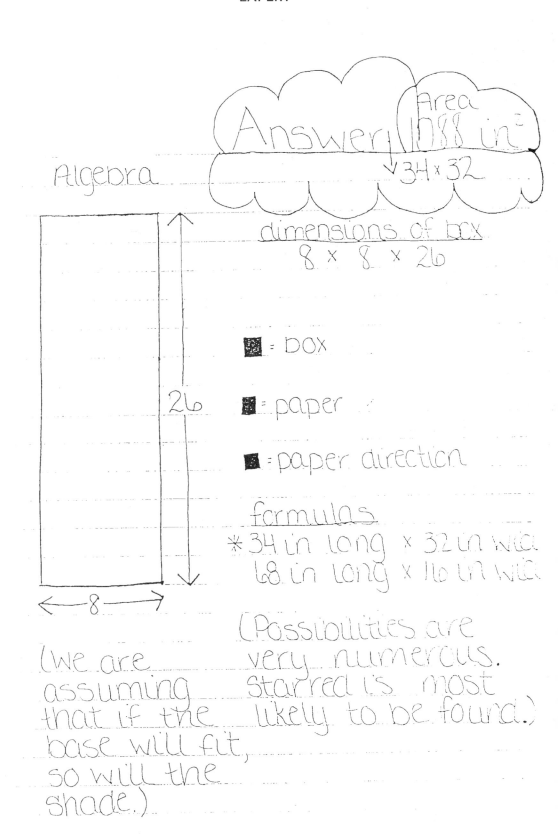

Answer! Area 1088 in²

Algebra

↓ 34 × 32

dimensions of box
8 × 8 × 26

■ = box

■ = paper

■ = paper direction

26

formulas
* 34 in long × 32 in wide
68 in long × 16 in wide

← 8 →

(Possibilities are
very numerous.
starred is most
likely to be found.)

(we are
assuming
that if the
base will fit,
so will the
shade.)

Diagram

A = covers top & bottom of box (34)
B = covers height of box (32)

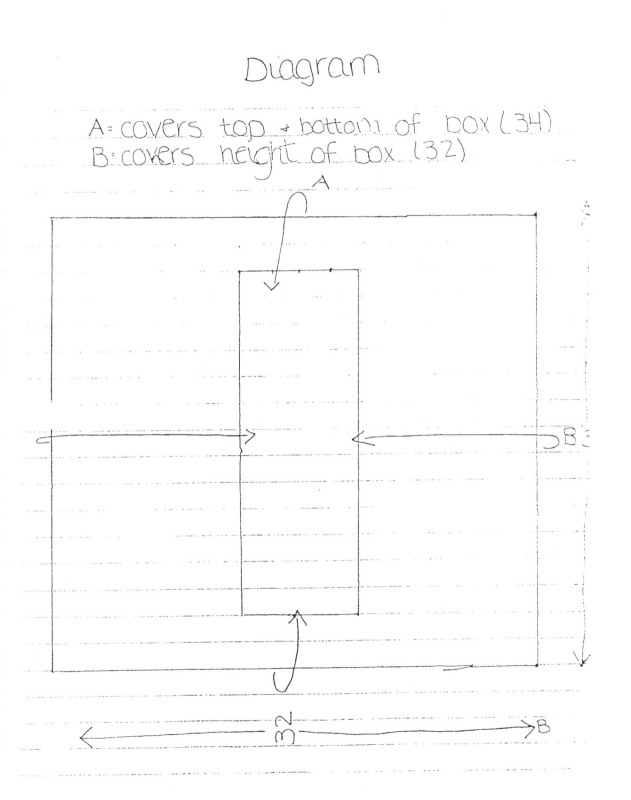

Explanation

A. 26 inches is height of box. You must have this number in this part of the equation so the box heighth will be covered. This is only added once because it will make the whole paper this heighth. Then you add 1/2 of the boxes width, which is eight, so you add four. You do this to cover the top of the box; do the same (1/2 of width) once more to cover the bottom. You only add half, because again, it makes the whole paper 34 inches tall, and when wrapped around, it will cover the other half of the top + bottom of the box.

B) To get 32, you notice that the length of the box is eight. You must simply multiply this by four. You do this because the box has 4 sides that are this length, and not yet covered. This will cover the remaining uncovered part of the box.

Association

On birthdays this is a problem we all face. I never go into this much detail about this much wrapping. I think I don't need to explain a real life association because this is one.

Source Materials on Assessment

Airasian, Peter W. *Classroom Assessment*. New York: McGraw-Hill, 1991.

Allard, Mariella, et al. *Getting Started with Portfolios in Needham*. Needham, Mass.: Needham Public Schools, September 1993.

Archbald, D., and F. M. Newmann. *Beyond Standardized Tests: Assessing Authentic Academic Achievement in Secondary School*. Reston, Va.: National Association of Secondary School Principals, 1988.

"Assessment in STC Units." *National Science Resources Center Newsletter* 6, no. 1 (Spring 1993).

Baker, Eva L. "Making Performance Assessment Work: The Road Ahead." *Educational Leadership* 51, no 6 (March 1994).

Baker, Eva L., et al. *CRESST Performance Assessment Models: Assessing Content Area Explanations*. Los Angeles: UCLA Center for the Study of Evaluation, April 1992.

Baron, Joan Boykoff. "Performance Testing in Connecticut." *Educational Leadership* 46, no. 7 (April 1989).

Bembridge, Teri. "A MAP for Reading Assessment." *Educational Leadership* 49, no. 8 (May 1992).

Bloom, Benjamin S., George F. Madaus, and J. Thomas Hastings. *Evaluation to Improve Learning*. New York: McGraw-Hill, 1981.

Bonnstetter, Ronald J. "Where Can Teachers Go for More Information on Portfolios?" *Science Scope* 15, no. 6 (March 1992).

Bracey, Gerald W. "A Critical Look at Standards and Assessments: Do They Go Together Like Love and Marriage—or Oil and Water?" *Principal* 73, no. 3 (January 1994).

Bradley, Ann. "In Connecticut, Moving Past Paper and Pencil: Teachers Evaluated on Class Behavior." *Education Week*, September 13, 1989.

Brandt, Ron. "On Creating an Environment Where All Students Learn: A Conversation with Al Mamary." *Educational Leadership* 51, no. 6 (March 1994).

———. "On Performance Assessment: A Conversation with Grant Wiggins." *Educational Leadership* 49, no. 8 (May 1992).

———. "On Misuse of Testing: A Conversation with George Madaus." *Educational Leadership* 46, no. 7 (April 1989).

Brown, Rexford. "Testing and Thoughtfulness." *Educational Leadership* 46, no. 7 (April 1989).

California Assessment Program Staff. "Authentic Assessment in California." *Educational Leadership* 46, no. 7 (April 1989).

California Learning Assessment System. *1991 Performance-Based Assessment Grade 11 Science: A Criminal Investigation.* Sacramento, Calif.: California Department of Education, 1993.

Campbell, Jo. "Laser Disk Portfolios: Total Child Assessment." *Educational Leadership* 49, no. 8 (May 1992).

Collins, Angelo. "Portfolios: Questions for Design." *Science Scope* 15, no. 6 (March 1992).

Corbett, William D. "Let's Tell the Good News About Reading and Writing." *Educational Leadership* 46, no. 7 (April 1989).

Costa, Arthur L. "Re-Assessing Assessment." *Educational Leadership* 46, no. 7 (April 1989).

Crooks, Terence J. "The Impact of Classroom Evaluation Practices on Students." *Review of Educational Research* 58, no. 4 (Winter 1988).

Culp, Linda, and Virginia Malone. "Peer Scores for Group Work." *Science Scope* 15, no. 6 (March 1992).

Curry, James, and John Samara. Workshop handouts at the National Staff Development Council Annual Conference, December 1994.

Davis, Alan, and Catherine Felknor. "The Demise of Performance-Based Graduation in Littleton." *Educational Leadership* 51, no. 6 (March 1994).

Diez, Mary E., and C. Jean Moon. "What Do We Want Students to Know? and Other Important Questions to Ask." *Educational Leadership* 49, no. 8 (May 1992).

Doran, Rodney L., and Nicholas Hejaily. "Hands-On Evaluation: A How-To Guide." *Science Scope* 15, no. 6 (March 1992).

Doran, Rodney L., et al. "Successful Laboratory Assessment: A Performance-Based Lab Tool." *The Science Teacher* (April 1992).

Doran, Rodney L., et al. "Authentic Assessment: An Instrument for Consistency." *The Science Teacher* (September 1993).

Dorsey, Valerie Lynn. "Women Find Perfection in NCAA at Last." *USA Today*, April 1, 1992.

Dweck, Carol S. "Self-Theories and Goals: Their Role in Motivation, Personality and Development." In R. Dienstbier, ed., *Nebraska Symposium on Motivation (1990)*. Lincoln: University of Nebraska Press, 1991.

Finson, Kevin, and John B. Beaver. "A Litmus Test for Performance Assessment." *Science Scope* 15, no. 6 (March 1992).

Fleming, Margaret, and Barbara Chambers. "Teacher-Made Tests: Windows on the Classroom." *New-Directions-for-Testing-and-Measurement: Testing in the Schools* 19 (September 1983): 29–38.

Fleener, M. Jayne, and Edmund A. Marek. "Testing in the Learning Cycle." *Science Scope* 15, no. 6 (March 1992).

Frazier, Darlene M., and F. Leon Paulson. "How Portfolios Motivate Reluctant Writers." *Educational Leadership* 49, no. 8 (May 1992).

Gaffney, Kerry E. "Multiple Assessment for Multiple Styles." *Science Scope* 15, no. 6 (March 1992).

Germann, Paul J. "A Model Method." *Science Scope* 15, no. 6 (March 1992).

Glassie, Henry. *Passing the Time in Bellymenone.* Philadelphia: University of Pennsylvania Press, 1982.

Goldberg, Mark F. "Portrait of Gordon Cawelti." *Educational Leadership* 49, no. 8 (May 1992).

Goodlad, John. *A Place Called School.* New York: McGraw-Hill, 1984.

Goodman, Kenneth S., et al. eds. *The Whole Language Evaluation Book.* Portsmouth, N.H.: Heinemann Books, 1989.

Guskey, Thomas R. "What You Assess Might *Not* Be What You Get." *Educational Leadership* 51, no. 6 (March 1994).

———, ed. *Communicating Student Learning.* Alexandria, Va.: Association for Supervision and Curriculum Development, 1996.

Gustafson, Chris. "A Lesson from Stacey." *Educational Leadership* 52, no. 2 (October 1994): 22–23.

Hansen, Jane. "Literacy Portfolios: Helping Students Know Themselves." *Educational Leadership* 49, no. 8 (May 1992).

Hebert, Elizabeth A. "Portfolios Invite Reflection—from Students *and* Staff." *Educational Leadership* 49, no. 8 (May 1992).

Henning-Stout, Mary. *Responsive Assessment: A New Way of Thinking About Learning.* San Francisco, Calif.: Jossey-Bass, 1994.

Herman, Joan L. "What Research Tells Us About Good Assessment." *Educational Leadership* 49, no. 8 (May 1992).

———, et al. *A Practical Guide to Alternative Assessment.* Alexandria, Va.: Association for Supervision and Curriculum Development, 1992.

Hetterscheidt, Judy, et al. "Using the Computer as a Reading Portfolio." *Educational Leadership* 49, no. 8 (May 1992).

Hiebert, Elfrieda H., et al. "Advancing Academic Literacy Through Teachers' Assessments." *Educational Leadership* 46, no. 7 (April 1989).

Hill, Bonnie Campbell, and Cynthia Ruptic. *Practical Aspects of Authentic Assessment: Putting the Pieces Together.* Norwood, Mass.: Christopher-Gordon Publishers, 1994.

Holm, Jane et al. "The Mind Is Not a Vessel to Be Filled But a Fire to Be Kindled—Plutarch: Assessment by Exhibition." Los Naranjos School, Irvine Unified School District, 1992.

Jamentz, Katherine. *Charting the Course Toward Instructionally Sound Assessment.* San Francisco, Calif.: California Assessment Collaborative, September 1993.

————. "Making Sure That Assessment Improves Performance." *Educational Leadership* 51, no. 6 (March 1994).

Jervis, Kathe. "Daryl Takes a Test." *Educational Leadership* 46, no. 7 (April 1989).

Jones, M. Gail. "Assessment Takes Wing." *Science Scope* 15, no. 6 (March 1992).

Kallick, Bena, and Ross Brewer. *Exemplars: A Teacher's Solution.* Volume 1, nos. 4–12. Underhill, Vt.: Exemplars, 1994

Knight, Pam. "How I Use Portfolios in Mathematics." *Educational Leadership* 49, no. 8 (May 1992).

Kohn, Alfie. "From DeGrading to DeGrading: Basic Questions About Assessment and Learning." Audiotape 95-3213. Alexandria, Va.: Association for Supervision and Curriculum Development, 1995.

Lewis, Melva, and Arnold D. Lindaman. "How Do We Evaluate Student Writing? One District's Answer." *Educational Leadership* 46, no. 7 (April 1989).

Liftig, Inez Fugate, et al. "Making Assessment Work: What Teachers Should Know Before They Try It." *Science Scope* 15, no. 6 (March 1992).

Livingston, Carol, et al. "Testing and Curriculum Reform: One School's Experience." *Educational Leadership* 46, no. 7 (April 1989).

MacIver, Douglas J., and David A. Reuman. "Giving Their Best: Grading and Recognition Practices That Motivate Students to Work Hard." *American Educator* (Winter 1993–1994).

McDonald, Joseph P., et al. *Graduation by Exhibition: Assessing Genuine Achievement.* Alexandria, Va.: Association for Supervision and Curriculum Development, 1993.

McTighe, Jay. "Toward More Thoughtful Assessment: Principles and Practices."' Paper presented at the National Staff Development Council Annual Conference, December 7, 1992.

Maeroff, Gene I. "Assessing Alternative Assessment." *Phi Delta Kappan* (December 1991).

Martinez, Michael E., and Joseph I. Lipson. "Assessment for Learning." *Educational Leadership* 46, no. 7 (April 1989).

Marzano, Robert J. "Lessons from the Field About Outcome-Based Performance Assessments." *Educational Leadership* 51, no. 6 (March 1994).

Marzano, Robert J., Debra Pickering, and Jay McTighe. *Assessing Student Outcomes: Performance Assessment Using the Dimensions of Learning Model.* Alexandria, Va.: Association for Supervision and Curriculum Development, 1993.

Mathematical Sciences Education Board. *Measuring What Counts: A Conceptual Guide for Mathematics Assessment*. Washington, D.C.: National Academy Press, 1993.

Meisels, Samuel J. " High-Stakes Testing in Kindergarten." *Educational Leadership* 46, no. 7 (April 1989).

———. "The Work Sampling System: An Authentic Performance Assessment." *Principal* 72, no. 5 (May 1993).

Messick, Samuel. "The Interplay of Evidence and Consequences in the Validation of Performance Assessments." *Educational Researcher* 23, no. 2 (March 1994).

Meyer, Carol A. "What's the Difference Between Authentic and Performance Assessment?" *Educational Leadership* 49, no. 8 (May 1992).

Mirando, Peter A. "Microscale Assessment: Performance, Evaluation, and Chemistry." *Science Teacher* (January 1994).

Mitchell, Ruth. *Testing for Learning: How New Approaches to Evaluation Can Improve American Schools*. New York: Free Press, 1992.

Moran, Stephen B., and William Boulter. "Step by Step Scoring." *Science Scope* 15, no. 6 (March 1992).

National Council of Teachers of Mathematics. *Assessment Standards for School Mathematics*. Working draft. October 1993.

NAEP. *Learning by Doing: A Manual for Teaching and Assessing Higher-Order Thinking in Science and Mathematics*. Study supported by the National Science Foundation through a grant to the Center for Statistics, Office for Educational Research and Improvement, U. S. Department of Education, 1987.

Nott, Linda, et al. "Scoring Rubrics: An Assessment Option." *Science Scope* 15, no. 6 (March 1992).

Nuttall, Desmond L. "Performance Assessment: The Message from England." *Educational Leadership* 49, no. 8 (May 1992).

Obechki, James. *Tenth Grade Science Performance-Based Assessment*. Sacramento: California Department of Education, 1993.

O'Neil, John. "National System of Standards, Exams Piloted." *ASCD Update* 34, no. 8 (October 1992a).

———. "Putting Performance Assessment to the Test." *Educational Leadership* 49, no. 8 (May 1992b).

———. "The Promise of Portfolios: Vermont Effort Reveals Benefits, Shortcomings." *ASCD Update* 35, no. 7 (September 1993).

Ostlund, Karen L. *Science Process Skills: Assessing Hands-On Student Performance*. Menlo Park, Calif.: Addison-Wesley, 1992a.

———. "Sizing Up Social Skills." *Science Scope* 15, no. 6 (March 1992b).

Perrone, Vito. *Expanding Student Assessment*. Alexandria, Va.: Association for Supervision and Curriculum Development, 1991.

Pollock, Jane E. "Blueprints for Social Studies." *Educational Leadership* 49, no. 8 (May 1992).

Pytowska, Ewa. "Success-Oriented Classroom: An Alternative Approach to Grading through Performance Assessment." Unpublished paper, Boston, 1993.

Quigley, Michael E. "Grading Students: A Practice Without Theory." *Critical Linkages II Newsletter* 1, no. 2 (April 1994).

Rackow, Steven J. "Assessment: A Driving Force." *Science Scope* 15, no. 6 (March 1992).

Redding, Nora. "Assessing the Big Outcomes." *Educational Leadership* 49, no. 8 (May 1992).

Roeber, Ed, and Peggy Dutcher. "Michigan's Innovative Assessment of Reading." *Educational Leadership* 46, no. 7 (April 1989).

Roth, Wolff-Michael. "Dynamic Evaluation." *Science Scope* 15, no. 6 (March 1992).

Rothman, Robert. "In Connecticut, Moving Past Paper and Pencil: Student Assessment Rates Performance." *Education Week,* September 13, 1989.

———. "Testing Smarts: Boston Schools Pilot Urban Assessments." *Education Week*, June 16, 1993.

Samson, Gordon E., M. Elizabeth Graue, Thomas Weinstein, and Herbert Wahlberg. "Academic and Occupational Performance: A Quantitative Synthesis." *American Educational Research Journal* 21, no. 2 (Summer 1984): 311–321.

Saphier, Jon. "Bonfires and Magic Bullets." Carlisle, Mass.: Research for Better Teaching, 1994.

Saphier, Jon, and D'Auria, John. *How to Bring Vision to School Improvement*. Carlisle, Mass.: Research for Better Teaching, 1993.

Saphier, Jon, and Matthew King. "Good Seeds Grow in Strong Cultures." *Educational Leadership* (March 1985): 67–74.

Seidel, Steve. "How to Change Our Schools in Just One Day: An Educational Researcher's Open Letter to the President of Harvard University." *The Harvard Education Letter* (March–April 1994).

Shavelson, Richard J., et al. "Performance Assessments: Political Rhetoric and Measurement Reality." *Educational Researcher* 21, no. 4 (May 1992).

Shavelson, Richard J., and Gail P. Baxter. "What We've Learned About Assessing Hands-On Science." *Educational Leadership* 49, no. 8 (May 1992).

Shepard, Lorrie A. "Why We Need Better Assessments." *Educational Leadership* 46, no. 7 (April 1989).

Sizer, Theodore R. *Horace's School: Redesigning the American High School.* Boston: Houghton Mifflin, 1992.

Small, Larry, and Jane Petrek. "Teamwork Testing." *Science Scope* 15, no. 6 (March 1992).

Smith, Sidney. "The Position Paper: English High School, Boston." In *Graduation by Exhibition: Assessing Genuine Achievement.* Alexandria, Va.: Association for Supervision and Curriculum Development, 1993. Pp. 14–23.

Spandel, Vicki, and Richard J. Stiggins. *Creating Writers: Linking Assessment and Writing Instruction.* New York: Longman, 1990.

Sparks, Dennis. "Dennis Sparks Interviews Judith Warren Little on Professional Development in School Reform." Audiotape. Oxford, Ohio: National Staff Development Council, 1993.

Sperling, Doris. "What's Worth an 'A'?: Setting Standards Together." *Educational Leadership* (February 1993).

Stiggins, Richard. *Classroom Assessment Video Training Program: Using Portfolios in Assessment and Instruction.* Portland, Ore.: Northwest Regional Educational Laboratory, 1992.

Stiggins, Richard J., and Nancy Faires Conklin. *In Teachers' Hands: Investigating the Practices of Classroom Assessment.* Albany: State University of New York Press, 1992.

Strong, Richard W. "Developing a Unified Mathematics Curriculum." Workshop presented for the Catskill Central Schools, Catskill, New York, September 2, 1982.

Strong, Richard W., and J. Robert Hanson. "The Authentic School: How to Integrate New Forms of Assessment into a Comprehensive Plan for School Improvement." Paper presented at a National Staff Development Council Workshop, December 7, 1992.

Szetela, Walter, and Cynthia Nicol. "Evaluating Problem Solving in Mathematics." *Educational Leadership* 49, no. 8 (May 1992).

Tetenbaum, Zelda. "An Ordered Approach." *Science Scope* 15, no. 6 (March 1992).

Tippins, Deborah J., and Nancy Fitchman Dana. "Culturally Relevant Alternative Assessment." *Science Scope* 15, no. 6 (March 1992).

Valencia, Sheila W., et al. "Theory and Practice in Statewide Reading Assessment: Closing the Gap." *Educational Leadership* 46, no. 7 (April 1989).

Vargas, Elena Maldonado, and Hector Joel Alvarez. "Mapping Out Students' Abilities." *Science Scope* 15, no. 6 (March 1992).

Viadero, Debra. "Teaching to the Test." *Education Week*, July 13, 1994.

Virginia Education Association and Appalachia Educational Library. *Alternative Assessments in Math and Science: Moving Toward a Target.* Washington, D.C.: Office of Educational Research and Improvement, U.S. Department of Education, October 1992.

Waters, Faith, Margaret MacMullen, and John Glade. *Intelligent Learning: Thinking and Writing.* Unionville, N.Y.: KAV Books, 1992.

Weissglass, Julian. "Constructivist Listening for Empowerment and Challenge." In Sciences Education Board, National Research Council, *Measuring Up: Prototypes for Mathematics Assessment.* Washington, D.C.: National Academy Press, 1993.

Wiggins, Grant. "Teaching to the (Authentic) Test." *Educational Leadership* 46, no. 7 (April 1989).

———. "Creating Tests Worth Taking." *Educational Leadership* 49, no. 8 (May 1992).

———. *Assessing Student Performance: Exploring the Purpose and Limits of Testing.* San Francisco: Jossey-Bass, 1993a.

———. "Honesty and Fairness: Toward Better Grading and Reporting." In Thomas Guskey, ed., *1996 A.S.C.D. Yearbook.* Alexandria, Va.: Association for Supervision and Curriculum Development, 1996.

Wiggins, Grant, et al. *Standards, Not Standardization* (videos and print). Geneseo, New York: CLASS, 1993b.

Wolf, Dennie Palmer. "Assessment as an Episode of Learning." Unpublished paper. Cambridge, Mass.: Harvard Graduate School of Education.

———. "Portfolio Assessment: Sampling Student Work." *Educational Leadership* 46, no. 7 (April 1989).

Wolf, Dennie Palmer, et al. "Good Measure: Assessment as a Tool for Educational Reform." *Educational Leadership* 49, no. 8 (May 1992).

Worthen, Blaine R. "Critical Issues That Will Determine the Future of Alternative Assessment." *Phi Delta Kappan* 74, no. 6 (February 1993).

Zessoules, Rieneke, and Howard Gardner. "Authentic Assessment: Beyond the Buzzword and Into the Classroom." In Vito Perrone, ed., *Expanding Student Assessment.* Alexandria, Va.: Association for Supervision and Curriculum Development, 1991. Pp. 47–71.

17

Curriculum Design

How do I build and adjust the curriculum for maximum effectiveness?

Continuity

Sequence

Integration

I n the last several chapters, we covered parameters that are basic building blocks of curriculum: Objectives, Learning Experiences, and Assessment. This chapter introduces the fourth, and the one least discussed in schools: the Design of Curriculum.

Objectives tell you where you are going and what you are going to achieve. Learning Experiences tell you what you are going to do to get there. The Design of Curriculum tells you how to arrange Objectives and Learning Experiences for a cumulative effect.

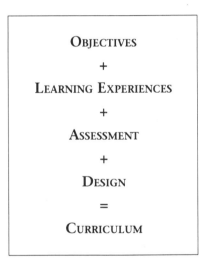

OBJECTIVES

+

LEARNING EXPERIENCES

+

ASSESSMENT

+

DESIGN

=

CURRICULUM

The actual things that get organized in curriculum are objectives, content (meaning information), and learning experiences. Skill at selecting objectives, isolating content, and picking appropriate learning experiences to go with them is not enough to ensure good curriculum. The design of how those things are organized in curriculum is important because it has a lot to do with making learning stick. It also has a lot to do with the quality, breadth, and depth of the material that is learned. Good design has its own impact. And knowing what well-designed curriculum looks like is something teachers need to know. As consumers of curriculum, teachers choose among competitors in the marketplace and need knowledge of what good curriculum is to discriminate the poor from the good from the better. Implementing a curriculum maximally requires an understanding of the design behind it, so that timing can be appropriate and choice points taken well.

Teachers are sometimes asked to design curriculum themselves and often to explain what they are doing to such groups as parents and school committees. For all of these reasons, basic knowledge about curriculum design and organization has been included among the parameters of teaching.

The design is the blueprint of the larger effort, the sum total of all the experiences the student has in a given curriculum. It is the broad pattern of instructional events and encompasses what we see students and teachers doing—their materials and spatial arrangements. When these patterns are well constructed, they help teachers achieve the higher-level objectives of the curriculum like critical thinking. Individual learning experiences can achieve small, short-term objectives, such as "understanding the traditions of the Puritans." The larger ones, however, such as "understanding the role of traditions in society," are achieved only if curriculum is designed well.

The following aspects of curriculum design are key when reviewing, purchasing, or designing curriculum:

- The building blocks of curriculum as learning experiences (described in Chapter 15; i.e., complex entities with many controllable attributes).

- The structuring of curriculum through arranging entities of different sizes and duration (learning experiences, lessons, units, courses, programs).

- The use of key concepts or essential questions around which subordinate main ideas and specific facts or operations are developed (rather than organizing around topics).

- Returning to or recycling through key concepts in spiral fashion again and again over time, so that each time they are dealt with students treat them with more abstractness, generality (applying in new contexts), and complexity. This is the principle of continuity.

- The organization of learning experiences in sequence so that each experience builds on previous learning and provides a basis for a subsequent one.

- The principle of integration, by which students apply or see the knowledge from one area as it operates or relates in another area.

For a full set of examples of these principles in action, we refer readers to Ralph Tyler's classic *Basic Principles of Curriculum and Instruction* (1949). It is interesting how often one hears the "Tyler rationale" discussed by people who have not read this central work. It is one of the most cited and least read books in the business and comprises a most useful part of our professional knowledge base. ❧

Source Materials on Curriculum Design

Gagne, R. M., and L. J. Briggs. *Principles of Instructional Design.* New York: Holt, Rinehart and Winston, 1974.

Taba, H., M. C. Durlin, M. C. Prenhul, and A. A. McNaughton. *A Teacher's Handbook for Elementary Social Studies.* 2d ed. Reading, Mass.: Addison-Wesley, 1971.

Tyler, R. *Basic Principles of Curriculum and Instruction.* Chicago: University of Chicago Press, 1949.

18

Overarching Objectives

Interactive Teaching

Curricular Choices and
    Materials

The Hidden Curriculum

Many of you reading this book came into teaching because you had something very particular you wanted to give to students. You had a passion for it, and you built everything you did around it. You had an overarching objective.

Maybe what you wanted was that your students would leave loving books and believing that books had something of value for them. Or maybe you wanted your students to be critical thinkers who could size up situations with care and be deliberate in their decisions. Or maybe you wanted your students to know what it is like to walk in someone else's shoes: developing empathy for other humans. No matter what else you were teaching, that was always in the back of your mind and somehow visible in your choices.

Not all teachers have overarching objectives, but those who do stand out from the crowd. Overarching objectives are those big picture outcomes for students which, if a teacher actually has them, shape core practices and account for much of what we see in their classrooms. They come from teachers who have asked themselves: "What do I most want for my students? When they leave me at the end of the year, what is the most important thing I want them to carry away from the experience?" These overarching objectives may not show up in unit or lesson plans, but they permeate everything the teacher does. They show up in interactive behavior and in decisions about learning experiences. Overarching objectives are stated in sentences like the following:

"When my students leave me at the end of the year,

- they will know how to work effectively in groups.
- they will have the motivation and the skills to be lifelong learners.
- they will be slow to judge and adept at critical thinking.
- they will know how to confront without hostility and resolve conflicts without rancor.
- they will understand the balance of life on the planet and be willing to do their part to preserve it.
- they will understand and appreciate the differences between people in the world—differences of color, culture, language, thinking style—and respond with tolerance and inclusion rather than with prejudice and exclusion."

This list is meant to exemplify the concept of overarching objectives, not be an inclusive or a recommended list. Though one may value all the statements above, it is rare that an individual will really be seen in practice to stand for more than one of them. If you really *stand* for an objective, it permeates your practice and influences everything you do. It is always in the back of your mind and serves as a backboard against which you make all your decisions.

One can have only a very few overarching objectives at this level of commitment—usually one and maybe two or three at most. Otherwise one becomes simply too diffuse in one's efforts and makes little progress on any front.

Individual teachers who have overarching objectives may give lasting gifts to their students. It would be possible also for teams of teachers or "houses" within a larger school to have an overarching objective in common and achieve even more by virtue of their consistency and congruence with one another. And beyond that, it would be possible, indeed, for a whole school to share an overarching objective and create an environment so supportive and total in its commitment as to be an incredible engine for change. In such places the objective becomes a beacon for structuring arenas throughout the school that go well beyond individual classroom practices—arenas like the cafeteria, school reward systems, faculty meeting time,

> *Individual teachers who have overarching objectives may give lasting gifts to their students.*

extracurricular activities, student government. We have written elsewhere in detail (Saphier and D'Auria 1993) about the process of creating such a school. It is not easy or quick, but it can be done. In this chapter, however, we wish to focus on the classroom dimension of overarching objectives.

How does a teacher go about pursuing such a large objective in his or her own classroom? How does it influence interactive teaching, his or her choices of strategies from the other parameters? How does it influence the way a teacher treats curriculum if the overarching objective is unique to that teacher and is not part of the curriculum as written?

Interactive Teaching

The overarching objective becomes the set for instruction, the charter, the guidelines for which items to pluck from the repertoires of each parameter. And the overarching objective highlights certain parameters themselves. The following section shows how the light from an overarching objective illuminates choices from the repertoires in certain parameters. Because we will run only one overarching objective through this exercise, we will highlight only one set of choices. It is our hope that readers, either singly or in groups, will repeat the exercise for different overarching objectives that represent their personal commitments.

Suppose a teacher has an overarching objective that students leave at the end of the year with an appreciation of human differences so that they not only tolerate differences but embrace them. This teacher will be particularly active with the Classroom Climate parameter. Developing strand 1, community among the students with acceptance and inclusion, will be particularly important to this person. This teacher will also want to recognize differences in learning style among students and have the students themselves understand how learning styles influence behavior and students' reaction to different kinds of tasks. Thus this teacher might explicitly teach the students about learning style, their own and others, and be explicit about calling for the students to value and honor the differences between themselves and their peers.

Those Models of Teaching that bring students together in groups and teach them how to work well with those different from themselves will be prized by this teacher. Thus Group Investigation, the Johnson Brothers version of cooperative learning with social skills training, and Slavin's S/T/A/D will be valued. Certain strategies from Clarity that bring students together with peers will be used often because this teacher will see them as an opportunity to bring students from different backgrounds into joint work situations where they need and can help one another. This teacher would tend to choose strategies like Round the Clock Learning Buddies and numerous other Activators and Summarizers.

Classroom routines might be structured with content that emphasizes the human differences theme. For example, a daily news routine may highlight events from around the world where racial or ethnic differences have been respected or disrespected. Students could be expected to bring in clippings or articles for posting on a bulletin board and later discussion in the class.

Routines might be created for students to get help from one another where kids with different strengths—art, organization, video editing, writing— were available to peers to help with projects and assignments.

The Personal Relationship Building parameter would be important to this teacher. The teacher's desire to value differences would require as a foundation that each student felt acknowledged and valued personally by the teacher. This teacher would rank high on the application of fairness, respect, and active listening with all students, and especially those who might be different—physically or mentally disabled, learning disabled, or racial minorities.

In addition to choices like those within parameters profiled above, an overarching objective will influence choices of curriculum units and materials and how a teacher deals with the materials.

Curricular and Materials Choices

A teacher who has respect for human differences as an agenda might be expected to highlight issues of race in social studies or in literature and deal with them up front in a way that forced students to think. For example, characters or episodes in *Huckleberry Finn* could be placed on a grid as they came up during the novel and discussed in terms of racist or antiracist behavior. One of the revelations in this particular exercise is that there is no such thing as "passive antiracist" behavior. Being passive in the presence of racism and disapproving without speaking or acting actually supports and perpetuates the racism. These discussions would not replace, but would be woven throughout the unit on *Huckleberry Finn* by a teacher who had an overarching objective pertaining to human differences.

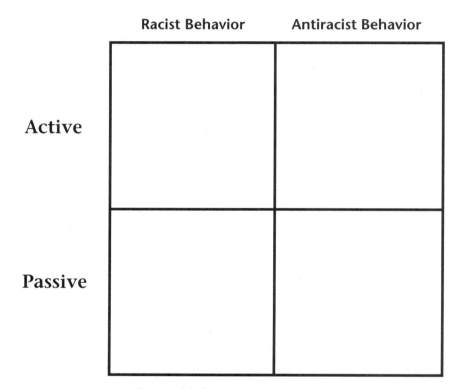

FIGURE 18.1: RACIST AND ANTIRACIST BEHAVIOR*
Source: Beverly Daniel Tatum and Andrea Ayvazian,
Mount Holyoke College, South Hadley, Massachusetts.

Both the racist and antiracist actors and actions in this book could be addressed within a context of understanding and dismantling racism.

The stories and novels a teacher chooses for students is an obvious place to locate an overarching objective. Whether it be courage, perseverance, respect for difference or any other character trait, excellent bibliographies can be found to aid selection of books (Developmental Studies Center 1994).[1]

[1] *Developmental Studies Center K-8 Curriculum Materials Catalog.* 2000 Embarcadero, Suite 305, Oakland, Calif. 94606

*Reprinted with permission. Beverly Daniel Tatum and Andrea Ayvazian, Mount Holyoke College, South Hadley, Massachusetts.

Overarching objectives that pertain to attitudes and habits of mind tend to show up in specific skill lessons and units. For example, if the overarching objective is love of learning and the skills to pursue one's own questions, the teacher is likely to teach interviewing skills explicitly to children because interviewing is a major way to find out what one wants to know. This same teacher is likely to make it a high priority that students learn how to use library resources, online services, and Internet browsers. These skills are in direct support of the overarching objective and might not have entered the curriculum at all but for the big picture objective The larger point here is that a teacher's overarching objective may easily have direct implications for the skills that the teacher chooses to emphasize or teach at all.

The Hidden Curriculum

Overarching objectives may be understood and classified through a set of lenses set forth by Gower and Scott (1977). They describe five realities present in any classroom (or, for that matter, any other human interaction) at all times: social, personal, moral, political, and information processing realities. These same five dimensions could be used to classify overarching objectives teachers may have for individuals. Objectives may be primarily social in nature (e.g., students learn to resolve conflicts nonviolently) or moral (respect for human differences). These objectives can be aimed at personal development (students become risk takers) or political outcomes (students will become active environmentalists). Finally these objectives may aim to develop certain thinking skills or ways of processing information that students use whatever the content they're studying (e.g., students will be able to restrain the rush to judge and exercise critical thinking skills).

Another way to use these five lenses from Gower and Scott is to analyze the classroom realities that teachers create on each of the dimensions from an inductive point of view. Even without a deliberate overarching objective in any of these five categories, a certain reality for students in each of the five dimensions is created in every classroom by every teacher. Each has attributes and each can be described. Switching gears now from the prescriptive and intentional (overarching objectives) to the descriptive and perhaps unintentional, let us examine these five realities. They do, after all, form a hidden but describable curriculum in every classroom in every school.

Classroom Realities

Social Reality
What is the social reality in a class at any given moment? Social reality has to do with the way people interact. We can inquire into group dynamics, norms, roles, expectations, and interpersonal transactions from any one of a number of points of view. But the point remains that at every moment there is a social reality present, whether or not we attend to it. It has been constructed or allowed to develop, and can be described. And its form may

or may not be a deliberate creation of the teaching. Students working together cooperatively on a group project constitutes a very different social reality with respect to norms, roles, and interpersonal transactions from the same group working with a teacher as director.

Personal Reality

Every one of us has a personal reality at any moment that consists of how we are feeling and reacting. Our hopes, fears, dreams, and goals, which we carry with us at all times, are touched, to a greater or lesser degree, by the events of the moment. Each student in a classroom, at every moment, has a personal interior state of feeling. That state is complex, changeable, and real. Each individual's feelings at the moment are the personal reality for him or her. When we seek to understand or provide for personal reality in the classroom, we are examining the changeable, interior, personal world of individuals and their feelings of well-being.

> *Each student in a classroom, at every moment, has a personal interior state of feeling. That state is complex, changeable, and real.*

Moral Reality

We enter the moral dimension in a classroom when we ask about the concepts of right and wrong, of duty, justice, and obligation, that exist—that are embedded in curriculum materials, in teacher behavior, in class norms and procedures, and in students' judgments and choices. Such concepts exist, they function, and they are describable and analyzable in any class, whether or not the teacher is aware of and deliberate about them. Sometimes in more modern curriculum packages moral considerations are taken up head-on in learning experiences (Shaftel and Shaftel 1967; Lickona 1972, 1991).

Political Reality

The political dimension of reality has to do with power, influence, and control. When we examine this dimension we ask questions like: Who has power? How is influence exerted? On whom, by whom? How are decisions made? Who influences the course of events and their form? How does one person (the teacher or a student) get another to behave in a certain way? Who decides what will be done next? What are the students learning in this class about their role in relation to power?

Information Processing Reality

The information processing reality in schools has to do with academics. How is information dealt with? How is it presented, acquired, received, manipulated, used? The answers are quite different when one contrasts a discovery orientation with an advance organizer orientation, or a Socratic discussion with a laboratory experience, or programmed instruction with self-directed research.

The nature of each of these five realities can be described for a given class period. In addition, one could comment over time on how much variance there was within each of the five dimensions. By variance we mean the range of ways to be on one dimension, the number of different realities observable over time when the classroom is examined through a particular dimension's lens. The social reality of a class may remain constant, such as always one large teacher-directed group; or it may have two social realities: large teacher-directed group, and large democratic discussion group with emphasis on interpersonal transactions. (This distinction is not one that would be picked up by the attribute Interpersonal Complexity of Learning Experiences.) One may see a variety of social realities over a class day or week or year. The social reality within a small group changes if the teacher ceases being a direct skill lesson leader and becomes an equal participant and facilitator in a discussion of, say, states' rights.

Moral reality may be invariant: community norms and expectations that students do their work (the good, duty, obligation) are maintained and enforced by the teacher without discussion. Or, a different moral reality may be observed at different times as, for example, when children consider ethical issues as a learning activity or when groups are permitted to problem solve with the teacher acting as a mediator.

Emphasis Within Dimensions

The hidden curriculum can be seen as those social, personal, moral, and political learnings that accrue to students as a result of the environment in which they function, both in the classroom and in the broader school at large. These learnings may be built in unconsciously, or they may be deliberate and orchestrated by the teacher. Either way, they are happening and in all five dimensions.

When they are deliberate, we find teachers who can talk explicitly about their ideas of social curriculum, personal or psychological curriculum, and, less often, moral curriculum, and political curriculum. These people may be so clear as to have an overarching objective related to that dimension and curriculum to go with it. This curriculum may evince itself in explicit learning experiences or, more subtly, in intentional aspects of the learning environment the teacher constructs or allows to exist (for reasons he or she attributes to social goals or moral goals). Emphasis in any dimension usually manifests in awareness, deliberateness, and objectives for that dimension. As we observe teaching and interview teachers about their teaching, we have found that we can identify dimensions that are being emphasized either in the design of the learning environment or in personal interactions with certain students.

We commented before that there is some describable reality on each dimension at all times, regardless of the teacher's awareness or deliberateness about what it is. When a dimension is emphasized, even if it has only one form, it means that the dimensional reality figures prominently in learning experiences and one would expect the teacher to be able to say why. For example, some teachers may provide for a high frequency of negotiation and choices by students because they have a philosophical commitment to developing student ownership and influence (a commitment from the political dimension). If we observe students in frequent debate, stating and defending positions on issues with the teacher as facilitator and clarifier, we would expect the teacher to have something to say about getting students to be independent thinkers, or critical thinkers, or effective speakers, or some such goal.

Matching Dimensions to Needs of Classes or Individuals

While they stop short of forming overarching objectives, there are many teachers who pursue personalized objectives for particular students that are outside the formal boundaries of their academic agendas. These goals could be from any of the five dimensions and could show up in individual choices or interactions. They are, in fact, usually highly personalized moves and reflect a high level of matching.

For many teachers these moves are quick and spontaneous. Though it often takes probing to get people to even remember they did them, the moves may come from deep and consistent wells. Experienced and well-developed teachers may have a large number of such individual objectives from the five dimensions for different students.

If a teacher has a social goal for a child, that teacher wants the student to develop or increase some particular interpersonal capacity or insight. "Well, I stopped and asked Jane how she saw the issue because I wanted her group to hear her thinking. She's too shy to offer it on her own and needs an opening. I want to help raise her status in her group." This teacher has a social goal for the student.

If a teacher has a personal goal for a student, that teacher wants the student to develop some personal capacity or inner strength. "Jimmy, I'd like you to see if there is any pattern to the ones you got wrong. If there is, how about setting a goal and checking it out with me before lunch?" This teacher has a personal objective for Jimmy to learn how to self-analyze and set goals.

If a teacher has a moral goal for a student, that teacher wants the student to learn something about justice, right, duty or obligation. Charmaine has several students sent to her today for help during the 90-minute period. The teacher has arranged in advance with Charmaine by negotiation that she, who is skilled at analyzing and setting up word problems, will be willing to help others in this difficult problem set. This arrangement is not an attempt to boost Charmaine's self-esteem. Her self-esteem is already at the point of arrogance. The teacher is systematically trying to help Charmaine develop a sense of responsibility for the success of others. This is a moral objective.

When a teacher has a political objective for a child, that teacher wants that student to learn something about power or influence. Mrs. James has had Peter read a chapter on mediation during the class study of the labor movement. She has asked him to conduct a mock mediation in front of the class in which he explicitly models the mediation skills in the chapter. Later when Peter gets into one of his frequent high-pitched arguments with a classmate that he usually wins by bullying, Mrs. James intervenes and says, "Peter, let's mediate. Coach me through the steps." She does this frequently over the first term in an attempt to teach Peter an alternative way to exert his influence in a dispute.

Notice that in these examples, some of the teachers' actions were spontaneous, as in the case of Jane and the goal to increase her status in the group. Others were deliberate and planned, such as the last example with Peter. What all the examples share in common, however, is individualized thinking about objectives for the child's growth. These objectives are in realms that include academic and thinking skills, but also go beyond into other dimensions.

In the teaching ranks of our schools there are thousands of unheralded virtuosos of the five dimensions profiled in this chapter. These people make subtle and deliberate on-the-fly moves with individual students. These moves are keyed to social, personal, moral, and political objectives that rarely show up in lesson plans, but are alive as perceptual filters the teachers use to catch teachable moments with particular students. These teachers are complex thinkers who can and who do address multiple objectives simultaneously.

Understanding this aspect of sophisticated teaching may give observers a new lens for inquiring into those quick little comments and moves that teachers make almost in passing with individual students. This lens can serve as a foundation for interesting questions in conferences as observers help teachers debrief and interpret the incredibly complex reality of interactive classroom teaching.

For teachers this chapter may provide a frame for thinking about their students, one by one, and for sorting through the multiple ways their teaching can match the needs of individuals. 🐦

Source Materials on Overarching Objectives

Gower, R. R., and M. B. Scott. *Five Essential Dimensions of Curriculum Design.* Dubuque, Iowa: Kendall Hunt, 1977.

Lickona, T. *Educating for Character.* New York: Bantam Books, 1991

Lickona, T. *A Strategy for Teaching Values.* Pleasantville, N.Y.: Guidance Associates, 1972.

Saphier, Jon, and John D'Auria. *The Core Value Process: Bringing Vision to School Improvement.* Carlisle, Mass.: Research for Better Teaching, 1993.

Shaftel, G., and F. Shaftel. *Role Playing for Social Value*s. Englewood Cliffs, N.J.: Prentice Hall, 1967.

Stanford, G. *Developing Effective Classroom Groups.* New York: Hart Publishing Co., 1977.

Tatum, Beverly Daniel, and Andrea Ayvazian. Mount Holyoke College, South Hadley, Mass.

19

Opening Wide the Gates

Building a professional
development culture that
incorporates optimal
conditions for
teacher learning

The best staff development creates an environment that treats teachers as thinking, reflective, and responsible professionals.

Wildman and Niles (1987)

One rarely has optimal conditions for anything in this life. Recent research on school change and teacher development, however, has made it increasingly clear that certain key conditions open wide the gates for all the improvements we dearly wish in professional development. Our starting premise is that increasing teacher capacity through knowledge is the most important lever for improving schools (Saphier 1994). In this chapter we highlight and then examine seven conditions that are vital to teacher learning in the workplace and connect those conditions to the purposes and uses of this book.

1. Teachers engage in self-study of their own practice. This condition grounds the work of teacher improvement.

2. Schools contain within them both collegial structures and personal support for reflection and for study of the knowledge base on teaching.

3. The knowledge base on teaching is construed as areas of performance, repertoires, and matching, not "effective behaviors."

4. The risk taking and vulnerability conducive to teacher growth and learning are successfully managed.

5. There is systematic and varied access to two kinds of professional knowledge:

   (1) one's own personal practical knowledge and that of one's colleagues

   (2) the public domain research-based knowledge on teaching.

6. Professional knowledge and data about student needs should inform teachers' choices regarding the content and process of their own learning.

7. Leaders act in congruence with the previous six conditions and explicitly support them.

Let us now expand a bit on each of these conditions.

1.   Teachers engage in self-study of their own practice.

> ## *It is thoughtful, lived experience that gets one to expert performance.*

Many thoughtful writers agree (Edwards 1994; Darling-Hammond and McLaughlin 1995; Wildman and Niles 1987) that improved teaching begins with teachers' analyzing their own practice. For deep and lasting change to happen, teachers must be engaged "in concrete tasks of teaching, assessment, observation, and reflection that illuminate the processes of learning and development" (Darling-Hammond and McLaughlin 1995). In practice, however, professional development is usually based on outside input that teachers are expected to receive and incorporate into their practice. John Edwards (1995) writes, "Most staff development and management training works on the naive belief that if you present people with new knowledge they will change their current thinking and practice. For most people, in most situations, that simply is not the case. It is thoughtful, lived experience that gets one to expert performance. You learn by studying yourself, what you do and think. You become self-aware, and then you work on improving."

Certain skills are indispensable for studying one's own practice:

(1) observation and analysis tools that eschew the judgmental (these encompass getting literal data, using students as sources of data, and making the tacit explicit) and (2) cognitive coaching skills (Costa and Garmston 1994).

Observation and Analysis Tools

Wildman and Niles (1987) have pointed out the overpowering tendency educators have to be judgmental of observed teaching and how often their conclusions cannot be substantiated from the data. In their study, Wildman and Niles watched teachers "react with varying degrees of surprise when we asked them to examine their own descriptions of teaching events in terms of the evidence they drew upon and the conclusions and judgments they reached. Initially, the teachers were astounded to find that most or all of their statements were judgmental in nature and not tied to objective evidence."

Total objectivity may be unattainable, but self-study can begin with plentiful bodies of actual data about teacher behavior and student performance. In our fifteen years of training teachers and administrators to be good observers, we have found that developing the ability to collect real data on teaching takes considerable time—Wildman and Niles claim up to 20 hours of training and practice. First, it takes restraint—restraint of the rush to judgment, and nourishment of the desire to inquire. Then it needs an attitude shift that comes from an investment in observation skills and posing questions about practices and effects rather than rushing to judgment.

Groups of teachers can study the links among their objectives, their learning activities, and the samples of work the students produce; then they can go back to an examination of their own teaching behaviors to determine what the actual effects were in comparison to what they intended.

Cognitive Coaching Skills

Cognitive coaching skills give teachers a framework and a set of skills for helping each other analyze data about classroom events. The formats for conferences provided in the training ensure that these meetings stay data oriented, that the teacher is the owner of the conclusions, and that both teacher and observer inquire into the links among objectives, activities, and student performance. By active listening and probing for specificity, teachers learn to elaborate their thinking and maintain an analytical cast, not a judgmental one.

2.   Schools contain within them both collegial structures and personal support for self-study.

If teacher self-study is to flourish, support structures must be in place so that teachers get together to do the necessary observing, coaching, and data analysis. Four factors are critical here, and they are interdependent:

1. Structures. Teachers can talk and work together in structures such as study groups, grade-level and department meetings, and workshops .

2. Time. The time for these structures to operate exists and/or is built into each teacher's schedule.

3. Administrative support. This support for the teacher's professional learning is verbally and tangibly expressed.

4. Personal support. Each teacher has a critical friend (inside or outside the institution) who is interested in and committed to the teacher's growth.

Special structures can be created to facilitate teachers' doing experiments and self-study—for example, schoolwide study groups or departmental study groups—but most schools already have adequate structures in place: faculty meetings, department meetings, grade-level meetings, and team meetings. It is the pull of the past and old models of doing business that prevent us from using these structures for self-study and teacher improvement. Administrative commitment and leadership are essential to break out of these habits.

Elsewhere (King and Saphier in press) we have written at length about specific ideas and strategies for creating collegial conditions in the workplace. We believe readers of this book can be equally as creative as the many fine educators who have contributed to our own bank of how-to ideas. The point we are making here is that leaders must make a deliberate commitment to create the time and structures required for teachers to do self-study. They are not currently built into either the ethos or the structural design of American schools. One way to nourish this commitment is to tie it to the training and certifying of administrators. In other words, administrators should be evaluated on their ability to nourish collegiality in their institutions.

> *Leaders must make a deliberate commitment to create the time and structures required for teachers to do self-study.*

Personal support is an important component here. Having a friend who will periodically ask how you are progressing and then provide assistance is more than just support; it is a form of gentle push. This combination of qualities is vital—someone who is interested in your growth, cares about you, and challenges you to self-evaluate and ask, "What's next?" Good mentors embody all of these qualities.

One of us once had a line job in an urban district to play this role—"staff developer," it was called. Most "staff developers," however, usually have a mission more associated with system-wide training, curriculum implementation, or program development. A staff developer whose mission is to support individual professional growth of teachers is rare indeed. Yet we can think of no other position that would be more powerful for increasing teacher capacity if its mission were construed properly. (And what a wonderful role it would be for senior teachers to aspire to, be trained for, and use to leave a legacy of their work.)

3.   **The knowledge bases on teaching are construed as areas of performance, repertoires, and matching, not "effective behaviors."**

Being open to studying one's own practice and the knowledge base on teaching requires a particular view of what the knowledge is like—and it requires an explicit disavowal and rejection of the current view of what knowledge on teaching is like.

We need an acknowledgment and understanding within the school that teaching is intellectually complex, difficult, and demanding work and that the nature of the knowledge is not a list of effective behaviors that everyone should learn and do. Rather, the knowledge base is a value-neutral and ever-increasing repertoire of approaches that can be categorized according to their function (e.g., clarity, communicating expectations, maintaining momentum). Teacher judgment developed through experience is the source of wisdom about which strategies to use for a particular child, situation, or curriculum. There are no best strategies or governing rules or formulas that dictate which strategies to use in which situations (though some generalizations and rules help novices in getting started). It is important to have a repertoire of skills, not just one way of dealing with each basic function of teaching. And it is important to keep adding to one's repertoire.

This view of the nature of teaching knowledge is essential to developing a collegial, open, risk-taking environment. Unfortunately, the prevailing "effectiveness" view about teaching knowledge sabotages risk taking and obstructs teacher learning. This view holds that there exists a list of "effective behaviors" that define good teaching. This right-wrong, effective-ineffective image tends to support polarized discussions between teachers about how to handle instructional situations—polarized in that when there is a difference of practice or a difference of

> *Teaching is intellectually complex, difficult, and demanding work.*

opinion, the implication is they both can't be right. Another consequence of the effectiveness view of teaching is that it prevents discussions about teaching at all, for fear we might disagree. A third consequence is to truncate discussions about different approaches because people tend to say, "Well, it's fine if that works for you; but it's not my style." Successful teaching is not a matter of style but a matter of matching, a matter of appropriateness for the child, the situation, or the curriculum.

4. The risk taking and vulnerability conducive to teacher growth and learning are successfully managed.

An acceptance of the "areas of performance-repertoire-matching" view of professional knowledge is the basis for talking openly with colleagues about problems and for sharing strategies. Still, there is no guarantee that collegiality and experimentation will flourish as school norms. More is needed.

If teachers are meeting together in collegial structures (point 2) and engaged in self-study (point 1), the odds for teacher learning are climbing fast. Now suppose these teachers work under the leadership of a person who is honest about his or her own areas of vulnerability, is clearly in search of new learning, and models taking risks openly. Suppose further this leader/facilitator helps the teachers solve problems with colleagues and in the process surfaces teacher beliefs, values, and assumptions that may differ—differing world views, as it were. Suppose, finally, that it becomes apparent that the way in which all this happened was respectful and safe (though occasionally challenging). Now the odds for teacher learning skyrocket.

The point about surfacing teacher beliefs, values, and assumptions bears consideration in the light of what we know about the power and stability of teacher beliefs because "personal predispositions...stand at the core of becoming a teacher" (Lortie 1975). Teachers' worlds are anchored not only in their daily experiences and their concerns for students but also in their personal beliefs and assumptions about children, teaching, and learning. Change comes when teachers are willing to recognize these assumptions and discuss them with others. That requires trust in one's fellows to respect those views and an openness to questioning some of those long-held assumptions and beliefs. When this happens, profound changes can occur in teaching practices. Edwards (1994) writes: "While it is a difficult area to work in, because many people regard it as totally private, it is important to encourage people to become more aware of their world views at an explicit level and to explore their influence on their thinking and actions. Our experience has been that if trust is developed through the careful forming of the group, and if the activities are at the right level of openness, most people are willing to look at some of their world views."

In the framework we are developing here, the study of one's own beliefs becomes an element of the self-study that grounds teacher development. Such study is carried on in collaboration with peers. Revealing these innermost beliefs about professional practice makes all of us feel vulnerable. Nevertheless, entering this dangerous territory enables us to approach some of the most powerful levers to change and improvement.

Frank Pajares (1992) has summarized some of the strongest findings in research on teacher beliefs:

- Educational beliefs of preservice teachers play a pivotal role in their acquisition and interpretation of knowledge and subsequent teaching behavior. Unexplored entering beliefs may be responsible for the perpetuation of antiquated and ineffectual teaching practices.

- Beliefs are formed early and tend to self-perpetuate, persevering even against contradictions caused by reason, time, schooling, or experience.

- Belief systems help individuals define and understand the world and themselves.

- Thought processes may well be precursors to and creators of beliefs, but the filtering effect of belief structures ultimately screens, redefines, distorts, or reshapes subsequent thinking and information processing.

- Beliefs are instrumental in defining tasks and selecting the cognitive tools with which to interpret, plan, and make decisions regarding such tasks; hence, they play a critical role in defining behavior and organizing knowledge and information.

- Beliefs strongly influence perception, but they can be an unreliable guide to the nature of reality.

- Beliefs about teaching are well established by the time a student gets to college.

Can data about student learning and self-study of one's own teaching practices create sufficient cognitive dissonance to cause a reexamination of one's beliefs? Can sharing with colleagues one's deepest goals for students and one's approaches to meeting those goals enable new insights that lead teachers to reach out to the repertoires?

We believe that without this examination of beliefs, any change may be superficial. In fact, the absence of such examination accounts in part for the failure of good teaching practices to transfer beyond the site where they were created, no matter how many articles and workshops are generated about them.

5.   There is systematic and varied access to two kinds of professional knowledge:

> (1) one's own personal practical knowledge and that of one's colleagues and
> (2) the public domain research-based knowledge on teaching.

Personal Practical Knowledge

Edwards's (1994) point of view on teacher development is that "it is thoughtful, lived experience that gets one to expert performance. You learn by studying yourself, what you do and think. You become self-aware, and then you work on improving." Edwards christens this knowledge born of lived experience and reflection on that experience one's "Personal Practical Knowledge (PPK). It is unique to you. It is largely implicit and difficult to articulate and it is very resistant to change."

"Trainers or staff developers who desire to promote reflection...will also value what teachers know in addition to scientific evidence [i.e., research-based findings about teaching] and will communicate in such a way that teachers will be encouraged to reveal their private worlds of teaching. Thus, the relationship between trainer and teacher is one of reciprocity where the goal is personal growth rather than compliance" (Wildman and Niles 1987). In this way of thinking, teacher development will proceed optimally if we "put people in touch with their personal power and convey utmost respect for their lived experiences" (Edwards 1994).

These authors convey a potent message. They argue for acknowledging the huge reservoir of knowledge that resides in the experience of teachers and remains untapped by virtue of the isolation in which they typically work. They argue that unless the personal practical knowledge of teachers is acknowledged and included in the development process, teachers cannot truly change by integrating ideas from outside into their practice. Although there is evidence that change and even attitude and belief shifts can occur as a consequence rather than a forerunner of behavioral change (Guskey 1995), we believe too that respecting teachers' experience and using their personal practical knowledge are essential to building powerful staff development cultures.

> *The huge reservoir of knowledge that resides in the experience of teachers remains untapped by virtue of the isolation in which they typically work*

All teachers over their careers are continually filling their personal treasure chest with knowledge about children, knowledge about content, and knowledge about how to teach that content. This knowledge is their personal practical knowledge derived from their own reactions to challenges, their own discoveries, their own experiments. It comes at different rates to different people depending on how reflective and resourceful they are. It also contains items of knowledge that have been discovered (and rediscovered) by many others but have not entered the public knowledge base; thus, these items are reinvented through personal practice in random places over and over again through thousands of career histories.

In workplaces that optimize conditions for teacher learning, teachers have access to their own personal practical knowledge and that of their colleagues through a variety of channels: study groups, grade or department meetings, observations of one another's classes, demonstrations by others in their own classrooms. In this way, private and idiosyncratic knowledge is shared and multiplies the collective power of a faculty.

Public Professional Knowledge on Teaching

In addition to the tremendous resource in every school of the personal practical knowledge of individual teachers, we must also acknowledge and reach out to the huge reservoir of available strategies and skills for teaching that exists in what Edwards (1994) calls public knowledge: the common knowledge of the field available from books, workshops, and courses. Because of widespread denial of the existence of a knowledge base on teaching, many teachers, and probably most of them, are unaware of many of the powerful teaching strategies that exist. The mission of Research for Better Teaching and the authors of this book has been to get widespread awareness and understanding of the huge knowledge base on teaching that is outlined in this book. It is imperative that teachers reach out to this base, and the repertoires in it, and expand their own repertoires by learning new strategies and new ways of thinking.

This book sets out what is in the repertoires. Because universities and colleges of education have not taken it upon themselves to be repositories of professional knowledge on teaching as universities have in architecture, law, and medicine, *there is no place to go to see what one does not yet know about pedagogy.* No one can chart an intelligent course of self-development without knowing what is out there to learn: the personal practical knowledge of our colleagues and the repertoires of public knowledge profiled in this book.

This book contains enough material for any practicing teacher, no matter how experienced or competent, to find new and useful tools and ways of approaching the teaching issues that arise daily. More important, it contains a framework for the knowledge base itself, which acknowledges that its creators have been practitioners. Its productive use is based on professional judgment, not application of universal rules. Learning about teaching never ends for professional teachers. If matching is the name of the game, as we have been saying since Chapter 1, then each of us must be constantly expanding our repertoires if we are to meet the needs of ever more diverse learners.

Faculty members must have systematic and regular access to the repertoires of strategies in the public knowledge base. Such access requires a map of the knowledge base that is organized according to rational categories and constantly updated. Every true profession has such a schema for organizing its professional knowledge. It is in the service of offering such a map for teaching that this book has been written. The map makes it easier to identify areas of development and underdevelopment in one's personal capacity and lays out the menu of things yet to learn for novice and expert practitioners alike.

Novices and experts learn differently. Novices need more rule-bound guidance to get started (Dreyfus and Dreyfus 1986.) They benefit from being told what parameters of teaching to focus on and what repertoire items to learn in their first years. More developed, competent teachers tend to learn through analysis of their own experience and by making choices about what to learn next. And experts tend to develop through an inner process of drawing on intuition, active experimentation, and dialogue. The way teachers contact the public knowledge base and draw upon it changes as they mature professionally. But some things never change: having access to learning new items from the repertoires, access to different models of teaching, different models of discipline, new explanatory devices, deeper insights into how to build community and ownership into classroom life for students, into how to support risk taking and confidence building for students—these things never become obsolete. No one of us ever knows enough about any of them to quit learning.

None of the parameters of teaching in *The Skillful Teacher* is a fad; every one of them, from classroom climate to principles of learning, is a variable, present in every classroom all the time, and accounting in part for how the learning is going for the students. Teachers do, in fact, already have repertoires, however large or narrow, on each of the parameters. But there are none among us who could not reach more students more effectively if we had broader repertoires and more developed wisdom about matching.

The public knowledge base on teaching, organized into the eighteen parameters pictured in the triangle in FIGURE **1.2** of Chapter 1, is a set of dynamic categories holding ever-growing repertoires. High-grade professional practice requires that each of us continually reach out to these repertoires and enlarge our capacity with them.

6. Professional knowledge and data about student needs should inform teachers' choice regarding the content and the process of their own learning.

Consider this conventional wisdom about staff development:

- ▶ If individual teachers select their own staff development options, their buy-in will ensure satisfaction and implementation.

- Staff development should be based at the school site, with the faculty making the decisions about directions and how to get there.

- Centralized initiatives are doomed to fail because of resistance and lack of buy-in.

- Knowledge is personal and situation specific. External sources provide little of value to local problem solving.

Surprisingly, however, a recent review of the literature on staff development found *no support* for these points and discovered a number of projects where school improvement efforts did successfully affect student learning using knowledge generated elsewhere (Joyce and Showers 1995). These authors demonstrated that staff development orchestrated from the central office can be quite effective in altering teachers' repertoires and influencing student achievement.

Teacher choice, in fact, is no guarantee of buy-in or of fruitful work. Faculty decisions about what to take on for staff development may be myopic or diffuse. Centralized initiatives, as Joyce and Showers showed, can be wonderfully effective if the decision-making process is inclusive and well conducted and the staff development design includes adequate dialogue, feedback, and coaching. So for optimal teacher learning, then, what should be the position regarding teacher ownership of staff development choices? This is a complicated question.

Adult learning theory is clear and consistent that adults do need to "own" their learning (Knowles 1984). But that ownership does not mean unbridled or unguided choice, and it does not mean making choices in a vacuum. A premise of this book is that dynamic professional development must make the public knowledge base on teaching available and put the map of its contents in front of people so they are not forced to rely solely on inner resources and invention when there is a wealth of material to choose from. The thrust of this chapter, however, has been to say that the selection of *what* to study from that knowledge base and, indeed, *how* to study it should be in the hands of teachers.[1] We have gone on to argue that starting with the study of their own work with children gives meaning, motivation, and direction to the definition of problems or the posing of questions that teachers may seek to answer by reaching out to the public knowledge base. This kind of inquiry will, in fact, identify their own entry into the public knowledge base.

---

[1] This position is taken with experienced teachers in mind. Here we need to acknowledge that beginning teachers may need direct intervention by mentors or others to teach them things they do now know and would not have been able to choose. You can't choose to study things if you don't know they exist. Likewise beginning teachers and advanced beginners benefit from the guidance of supervisors and mentors who can lead them in proper sequence through learning strategies for classroom management and content-specific pedagogical techniques.

Though our position here does authorize being more directive with beginners in choosing what they should learn, we still wish to recognize the value of problem-centered learning. Beginners will usually identify their own problems to mentors and supervisors; and these problems can still be the springboard for their best professional learning.

Putting these two ideas together leads to the position that teachers' choices for what to study and add to their repertoires should be (1) exercised against a backdrop of student needs and (2) informed by a comprehensive systematic map of what is available to study in our professional knowledge base.

Wildman and Niles write (1987):

> In settings where teachers are in control of their own reflective processes, we find that the content of that deliberation is primarily student centered. This is in contrast to most inservice efforts which emphasize the what and the how of teaching. Teachers, when guided by their own needs, seem to use the who as the fulcrum of their thought. That is, "How is what I am doing affecting my students?" It becomes clear when listening to teachers talk that individual students occupy large amounts of their thinking time. This "student centeredness" is an important feature to keep in mind when trying to promote reflection among teachers. To ignore natural interests and instincts may lead to unnecessary tension if teachers are forced to consider ideas, techniques, or research findings that are fundamentally at odds with, or irrelevant to, their own conceptions of teaching.

We might conclude that we should start with the immediate—with the students, the current issues of teachers—and from that context take direction about what parts of the knowledge base to tap. Thus, both the personal practical knowledge of teachers and the public knowledge base of the field can be drawn upon: for example, a team of sixth-grade teachers examining student work sees that many students are getting large amounts of information in their notes but not recognizing the connections among items. One of the teachers recommends the team learn more about graphic organizers and start building them into practice, with a goal of eventually getting the children to take notes in graphic organizer form. Three of them sign up for a one-day institute on graphic organizers that one of them has heard about. Afterward they set up a study group with peer observations and feedback for the fall semester to support one another's learning about how to use these graphic organizers.

This example shows the ownership by teachers of the direction for their learning, formed from an analysis of their needs with current sixth-grade students. Note that one of their members knew of a skill from the public knowledge base on pedagogy, graphic organizers, and suggested it for further study.

We believe the best professional learning comes from a mindful weaving together of internal and external sources of knowledge. And teachers, either alone or in groups, are the ones who should make those mindful choices about where and when to reach into those two sources.

Our final position about optimal conditions for teacher learning, then, is this:

- The teacher defines and owns the issues to work on for his or her own improvement.

> ◗ The teacher chooses the forms of support for this learning.

Of course, these choices should be made against a backdrop of an informed and systematic map about what is out there to learn, or what is out there to help solve a problem defined in the classroom.

7. Leaders act in congruence with the six previous conditions and explicitly support them.

What do leaders do to nurture these six and act in congruence with them? We like Edgar Schein's (1985) formula for approaching this leadership task. He says that a leader who is successful in changing a cultural norm (which is what is happening when a school becomes a good learning environment for adults) does the following things with respect to the new norm:

◗ say it

◗ model it

◗ organize for it

◗ protect it

◗ reward it

"Say it" means acknowledging to others in every appropriate setting the importance of these conditions: collegial behavior, self-study, the importance of reaching out to the knowledge base, and teacher choice. Opening-of-the-year speeches are typical occasions for leaders to introduce these commitments and reinforce them. Continually using the language of the new norm is important. It needs to become integral to dialog in the school.

"Model it" means leaders' practicing what they preach—and visibly. Thus, a principal might be doing a self-study, be in a principals' study group, and reach out for new leadership knowledge through reading, workshops, and conferences.

"Organize for it" means creating structures and groups and providing time for them to work together. For numerous examples, see King and Saphier (in press). One way might be to hire a permanent sub for every Wednesday who substitutes only for teachers doing peer observations. This sub might be a competent, recently retired teacher who brings his or her own lessons that provide enrichment and extension for the children in ways tied to schoolwide curriculum themes. Another way is to build in the schedule common blocks for groups of teachers to work together (Tanner, Canady, and Rettig 1995). Organizing the schedule to support teacher learning time together can liberate large amounts of energy for professional development.

"Protect it" is vital because, as Roland Barth (personal communication 1984) says, there are powerful antibodies against change in school organizations. Teachers who take the risk to share openly and make vulnerable their belief systems must be protected from sarcasm, ridicule, or other putdowns. The "guardian principal" or department chair is not the only person on whose shoulders this work falls, but it must clearly be modeled there.

"Reward it" can take many forms. At one level it means that administrators make resources available to faculty members who take risks, speak openly, and model the self-study behaviors of healthy staff development. At another level it means showing approval. At still another it means generating opportunities for teachers who are learners to share their new learning with other colleagues around the district or state.

When our society takes teacher learning seriously—that is, when our citizenry as well as our profession see the effect on student achievement of powerful learning conditions for teachers—then leadership for these conditions will be built into the training, licensing, certification, evaluation, and continuing education of American school administrators. It is ironic but consistent that in a chapter featuring the role of choice, we end with the position that learning to lead for strong school culture should be required. ❧

> *When our society takes teacher learning seriously, leadership for powerful learning conditions for teachers will be built into the training, licensing, certification, evaluation, and continuing education of American school administrators.*

Source Materials on Opening Wide the Gates: Conditions for Teacher Learning

Barth, Roland. Personal communication, 1984.

Costa, Arthur L., and Robert J. Garmston. *Cognitive Coaching: A Foundation for Renaissance Schools*. Norwood, Mass.: Christopher Gordon, 1994.

Darling-Hammond, Linda, and Milbrey W. McLaughlin. "Policies That Support Professional Development in an Era of Reform." *Educational Leadership* (April 1995).

Dreyfus, H. L., and S. E. Dreyfus. *Mind over Machine*. New York: Free Press, 1986.

Edwards, John. "Thinking, Education and Human Potential." In J. Edwards, ed., *Thinking: International Interdisciplinary Perspectives*. Melbourne: Hawker Brownlow Education, 1994.

Guskey, Tom. Audiotape interview with Dennis Sparks, National Staff Development Council, 1995.

Joyce, Bruce R., and Beverly Showers. *Student Achievement Through Staff Development*. White Plains, N.Y.: Longmans, 1995.

King, Matthew, and Jon Saphier. *Strengthening School Culture*. Carlisle, Mass.: Research for Better Teaching, in press.

Knowles, Malcolm S. *The Adult Learner: A Neglected Species*. 3d ed. Houston: Gulf Publishing Co., 1984.

Leiberman, Ann. "Practices That Support Teacher Development." *Educational Leadership* (April 1995).

Lortie, Dan C. *School-Teacher*. Chicago: University of Chicago Press, 1975.

Murphy, Carlene. "Study Groups Foster Schoolwide Learning." *Educational Leadership* 50, no. 3 (November 1992).

Pajares, Frank. "Teachers' Beliefs and Educational Research: Cleaning Up a Messy Construct." *Review of Educational Research* 62, no. 3 (Fall 1992).

Saphier, Jon. "Bonfires and Magic Bullets." Carlisle, Mass.: Research for Better Teaching, 1994.

Shein, Edgar. *Organizational Culture and Leadership*. San Francisco: Jossey-Bass, 1985.

Tanner, Brenda, Robert L. Canady, and Michael D. Rettig. "Scheduling to Maximize Staff Development Opportunities." *Journal of Staff Development* 16, no. 4 (Fall 1995).

Wildman, Terry M., and Jerome A. Niles. "Reflective Teachers: Tensions between Abstractions and Realities." *Journal of Teacher Education* (July-August 1987).

Teacher Beliefs

About intelligence and
    children's capacity to learn

About learning itself

About teachers and teaching

About schools and schooling

This has been a book about the knowledge base on teaching that attempts to make it more accessible. One way we have done this is to build a construct of teaching that attempts to be comprehensive but not prescriptive. This construct has organized the practice of teaching into categories which we have called Parameters like Clarity, and subcategories such as Activating and Summarizing. So what place, one might reasonably ask, does a section on beliefs have in a book that aims to profile the repertoires of strategies and ways of thinking that exist within each of these parameters?

Our answer is this: *The Skillful Teacher* is also a book about teacher learning and, we hope, a resource for it. There are certain beliefs about children, beliefs about teaching and learning, and beliefs about schools that bear heavily on one's willingness to learn and what it is one feels impelled to seek to learn. We are convinced—this is our belief system you're getting now—that a few particular beliefs are essential to teacher learning and that without them teachers will not be able and/or committed to stretching themselves fully. One of these beliefs is about the nature of the knowledge on teaching itself.

If one believes there is no real knowledge base on teaching, then it is easy to cruise on intuition and rely on the muse to inspire you toward improved performance. It is also easy to take the position that one needs only to recruit superior people to improve schools. "Any capable person can do it if they know their content." This nonbelief in teaching knowledge devalues the complexity of the work and hobbles teacher learning. And let there be no mistake, this nonbelief is abroad in the land and articulated frequently from pulpits of high visibility.

Another stance is to believe that the only real knowledge about teaching is one's internally generated knowledge through experience; therefore one need only reflect or join with others to reflect on one's own actual teaching experience. The only knowledge worth having will come from within and from reflective interaction with one's peers. Though this view is based on the valuable commitment to practice-based learning, it ignores the resource of public knowledge described in the previous chapter and consigns teacher learning to the half-a-loaf syndrome. Half a loaf is better than none, but there is no reason to forgo the full meal.

If one believes teaching knowledge consists of "effective behaviors," then yet another unproductive mind-set is created. The nature of learning about teaching becomes reduced to the workmanlike task of following others' prescriptions about how to teach. Learn what the "effective behaviors" are, the story would go. Practice them and get good at them. Then one will be a good teacher. We have written at length about the negative consequence of this belief.

If, on the other hand, one believes that our work is intellectually complex, difficult and demanding, and that like any other true profession, its knowledge is based on repertoires and matching, then the doors of professional dialogue are opened wide; the need to learn *with* colleagues in examination of situation-specific questions comes to the fore, as does the need to reach out for new strategies and ways of thinking in the public knowledge base.

Think about this notion for a minute: why is it so difficult to get teachers to share openly their good ideas and successful practices at faculty meetings and other forums? If one believes in the "effectiveness" paradigm, then there are assumed to be right and wrong ways of doing things—effective and ineffective (or at least less effective). Suppose you share a "successful practice" that is different from what I do. The tacit inference, based on my "effectiveness" belief system, is that either you are right or I am—and you are either showing me up or trying to tell me how to do it right—which I'm not doing now. If, on the other hand, our school culture has internalized the belief in the complexity of teaching and the view of professional knowledge posed in this book, then I can hear your "successful practice" as an interesting alternative for my consideration, not a prescription for how to do it instead of the way I employ. So one belief essential to fruitful teacher learning is a belief about the nature of professional knowledge itself—namely, that its nature is based on repertoires and matching, not effective behaviors.

In the previous chapter we presented some points of view about the interaction of beliefs and behavior. Beliefs drive behavior, are often unexamined, and are certainly resistant to change. The connection here is that without understanding one's beliefs, it is impossible to understand one's attitude and motivation to learn new approaches to teaching.

So now let us now examine a few beliefs which we think are pivotal to teacher learning—beliefs which may be necessary to unleash curiosity and energy for teacher learning.

Belief About Intelligence and Children's' Capacity to Learn

1. **"You can get smart." Children's learning is primarily determined by their effort and use of effective strategies. "Intelligence" is not a fixed inborn limit on learning capacity. All children can do rigorous academic material at high standards (Howard 1993).**

If I have internalized this belief, there are direct consequences one would see in my teaching. I would believe it to be my responsibility to:

- communicate the three expectation messages to all students
- constantly reexamine my practice
- explicitly and implicitly teach my students how to mobilize effective effort and
- teach my students strategies for successful learning.

Most Americans believe in the concept of "intelligence" as a fixed innate entity that is unevenly distributed and that determines how well a student can do. The belief in the "bell curve" of intelligence has huge implications for teaching and learning—namely, that only a few students are "smart" enough to learn sophisticated academic material at high standards.

If, on the other hand, one believes that almost all his or her students can achieve at a high level given the right conditions, that is, that students can actually *increase* their ability through application, focus, and good strategies, then one is almost driven to reconceptualize one's role as a teacher. That reconceptualization would include being a teacher of strategies as well as a teacher of an academic discipline; it would include an implied obligation to diversify one's teaching so as to match different student learning styles. And it would certainly imply developing one's commitment to and repertoire for conveying high positive expectation messages to students.

Others (Gould 1983) have documented the sorry history of our unique and limiting view of intelligence in this country with its sad consequences for students. There is not room here for us to make the contrary case in any more detail—namely, the case that intelligence can, indeed, be developed, and that effective effort and good strategies are the principal determinants of academic success. We refer readers to other articulate proponents (Howard 1993 , 1995; Resnick 1995). Our point here has been that one's belief about the nature of intelligence and its limits (or limitlessness) form a powerful frame around teachers' motivations to expand their repertoires. Anyone serious about professional development must address this belief system if they wish to unleash the full energy of adults to expand their capacity to reach all students.

Beliefs About Learning Itself

2. Learning is constructed as learners assimilate new experience with prior knowledge.

If I accept this belief, then I must construct learning experiences where the learners are active, doing and applying knowledge and reflecting on its meaning out loud or in writing. It is my responsibility to create a balance between students' time *receiving* information and practicing skills and their time actively *constructing*, assimilating, and applying information in real contexts. This implies I learn a variety of models of teaching and take it upon myself to learn how to develop the "influence" strand of classroom climate in this book.

3. Learning varies with the degree to which learners' needs for the following are met: inclusion, influence, competence, confidence.

Therefore, since I create a psychological and cognitive milieu that has an enormous impact on what and how children learn, it is my professional responsibility to deliberately design an environment in which each child can succeed. Such an environment is characterized by community, mutual support, risk taking, and higher-level thinking for all. I cannot narrow my self-definition to being a representative of my academic discipline. I must think of myself as a teacher of *students* as well as a teacher of my discipline.

Beliefs About Teachers and Teaching

4. The nature of professional knowledge is "areas of performance, repertoire, and matching," not "effective behaviors."

Therefore my learning can never be considered finished. I must constantly enlarge my repertoire, stretch my comfort zones, and develop my ability to match students so I can reach more kids with appropriate instruction.

5. Professional capacity of a teacher requires systematic and continual study of diverse knowledge bases.

These knowledge bases include continuing development in one's knowledge about (1) content; (2) pedagogy; (3) content-specific pedagogical knowledge; (4) children and their differences; (5) behaviors of individuals in effective organizations; and (6) parent and community involvement. For purposes of the category system here, "pedagogy" will include the study of curriculum design and planning. All of these are important areas of teacher knowledge in addition to interactive teaching skill.

Therefore I must broaden my concept of professional development to include these other domains and find ways to build repertoires in them.

Beliefs About Schools and Schooling

6. The total environment of a school has a powerful effect on students' learning.

Therefore I must participate actively with my colleagues as a shaper of the school-as-learning-environment; I must learn how to play a role in strengthening the institution; I must see myself as a player beyond my classroom and responsible for the "system" of the school. For this to happen, collegiality and interdependence need to be built into the fabric of our working relationships. Interdependence requires that I function as both a leader and a team player, and that I support a balance of autonomy and cohesion in curriculum and teaching practices.

I am a leader in that I take initiative to influence colleagues toward ideas I value and move the school toward practices I believe will strengthen us. I am a team player in that I collaborate with colleagues to improve the school and help individual students. I am also a team player in that I am willing to give up some autonomy for actions implied by common visions and agreements.

The connection between teacher learning and this belief in interdependence and collegiality is this: only if I have regular interaction with my colleagues through joint work can I experience the benefit of their knowledge and the synergy of creating new knowledge with others.

7. Racism in our society exerts a downward force on the achievement of students of color that must be opposed by active antiracist teaching.

Racism is invisible to whites because as the dominant group they enjoy the "white privileges" (McIntosh 1993) of not being followed in stores, of taking a walk at night without being stopped by police, of getting credit and loans more easily and more quickly, and a thousand other unseen privileges they experience as "normal." The cultural and institutional manifestations of racism get carried over into school as the stereotypes, distortions, or omission of cultures other than Western European from curriculum.

The American view of intelligence as innate, fixed, and deterministic compounds the problem. It mingles with racism and creates the secret belief, articulated about once a decade (Jensen 1969; Murray and Herrnstein 1994) that people of color (particularly African-Americans) are less intelligent than whites. This induces differential teacher behavior toward students of color (Rist 1970) and stereotype vulnerability (Steele 1992) among the students themselves—that is, actual lower performance in situations where their race even subtly calls their ability into question.

All our teachers need thorough education about these issues. We all need information and experiences that will cause introspection into our tacit beliefs about people of color and the practices of society that reinforce them. And above all, we need to build culturally relevant teaching (see Classroom Climate chapter) into our practice.

Readers could probably make the case for including other beliefs in the framework above. Any belief that leverages teachers' behavior toward curiosity, sharing, reaching out to the knowledge base, and expanding repertoires would be an easy sell to us. Our concern here is not to lay out a definitive set of beliefs; it is in posing the question, "How can we nurture beliefs that foster teacher learning and build supports for them into the cultures of our schools?" For without doing so, professional learning (and enduring school progress) is hamstrung.

We urge all our readers to join us in pondering this question and in framing responses in action at their worksites, as we ourselves are trying to do at schools where we work. In addition, we offer one concluding thought.

The most powerful lever for influencing teacher learning and beliefs may be teacher induction programs. In the decade following the publication of this book, two-thirds of the American teaching force will turn over. In 2006 two-thirds of the teachers working with our children will be new to the profession. Over their first three years their beliefs about teaching knowledge and its nature, about collaborative work, about how students learn, their conception of the role of a teacher, their place in the ecosystem of the school—all these beliefs will be formed and solidified through what they see modeled by significant figures around them, by what mentors tell and show them, by what colleagues help them discover, by what messages their administrators send to them about openness and seeking help, and by what support they themselves experience for their own learning from the institution in which they find themselves. Therefore among all the possible avenues for teacher development, we would put induction programs at the top of the priority list. Specifically we would recommend:

1. Train a large and dedicated corps of mentors to be knowledgeable in adult development, observation and coaching skills, differential conferencing skills, and above all, the knowledge bases of professional teaching. Expect them to spend three hours per week with their new teacher colleagues, and to learn how to use teachable moments to help new teachers develop the beliefs described above.

2. Redefine building leadership (i.e., the principalship) to include leadership for strong culture with emphasis on collegiality, experimentation, and reaching out to the knowledge base. Train, support, and evaluate leaders on their ability to deliver such leadership. ❧

Source Materials on Teacher Beliefs

Gould, Stephen Jay. *Mismeasure of Man*. New York: W. W. Norton, 1981.

Herrnstein, Richard J., and Charles Murray. *The Bell Curve*. New York: Free Press, 1994.

Howard, Jeff. "You Can't Get There From Here." *Daedalus* 24, no. 4 (Fall 1995): 85–92.

———. "The Social Construction of Intelligence." Lexington, Mass.: Efficacy, Inc., 1993.

Jensen, Arthur R. "How Much Can We Boost IQ and Scholastic Achievement?" *Harvard Education Review* XXXIX (Winter 1969): 1–123.

McIntosh, Peggy. "White Privilege: Unpacking the Invisible Knapsack." *Peace and Freedom* (July–August 1989): 10–12.

Resnick, Laurence. "From Aptitude To Effort: A New Foundation for Our Schools." *Daedalus* 124, no. 4 (Fall 1995): 55–62.

Rist, Ray. "Student Social Class and Teacher Expectations: A Self-Fulfilling Prophecy in Ghetto Education." *Harvard Educational Review* 40, no. 3 (August 1970): 411–451.

Steele, Claude. "Race and Schooling of Black Americans." *The Atlantic Monthly* (April 1992): 68–78.

Two indexes are provided for your use: a Subject Index and an Author/Title Index. The Subject Index presents all topics discussed in this book. The Author/Title Index lists all authors and books discussed in this book. Page references followed by "n" indicate textual material in footnotes.

SUBJECT INDEX

AUTHOR/TITLE INDEX

▲ **THE SKILLFUL TEACHER:** *Building Your Teaching Skills*   5ᵗʰ edition • 1997
by Jon Saphier & Robert Gower

This book has become a standard text in many teaching courses. Designed for both the novice and the experienced educator, *The Skillful Teacher* is a unique synthesis of the Knowledge Base on Teaching with powerful repertoires for matching teaching strategies to student needs. Designed as a practical guide for practitioners working to broaden their teaching skills, the book focuses on 17 critical areas of classroom performance. Numerous examples illustrate teaching approaches, and chapter-by-chapter bibliographies provide additional sources for further research. This expanded fifth edition includes new chapters on Assessment, Expectations, Classroom Climate, the Importance of Teacher Beliefs, and Conditions for Teacher Learning.

▲ **HOW TO MAKE SUPERVISION AND EVALUATION REALLY WORK:**
Supervision and Evaluation in the Context of Strengthening School Culture   1993
by Jon Saphier

This book offers school leaders a carefully integrated approach for transforming often divisive supervision and evaluation systems into a positive force for strengthening school culture. Specific guidelines lead to meaningful, multifaceted teacher evaluation systems.

▲ **THE SKILLFUL LEADER:** *Confronting Mediocre Teaching*   1ˢᵗ edition • 2000
by Alexander D. Platt, Caroline Tripp, Wayne R. Ogden, & Robert G. Fraser

Based on *The Skillful Teacher* framework, this book is targeted to evaluators and supervisors who want a field-tested tool kit of strategies to improve, rather than remove underperforming teachers. The text includes valuable legal notes and a model contract, case studies, assessment tools, and personal accounts of leaders in action.

▲ **ACTIVATORS:** *Activity structures to engage students' thinking before instruction*   1993
by Jon Saphier & Mary Ann Haley

This book is a collection of classroom-tested, practical activity structures for getting students' minds active and engaged prior to introducing new content or skills. Each structure is designed to elicit what students already know about a topic, to surface misconceptions, and to create cognitive hooks when new material is presented.

▲ **SUMMARIZERS:** *Activity structures to support integration and retention of new learning*   1993
by Jon Saphier & Mary Ann Haley

This book is a collection of classroom-tested, practical activity structures for getting students cognitively active during and after periods of instruction. Each structure provides a framework for guiding students to summarize for themselves what was important, what they have learned, how it is important, and/or how it fits with what they already know.

▲ **HOW TO BRING VISION TO SCHOOL IMPROVEMENT**   1993
Through Core Outcomes, Commitments and Beliefs
by Jon Saphier & John D'Auria

This practical guide provides a proven step-by-step sequence for generating consensus among parents and staff about a few valued core outcomes they want for all children. Then it shows how to achieve them through concrete areas of school and family life.

▲ **HOW TO MAKE DECISIONS THAT STAY MADE**   1993
by Jon Saphier, Tom Bigda-Peyton & Geoff Pierson

This brief guide, first published in 1989 by ASCD, offers administrators and staff twelve clearly defined steps for making better decisions in schools. A case study illustrates how each step would work in an actual school setting.

RESEARCH FOR BETTER TEACHING
One Acton Place • Acton, MA 01720-3951
978.263.3280 *voice* • 978.263.9959 *fax* • rbteach@tiac.net *email*